# Landscape Design with Plants

## SECOND EDITION

*Edited by*
BRIAN CLOUSTON

*Published for*
THE LANDSCAPE INSTITUTE

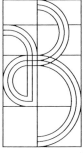

D1341461

Butterworth Architecture
An imprint of Butterworth-Heinemann Ltd
Linacre House, Jordan Hill, Oxford OX2 8DP

A member of the Reed Elsevier plc group

OXFORD    LONDON    BOSTON
NEW DELHI    SINGAPORE    SYDNEY
TOKYO    TORONTO    WELLINGTON

First published 1977
Reprinted 1979
Second edition 1990
First published as a paperback edition 1994
Reprinted 1996

**British Library Cataloguing in Publication Data**
Landscape design with plants – 2nd ed.
1. Landscape design. Special features.
Plants. Manuals
I. Clouston, Brian. II. Landscape Institute 716

ISBN 0 7506 1962 7

Printed in Great Britain by
BAS Printers Limited, Over Wallop, Hampshire

# FOREWORD

The need for a second edition of *Landscape Design with Plants* bears witness to the success of the book. Its form explains its particular role. The first part discusses design with plants as the raison d'être of technique, demonstrating how this book is something completely different from a horticultural manual or gardening book. It proposes an approach to making landscapes which is based on design. This is a tradition deep-rooted in British culture, which has long perceived the importance of incorporating intellectual and emotional values into the process of forming man-made landscapes.

The landowner's picturesque demesne, the vernacular landscape around comfortable farmsteads, the urban recreation parks created for the populace as cities grew have all expressed this fundamental belief in the conscious creative use of vegetation. Plants are perceived as a 'material' to enclose space, to give shelter and shade or to frame pleasing views as well as being shown off in their own right for their individual beauties, a design skill in itself. What was said on the background of the subject a decade ago addressed long-lasting values, still as true today, and so the first part of the book is little changed since the first edition.

The second part of the book concerns the techniques to be used in the modern application of landscape design with plants. This is a subject in which knowledge is moving forwards tremendously fast in response to an increasing need for well-designed landscapes. Recent years have offered immense new opportunities. Therefore the second part of the book has been substantially revised and updated to make available contemporary knowledge and thought about the subject. A much broader spectrum of techniques is now included. The material is more incisive.

The book had been first conceived as a vehicle for the publication of the plant information sheets which had appeared regularly in the *Journal of the Institute of Landscape Architects* (now *Landscape Design*). The new edition takes another great step forwards producing a book altogether more sophisticated in intention. The series of technical chapters, including such subjects as the role of vegetation in land engineering, makes the book one of the handbooks of the landscape profession.

This new updated edition is a yet more powerful tool with which to continue into the future the long tradition of designing landscapes with plants.

*Hal Moggridge*

**Autumn Mood.** (*Maurice Nimmo*)

# PREFACE

Much of our physical environment is of man's own making. Cicero has Balbus say in his discourse 'We enjoy the fruits of the plains and of the mountains, the rivers and lakes are ours, we sow corn, we plant trees, we fertilise the soil by irrigation. We confine the rivers and straighten their courses. By means of our hands we try to create, as it were, a second world within the world of nature'. It is the creation of that second world within the natural world, by design, that the profession of landscape is about.

*Landscape Design with Plants* was commissioned by the then Institute of Landscape Architects in 1975, published in 1977, and enjoyed considerable success. The original book combined both the theoretical and practical aspects of landscape design with plants into a single book and provided, for the first time, a comprehensive handbook for landscape architects and others concerned with the creation of new landscape and the rehabilitation of degraded landscape.

Much of the illustrative material for the first edition was drawn from examples of work of preceding years and therefore dated back to the mid 1960s and beyond. Thankfully the practice of landscape in Britain and overseas has thrived over the past twelve years. We can now draw on illustrations of recently implemented designs by a new generation of landscape architects: designs achieved through the provision by clients of realistic budgets. New illustrative material demonstrates the wide scope of work now being undertaken by the profession in Britain and increasingly overseas.

Part I deals with the use of plants in landscape design and remains little changed. All chapter authors have brought up-to-date matters which do become outdated over a decade or more, such as reading lists and the like. Perhaps it is a tribute to the authors (all of whom, with the exception of Brenda Colvin who died in 1981, remain in practice) of this sextet of chapters that so few amendments were needed. Design principles change slowly. It is the kind and combination of plants which change. Over the past ten years or so we have seen more use made of colour in the landscape and of

hedging, but these are matters of fashion and cannot really be dealt with in a book of this kind.

Part II is concerned with techniques, matters about which, if there were no real advance over a decade of time, any profession would become concerned. New chapters (18, 19 and 20) have been introduced dealing with the establishment of trees and shrubs from seed (Chapter 18), recent research into techniques concerned with the establishment of trees and shrubs (Chapter 19), and interior planting (Chapter 20). All three chapters introduce techniques which were not part of contemporary practice ten years ago. Christine Avis and Jim Mitchell's chapter, which deals with Australian arid and semi-arid native plants (now much used by landscape architects working in the Middle East), extends the range of material describing the use of plants into regions distant from Britain, and regions of the world which are now the work place of many British trained professionals. The profession is becoming more international and a third revision of the book will no doubt extend these geographical boundaries further still. All the chapters in this second part of the book have been extensively revised. Whereas design principles change slowly, techniques related to planting evolve relatively quickly.

Ralph Cobham's material (Chapter 17) deals with landscape management and maintenance and reflects those changes in techniques and practice affecting the newer management class of the Landscape Institute — an area of practice which has expanded rapidly in recent years.

My thanks must go to all the chapter authors for participating so cheerfully in the preparation of new and revised texts and for coming up with such splendid illustrations. For those concerned with chapter revision, I appreciate their difficulties in finding time within busy professional lives to bring up to date those chapters published so long ago. Those who provided new work had perhaps an easier task. They, nevertheless, had to put up with their share of bullying and enticement from the editor's desk.

My thanks also to John Welsh and Lucinda Gresswell of my London office who did sterling work in organizing the revision with me and to Stephen Pevsner who assisted with the final editing of chapter texts. Thanks also to Sheila Harvey of the Landscape Institute for her work in indexing; to all the organizations who have so generously supplied illustrations; and to Bridget Buckley of Heinemann for her patience and most excellent professional guidance.

*Brian Clouston*

# PREFACE TO THE PAPERBACK EDITION

The two hardback editions of this book were successful. When the second edition was published in 1990 reviewers accepted the revisions and additions with enthusiasm. In an endeavour to bring the book to a wider audience the publishers have now decided to produce the book in paperback – omitting Part III Plant and Tree Information Sheets. This part of the book was originally published over a period of years in *The Journal of the Institute of Landscape Architects* (now *Landscape Design* magazine).

A dramatic reduction in price will bring the paperback edition of the book within reach of landscape students and young professionals alike. The book was originally conceived as a desktop manual – accessible as an everyday reference for designers and landscape managers.

In recent years a number of new courses have been established which embrace environmental science, applied ecology, garden design and landscape husbandry. *Landscape Design with Plants* – in an inexpensive format – will furnish students of these emerging courses with important information. A number of the chapters in Part II of the book are of equal importance to the designer or to the ecologist creating a new habitat on contaminated land.

With each year that passes the work of the landscape profession and the industry which supports it increases in both scale and scope. Fashions in planting design change gradually. However, the essential principles which underlie design with plants change slowly. For this reason no amendments have been included in this paperback edition. Another decade may pass before the book will require updating and major revision.

*Brian Clouston*

# CONTENTS

# THE AUTHORS

**Penny Beckett**, Dip LA, ALI
Landscape architect with Brian Clouston and Partners. Eight years' experience in private practice covering a wide range of projects, including large-scale land reclamation and urban landscape design. Committee member of the North West Chapter of the Landscape Institute.

**Professor A. D. Bradshaw** MA (Botany, Cantab), PhD (Wales). FRS
Professor Bradshaw started as an ecologist interested in plant growth on problem soils, and for the last twenty years has been much involved in land reclamation work. He has been the Professor of Botany at Liverpool University since 1968. He founded the Environmental Advisory Unit to Liverpool University in 1976. He was formerly a member of both the NERC and the NCC, and was instrumental, with Sir Norman Rowntree and Duncan Poore, in pioneering reservoir margin work.

**Colin Brown** BSc (Hons), DipMALD
Worked as a landscape architect for the Milton Keynes Development Corporation and Central Lancashire Development Corporation before joining the Lisney Associates practice in 1987, as an associate.

**Ralph Cobham** BA Agr B, Dip Agr Eco, MSc
Ralph Cobham is the Senior Partner of Cobham Resource Consultants. He was a founding member of the Management Branch of the Landscape Institute. He is also a Fellow of the British Institute of Agricultural Consultants and a Member of the Institute of Leisure and Amenity Management. He has extensive experience of landscape management and maintenance in the UK, North America, Middle East and Far East.

**Brenda Colvin** CBE, PPILA
Landscape architect in private practice from 1925. In partnership with Hal Moggridge, AILA, ARIBA involved mainly in rural planning, such as reservoirs and agricultural problems in England and Wales, and work overseas. Founder member of ILA and IFLA. Landscape consultant to CEGB, Birmingham Water Board, new towns, universities, and various other educational establishments. Author of *Land and Landscape* and *Trees for Town and Country*. Died in 1981.

**Nick Coppin** MSc, ALI, CBiol, MIEnvSci, AMIQ
Landscape scientist in private practice, currently an Associate with Wardell Armstrong (Mining, Minerals and Geotechnical Consultants) and Manager of the Environmental Consultancy Unit. Principal work includes land restoration and revegetation of difficult areas. Currently working on a keynote report for the Construction Industry Research and Information Association on 'The Use of Vegetation in Civil Engineering', a guide for the construction industry on the application of vegetation in a functional role on engineering structures.

**Alan Cornford**
Executive Director of Rentokil Tropical Plants — Britain's largest interior landscape contractor — and arguably one of this countries most knowledgable exponents of interior landscaping. From an initial involvement in office planting he visited America in the 1970s and saw the developments there in the creation of space and the interior landscape treatment within new office buildings and shopping malls. From that moment on, through his work with the British Association of Landscape Industries in developing a *Guide to Specification for Interior Landscape* and through promoting A. C. Rentaplant, his former company, he has been a major contributor in developing this new landscape discipline.

**Sylvia Crowe**, DBE, PPILA, Hon. FRIBA, Hon. MRTPI
Landscape architect in private practice since 1945. Landscape consultant to Forestry Commission until 1974; CEGB, new towns, water authorities and many local authorities. Chairman of the Tree Council. Author of many books and papers including *Tomorrow's Landscape; Landscape of Power; Landscape of Roads;*

*Relation to Landscape and Amenity* (paper to The Royal Society).

**Stephen Dale**
Associate of the Landscape Institute and the Director of A. C. D. Landscape Architects Ltd. He studied at Thames Polytechnic, has since worked for West Sussex County Council and the London Borough of Haringey and was senior landscape architect for the Alexandra Palace Development team before establishing his own practice at Dale Landscape Associates. He formed A. C. Design Landscape Architects with Alan Cornford, in order to develop a practice with a full knowledge of interiors and the specialist design principles required for them.

**Christopher Driver**, Dip L.A. (Leeds), A.L.I.
Landscape architect with Brian Clouston and Partners. Previous experience in private practice and Central Lancashire New Town. Spent three years in Sultanate of Oman, as resident landscape architect on Sultan Qaboos University Project (completed in 1987). He has also worked on projects in Saudi Arabia and Egypt.

**Ray Gemmell**, BSc, C Biol, MI Biol, PhD (Wales), ALI Land Science
Consultant ecologist and partner in the Environment Research and Advisory Partnership. He has worked on the reclamation of derelict land, including collier spoil, metalliferous wastes, chemically polluted land, refuse disposal sites and urban wasteland. He is now increasingly concerned with wildlife issues and assisting developers in the planning and reconstruction of wildlife habitats. He has advised on the ecological and environmental aspects of major developments, such as landfill sites, mineral workings, gas pipelines, housing estates and road schemes.

**Christopher J. Gill**, MA (Agricultural Sciences, Cambridge), PhD (Liverpool)
Deputy Director of the Timber Research and Development Association. PhD thesis on 'The Revegetation of Reservoir Margins' at Liverpool University Botany Department and continued research in same field at Cambridge for four years. Involved in planting schemes for Rutland Water, Brenig and CEGB reservoirs.

**Allan Hart**, AILA, AIPRA (Dipl.), DH (Kew)
Landscape architect in own private practice since 1968. Experience includes landscape work with commercial firms, local authorities and central government, including extensive projects, design and management in Cyprus, Gibraltar, Libya and Hong Kong. Author of *Use of Plant Material – Handbook of Urban Landscape*; co-author of *Select List of Plants Suitable for Landscape Work in Hong Kong* (Department of the Environment).

**Ronald L. Hebblethwaite** BSc, FLI
Principal of Hebblethwaite Landscape Consultants, Cheltenham. Former Principal Landscape Architect to CEGB. Considerable experience in the United States of America. Former Landscape Architect to Hampshire County Council. Former LI Council Member and Chairman of the LI Research Committee; research on reclamation of pulverized fuel ash, trees in 'draw down' areas, transplanting semi-mature trees, qualitative analysis of the countryside and computer analysis 'Zone of visual influence' studies.

**John L. Innes** BA PhD
Research scientist with the Forestry Commission, stationed at Alice Holt Research Station in Surrey. He joined the Commission in 1986, specifically to work on problems related to air pollution. Currently he is responsible for the surveys of forest health undertaken by the Forestry Commission and for international liaison on the problem of forest decline. He has written numerous papers and articles on the subject, many of them in international scientific journals.

**Preben Jakobsen**, RA Dip (Copenhagen), DH (Kew)
Landscape architect in private practice since 1969. Experience includes landscape work for various government bodies, local authorities and industrial concerns, consultant to new towns, hospitals, universities, and projects in Europe and the Middle East. Formerly part-time lecturer and studio instructor at Thames Polytechnic Landscape Architecture diploma course. Has given lectures and papers on landscape design to various courses and professional groups, and written reports, articles and reviews in professional journals and magazines.

**Cedric Lisney** DipArch, RIBA, DipLA, PLI
Principal of Lisney Associates, Bath. As a former chairman of the LI Technical Committee he organized the very successful and repeated technical symposium 'Tree Establishment' at the University of Bath, which led to improved practical standards set out in the linked documents, 'Frost Damage to Trees and Shrubs' and 'Plant Handling'. He has been President of the Landscape Institute (1987–1989) and Vice Chairman of the Joint Council for Landscape Industries.

**James Mitchell** Pip, LD (NSW), Dip Hort (Kew), AAILA, ARAIPR
Jim has practised landscape architecture in Australia for twenty years and has travelled widely throughout this vast continent. He completed his horticultural training at the Royal Botanic Gardens, Kew, and studied landscape design at the University of New South Wales, Australia. Earlier, he attended the Lancashire College of Agriculture. He was employed as landscape planner by the Electricity Commission of New South Wales for six and a half years. In 1974 he set up the office of James Mitchell and Associates Pty Ltd, and has completed many significant projects throughout the three eastern states of Australia. Jim was actively

involved with the design documentation and supervision of the Darling Harbour Redevelopment Project, part of New South Wales' largest urban renewal programme and Australia's Bicentennial project of 1988.

**David Parker**, BSc, PhD, ALI (Landscape Science Division)
Senior Consultant in the Environmental Advisory Unit, University of Liverpool. Seven years' professional experience in advising the public and private sector on the integration of development with environmental conservation and protection, both in the UK and overseas.

**A. du Gard Pasley**, FILA
Landscape architect in private practice. Author and lecturer on various aspects of landscape design.

**Gordon Patterson**, Dip LA (Reading), AILA
Senior Partner, Gordon Patterson & Partners, Landscape Architects. Principal work includes landscape of Stevenage New Town, various health authorities and government agencies. Formerly in charge of Landscape Department at the School of Architecture and Landscape, Gloucestershire College of Art and Design. Consultant to the Forestry Commission. Secretary to *Landscape Design* Trust. Co-author of *Mughal Gardens of India*.

**Stephen Scrivens**, BSc (Horticulture, University of Bath), Dip LA (University of Sheffield)
Principal of Technical Landscapes Ltd since 1981, specializing in the design of high technology landscapes, especially interior landscapes. Post-graduate research into water retention in roof gardens, current MSc/PhD at the University of Bath on 'The Effect of Certain Light Sources and Pre-trial Treatments upon the

Growth and development of *Cordylin terminalis, Dieffenbachia maculata, Schefflera actinophylla* and *Ficus benjamina*'. Author of *Interior Planting in Large Buildings* and *Roof Garden Technology*. Also approximately fifty technical articles on various aspects of roof gardens and interior landscape technology in *The Architect's Journal, Building Magazine, GC* and *HTJ* and *What's New in Building*.

**Mark Smeeden** BA, HND (Hort), Dip LA (Leeds), ALI, MI Hort
Landscape architect and horticulturalist with Brian Clouston and Partners. Previously, landscape architect for Cambridge Direct Tree Seeding Ltd. Worked on applying and developing the techniques of establishing woody vegetation from seed on a wide variety of waste materials, and derelict land sites throughout Britain.

**Henry Steed**
Henry Steed has been working in Tropical Asia as a landscape architect for nine years. He is a director of Brian Clouston and Partners' Singapore, Malaysia and Hong Kong offices, operating out of Singapore. While his experience is mainly in the Asian tropics, he maintains a great interest in the landscape of all tropical areas, especially the threatened rain forests.

**Richard Stiles** MA (Oxon), Dip LD (Newcastle), ALI
Lecturer in Landscape Design at Manchester University. Trained originally as a biologist. Experience as a landscape architect working on a wide range of projects in both private practice and the public sector in the UK, as well as several years working with private practices in West Germany. Recent publications include articles in *Landscape Design, Landscape Research, Garten und Landschaft* and the *Oxford Companion to Gardens*.

*Overleaf*: **St Dunstans in the East, London.** (*John Chitty*)

**Snowdrop in winter.** (*Dick Hoyle*)

# Part I
# DESIGN

# Design: Introduction

## BRENDA COLVIN

### WHAT THE EYE WILL SEE, THE IMAGINATION FORESEES

Design implies purpose: the adaptation of means to an intended objective. It implies change from that which has been to that which will be under new circumstances.

All man-made changes to our environment involve design — whether with or without artistry — often almost unconsciously. Today much of our too-hasty design is influenced only by necessity, short-term economy or greed. In the landscape, the lack of thoughtful, sensitive design leads to lowering of civilized standards and to degradation of human life.

Landscape architecture seeks to apply design in its fullest sense: in order to ensure the best possible adaptation of the means to an intended, carefully considered end in the new scene, we find that artistry, or visual appreciation, must act in unison with the sciences of the earth. Humanity, using the earth both as a palette and a means of livelihood, comes to see the necessity of designing creatively, not only in three dimensions but in the progression of time and change — the dynamic necessity of landscape change — depending, like evolution itself, on movement in time. Landscape growth is a long slow process: those who profess to design it need patience and experience. They have to develop a four-dimensional imagination.

In three dimensions, the artist expresses design through the media of form, colour and texture, in varying proportions related to his objective and his materials.

All these apply equally to landscape design, and though devices such as grouping, contrasts of light and shadow, punctuation and materials used are of a different scale, the artist's individual style and his power of appreciation influence all his work as in any three-dimensional design.

### RELATING FUTURE TO PAST — A FUNCTION OF DESIGN

The time dimension is an additional problem, more critical perhaps in this than in the traditional arts, because our material constantly undergoes change. The seasonal changes, the growth and ageing of plants, the effects of climate and erosion, provide problems more critical and immediate for us than for designers in other fields.

In landscape design, past and future must be related. We think not just of an area or region as now seen, but of how it came to be so: what has been its history, and how it will develop when it passes out of the designer's hands. The present is the link between past and future. Good design should ensure a stable link in the time chain so that the theme or pattern of the intention influences the whole concept and relates the new movement to its origins and general objective. The continuity of the theme, from the former changing pattern to that which will follow, and to the total heritage of civilized life, depends on the link our design forges in the chain.

Landscape design differs from other arts in that after implementation in three dimensions, the design is still immature and can only develop its full potential in course of time. The project when completed is newborn, requiring parental care to ensure its survival and development. Our designs must be adapted to the future use of the site and to the system of maintenance responsible for its care.

Design and after-care are complementary in a sense different from that of inorganic structures, because change begins inevitably from the time of planting. This time factor influences landscape design from the earliest stage, since we have to foresee not only the vegetation changes, due to season and age, but also the effects of erosion and sedimentation of land form. The future use of a landscape must determine the new form, just as much as the future use of a building determines the architecture. The vague specification 'restoration of landscape' sometimes given in planning consents is as meaningless as if an architect were required to build a structure without a brief. Is it to be a hospital, a school or a cathedral? Is the landscape to be a farm, a forest or a mountain?

## THE EARTHY PATH TO TRUTH

The skills of landscape design are largely concerned with what our eyes can see, but our work is of the Earth, earthy. Throughout the centuries of western civilization, artists have been inspired by the belief that beauty is a means of approaching truth:

'Phaedrus learnt what beauty is from
Socrates beneath the tree:
Beauty is the only form
Of spirit that the eyes can see
So brings to the outcast soul
Reflections of Divinity.'[1]

Sir Kenneth Clark in his personal view of civilization (quoting Bishop Sugar, one time Regent of France) said: 'The dull mind rises to truth through that which is material', and noted that this idea, whose western origins are seen in early Greece, is the philosophy on which our civilization was nourished.[2]

This concept is consoling for landscape architects, whose art can only be expressed in material things with definite limitations of climate and soil conditions. Other designers today may be able (and content) to express *themselves*, seeking above all originality. Instead of seeking truth in the mysterious outer world, it is being sought in the even more mysterious sub-conscious mind, which may be far from that 'beauty which our eyes can see'. By overstressing individuality and originality, the natural standard of appreciation of nature, by which truth was judged, is lost and new standards are sought.

But for all artists, including landscape architects, it is essential to find the relationship of the part to the whole: to express the truth that the whole is greater than the sum of the parts. The successful solution of this problem is, I believe, the quality above all others to which our emotions respond in any great work of art.

Landscape design recognizes in the science of ecology — that is, in the relationship of living things to their surroundings, to the other forms of life depending on the same air, soil, food and water which support all of us — the essential need to relate ourselves and our work to that greater whole. We have learnt that 'Man is one among other groups of living things, each equally important in an integrated system'. We can think of the biosphere as a single entity. That envelope of soil, air, water and all the life it supports is the flesh on the earth's rocky crust, without which the planet would be a dry skeleton like the moon; its parts, its molecules, atoms and protoplasm are interchangeable in time — and all living forms are literally in actual fact 'members one of another'.[3]

Man is a late-comer whose demise or extinction would scarcely be missed in the slow processes of evolution.

## INDIVIDUAL RESPONSIBILITY AND TEAMWORK

Dr. Bronowski has pointed out, however, that man is the only animal that is faced with a dilemma between his wishes and his integrity. We now have the power, through modern technology, to destroy ourselves and perhaps much other life in the process, if we so wish. The question we face now is: can technology be relied upon to steer us between our wishes and our integrity to safe survival? Could it be that man's future depends more than we like to admit on the quality of work and the integrity of individual decisions in every field? I believe that Clifford Tandy's presidential address to the Institute of Landscape Architects on 8 October 1973 put this same question less bluntly and with far greater artistry.[4]

We are apt to leave too much to 'them' — to the technologists and politicians — but surely it is true that each has responsibility in some degree and that at least amongst landscape architects, individuals who advise on the design and use of land, however small or however extensive, can contribute to future quality of life by creating fine and healthy landscape in the areas they influence, aiming so far as possible to conserve and promote vegetation and other forms of life. We know that animal life depends on plant life. The trees and plants we use serve to purify the air, the crops serve to provide food, but the total scene should serve not only to ensure survival, but also to bring to humanity those 'reflections of Divinity' and the consolations and joy of nature.

Although this book deals with vegetation rather than land form and all the human artefacts and other things composing the total landscape, it is essential at the start to consider landscape design 'in the round' because landscape is the setting for our lives.

Now that we are realizing this, and the rate at which the scene is being changed by human action, whether for new use or for restoration after past misuse, all changes under our control should be done as a process of conscious design, using to the full our appreciation of art as well as the best available scientific knowledge. Those of us in the land-based professions can contribute much from our various fields to the teamwork — the multiple skills of design and after-care needed to ensure development of the intention, founded on the designer's imaginative foresight.

The principles and philosophy underlying our task should be dwelt on and understood by all, whether designers, scientists or managers, however specialized their own contribution.

Unlike most other expressions of art, the basic material of design in this case is the *land* as it exists beneath our feet and on which our subsistence depends. Full appreciation of its character and needs and conditions is the foundation of our studies, as its capacity affects the future potential use.

The artist's eye can often see beneath the superficial and so sense, instinctively, further than the intellect can as yet analyse. While we make use of all that can be learnt from scientific studies, inborn instincts of balance and beauty are still the artist's lodestar.

## REFERENCES

1. Piper, M. Libretto for *Death in Venice*, opera by Benjamin Britten (London: Faber Music Ltd 1973)
2. Clark, K. *Civilisation — A Personal View* (British Broadcasting Corporation and John Murray; 1969)
3. *The Bible* — Romans Ch. 12. v.5
4. Tandy, C. R. V. 'Presidential Address to the Institute of Landscape Architects', 8 October, *Landscape Design* — Issue No. 104, November 1973.

**Aztec West Business Park, Bristol.** (Landscape Architects: *Brian Clouston & Partners*; Photograph: *Margaret Turner*)

CHAPTER 1

# Trees in the Countryside

## BRENDA COLVIN

## 1.1 ADAPTATION TO LOCALITY

The landscape architect's choice of tree species must in all cases be influenced by ecological facts. The person choosing the plant has either to limit the choice to species that are naturally adapted to the site, or else adapt the site to the species required for some other reason, whether it be aesthetic or functional. Adaptation of the site to the selected vegetation is suitable only for small plantations, usually in urban situations or areas closely related to buildings. It may involve the provision of special soil, irrigation and drainage, all to be recognised as artificial, and therefore requiring constant attention and care. The former choice, that of choosing species which are adapted to the situation, is applicable on the broad scale and is visually better suited to large scale projects, especially in open countryside. Maintenance of natural planting in the short term is less demanding, and in the long term it can be reduced to the minimum. In this chapter we are concerned with natural planting, and refer to it as ecological planting.

In the past, most conscious design of gardens and landscape was on a very small scale by comparison with the needs of the present day. The tendency to design in harmony with local conditions rather than impose a conception based on our power to dominate nature is not just a modern fashion; rather it is the result of working on this large scale. The designer may have to decide between ecological and artificial planting according to the circumstances of each project, but as our understanding of the relationships between the plant and its environment grows, so we come to a greater appreciation of the visual value of the diversity indicated by ecology. Horticulturalists and owner-gardeners seem slow to see that garden-type planting overlays and

masks nature's own scheme of diversity and interest. For that reason, if for no other, it is appropriate only on a small scale and in artificial surroundings. It is to be hoped that the general public is coming to see the importance of conserving the wonderful diversity of character in the wider landscape which is founded on the ecological facts of the land.

## 1.2 LET THE HISTORY OF THE LAND BE SEEN

Landscape reflects its geological structure and history to all who trouble to read the signs. We can help to preserve the record in our new creative work just as much as we can by simple preservation of existing features. On all large sites, especially those in or adjoining rural scenery, the outer plantations, seen from roads, railways and areas of water and from local views, can be planted according to ecological principles even if, in the interior details, concessions to popular taste are required. A graduation from 'pop planting' near the buildings to classic ecological truth on the fringes is a reasonable compromise. The function of horticultural flamboyance is to provide decoration that is pleasing to the clients and to any users of the site, and perhaps to inspire designers and test their horticultural skills. All planting should in some degree be functional, and artificially decorative planting of a garden-type is an interesting challenge which can stimulate us to demonstrate the need for good design in any medium.

In every case we should be clear in our own minds as to which function we are serving, and of the reasons for our choice, so that the long-term intention can be understood by clients and maintenance staff, and can be followed accordingly. Verbal expression of this intention should also be stated, either in the form of a report or in the plans, which will serve as a record and guide for those responsible for maintenance as the scheme matures.

For most of the British Isles, tree cover is the normal condition. Any area below the five hundred metres contour that is left to itself and protected from vandalism, grazing or other biotic factors, will revert to forest unless exposed to high gales or salt spray. It is not sufficiently recognised that trees that grow under natural conditions like these mature faster and are more securely rooted than are transplants. The only maintenance required to produce good specimens from self-sown seedlings or sucker growths is protection from damage and undue competition. Adequate protection in the early years is usually essential until the trees are well established. Self-propagated groups of this type that are protected and thinned to selected specimens should give excellent and natural-looking spinneys and woodland. In the UK the Forestry Commission and other landowners are realising the advantages of the system: under suitable circumstances, timber of economic value can be produced, but for amenity and landscape values, where timber is of secondary importance, natural regeneration has a greater potential which has too often been overlooked.

PLATE 1.1 **Natural regeneration of beech woods showing two different stages of growth.** *(Forestry Commission)*

## 1.3 SELF-SOWN VEGETATION

The general public and others, such as architects, developers, engineers and even planners, tend to regard all young growth as scrub to be cleared before starting new work. Amenity societies often advise planting new trees in places where unnoticed, existing saplings would serve their purpose better. Many of our older hedgerows contain thousands of young ash, field maple, oak or other saplings which could develop into fine tree groups if not quite to fine timber. Disused waste ground, when it is closely examined, will often be found to contain enough seedling trees to form effective woodland without further planting. Old railways, parade grounds and marshalling yards harbour saplings capable of fine maturity if they are protected and are cared for properly. These natural growths do not transplant well, and they can only survive if ground levels remain unchanged, but their existence should be recorded in preliminary site investigation and appraisal. Existing features can in many cases influence the design and treatment of new developments. Given due care and attention, undisturbed areas with their ability to regenerate can speed up the establishment of new landscapes and can reduce planting costs.

Young trees adapt more easily than old trees to conditions of changing drainage and irrigation. Much of the trouble that is taken to preserve old established trees can be wasted if the tree is unable to adapt to drier conditions due to changes in drainage levels in the course of development. Where any such risk is apparent, understudy planting of similar species is advisable. In many cases, it would be wise to adapt the layout of the design to existing young saplings rather than to the older mature trees. For the short-term effect, we can add large nursery-grown trees, remembering that even these would be outstripped by self-sown or sucker growths in, say, about fifteen years.

## 1.4 DESIGN FOR BOTH SHORT-TERM AND LONG-TERM EFFECT

For the sake of ensuring quick effects as well as long-term growth, we can use more than one method to start with (such as a mixture of large stock and forest seedlings); on the assumption that time will prove which is best and that those responsible for maintenance will decide on the correct thinning to bring about the designer's intention. Maintenance schedules that indicate this are essential in such cases, but since even the most detailed instructions cannot ensure the development of long-term schemes, designers tend to rely on permanent planting of semi-mature trees at the outset. Improved training of landscape managers and closer co-operation between them and designers should advance the art of landscape design in the future. Designers could make much better use of mixed systems

PLATE 1.2 **Trimbley Reservoir. New use of previous farmland on the River Severn, combining industry and recreation in what can still appear as a clearing in a forest. Public footpaths do not conflict with sheep grazing so that some agricultural use can continue, and the cost of maintenance of the land is reduced.** *(Hal Moggridge)*

of planting if they could feel sure that their final intention is understood and likely to be correctly developed by the maintenance team. As an example of past failures in this respect, the case of a war memorial garden on Wimbledon Common in South London can be quoted. Miss Madeline Agar was commissioned in the 1920s to design the grounds around a First World War memorial. She planned concentric rings of English oak with a lot of undisturbed ground between for its long-term objective, but for short-term, public use she super-imposed over the long-term plan an additional scheme of winding paths with flowering trees and shrubs to make an immediate effect. That was before the days of semi-mature tree planting. The short-term scheme was intended to be temporary, and should have been removed when the oaks were nearing maturity. Instead, the small oaks were sacrificed as soon as they began to threaten the lilacs and laburnums, although sensitive thinning could have preserved both until the oaks, nearing maturity, could have proved the long-term value of her choice.

Moisture conditions are a governing factor in choosing species, and are often of more importance than soil types. Species such as willow, alder and poplar, commonly found along the banks of rivers and streams, create the character of many valley regions. Their appearance suggests the lush fertility of waterbone soils that are deep, moist and rich in humus and minerals, just as the appearance of gorse and pine suggests the sandy uplands and thin soils which are periodically dry. Their use in design conveys a mood and sets the scenic character of an area. Even if, for special reasons, we do not keep strictly to native species, the character can be retained by the use of introduced species which harmonise so well with the native plants that they do not appear intrusive. This, however, calls for experience and sensitive judgment on the part of the designer.

## 1.5 LOCAL CHARACTER

There are obvious advantages in keeping to the local species in many cases: they blend well with the scenery and help to give new projects the appearance of belonging to their setting, and they are more likely in many

9

instances to suit local conditions than are introduced species. This, however, is not a rule to be applied under all circumstances: there may be excellent reasons for preferring exotics in special cases, where their appearance does not strike a discordant note and when they have become adapted to the local ecosystem. In the UK many species (like the sycamore) have become firmly established and are quite capable of competing with species which are strictly indigenous even though they were probably introduced by man. Many introduced trees and shrubs endure sea gales as well as, or better than, natives. Several introduced pines are invaluable for shelter, as is the evergreen oak, *Quercus ilex*, in coastal areas not liable to very severe frosts, and provided that these are not planted in a way to dominate or eliminate the local vegetation, our mild interference with an ecosystem is no more than a normal biotic factor.

It may be more useful to study the natural habit of growth of local vegetation than to note the particular species of which it is composed. The grouping, and the way groups are shaped by wind, give us clear indications of the spacing, sizes of plants needed, and the width of plantations in windswept sites. In windy sites it is also important to note the extent and direction of shelter provided by plantations. Local observations of this sort are usually a better indication of which species to plant and how to adjust to special sites than all the books and scientific research on the subject, as every site has individual and special circumstances which must influence our designs and choice of species. These circumstances are often well known to local inhabitants, and their opinions can thus be of great value.

Some general characteristics of native vegetation are generally applicable, however, being the result of the climate and soils of our land. For example, the fringes of woods and open glades harbour a richer variety of smaller trees, shrubs and herbs than the forest interior which may be composed mainly of tall timber trees without shrubby undergrowth. In this case the woodland fringe provides the chosen home for the great majority of wildlife, birds, insects and mammals. It also provides shelter for the ground inside and encourages the growth of seedling trees. The close compact grouping of these fringes provides an example we do well to follow when possible, especially where wind shelter is needed. It helps to deter trespass, to encourage the establishment of songbirds, butterflies and all the rest of the wildlife now threatened with extinction, and in many cases it enables the designer to give pleasing definition to the shapes of open spaces such as playing fields and community grounds whose pragmatic outlines are apt to be visually boring and monotonous. Our open spaces can be designed as the equivalent of the glades formed in the forest under natural conditions by the decay of ancient tree groups or changes of groundwater level, gales and other natural events.

Another characteristic of natural grouping which we would do well to study is the interrelation and mixture of species, usually found in groups which have become self-established. Pure stands or monocultures, as we have seen, are rare in nature: yet the mixture is usually formed of groups rather than of individuals. The groups may show strong contrasts and diversity, depending on small-scale local differences of land form, soil type, drainage, temperature and so on. Such ecological guidelines are an excellent example worth studying for application in our designs.

## 1.6 ECOLOGICAL PLANTING

Our reasons for ecological planting, especially in the case of trees, may be summed up as follows:

1. Conservation
2. Appearance
3. Diversity
4. Economy (capital cost and long-term maintenance).

These four reasons are closely linked, but while for the purposes of future maintenance the first and fourth are to be stressed, all four should be considered in any design.

## Conservation

In landscape, conservation implies the design and maintenance of a self-perpetuating environment — not changeless, since all life implies change, but in perpetual balance as it exists in nature. *Homo sapiens* evolved along with other forms of life in the primitive environment which nature provided: the species has recently acquired the power to disturb the balance of nature. Arrogant in our power, we forget that our race was cradled in that natural setting and that while life could continue to exist without our 'sapience' we cannot survive alone. We can destroy in a few years the conditions which through untold millennia adapted nature to our existence.

## Appearance

The link between conservation and visual appearance is the fact that the human ambition to dominate nature can only partly be indulged by working with natural forces. The most successful landscape creations, whether they be the gardens of Buddhist temples, the parks of Le Nôtre or the English landscape gardens of Kent, Brown and Repton, are capable of survival in so far as they were designed with understanding of the forces of nature and obeyed nature's laws: that is to say on an ecological basis.

The more we learn about the working of the life cycle, the greater grows our appreciation of the visual results in the landscape. With greater understanding, we come to feel the meaning of the natural grouping more deeply. Understanding of the relationship between vegetation and ground formation to the structure and nature of the underlying rocks, and to climatic influences, reinforces and develops our natural appreciation. It appears that many intuitive responses are based on our physical relationship to all that lives and breathes, and to human dependence on the same material things and unchanging laws that govern the rest of life.

## Diversity

The third reason for ecological planting is the need for broad scale diversity. Diversity is not the least important of nature's laws. Its relationship to scale is perhaps the most difficult problem for man to master. We know that monoculture is unhealthy, but how large an area do we regard as monoculture? Nature's diversity is not a haphazard mixture, it is all organized in a cellular pattern, but in a pattern with no tiresome repetition: no two crystals are alike. The perpetuation of natural forest depends on constant variation in the size and shape of the open glades and fringes, lakes and river valleys in a long, slow cycle of alternating mass and void. The human eye responds instinctively to this natural fact, but our minds are still struggling to learn how it can be applied in planting design. We are aware that monotonous repetition of a form, of a sound or of any unit, however beautiful in itself becomes unbearable to our senses if it is repeated endlessly. Yet our housing estates and our factories (urban and rural)

prove our present inability to design diversity on the scale of natural laws. Painters, sculptors and other artists make full use of diversity within a whole conception on that scale: the difficulty arises when the scale of the whole gets beyond their experience. Then we reach the scale of natural landscape and find that a new approach and a new art is needed, and that the future of our race depends on our ability to adapt our creative faculty to nature's laws in the development of that art. Our diversification must not be haphazard: each unit must have a clear relationship to a whole, but unlike the edge of a canvas or the mass of sculpted stone, the boundaries, limitations and the scale of the whole are often indeterminate or controversial.

One of the limitations is the passage of time, and here the aesthetic design is linked to our fourth down-to-earth reason for ecological planting, namely economy.

## Economy

This fourth reason depends on those given above. If our objective, for the other reasons listed, is that of a self-perpetuating environment, then economy can reinforce and strengthen the reasons for ecological planting in the long term, if not in capital cost, though both should play a part. In the longer cycles, economy in landscape maintenance far outweighs capital cost, and though as yet proof of this statement may be lacking, those experienced in the field cannot doubt that research could provide and will be available, to give authentic figures to illustrate its truth.

In the wild, nature ensures a self-perpetuating system

PLATE 1.3 **View towards White Horse Hill. On the slopes the typical chalkland vegetation is seen, including juniper on the left. In the distance, the lines of hedgerow and roadside verge link spinneys and shelter groups, forming a green network which favours wildlife of all kinds and creates a lovely scene.** *(Hal Moggridge)*

through reproduction by seed or suckers from parent plants. Of course, the system works only if the parent plants are suited to the soil and other environmental factors. Evolution through countless generations has brought this about and each local ecosystem is a balanced continuum, with flora, fauna and all forms of life adapted to its soil and climate and to each other's survival. Human needs for changes of land use disrupt this balance and, impatient for quick results, we often fail to see the need to preserve or reinstate it even where that would be an economic possibility. We could make much better use than we do of nature's extravagance by following the local ecosystem as far as other circumstances of the project permit.

The shapes resulting from existing local differences, so different from the geometric shapes of human habit and habitation, are typical of new attitudes towards landscape design. Approaching the problem with an understanding of the advantages of working with, rather than against nature, a more humble view of our relationship with nature opens up a vast field of new discovery and endeavour to us.

Vegetation relates closely to ground shape. Even half a metre of vertical difference may indicate a change of planting in low-lying land. The interesting curve of a contour line may be emphasized by a change of vegetation, and such effects can be purposely designed to suit the pragmatic requirements of the plan. As an example of this kind, I would mention a site where the ground level of a car park was so close to a saline water table that shrubs and trees could only thrive if they were planted on raised ground. The screening required for the car park indicated modelling of surrounding banks to give enough dry root run to suit the shrubs and trees that were needed.

## 1.7 PLANT ASSOCIATIONS

The typical plant associations found on most British landscape types have a characteristic charm so differentiated that one can judge most soil types by their vegetation, and even assess fairly closely the pH value of a given area. The lovely mixture of yew and whitebeam accompanied by wayfaring tree, spindle and blackthorn occurs typically on the shallow soils of chalk hillsides, just as pine and heather typify thin acid soils and podsols, while oak, holly and hazel thrive on the heavier clays. The field maple occurs most abundantly on various limestones, with crab-apples and honeysuckle. The valleys and water courses, the marshes, fens and commons, each have their typical trees and shrubs accompanied by herbaceous species and ground flora associated with the familiar trees. This aspect of the subject cannot be covered in depth in a brief chapter. We can all learn from the landscape we see, and by reading the work of ecologists such as Tansley, whose *The British Islands and their Vegetation* is a mine

of information invaluable for the British landscape designer. Ian McHarg's book *Design with Nature* is a thought-provoking inspiration for landscape architects and points the way to improvement of our professional work.

## 1.8 HEDGE HISTORY OF THE UK

Much new knowledge available recently, particularly in regard to the historic associations and relics of former forest vegetation, enables us to date the hedges and, through them, the land tenure and parish boundaries of former settlements. A whole new range of knowledge on these matters is opening up which may influence our thinking on matters of design. Of the former forest once covering the British Isles, these relics in the form of hedges, shelter belts, woods and parks remain, and are a last refuge for the wildlife of the old forests. We now know that the older a hedge is, the greater its wealth of native vegetation and fauna. Hedges and the verges of roads, railways and waterways are important links in a web enabling the movement and migration of many living species which are unable to cross large unbroken tracts of urban development or cultivated areas. The continuity of a web or network of vegetation, connecting town and country, from coast to coast, has great conservation value. In many areas the fields are too small and the hedges too abundant for modern needs. Often larger enclosures may be visually preferable, but to destroy the whole pattern is a ruthless and unnecessary extreme that will surely be regretted in the future: the broad national implications of conservation are not at variance with fine landscape. Farmers, planners and landscape designers can seek the proper balance in their individual areas, respecting the economic sizes of enclosures, but aiming to keep the older historic hedges as links in the web of conservation. The green lines of shelter belt, hedge or towpath, linking spinneys, woodlands and parks, give a more pleasing composition than unrelated scattered items.

This is a case where experience and study reinforce the artist's intuitive response. Intellect and intuition are not always so clearly in step, but this checking of the relationship between art and science is inherent in the discipline of landscape design.

### FURTHER READING

Colvin, B. *Land and Landscape* (London: John Murray, 2nd edition 1970)

Colvin, B. *Trees for Town and Country* (London: Lund Humphries, 4th edition 1972)

Fairbrother, N. *The Nature of Landscape Design* (London: Architectural Press 1974)

Haywood, S. M. *Quarries and the Landscape* (London: The British Quarrying and Slag Federation Ltd 1974)

Hoskins, W. G. *The Making of the English Landscape* (London: Hodder and Stoughton 1955)

Jellicoe, G. *Studies in Landscape Design* (Oxford: University Press 1960, 1966, 1970)

Lovejoy, D. (Ed.) *Land Use and Landscape Planning* (Aylesbury: Leonard Hill 1973)

McHarg, I. L. *Design with Nature* (New York: The Natural History Press, Garden City 1969)

Mitchell, A. *A Field Guide to the Trees of Britain and Northern Europe* (London: Collins 1974)

Rackham, D. *Trees and Woodland in the British Landscape* (London: Dent 1976)

Rackham, D. *Ancient Woodland: Its History, Vegetation and Use in England* (London: Edward Arnold 1980)

Rackham, D. *The History of the Countryside* (London: Dent 1986)

Tansley, A. G. *The British Islands and their Vegetation* (Cambridge: University Press 1939)

13

# CHAPTER 2

# Planting for Forestry

## DAME SYLVIA CROWE AND GORDON PATTERSON

Forests are no exception to the rule that the beauty of the landscape and ecological health go hand in hand. Their contribution in both respects can be very great, provided that planting and maintenance are directed to these ends.

## 2.1 THE NEED FOR AFFORESTATION

In the present man-eroded landscape of countries such as Britain, strong positive action is needed to reverse the impoverishment of what was once a well-forested country.

Under favourable and stable conditions, forests are self-perpetuating and will develop and retain the climax vegetation for their particular environment. However, even without direct human action, this climax may be arrested or regeneration prevented by some outside intervention; for instance grazing animals, usually but not necessarily introduced by man, may prevent regeneration. There may be climatic changes or other natural hazards; for instance, certain forests in the western United States, whose true climax species is spruce, remain permanently at the arrested climax of Lodgepole pine (*Pinus contorta*) owing to naturally-generated fires.

PLATE 2.1 **Different species drifting into each other, Aberfoyle.** (*Sylvia Crowe*)

PLATE 2.2 **Indigenous silver birch giving light to a conifer crop. The effect would be better still if the birch had been allowed to drift into the forest on the far side of the road. Allen Forest, Perthshire.** *(Forestry Commission)*

It cannot therefore be assumed that a forest will necessarily either perpetuate itself or develop into its climax vegetation, even in a state of nature. When the effects of human intervention are taken into account, the prospects of regeneration are much reduced, and man must often take steps to counteract the effects of his past actions. A typical case is that of the Scottish Highlands, where regeneration is prevented both by grazing of sheep and deer and by the degraded condition of the soil, caused by generations of over-grazing and over-burning. Forest planting must therefore be seen as a means of repairing past ecological impoverishment as well as maintaining and increasing the biological richness and landscape quality of such woodlands as still exist.

Perhaps the most significant aspect of our appreciation of the woodland scene lies in its shape. The size and outline of a component element of the forest will often determine its character.

The shape of the outer edge of a plantation also has important consequences, not only for the satisfactory appearance of individual parcels of forest, but also, and often more importantly, in helping to link the forest with its neighbouring areas.

## 2.2 THE FOREST HABITAT

Forests provide a greater range of habitats than any other type of plant association. Their vertical range extends from deep into the soil up to one hundred feet above ground level. Within this area, dependent life-forms range from organisms on the roots to birds roosting in the tree tops.

The main divisions of the forest habitat are classified by Tansley in his book *Britain's Green Mantle* as the canopy, the shrub layer, the field layer and the ground layer. To this should be added the root system, which, functioning at varying depths, plays a vital part in recycling the water and nutrients upon which all plant growth depends. The ecological richness of woodlands depends on their composition both in species and age. The variations between different species in this respect is considerable. The oak has by far the greatest number of associated species. It is host to a great many insects (and hence to birds), its leaf-fall is rich and its open canopy encourages the growth of shrubs and a field layer. Ash is less prolific in the number of organisms that it supports directly, but its light foliage also encourages growth on the forest floor.

Beech scores only moderately as a host, and its deep shade excludes all but a few shrubs and forest flowers. Its leaf-fall, while enriching alkaline soils, does less to improve acid soils. Spruce is even more inhibiting to undergrowth since its shade persists through the year and also contributes little to soil improvement. Larch, on the other hand, with its deciduous nature, lighter foliage and softer needles, is far more hospitable and produces a richer field layer and greater soil improvement.

Diversity in the age of trees adds to the richness of the forest's ecology. Some wildlife favours young trees in the thicket stage, birds nest high in the branches of tall trees and some, such as the woodpecker, need old dead wood. The shrub layer and the edge bordering open glades are favoured by a great variety of birds.

The wide range of habitats provided by a mixed-age natural forest, or by one managed on a system of selective felling, may be equalled or even exceeded by a timber forest managed on a system of clear felling, provided this felling is planned in size and shape on a basis of conservation. A maximum of edge can be provided by well-contrived felling coupes, and the clear-felled areas will produce a spectacular flush of forest flowers.

Remnant trees, that is those trees that are often left in isolation after a crop has been harvested, can sometimes provide a resting place for larger visiting birds. Raptors will often take refuge in solitary coniferous species. Older deciduous trees, as well as attracting a great variety of insects and lower plants, have a charm which adds greatly to a sense of place in an otherwise new plantation.

## 2.3 THE SCALE OF THE FOREST MOSAIC

A mosaic of different-aged stands of trees gives great beauty as well as the widest range of habitats. This mosaic, however, can work on varying scales, and it is in the interests of the landscape that it should do so. The smallest scale is one of mixed-age, mixed-species woodland on a fertile soil, which will support a wide range of plant species which, it their turn, will support a wide range of fauna. Visually, such a woodland will be interesting and pleasant and will almost certainly fit easily into its surroundings. But if all forests were of this type we should lose some of our most satisfying landscapes, and certain bird and animal species might lose the particular type of habitat they need. Pure, or almost pure stands of a single species can have a beauty and character of their own. A beech wood may have a limited range of associated species, but it is surpassingly beautiful, seen both from within and without. The clear statement of beech climax forest could only be lessened by introducing mixed planting. The occasional sub-dominant gean (*Cerasus avium*), however, is insufficient

PLATE 2.3 **Indigenous species adding conservation value to a forest. Soudly Ponds, Forest of Dean.** *(Forestry Commission)*

PLATE 2.4 **A single species forest has a different type of beauty than does one of mixed species.** (*Forestry Commission*)

to break the unity of the beech canopy, and can be an added spring delight. On chalklands, whitebeam and yew will often colonize the edge of the beechwood, giving a perfect transition to the surrounding landscape.

A closed canopy of oak may be less spectacular than beech, but it has great character in texture and colour. Sessile oakwoods, clothing steep hillsides, can be a vital part of a strong hill landscape, which would be weakened by breaking up the closely patterned texture of the oak canopy. The same clear statement, which needs no blurring, can be found within a stand of mature Douglas Fir or spruce and, as a final example, the Redwood grove in California has the majesty and splendour of a cathedral.

Pure stands are still part of a mosaic, but in larger units than that of a mixed forest. The precise scale of the mosaic in every case needs to be studied from both the visual and ecological angle. Close attention to change of soil and micro-climate will often provide the guide.

Unforeseen circumstances, such as windblow or fire, can play havoc with considerations of scale as it affects our appreciation of the forest scene. If this occurs with unsatisfactory results, it may become necessary to fell or reshape adjacent or additional areas, in order to re-establish balance.

It has not always been considered expedient, for largely economic reasons, to retain trees beyond their normal rotation period. However, the benefit of doing this in landscape terms in maintaining stately veteran trees should not be underestimated. The Californian Redwoods may seem a far cry, but the magnificence of the large Douglas Fir in Coed y Brenin or the great Scots Pine of Glen Affric are markers for a future heritage.

## 2.4 THE DIFFERING ROLES OF FORESTS

Whether planting new woodlands or managing and restocking old ones, the particular contribution which they can make to the landscape, the community and to conservation should be decided. Soil improvement, shelter, wild life conservation and appearance can and should be served by all woodlands whatever their other functions. Additional values will usually include timber production and often recreation. The relative weight given to these objectives will vary, and will influence forest planting and management. A natural forest managed as a nature reserve will require very different treatment from that appropriate to a timber-producing forest.

## Timber-producing forests

In forests planted and managed primarily for timber there are obviously constraints which do not arise if the prime objects are landscape beauty and conservation.

PLATE 2.5 **Forests provide an interior landscape. New Forest, ancient and ornamental.** *(Forestry Commission)*

PLATE 2.6 **Interior landscape: the Lime Avenue, Santon Downham, Thetford.** *(Forestry Commission)*

The degree of these constraints will vary according to the species of the timber crop. It is much easier to achieve a richly varied woodland, fitting naturally into the landscape, in those areas where oak can be grown as the timber crop, rather than where spruce is the only viable choice. Nevertheless, some practices are applicable to all forests. The varied age group and carefully designed felling coupes are cases in point. (A large square area of thicket-stage oak is no more beautiful than one of thicket-stage spruce.) The admission of light to edges, thinning trees at the sides of rides, giving space and light to stream sides, leaving certain topographical features unplanted and encouraging the 'volunteer species' which may appear, such as rowan or birch, are all practices which add to the landscape and conservation values of forests, whatever the timber crop may be. Fine examples may be seen in some of the newer forests of East Anglia, at Thetford and Alder Wood.

However, since a species such as spruce will not by itself encourage the diversity or, to most eyes, provide the beauty of a deciduous forest, more positive action needs to be taken to ensure changes of species to give visual and ecological diversity. Birch and rowan on the poorer outcrops, alders in the wet hollows or larch on bracken-covered hillsides, can transform a monotonous spruce forest into a place of interest and bring the landscape to life by responding to the changing seasons instead of maintaining the same general tone throughout the year, as well as emphasizing the subtle changes of terrain.

The deciduous leaf-fall will enrich the degraded soil and there are other ecological advantages in diversity, as well as the obvious reduction in fire and pest risk. For instance, it has been found that clearings forming deer lawns that are planted with alder and willow will provide browse for the deer, thereby diverting them from the young crop trees.

## 2.5 WOODLANDS AS VISUAL ELEMENTS IN THE LANDSCAPE

There are two visual aspects of woodland: one is the interior, to be experienced by walking within the canopy of trees, and the other is external, seeing the woodland

19

as part of a wider landscape. Forests are the only type of landscape, except perhaps canyons, which can be enjoyed from within, giving the same sense of containment as the interior of a great building. The closed, high canopy of trees nearing maturity gives this sensation to the full. This interior view is looked after almost entirely by following the precepts of sound conservation and providing the varied experiences given by the mosaic patterns previously mentioned.

Passing from the enclosure of high forest to open views over unplanted land or young crops is an aesthetic experience of high quality. The external view requires, in addition, careful attention to the siting, shape and composition of the wood. Since woodlands form a definite, three-dimensional element in the landscape, they are a dominant feature and need to be related sympathetically to the land form and the general landscape pattern. Their colour and texture is almost as important as their shape.

PLATE 2.7 **Sheep and deer grazing have prevented natural regeneration of the Old Caledonian Pine Forest. It can be restored by protection and replanting.** *(Forestry Commission)*

Deciduous woodland in an agricultural landscape, similar in texture to the network of hedges in which they stand, forms nodal points in a unified pattern. The continuing loss of hedgerows in agricultural land is eroding this network and node pattern. However, in some parts of the country an enlarged alternative can be seen, with belts of trees and scrub drifting out from small areas of woodland, along gullies or on thin-soiled ridges. If the nodal woodlands in either pattern are of conifers they will form a strongly accented and less restful pattern. Alternatively, there may be a pattern formed by drifting the deciduous trees into the mainly coniferous heart of the woodlands. In a landscape predominantly of hardwoods, a group of Scots pine on a hilltop can form the strongest feature for miles around. An almost equal accentuation of topography can be given by a drift of dark Douglas fir in the re-entrant of a valley. In conifer country, the deciduous relief of larch drifting over the breast of a hill can lighten a whole landscape, as can the native birch and rowan clothing the rocky knolls on a mountainside.

Examples of this blending of timber crop and native vegetation can be seen on some Scottish hillsides, such as those flanking Loch Garvie, a welcome contrast to other hillsides completely blanketed by conifer crops, and at Grizedale Forest in the Lake District National Park.

There are, however, some strong, hard, landscapes such as the Border country, where clean-cut windbreaks of conifers, provided they are well-placed and shaped, are as much in character with their surroundings as are the deciduous small woodlands of southern England with their softer landscape.

## 2.6 PLANTING MIXTURES

The object of planting in mixtures may either be to produce a mixed woodland, or to raise the climax tree within a nurse crop which will subsequently be removed. A nurse crop is desirable for many hardwoods, and necessary for beech. The silvicultural reason for the nurse crop is to protect and draw up the main crop. The economic reason is to provide a short-term timber crop by felling the nurse trees when they have achieved their silvicultural purpose.

Various methods of mixture by lines or groups are practised. The worst from a landscape point of view is the vertical 'pyjama stripe', which should never be used and is particularly unfortunate when seen on steep hillsides. In a permanently mixed forest, there may be either an overall mixture of species, or separate areas of each species. Either method can form a good landscape, but in the case of separate blocks the shapes need to be well related to the topography and landscape pattern, and the species drifted into each other as would occur in natural woodland. Separate hard-

PLATE 2.8 **Pine tree over Maddum Lake, North Jutland, Denmark.** *(Preben Jakobsen)*

outlined compartments of different species never look natural, and when the shapes fail to accord with the land form they can be positively ugly.

Where a secondary species is planted to improve the appearance and ecological diversity of the main timber crop, the secondary species should be carefully sited for maximum effect. A narrow fringe of hardwoods round a conifer plantation should be avoided. Drifts breaking into the main crop from the edge will be more effective. These drifts should relate to topography, accentuating ridges, valleys, stream sides and other natural features.

Planting should thin out at the edge of plantations, allowing indigenous species to establish themselves and give a natural transition to the surrounding landscape. This practice also helps to establish a wind-firm edge and a very rich wildlife habitat. A forest managed for timber on a felling and replanting regime can incorporate a network of permanent cover along exposed margins, the sides of rides, steep valleys and rocky ridges. This ecologically rich network will serve equally the interests of conservation and good landscape.

## 2.7 SPECIES NATIVE TO BRITAIN

The list of native trees commonly planted in UK forests is very short: oak (*Quercus* species), beech (*Fagus sylvatica*), ash (*Fraxinus excelsior*), Scots pine (*Pinus sylvestris*), to which may be added the old-established aliens, sycamore (*Acer pseudoplatanus*) and sweet chestnut (*Castanea sativa*). If dutch elm disease dies out, elm can be added to the list of native timbers, while aspen and lime are grown locally.

There is, however, a far wider range of native forest shrubs and smaller trees which form the associated plant communities of the climax trees and which can be introduced and encouraged in new plantations. Many of these are both beautiful and very rich providers for wildlife.

Alder (*Alnus glutinosa*) will colonize stream sides and damp hollows over a wide range of soil and climate. It is a soil improver and a source of food for wild fowl and deer. The flat-topped growth of the mature tree and the pattern of its catkins have the quality of Chinese

21

painting. *Salix caprea*, often its companion in the damp valleys, is spectacular in the spring and an attraction to bees. It is also the food plant of the Purple Emperor butterfly. *Viburnum opulus*, a native of damp oak-woods, is equally attractive. Where light penetrates the forest edge hawthorn, wild rose and blackthorn will be found, while throughout the oak forest hazel and the occasional wild crab, both important sources of food for wildlife, may be seen.

While these attractive native shrubs can easily be recognized as desirable plants for the forest, it should also be realized that plants that are often regarded as weeds are vital to wild life. The common bramble is one of the richest sources of food, providing winter browse for deer among other things.

In the highland regions, birch (which is second only to the oak in richness of associated species) and the beautiful rowan will colonize the poorest ground. Given time and helpful management, a newly planted forest will develop the shrub and field layer and associated trees natural to the soil and climate. In the case of birch and rowan, if seed parents are present, the colonization will be so speedy that it is only necessary to leave appropriate areas free from the crop tree and protected from grazing. Any unplanted area within the forest fence will quickly be colonized. In other cases, where seed parents are absent or propagation of the species by seed is less prolific, the plant associations can be planted to hasten the establishment of a whole and balanced forest ecology.

## 2.8 SPECIES INTRODUCED TO BRITAIN

Great Britain has an unusually short list of native species. This is due to severance from the European land mass before species driven south by the last ice age had time to recolonize in the wake of the retreating ice. On the other hand, the temperate climate and great variety of soil types provide favourable conditions for growing a very wide range of species from other parts of the world. Under these circumstances it is inevitable that many species from overseas have been introduced. A correct decision on when and where to plant the introduced species is not always easy. Arguments against introductions can be both visual and ecological, but they may also be the result of prejudice.

Established native ecosystems may be thrown out of balance by introduced species. One example is the introduction of *Rhododendron ponticum* into woodland where it has become an invasive weed, stifling forest flora and preventing natural regeneration of the trees. Other introductions have been assimilated without detriment to the ecology and with benefit to the landscape. We would be sorry to lose the sweet chestnut or the walnut.

For visual as well as scientific reasons, there are advantages in retaining different types of native wood-land in different situations, thus ensuring the survival of special ecosystems and giving a sense of place to different parts of the world. Introduced species can blur these distinct characteristics and end by creating a dull similarity everywhere. This has happened to a large extent over the last few decades in Great Britain by the 'enrichment' of lowland hardwood forests with introduced conifers; it must be hoped that this trend will cease and that the typical hardwoods will be given pride of place, but this is unlikely to occur unless sound financial incentives are provided.

There are, however, situations where introduced species will serve some specific purpose for which no native plant is suitable. *Robinia pseudoacacia* is a valuable tree for restoring lost fertility and Corsican pine is usually a better species for stabilizing sand dunes than the Scots pine, and also withstands pollution better in industrial areas. Overgrazed and overburnt areas in the Highlands will not allow the species which once grew there to develop into timber trees, but these lands can be far more easily colonized by species from the Pacific coast of America, notably Sitka spruce on wet peat and Lodgepole pine on harder ground. *Nothofagus* in the Welsh hills, red oak (*Quercus rubra*) on drier soils or Norway maple (*Acer platanoides*) on alkaline soils, have all been found capable of producing better timber than native hardwoods in similar situations, and can all be considered welcome additions to our forest trees.

In all these cases where a new need or changed growing conditions make introduced species more suitable than natives, it is reasonable to plant them, and indeed to search out any new source of supply which may fill genuine need. But where the native species will flourish they should be given preference and allowed to form the characteristic landscapes of the countryside, otherwise there is danger that our whole landscape will merge into one huge, muddled arboretum. Where there is a valid reason for using exotics, their effect on the soil and the ecological systems should be carefully watched so that any harmful side effects may be counteracted.

The few remaining natural woodlands should certainly be conserved, although to achieve this replanting may be necessary. In the case of the Caledonian pine forests, the degeneration of the ground and depredations of deer have prevented regeneration, and seedlings have to be raised in a nursery and planted out.

A truly natural condition scarcely exists in the British Isles, where the choice is either to work with the inherited forest ecology or, where necessary, to change it deliberately. Wistman's Wood on Dartmoor is perhaps the best example of a primeval deciduous oak woodland. The timeless quality of the pines of Glen Affric has already been mentioned, and the dangers of a 'do nothing' policy should be apparent enough.

We have a responsibility to plant and manage forests in a way which will increase the richness and the stability of the land, while adding to its beauty and providing an awareness towards the need for living landscapes for the future.

## FURTHER READING

Campbell, D. 'Landscape Design in Forestry', *Landscape Design* No. 166 (April), p. 31 (1987)

Countryside Commission *Forestry in the Countryside* (1987)

Crowe, Sylvia *Forestry in the Landscape* (London: HMSO third impression with amendments 1972)

Crowe S. *The Landscape of Forests and Woods*, Forestry Commission Booklet No. 44 (1978)

Edlin, H. *Broadleaves*, Forestry Commission Booklet No. 20, 2nd edition (1985)

Forestry Commission (undated) *Forestry Facts* (leaflet series) : (1) 'Forestry Policy since 1919', (2) 'The Forestry Commission', (3) 'Timber Production in Britain', (4) 'Forestry in the Environment'

Forestry Commission *British Forestry* (1986)

Hibberd, B. G. *Forestry Practice*, Forestry Commission Bulletin No. 14 (1986)

Holliday, S. 'In Defence of the Forests', *Landscape Design* No. 166 (April), p. 37 (1987)

Mitchell, A. *Conifers*, Forestry Commission Booklet No. 15, 3rd edition (1985)

Steele, R. C. *Wildlife conservation in woodlands* (London: HMSO 1972)

Tansley, A. G. (Ed. Proctor, M. C. F) *Britain's Green Mantle* (London: George Allen and Unwin Ltd, 2nd edition, 1968)

CHAPTER 3

# Trees in Urban Areas

## GORDON PATTERSON

### 3.1 INTRODUCTION

Most of us gladly accept the tree as part of the urban scene. Many of our cities, towns and, especially, our villages owe much of their character to the incidental use of vegetation within them. Trees are an important part of the townscape, and one of the most interesting and effective design elements which the landscape architect has at his or her disposal. Perhaps this happy acceptance of something seemingly so inessential to the basic business of living (although many of us have enjoyed tree houses in our time) stems from some deep desire within all of us, if not to get back to the primaeval forests, at least to identify with the natural order of things. We all feel the need to be made aware from time to time of the way the seasons alter, contrasting with the otherwise dull repetition of the everyday routine and scene. How often we hear the more fortunate city dweller praising the virtues of a tree-lined boulevard or the seclusion and privacy afforded by a tree-bound square. Such delights should be regarded not as the privilege of the few but as a universal necessity to be found in all parts of our towns and cities.

Many of our ideas about the place of trees in the

PLATE 3.1 **Heavy shade provided by lime trees in Tivoli Gardens, Copenhagen, contrasts with the bright sunlight of the space around the fountain, and frames the view.**

PLATE 3.2 **A row of willow trees recently planted in paving at Surrey Quays, London Docklands.** (Landscape Architects: *Brian Clouston*; Photographer: *K. Stansfield*)

urban environment stem from the traditions of the past, and in this respect England has a particularly rich heritage. The open quality of Cambridge and Bath or the London parks immediately springs to mind, and the great tract of river and downland which runs into the heart of the city of Bristol is an inspiring example of the integration of town and countryside.

Not all towns have been so fortunate, but most exhibit some feature of landscaping with trees and with natural attributes, whether it be in the form of the tree-lined avenues once so popular in towns that streets were lined to the horizon, or whether it is in the one fair-sized park which served the whole of an industrial town. In this way the patterns of open space in towns have been created. Changing fashions and opinions limit the extent to which the past can provide inspiration for the future, but we should not ignore the many historical examples which owed their creation to a vision and a genius which have stood the test of time.

## 3.2 THE EFFECT OF TREES ON THE URBAN ENVIRONMENT

There are, of course, purely visual pleasures to be derived from looking at individual trees. But in urban scenes it is more often the visual play of a mass of natural foliage contrasted with the built forms which is important and which adds up to a sum that in total is greater than that of its parts.

Trees provide contrasts of colour, texture and form in a built environment, introducing the shapes, colours and feelings for nature into the man-made geometric patterns of roads and buildings.

In the change of colour with the passing of the seasons, trees provide endless variety and delight, with fresh greenery and gay blossoms in spring, swollen globes of foliage casting heavy shade in summer, ripening fruit and seed and vivid autumn colours. Even in winter, those which shed their leaves still provide visual pleasure in the delicate sculpture of naked branches casting intricate shadows on brick or concrete walls and pavings or silhouettes against the sky.

Trees also often have particularly evocative qualities or associations. Noble trees such as the oak and beech remind us of deep forest, tall uncompromising poplars echo the columnar structures of surrounding buildings and willows, traditionally associated with water, create an impression of softly falling rain from their light-coloured pendulous foliage.

Trees have more than simply a visual appeal. The

25

wind rustling through leaves is a sound evocative of the countryside, and a welcome diversion from city noises. The smell of their flowers, ripening fruit or dying leaves all have their associations with nature, and temper the artificial appearance of urban surroundings.

There is another aspect of considerable importance, and partly psychological in its effect. Trees contribute to the well-being and comfort of the town dweller in replacing oxygen, recycling water and improving the soil and they are capable of absorbing large quantities of dust from the atmosphere. Some species, notably conifers and evergreens, can trap dust and other forms of air pollution on the surface area of their leaves (see Chapter 12, Plants and Air Pollution). Although the residue is washed off during rainy periods, the ground beneath the canopy benefits during long, dry spells.

Some benefit is claimed both from the cooling effect of trees on their surroundings by the shade they afford and by the temperature reduction produced as the result of evapotranspiration. This is of particular importance in hot climates. There can also be no doubt that, in general terms, the surrounding soil is improved. This benefit can be gained more especially where the ground is open and the recycling process provided by leaf-fall is completed. It is, however, likely to prove unimportant in most fully urban conditions, where it is usually necessary to provide a good soil at the outset.

To a limited extent, depending upon the amount of planting relative to built areas, trees can provide a valuable habitat for wildlife, linking open spaces and parks within the urban framework.

There are also certain disadvantages to planting trees within urban areas which must be taken into account in all landscape schemes. Those who have responsibility for clearing streets, gulleys or gutters of leaves may well feel that many of these counter-considerations are paramount. Nor do the disadvantages stop at annual leaf-fall. Roots can get into drains and foundations, and certain trees, such as some species of lime, exude sticky substances which can cause nuisance and even accidents to passers-by. Trees in an unsafe condition can fall, and even those that look in good health can sometimes do the unexpected. All this should not, however, deter us or detract from the very tangible advantages which trees can bring to an everyday scene. The disadvantages can be avoided by careful selection of species to suit the particular requirements and conditions of the site.

## 3.3 REQUIREMENTS

Trees in urban areas exist in a largely artificial environment, and their physiological needs must be met if

PLATE 3.3 **A single splended specimen of beech makes an effective landscape for private flats in Twickenham, supplemented though it is by the more intimate shrub planting outside the houses.** (Landscape Architects: *Eric Lyons Cunningham Partnership*)

planting is to be successful. These include paying attention to soil, water, microclimate (shade and shelter), supply of nutrients and drainage. The particular needs and problems associated with transplanting semi-mature trees are the subject of Chapter 9.

Trees also require space. Not only do they require room enough to grow upwards, but usually a certain freedom to expand downwards and outwards. The spread of a large, mature tree may be 20 m or more. Planting in accordance with minimum space recommendations is seldom advisable, for if a tree outgrows the space provided it may cause damage to buildings and have to be felled.

## 3.4 TREES AND THE TOWNSCAPE

Trees should be seen as an integral part of the total three-dimensional urban structure, giving definition and meaning to the spaces between buildings, and enhancing the buildings themselves. There is an endless variety of tree forms which can be used to define spaces, to provide a natural focal point to a view or to soften the impact of built forms − as individual specimens, in small groups or massed to form green swathes. The selection of tree species should reflect the designer's understanding of the purpose of the site and its architectural character, the trees being of the appropriate scale, shape, texture and colour. Trees may be required simply to enhance urban developments, or for more functional purposes, such as:

(i)  to block out undesirable features, e.g. industrial areas or car parks;
(ii)  to indicate changes in use, for instance as the demarcation line between traffic and pedestrian routes;
(iii)  for emphasis and direction, as in avenue planting for enclosure of seating areas, children's play areas and so on;
(iv)  individual specimens or trees with special character can be used for more formal ornamental purposes, as living sculptural elements in town squares or courtyards.

Trees have a time scale of their own; they are part and parcel of a naturally recurring cycle and should always be seen as dynamic rather than static entities. Growth and changeover time should be anticipated by the designer if he or she is to make the most of trees in a landscape scheme. Trees should be regarded as part of a continuing process of planting, growth to maturity and removal, otherwise there will be a lack of succession, and possibly even total disappearance of trees in some parts of our towns. In some urban situations, arboriculture has been looked at in terms of a rotational crop and this technique, perfected in many Dutch towns, can often give very reassuring results.

Trees in cities need to be kept under continuing surveillance. The recent scourge of elm disease has brought this fact home to many, since virtually overnight a useful and beautiful feature has become a liability. The occurrence of the attack pinpoints the desirability of having on hand a continuous brief of stewardship and husbandry and the need for planting younger trees to replace those which have to be felled. Only in this way can we hope to predict with any reliability what the state of either individual trees or the overall vegetation cover is likely to be at any point in time.

It is very important to see tree planting in our towns and housing estates as an organic process. With such an emphasis, planting design can take on something of the expanding quality of town building itself, and can be seen as an integral part of the townscape rather than merely as a decorative addition to the urban form. This does not necessarily exclude the placing of individual specimens, but for cultural and visual reasons trees in an urban setting may have the greatest impact when seen as a collective mass against the façades of bricks and mortar, or running through and against the more open fabric of townscape. Where space permits, groups of trees can be allowed to coalesce into quite significant knots of foliage, taking on the appearance of small plantations or spinneys. When these are visually linked with associated clumps, the strands of green can form the basis of that overriding cellular structure so important to the successful townscape pattern.

This approach of course is not new. It owes its origins to the early landscape traditions 'of joining willing woods', so effectively begun by Earl Bathurst at Cirencester in the early eighteenth century. It is a technique of design, however, which has had a fair measure of success in its application in many of the early new towns where small scale and repetitive housing units have been effectively landscaped. Some of these town sites were fortunate in embracing tracts of existing woodland, and these in turn have helped to form the nucleus of an extended series of belts of tree planting which now run right through the middle of many housing areas. These plantations give an overall green structure to the town and also provide compartments in which varied development can often take place without wrecking the total picture. Such estates enjoy a very satisfactory measure of landscape enclosure. When trees grow higher than the roof ridges, the whole housing landscape immediately benefits from a sense of containment.

Trees should be carefully selected for the effect or use desired; too wide a range of species should be avoided as the different shapes, textures and colours are likely to result in a restless composition. The best effects are generally achieved with boldness and simplicity, as in mass, closely spaced planting of a single species or of a few species with similar texture, form and colour. Some trees may be selected to act as foils to

27

PLATE 3.4 & 3.5 **The importance of imaginative landscaping around trees can be seen in this urban rehabilitation scheme of interwar housing in Islington, London. The modern landscaping makes use of the existing group of cherry trees but injects an atmosphere of informality and privacy.** (Landscape Architects: *Brian Clouston & Partners*; Photographer: *Peter Lake*)

existing buildings, enhancing rather than obscuring the architecture, or as elements in a formal design. It is necessary to consider the seasonal variation in order to design a scheme which will be effective and harmonious throughout the year. Evergreens will provide colour and strongly-defined natural forms during the winter, which may be of particular value in areas where buildings lack variety. Trees with colourful foliage or blossom will generally be more effective if they are planted in groups, provided that the range of colours is limited to those which blend together well and are appropriate for the site.

The landscape architect must devise a design which works in both time and space, trees being so placed that they achieve the desired effect from all angles. This can often only be achieved by working on the site as the trees are being planted and viewing them critically as they are placed. The views of the pedestrian should be taken into account so that the design reflects an under-standing of progression through space — from light to shade, unfolding and concealing views and enclosing and opening up spaces.

## 3.5 TREES IN HOUSING AREAS

## Existing trees

Existing trees have many advantages if they are carefully incorporated into housing layouts. The retention of the trees can add immeasurably to the sense of age of the place and give it a quality that would have taken many years to develop otherwise, although there are problems concerning the use of large trees in housing layouts. Much depends on the physical condition as well as on the nature of the particular tree involved. Elms, for example, although handsome adjuncts to housing are notoriously undependable. They can shed branches

PLATE 3.6 **Some trees owe their character to their form, and none perhaps more so than this pine growing from an island in the courtyard of a Technical College in Copenhagen. It is, of course, a highly contrived situation, but is none the less attractive for this.** *(Gordon Patterson & Partners)*

29

PLATE 3.7 **An eighteenth-century landscape formula applied to the modern context to provide a park on previously derelict land.** (Landscape Architects: *Brian Clouston & Partners*; Photographer: *Ian Bruce*)

without warning and their roots can be troublesome in relation to drains and footings. On the other hand a mature oak, will often grow quite happily beside a road or building, provided it is not affected by change in water relation, drainage or water table.

The existing trees on the site should be carefully identified and surveyed before a final selection of those to be retained is made. This appraisal should include the condition of the tree, its probable life expectancy, susceptibility to disease and maintenance requirements. The position of existing trees relative to new buildings and roads should be most carefully assessed so that the trees that are retained are of maximum value to the overall design and are allowed to continue to grow as freely as possible. Whilst existing beautiful trees can form the focal point of a new design, it is useless to expect them to survive changes in water table and large civil engineering works unscathed, unless adequate protection is provided during building operations. Trees must be protected against damage by fencing off groups or cladding single specimens prior to any work on a site. The roots should be protected from pollutants, vehicles and building materials. All construction activities, storage and so on should be kept a safe distance beyond the spread of the crown. Trees vary considerably in their reaction to changes in surrounding soil levels and professional advice should be taken in each case; deep-rooting trees are generally more tolerant of a lowering in soil levels than shallow-rooted species. As far as possible soil levels around the tree boles should be maintained and the level of water table kept constant by using revetments or retaining walls (which should be at least 3 m away from the tree). As a last resort, if the soil level has to be raised, this should be done only with light, sandy soil or ballast at a rate of between 80–150 mm per annum. Alternatively, the soil can be held back with revetments or retaining walls.

## Density and building types

The density and type of building will determine how much land is available for tree planting – mostly in

PLATE 3.8 **Shadow effect of semi-mature trees on the paving of Leeds University precinct.** (Landscape Architects: *Brian Clouston & Partners*; Photographer: *Vince Chapman Studios*)

areas of common open space. For instance, in low density developments there may be scope for forest trees and in medium density layouts, lines or groups and massed belts of trees may be more appropriate. In high density schemes with high-rise buildings, single trees of forest dimensions will be more effective as a foil than will smaller trees.

The scale and character of the trees must be related to the scale of the buildings and spaces. A tree which eventually grows above the roof line gives a most satisfying effect, and if small trees are used they are generally more effective in groups.

The purpose of the spaces may determine the type of tree planting that is carried out. In play areas within residential developments, groups of trees which can withstand more than average interference are most likely to survive. In areas designed for sitting shade and protection from wind will be important; the seating, paths and tree layout are interdependent and should be designed together. Pedestrian movement should be kept a safe distance from the boles of trees, however.

Tree planting in private gardens will depend very much on the space available, but there is a considerable amount of choice, even for smaller gardens. Trees with open, light foliage or narrow spreads are generally suitable, as well as small fruit and flowering trees, though the latter are perhaps too strongly favoured in many areas unless they are visually supported by other trees of greater stature.

## Proximity to buildings

Trees continuously change in shape and size both above and below ground, and sufficient space must be allowed

PLATE 3.9 **Young elm trees which have grown out from an old hedge furnish these early New Town houses with a foil and screen in scale with the layout. They will, however, need to be carefully trimmed and pruned.** (Landscape Architect: *Gordon Patterson & Partners*)

**PLATE** 3.10 & **FIGURE** 3.1 **Goldswork Park, Surrey. A large housing scheme showing the successful use of extensive tree planting.** (Landscape Architects: *Brian Clouston & Partners*; Photographer: *Peter Lake*)

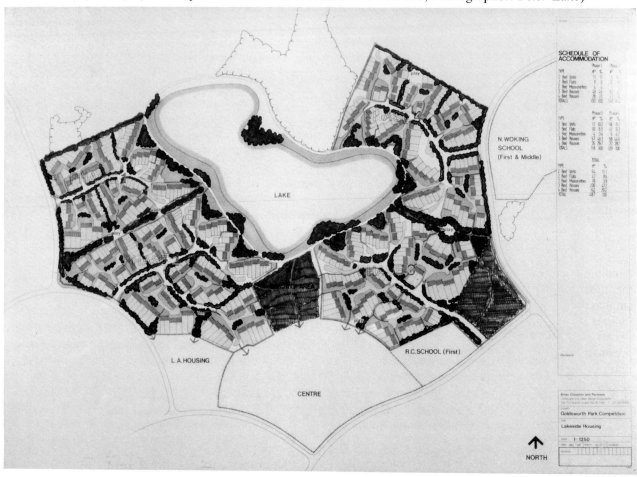

for the likely spread of roots and branches. Roots may cause contraction of the soil by extracting soil moisture, and this in turn may cause cracks to appear in nearby buildings, particularly on heavy clay soils. Elm, poplar, willow and ash are the most likely offenders and should be planted at least as far away from a building as their estimated mature height. Other trees can be planted up to about two-thirds of their height away, or closer if the building foundations reach to a depth of 2 m or more, or other precautions are taken such as an underground wall barrier or raft foundations. Roots may deflect or grow into pipes which should be protected by concrete casting or made of cast iron if they are placed near to existing trees. In addition, root suckers may penetrate soil and grass, and break up hard surfaces – particularly poplars and elms. Thus sucker species should be avoided.

Trees which are to be placed close to buildings should be selected for their light foliage, or carefully sited away from windows. Where mature trees have blocked out the light, a tree surgeon can be called in to solve the problem while maintaining the shape and character of the tree by careful pruning. In all cases of planting trees close to buildings, careful note should be taken of any recommendations that are made in the *NHBC Code of Practice Notes*.

## 3.6 TREES IN STREETS AND SHOPPING AREAS

There are limited opportunities for tree planting along existing streets and this option is rarely considered at the design stage. Planting is generally confined to specimen trees in odd corners, with formal avenues or group planting where space allows, for example on roundabouts. Tree planting along streets can accomplish more than any other planting in visually breaking up the hard lines of road surfaces and buildings and in dividing pedestrian footpaths from the traffic flow. Suitable trees should be planted far enough from the kerb to allow them to spread without too much pruning, and they should be kept clear of overhead wires and underground services. In avenue planting, single trees interspersed with groups will often achieve more satisfying informal results than trees that are spaced evenly, and trees can be used to great effect in framing views or buildings. Variation of species and scale can help relieve the monotony of city and suburban streets and to emphasize a particular building or space. The opportunities are greater in pedestrian areas such as shopping streets where little or no traffic is permitted, or in precincts which have been designed for pedestrian use only. In Stevenage New Town shopping centre, trees are an integral part of the design, affording shade and shelter in sitting areas and enriching the scene for pedestrians.

City conditions are often unfavourable for tree

PLATE 3.11 **This housing scheme provides small-scale intimate space with generous provision for private gardens. Robust, quick-growing shrubs and trees have been used, planted in raised beds where possible. They include species of** *robinia, rhus* **and cotoneaster. Mozart Street Housing, Westminster Council.** (Landscape Architects: *Michael Brown Partnership*; Photographer: *Anthony Blake*)

growth, and species must be selected which can tolerate air pollution, dry conditions, limited light, glare from pavements and so on. It is essential to maintain the balance between water absorbed into the root system and that evaporated from the leaves. This can be done by pruning to remove excess leaf growth or by cutting back the branches each year. Trees will require annual application of fertilizers in late autumn or early spring, and protection against pests.

33

FIGURE 3.2 **Artist's impression of trees used to frame views along pedestrian ways in housing in London.** *(Andrew Donaldson)*

PLATE 3.12 **Silver birch form an attractive feature of the town square in Stevenage, set at intervals along a paved pedestrian street.** *(Cement and Concrete Association)*

PLATE 3.13 **Young trees and shrubs as part of a car park design for a new shopping centre in the heart of Leeds.** (Landscape Architects: *Brian Clouston & Partners*; Photographer: *Simon Miles*)

## 3.7 TREES IN CAR PARKS

Car parks impose a particular set of restrictive conditions in their design which are not always fully appreciated at the outset. Although they can provide a useful space within the urban framework in which to plant trees, the task of accommodating trees in these surroundings is not always as straightforward as it may seem. The difficulty experienced in establishing individual trees or groups of trees, especially in large areas of unrelieved hard surfacing, is often due to the dry conditions, lack of air and the intensity of the light which is thrown up from the ground to the tree, which can cause leaf scorch and abnormal transpiration rates.

Even after satisfying the minimum loss of parking spaces (usually a prerequisite in urban space planning), a disjointed fashion of planting often results, failing to provide a satisfactory visual flow to a scheme. Damage may be caused to tree boles (and lower branches) by vehicles backing into them, and tree roots may be poisoned if fuel run-off gets into the water supply. To avoid these hazards it is usually suggested they should be planted between raised kerbs or in elevated boxes. Here again, however, discontinuity of the ground sur-face can lead to an artificial appearance, and it will usually be found that trees look better and more natural if the base of the tree is visible. Therefore, whilst hazard fencing at bumper height can go some way to meeting practicalities, it is more frequently the careful siting of trees in relation to the overall car park design which gives the best solution, rather than the *ad hoc* filling with trees that is so commonly practised.

## 3.8 TREE SELECTION

Local soil and water characteristics should be thoroughly investigated before selecting which trees to plant, for instance the type and depth of soil and sub-soil and level of the water table. The site may be prone to frost, air pollution or other microclimatic influences which will affect tree selection.

The size of the trees relative to the space available and the rates of growth of the proposed trees must be taken into account. It is misleading to show the mature size of the tree on a landscape plan, particularly if it is very slow growing.

The general appearance and character of the tree is important, whether individual specimens or groups are

35

PLATE 3.14 **The value of existing trees, both as specimens and in groups is illustrated by this new office in Solent Business Park, where the building was designed specifically to retain and surround the oaks.** (Landscape Architects: *Brian Clouston & Partners*; Photographer: *Alistair Hunter*)

being considered. Tall, narrow trees may be appropriate in restricted spaces such as central road reserves where spreading trees could be dangerous. Weeping or pendulous species provide contrast and movement and small-scale trees would be useful where a limited space is available, for instance if trees are to be planted in small scale residential areas. The effect of seasonal changes can be very important where colour and variety are lacking in the built environment: the winter effect of bare branches and bark texture or evergreen leaves, autumn colouring, fruit and seeds, summer leaf shade and density and new leaves and blossom in the spring can all add something particular to a design.

Length of life and availability are important factors in tree selection. For instance, birch, willow and poplar will grow quickly, but for long-lasting effects, in parks perhaps, slow-growing, long-living species may be more appropriate.

In the past, urban tree planting has probably embraced, if anything, too wide a choice of specimens,

with the result that planting schemes have often lacked an overriding sense of unity. The common desire has been to include one of everything, and this approach is unlikely to lead to the best results, at least in visual terms. This way of thinking has arisen in part from a gardenesque approach; that is, identifying the solution in terms of what we recognize in our own back gardens. In fact, there are relatively few trees which meet all the design criteria for truly satisfactory urban growth, in much the same way as there are relatively few tree species which form the climax of our deciduous semi-natural English woodlands. This is why so much of our countryside takes on its characteristic, much admired, unified appearance.

There are, in addition, many other cultural, technical and traditional reasons for limiting the number of species within urban planting schemes. If the quest for variety has to be satisfied, then this particular problem would best be met in the context of the wider issue of a truly ecological selection. Seen in this particular way there are, again, relatively few trees which meet the rather stringent requirements of cities and towns. The success of the London plane (*Platanus hispanica*) in meeting the very rigorous demands made upon it is a fine example of a tree that is well adapted to urban conditions. The Norway maple (*Acer platanoides*), though it cannot claim the stature of the plane, adapts well to urban surroundings. It is not particularly demanding regarding water conditions or as a feeder, and so far has remained relatively free from pests and diseases. It is a tree with a considerable degree of natural variety in its form and colours, as well as creating interest because of its dumpy massing, branching and autumn colour. It is also decorative during its flowering period. It can therefore lay some claim to being seen as a ready alternative dominant for general purposes in urban areas.

The common lime (*Tilia x vulgaris*) has some claim to precedent in use as a town tree. Certainly its size and grace as well as the delicate green of its foliage and flowers do much to commend it in this respect. It does, however, have a number of serious disadvantages. Some trees will sucker profusely or encourage aphids and drop sticky substances and nectar from their flowers. They are tolerant of a wide variety of soils, though less likely to adapt to particularly dry conditions than maples and planes. They also have a tendency to die back in the head, particularly after they have attained a considerable size. *Tilia x euchlora* is possibly the most suitable lime for urban planting as it has none of these disadvantages.

These trees, along with a handful of others, such as the tree of heaven (*Ailanthus altissima*), native cherry (*Prunus avium*) and black pine (*Pinus nigra*), and in some places the sycamore (*Acer pseudoplatanus*), can be relied upon to provide a good backbone to urban planting.

Table 3.1 lists trees that are suitable for planting in urban areas, along with their main characteristics. It contains many specimens described in further detail and illustrated in the Tree Information Sheets at the end of the book.

## 3.9 MAINTENANCE AND MANAGEMENT

The long-term success of tree planting in urban areas, as in any landscape scheme, depends on the quality of the ongoing maintenance and management. Trees planted in urban areas require more care than those in rural or natural conditions if they are to survive, develop, and grow to their full stature. It is important, therefore, that the appropriate size and species of tree be selected to fulfil the designer's requirements and the site conditions, so that the tree has the best possible chance to develop from the start. The larger the tree is when it is planted, the less prone it will be to damage by vandals, which is a regular hazard in urban areas. A semi-mature tree will, therefore, be more likely to survive attacks by vandals, although it will require a considerable amount of care and attention if it is to be transplanted successfully (see Chapter 8).

PLATE 3.15 **The stature of one tree can often support a whole scene so long as it survives. This plane tree, although isolated, acts as a pivotal point between the lake and library, bringing unity to the whole scene. Elsinore, Denmark.** *(Gordon Patterson & Partners)*

TABLE 3.1
**Trees suitable for urban use**

| Latin and common name | Use, tolerance, qualities | Latin and common name | Use, tolerance, qualities |
|---|---|---|---|
| *Acer platanoides** Norway maple | Streets and parks. Tolerates polluted atmosphere. Early spring flowers and good autumn colour | *Fraxinus excelsior** Common ash | Cold urban sites; where subtle effects required. Withstands smoke and exposed sites. Light shade, hardy. Graceful and decorative. Winter, sculptural effect. Keep away from buildings |
| *Acer pseudoplatanus** Sycamore | Difficult urban conditions. Wind and salt resistant. Fast growth, free seeding. Excessive fertility can be a nuisance. Coarse foliage can attract pests in summer | *Ilex aquifolium* Holly | Understorey planting; hedges, ornamental. Withstands smoke and wind. Evergreen; winter colour |
| *Aesculus hippocastanum* Horse chestnut | Ornamental; parks and avenues. Impressive spring flowers and autumn colour | *Picea omorika* | Groups, specimen − parks and open spaces. All year round interest. Good form and colour near buildings |
| *Ailanthus altissima* Tree of heaven | Urban squares and streets. Smoke resistant; grows on poor soils. Bold foliage; open forked branches | *Platanus hybrida** x acerifolia, x hispanica London plane | Industrial sites; street tree. Tolerates polluted atmosphere, cold winds, compacted soil and heavy pruning. Large leaves, dappled bark, globular seeds remain all year. Forest stature. Open leaf, branch network. Decorative and elegant |
| *Alnus glutinosa* Common alder | Urban river and lakeside; slag heaps; group or coppice planting. Spring catkins | | |
| *Betula verrucosa* Silver birch | Groups. Domestic areas; near buildings, in limited space. Small scale; quick growth, short-lived. Needs plenty of light; moist or dry conditions; all year round interest. Slender branches, light leaves, attractive bark. Spring catkins | *Populus* 'Serotina' Black Italian poplar | Quick screening for tall buildings, industries. Tolerates polluted atmosphere. Fast growth. Red-brown leaves early. Keep away from buildings |
| *Carpinus betulus* Hornbeam | Cold exposed sites; streets; shelterbelt. Hardy. Winter colour; retains brown leaves | *Prunus avium** Wild cherry | Parks, open spaces, streets. Attractive blossom, bark and autumn colour |
| *Crataegus monogyna** Common hawthorn | Street, park, development schemes. Interest all year round, flowers, fruit | *Quercus robur* Oak | Park − specimen, small group, avenue. Requires large space. Traditional; very decorative; light shade. Interesting leaf shape and acorns |
| *Fagus sylvatica* Beech | Groups, park − requires large space. Shelterbelt. Hardy; wind firm, forest tree. Delicate green, spring; gold autumn. Interesting varieties for shape and colour | *Robinia pseudoacacia* False acacia | Paved courtyards, streets. Hardy, smoke resistant. Open, light, attractive foliage and flowers. Shallow roots. Brittle branches |

| | | | |
|---|---|---|---|
| *Salix x chrysocoma* Weeping willow | Specimen, waterside. Requires large space. Urban lakes and riversides. Quick growth. Good winter stem colour. Wind movement. Many varieties | *Sorbus aucuparia** Rowan; mountain ash | Small scale – good for small spaces. Attractive pinnate leaves; winter berries; white flowers in spring |
| *Sorbus aria** Whitebeam | Street, restricted sites, near buildings. Upright, wind resistant. Attractive foliage especially in wind | *Tilia x euchlora** Common lime | Parks and open spaces. Requires large space. Magnificent specimen tree; groups and avenues. Fresh pale green leaves, yellow in autumn. Long-lived; tolerates pruning |

\* Most commonly planted species.

## 3.10 CONCLUSION

It takes years, sometimes generations, to replace a mature tree, and a complete change of heart to prevent unnecessary felling and vandalism. Our present urban environment would benefit from the planting of many thousands of trees, some to replace mature specimens, others to create beauty in newly-built developments. The importance of trees as supremely useful elements in planting schemes for urban areas cannot be over-emphasized. No other form of planting brings the presence of nature so forcefully into our man-made environment, or does so much to conceal the ugliness and to enhance the beauty of our urban surroundings.

## FURTHER READING

Arnold, H. F. *Trees in Urban Design* (New York: Van Nostrand Reinhold 1980)

Burrows, G. S. *Tree Planting in Urban Areas* (West Sussex County Council 1972)

Clouston, B. and Stansfield, K. *Trees in Towns* (London: Architectural Press 1981)

Colvin, B. *Trees for Town and Country* (London: Lund Humphries, 4th edition 1972)

Fairbrother, N. *New Lives, New Landscapes* (London: The Architectural Press 1971)

Higson, N. 'Milton Keynes: City of Trees', *Landscape Design* No. 168 (August, p. 24 1987)

Johnson, H. The International Book of Trees (London: Mitchell Beazley Ltd 1973)

McCullen, J. and Webb, R. *A Manual of Urban Trees* (Dublin: An Foras Forbatha 1982)

Morling, R. J. *Trees* (London: Estates Gazette Ltd., revised edition 1963)

Zion, R. L. *Trees for Architecture and Landscape* (New York: Van Nostrand Reinhold Company 1968)

CHAPTER 4

# Shrubs and Groundcover

## PREBEN JAKOBSEN

## 4.1 INTRODUCTION

The terms 'shrubs' and 'groundcover' may mean different things to different people. In the widest sense groundcover can be of any height, depending upon the vantage points. The common characteristic, whatever the height, is that the plant covers the soil with its leaves. The more rigorous definitions given below, however, should serve to indicate how they relate in height to other plant material and to clarify their meanings in the context of this chapter.

The *Oxford Dictionary* defines a shrub as a woody plant of less size than a tree and usually divided into separate stems from near the ground (OE *scrybb* brushwood).

*Webster's Dictionary* defines groundcover as: the small plants in a forest except young trees; a low plant (as ivy) that covers the ground in place of turf; a plant adapted for use as groundcover.

Professor R. W. Curtis of Cornell University gives the following range of heights for shrubs and groundcover:

| | |
|---|---|
| Groundcover | 150−300 mm (6−12 in.) |
| Low shrub | 450−1000 mm (18−36 in.) |
| Small shrub | 1−1.5 m (approx. 4−5 ft) |
| Medium shrub | 1.5−2.5 m (approx. 6−8 ft) |
| Large shrub/small tree | 3−7.5 m (10−25 ft) |

## 4.2 HISTORICAL BACKGROUND

A traditionally popular form of planting in England can be described as mixed or *mélange* planting where different varieties of natural and exotic groundcovers and shrubs are combined. The late Margery Fish was one of the greatest popularizers of this type of planting, which, it should be stressed, includes a high proportion of native plant material or selected forms therefrom.

Another type of groundcover planting in the United Kingdom can be traced from the period between the wars, when Michael Haworth Booth coined the word *boscage* planting, and put this into effect in his own nursery near Haslemere and later in his clients' gardens. This method did not become generally recognized until after the Second World War. He became an authority on and exponent of a type of planting which can best be described as anti-bare earth policy, where the plant material totally covers the ground. The majority of material used consisted of Japanese Kurume azaleas with hummock forming plants such as various species of genista, cytisus, hebe, hydrangea and viburnum, all being allowed to 'knit' together.

A third form of planting is woodland-paradise planting, which uses an exuberance of plant material and is a combination of boscage and *mélange* traditions of which the Savill Garden in Windsor Great Park is an outstanding example. There are also many National Trust properties and private estate gardens where this form of planting is accepted as the norm. Successful as these plantings may be, however, there are signs that this style has passed its peak.

Cyclical movements can be discerned in the design and use of different types of shrubs and groundcovers in landscape design. There is currently a commonly held view that much of the inspiration in Britain during the last twenty years has been derived from America and the continent of Europe. Looking back into the past, however, similar movements can be discerned in England in Victorian times and during the earlier part of the twentieth century. The use of ivy as a groundcover can be seen as an example of this cyclical change. Ever since the Victorian writer Shirley Hibberd first published his monograph on the ivy, the gardeners of the British Isles have led the world in the use of groundcover. Perhaps no other individual plant is better suited to this climate as a groundcover. From Victorian times to the late 1920s saw the heyday of its use and from this stems the popularization of ivy in the United

40

PLATE 4.1 **Lavender groundcover used in the manner that an artist applies paint to a canvas, mauve high-lighted by accents of** *Cortaderia*. **Templemere, Weybridge 1965.** (Landscape Architect: *Preben Jakobsen*)

PLATE 4.2 **Cool, structured, circular grass bowl and hedge juxtaposed with exuberant amoeba-shaped shrub and herbaceous planting beds at Broadwater Park, Denham.** (Landscape Architect: *Preben Jakobsen*)

States. The ivy including its variants and foreign counterparts is perhaps the archetype of all native groundcovers; it is heartening to note the renaissance in its use which is now occurring.

Landscape design is influenced by movements in architecture and art. The influence of cubism, for example (by such notable artists as Mondrian and Klee in particular) on the use of shrubs and groundcovers, is particularly obvious when one analyses the work of the renowned Brazilian landscape architect Burle Marx, who paints great brushstrokes with groundcovers on which a limited amount of statuesque accent and emphasis planting is carefully displayed.

## 4.3 DESIGN DISCIPLINE

No one part of planting design can be viewed in isolation. Shrubs and groundcover form an integral part of the overall design in which trees, by virtue of their size, are often considered to be dominant features. The

PLATE 4.3 **Trees used as an exclamation mark and pivotal point in Brussels. Note the simple banks of monoculture groundcover.**

lower planting levels with which we are primarily concerned in this chapter and the two following chapters on Herbaceous Plants and Bulbs and Water Plants, complement the design. They form linking areas of focal elements, and create diversity and kinetic impact.

Landscape architecture is an art form in which planting design plays a major role. The great challenge is to make effective use of such ephemeral material within a disciplined design framework. The supreme quality in most art forms is self-restraint and purity of design intent. It is well to bear in mind at the outset Mies van der Rohe's comment 'less is more' and guard against a natural inclination towards artistic self-indulgence.

The good designer will be the first to acknowledge and seek to use to effect the individual design characteristics of the plant material with which he is working. The dogmas and rules associated with landscape design, however, are not so rigid that they must remain unbroken and a design may benefit from an ingenious or daring departure from conventional principles. The application of creative thought processes will help to provide inspiration.

## 4.4 DESIGN PRINCIPLES

The importance of creating a structured skeleton for the design cannot be overstressed. This provides a framework for the planting composition and space definition, by means of open and closed hierarchical landscape cells.

When composing a design one is essentially juxtaposing one or several volumes against each other, creating positive and negative volumes, or solid and void spatial compartments or cells.

The architect Sir Edwin Lutyens was a great exponent of the compartmentalization of external spaces relative to his buildings. He created cells of yew hedges which in essence are outdoor rooms forming a continuation of the building into the landscape, thus skilfully containing the excesses of Gertrude Jekyll's colourful herbaceous borders (see 4.7).

If one analyses the landscape of the British Isles it will be found that it consists of a structured network of cells, based on boundaries of field ownership, roads, railways, rivers, canals, geological formations, etc. Therefore in landscape design terms one is working with a hierarchy of cells: the cell enclosure can consist of shelterbelts, hedgerows, edges of woodland and so on. Buildings sited within these cells form nuclei within more refined cells, and more obvious segmentation is formed by the cell enclosing elements – hedges, borders and other delineating distinctive plant material which is more carefully maintained.

Apart from the visual containment of plants, the formation of cells can be seen as a self-perpetuating need for improved microclimatic conditions.

It follows that space and volume are closely related.

PLATE 4.4 **Classic lines of beauty still hold true. Courtyard at Jutland Telephone Exchange, Denmark.** (Landscape Architects: *Arevad Jacobsen*)

PLATE 4.5 **Spiky** *Phormium* **sp. set against domeshaped** *Hebe* **sp., creating an exotic, exuberant mood. Willingdon Trees, East Sussex.** (Landscape Architect: *Preben Jakobsen*)

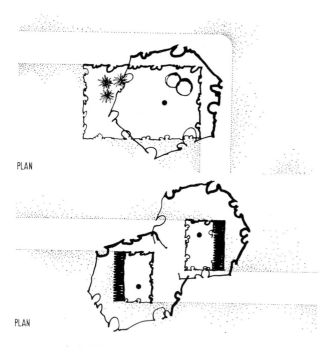

PLAN

PLAN

FIGURE 4.1 **Pivot point, illustrating physical and visual change of direction.**

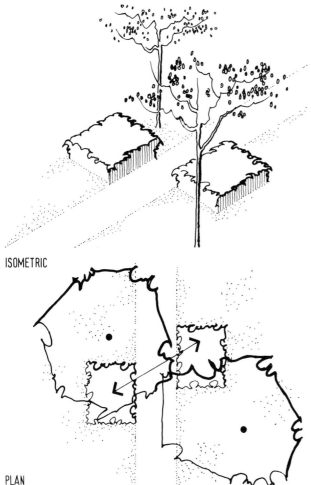

ISOMETRIC

PLAN

FIGURE 4.2 **Bridging point. The balanced tension is created simultaneously at different levels, forming a harmonious whole.**

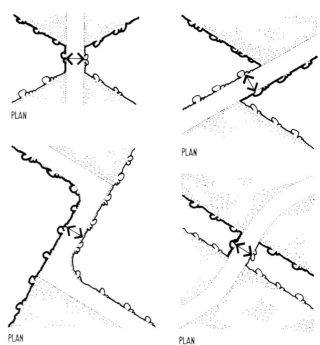

PLAN

PLAN

PLAN

PLAN

FIGURE 4.3 **Tension points. The figure shows the simplest solution: an offset view, a deflected view and a tension point created by opposing areas of planting. The principle also applies to roads.**

This concept, sometimes termed *volumetrics*, can be applied both in the early stages of the design, to create the framework and spatial relations, and at later stages when plant material is being selected. All plant material can be seen as positive volumes, as can architectural elements such as buildings or walls. Spaces can be described as negative volumes, although if one tries to imagine a cube of air, it becomes positive as soon as the space is enclosed or surrounded by plant material. Certain plant material, depending on the density of foliage and branch system, can be a combination of both positive and negative volume — that is, solid organic matter and air.

## Design dynamics

Architectural theories concerning the relationship between the moving observer and his immediate environment have equal application to landscape design. Plant material can be effectively used to create a kinetic relationship between the pedestrian observer and the landscape, unfolding views and enclosing spaces along paths in a carefully designed sequence, or applied on a larger scale to the movement of people in cars, such as the design of motorway planting for viewing at high speeds.

Unlike architecture, landscape design is concerned with living material which not only grows and changes during the seasons and over time, but moves in response to wind or to the touch. Thus the kinetic experience is enriched and made more intimate and varied.

The movement of the observer can be influenced by the positioning of groups of planting relative to the path. Where a change of direction is desired, groundcovers as well as trees and accent shrubs can be used to create pivot points at which one is physically and visually forced to change direction. Pivot points can be extended to form bridging points across paths and roads (*see* Figures 4.1 and 4.2). If the bridging points are sited close together, these in turn create tension points in the design where the space is narrowed down or constricted before opening up and expanding into another space (*see* Figure 4.3).

When composing and making design statements with groundcovers and shrubs, certain rules governing artistic line movements may be considered. Classic lines of beauty still hold true. They are largely based on the historical orders of Greek and Roman architecture and most are applicable to planting design. Examples of ogee curves, more correctly known as cyma recta and cyma reversa, shown in Figure 4.4 indicate how they are most commonly used in landscape architecture.

Using the idea of line movement, the design can be given a momentum of its own which can be described as a 'design speed'. This can be static, slow, moderate or fast. The inherent design force built into any line movement is self-expressive, as is shown in Figure 4.5.

Certain misconceptions exist relating to design line movement. All too often designers seek to create line movement by giving a wavy outline to planting beds (Figure 4.6). Tree and shrub planting will itself create all the wavy line movement at a higher level as it grows.

Plant material junctions should not be too acute (Figure 4.7). Where the design line movement abuts a building, or two converging paved areas meet grass areas, the acute point formed results in an awkward space for planting, and should be avoided where possible.

A landscape designer's flair may be judged in part by his attention to detail – in particular how he separates, defines and juxtaposes the different hard and soft landscape materials. Certain designs require sharp edge delineation and definition, which will either mean high maintenance or raising the paved plane considerably above the planting area. Some rampant groundcovers such as *Rubus tricolor* will produce a serrated edge. Ascending ones such as *Lonicera pileata* and *Prunus laurocerasus* 'Otto Luyken' or neat but prolific *Stephanandra incisa* 'Crispa' will cover the edge of paved spaces, producing an irregular but constant delineation.

FIGURE 4.6 **The planting beds are given bold, free-flowing continuous curves, respecting free growth of plant material.**

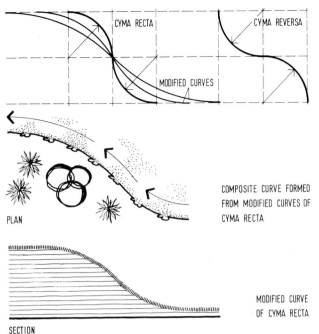

FIGURE 4.4 **The ogee is a double continuous curve (cyma recta and cyma reversa), concave below, passing into convex above. It can be used in plan or sectional form.**

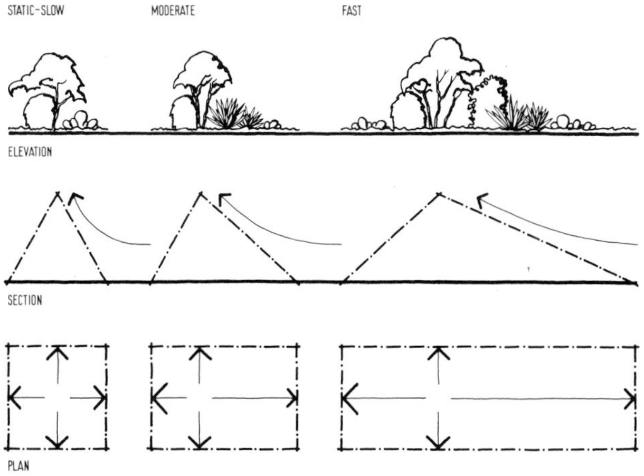

FIGURE 4.5 **Design speeds. In terms of volumes, the more extended the shape of the triangle and the square, the faster the design speed. The principle still applies to circular or informally shaped beds.**

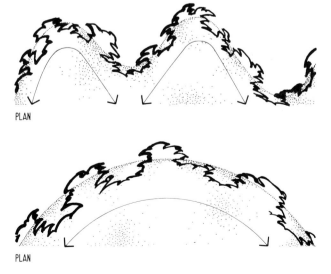

PLATE 4.6  **A basic 1:2:3 relationship — a base of ivy groundcover with accent trees** *(Alnus cordata)* **and sculptural cubiform, dwarf hedge** *(Ligastrum vulgare 'Lodense')*. **University of Strathclyde, Glasgow.** (Landscape Architect: *Preben Jakobsen*)

PLATE 4.7  **Contra-jour lighting effect of foliage. Templemere, Weybridge 1965.** (Landscape Architect: *Preben Jakobsen*)

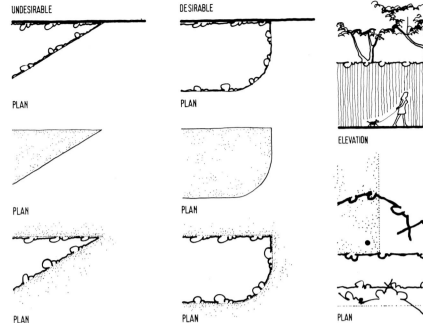

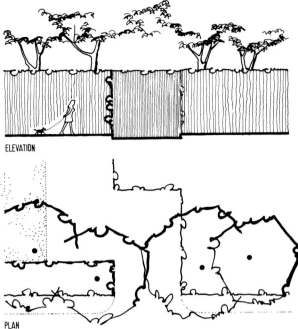

FIGURE 4.7 **Avoidance of acute plant material junctions. The diagram shows paving to wall, paving to paving and paving to grass situations.**

FIGURE 4.8 **Concealed access; the bridging point at the site entrance completely obscures the view into the site.**

Care should be taken when showing edge definition on plan. A neat drawing with straight lines to indicate overhanging paved edges may be wrongly interpreted.

Lawn mowing strips and groundcover separation are clearly defined directional line movements. Their inclusion is often deemed desirable when easier and more economical maintenance is envisaged, but should be avoided if possible because of the unpleasant effects of parallelism. In tropical climates, however, they may be necessary to prevent two different species from becoming too entangled. Rough cut grass affords a more romantic edge definition with an appropriately slow design speed, when allowed to define its co-existence with groundcover and shrubs of its own accord.

## Access, vistas and enframement

The point of entry into any given space is always of crucial importance in the design. For instance, one may choose to make it discreet or emphasize it by enframement. A drive or access road into a site may have predominantly vistalike qualities which can be reinforced with banks of tall and medium shrub and groundcover planting flanking each side. The long accepted tradition that when one entered a site, part of the building was first seen and then lost from view, to re-emerge later, still remains an effective design technique. Surprise and expectation have been important design concepts in landscape since the days of such well-known exponents as Brown, Repton, Puckler,

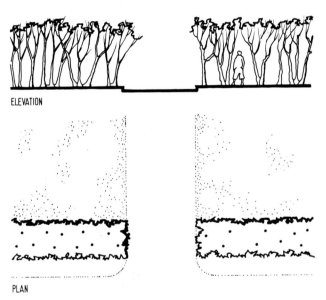

FIGURE 4.9 **Filtered access: a visual filter of tree trunks allows a partial view.**

Andrée, Kemp, Miller and Mawson. See Figures 4.8 to 4.11.

The principle of enframement can be used effectively to draw attention to specifically desirable views and possibly to block out the less desirable elements. For instance, massed foreground planting may be used to screen the near view, larger framing plants placing the emphasis on the distant view.

47

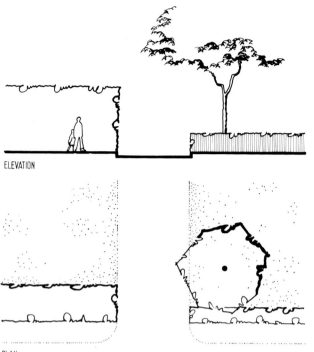

ELEVATION

PLAN

FIGURE 4.10 **Semi-closed access provides a screen at one side and partial vision at the other.**

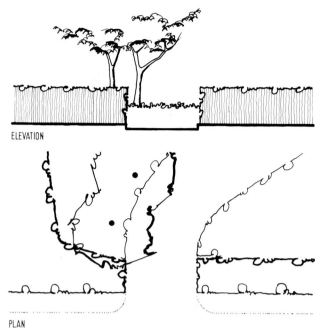

ELEVATION

PLAN

FIGURE 4.11 **Deflected access: the planting exerts a directional influence.**

Enframement of certain views (Figure 4.12) in connection with doorways or atrium courtyards can best be achieved by the use of large vertical shrubs or small trees with a horizontal branch structure such as *Cornus controversa*, *Cercis canadensis*, etc. Anchoring as a design technique is akin to enframement in so far as it has a similar design purpose, that is, to control corners and portions of the design which need reinforcement.

The planting of dome-shaped shrubs at the base of a small sculptural tree or shrub is another form of anchoring.

## Scale, proportion and balance

Once more a comparison with architectural design is useful. In interior spaces the proportion of room height

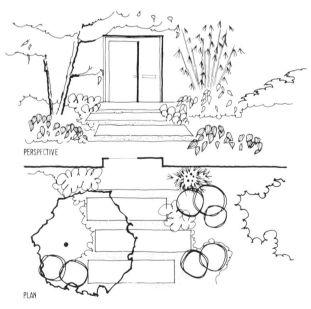

PERSPECTIVE

PLAN

FIGURE 4.12 **Enframement of an entrance, using plants of different heights.**

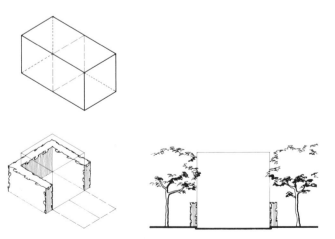

FIGURE 4.13 **The double cube provides a plan or three-dimensional shape of pleasing proportions, which can be used to structure landscape cells.**

48

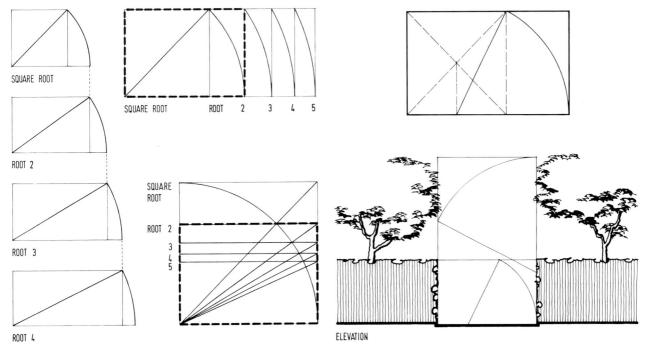

FIGURE 4.14 **The sequential formation from the square root.**

FIGURE 4.15 **The golden section and its application in landscape architecture.**

to area is important, and the architect works with geometric principles such as double cubes (Figure 4.13), root cubes, the golden section (Figure 4.15), and the logarithmic spiral (Figures 4.16 and 4.17). This has application in landscape architecture in the creation of spaces, many of which are literally outdoor rooms or cells. For example, in a courtyard the proportion of floor space should be relative to wall height.

Scale and proportion together constitute perhaps the most abused and misunderstood aspects of planting design. The failure to assess the proportion of one groundcover such as grass against other groundcovers and shrubs often results in unbalanced planting. Sometimes the landscape architect has little choice in the matter; for example, on housing estates where the roadway and footpath layouts are often determined without prior consultation, it may be difficult to harmonize the planting of the disproportionate left-over spaces.

Equal proportions may be acceptable in a formal design, but in informal schemes the normal rule of thumb proportion of shrubs and groundcover to grass would be between 1:5 and 1:7. For reasons of economy, the designer may be forced to accept a larger area of grass to groundcover and shrubs than desired. Where there is some doubt, as when road and footpath layouts create left-over cells, then these should be fully planted to give visual cohesion and facilitate maintenance. Initial design concepts can sometimes be maintained in these cases by compromising on planting distances and cheaper plant material. There are limits, however, to how far one can go without prejudicing the scheme.

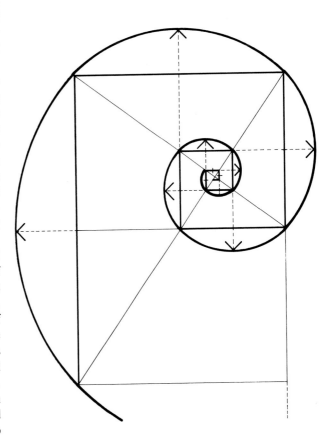

FIGURE 4.16 **The logarithmic spiral.**

49

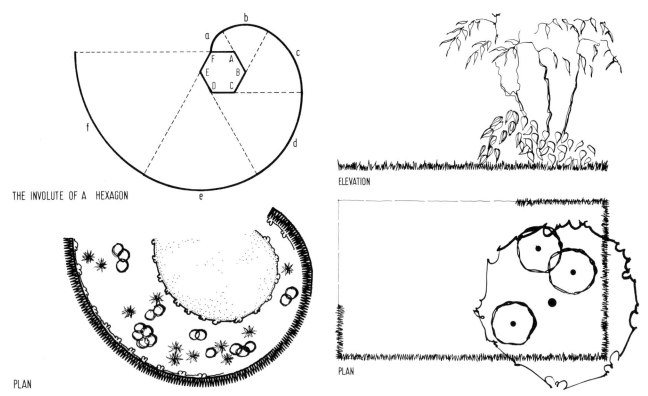

THE INVOLUTE OF A HEXAGON

PLAN

FIGURE 4.17 **Involute of a hexagon, demonstrating use of logarithmic spiral.**

ELEVATION

PLAN

FIGURE 4.19 **Accents and emphasis 1:2:3 relationship.**

## Juxtapositioning

Juxtapositioning is the essence of all planting design. The principles already described relating to bridging and tension points, pivot points and enframement are in effect a large scale form of juxtaposition. Where two or more kinds of the same planting material are used

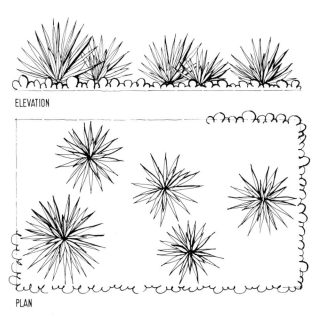

ELEVATION

PLAN

FIGURE 4.18 **Accents and emphasis 1:2:3 relationship.**

50

repetitively across a footpath or road or diagonally across a viewpoint etc, a sequential rhythm is set up, but the designer should beware of overstating and overbalancing volume relationships.

The dynarhythmic force described on page 45 is created by the art of juxtapositioning. Basic plant compositions of different design speeds may be based on Euclidian geometric shapes – the circle, square, and triangle (used by the Bauhaus which so impressed many designers). A dynamic design speed can be built up in three dimensions by increasing the number of accent plants and the way they are sited (see Figure 4.5).

Different accents and emphasis can be created by the ways in which shrubs and trees are placed in relation to each other and the ground plane. Some examples are shown in Figures 4.18–4.21. In each case the base plane is the groundcover. Figure 4.18 shows a simple 1:2 relationship; Figure 4.19 indicates the well-known 1:2:3 relationship, where the tree is the dominant and the lower shrubs are co-dominants. The remaining two figures show variations on this theme. A basic triad plant composition could consist of a sculptural, multi-stemmed *Aralia elata*, a dome shape or hummock of *Hebe rakaiensis* and a spiky linear form such as *Phormium tenax*.

Accent planting may consist largely of distinct bold planting, which may be linear and spiky in form yet with an hemispherical outline, such as *Cortaderia*

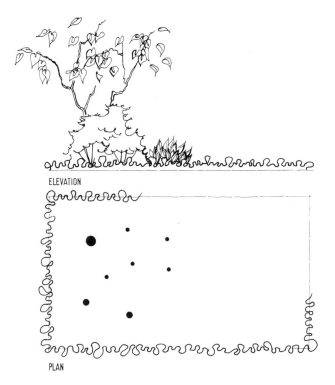

ELEVATION

PLAN

FIGURE 4.20 **Accents and emphasis. A single dominant, two co-dominants and five subservient shapes on the horizontal plane.**

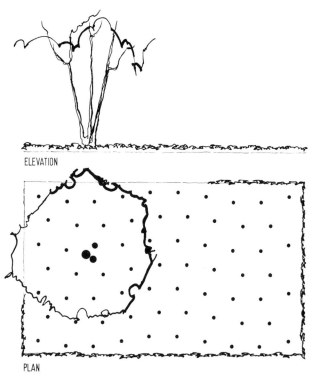

ELEVATION

PLAN

FIGURE 4.21 **Accents and emphasis. A single multi-stemmed tree or shrub with low level groundcover. Note proportional stagger of setting out.**

*argentea, Yucca gloriosa* and *Phormium tenax*. The dominant accent may be a large sculptural foliage shrub such as *Fatsia japonica* which, together with the spiky accents, acts as a pivotal point.

When working with long, linear groundcover and shrub borders, the use of distinct 'facers' and foreground plant material is necessary (Figure 4.22). This may be linear vertical such as *Libertia* spp, *Iris* spp or linear foliage of bold outline such as *Hosta* spp and *Viburnum davidii*. (The latter is useful as both an individual dome shape, or used *en masse*.) The 'facer' may have rotund foliage such as *Senecio greyi*, or crisp, ferny leaves such as *Stephanandra incisa* 'Crispa'.

'Fillers' is the term (Figure 4.22) used to describe background plant material which plays a subservient role, in a position where it is obscured to a large extent, and where bold and distinctive planting material of quality (often expensive) would be wasted. Invariably the designer will select cheap easily propagated plant material for this situation, for example *Spiraea* spp.

*Drift planting.* This is a type of planting where a distinct linear flow is aimed at, contrasting linear carpets of groundcover with each other. Drift planting can be used with or without accent planting and emphasis and may be of varied height (see Figure 4.23). Interlocking and overlapping planting is similar in many respects to drift planting, but usually the material is of higher stature and there is a greater change of textures (see Figure 4.24).

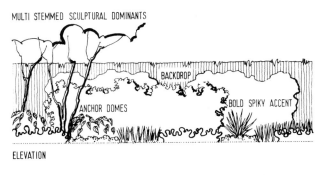

MULTI STEMMED SCULPTURAL DOMINANTS

BACKDROP

ANCHOR DOMES

BOLD SPIKY ACCENT

ELEVATION

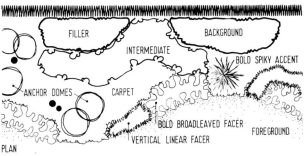

FILLER

BACKGROUND

INTERMEDIATE

BOLD SPIKY ACCENT

ANCHOR DOMES

CARPET

BOLD BROADLEAVED FACER

VERTICAL LINEAR FACER

FOREGROUND

PLAN

FIGURE 4.22 **General illustration of basic planting terminology.**

PLATE 4.8 **An effective foliage combination of** *Jeffersonia disphylla* **with a fern sp. Zurich Botanic Garden.**

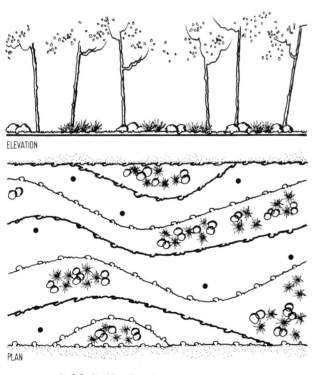

FIGURE 4.23 **Drift planting.**

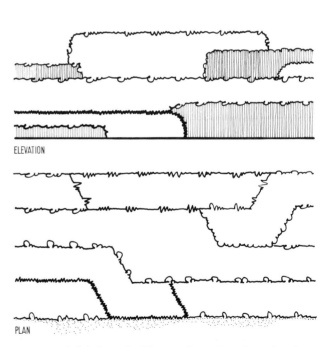

FIGURE 4.24 **Interlocking and overlapping planting.**

# Functional use

The functional requirements of landscape design can be met by relating the planting and arrangement of spaces (Figures 4.25 and 4.26) back to the average size of the user and the objects brought into any given space. From Leonardo da Vinci and the Renaissance to Corbusier and the twentieth century, this has been of major importance in making analytical assessments in design terms. The designer is thus able to influence the movements of the user. The following list indicates the ways in which plants can be used for different functions:

(i) channelling and directing traffic;
(ii) protection against vandalism;
(iii) emphasizing desire lines;
(iv) prevention of short cuts;
(v) specific spatial requirements – especially enclosure;
(vi) curtailment of access and vision;
(vii) positive camouflage – used to improve the design;
(viii) negative camouflage – less acceptable when used to cover up errors which come to light when buildings are constructed etc.;
(ix) deliberate emphasis or distortion of space;
(x) containment, compartmentalization and creation of landscape cells with a large structural framework, be it organic or not. For example, in plan diagrammatic form a cellular network of footpaths will create islands which need not necessarily be enclosed by shrubs and other forms of planting, groundcover being ideal.

When shrubs and groundcover are related to the heights of the human figure, the design possibilities for different plant heights become clearer (see Figure 4.27).

(i) *Ground level.* Groundcover is primarily used to create a ground plane or carpet which links and defines spaces without impeding views, and as a base or platform on which to display accent planting. It may also be used to prevent access. In some cases groundcovers can be effectively used as climbers as well, being continued from the horizontal to the vertical plane and thus masking the meeting point between a building or wall and the ground (see Figure 4.39).
(ii) *Knee height.* Medium to large scale groundcovers are generally used where a taller and more positive definition of space is required. They can be used as part of a gradual build up of planting from lower to higher levels.
(iii) *Waist height.* Plants of this height can be used more directionally for distinction and edge definition. The height begins to impede the view, depending on the distribution and the obser-

PLATE 4.9 **To optimize foliage compositions, contrast the bold with the refined.** *Bergenia ciliata* **versus** *Senecio bicolor ceniraria 'White Diamond'.* **Knightshayes Court, Devon.**

vation point. This group can be used to prevent short cuts being taken and may provide a protective barrier against vandals. They can be used as part of a gradual build up, as described in (i).

(iv) *Eye level*. Medium to large shrubs are used largely to give direction, provide enclosure and privacy and to obstruct or frame a view. Thorny material can be a useful access barrier or boundary definition and a deterrent to vandals.

(v) *Above eye level*. Large shrubs and small trees are chiefly used to create landscape cells, to give direction and provide screens for shelter and privacy. Really tall plants and trees can be used for emphasis, enframement and special effects, such as reflection in water.

## Planting centres and setting out

This subject is always controversial. German speaking landscape architects refer to plant material as the *lebende Baustoffe*, literally 'living (organic) building material'. This is an appropriate analogy as the designer needs to be just as aware of the behavioural patterns and performance of organic material as of inert material, particularly spread and growth rate. These become extremely important when selecting suitable planting centres. The spread of the plant material needs to be considered, and whether it will 'knit' sufficiently to conceal all patches of bare earth between the plants.

Most landscape architects develop their own system of spacing and setting out. Richard Sudell maintained that a good rule of thumb is to plant at the same distance as ultimate height. Thus if the mature height is 1 m, the planting centres should be 1 m apart; this is presumably on the basis that most shrubs and groundcovers are slightly wider than tall.

Another concept which has been developed over the years is that when forming planting associations where the span coverage of two shrubs and groundcovers differ, say a 2 m and 1 m diameter, then the following equation should be applied:

$$\frac{2\text{ m} + 1\text{ m}}{2} = 1.5 \text{ m planting centres}$$

When dealing with herbaceous and mat-forming groundcovers, the method of allocating a specific number of plants per $m^2$ is useful, but demands a good knowledge of plant material. This method would involve categorizing plants in broad groups, such as weak, moderate and fast growers. The weaker the plant's growth rate and mature state, the higher number per $m^2$, and conversely the bulkier, coarser and faster growing the plants, the less number per $m^2$.

Fortunately most groundcovers and shrubs can be classified into groups as far as planting centres are concerned. For general working purposes the doubling of centres for setting out seems practical. Figure 4.27

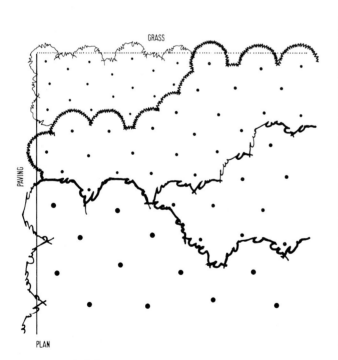

FIGURE 4.25 **Progressive transition of setting out. Spacing between different plant groups equals 1.5 × planting centres of the smaller species.**

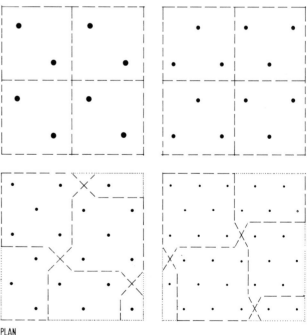

FIGURE 4.26 **Allocation of specific number of plants per square metre.**

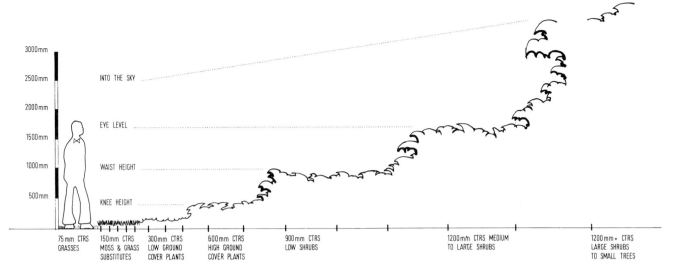

FIGURE 4.27 **Shrubs and groundcover related to the human figure.**

shows the planting centres generally used and gives the height of each group relative to the human figure. Note that the proportional distance increases between plant groups, relative to size. Examples are given below:

(i) 150 mm planting centres
Within this group falls *Cotula squalida*, and species of *Festuca* and *Sagina*.

(ii) 300 mm planting centres
The basic distance for mat-forming groundcovers such as *Vinca minor, Hypericum calycinum, Euonymus gracilis, Erica vagans, Hebe propinquum, Pachysandra terminalis*, etc.

(iii) 600 mm planting centres
Examples include *Vinca major, Viburnum davidii, Stephanandra incisa* 'Crispa', *Lonicera pileata* and *Symphoricarpos* x *chenaultii* 'Hancock'.

(iv) 900 mm planting centres
Examples include species of *Cotoneaster, Berberis, Spiraea, Cornus* and *Viburnum*.

(v) 1200 mm planting centres
This group includes taller species of those in (iv) and species of *Pyracantha, Ligustrum, Syringa, Buddleia*.

The above method of spacing will give a close-knit appearance in about three to five years. By compromising on wider spacing, an equally good groundcover will be obtained over a longer period.

It is difficult, however, to generalize about plant material, because growth patterns are so varied. *Cotoneaster* 'Herbst Feur', for example, will spread at least 2 m from the planting centre, rooting as it grows, and is self-layering while certain types of leggy and spindly shrubs with a vertical emphasis,

such as *Rubus cockburnianus, Hippophae rhamnoides, Philadelphus* and *Rosa* spp require a secondary mat-forming groundcover underneath to be effective. These are not suitable where economies are desirable as one has to pay twice to cover the same area of ground.

A very common practice consists of laying out the plants in straight rows, or on a grid known as the quincunx, as in an orchard or using forestry planting techniques. A common layout is shown in Figure 4.28; this is not to be recommended except where a formal layout is intended. Much more subtle effects can be created with a little time and effort, which are closer to the patterns and structures found in nature. Using equidistant lines on paper (strings along the ground) as a base, the distance of the plant from the lines can be varied according to a predetermined pattern. The simplest method is shown in Figure 4.29 where the planting along the first row ranges between 0–50 mm on each side of the base line, and that along the second follows the same layout with planting commencing a third of the way between the first two plants on the first row. Figure 4.30 shows more complex variations of which there are an infinite number.

Planting centres chosen for climbers along walls (Figure 4.31) and fences will depend on the design effect required from the inert materials, such as brick or timber. If planting against a given length of fence or wall, for example, or the end elevation of a building, one-third planting to two-thirds wall from corner or end creates a harmonious asymmetric composition. The golden rule when planting climbers is to plant in twos (one extra as an insurance policy), no closer than 1.2 m.

Harmonious sequential rhythms are necessary in order to achieve a natural look when selecting planting

55

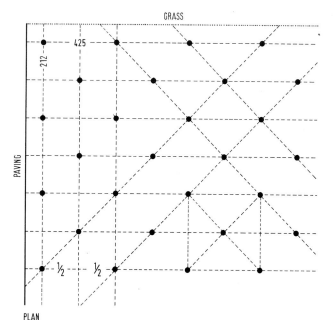

**FIGURE 4.28 Setting out: quincunx (an arrangement of five objects in a square, one at each corner and one in the middle).**

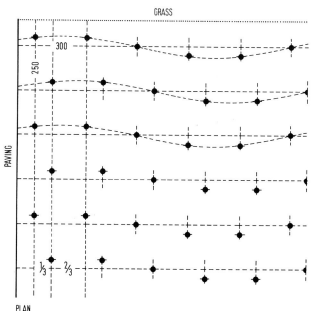

**FIGURE 4.29 Setting out at average 300 mm centres: asymmetrical stagger.**

centres for accent groups of plant material used with or without mat-forming groundcover. In Japanese garden design the ratio of 2:3:5:7 is always discernible (Figures 4.32 and 4.33). Even numbers tend to appear regimented. Another useful concept to apply when grouping plant material and selecting planting positions is to stipulate that no three plants, shrubs or trees should be

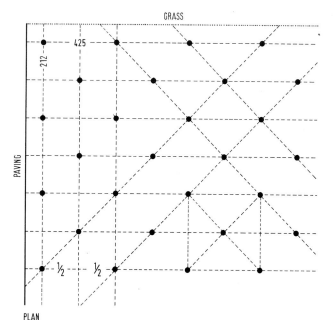

**FIGURE 4.30 Setting out: asymmetrical stagger.**

planted in a line (Figure 4.34). This is particularly applicable to trees where it shows most with tree trunks, but also applies to any distinct plant material which is compact or vertical.

A 'natural' asymmetric effect can be obtained particularly when planting bulbs in grass by simply scattering them by hand, and planting them where they fall. A handful of pebbles could be substituted to locate groups of other plants.

## 4.5 DETAILED DESIGN CONSIDERATIONS AND PLANT SELECTION

In this section more detailed consideration is given to aspects of design, and the ways in which these will affect plant selection.

To ensure that the planting design will work and that a good effect can be achieved, plants must be chosen which suit the site conditions − the soil characteristics, light, degree of shelter or exposure, and so forth.

Having analysed the site conditions and determined the design skeleton, the designer will be in a position to select the plants which will meet his needs.

Understanding of the natural biodynamic processes and ecological inter-relationships between different plants and plant communities will provide valuable information and inspiration for the landscape architect. It is useful, perhaps, to recall the Shakespearian

56

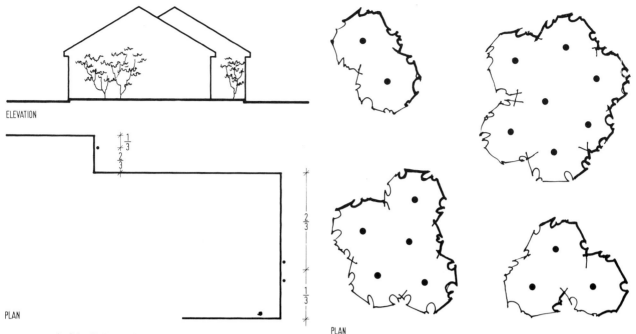

FIGURE 4.31 **Siting climbers.**

FIGURE 4.32 **Plant grouping 2:3:5:7 for harmonious sequential rhythm.**

quotation used by William Robinson to preface every issue of his renowned magazine *The Garden*: 'This is an art which does not mend nature: change it rather: but the art itself is nature.'

The designer may wish to impart symbolic or stylistic expressionism in the choice of material. On occasions he may arbitrarily choose plant material from another country or continent to meet his requirements, providing that the ecological acceptability of plant species selected relative to the location is ascertained. Without wishing to add to the existing controversy between some designers and co-professionals in allied fields of botany, ecology, forestry, and so forth, it is perhaps worth pointing out that much alien plant material is visually indistinguishable from indigenous plant material, while many native plants look distinctly exotic and foreign. This is shown in Frederick Law Olmsted's experiment with apparent 'exotics', in actual fact hardy native plants with striking foliage, in Central Park, New York.

It is well known that the bulk of shrubs and groundcovers in general use in North America and Northern Europe originated from South East Asia. While one country's weeds may be used as another country's groundcover, there is a danger in introducing alien species. Some have become so adept in naturalizing themselves, like Japanese Knotweed, *Polygonum cuspidatum*, that they have become pernicious weeds which have proved almost impossible to eradicate and have spread uncontrollably in parts of the British Isles.

## Size, life span and growth rate

When designing with shrubs and groundcover an effect of maturity and permanence can be achieved in a relatively short time; the minimum is one year but more often will be three to five years. It is worth stressing that, in planting design, forward planning on the basis of what the design will look like in five, ten and twenty-five or more years is desirable.

The growth rate of groundcover and shrubs should never be considered out of context to the growth rate of trees. In the formative years the growth rates are out of step; ground cover planting under a young tree has plenty of light, but as the tree grows this will gradually change to deep shade. In maturity, light may once more penetrate beneath the tree, as shown in Figure 4.35. It is important therefore to choose plants which will grow in the changing conditions, unless replanting with different species is anticipated. Suitably tolerant groundcovers are *Vinca minor*, *Hypericum calycinum* and *Epimedium*.

Inexperienced designers often rely on nurserymen's descriptions relative to height and this can cause some nasty surprises. Take for example a shrub like *Cotoneaster serotinus*, often described by nurserymen as $2 \times 2$ m high. At Highdown, Goring-by-sea it is approximately $13 \times 13$ m, enough to cover an average housing unit of today, including its patio garden. Another example is the now widely planted groundcover *Prunus laurocerasus* 'Zabeliana' of which

57

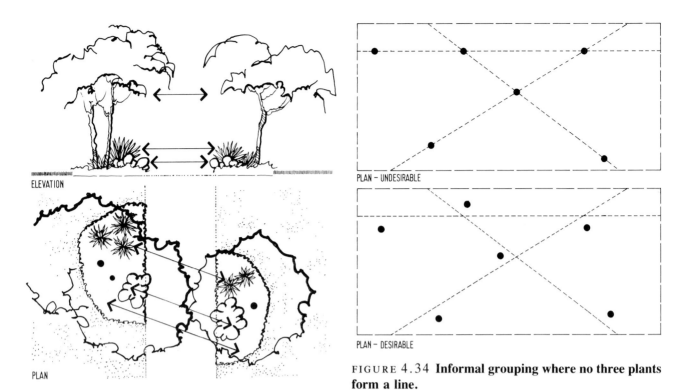

ELEVATION

PLAN

FIGURE 4.33 **Balanced bridging point using 2:3:5:7 ratio.**

PLAN – UNDESIRABLE

PLAN – DESIRABLE

FIGURE 4.34 **Informal grouping where no three plants form a line.**

there is a specimen at Nymans in Sussex, approximately 3 × 3 m and still remaining horizontal. It is as well to have access to several authoritative sources of written information in order to have as many comparisons as possible, but there is no real substitute for practical experience.

Planting for immediate effect can be acceptable when working on major exhibition projects or landscape areas to be laid out for temporary use, or where the required plant material cannot readily be obtained. Some of the best rapid growing groundcovers and shrubs are listed below:

SECTION

FIGURE 4.35 **Growth rate of tree on groundcover affecting light penetration.**

58

*Euonymus fortunei* 'Emerald Gaiety'
*Hypericum calycinum*
*Rosa virginiana* 'Harvest Fire'
*Rubus tricolor*
*Stephanandra incisa* 'Crispa'
*Symphoricarpos* × *chenaultii* 'Hancock'

In Scandinavia, fast growing and often short-lived shrubby, multi-stemmed willows or other plants are used on major landscape projects as temporary 'fillers', sometimes along the outer row of a shelter belt, until the slow-growing plant material becomes established.

## Characteristics and habit

The shape and growth characteristics of plants under the ground is as important as that above ground. The underground spread of plant roots, for instance, may be very considerable.

An understanding of the shape or form in which the plants grow and spread will help the designer not only in selection, but in layout. When choosing a groundcover, for instance, the plant's ability to colonize and spread over an area relative to its centre of planting will be important.

The compatibility of the plant material to be used should be ascertained. Certain plants need to cohabit and become entangled with each other in order to flourish satisfactorily, whereas other plants have a detrimental effect on each other, to the extent that the other species is severely weakened and in some cases completely destroyed. The foliage of *Artemisia*, for example, contains absinthium which, when deposited on the ground near adjoining plants, will severely weaken certain species, such as *Hypericum*, when it rains.

In temperate climates the marked differences between the seasons will influence the selection of plants to a considerable degree. The ideal plant will provide interest throughout the year – flowers in spring; foliage in summer; colour and berries in autumn; and branches, bark and evergreen foliage in winter. Flowers are the least important in design terms – plant form and foliage having a greater impact for a longer period.

In tropical climates the seasons are less clearly distinguished, and flowering seasons may be much longer, thus the selection of plants for seasonal variation and characteristics may not be so important.

Many groundcovers are exceptionally hardy, and will withstand average wear and tear, once established. Greater advantage should be taken of this fact, allowing planting design compositions to be made more serviceable. The amount of wear that a groundcover exposed to walking can stand varies enormously, depending on the species. The Arnold Arboretum in America has for several years been conducting trial plots of both cultivated and species groundcovers, including lawn substitutes, which will withstand close cutting and

TABLE 4.1
**Examples of different structure and branch forms**

| 1. Vertical linear | *Cytisus*<br>*Ephedra*<br>*Phormium*<br>*Salix purpurea* 'Nana' |
|---|---|
| 2. Horizontal tabulate | *Cornus controversa* and other variegated spp<br>*Emmenopterys henryi*<br>*Enkianthus campanulatus*<br>*Trochodendron aralioides*<br>*Viburnum plicatum* 'Mariesii' |
| 3. Ascending horizontal | *Lonicera pileata*<br>*Prunus laurocerasus* 'Otto Luyken' |
| 4. Bizarre and sculptural | *Acanthopanax sieboldianus*<br>*Aralia elata*<br>*Colletia cruciata*<br>*Corylus avellana* 'Contorta'<br>*Euonymus alatus*<br>*Fatsia japonica*<br>*Poncirus trifoliata*<br>*Rosa omeiensis pteracantha* |
| 5. Hummock, dome shaped | *Hebe anomala*<br>*H. rakaiensis*<br>*Picea abies* 'Nidiformis'<br>*Rhododendron williamsianum*<br>*Salix lanata*<br>*Stephanandra incisa* 'Crispa'<br>*Viburnum davidii* |
| 6. Pendulous | *Buddleia alternifolia*<br>*Genista aetnensis* |

trampling without harm. A serious attempt to institute similar trial plots should be instigated by some of the horticultural establishments in this country.

Most shrubs and groundcovers, like trees, possess a distinctive form and branch structure, some examples of which are given in Table 4.1. The way in which this is perceived will vary according to the season, and the distance from which the plant is viewed. The clearest effect will be that of deciduous material in winter. Shrub forms may be part hazy and part solid where there is a mixture of evergreen and deciduous material, becoming more distinct during the spring and summer. An example will serve to show the variety in structure and outline in a single species. A large group of ghost brambles during the summer can be likened to a nimbus cloud formation. In winter their elegant, multi-stemmed arching, bluish-white branches will have a lighter but none the less distinct volume, despite the loss of foliage, allowing a *clair voyée* through to the groundcover beneath and beyond. From middle distance the ferny texture of the foliage billowing in the wind will be very apparent; close up it has a strong impact, with its heavily indented foliage elegantly drooping down in cascading plumes.

The time of day and light conditions will also affect the way in which a plant appears to the observer. At twilight, the outline becomes black and more rounded, depending on viewing distance. *Contrajour* effects (against the light) may be particularly noticeable in stormy weather, or where light coloured foliage is displayed against dark hedges, trees or a building.

Bold and architectural plants have in recent years had an unparalleled vogue, for obvious reasons; they are distinct and lend themselves to use for accent and emphasis. William Robinson was perhaps the first great exponent of foliage planting design. Although he abhorred architectural design and carpet bedding, he was one of the first to select bold, statuesque architectural plants and to introduce them into the countryside and woodland to afford naturalization.

All plant material can be graded according to texture of foliage, branches and bark. Leaves may be rotund, cordate, oval, oblong, or acuminate and so forth in shape with smooth, glossy or hairy surfaces; branches and bark may be rough or smooth, thin or thick, etc.

The range of opposing textures should be sufficiently distinct to obtain the desired contrast, which may be reinforced by the overall shape of the plant and its colour.

Colour is of great importance to the planting scheme, but should form part of a carefully considered design in which the form, structure, texture and density all play their part. Shrubs and groundcover dissimilar in shape may not be so in colour, and this may result in a blurring of the design if not considered. Similarly plants having dominant characteristics may be far from dominant in colour.

Colour in plant material is not an inert pigment. It is a culmination of the light-reflective and light-absorptive qualities of the foliage, the former being seen to particular effect in shiny foliaged evergreens such as *Prunus laurocerasus*, or *Ilex* spp where the foliage may appear silvery and metallic. Another good example is *Nothofagus cliffortioides* which, when sited in the sun against a dark background or shaded area, looks like floating, horizontally stratified, sparkling silver coins.

When using colour in a design, spottiness should be avoided by providing sufficiently large units of colour. Gertrude Jekyll affirmed that colour in the garden should not consist of mere dabs set out on a palette. To use plants correctly they should form 'beautiful pictures'.

The most common colours of indigenous plant material in the country concerned will form a guide to the range which may be suitable. In Britain, for example, a large percentage of the native flora is predominantly white or near white, followed by yellow and blue. In tropical climates the range of colours will be far greater and the strong sunlight will display vibrant colour to great effect.

Strong colours should be used with care: red, for example, although a complementary colour of green, can completely destroy a spatial composition by overpowering the greens. Neutral white or cream is a useful transition element from light to dark blue, or yellow to orange and red. Strong plant colours may have limited uses except in urban situations where bold colours are used to enliven the exterior of buildings. Similarly colourful groundcovers can be used to form large-scale abstract patterns, akin to Victorian carpet bedding adapted to the use of permanent groundcovers.

When using colour in planting design one is able to accentuate three-dimensional volumes by over- and under-stressing their visual impact, but a balance in the choice of warm and cool hues should be achieved. Leonardo da Vinci observed that 'colours seen in shadow will reveal more or less of their natural beauty in proportion as they are in fainter or deeper shadow'.

Colours exert a strong psychological effect upon the observer, affecting both mood and attitude to environment. Care should be exercised with the use of strong colours in confined areas and spaces. In courtyard planting design, for example, only a minimum of strong colour should be used for direction and emphasis. Harsh colours in confined spaces exert an overpowering, depressive influence. Colour can be used in the landscape in much the same way as an architect or interior designer might use it, to define spaces and give them a special character.

A thorough knowledge of the colours and textures of building materials and landscape artefacts such as fences, gates, seats, etc. plays an important role in the choice of colour when selecting suitable plant material. A blue-black semi-engineering brick suggests the use of silvery white and yellow, including light green and lemon green, whereas a dark red brick suggests deep, dark evergreens or blue, blue-grey and grey which are able to offer a sufficiently strong contrast. A fence stained dark blue or brown associates well with silver, white and yellow flowered and foliaged plants.

## Special requirements

The sociological aspect of planting design is little understood, but there are definite effects upon the psychological well-being of individuals and the subsequent effect on their social behaviour. Some of the effects of colour have already been noted, and it has been shown that the landscape architect can influence the movements of an observer by the use of planting material.

PLATE 4.10 **Intrinsic geometry of rectangular wood paviors and orbicular nasturtium leaves. Bonn Bundesgartenschau 1979.**

PLATE 4.11 **Land art — the amphitheatre treated as a giant sculpture using the universal ground cover: grass. Sun life of Canada National HQ, Basingstoke.** (Landscape Architect: *Preben Jakobsen*)

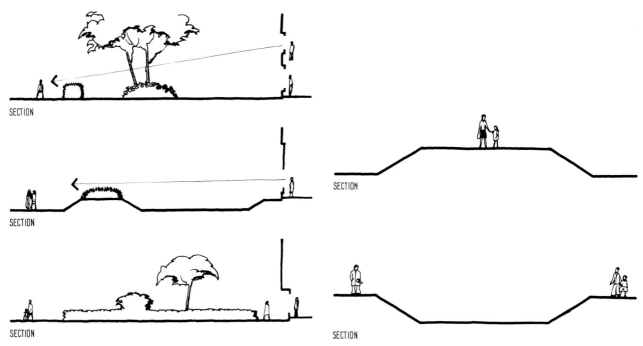

FIGURE 4.36 **Defensible space. Psychological effect of landform, shrubs and groundcover discourages intruders in overlooked areas.**

FIGURE 4.37 **Effects of depressions or mounds on movement.**

FIGURE 4.38 **An artist's impression of a garden for blind people. Whitley Park, Ellesmere. The plants are aromatic and a handrail surrounds the planted areas.** (Landscape Architects: *Donaldson/Edwards Partnerships*)

These facts can be used in a landscape design to discourage public access to semi-private areas overlooked from windows, as shown in Figures 4.36 and 4.37. People will normally tend to cross in a direct desire line between two points, but there is a distinct psychological objection to crossing dished or sunken grass areas. People will generally skirt the edge of a depression. The converse is true of a raised mound of grass, provided that the slopes are not too steep.

Planting can be specially selected for groups of people such as the blind (Figure 4.38) or deaf. The blind appreciate rough and smooth textured bark, coarse and smooth foliage, aromatic shrubs and groundcovers, and the rustling of foliage in the wind, etc. The deaf, whose optical perception is sharpened, may particularly appreciate *contrajour* lighting which tends to highlight well sited multi-stemmed shrubs with distinct foliage.

## 4.6 GROUNDCOVERS

## Grass, the universal groundcover

Throughout the world grass is the most commonly used groundcover, but perhaps nowhere more so than in

62

Britain, where the climate is particularly well suited to turf culture. Its prime use is to cover the ground and provide a horizontal plane. The landscape architect in his role as landscaper, landshaper and land sculptor has in grass, when used in conjunction with contouring and earthworks, a tool well suited to the manipulation of spatial changes in level. The creation of grassed mounds and other features is also a useful way of disposing of surplus topsoil and subsoil.

The combined practical and ornamental values of a close-cropped sward of grass can be appreciated in a variety of ways, from the landscaping of historic ruins and monuments, to the grounds of stately homes, to the creation of modern grass amphitheatres. The list below is presented to indicate where grass cover has in the past been used to particular effect, in the hope that it will stimulate the imagination and perhaps suggest new ways of using grass effectively as groundcover.

| | |
|---|---|
| Neolithic, religious | Ornamental hill figures |
| Viking | Fortresses and domestic hill settlements |
| Iron Age | Fortresses and tumuli (e.g. Silbury Hill) |
| Roman villas | Hill forts, dykes (e.g. Offa's Dyke) |
| Medieval castles | Moats, dykes and seats |
| Renaissance | Ideal towns in Italy, French engineers |
| Sixteenth century | Le Nôtre, *tapis vert* |
| Seventeenth and eighteenth century | Repton and Brown's great rolling landscapes |
| Puckler | Pyramids of grass |
| Victorian and Edwardian | Jekyll, Lutyens; unmown grass, mown grasspaths, waterworks, bridge abutments. |

A modern movement in the use of grass and earth sculpture can be discerned from the end of the nineteenth century, gaining popularity in the twentieth. This includes grass amphitheatres in Scandinavia in the 1940s, the Aspen Memorial, Colorado in 1955, the Zurich Horticultural Exhibition in 1959, and the grass gardens of Burle Marx in the 1960s.

## Mosses, lichens and ferns

Mosses and lichens are considered by some to be undesirable weeds. In Japanese gardens, however, moss has always been appreciated as a groundcover; some consist almost entirely of moss, with a few maples and bamboos juxtaposed against round boulders, formal or informal paving and buildings.

In Britain one of the most notable examples of the use of moss is in the Savill Garden at Windsor, under mature beech trees. Indeed, we may be about to see the

PLATE 4.12 **Stylized step formation incorporating inert stone mosaic and grass groundcover. Zurich Botanical Garden.**

PLATE 4.13 **Stratified, landscape-integrated steps, using the planting to create a zig-zag bridging effect. Westmill, Hertfordshire.** (Landscape Architect: *Preben Jakobsen*)

PLATE 4.14 **Inert groundcover of stepping stones and beach pebbles contrasted with layers of organic ground cover plants – giving an effect like a dry river bed. Broadwater Park, Denham.** (Landscape Architect: *Preben Jakobsen*)

PLATE 4.15 **Roses as groundcover at Meilland et Cie demonstration gardens at Cannet des Maures, Var, Provence.**

revival of moss growing on a large scale. It has been fostered in the USA for some time. There are a number of Victorian gardening books on mosses, lichens and ferns which indicate the former popularity of these plants.

Whilst paving full of moss on a public path can be dangerous, in a less accessible space it can be used effectively in paving joints to create a feeling of age and mystery. Perhaps one of the most effective moss plantings of this type is at Dartington Hall, where moss on both the stone paving and walling is juxtaposed with large *Fatsia japonica*.

Good moss substitutes are *Sagina subulata*, *Arenaria* spp, *Saxifraga* spp, and *Cotula squalida*. In milder parts *Helxine solierolii* will rapidly spread to form close mats in semi-shaded areas, and in sunny sites *Bolax glebaria* can be used.

Lichen is not often considered as a groundcover but in a suitable climate, such as in Cornwall, where stony and rocky ground, roofs and walls often become invaded with lichen, the effectiveness of the plant as a cover can be seen.

Ferns are becoming more widely used amongst land-scape architects. They have been used along the frontage of York University's Institute of Architectural Studies, and in courtyard design and exhibition areas.

Several ferns are low and ground-hugging, notably *Scolopendrium vulgare and Polypodium vulgare*. *Polystichum angulare* 'Proliferum' has a spreading habit and displays a neat rosette that when used *en masse* appears like a carpet of filigree snow crystals.

## Weeds as groundcover

The accepted definition of a weed is a plant in an unwanted place. To a landscape architect plants which are native to a locality or which adapt so well that they grow rapidly and with little maintenance can form useful and attractive groundcovers particularly where the need for economy is uppermost or where there is a concern to foster the use of native species and their associated wildlife (see Chapter 7). An example is shown in Plate 4.17 where *Petasites fragrans* grows naturally in a Cornish graveyard. It is a rampant ground cover which can sometimes be a nuisance, but if kept

65

**PLATE** 4.16 **Roses fully established as groundcover at a junction of the Parkway, Durham.** (Landscape Architect: *Brian Clouston & Partners*; Photograph: *Peter Lake*)

**PLATE** 4.17 *Petasites fragrans* **growing wild in Madron Churchyard near Penzance. Design despite neglect.**

under control can in certain conditions be extremely effective and cheap.

Plate 4.18 shows how well the South African Hottentot fig *Carpobrotus edulis* has adapted to become a typical groundcover on the rocky coasts of Devon and Cornwall. Once more, it can become invasive and its spread should be controlled.

## Climbers and ramblers

The early groundcover trials at the Arnold Arboretum in America did a great deal to indicate the possibilities of climbing and rambling plants as groundcovers.

They are useful in constricted urban situations to fuse the horizontal and vertical planes. *Hydrangea petiolaris* was used for this purpose in Arne Jacobsen's Harby School. Climbers and ramblers can also be used to good effect in permanent planting containers on overhanging parapets or balconies (*see* Chapter 9 and Figure 4.39).

On motorway banks in the USA various vines have been used extensively as an effective method of erosion control. The Road Research Laboratory in Britain has conducted tests to ascertain the shock absorption and impact resistance of shrubs, notably with a rambler *Rosa multiflora japonica*, with a view to using them as a buffer for central reserves.

## Vegetables and herbs

A recent trend in Scandinavia has been to accept vegetables in their own right as part of landscape design. Perhaps the emphasis on economy and wholesome

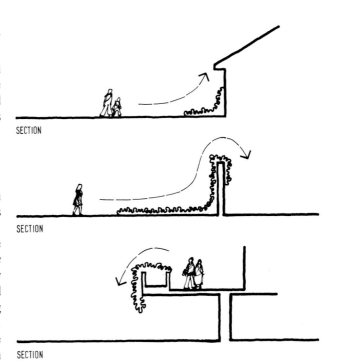

SECTION

SECTION

SECTION

FIGURE 4.39 **Use of climbers and ramblers to fuse vertical and horizontal planes and on balconies.**

foods has helped this trend; no longer need it be considered socially and visually unacceptable to grow vegetables in the front garden. A well tended kitchen or herb garden is culturally and aesthetically as acceptable as ornamental groundcover and shrubs. Aromatic groundcovers include many culinary varieties and are of special value when designing for the blind.

PLATE 4.18 **South African Hottentot fig naturalized on rocky coast of Cornwall.**

## Inert materials

The use of inert materials in conjunction with plant material stems from oriental landscape design, notably the stylized Japanese garden. Oriental designs featuring a miniature river bed with carefully chosen and sited plant material, have been instrumental in the development of the typical American west coast garden. Although much larger in scale than those from which they derive inspiration, these gardens adhere to the basic stylistic principles of the oriental garden. The idea of simulating beaches or dry river beds following the Californian example has won many ardent admirers in Europe, particularly amongst Swiss and German landscape architects.

The acceptable proportion of pebbles to planting can be critical, for example 1:1 is never very satisfactory; either plants or pebbles should appear to dominate. Russell Page in his *Education of a Gardener* declares that if he were given a white walled courtyard, a load of gravel as ground cover, and a golden elderberry bush, he could provide an effective landscape composition relying almost totally on the inert gravel.

Through close observation of nature one can arbitrarily create a particular landscape type within an enclosed and confined environment such as a courtyard. Sand, gravel, pebbles, cobbles and boulders are just as much groundcover as the plants themselves, their function being decorative and to act as a foil to the plant material.

The courtyard gardens of the Gulbenkian Museum in Lisbon by Professor Cabral are some of the more recent successful European examples of the use of inert materials and plants, relying mostly on tall grass species and pebbles.

Although bark mulches have been introduced primarily as a weed suppressor, their decorative aspects offer possibilities for wider use for offsetting plants, similar to the technique in interior planting where a terracotta 'leca' type aggregate is used for offsetting dark evergreen foliaged plants.

## 4.7 DESIGNING WITH GROUNDCOVER, SHRUBS AND CLIMBING ROSES

### Shrub, wild and park roses

The park roses, which include shrub roses, species roses (botanical roses) and thicket roses, are hardy and strong in growth. They are admirably suited to foreground planting in shrubberies, and planting on slopes and contoured mounds, as well as in solitary groups and as specimens in lawn areas. They often have decorative growth, rich flowering periods and, in certain species, strongly coloured hips and autumn colouring. Pruning is generally unnecessary. The species is usually wind-resistant and extremely tolerant of severe drought.

The rose family comprises some 400 species which are globally distributed in the temperate and cold temperate zones of the northern hemisphere. In the tropics and subtropics roses only grow in mountainous areas. The roses used today originate from middle and south-western Asia. Roses are both evergreen and deciduous and some climbing varieties are known to exceed 20 m in height: the famous *Kiftsgate* rose at Kiftsgate Court in Gloucestershire is some 14.5 m high and occupies almost 1/10 ha. With few exceptions, the species, shrub, park shrub, groundcover and thicket-forming roses are extremely hardy. Most of them will withstand $-15°C$, and the species will even withstand $-30°C$. They are adaptable to most soils, tolerating a pH ranging from neutral to alkaline.

## Designing with native rose species

In the UK there are approximately six native species of wild rose (Europe 44), *Rosa canina* (the dog rose) which is 3 m high, being the most common in the south in hedgerows and scrubland. *R. arvensis* (the field rose), 1 m high, found in hedges and woods; *R. pimpinellifolia* (burnet rose), 0.5 m high, found in dry places and on coastal dunes; *R. tomentosa* (downey rose), 2 m high and *R. rubignosa* (sweet briar/eglantine), 2–3 m high, are found in hedges and scrub on northern hills. The indigenous species are particularly useful for dune stabilization. The salt-tolerant Japanese 'sea tomato' *R. rugosa* (or Nordic apple rose) is naturalized throughout the sandy Baltic coastlands as a permanent pioneer species, with unequalled spreading ability; the creeping North American *R. virginiana* 'Harvest fire' with its widespread arching growth, good autumn colour and red stems in winter, should be specified more often for game coverts and the like.

## Groundcover roses

The qualities required of a good groundcover rose ranging in height from 40 to 60 cm are manifold. Most importantly it should have an economical establishment cost and a long combined season of interest. After this structural form, stem shape and colour, foliage shape and colour, good large or small single flowers in a variety of colours, hips and finally scent should be considered. Hardiness and tolerance of poor site conditions are a prerequisite. Low maintenance cost, weed suppression, non-suckering on its own roots and resistance to pests and diseases, including the dreaded mildew, are also all essential requirements. The increasing popularity of groundcover roses is linked to a low purchase cost and high site performance. Quite a few groundcover roses need to be planted, at two plants per m[2]. Average supply cost varies with varieties, scarcity and numbers to be supplied.

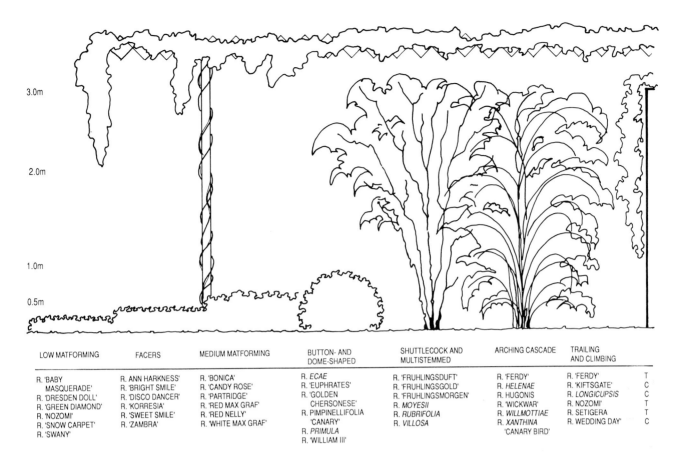

| LOW MATFORMING | FACERS | MEDIUM MATFORMING | BUTTON- AND DOME-SHAPED | SHUTTLECOCK AND MULTISTEMMED | ARCHING CASCADE | TRAILING AND CLIMBING | |
|---|---|---|---|---|---|---|---|
| R. 'BABY MASQUERADE' | R. ANN HARKNESS' | R. 'BONICA' | R. ECAE | R. 'FRUHLINGSDUFT' | R. 'FERDY' | R. 'FERDY' | T |
| R. 'DRESDEN DOLL' | R. 'BRIGHT SMILE' | R. 'CANDY ROSE' | R. 'EUPHRATES' | R. 'FRUHLINGSGOLD' | R. HELENAE | R. 'KIFTSGATE' | C |
| R. 'GREEN DIAMOND' | R. 'DISCO DANCER' | R. 'PARTRIDGE' | R. 'GOLDEN CHERSONESE' | R. 'FRUHLINGSMORGEN' | R. HUGONIS | R. LONGICUPSIS | C |
| R. 'NOZOMI' | R. 'KORRESIA' | R. 'RED MAX GRAF' | R. PIMPINELLIFOLIA 'CANARY' | R. MOYESII | R. 'WICKWAR' | R. NOZOMI | T |
| R. 'SNOW CARPET' | R. 'SWEET SMILE' | R. 'RED NELLY' | R. PRIMULA | R. RUBRIFOLIA | R. WILLMOTTIAE | R. SETIGERA | T |
| R. 'SWANY' | R. 'ZAMBRA' | R. 'WHITE MAX GRAF' | R. 'WILLIAM III' | R. VILLOSA | R. XANTHINA 'CANARY BIRD' | R. WEDDING DAY' | C |

FIGURE 4.40 **Form studies diagram.**

## Form and colour studies of roses

Plant form and colour studies are essential ingredients for any landscape designer. With roses they are of paramount importance, and as designers are spoilt for choice, it is essential to select the correct clone, species and cultivar to suit the site from the fairly wide form spectrum (see Figure 4.40). For mat-forming groundcover the white-flowered R. 'Swany' and pink R. 'Nozomi' are typical; for dome shapes the primrose flowered R. ecae and R. primula can be used; and the maroon R. 'William III' is useful in foreground landscape step designs juxtaposed with spiky accents and boulders. For solitary accent display or group planting, R. rubrifolia, with a distinct multistem rising from the base, typifies the shuttlecock shape. There are numerous selections in the multistemmed arching cascade group, including R. 'Ferdy', R. 'Helenae' and R. 'Wickwar'. Many of the groundcover roses have a dual or multipurpose use. For retaining walls the trailing cascade R. 'Nozomi' is outstanding, R. 'Ferdy' equally good, and many of the climbing roses will adapt for trailing over retaining walls.

## Roses for foliage composition

The palette of rose foliage and stem colours is very wide. The best known is the grey–purple R. rubrifolia, with its distinct multistem shuttlecock shape, useful for solitary display on a carpet-forming groundcover. The colour associates well with the silver–greys of the Elaeagnus and Senecio species, and other purple foliaged shrubs such as Cotinus 'Grace'. Of the grey-leaved shrub roses three are outstanding, namely R. fedtschenkoana, R. murieliae and R. soulieana. All are white-flowered and associate well with purple-foliaged plums such as Prunus cistena. The shrub rose R. 'Isphahan' and the historic rose R. alba 'Celeste' are both magnificent pink-flowered, self-complementary, grey-leaved foliage plants. The glossy leaves of the groundcover rose R. nitida at 0.5 m high, positively reflect light, whereas R. scabrosa, with its matt-corrugated leaves, appears to absorb light. One of the best roses for autumn is R. virginiana 'Harvest Fire', with its bronze, purple and red colour. Many rose species, notably R. rugosa, retain deep yellow and green autumn leaves simultaneously. The glossy, light-

69

reflecting leaves and stems of the evergreen roses are a good design attribute.

## Roses for selected design effects

For colourful transparent scarlet thorns nothing quite equals the red barbed wire, R. omeiensis 'Pteracantha'. For shaggy, peeling bark and large round brown hips the Burr or Chestnut rose R. roxburghii is unusual. The Mexican Sacramento rose, R. stellata mirifica, and the prairie rose, R. setigera, are ideally suitable for hot, dry desert-like conditions. For fragrance, the pale yellow R. rugosa 'Dr Eckner' and the double lemon yellow R. Frühlingsduft are highly scented. R. 'Fritz Nobis' is a light salmon-coloured, clove-scented rose, and R. 'Parfum de l'Hay' is a highly scented, hybrid rugosa much in demand. For shade tolerance, R. wichuriana and R. 'Max Graf' are among the best. One of the most attractive design qualities of roses is the autumn and winter effect of hips, which range from the tiny red cherry-like R. Carolina to the huge orange, potato-like R. rugosa, the bright orange bottleshape of R. moyesii, the scarlet hips of the Alpine rose R. pendulina, the distinctive jet black hips of R. spinossissima and the myriads of orange, pea-sized hips on R. souliana. Roses with aromatic foliage include the incense roses R. primula and R. rubiginosa, and if you want a rose without thorns, the Danish R. 'Lykkefund' is one of very few. In value for money, R. helenae is hard to beat, with a 5.5 m spread per plant. For solitary accent specimens the eyecatching R. 'Ballerina' and showy R. 'Eyepaint' are especially good.

## Rose hedges, fedges and walls

Roses are ideally suited to hedge design. In the 1940s Danish landscape architects promoted the primrose-coloured R. hugonis as being the hedgerow rose par excellence, and it has also been used in group planting with dwarf dark mountain pine and white-stemmed birches to such as extent that it has become a Danish stereotype. The similar and perhaps superior R. xanthina 'Canary bird' also makes a splendid hedge and can be perfectly matched against a foil of bronze and purple-leaved elder (Sambucus nigra atropurpurea). The ubiquitous R. rugosa can be seen in many northern European housing estates, where it is used to define road layouts and for traffic and pedestrian segregation. In recent years the compact, low North American R. carolina has gained popularity for this purpose in Denmark. Mixed hedgerow design is a dying art; species diversity is essential in all forms of ecological planting design, even if it means having to introduce alien species at times.

The re-emergence of the fedge (fence and hedge) as an element in planting design is fortuitous. Industrial and hi-tech projects requiring enclosure by ugly chain-link security fences are ideally suited to camouflaging with thorny rose species. On a recent scheme, a green plastic chain-link fence was interwoven with R. wichuriana, a robust, glossy-leaved Japanese scrambler, as the plants grew. In public design there is a great future for sculptural rose features, using weld-mesh, both free-standing and compost-filled. For a floriferous wire or chain-supported rose hedge, R. 'Penelope', R. 'Felicite et perpetue', R. 'Joseph's coat' and R. 'Masquerade' are hard to beat.

## Roses for pergolas, spaceframes and trees

Pergola and spaceframe designs are popular all over Europe. There is, however, a lack of suitable new climbing varieties. R. 'Delbards Orange', a vigorous, clear-foliaged newcomer from France, 2–3 m high, and the dazzling crimson evergreen climber 'Cadenza' are more suited to the warmer climes of California, Australia and the Mediterranean. The R. wichuriana hybrids 'Bonfire' and 'Lady Gay' are extremely hardy, and will grow in adverse conditions to reach 3–6 m in height. The well known 'Kiftsgate' and white-flowered 'Synstylae' roses can be seen in National Trust gardens scrambling up trees and forming useful backdrops to shrub and herbaceous borders. For small pergolas the amber-coloured R. 'Lady Hillingdon' and R. 'Emily Gray', and for pillars and columns the pink R. 'Rosanna', and R. 'Lavinia' plus the red R. 'Altissimo', are suitable.

Climbers introduced in the 1980s include R. 'Breath of life', a rose with a future, and 'Golden showers' which associates well with blue clematis. Another recent favourite is the uniquely chocolate-coloured 'Harpippin' from Harkness, first seen at the Liverpool Garden Festival in 1984. This new climber juxtaposes rather well with the white R. 'Wedding day'. Another older, unusual-coloured rose is the slate-purple R. 'Veilchenblau'. Of the newer varieties, the single-flowered red R. 'Sweet Sultan' which is 2–3 m high, is suitable for posts and pillars. One of the best American varieties is the pure yellow R. 'High Moon', and the popular orange flame-coloured R. 'Danse de feu' will be around for some time yet. R. 'Albertine' with its vicious thorns, salmon flowers and plum red stems is one of the best rambling roses. R. 'The Garland', an old vigorous variety with small, fragrant, white daisylike flowers, should not be forgotten. R. 'Amadis' is an old thornless climber with crimson flowers.

## Roses for interior malls and atria

The vigorous evergreen roses, both the hardy and the more tender varieties, are eminently suited to interior mall and atrium designs. The yellow banksian rose R. banksiae lutea reaches a height of 7.5 m and is particu-

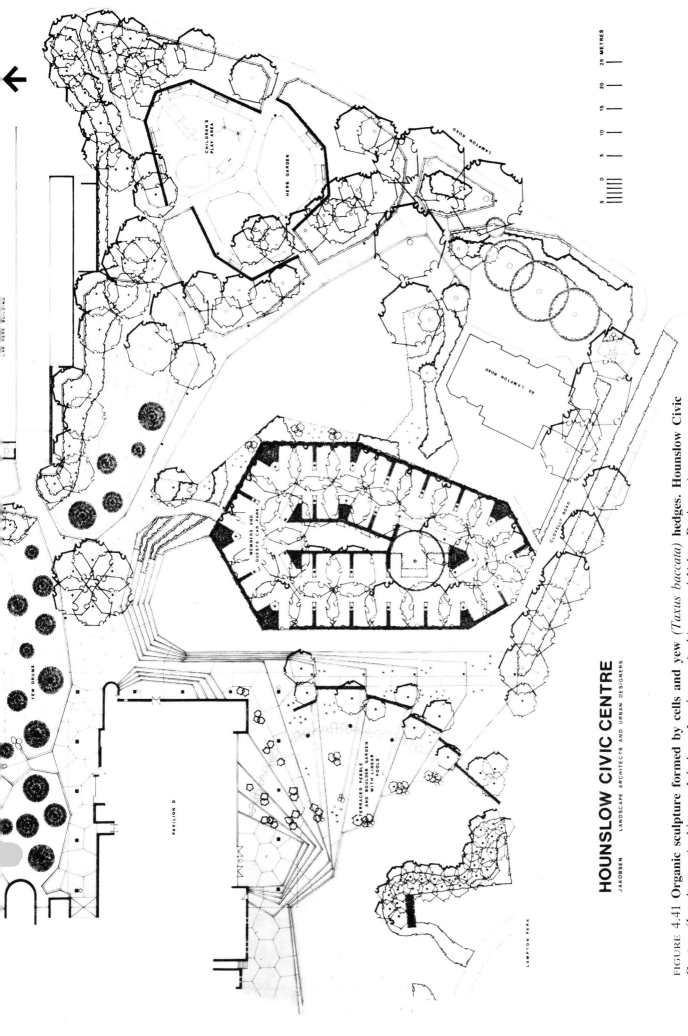

FIGURE 4.41 **Organic sculpture formed by cells and yew (***Taxus baccata***) hedges. Hounslow Civic Centre.** (Landscape Architects: *Jakobsen Landscape Architects and Urban Designers*)

**HOUNSLOW CIVIC CENTRE**
JAKOBSEN LANDSCAPE ARCHITECTS AND URBAN DESIGNERS

CHILDREN'S PLAY AREA

HERB GARDEN

MEMBERS AND GUESTS CAR PARK

PAVILION D

YEW DRUMS

CAR PARK BUILDING

TERRACED PEBBLE AND BOULDER GARDEN WITH LINEAR POOLS

LAMPTON PARK

CLOVELLY ROAD

LAMPTON ROAD

88 LAMPTON ROAD

5  0    5    10    15    20    25 METRES

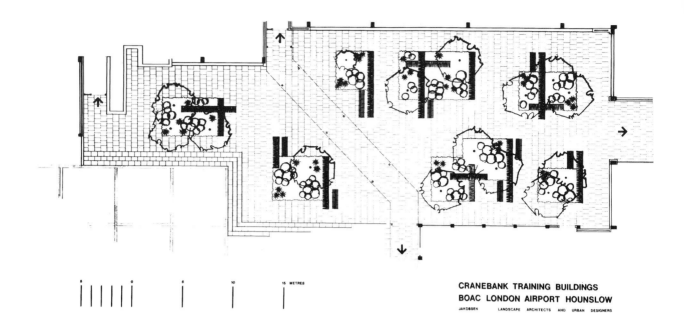

FIGURE 4.42 **Organic sculpture with constructivist influence. Tall dark green yew** *(Taxus baccata)* **hedges with penetrating lower, yellow-green** *Lonicera* **'Baggessen's Gold'. BOAC Training Centre.** (Landscape Architects: *Jakobsen Landscape Architects and Urban Designers*)

larly useful for columns and spaceframes. If a warm, sunny wall is available, the lemon-scented white Macartney rose *R. bracteata* is excellent. The rampant Himalayan white-flowered *R. brunonii* reaches a height of 9–12 m, as does the vigorous white Burmese rose *R. gigantea cooperii* in ideal conditions. The semi-evergreen fragrant white Cherokee rose *R. laevigata* is a Chinese species naturalized in south-east USA. Of the bold 'Synstylae' roses, the remarkable white banana-scented *R. longicupsis* and the related white-flowered *R. sinowilsonae*, introduced by 'Chinese Wilson', the well-known plant collector, are superb performers for a jungle-like look.

## Roses and herbaceous plants, shrubs and bulbs

In Europe it is a long established design tradition to mix roses with herbaceous plants and shrubs. Dark red roses associate particularly well with dark blue lavender, such as *L. Hidcote*, and low, dark blue mound-forming *Ceanothus thyrsiflorus* 'Repens' and *C.* 'Blue Mound', as well as with many grey-leaved herbs and plants. Blue grasses such as *Avena candida* and *Festuca glauca* are also most effective, and companion plants such as *Nepeta* 'Six Hill Giant' are superb with yellow

and orange polyantha roses, usually in foreground designs. As facers in shrub and herbaceous borders, the polyantha roses *R. koressia* and *R. zambra*, with their low, compact, healthy foliage and pure colour, are superb. The cool blue–grey broadleaved hostas are very good with the warmer colours. For linear verticality and contrast the blue-grey leaved alliums and *Iris pallida* 'Dalmatica' are excellent. Blue scilla and muscari associate well with salmon- and pink-flowered roses. For ecological planting the native white *Allium ursinum*, *Endymion nonscripta* (bluebell) and *Ornithogalum nutans* are eminently suitable.

## Roses in motorway design

The greatest potential use of the new groundcover and shrub roses lies in the new colourful designs for the motorway network. The 'Meidiland', 'Kordes' and 'Poulsen' varieties particularly lend themselves to fluid linear brushstroke compositions. Bridge abutments and tall retaining walls are ideal for ramblers and climbers, and use of colour and shape would be a clear way of signalling change and variety in the roadscape. Research reported by the American architect Kevin Lynch in his book *The View From The Road* helps to explain how colour is perceived when travelling at speed in a car.

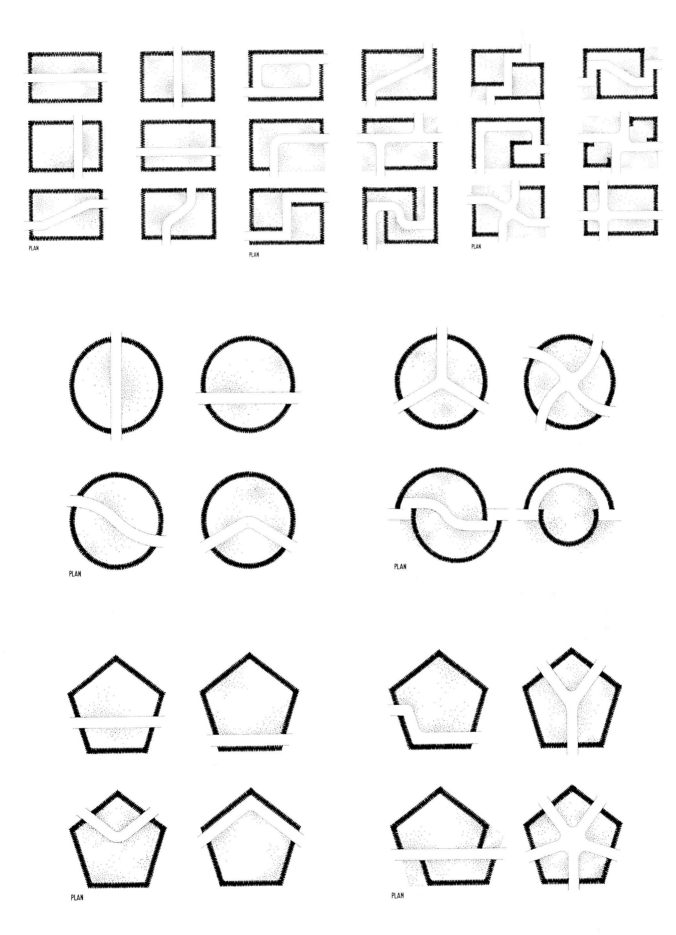

FIGURE 4.43, 4.44 and 4.45 **Sequences showing variations on hedge treatment.**

73

## Abstract painting with groundcover roses

The compact weed-suppressing groundcover roses, including the low polyantha cultivars, lend themselves to colourful abstract interpretations. Burle Marx, the well known South American landscape architect, has indicated how painting with plants heightens the perceived landscape experience; in the UK the late Percy Cane, garden designer, wrote 'The bare ground is our canvas, and shrubs, trees, flowers and stones are the paints. The cubistic and supremacist styles are perhaps the most adaptable. Care should be taken to select enclosed courtyard spaces where the design may be viewed from above; small inner urban parks overlooked by tall buildings and flats are particularly suitable.

## 4.8 DESIGNING WITH HEDGES AND OTHER CLIPPED AND PRUNED ELEMENTS

Throughout the history of landscape gardening the hedge has in its many forms played an important role in aspects of planting design (Figures 4.41 and 4.42). Initially the function of the hedge was to define land ownership, create shelter and prevent stock from trespassing. Later, the hedge surrounding the main house, castle, or cottage became largely ornamental culminating in the elaborate *broderie parterres* associated with seventeenth-century French and Dutch gardens in particular.

Scandinavian landscape architects have relied heavily on inspirations from the past and still do with regard to low and tall hedges in clipped and semi-clipped form. A notable departure is the hedge in depth principle (giant groundcover) used in Denmark by both Arne Jacobsen in Klampenborg school, and Jørn Utzon at 'Kingo' Houses, Helsingor. They both planted common beech *Fagus sylvatica* to be clipped at a height of approximately 1.2 m. Such large-scale clipped groundcover, regrettably, requires intensive maintenance. These two schemes are distinctive and appear to work well. In the Jørn Utzon scheme particularly the idea 'less is more' has been taken to its ultimate — only two species, *Fagus sylvatica* and *Vitis quinquefolia*, appear to dominate the scene.

Another distinctive departure is the use of the simulated hedge, really 'fedge' which is an Old English term for a combined fence and hedge. Such a fedge was deliberately created in the sculpture garden of Louisiana Museum near Copenhagen and consists of a leaf mould container made of impregnated soft wood with open gaps between the boards. This has been planted with common ivy and the boards are now totally covered.

The cubistic clumps of box used by Gunnar Martinsson and S. I. Anderson in the Outdoor Room

exhibition at Bastad in 1961 showed how this planting technique could be successfully used in the small private garden. C. Th. Sorensen made a notable contribution in front of Kalundborg Cathedral, with a design which changes with the height of the viewpoint. Due to its horizontal and simple layout the design avoids destroying the architectural unity of a distinctive townspace. The recent revival of labyrinths and mazes has a direct bearing for the landscape profession in the future, particularly in urban design. There is no doubt that hedges are a form of organic sculpture and their use is as varied as the designer's inventiveness. See Figures 4.43 to 4.45.

Apart from being pure space-enclosing elements, shrubs used as hedges can serve a multiplicity of design purposes within an overall planting design. Hedges can be seen as sculptural volumes affording a neutral background against which to display a shrub or tree for emphasis, or to make carefully controlled design statements with other plants. They allow free use of herbaceous borders and colourful planting schemes which can be concealed within landscape cells formed by hedges so that they do not detract from the purity of the overall design. Lutyens' work with Gertrude Jekyll is an example. His sombre dark yew hedges provided the perfect background for her herbaceous borders and shrub planting.

## ACKNOWLEDGEMENT

All drawings and sketches in Chapter 4 were produced by Jakobsen Landscape Architects.

## FURTHER READING

# 1. Design appreciation

Albarn, K. *et al. The Language of Pattern* (London: Thames and Hudson Ltd 1974)

Arnheim, R. *Towards a Psychology of Art* (London: Faber and Faber 1966)

Austin, R. L. *Designing with plants* (New York, Van Nostrand Reinhold 1982)

Bagger, B. *Nature as Designer* (London: Frederick Warne and Co. Ltd 1961)

Clark, K. *Landscape into Art* (Harmondsworth: Penguin Books Ltd 1949)

Critchlow, K. *Order in Space* (London: Thames and Hudson Ltd 1970)

Edwards, E. B. *Pattern and Design with Dynamic Symmetry* (New York: Dover 1967)

Ehrenzweig, A. *The Hidden Order of Art* (London: Weidenfeld and Nicolson 1967)

Goodman, N. *Languages of Art* (London: Oxford University Press 1969)

Gregory, E. L. and Gombrich, E. H. *Illusions in Nature and Art* (London: Gerald Duckworth and Co. Ltd 1973)

Grillo, P. J. *Form, Function and Design* (New York: Dover 1960)

Hackett, B. *Planting Design* (London: E. and F. N. Spon 1979)

Langer, S. K. *Philosophy in a New Key* (New York: Mentor Paperback 1954)

Matthews, W. H. *Mazes and Labyrinths, their history and development* (New York: Dover 1970)

Robinette, G. O. *Evergreen Form Studies* (New York: Van Nostrand Reinhold 1983)

Vernon, M. D. *The Psychology of Perception* (Harmondsworth: Penguin Books Ltd 1962)

Walker, T. D. *Planting Design* (Arizona: PDA Publishers Corporation 1985)

White, L. L. *Aspects of Form* (London: Lund Humphries 1968)

Wilson, F. A. *Art as Understanding* (London: Routledge and Kegan Paul 1963)

## 2. Landscape design

Allen, G. *The Colours of Flowers* (London: Macmillan and Co. Ltd 1882)

Booth, N. K. *Basic Elements of Landscape Architectural Design* (New York: Elsevier Science Publishing 1983)

Brooklyn Botanic Gardens *Creative Ideas in Garden Design* (Brooklyn Botanic Gardens 1965)

Carpenter, P. L., Walker, T. D. and Lanphear, F. O. *Plants in the Landscape* (San Francisco: W. H. Freeman & Co. 1975)

Chijiiwa, H. *Color Harmony* (Minehead, Somerset: Greenwood Publishing 1987)

Doczi, G. *The Power of Limits* (Boulder and London: Shambhala Publications 1981)

Eaton, L. K. *Landscape Artist in America: The life and Work of Jens Jensen* (University of Chicago Press 1964)

Grant, J. A. and C. L. *Garden Design Illustrated* (University of Washington Press 1954)

Hubbard, H. V. and Kimball T. *Landscape Design* (New York: Macmillan 1917)

Kramer, J. *Gardening with Stone and Sand* (New York: Scribners 1972)

Robinette, G. O. *Plants, People and Environmental Quality* (Washington, DC: US Department of the Interior 1972)

Wong, W. *Principles of Color Design* (New York: Van Nostrand Reinhold 1987)

## 3. Shrubs and Groundcover

Boddy, F. A. *Foliage Plants* (Newton Abbot: David and Charles 1973)

Boddy, F. A. *Groundcover* (Newton Abbot: David and Charles 1974)

Brooklyn Botanic Gardens *Tree and Shrub Forms: Their Landscape Use* (Brooklyn Botanic Garden 1972)

Duffield, M. R., and Jones, W. D. *Plants for Dry Climates* (USA: HP Books 1981)

Fish, M. *Ground Cover Plants* (London: W. H. Collingridge Ltd 1964)

Foley, D. J. *Groundcover for Easier Gardening* (New York: Dover 1961)

Gorer, R. *Hardy Foliage Plants* (London: W. H. Collingridge Ltd 1966)

Gorer, R. *Climbing Plants* (London: Studio Vista 1968)

Gorer, R. *Multi-Season Shrubs and Trees* (Newton Abbot: David and Charles 1971)

Haworth-Booth, M. *The Flowering Shrub and Garden* (London: Country Life 1938)

Hillier, H. G. *Hilliers Manual of Trees and Shrubs* (Winchester: Hillier and Sons catalogue, published annually)

Lloyd, C. *Foliage Plants* (London: Collins 1973)

Paturi, F. *Nature, Mother of Invention* (London: Thames and Hudson Ltd 1978)

Philbrick, H. and Gregg, R. B. *Companion Plants* (London: Stuart and Watkins 1967)

Robinette, G. *Design Characteristics of Plant Materials* (American Printing and Publishing Inc. 1967)

Robinson, W. *The Subtropical Garden* (London: John Murray 1879)

Seabrook, P. *Shrubs for your Garden* (France: Editions Floraisse 1973)

Sinnes, A. C. *Shade Gardening* (San Francisco: Ortho Books 1982)

Sunset Books *Lawns and Groundcovers* (California: Lane Magazine and Book Co. 1964)

Thomas, G. S. *Plants for Ground Cover* (London: J. M. Dent and Sons Ltd 1970)

Thomas, G. S. *Colour in the Winter Garden* (London: Phoenix House, 1957; Newton Centre, Mass.: Charles I. Blandford Co. 1957)

Wyman, D. *Ground Cover Plants* (New York: The Macmillan Company 1956)

# CHAPTER 5

# Herbaceous Plants and Bulbs

## A. DU GARD PASLEY

## 5.1 INTRODUCTION

Within the time scale of the landscape, herbaceous planting has a place as fleeting as the shadows of the clouds drifting across the face of some ancient rock formation. As fleeting, and as important, for it is just those chance shadows which give added richness to the texture of landform, revealing new depths until that moment unperceived. The transitory nature of such planting has both dangers and rewards. Forgotten for a year or two, some cherished effect may vanish into bindweed and desolation. But how easily it can be replaced or altered, unlike the wrongly shaped oak wood or misplaced cedar standing for centuries in mute reproach to their planter.

The possibility of change and experiment is an essential element in designing with herbaceous plants – a constant process of evolution, impelled not so much by a desire for novelty as by a wish to express a little better some cherished vision or idea. To have the vision is one thing, to try to capture it in materials which not only change constantly, but are at the mercy of pests and diseases, sudden storms and late frosts, is another. As Gertrude Jekyll wrote: 'Those who do not know are apt to think that hardy flower gardening of the best kind is easy. It is not easy at all. It has taken half a lifetime merely to find out what is best worth doing, and a good slice out of another half to puzzle out the ways of doing it.'[1]

As with any other medium, it is first essential to understand its limitation, which in this case is an inability to provide permanent structural form. However solid the pattern at high summer, any scheme relying entirely on herbaceous planting will inevitably lack height and firm structure in winter. Whether it is the box patterns of a parterre, the informal groupings of rhododendrons and trees at a woodland edge or the subtle arrangements of dwarf evergreens and bold foliage shrubs in the border, all herbaceous planting needs a frame and a background. Although the details of such planting are considered elsewhere, its presence remains implicit throughout this chapter.

Within the short span of a lifetime, changing social and economic conditions, to say nothing of the strange tides of fashion and ideas, can overturn accepted attitudes and just as easily reinstate them later. In the garden, scientific or mechanical advance may simplify an apparently complex process, making the practical and labour-saving ideas of the previous decade appear merely boring and sterile. While the long-term plans of the tree and shrub planter may not be much affected by these considerations, the question of maintenance vitally affects the use and extent of herbaceous planting. Not long ago it seemed that the day of the herbaceous plant – apart from those rampant enough to become groundcover or stolid enough to require little attention when once established – was over. Now new techniques and changed conditions have altered the situation and it is worth while considering those areas in which such planting is most appropriate today.

## 5.2 THE USE OF HERBACEOUS PLANTS AND BULBS

The term 'herbaceous border' has long been a household phrase – indeed a music hall joke in some circles – so it is perhaps justifiable to consider this feature first. At their best, in the hands of such sensitive artists as William Robinson, Gertrude Jekyll and Vita Sackville-West, these borders were beautifully controlled compositions in which trees, large shrubs, both deciduous and evergreen, shrub roses and drifts of small shrubs formed a constant framework to broad groups of plants, many of which were grown as much for their foliage colour and form as for their flowers. To such borders were admitted anything which could help the picture. Bulbs,

PLATE 5.1 **Bold architectural foliage of** *Rheum palmatum* **'Atrosanginium' contrasting with low hammock-forming geraniums and myosotis.** *(Anthony du Gard Pasley)*

PLATE 5.2 **A clear-cut rectangular pattern often proves a better setting for low herbaceous plants than the vaguely amoebic forms of 'island beds'.** *(Susan Jellicoe)*

PLATE 5.3 **In the wild garden, herbaceous plants take on a new dimension.** *(Susan Jellicoe)*

lilies, annuals, tender bedding plants, and even vegetables had their place. The possibilities for experiment were almost limitless and there is nothing to invalidate this style of gardening today. Indeed, there has probably never been a better vehicle for the garden genius. Love of flowers, colour and endless variety of material can have full rein, while a strong basic composition holds the whole together.

The mixed border, then, has an important place in our gardens, although different emphasis may change its basic character. It is impossible to keep such a border in full bloom for more than two months, so that before any consideration is given to detailed planning a preliminary decision must be made about the purpose which it is to fulfil. In general terms, a border which relies largely on a good structure and where sculptural forms, foliage contrasts, and tone values predominate, will be the most satisfactory because they remain constant, while flower colour can create special effects and be used to highlight particular times of year.

Where space is available or other considerations

allow, borders created for particular seasons of the year can be very effective. In this case, plant material need be considered only in relation to the chosen period and excellent effects can be obtained by using plants which have only a short season of beauty and are otherwise gross or unattractive – it is surprising how many of these there are. Such seasonal planting needs to be placed so that it does not appear obtrusive in its off periods, a problem particularly acute in the case of monocultures such as the iris garden, which is a dream of beauty for two weeks and either boring or hideous for the remaining fifty.

A later development of the old herbaceous border has been the island bed. The theory of fairly low-growing plants set out in the open away from down-draughts and problems of light caused by adjacent walls and hedges, and easily accessible on all sides, is an excellent one. As practised, the result – a selection of ill-assorted kidneys and amoebic shapes uneasily afloat on a sea of grass – has been deplorable. A simple dignified pattern of square or rectangular beds planted

PLATE 5.4 **Strong, well arranged contrasts of form and texture are quite as important as colour in the border. Here the interplay between rounded and spiky forms is particularly effective.** *(Anthony du Gard Pasley)*

with these same low-growing perennials, perhaps with an asymmetric counterpoint of evergreen shrubs and foliage plants, would be exceedingly effective. If the beds could be edged with bands of brick or stone, at once emphasizing the pattern and reducing grass cutting problems, they would also be very easy to keep. Such an arrangement on a large scale was created by Norah Lindsay in the 1930s to replace the old Victorian parterre at Blicking Hall in Norfolk, and to this day it remains the most spectacular feature of that garden. There are also many old paved rose gardens, where the soil has become rose sick, to which such a solution could be applied with advantage.

How often have Victorian and other parterres been swept away under the plea of saving labour, and stretches of tedious grass remained to bore the eye thereafter? Sometimes, of course, such parterres were added to landscape gardens in which they had no place, and consequently they are better gone, but where parterre and setting were designed together, the loss is all too obvious. Now that mechanical and chemical aids have reduced the problem of maintenance, there is a good case to be made for restoring the balance of these gardens by re-creating, perhaps in a simplified form, the old parterres and filling them with carefully chosen perennials rather than with time-consuming and gaudy bedding plants. A careful choice of good foliage plants, interspersed with suitable bulbs, would provide interesting contrasts of texture and colour, while the usual problem of too much bare earth in winter would

not arise, since at that season the exact pattern of the cut box-work would be seen to its greatest advantage.

The old knot garden, too, might well be revived, since in its earliest form the 'open knot' was planted with herbaceous perennials, bulbs and lilies rather than concentrated bedding schemes. Such knots are well adapted to present conditions as they often formed the major part of gardens even smaller than many of those current today, and their firm simple patterns have a calming effect on the magpie collections of plants to which the average gardener is so addicted.

Outside the confines of the formal garden, herbaceous plants take on a new dimension. In the woodland and wild garden they are, or can seem to be, in their native habitat, grouped naturally in long drifts under the trees, running out under shrubs and through the thin grass at the woodland edge. Apparently self-sown, certainly self-perpetuating and requiring a minimum of maintenance, many of the plants which are too rampant for the garden proper can find an ideal home there. As one eighteenth-century writer explains: 'Art should never be allowed to set foot in the province of Nature otherwise than clandestinely and by night', so however much nature is improved by art, the results must still appear natural, and this is one of the most difficult effects to achieve artificially. However carefully arranged, our groups tend to look stiff and lumpish, lacking the spontaneous flow of plants in the wild. Observation, aided by notebook or camera, and a careful study of plant groupings which please us, are

79

PLATE 5.5 **The natural method of one major effect at a time always looks impressive if there is sufficient space available, but it must be comprehensive. Mixed daffodils sold for naturalizing would have created a visual disaster instead of a harmonious unity. Hampton Court.** *(Preben Jakobsen)*

essential if we are to achieve really satisfactory effects. Once again the most worth-while advice comes from Gertrude Jekyll, whose trained eye and meticulous power of observation produced some of the most penetrating examinations of the use of plant material. She it was who noted the proportions of dominant and subdominant plants in their natural setting and the way in which plant associations ebb and flow in the wild, the dominants reversing roles, meeting, mingling and dividing again as soil, exposure or mere chance have affected them. She shows, too, how plants will grow in layers, their roots being at different levels, an important fact which we can use not only in the wild garden but also within the confines of our cultivated borders.[1]

Where the woodland opens to areas of rough or seldom mown grass, in the orchard or where the garden merges into paddock or parkland, there is an opportunity to practise that form of flowery meadow gardening beloved of William Robinson and described in his book *The Wild Garden*.[2] He was perhaps the first — although by no means the last, as it has become a very popular form of modern gardening — to point out the infinite charms of the flower-filled alpine meadow. This concept of the garden as an idealized meadow had a much earlier application in the 'flowery mead' of medieval romances and paintings, where so often the Virgin sits upon a carpet of grass scattered with flowers, each placed singly like the fleurettes of the tapestries. 'The orchard was fair beyond content. Herbs grew there of every fashion, more than I am able to name...'[3] In fact, massed planting was as alien to the vision of Botticelli as it was to Berthe Morisot, whose women rest in softly flowering meadows, enshrined in a sunny nineteenth century world before the hay was cut. Into a silvery carpet of grass are woven pointilliste spots of colour which form a complementary effect to balance the solid wood of bluebells or the bank of primroses.

However carefully we analyse, however objective our approach, our vision is influenced inevitably by subjective things — the half-remembered lines of Wordsworth (and I for one will always reject those great armies of brazen trumpets which march across our grass in springtime, simply because they spoil a cherished childhood vision; my heart could never dance with such rigid flowers and I am unable to see them for what they are, only for what they are not), the painting in some forgotten exhibition, the memory of a distant conversation. These echoes, just as much as our horticultural knowledge and our power to appreciate light, form and colour, will influence both our planting and that ideal of perfection which we try to achieve. For this reason there can be no absolute, merely a search for an ideal which may perhaps illuminate the lives of others beside ourselves, and in this respect the herbaceous planter has an advantage. The imagination can perceive the oak, but its planter will never live to see its perfection, whereas in a year or two the results of *Iris pallida* 'Dalmatica' spearing up beside a drift of *Ruta graveolens* can be seen, assessed and accepted or altered as our taste dictates.

## 5.3 WHAT TO PLANT

The possibilities are infinite, but are conditioned by various limiting factors which affect all forms of planting design. Soil, climate and exposure will force rejection of many plants which might otherwise be suitable, or at least they should do so. It is probably possible to grow anything anywhere, after a fashion, but to what purpose? Those who practise such gardening are no more than Commandants of concentration camps full of ailing and unwilling prisoners, and the visual results of such methods are little more agreeable. Then there is the human element which may reject otherwise desir-

80

able plants for purely personal reasons, but even so an almost daunting choice remains.

## Colour, shape and texture

Every plant has form, texture and colour and of these elements it is the first two which are more important because if they are not fully considered any planting scheme will become a formless jumble. Only careful observation at every season — for effects change so markedly with the passage of the months that each plant can appear in half a dozen different guises — will make us fully aware of the quality and of the possibilities of each plant. Some are sculptural, holding shadows even deeper than those within carved stonework, others are pure form or pure texture, or some balance between these things. Each needs to be placed to make full use of its potential, whether it be striking or recessive, either by direct contrast or the juxtaposition of like and like. One can contrast form and texture, texture and colour, colour and form, but seldom all three elements at once or the planting will become like a Victorian letter, so full of underlinings and exclamation marks as to be incapable of any emphasis at all.

The ease and popularity of colour photography has brought many problems in its wake, not least an inclination to play down the importance of composition. Pleasing colours agreeably grouped may seem to make a picture, whereas if the scene is reduced to black and white a satisfying composition of forms and proper balance of light and shadow will be found to be lacking, with a resultant loss of effect. At the outset it is useful therefore to think of any new planting in terms of black and white, infilling the major structure of trees and shrubs with abstract compositions whose form, texture and tonal values are fully developed. When the abstractions are considered satisfactory, it is not difficult to turn these formal elements into plant material, remembering that any group of plants takes on the basic outline and quality of a single plant of the same species. Even at a distance too great to observe any detail of leaf or branch structure, a clump of oak could not be mistaken for a clump of beech because the shape of the two trees, individually or grouped, is different.

For some strange reason, colour seems to be regarded by many people as a pure end in itself, without regard to what effect is being achieved. The results too often remind one of Elvira's exasperated remark in Noel Coward's *Blithe Spirit*: 'The border by the sundial looks like a fruit salad. . .' But green is also a colour, or more strictly an almost infinite variety of colours, and remains the most important because, as far as this country is concerned at least, it is predominant. 'No white nor red was ever seen as amorous as that lovely green' wrote Andrew Marvell and although our colour planting may not be dictated by its amorous quality, green has other advantages.[4] 'Annihilating all that's made to a green thought in a green shade'. . .what could be more restful in our frenetic age than that? The relief to the eye provided by a single stand of cool green aquatic plants in the big marquee at Chelsea Flower Show was very great, after the concentrated blast of multicolours everywhere else.

What then is colour to do, and how is it to be achieved? Colour can be soothing or stimulating, can create warmth or coolness, introduce light or shadow, create or emphasize a mood, underline the good or play down the bad points of a site, but it can do none of these things unless it is used with sensitivity and care. In general we will want our effects to be as long lasting as possible, and for this reason will make the greatest use of foliage which lasts for most of the season rather than flowers which have a fairly short life. This brings us back to green — or silver, grey, blue, yellow, white, purple, crimson, pink, apricot, and more besides — which leaves can provide. Indeed, one can make very satisfactory compositions from foliage plants alone, full of colour and interest without the rather ephemeral help of flowers at all.

There are two basic ways of using colour: by direct contrast (which produces a very restless picture if overindulged) or by building up a series of related tones and shades, with occasional contrast for dramatic effect. The easiest and safest way to handle it is to decide on one theme colour and then use it in a series of variations against some neutral background. This can be most effective in a small garden or as part of a large one: the results will seem clever and original while in fact it is difficult to go wrong.

A yellow garden, with flowers and leaves in every available shade from cream to near orange against either a dark green or silver background, is always satisfying, especially if the strong colours are kept to the centre of the beds, working out to paler tones at the edges. A red garden, in a setting of dark green or purple leaves, is very stimulating, as the great red borders at Hidcote prove, while a purple garden can seem a little sombre, although the magnificent purple border at Sissinghurst Castle proves that it can be carried through with success. Blue or white gardens are cool and fresh, the first for a sunny, the second for a partly shaded position because while blue seems to absorb sunlight and looks drab without it, white flowers look best in partial shade or at least against a background of shadow.

When using a number of different colours it is best to keep to those which incline towards yellow or those which are based on blue. Although flower colours appear to be almost limitless in their variety, when one comes to examine them carefully it becomes obvious that very few of them are so pure that they do not have a touch of either blue or yellow in their make-up. Taking an absolutely pure white base and adding yellow to it produces first a warm white in which there is a hint

PLATE 5.6 **The close, matt texture of clipped yew is a perfect background to detailed planting placed in front of it, particularly if this is of a pale and light reflecting nature. Great Dixter, Luytens House.** (*Preben Jakobsen*)

of cream, then cream of deepening intensity, then yellow. Progressively adding red will produce all the oranges, salmons, apricots and orange pinks (which do contain a little blue also, but the yellow is dominant) until in the end there is pure scarlet. In the other range there are cold bluish whites working up to pure blue which, with a varying addition of red, will produce all the pinks varying from apple blossom to deep rose and through crimson to violet and purple. Even if there is no direct blue or yellow in the scheme, the flowers based on one or the other have a natural affinity and always look well together.

Working within one range of colour in a setting of complementary or carefully contrasted foliage, the results can be very harmonious, but it must be remembered that the eye needs a space of rest and refreshment before another colour group can be appreciated. It is here particularly that the cool grey, silver and bluish foliage plants come into their own, helping to clear from the eye the impressions from one set of colours before the next, which may not necessarily be in violent contrast, is introduced. The light in this country is always blue — visibly so on some days — and the blue atmosphere has a dramatic effect on flower colour, intensifying pale colours, particularly if they are blue based, and giving them a vibrant depth which they would never have under a harder, yellower sun. That is why all those sweet pea colours, swooning mauves and greyish pinks, blues and silvers, look so wonderful in our borders and so frightfully limp and washed out when similar effects are attempted in some less misty climate. Likewise, many of the dashing colour contrasts which look so stimulating under a southern sun appear tawdry and vulgar if copied here. Bright colour should always be seen in full sunlight, pale colours (other than certain blues) gain from a measure of shade or from being seen against a shadowy background. In fact certain plants (mostly those with white or pale yellow flowers) actually seem to glow in the dark and this ability can be used to create special effects where the garden is going to be used at night.

Sometimes it is possible to rely on a single sweep of unadulterated colour, an effect to which bulbs lend themselves particularly well. The bluebell wood, the orchard of daffodils, the churchyard carpeted with snowdrops, have a pure impact which any additional element would destroy. Except on a limited scale within a firm framework, the mixtures which are so often all that can be obtained are most unsatisfactory. The mixed daffodils, too much alike yet too different,

82

and the mixed bedding plants which are guaranteed to destroy any carefully composed scheme of planting. The flowery mead works because the flowers are various, and set in a common matrix, but in the case of these mixed bags and boxes the flowers are all alike and the colours appear merely muddled.

## 5.4 PLANTING AND MAINTENANCE

The purely formal garden is the easiest of all types to make and to maintain. Single species planted at regular intervals and kept in a consistent way require a degree of labour but very little thought, an important factor today when it is easier to get help from an unskilled labourer than a professional gardener. With this in mind, the placing of blocks of plants, either symmetrically or asymmetrically, has much to commend it. Variations can still be obtained from the contrast of height, colour and texture, but the importance of a neat habit of growth, regular flowering pattern and interesting foliage, preferably evergreen but at least long lasting, is obvious. Obvious too is the desirability of plants which remain growing happily in one place without a constant need to lift and divide. In some cases it is perfectly possible to use plants with invasive tendencies, such as *Stachys lanata* for instance, by cutting round them every year to maintain the shape of the group, though of course in time the centre will become woody and the clumps will need division and replanting.

In association with static plant groups, which need little attention apart from the removal of weeds and the application of a yearly mulch, bulbs of various kinds come into their own in a way which is impossible in most areas of cultivated ground. The dying foliage of many bulbs is rather disagreeable, and it is a great help if it can be hidden by the new growth of associated plants. Early crocus and most small bulbs come well through thymes, dwarf campanulas, ajuga and similar things, while larger bulbs like narcissus, tulips and hyacinths tend to do better if the host plant is scarcely visible at their time of flowering but comes up later to engulf their fading leaves. Hostas, small geraniums, pulmonaria and many others are good in this way. Not only spring bulbs but alliums, autumn crocus and similar subjects can be used, often in the same group but planted in layers (although of course not directly on top of one another) to maintain a constant succession of interest through the season.

In the border the ability to plant in layers is important as it helps to prolong the season of full beauty or to create incidents of interest outside the major period of display. For instance, a group of Chinese paeonies could make the basis for three quite separate effects needing the minimum amount of labour and maintenance. In spring, the richly coloured young shoots might form an ideal setting for those white or white and salmon-pink daffodils which tend to look so artificial in the wild garden, together perhaps with tulips of an associated colouring which would extend the flowering period until the expanding paeony leaves concealed the unsightly dying foliage of the bulbs. In June, of course, the paeony flowers would be in full beauty, while later in the season the leaves, by now beginning to assume their fine autumn colouring, could make a base for a bold group of late orange lilies and later still a foreground to a drift of chrysanthemum or richly coloured asters. In this way the same area of ground might make an almost continuous contribution to the general effectiveness of the border while providing ideal growing conditions for a number of subjects all of which resent root disturbance.

With care, and understanding of the basic needs of various plants, any number of similar associations may be built up. Nor is it necessary to deal solely with purely hardy subjects, since in the warmer parts of the country at least, gladioli, dahlias, ixias and other half-hardy things can be overwintered outside with a little protection, and in colder parts they can always be lifted and replanted each year in the conventional way. When planting the border it is essential not to be dominated by preconceived ideas, and the use of dahlias and gladioli is a case in point. They are regarded as being stiff and ugly simply because they are associated with rows of bamboo canes, or with green-painted stakes crowned with straw-filled flower pots, while the flowers themselves are thought of in relation to the show bench or the market stall. Such thinking is very limited and lacks perception since there is scarcely any plant which is truly ugly or which cannot be grown to great advantage somewhere providing the setting and the method of cultivation are right. Smoky violet and rich purple gladioli rising through and supported by a strong drift of common lavender, the weight of the heads making them bend forward and sideways in graceful sheaves above the grey foliage, must surely banish all memories of bamboo canes and green twine, while crimson dahlias similarly supported by the lower branches of *Cotinus coggygria* 'Atropurpureus' are equally stunning.

Similarly, spaces can be left for the inclusion of bedding plants and annuals, spaces which in themselves need not be noticeable since thin drifts rather than large clumps are required. Geraniums of the right colouring can be very effective used in this way, and often old straggly plants, perhaps drawn up by being kept too long in the house and therefore of no use for bedding schemes, are ideal for the purpose. Other house plants can also be used, either plunged in their pots or set out and repotted again before the onset of winter. The tender plumbago, easily increased from cuttings, will introduce a note of clear pale blue which could be picked up and repeated in other parts by drifts of Cambridge blue lobelia. In the same way, many of

83

the tender silver and grey leafed sub-shrubs can be propagated and planted out where time allows. Even a small greenhouse, or a house with sufficient broad window ledges, can provide a good variety of less hardy plants to increase the border's range in summer. Naturally hardy annuals, preferably grown in a patch of reserve ground and later planted out, or boxed bedding plants from the florist, can be used in the same way. In the latter case, however, it is essential that the exact variety of plant is known, since all too often the plants available commercially are only in colourings or mixtures which are difficult to use.

In an established garden nature itself takes a hand, often producing self-sown groupings which, if thinned out and reshaped, can become an agreeable feature of border or wild garden. To take advantage of such chance effects, it is essential that all weeding should be done by hand and with the greatest care, only known weeds being removed and all other seedlings being allowed to remain until they prove their worth. Even when misplaced such seedlings can be lifted and used elsewhere or passed on to others who are in need. This principle of self-seeding can be encouraged by removing plants which have reached the seeding stage, or cutting off the seed heads as the case may be, and throwing them down in a spare corner or between other plants where they will remain out of sight. Many chance seedlings can be obtained in this way without trouble although of course the seed can be allowed to ripen and then sown in a more conventional way where time and space allow.

Both in the border and in the wild garden the removal of fading flowers, foliage and excessive growth is im-portant since even a few groups obviously past their prime can destroy the good effect of others still in bloom or yet to come. This is a task which is best undertaken daily and just ten minutes after breakfast or before dinner can make all the difference even to a large area of planting. No plant should ever look as though it has been cut back severely, but many can be cut back to half their size after flowering by careful reshaping, the complete removal of some growths and the shortening of others to points concealed by leaves either on the plant itself or on its neighbours. In this way natural outlines can be maintained and yet more space provided for the expansion of those plants which will produce their effects later in the season. Although these techniques are most necessary in the border, they can be extended to the wild garden, since even in an informal setting it is often necessary to remove excess leaves or shoots, or get rid of withered flowers in order to maintain the characteristic appearance of certain plan groupings.

Continuous adjustment and shaping do not only apply to the removal of fading material but also to the adaptation of plants to their positions as they grow. It is not always realized how many herbaceous plants can change their appearance, depending on the way they are treated. With some tall growing perennials, such as many of the asters, the height of flowering can be controlled by pinching out the shoots as they develop, and a sweep of a particular colour rising at different levels through the border can be achieved in this way. Other plants like helianthus and rudbeckia can be pulled forward and held down with long wire loops to cover bare spaces where oriental poppies, or even

PLATE 5.7 **An occasional tall plant of strong character, used near the front of the border, creates a three-dimensional effect which is helped considerably by the low planting below it.** *(Anthony du Gard Pasley)*

bulbs, flowered earlier in the season. These normally tall plants when grown almost horizontally form sheets of bloom from freely produced short side shoots. This habit allows groups of early flowering plants like lupins (which subsequently leave untidy gaps) to be grown quite far back in the border as the spaces can be covered from behind. Once again, even the wild garden can benefit from the possibility of creating sheets of colour rather late in the season when they might not be obtainable by more conventional means. In this, as in so many other realms of life, it is illusion rather than reality which is all-important.

Nothing is so boring as the old concept of the herbaceous border as a kind of highly coloured railway embankment, the plants all evenly graded from back to front in ever diminishing size, each group being neatly held in place with a ring of canes and string. The use of shrubs, trees, climbers and roses in the border helps to prevent this dreary effect, since low plants used as groundcover can sometimes sweep almost through to the back of the border, underplanting some shrub which is at once tall and bare below, while in other places tall plants can surge towards the front of the border like a wave, giving a three-dimensional effect. Staking and support will still be necessary, although the development of many varieties which are self-supporting has helped to reduce the extent of the problem. In some cases plants can help to support each other, bands of low shrubs helping to restrain the plants behind them, while the stout stems of delphiniums cut back to the right height could hold up weaker growths of asters or helianthus leaning forward over them. Otherwise there is really nothing to compare with brushwood inserted as the plants begin to grow in spring, any surplus pieces being cut out when full growth has been achieved, the whole aim being to ensure that the plant shows itself off to the best advantage without any appearance of artificiality.

The flowering orchard or meadow is perhaps the least affected by considerations of detailed maintenance, since this is largely a question of knowing exactly when to cut the grass to preserve order but to do the least damage to the various plants involved. However, flowering meadows do not spring up of their own accord and it is generally best to strip the grass from the required areas and resow them with a finer mixture to which the seeds of wild and suitable garden flowers, either bought from the seedsman or self-collected, have been added. Before sowing, bulbs can be planted and groups of plants put in to establish colonies which will then spread themselves gradually outwards by rooting and seeding. For the first few years undesirable weeds will have to be removed by hand but thereafter probably no more than a twice yearly cut will be necessary. Where it is not possible to treat the whole area in this way, it is best to prepare strategically placed patches to be planted and sown, so that plants and young seedlings do not have to contend with tough meadow grass until they are established. If the right species have been chosen, the plants will spread slowly to the untreated areas.

## 5.5 CONCLUSION

The effects to be achieved with herbaceous plants and bulbs are almost limitless in their variety, the only limiting factors being the extent to which we study their needs and habits of growth, and our perception of their visual qualities. Although plenty of information exists in the form of books and articles, there is no substitute for personal experience, observation and experiment, for all too often the writers merely follow one another and there is little advance in understanding. Never choose a plant or bulb solely from a catalogue description or the evidence of a specimen at a flower show, unless it is bought purely for experimental purposes to study its year-round effects and habits of growth, for otherwise time, money and effort may be wasted on something entirely unsuitable for its purpose.

The use of plants is not a purely practical matter, for scent, colour and form have an emotive power which can touch the springs of memory and emotion, giving an added dimension to our work and linking it firmly to the world of ideas. Plants are just as much the raw materials of art as are paint, bronze and marble. With these materials, the practical hands of the gardener and the trained eye of the artist achieve results as satisfying to the human spirit as anything to be found in the museums and art galleries of the world.

## FURTHER READING

Fairbrother, N. *Men and Gardens* (London: Hogarth Press 1956)

Hobhouse, P. *Colour in your Garden* (London: Collins 1985)

Jekyll, G. *Wood and Garden* (London: Longmans, Green and Co. 1914)

Robinson, W. *The English Flower Garden* (London: John Murray 1883)

Sieveking, Albert Forbes *In Praise of Gardens* (London: J. M. Dent & Co. 1899)

Thomas, G. S. *Perennial Garden Plants* (London: Dent 1976)

Thomas, G. S. *The Art of Planting* (London: Dent 1984)

## REFERENCES

1. Jekyll, G. *Colour in the Flower Garden* (London: Country Life, 1908)
2. Robinson, W. *The Wild Garden* (London: John Murray, 1894)
3. Anon. *Aucassin and Nicolette* (Thirteenth century)
4. Marvell, A. *The Garden* (Seventeenth century)

CHAPTER 6

# Water Plants

## ALLAN HART

## 6.1 HISTORICAL BACKGROUND

The water lily is unique in having been an object of veneration for almost four thousand years. There is evidence that members of Egyptian royal families and priests of the nineteenth and twenty-first dynasties were buried with petals of the water lily covering their bodies. The religious significance of this plant was attributed to its ability, after the rainy season, to arise anew in all its purity from a resting place of dank, evil-smelling mud.

This lily was called the Nile Lotus, and the name was attributed to both *Nymphaea coerulea* and *Nymphaea lotus* – a white scented species. Authorities suggest that the true lotus, *Nelumbo nucifera*, was included within the all-embracing name of Nile Lotus. Nelumbo has many associations with Buddhism and was taken from India to China, and from there to Japan in the sixth century A.D. The flower has been formalized in many different ways; basins derived from the shape of both the closed bud and the open flower are to be found in the Court of the Lions at the gardens of the Alhambra in Spain.

There is little evidence to show that other water plants were held in such high esteem, and it is unlikely that there was any deliberate planting of aquatics until the mid-nineteenth century, when the discovery of the giant water lily (*Victoria amazonica*) aroused great interest. Its first flowering in 1849 started a craze amongst wealthy garden enthusiasts for the cultivation of tropical water plants, all trying to find and flower other rarities. In most cases any artificially constructed lakes, pools and canals would have been colonized naturally where the conditions were suitable, particularly around the margins, if the sides were not too steep or the bottom too deep. The great stimulus for water gardening and planting came about as a result of four separate influences arriving on the scene at about the same time.

(i) The first influence was that of William Robinson, who passionately advocated the natural approach to planting using materials hardy to soil and climate. The publication of his book *The Wild Garden* in 1894 brought attention to the striking character of many indigenous foliage plants, in particular those associated with water.[1]

(ii) This new awareness of native species was also felt by Gertrude Jekyll, who by writing *Wall and Water Gardens* and by her example was able to influence a wider sphere of appreciation.[2] The majority of her observations on the siting and dispositions of hardy plants are still valid today.

(iii) Meanwhile, botanical and biological research was bringing to public attention the close interrelationships between aquatic flora and fauna, and particularly the effect of the delicate balance between a host of organisms on the health of a pool or pond.

(iv) Perhaps the greatest influence resulted from the pioneer hybridizing by Joseph Latour-Marliac of Temple-Sur-Lot in France. His name is now synonymous with water lilies, as a result of his carefully guarded methods of crossing North American species such as *Nymphaea odorata* and *Nymphaea tuberosa* with *Nymphaea alba-rubra* from Sweden and others, to introduce pink, red and yellow pigments. (It is interesting to note that Marliac's methods died with him, and Frances Perry records that the hybridizing of water lilies is generally so much fruitless labour; the efforts of her father-in-law, Amos Perry, a renowned horticulturalist, were to all intents and purposes a total failure.) The advent of striking shades and colours fostered a wave of interest in water lilies and their associated allies, and many gardens were designed to exhibit the rarities.

PLATE 6.1 **Willow trees framing a view at Aztec West Business Park, Bristol.** (Landscape Architects: *Brian Clouston and Partners*; Photographer: *Margaret Turner*)

PLATE 6.2 **A narrow stream is given a greater impression of apparent width by low profile contouring. Aylington Park near Winchester.** *(Allan Hart)*

## 6.2 THE USE OF WATER PLANTS IN GARDEN DESIGN

In addition to aquatics (plants growing freely on or within the water) the subject of water plants includes those plants which inhabit the margins of streams, ponds or lakes, which are of a herbaceous and semi-woody nature. It excludes trees and shrubs, several of which will grow at the water's edge − for example, swamp cypress (*Taxodium distichum*), the wing nut (*Pterocarya* × *rehderana*), swamp birch (*Betula nigra*), although the planting of any such trees or shrubs should always be in sympathy with the water area and its margins, both aesthetically and ecologically. The design principles and the method of handling water plants are very similar to those used for other plant materials, with the exception that the great majority of aquatics die down in winter, and therefore a particular effect may be lost temporarily, until the following spring.

The art of the use of shadowed water was outlined by Sir George Sitwell in his book *On the Making of Gardens* in which he illustrated how dark evergreens were invaluable as a background to water; by the simple expedient of truncating the suns's lateral rays, they help to concentrate the deep blue of the water when the sun is directly overhead.[3] It is also possible to increase the apparent size of an area of water by designing grass banks which slope gradually down to the water's edge − this gives less shadow than planted banks.

In a climate such as that of the British Isles, water for reflection has limited uses and must be carefully sited to take maximum advantage of a small amount of sunshine to realize its sparkling quality, otherwise it may appear dark and sombre. Water in Britain generally gives the impression of fading away into mist and trees, and a careful selection of plant materials can enhance this effect.

It is the quintessence of all design that the desired visual effect is determined as early as possible. In certain types of water features, particularly those in full sunshine, and where the reflective qualities of the surface are sought, aquatic planting must play a subordinate part, carefully located to add to rather than detract from the composition.

It is essential that the proportions of surface plant cover to open water are carefully determined, and that the aquatic plants are in scale with the surface area. Unless this balance is maintained, the surface of a sheet of water will be little different from that of an area of dry land covered with vegetation. The final effect of free growing plants can appear to reduce the apparent size.

Dramatic effects evoking a variety of moods can often be achieved by the simplest of detailing. The strong, arrow-like foliage of the giant rush (*Typha latifolia*) or common phragmite (*Phragmites communis*) standing in water, either reflected in sunshine or rising from a mist-covered lake, is an inspiring sight. A simple arrangement of the leaves of a solitary water lily or a total covering of duckweed (*Lemna minor*) on the surface of a still pool or basin in a shadowy glade can create a situation charged with mystery.

The tropical lushness of the huge leaves of *Gunnera*

PLATE 6.3 **Water, clear of vegetation, reflects the sky overhead.** *(Allan Hart)*

PLATE 6.4 **The qualities of both planting and open water are negated when vegetation covers the whole surface.** *(Robert Adams)*

*manicata*, suddenly revealed, excite the imagination with the thoughts of its Chilean jungle home. The same sense of wonder can be created by the first sight of the native great water dock (*Rumex hydrolapathum*) which usually reaches 15 m in height, particularly when the exotic size and shape of its leaves are transformed with its breathtaking autumn colour.

The composition of planting in and around the moat at Scotney Castle in Kent is a superb example of an idealized romantic setting for the ruins of the old castle, which would do credit to any of the artists of the pre-Raphaelite Brotherhood.

Britain has its own richly unique collection of indigenous water plants many of which possess particularly handsome foliage. This is a fact which may surprise many who think that lush foliage is usually associated with hot jungle climes. Many of our finest herbaceous plants grow by the waterside, and may be thought of as escapees from some distant country. Such a plant is the

PLATE 6.5 **Balanced proportions of planting to surface area at Sutton Palace, Surrey. The pond, designed by Susan Jellicoe, reflects the Ben Nicholson wall.** *(Maurizio Zorat)*

PLATE 6.6 **Romantic water associations. Scotney Castle, Kent.** *(Allan Hart)*

flowering rush (*Butomus umbellatus*), which has been favourably compared with the sacred lotus of ancient Egypt.

The grouping of *Butomus* with *Equisetum telmateia* by Robinson has almost become a classic. *Equisetum telmateia* may reach 1 m in height in deep shaded soil, and has long, closely grouped, slender branches, set in whorls. Similar to the flowering rush is the buckbean or bogbean (*Menyanthes trifoliata*), which has long stalked leaves topped with three leaflets, like a giant clover.

The yellow iris (*Iris pseudacorus*) and sweet sedge (*Acorus calamus*) exhibit strap-shaped leaves, the former displaying bright red seed capsules in the autumn, and the latter producing a sweet scent when the foliage is bruised. It also has a curious horizontal ribbing on the stems which is an aid to identification. The branched bur-reed (*Sparganium erectum*) has sword-like leaves, with its flowers grouped in globular bur-like masses on the branches at the top of the stalk. The arrowhead plant (*Sagittaria sagittifolia*) has lanceolate leaves above the water, its submerged leaves being linear. This is a most handsome plant at the water's edge. Two plants which are often found growing naturally together and which complement each other perfectly are the yellow loosestrife (*Lysimachia vulgaris*), a member of the primrose family, and purple loosestrife (*Lythrum salicaria*).

Greater emphasis is now being placed on ecologically based planting, the principles of which must be thoroughly understood if the designer is to achieve the desired effect. Submerged and floating aquatics play an essential role in the maintenance of a correct ecological balance, without which the water would become cloudy and foul. The correct 'mix' of plants, animals, fish, micro fauna and flora gives a self-maintaining environment. Submerged plants release oxygen into the water for use of fish and insects — they also deprive algae (unicellular plants) of light and mineral salts. Aquatic plants provide food for insects, which in turn provide food for fish which find nesting places in the leaves and stems. The young fish are able to hide and shelter from predators. The protective aspect of underwater planting is therefore important.

## 6.3 AQUATIC COMMUNITIES

Perhaps with aquatic plants more than any other group, the designer must realize that the relationships between various groups of plants are rarely fixed or permanent but continually changing. The natural succession is a 'hydrasere', in which there is a progression from deep open water, through to marsh and finally to dry land. This is brought about by silt and dead organic material accumulating in depth on the bottom, so gradually reducing its suitability for deep-water plants, but making it more habitable for shallow-water species.

Eventually, if the process continues, only dry land species will find a home there. It is possible to see zones of vegetation around ponds and lakes, and these usually indicate the various stages of succession.

The main varieties of water plants described below are listed in Table 6.1. Most of the limited selection of plants are native British species, rather than exotic varieties.

### (a) Plants growing adjacent to water

*Mixed herbaceous plants.* The plants adapted to this situation include many which are renowned for their bold foliage and architectural form and are used for mixed herbaceous plantings. For example, goat's beard (*Aruncus sylvester*) has very distinctive plumes of creamy-white flowers, tall and arching, over multipinnate foliage, a more aristocratic version of the native meadowsweet (*Filipendula ulmaria*). Spiraeas or false goat's beard (*Astilbe* × *arendsii* and *Astilbe japonica*

PLATE 6.7 **Riverside marginal plants including** *Butomus umbellatus*. *(Robert Adams)*

hybrids) in shades of white, through pink to red, and in heights ranging from 600–900 mm, make very effective groundcover. In complete contrast is that most delicate looking but persistent plant, lady's smock (*Cardamine pratensis*), surely one of our most beautiful native plants and best seen in association with grasses.

There are several bulbs adapted to these conditions, including snowflake (*Leucojum aestivum*), found along the banks of the Thames, and quamash (*Camassia quamash*), a native of North America, which can seed and colonize in water meadows if undisturbed. The various forms of plantain lily (*Hosta* spp) associate well with the day lily (*Hemerocallis* varieties), though it is better to avoid the harsher tones of many modern varieties.

*Foliage trees and shrubs.* Hazel, willow and poplar, water birch (*Betula nigra*) together with dwarf species of willow, sweet pepper (*Clethra alnifolia*), a vastly underrated shrub, and tupelo (*Nyassa sylvatica*) are some of the trees and shrubs which would be found adjacent to water.

## (b) *Marsh plants*

These require moist soil conditions at all times. The sides of a pool can be stepped to provide pockets of soil at water level, or the banks of a river, stream or lake can be graded or excavated to provide similar conditions. It will be found that the stems and foliage will be more lush and exotic, none more so than the Chilean rhubarb (*Gunnera manicata*) and its visual

TABLE 6.1
**Plants associated with water**

| Location | Latin Name | Popular Name |
|---|---|---|
| **1. Adjacent to water** | | |
| Mixed herbaceous | *Aruncus sylvester* | goat's beard |
| | *Astilbe × arendsii* | spireas or false |
| | *Astilboides tabularis japonica hybrids* | goat's beard |
| | *Cardamine pratensis* | lady's smock |
| | *Hosta* spp (various) | plantain lily |
| | *Ligularia clivorum* | giant groundsel |
| Bulbs | *Camassia quamash* | quamash |
| | *Hemerocallis* var. | day lily |
| | *Leucojum aestivum* | snowflake |
| Trees and Shrubs | *Alnus* spp | alder |
| | *Betula nigra* | water birch |
| | *Clethra alnifolia* | sweet pepper |
| | *Corylus* spp | hazel |
| | *Nyssa sylvatica* | tupelo |
| | *Populus* spp | poplar |
| | *Pterocarya fraxinifolia* | wing nut |
| | *Salix* spp | willow & dwarf spp |
| | *Taxodium distichum* | swamp cypress |
| **2. Marsh Plants** | *Carex* spp | sedges |
| | *Eupatorium cannabinum* | hemp agrimony |
| | *Filipendula ulmaria* | meadow sweet |
| | *Gunnera manicata* | Chilean rhubarb |
| | *Iris kaempferi* & var. | Japanese water iris |
| | *I. sibirica* | |
| | *Juncus* spp | rushes |
| | *Lysichitum americanum* | skunk lily |
| | *Lysimachia nummularia* | creeping jenny |
| | *Peltiphyllum peltatum* | umbrella plant |
| | *Rheum palmatum* | |
| | *Rodgersia aesculifolia* | |
| | *R. podophylla* | |

| Location | Latin Name | Popular Name |
|---|---|---|
| 3. Marginal Plants | *Acorus calamus* | sweet flag |
| | *A. calamus* var. | |
| | *Alisma lanceolatum* | water plantain |
| | *A. plantago-aquatica* | |
| | *Butomus umbellatus* | flowering rush |
| | *Caltha palustris* | marsh marigold |
| | *Carex pendula* | sedge |
| | *C. pseudo-cyperus* | |
| | *C. riparia* | |
| | *Cotula coronopifolia* | brass buttons |
| | *Cyperus longus* | galingale |
| | *Epilobium hirsutum* | hairy willow herb |
| | *Galium* spp | water bedstraw |
| | *Mentha* spp | water mint |
| | *Menyanthes trifoliata* | |
| | *Myosotis palustris* | water forget-me-not |
| | *Oenanthe crocata* | hemlock dropwort |
| | *Orchis* spp | marsh orchids |
| | *Parnassia palustris* | grass of Parnassus |
| | *Ranunculus lingua* | great spearwort |
| | *Scutellaria galericulata* | skull cap |
| | *Senecio aquatilis* | water ragwort |
| | *Trollius* spp | globe flower |
| 4. Reed Swamp | *Phragmites communis* | common reed |
| | *Scirpus lacustris* | bulrush |
| | *Typha augustifolia* | |
| | *T. latifolia* | great reed mace |
| Sword-like foliage | *Acorus calamus* | sweet flag |
| | *Iris pseudacorus* | yellow flag |
| Arrow-shaped foliage | *Sagittaria sagittifolia* | |
| Submerged species | *Ceratophyllum demersum* | hornwort |
| | *C. submersum* | |
| | *Elodea canadensis* | Canadian pond weed |
| | *Myriophyllum verticillatum* | water milfoil |
| Attractive foliage & flowers | *Hottonia palustris* | water violet |
| | *Nasturtium officinale* | watercress |
| | *Ranunculus aquatilis* | water crowfoot |
| | *Utricularia vulgaris* | bladderwort |
| 5. Floating plants | *Aponogeton distachyos* | water hawthorn |
| | *Callitriche* spp | starworts |
| | *Glyceria fluitans* | flote grass |
| | *Hippuris vulgaris* | mare's tail |
| | *Hydrocharis morsus-ranae* | frogbit |
| | *Nuphar lutea* | yellow water lily |
| Native to Britain | *Nymphaea alba* | white water lily |
| | *Nymphoides peltatum* | fringed water lily |
| | *Polygonum amphibium* | floating persicaria |
| | *Potamogeton natans* | floating pondweed |
| | *Stratiotes aloides* | water soldier |

PLATE 6.8 **Early development of a typical hydrasere. Canal at Bath.** *(Robert Adams)*

PLATE 6.9 **Canal abandoned less than a decade ago, and already in the final stages of colonization.** *(Robert Adams)*

allies, *Rheum palmatum* which has large toothed, red leaves; the umbrella plant from California (*Peltiphyllum peltatum*) with parasol shaped leaves; *Rodgersia aesculifolia* with its dark green chestnut-like foliage; *Astilboides tabularis* with plate shaped leaves and *R. podophylla* with palmate leaves. The Japanese water iris (*Iris kaempferi* and its varieties) must surely be the star of this particular galaxy, with its clematis-like flowers in delicate shades of white, blue, pink and red. However, it does need a certain amount of cosseting and it is better to use *Iris sibirica*, a more hardy and easily grown species.

Hemp agrimony (*Eupatorium cannabinum*) is a very handsome foliage plant with large heads of composite flowers. One of the most showy marsh plants rejoices in the name of skunk lily (*Lysichitum americanum*) with a typical aroid-like bright yellow flower which appears before the very large and dark green foliage. Creeping jenny (*Lysimachia nummularia*, and the variety *aurea*) is found covering the ground between individual plants, hiding a soil which otherwise appears dank and unappealing.

## (c) *Marginal plants*

Marginal plants, or those requiring a water depth of up to 500 mm, include many striking foliage plants, mainly reed-like or arrow shaped.

Water musk, or monkey flower (*Mimulus luteus*) is a native of Chile, now naturalized in several English rivers. There have been fewer more beautiful acquisitions by the British countryside than this plant, which usually establishes itself on the banks of streams as they emerge from the hills. Bogbean (*Menyanthes trifoliata*), marsh marigold (*Caltha palustris*) and globe flower (*Trollius* spp) are all worthy companions. Examples may also include hairy willow-herb (*Epilobium hirsutum*), marsh orchids, water mints (*Mentha* spp), hemlock dropwort (*Oenanthe crocata*) (extremely poisonous and similar to water cress in spring), water bedstraws (*Galium* spp), water ragwort (*Senecio aquatilis*), water forget-me-not (*Myosotis* spp), grass of Parnassus (*Parnassia palustris*), great spearwort (*Ranunculus lingua*) and skull cap (*Scutellaria galericulata*).

## (d) *Reed swamp*

This zone of vegetation is generally a dense mass of plants with tall erect stems, the intermediate stage between marsh and water vegetation. As with most zones, it has no clear boundary, and one may find marsh plants on the land side and water plants on the other margin. For example the loose outer edge of reed swamp furthest from the pool or lake edge may have water lilies whose floating leaves occupy the spaces between the sparsely occurring shoots of the reeds. The floating leaves are thus protected from wave action. Generally, the plants are very vigorous and one species tends to become dominant, with others occurring locally and erratically.

Its associated plants include the common reed (*Phragmites communis*), which is readily recognized with its tall slender stem, 1.5–2 m high, with a grass-like leaf at each joint and flowers grouped into a plume-like paniche on top of the stem. The flowers are purple-brown at first, becoming silver as the seed ripens.

The great reed mace (*Typha latifolia*) is more commonly called bulrush (properly *Scirpus lacustris*) and requires plenty of room to develop as the rootstocks are very invasive. The reeds can reach a height of 5 m and are very handsome. It is possible, by creating an artificially restricted root run, to grow these majestic plants in fairly small pools. They may need replacing at intervals if the size of canes noticeably decreases.

Sweet flag (*Acorus calamus*) and its variety 'Variegatus', together with the yellow flag provide the sword-like foliage, *Sagittaria sagittifolia* the arrow shapes. This plant clearly exhibits the tendency of several of those plants growing partly submerged, to have more than one shape of leaf on the same plant. The aerial leaves are shaped like an arrow head, the floating leaves are lanceolate and those submerged are linear. The flowering rush is also an inhabitant of this area.

Submerged plants are of vital importance to the health and well-being of water. They generally have finely divided foliage below the surface: those species which grow above the water as well have a combination of dissected and entire leaves. Milfoil (*Myriophyllum verticillatum*) and hornwort (*Ceratophyllum demersum* and *submersum*) together with Canadian pond weed (*Elodea canadensis*) rarely appear above water, and consequently have little to contribute visually. The water violet (*Hottonia palustris*), water crowfoot (*Ranunculus aquatilis*), watercress (*Nasturtium officinale*) and bladderwort (*Utricularia vulgaris*) all possess very attractive foliage and flowers, and are all perfectly hardy plants native to Britain.

## (e) *Floating plants*

Floating plants obtain all their food by photosynthesis and have roots in the bottom of the pool or lake. They may be said to be the aristocrats of water plants, with their combination of handsome foliage and flowers. Native to Britain are the white water lily (*Nymphaea alba*) the fringed water lily (*Nymphoides peltatum*) — distinguished from the true Nymphaea by the frilled edges to its leaves and five fringed yellow petalled flowers — and the yellow water lily or brandy bottle (*Nuphar lutea*), the flowers of which have a strong alcoholic smell. There are many hybrids suitable for different depths or areas of water, ranging in colour from white to yellow, pink, red and blue, and many are scented. Discretion should be exercised concerning the setting and location of plants with the more strident colours.

There are other beautiful deep water aquatics. Floating pondweed (*Potamogeton natans*) has elliptic,

95

PLATE 6.10 **Marginal planting at a lakeside swimming lido, Zurich.** *(Ian Laurie)*

leathery leaves 75 mm long, and differs from other aquatics in that the veins are parallel and not netted. Frogbit (*Hydrocharis morsus-ranae*) produces strawberry-like runners with heart-shaped leaves in tufts at the ends of them. The flowers are three petalled, white and very attractive. Water hawthorn (*Aponogeton distachyus*) is one of the most sweetly scented of plants and is thought to smell like vanilla; the common name refers to the shape of the flowers. Floating persicaria (*Polygonum amphibium*), flote grass (*Glyceria fluitans*), starworts (*Callitriche* spp) and mare's tail (*Hippuris vulgaris*) may also be present.

## Controlling the cycle

If the designer wishes to maintain a certain effect, he must somehow contrive to halt the natural progression otherwise the next stage of the hydrasere will eventually be reached. This may be achieved by re-starting the cycle, or maintaining the *status quo* by sympathetic after management. A positive policy will be needed,

with allowance made for adequate funds to implement the after care. It is important to realize how quickly one group of plants may develop at the expense of others.

This is particularly the case with newly created water areas. During early stages of ecological succession there may be great invasions of colonizing species. The balance between species may fluctuate wildly, especially if there is a source of aquatic plants nearby. The chosen planting may be overrun, and then the permanent planting may have to be re-established at a later date when the ecosystem has achieved some kind of balance.

The degree and rapidity of change and succession will be dependent on a number of factors:

(i)   the presence or absence of running water;
(ii)  the depth of water;
(iii) the quality of water;
(iv)  the lack of toxicity;
(v)   the degree of alkalinity or acidity;
(vi)  the presence or absence of silt or decayed vegetation on the bottom;
(vii) light penetration and variations in temperature.

All factors must be carefully analysed, and planting proposals based on the result of that analysis. Too often plant types alien to the location are chosen in preference to those particularly suitable, on the grounds that they do not meet the designer's aesthetic or visual requirements.

The introduction of alien species can upset the delicate ecological balance between naturally associating plants. The dividing line between survival and extinction is a fine one. Recent examples of such introductions are Canadian pond weed, planted in British waterways in 1847 and rapidly reaching pest status. Subsequent research has shown that after a period of several years' intense activity, it declines. But this is of little solace to the owner of a new pond or lake which is becoming rapidly choked. The most up-to-date introduction is that of tape grass (*Vallisneria spiralis*), normally a plant for the tropical aquarist. It can be found in canals, particularly near warm water outfalls from factories, but it is thought unlikely that it will ever become thoroughly naturalized. Both of these examples pale to insignificance when compared to the notorious water hyacinth (*Eichhornia crassipes*) from tropical America. When ten plants were introduced to the St. Johns River in Florida they increased to half a million in eight months and seriously hampered navigation: similarly, plants introduced into gardens have escaped their confines and found the new habitat very much to their liking. The Indian balsam (*Impatiens glandulifera*), a native of the Western Himalayas, is a fairly recent addition to the British flora and has made rapid progress, spreading along water courses throughout the country. It is a very beautiful aromatic plant which extends its territory by the simple expedient of exploding its seed capsules and projecting the seeds a distance of several metres. The touch-me-not plant (*Impatiens noli-tangere*), a yellow flowered, smaller version, does not appear to be quite so invasive.

## Planting and maintenance

The supply of many garden and exotic species poses few problems. In Britain water gardening is showing an upsurge in popularity to which the trade is responding.

PLATE 6.11 **An example of water planting at York University.** (*Allan Hart*)

PLATE 6.12 **Typical example of a lake bed requiring dredging. Note the swollen underwater trunk of** *Pterocarya.* **Kew Lake.** *(Robert Adams)*

PLATE 6.13 **Dredging almost complete; clay base of lake exposed.** *(Robert Adams)*

But for those concerned with the establishment of indigenous species for large-scale planting of lakes and rivers, the situation is quite different. As with the production of hardy nursery stock, the range of plants being grown is becoming smaller with each passing year, and many native aquatics are no longer commercially available. Alternative sources of supply could be explored – local authorities and water undertakings may be sympathetic to a competent person taking samples of plants for re-establishment elsewhere; similarly, local field centres and the Nature Conservancy may be able to help, particularly if the new schemes and planting have a sound ecological and educational basis. (Such organizations are useful contacts, as they may be able to help with suggestions of plants in which they have a special interest and which they would like to see given a wider distribution. In certain cases they may suggest that a research student be appointed to collect and plant the vegetation and if possible to monitor the project over a period of time. Where such arrangements are made, they would have to be included within any contract specification for new works.)

Planting times are fairly critical for many of the heavily rooted species such as nuphars and pontaderias, and planting is usually carried out as they are emerging from their dormant period from mid-April to mid-May, with temperatures around 20–25°C. From May to June is the period of most active growth which is necessary for new planting to become established before winter. The lesser aquatics, submerged oxygenators and marginal plants can be planted at almost any time during the growing season.

The new growth of established water lilies is such that the new leaves do not unfold until they reach the surface. Plants may be purchased pot-grown, with young leaves just above the surface of the container. It would be a tremendous shock to the plant's system if it were to be placed at its ultimate depth. It is therefore necessary either to lower it gradually into the water as the stems develop, or to raise the level of the water in stages to correspond with the stem growth until the correct depth is reached. If the tubers are dormant it is usually sufficient to tie them to a heavy weight and drop them into position in the mud. This is the normal method of planting submerged aquatics. Cultural requirements are simple – heavy loam (free from organic matter to avoid decomposition and therefore pollution of the water) in open mesh containers of basketwork or plastic. For ease of operations, marginal planting may be carried out in prepared dry soil which is then allowed to become saturated.

The maintenance of water plants is relatively simple – smaller ponds may need emptying annually, while larger pools may need the removal of competing vegetation. It may be necessary to resort to dredging if the water area becomes badly silted. This can be a complicated and expensive operation.

There is a purely natural occurrence which causes concern, and that is the discoloration of the water. This is caused by algae, tiny unicellular plants which thrive on the soluble salts found in the new water, or soil and mud disturbed during construction or dredging operations. In severe cases this can result in low dissolved oxygen concentrations which increase the danger of fish mortality. The introduction of daphnia (water fleas) quickly brings about a reduction in their numbers. The growth of oxygenating and floating plants helps to exclude light from the water and in turn this prevents further growth. Similarly, blanket or flannel weed, which is a filamentous plant, is best removed periodically by hand until the main planting covers the water's surface.

Certain plants may grow at the expense of others, and may be removed by hand cutting in late June or early July, or by chemical means. The Toxic Chemicals and Wildlife Division of the Nature Conservancy are currently investigating new methods of controlling aquatic vegetation. The following is a list of chemicals with low toxicity:

| Chemical | Quantity | Controls |
|---|---|---|
| Simazine | 3–6 parts per million | Duckweed |
| Monuron | 4–12 parts per million | Underwater vegetation |
| Sodium arsenate | 10 parts per million | Underwater vegetation |
| Dalapon | 1 kg/litre of water sprayed onto foliage | Rushes, reed-mace, bur-weeds etc. |

In newly established areas the more vigorous species such as reed sweet mace (*Glyceria maxima*) may invade cleared waters, and to reduce this an attempt should be made to diversify the glyceria swamps by using selective systemic insecticides. The resulting dead foliage is formed into mounds on which nettles, willow herb and other colonizers may establish. This technique was originated by RSPB at the Rye House Marsh Reserve in Hertfordshire. The floral diversification attracts birds and provides nesting sites.

The extent of winter maintenance will depend on the situation and use. Water plants can look very depressing after the first frosts have blackened and destroyed their lush features, and consequently they are better cut down in an urban setting. This will also remove the overwintering habitat of water-lily beetles and other pests. The natural breakdown of plants under water releases toxic gases which can prove fatal to fish or at best lower their resistance to disease. This normally applies to small ponds and is not usually a problem with larger areas. It may not be visually desirable to remove vegetation, for reed stems piercing the water can give an extra dimension to a water surface in winter. Plants such as water plantains (*Alisma*), irises and reed maces (*Typha*) which seed readily should have the seeds removed. Certain of the semi-hardy marginal plants, such as Brazilean rhubarb, need protecting with straw or bracken against frost.

## 6.4 CONCLUSION

The use of water plants in landscape design can be most rewarding. They establish themselves quickly and can produce a mature effect within the first year of planting. A practical contribution to the conservation of native species can be made and justified, as many of these are aristocrats of the plant world and worthy of a place in any planting scheme.

It can be an intellectual exercise in management techniques in determining the best means of maintaining the desired effect. It may be that the natural expression of succession should be allowed, to achieve a balance between the different plant types; or perhaps the development should be arrested at a particular stage, to freeze the composition. It will only be possible to achieve the right effects by a full understanding of the plants' physical characteristics and cultural requirements. There is good documentation on the needs of most ornamental species, but for many of the native water plants, personal observation and research will be needed, which is the best way to know and understand any group of plants.

### FURTHER READING

Campbell, C. S. *Water in Landscape Architecture* (New York: Van Nostrand Reinhold 1982)

Chaplin, M. *Riverside Gardening* (Feltham: W. H. and L. Collingridge Ltd 1964)

Cook, C. D. K. *Water Plants of the World* (The Hague: Junk 1974)

Crowe, S. *Garden Design* (London: Country Life Ltd, 3rd impression 1965)

Haslam, S. M. *River Plants* (Cambridge University Press 1978)

Landphair, H. C. and Klatt, F. *Landscape Architecture Construction* (New York: Elsevier 1979)

Lee, M. 'Water Gardens, the University of York', *Concrete Quarterly* July/September, p.2 (1979)

Machin, T. T. and Worthington, E. B. *Life in Lakes and Rivers* (London: Collins 1951)

Mayson Whalley, J. 'Water in the Landscape', *Landscape and Urban Planning* No.16, p.145 (Amsterdam: Elsevier Science Publishers 1988)

Ministry of Agriculture, Fisheries and Food *Guidelines for the Use of Herbicides on Weeds In or Near Watercourses and Lakes* (Booklet No.2078 1979)

Newman, L. H. 'Wildlife in the Garden Pool', *The Garden*, June, p.229 (1982)

Peters, P. and Roemer, L. *Garden Pools for Pleasure* (London: Abelard Schuman 1972)

Rowbotham, R. 'The Construction of the Lake (Sutton Place)', *Landscape Design*, October, p.12 (1983)

Shinn, J. 'Cambridge Science Park', *Landscape Design*, December, p.32 (1986)

Spencer-Jones, D. and Wade, M. *Aquatic Plants: A Guide to Recognition* (ICI Professional Product 1986)

Teagle, W. G. 'The Water's Edge', *Landscape Research*, No.3, p.25 (1981)

Turrill, W. B. *British Plant Life* (London: Collins, 3rd edition 1962)

Wolf, A. 'A Garden Pond Habitat', *Garten und Landschaft*, June, p.443 (1979)

### REFERENCES

1. Robinson, W. *The Wild Garden* (London: John Murray 1894)

2. Jekyll, G. *Wall and Water Gardens* (London: Country Life 1901)

3. Sitwell, Sir George *On the Making of Gardens* (London: Gerald Duckworth Ltd 1951)

# Part II
# TECHNIQUES

# CHAPTER 7

# The Use and Management of Plant Species Native to Britain

## PENNY BECKETT AND DAVID PARKER

## 7.1 INTRODUCTION

Native plants have always had a place in British landscape design, though in recent years their use has become more general and almost demanded by environmentally aware sections of the public. Scientific research carried out mainly in the last twenty years has also demonstrated that the creation of ecologically interesting vegetation and wildlife habitats can be successfully carried out, both in urban and rural situations. Indeed there has been a recent explosion of urban ecology groups throughout the UK, groups that are pledged to create sites of visual and wildlife importance in urban areas. Native planting forms a key part of their philosophy, together with a policy of using sites of urban dereliction to create environments of real value to the local community and to wildlife.

Native plants are normally defined as those species that are naturally present in the British Isles, not having been introduced, either accidentally or deliberately, by man. Their use in landscape schemes, whether on large-scale reclamation sites or in small 'pocket parks' in cities, demands an understanding of a number of ecological principles which govern whether the establishment and growth of a particular species or association of species will be successful. These principles relate to such general site conditions as climate, soils and geographical location, as well as to an understanding of how native plant species occur in nature.

In all there are about 1800 native species in the British Isles, and many of these can satisfy the varied requirements of the landscape designer. Native species will not always be appropriate to a particular requirement, but a landscape designer should always be aware of the possibilities that the native flora provide. Perhaps the most important use of native species comes in blending rural reclamation schemes with the surrounding countryside. Despite the enormous changes that the activities of man impose on the landscape of the British Isles, much of the visual character of the rural landscape continues to result from the effect of native species of trees and shrubs. The landscape designer is increasingly asked to produce planting schemes which will be attractive to wildlife, and therefore eventually come to have some ecological value. Native species would have to form the bulk of such planting because native insects and other invertebrates are adapted to native flora and will often not live on non-native introduced species.

The next section describes and discusses the most important ecological principles which relate to the use of native plants. The British Isles are used as the example in this account, but the principles relate equally to the use of native plants in other parts of the world.

## 7.2 ECOLOGICAL PRINCIPLES

Ecology is defined as the interaction of living organisms with their environment. An understanding of the way plants exist in their natural environment is central to an understanding of the ways in which they can successfully be established and used in planting schemes. In the natural situation, uninfluenced by man, plants are found in associations known as plant communities. These can then be grouped to form different habitats or, more precisely, ecosystems.

Man has had a substantial influence on the natural vegetation cover of the British Isles over the centuries. Woodlands have been removed and replaced by grasslands and arable farmland and woodlands have been planted with non-native species. Wetlands have been drained and coastlands have been subjected to land reclamation for agricultural use or urban development. Despite these changes, which will be discussed in more

**Morwell Quay Woods.** (*John Chitty*)

detail below, the landscape designer needs to consider the native plants in their natural environment, or at worst in a very stable 'semi-natural' environment which may have been produced by many centuries of continuous land management. The topographic, climatic and soil conditions that support the ecosystems are also of fundamental importance to an understanding of the composition and mechanics of these systems.

## The natural and semi-natural vegetation of the British Isles

### (a) *Historical development*

The end of the last ice age, some 10 000 years ago, is normally taken as the starting point in the recent history of the vegetation of the British Isles. At this point the northern half of the UK was covered by an ice sheet, with the southern part of the country having low tundra vegetation dominated by mosses, lichens, ericaceous species and a locally rich flora of arctic–alpine plants. As the climate improved, the ice sheet retreated and the open tundra became colonized by shrubs and trees. The first colonists were what we now know as mountain willows (*Salix* spp), followed by birch (*Betula* spp) and then Scots pine (*Pinus sylvestris*). Pine forests covered great parts of the country, but today only survive in the central highlands of Scotland. The pine forests gave way to new colonists: elm, hazel, oak and ash, with the oaks forming the dominant forest type, known as the 'forest climax' vegetation. Many upland

areas above 600 m were never afforested and elements of the open tundra vegetation have survived in specialized environments, though most of the land became open moorland and bogs, dominated by heathers and *Sphagnum* communities.

From neolithic times to the present day, man has exerted a profound influence on this natural vegetation. Clearance of the forests created numerous areas of grassland, with heathland on the more acidic soils. Some of these areas developed a considerable variety of wildlife, owing to centuries of similar management. This is especially true in areas of grazing. Conversion of these lands to arable farming and, in modern times, the use of artificial fertilizers, have now greatly reduced the extent of grasslands and heathlands that are of major ecological interest.

### (b) *Woodland and scrub*

The original woodland cover of the British Isles has been considerably reduced and modified by man's activities to the extent that almost no 'natural' woodland now occurs, except on steep slopes, cliffs and in other small pockets. However, some areas of primary woodland, often referred to as 'ancient woodland', do remain, even though tree clearance, replanting, and coppicing have taken place (*see* Figure 7.1 and Plate 7.1). These woodlands retain much of their former ecological diversity and interest, including a characteristic woodland ground flora. They have also retained elements of their original tree species composition.

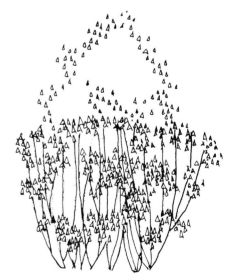

NEWLY COPPICED STOOLS. LIGHT DEMANDING GROUND VEGETATION BEGINS TO DEVELOP.

AFTER FIVE YEARS A THICK AND TANGLED VEGETATION DEVELOPS.

MATURE COPPICE, 15–20 YEARS OLD AND READY FOR CUTTING. LITTLE GROUND VEGETATION.

FIGURE 7.1 **Managed coppice-with-standards woodland preserves a variety of habitats, changing in location through time.**

PLATE 7.1 **Coppiced woodland, especially with standards above, provides a rich variety of habitats, and could be a good way of managing a visual screen (although hazel would be of much more benefit to wildlife than the sweet chestnut in the photograph).** *(C. Yarrow)*

The term 'secondary woodland' is used for deciduous woodlands that have had a period in their history during which the woodland was cleared and the land turned into pasture or given over to arable production. These woodlands tend to have less ecological value than the primary woodlands, as the continuity and diversity of species were lost during the agricultural period. Many species of woodland plant and animal are extremely poor colonizers and secondary woodlands only rarely regain many of their original species.

The landscape designer will want to have some kind of guidance as to the species composition of these woodlands, especially in terms of the major species of trees and shrubs, which can have great ecological value in their own right. The broad divisions of native woodland in the British Isles have been summarized by Peterken (1981), into twelve 'Stand Groups', as is shown in Table 7.1. The groups in the top half of the table are based on the presence of five species which rarely occur together. Those groups in the bottom half of the table form a hierarchical sequence down the

TABLE 7.1
**General classification of British woodlands (From Peterken, 1981)**

| | |
|---|---|
| Group 7 | Alderwoods (*Alnus glutinosa*) |
| Group 8 | Beechwoods (*Fagus sylvatica*) |
| Group 9 | Hornbeam woods (*Carpinus betulus*) |
| Group 10 | Suckering elm woods (*Ulmus carpinifolia*, *Ulmus procera*) |
| Group 11 | Pinewoods (*Pinus sylvestris*) |
| Group 1 | Ash−wych elm woods (*Ulmus glabra*) |
| Group 4 | Ash−lime woods (*Tilia cordata*) |
| Group 5 | Acid oak−lime woods (*Tilia cordata*) |
| Group 2 | Ash−maple woods (*Acer campestre*) |
| Group 3 | Hazel−ash woods (*Fraxinus excelsior*) |
| Group 6 | Birch−oak woods (*Quercus petraea*, *Quercus robur*) |
| Group 12 | Birch woods (*Betula pendula*, *Betula pubescens*) |

table in which those species closest to the bottom of the table are increasingly likely to be found within the groups above them in the table. Therefore the oaks and birches have the widest ranges of occurrence in native woodlands.

## (c) Grasslands and heathlands

Grasslands and heathlands form the second component of the vegetation of the British Isles. The major part of the grassland now consists of ploughed, reseeded and heavily fertilized pasture, known as 'improved grassland'. Much of this grassland was, until recently, of an unimproved, species-rich type, especially that which is found on calcareous and clay-rich soils.

These grasslands supported a wide range of wild plants, and their ecosystems were maintained by a regular pattern of grazing, often with annual hay production. Ploughing was rare and only organic fertilizers were used, mainly animal manure. The increasing intensification of agriculture, especially since the 1940s, has resulted in the loss of most of these species-rich grasslands. Many of the best examples now only occur in nature reserves, on very steep slopes which are difficult to plough and fertilize, or on roadside verges running through areas where unimproved grasslands used to occur.

The species composition of these grasslands depends on the underlying soils and their past management. The richest grasslands are generally found on chalk and limestone, though neutral to slightly alkaline clay soils can often support rich floras, such as at Eades Meadow in Worcestershire. Alluvial river floodplain soils that occur over gravels, such as in the Cricklade area of Wiltshire, support some of our richest meadows (see Plates 7.2, to 7.4).

On the most acidic soils in the UK a long history of grazing management has led to the development of vegetation that is dominated by heathers and other ericaceous dwarf shrubs. In the lowlands this vegetation is termed heathland, and in the uplands moorland. This dwarf shrub vegetation is usually highly important for wildlife, supporting rich communities of plants and animals. Much of the land that is now heathland was once forested, though some moorlands are above the maximum elevation at which trees used to grow, known as the tree line.

Heathland and, to a lesser extent, moorland have a tendency to become colonized by trees and shrubs very rapidly once grazing management ceases. There has been a substantial decline in the extent of heathland in the last fifty years, and much of this is due to a natural colonization, mainly by birch and introduced Scots

PLATE 7.2 **Unimproved species-rich hay meadow at Cricklade, Wiltshire, with abundant snake's head fritillary** *(Fritillaria meleagris). (David Parker)*

PLATE 7.3 **Scrub being cleared to restore part of a site to grassland after the lack of grazing management has allowed scrub to invade. The flail leaves a layer of chopped material which, unless removed, encourages worse 'waste ground' species.** *(F. L. Ryan)*

PLATE 7.4 **A site where part of the grassland is mown short, while other areas are left as long grass. Grazing animals are now absent and mowing is therefore necessary.** *(F. L. Ryan)*

PLATE 7.5 *Ammophila arenaria* (**marram grass**), **the most important stabilizing plant for sand dunes.** *(Dick Hoyle)*

pine. Many heathland and moorland soils are poorly drained, and communities of wetland plants can establish themselves on these sites. Perhaps the most spectacular of these are the large peatland areas that are dominated by extensive communities of *Sphagnum* mosses. These bogs cover large areas of uplands, but also occur in lowland areas such as the New Forest. Again, wet heaths and bogs are of great importance for wildlife.

### (d) *Coastlands*

The coastal vegetation of the British Isles comprises a number of plant communities, including salt marshes, sand dunes and cliffs. Salt marshes are intertidal habitats which are covered in water during the highest parts of most tides. They occur mainly in sheltered areas and are most extensive on larger estuaries such as the Dee, the Wash and the Solway Firth. The vegetation consists of salt-tolerant plants, known as halophytes, and includes both grasses and herbaceous species. These areas are of great importance for birds, especially wildfowl.

Sand dunes occur mostly above the high tide level,

and, as well as being ecologically important, they often have a vital coast protection function. The most important plant on the dune systems is marram grass (*Ammophila arenaria*), which is able to colonize and stabilize shifting sand (see Plate 7.5). Dunes are very sensitive to human pressure, and the removal of vegetation, especially marram, can lead to serious erosion problems. A diverse and specialized flora occurs on sand dunes, and the greatest richness is found in damp hollows, known as 'slacks', between the dunes, where dense colonies of marsh orchids and other uncommon species can be found.

Coastal cliffs, with their steep slopes and highly exposed environments, support vegetation that has been little influenced by man. There can be woodland, scrub, grassland or heathland, depending on local conditions.

### (e) *Wetlands*

The peat bogs of heathland and moorland areas have already been discussed. Here we consider the remaining types of wetlands, including rivers and streams, lakes and ponds and freshwater marshes.

Rivers and streams and their marginal vegetation

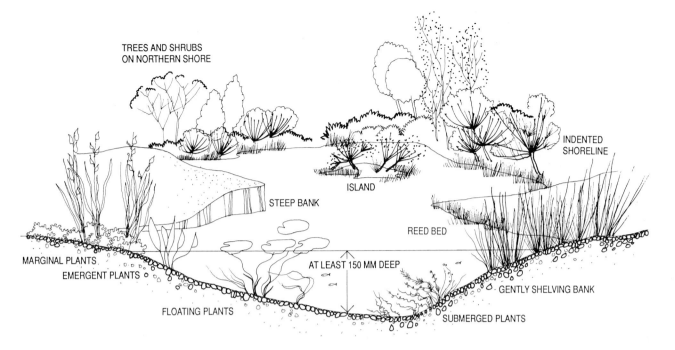

FIGURE 7.2 **Diagrammatic representation of habitats that would be found in an ideal pond.**

PLATE 7.6 **Pond in need of clearance to restore the habitats illustrated in Figure 7.2.**

form an important part of the natural habitats found in the British Isles. The trees and shrubs in these environments tend to be native species, alder and willow being the most important. Many river courses have been straightened to improve water flow and prevent flooding, and this has resulted in ecological damage. Despite changes introduced by man, rivers and streams still form wildlife habitats and corridors of immense importance.

Most of the lakes and ponds found in the lowland areas of the British Isles have been created by man. In the uplands and in restricted lowland areas, such as the Cheshire and Shropshire plain, there are natural lakes which have been produced by glacial action in the last ice age. All open water tends to be colonized by native wetland vegetation. This vegetation, with the exception of certain rare species, can easily be transplanted and established in new lakes, and ecologically interesting habitats can be rapidly created (see Figure 7.2 and Plate 7.6).

Many rivers, streams and lakes are associated with areas of freshwater marshes. Man has always tried to drain marshlands, and very little now remains of a formerly extensive habitat. Those that remain are often of high ecological importance and support uncommon species of plant and animal. Fortunately, as will be described in detail later, interesting marshland vegetation can be created by reproducing the correct physical conditions and by planting the appropriate species.

## (f) Farmland, hedgerows and verges

The greatest proportion of the land area of the British Isles consists of farmland. Hedgerows survive in good quantity, though there have been serious losses, especially in the east of England, which are continuing. In the past much of the permanent pasture in the British Isles was of the relatively unimproved, species-rich kind which has now been lost. Much of the ecological value of our farmed landscape now resides in the small areas of rich grasslands that remain, together with woodlands, wetlands and hedgerows. Hedgerows can be thought of as narrow strips of woodland or scrub, with native trees and shrubs growing together with herbaceous woodland species. The presence of these native species and the ability of hedgerows, for example, to connect woodlands and other features, confers great ecological value on them. It is for this reason that the future of hedgerows assumes such prominence in the environmental debate. It should be remembered that the majority of hedgerows have been planted, and this gives valuable encouragement to the modern land manager to do likewise and ultimately to create systems of value for wildlife.

Roadside and railway verges, which are often associated with hedgerows, can consist of species-rich grass-

PLATE 7.7 **A fine old oak that provides a valuable habitat for insects, birds and lichens (and will continue to do so even when dead).** *(D. Harvey)*

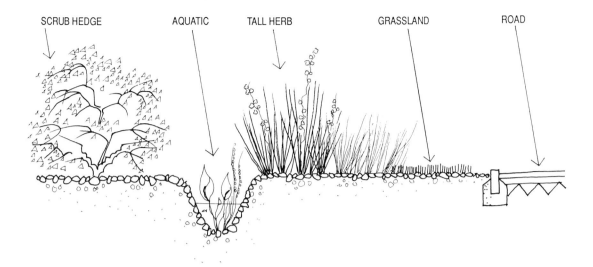

SCRUB HEDGE      AQUATIC     TALL HERB       GRASSLAND       ROAD

FIGURE 7.3 **Habitats represented in an ideal roadside hedgerow.**

lands and can be the only vestige of the unimproved grassland which used to occur widely in the locality (see Figure 7.3). The less species-rich grasslands are still of some ecological value and provide habitat for insects, birds and small mammals. Recent research has shown that interesting grasslands can be created along new roadside verges and similar sites; this will be discussed below.

# The intrinsic value of native plant species

The major reason for planting native species is to create new habitats which stand a good chance of being colonized by native animals, including invertebrates, birds and mammals. Although non-native planting will be colonized by animals, the native plant species have

PLATE 7.8 **Marbled white butterfly feeding on greater knapwood** (*Centaurea scabiosa*). **The caterpillar, in contrast, feeds on coarse grasses.** (*David Parker*)

111

TABLE 7.2

**The numbers of insect species associated with various deciduous and coniferous trees in Britain**

| Species | Number of insect species |
|---|---|
| Oak (*Quercus robur* and *Q. petraea*) | 284 |
| Willow (*Salix* spp) | 266 |
| Birch (*Betula* spp) | 229 |
| Hawthorn (*Crataegus* spp) | 149 |
| Sloe (*Prunus spinosa*) | 109 |
| Poplars (*Populus* spp) | 97 |
| Scot's pine (*Pinus sylvestris*) | 91 |
| Alder (*Alnus glutinosa*) | 90 |
| Elm (*Ulmus* spp) | 82 |
| Hazel (*Corylus avellana*) | 73 |
| Beech (*Fagus sylvatica*) | 64 |
| Ash (*Fraxinus excelsior*) | 41 |
| Spruce (*Picea abies*) | 37 |
| Lime (*Tilia* spp) | 31 |
| Mountain ash (*Sorbus aucuparia*) | 28 |
| Hornbeam (*Carpinus betulus*) | 28 |
| Field maple (*Acer campestre*) | 26 |
| Larch (*Larix decidua*) | 17 |
| Fir (*Abies* spp) | 16 |
| Sycamore (*Acer pseudoplatanus*) | 15 |
| Holly (*Ilex aquifolium*) | 7 |
| Sweet chestnut (*Castanea sativa*) | 5 |
| Holm oak (*Quercus ilex*) | 2 |

(*From Southwood, 1961*)

evolved with the native animals and are able to support many more species than the non-native plants (see Plates 7.7 and 7.8 and Tables 7.2, 7.3, 7.4 and 7.5). Native species can, especially in rural situations, be the most appropriate species to plant in order to allow a new development or a reclamation scheme to blend into its surroundings. In urban sites the use of native species can, apart from attracting wildlife into the city, form a valuable educational resource for the local population.

## Physical principles

The physical and chemical conditions that govern native plants' establishment, growth and associations with each other include climate, soils (including plant nutrient availability), geographical location and topography. The use of native plants calls for an understanding of the ecological factors of both the plant itself and of its relationship to the natural conditions.

Attention must be paid to soil and climate; together with the soil and water relationships, these will deter-

mine the type of native plants that can be established as well as their maintenance requirements and cost.

The most important parameters related to the soil are its particle-size composition (that is the proportions of sand, silt and clay), its organic matter content, pH, conductivity and the levels of nutrients, especially nitrogen, phosphorus and potassium, that are available to the plants. A knowledge of the physical and chemical characteristics of soils which support desired plant communities in nature can give guidance as to what remedial soil treatment is required on a particular site that is to be planted, or guidance on which native plants could be supported by the untreated on-site soils.

For the establishment of species-rich grassland communities the most satisfactory results will be achieved with soils that are poor in the major plant nutrients, especially nitrogen. Trees and shrubs will also grow on poor soils; evidence for this can be seen by observing the colonization of waste heaps and derelict land. Many substrate materials can provide the right growing conditions for these communities. Expensive topsoil is usually not required and would normally be too rich in plant nutrients, and therefore subsoils are usually preferable. Brick rubble, readily available in urban redevelopment areas, is an excellent growing medium for chalk and limestone flora provided, that is, it is sufficiently finely ground and retains sufficient moisture, and will often not need any improvement. Further practical research is required in the UK to explore the different forms of growing media for native species planting.

To prepare the site, the object is not to improve the soil but to prepare it as a base. Nutrient-rich topsoil, if present, will probably have to be replaced by low nutrient materials, and the top metre or so should be freed of all vegetation that is likely to cause later competition. Advantage should also be taken of existing site conditions, and every attempt should be made to retain not only the existing vegetation but also wet and dry areas, gradients and variable soil conditions to give as much variety to the planting conditions as possible. It is not usually possible, for economic reasons, to make great changes in the prevailing soil conditions, but localized variations can be made by introducing pockets of sand, brick rubble and ash, all with different pH levels and physico-chemical characteristics, for example.

A greater variation in the habitat can be achieved by varying the height of the soil surface in relation to the underlying water table. By the use of gradual gradients, up to 1 m in height above water level, it is possible to create a more diverse environment with a range of wet and dry habitats.

As well as the soil, the geographical location and topography of the site are great determining factors in what native species and communities can be established. Reference must always be made to the natural distri-

TABLE 7.3
**Food plants – shrubs (native or naturalized species)**

| Scientific name | Common name | Birds | Butterflies and moths Larvae | Butterflies and moths Adults | Rodents | Remarks on habitat etc. |
|---|---|---|---|---|---|---|
| *Buddleia davidii* | Buddleia | | | × | | Naturalized in S. England. |
| *Cornus sanguinea* | Dogwood | × | | | | Especially on calcareous soils. |
| *Corylus avellana* | Hazel | | | | × | Lowland woods and hedges. |
| *Cotoneaster simonsii* | | × | | | | Naturalized. |
| *Crataegus monogyna* | Hawthorn | × p | × | × | × | Hedging species. |
| *C. oxyacanthoides* | Midland hawthorn | × p | × | × | × | Mostly in S. and E., on clay and loam. More shade-tolerant, therefore found in woodland. |
| *Euonymus europaeus* | Spindle | × | | | | Especially on calcareous soils. |
| *Ilex aquifolium* | Holly | × | | | | |
| *Ligustrum vulgare* | Privet | × | × | | | Calcareous soils. |
| *Lonicera periclymenum* | Honeysuckle | × | | × | | Woods and hedgerows. |
| *Malus sylvestris* | Crab apple | × | | | | |
| *Prunus avium*, etc. | Cherry | × | × | | | |
| *P. domestica* | Plum | | × | | | |
| *P. spinosa* | Blackthorn | p | × | | | Chiefly calcareous soils in S. & E. |
| *Rhamnus catharticus* | Buckthorn | | × | | | |
| *Rosa* spp | Wild rose | × | | | | |
| *Rubus caesius* | Dewberry | × p | × | × | | Less vigorous form. Mainly basic soils. |
| *R. fruticosus* agg. | Blackberry, bramble | × p | × | × | | |
| *Salix caprea* | Goat willow | | × | × | | |
| *Sambucus nigra* | Elder | × p | | × | | |
| *Sorbus aucuparia* | Rowan | × p | | | | Mainly light soils. |
| *Symphoricarpos rivularis* | Snowberry | × p | | | | Naturalized. |
| *Taxus baccata* | Yew | × | | | | Calcareous soils. |
| *Viburnum lantana* | Wayfaring tree | × | | | | Not on acid soils. |
| *V. opulus* | Guelder rose | × | | × | × | Neutral or calcareous soils. |

p – berries eaten by pheasants.
Butterfly larvae – generally three or more species found on each plant or group mentioned.

bution of the native species being used to see whether their use is appropriate in a particular site (see Figure 7.4, showing three maps from the *Atlas of the British Flora*). For example, chalk grassland shrubs and herbs of southern England are unlikely to do well on an exposed hillside in the southern uplands of Scotland. Considerable research may therefore be necessary to match site conditions with appropriate native species.

## 7.3 HABITAT DESIGN AND MANAGEMENT

In order to design a given habitat it is important to understand both the habitat on which the design is to be modelled and the fundamental principles of ecology that govern it, such as the principles of succession and competition. The designer will often need to bring in

113

## TABLE 7.4
### Food plants – Herbaceous species (native or naturalized)

| Scientific name | Common name | Birds | Butterflies and moths | | Bees | Remarks on habitat, etc. | Height |
|---|---|---|---|---|---|---|---|
| | | | Larvae | Adults | | | |
| Ajuga reptans | Bugle | | | × | | Damp woods and fields. | L |
| Alliaria petiolata | Garlic mustard | | × | | | Hedgebanks, wood margins, damp places. | M-H |
| Anthriscus sylvestris | Cow parsley | × | | | | Undisturbed ground. | H |
| Armoracia rusticana | Horseradish | | × | | | | M-H |
| Aster spp | Michaelmas daisy | | | × | | Locally naturalized. | M-H |
| Cardamine pratensis | Ladies smock | | × | × | | Moist places. | M |
| Centaurea nigra, C. scabiosa | Knapweed | × | | × | | C. scabiosa especially on calcareous soils and dry places. | M-H |
| Centranthus ruber | Red valerian | | | × | | Naturalized on old walls, cliffs. | M |
| Centranthus cheiri | Wallflower | | | × | | Naturalized on cliffs and rocky places. | M |
| Cirsium and Carduus spp | Thistles | × | | × | | Cirsium vulgare and C. arvense are injurious weeds (statutory obligation to control spread). | M-H |
| Daucus carota | Wild carrot | × | × | | | Grassy places, especially on calcareous soils and near sea. | M |
| Dipsacus fullonum | Teasel | × | | | | Especially on clay soils. | H |
| Erica and Calluna spp | Heathers | | | × | × | Acid soils. | M |
| Foeniculum vulgare | Fennel | | × | | | Locally naturalized in waste places especially near the sea. | H |
| Heracleum sphondylium | Hogweed | × | | | | Rough grass. | H |
| Knautia arvensis | Scabious | × | | × | | Dry places, especially on calcareous soils. | M |
| Leucanthemum vulgare | Ox-eye daisy | | | × | | Basic soils, pastures. | M |
| Lotus corniculatus | Birds-foot trefoil | | × | | | Short grass. | L |
| Lupinus arboreus | Lupin | | | | × | Locally naturalized, dry and gravelly places. | H |
| Nepeta cataria | Catmint | | | × | | Calcareous soils. | M |
| Oenothera biennis | Evening primrose | × | | | | Dry places. | M |
| Origanum vulgare | Marjoram | | | × | | Usually calcareous soils. | L-M |
| Papaver spp | Poppy | × | | | | Mainly in dry places, disturbed ground. | M |
| Petasites fragrans | Winter heliotrope | | | × | | Naturalized in hedgebanks, etc. | L |
| Primula vulgaris | Primrose | | | × | | Woods, woodland margins. | L |
| Reseda lutea | Mignonette | | | × | | Chalky and dry places. | M |
| Rumex spp | Docks | × | × | | | Waste places. | M-H |
| Solidago virgaurea | Golden rod | | | × | | Dry places, cliffs. | M |
| Taraxacum officinale | Dandelion | | × | × | | Short grassland. | L |
| Thymus spp | Thyme | | | × | × | Calcareous and dry soils | L |
| Trifolium repens, T. pratense, etc. | Clovers | | × | × | × | Short grassland. | L-M |
| Urtica dioica | Nettle | × | × | | | Nitrogen-rich places. | M-H |
| Valeriana officinalis | Valerian | | | × | | Rough grassy places. | H |

L – Low growing (normally below 30 mm)   M – Medium   H – High (commonly reaching 1 000 mm or more)
Butterfly larvae – generally three or more species found on each plant mentioned
Rough grass is the food plant of many kinds of butterfly larvae.

TABLE 7.5
**Food plants − waterfowl**

| Scientific name | Common name | Habitat notes | Height |
|---|---|---|---|
| Marginal plants | | | |
| *Carex hirta* | Hairy sedge, hammer sedge | In damp grass and near ponds. | 0.3−0.6 m |
| *C. acutiformis* | Pond sedge | Fringes of still or slow moving water, swamps, especially in north. | 0.6−1.5 m |
| *Eleocharis palustris* | Common spike-rush | Tufted. Wet meadows, marshes, by ditches and pools. | 15−30 cm |
| *Glyceria fluitans* | Flote-grass | Common in stagnant and slow-flowing water. | 0.3−1.2 m |
| *G. maxima* | Reedgrass | Usually deeper water than *G. fluitans* | 1.2−1.8 m |
| *Polygonum hydropiper* | Water pepper | Marshy fields, shallow water by ponds and ditches | 0.3−0.6 m |
| *P. persicaria* | Redleg, redshank | Besides ponds and streams. | 0.3−0.6 m |
| *Ranunculus repens* | Creeping buttercup | Wet meadows by rivers and ditches. | |
| *Rumex hydrolapathum* | Great water dock | Wet places and shallow water. Rare in north. | 1.2−1.8 m |
| *Sagittaria sagittifolia* | Arrowhead | Best in silt or mud in approx. 15 cm of water. Rare in north. | 0.3−0.9 m |
| *Scirpus lacustris* | Common bulrush | Margins of silted lakes, ponds, rivers. | 1.8−2.4 m |
| *S. maritimus* | Sea club-rush | Brackish water. | |
| *Sparganium erectum* | Bur-reed | In water at edge of lakes, canals, rivers. | 0.6−1.2 m |
| *Typha latifolia* | Reedmace, bulrush | Invasive, growing down to at least 90 cm. At edges of ponds, canals, etc. | 1.2−2.4 m |
| TREES (SEEDS EATEN) | | | |
| *Alnus glutinosa* | Alder | | |
| *Betula pubescens* | Birch | | |
| *Quercus* spp | Oak | | |
| EMERGENT PLANTS | | | |
| *Hippuris vulgaris* | Marestail | Ponds, lakes, slow streams. Wide pH range. | |
| *Polygonum amphibium* | Amphibious bistort | Widespread and common. Pools, canals, etc. | |
| *Potamogeton natans* | Floating pondweed | Lakes, ponds, ditches. Prefers 0.3−1.5 m depths. More tolerant of acid conditions than other pondweeds. Likes highly organic substratum. | |
| *Ranunculus aquatilis* | Water crowfoot | Swift streams or bog water. Will tolerate moderate acidity. | |
| *R. baudotii* | Brackish-water crowfoot | Brackish water. | |
| FLOATING PLANTS | | | |
| *Lemna* spp | Duckweeds | *L. trisulca* will grow in acid water. | |
| SUBMERGED PLANTS | | | |
| *Chara* spp | Stonewort | Alkaline or brackish water. Still or stagnant. Very rapid growth. | |
| *Potamogeton pectinatus* | Sago pondweed | Rich fresh or brackish ponds, ditches, rivers. | |
| *Ruppia maritima* | Tassel pondweed | Brackish ditches and ponds. In soil or sand from a few inches to several feet. | |
| PLANTS GIVING MARGINAL COVER | | | |
| *Iris pseudacorus* | Flag iris, yellow flag | Marshes, shallow water. | 0.3−1.2 m |
| *Phragmites australis* | Common reed | Swamps and shallow water. Invasive. | 1.8−3.6 m |

* Species of particular value

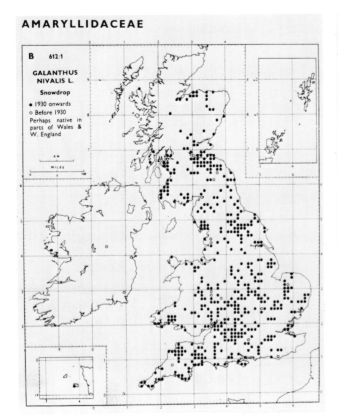

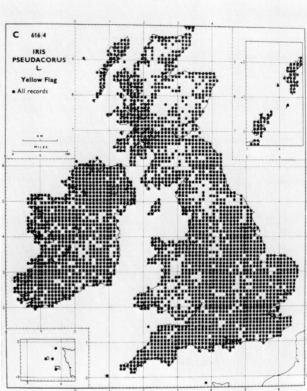

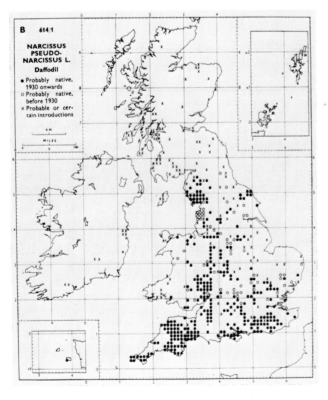

FIGURE 7.4 **Examples of the distribution of three native plants in the British Isles, as presented in the** *Atlas of the British Flora. (Courtesy of the Botanical Society of the British Isles.)*

or whether another habitat or several habitats suggest themselves, what are the soil types and what native plants are already there and whether there are features such as damp hollows or rock outcrops that, if retained or extended, would add to the richness of the site.

Any newly-built development creates a new habitat around it, even if this habitat is limited to a monoculture of rye grass and the occasional tree. More often, however, there is scope to create a much richer environment. For example, what in one engineer's eyes may be a dry storage pound for drainage run-off can, with the landscape designer's input, become a wet balancing pond with rich planted edges. The designer can do much to persuade both his fellow professionals and his client that the creation of more diverse habitats will be in the long-term interest of both the client and the site itself.

Assuming that the site in question is to be designed from scratch with no existing features worthy of retention, where does the designer start? As discussed under Physical Principles earlier, the soil and its preparation is fundamental to the success of habitat design.

Planting design and mix come next. In choosing native plant species the designer should be trying to make sure that they are typical of the chosen habitat,

specialists such as botanists, ecologists, landscape managers and scientists at an early stage of the design process to advise and carry out the specialist field work that may be required.

A field survey will establish the answers to questions such as whether a desired habitat is feasible on the site

116

TABLE 7.6
**Design check list**

*SITE SURVEY*: Thorough analysis of the native species that are present and their relationship with soil, slope, moisture and use.

*SITE ANALYSIS*: Explore the possibility of retaining areas with established and interesting vegetation cover.

*DESIGN STAGE*:

1. Consider the provision of a suitable growing medium and good ground preparation.

2. Consider the use of native plants as part of the design.

3. Consider supply and contract growing of species in phasing programme.

*CONTRACT STAGE*:

1. Protect existing habitats and plant species, including herb layers in woodland areas.

2. Use of material for contract growing taken from site prior to the start of the contract proper. Salvage plants for other jobs if they are not required, or turf pieces or use hay cut techniques from within the site boundary.

*COMPLETION AND MAINTENANCE*:
Draw up maintenance plan for successful establishment and perpetuation of the design.

---

and a greater percentage of normally dominant species should be chosen over those only occasionally present in natural circumstances. Diversity, both in age structure and plant type, should be the aim. This is particularly relevant to establishing woodland or shrub communities.

The edges between one habitat and another are often ecologically rich and, when dealing with an existing site, it is at the edge that species can indicate plants which may have covered a much wider area of the site. The gradual transition from woodland to non-woodland and the land/water boundary are often particularly rich, so whenever possible the edge between such habitats should be kept or maintained for as long as possible. Moreover, the edge should keep an irregular outline or boundary, since that way it is likely to be richer biologically than an area of the same size with a regular outline.

Links or corridors between several small areas of similar habitat will increase the effectiveness of that habitat in terms of wildlife and flora conservation. Links of a diverse habitat in an ecologically barren area, such as arable farmland, can help species to spread and populations to maintain themselves: hence the great ecological importance of hedges, railway embankments, road verges and even footpaths.

# Woodland and scrub

## CASE STUDY 1: Warrington and Runcorn Development Corporation

The structural woodland planting of Warrington and Runcorn New Town comprises 300 hectares (1987 figure) and provides one of the more impressive examples of woodland habitat creation using indigenous plant species that has been developed in the UK since the 1970s.

The aims of these 'natural' plantings are to produce:

1. A cost effective landscape structure for the New Town in terms of both establishment and maintenance.
2. Robust landscape that can withstand both public pressure and vandalism.
3. A replacement for the semi-natural woodland habitats that are fast disappearing in the area.
4. Amenity planting which does not look designed or planned (such as plantations planted primarily for timber production).
5. Structural diversity.

It was recognized at an early stage that simply planting native species would not be sufficient to establish new

117

areas of indigenous woodland and from the time of the first plantings at Warrington–Runcorn (1974 onwards) four elements for the successful establishment of native woodland were defined and adhered to. These are:

(a) ground preparation;
(b) design on an ecological basis;
(c) maintenance principles;
(d) management principles.

*(a) Ground preparation.* The principles behind the ground preparation policy were developed from the existing poor soil conditions at Warrington–Runcorn and the prohibitive cost of importing topsoil in quantity to provide a suitable growing medium. Instead of importing topsoil therefore, the ground preparation is carried out as follows:

(i) Deep ripping and the incorporation of a bulky organic ameliorant is combined in one operation by means of spreading a 150 mm layer of coarse, 'as dug' peat over the given area and cross ripping to a depth of 450 mm with machine tines set at 500 mm centres. This is normally carried out in August or September when the clay subsoil is reasonably workable.

(ii) Subsequent weed growth that develops is then sprayed in October with a total translocated herbicide such as Roundup.

(iii) The site is then prepared for planting over the dormant winter period.

*(b) Design.* Four basic plant mixes are used in the design where the planting bed is over 10 m in width (see Table 7.7).

(i) Woodland mix.
(ii) Light demanding mix.
(iii) Tall edge mix.
(iv) Low edge mix.

TABLE 7.7
**Warrington–Runcorn structure planting species mixes**

---

*Woodland mix*
1.5–2 m centres; group planted with trees at 10–50 per group and shrubs at 5–10 per group; *Alnus* and *Corylus* planted randomly with occasional group.

| Species: | | |
|---|---|---|
| | 25% | *Quercus robur* |
| | 20% | *Alnus glutinosa* |
| | 15% | *Corylus avellana* |
| | 12.5% | *Fraxinus excelsior* |
| | 12.5% | *Pinus sylvestris* |
| | 5% | *Prunus avium* |
| | 5% | *Ilex aquifolium* |
| | 5% | *Sambucus nigra* |

*Light-demanding mix*
1.5–2 m centres; all species group-planted at 5–100 per group; may occasionally form edge to plantation; mostly group-coppiced on rotation.

| Species: | | |
|---|---|---|
| | 17.5% | *Betula pendula* |
| | 17.5% | *Alnus glutinosa* |
| | 12.5% | *Populus tremula* |
| | 12.5% | *Sorbus aucuparia* |
| | 12.5% | *Corylus avellana* |
| | 12.5% | *Sambucus nigra* |
| | 10% | *Ilex aquifolium* |
| | 5% | *Acer campestre* |

*Tall edge mix*
1.5 m centres; group-planted at 5–50 per group; *Lonicera* planted randomly; frequently forms edge to planting; percentage of *Crataegus* increased when used as hedge.

| Species: | | |
|---|---|---|
| | 42.5% | *Crataegus monogyna* |
| | 17.5% | *Corylus avellana* |
| | 15% | *Prunus spinosa* |
| | 10% | *Alnus glutinosa* |
| | 5% | *Acer campestre* |
| | 5% | *Sambucus nigra* |
| | 2.5% | *Lonicera periclymenum* |
| | 2.5% | *Salix caprea* |

*Low edge mix*
1.5 m centres; all species group-planted at 5–30 per group; percentages and combinations may vary widely, depending upon effect required; small-scale variation important. *Rubus fruticosus* not planted, as it will rapidly colonize suitable areas.

| Species: | | |
|---|---|---|
| | 50% | *Rosa arvensis* / *Rosa canina* |
| | 30% | *Corylus avellana* / *Crataegus monogyna* / *Prunus spinosa* |
| | 20% | *Cornus sanguinea* / *Ilex aquifolium* / *Rosa pimpinellifolia* / *Ulex europaeus* |

WOODLAND CANOPY, PLUS UNDERSTOREY OF SAPLINGS AND SHADE TOLERANT SHRUBS AND GROUND VEGETATION

WOODLAND EDGE. LIGHT DEMANDING TREES AND SHRUBS

LONG GRASS

SHORT GRASS

FIGURE 7.5 **A woodland—grassland sequence giving a wide variety of habitats.**

Within each mix, single species group planting is employed both to reflect natural regeneration patterns and to overcome competition problems that arose in the earliest schemes at Warrington—Runcorn where the species were mixed together randomly (see Figure 7.5).

Spacing of species has likewise been modified from experience of the earliest planting schemes, and they are now set at 1.5—2.0 m spacing for both the woodland and light-demanding mixes, and both edge mixes are set at 1.5 m centres. Hawthorn (*Crataegus monogyna*), blackthorn (*Prunus spinosa*) and dogrose (*Rosa canina*) are planted at 2.0 m spacing to provide a physical barrier where public pressure is high. Where this pressure is not so great or where more time is available, these species are given a wider spacing.

*(c) Maintenance.* Maintenance is defined as 'operations to retain the status quo'.

The whole basis of the planting at Warrington—Runcorn is to establish planting quickly and ensure rapid growth. Transplants and whips in the 450—600 mm range are used, and competition from other 'undesired' plants is avoided by means of a clean-ground policy using herbicides. Fertilizers are used for the first two years following planting to ensure good plant development.

Trials carried out at Warrington suggest that this policy pays dividends. Initial plant losses on peat-ripped sites with a clean-ground policy are only 3—5 per cent, as compared to 15—20 per cent for areas where

no maintenance is carried out. In addition, growth rates are greater and the cost is one-fifth that using traditional methods of site preparation (with three years' maintenance).

*(d) Management.* Management is defined as 'the manipulation of the structural characteristics of a planting belt'. Fundamental to a successful management policy on woodlands is a thorough understanding of both successional change and the responses of plants to treatment in time and space.

The early planting schemes at Warrington used random mixes of species, with the result that the more aggressive species, particularly poplars, willows and elder, began to outcompete the long-term species, and heavy thinning became necessary after only two to three years. The result has been high maintenance costs on thinning alone and a decision that, unless exposure or poor soil conditions warranted them, nurse species would not be planted with the long-term species. A management plan is summarized in Table 7.8.

## Grassland and heathland

### CASE STUDY 2: The creation of species-rich grasslands at the Institute of Terrestrial Ecology, Monks Wood

The dramatic rate of loss of species-rich grasslands in the British Isles, owing to the intensification of agriculture, stimulated a research programme at Monks Wood

TABLE 7.8
**Warrington−Runcorn management plan***

| Year | Woodland mix | Light-demanding mix | Tall edge mix | Low edge mix |
|---|---|---|---|---|
| 1 | | | Heavily pruned to produce bushy plants | Initially hawthorn, blackthorn and dogrose are heavily pruned |
| 2 | Trees are thinned on commercial forestry lines to achieve broken canopy. Some groups of species are left unthinned and understorey species are coppiced | Coppicing begins by cutting to 75 mm. Thinning or coppicing plants creates three distinct phases within single-species groups: (a) Groups of between 5−20 of some species cut down to 75 mm. (b) Groups thinned out on commercial forestry lines (c) Groups left unthinned to fight among themselves. *NB* Stump treatments not normally necessary until after years 4 and 5. *Note* Coppicing begins in year 2, then every second or third year to year 10. Thereafter every third or fourth year | Year 3: Mix group coppiced every 2−3 years to varying heights between 300 and 600 mm to achieve uneven edge effect | 50% of plants are heavily pruned in groups to create uneven edge |
| 3 | | | | |
| 4 | | | | Year 4: Low edge is now impenetrable Sections pruned to retain uneven edge. Plants allowed to fight their way through |
| 5 | | | | |
| 6 | | | | |
| 7 | | | | |
| 8 | | | | |
| 9 | | | | |
| 10 | | | | |

* Drawn from text in *The Natural Approach to Structural Open Space at Warrington New Town* by Duncan Moffatt (Warrington and Runcorn Development Corporation).

which began in the late 1960s. It has been directed by Terry Wells, who established a large-scale field experiment which tested the creation of species-rich grasslands grown from seed. This work is reported in Wells *et al.* (1981). The seed was collected from unimproved meadows and a great deal of information was obtained on the germination biology of the various grassland species. The monitoring of the field plots has also provided information on the dynamics of the species composition of the grasslands. Differential management of the plots has yielded information on management techniques with which to improve the species diversity of the swards.

It is not possible by sowing grassland seed mixtures to recreate grasslands with the structure and floristic composition of long established grasslands such as chalk downland or old hay meadows. However, the research carried out at Monks Wood has shown that it is possible to create grasslands that contain many of the interesting species of the old grasslands and, given time and further research, these grasslands should further improve.

The seed of wildflower species is expensive and it makes both economic and ecological sense to sow these seeds with the seed of grasses that are commercially available. In the old grasslands, grasses can form up to 60 per cent of the above-ground cover and they add physical robustness to the sward. Aggressive grass species such as rye grass (*Lolium perenne*) are not used. Less competitive species which are available commercially and appear to be compatible with herbaceous species are used, including the common and fine-leaved fescues (*Festuca ovina* and *F. tenuifolia*), common bent (*Agrostis capillaris*) and crested dog's-tail (*Cynosurus cristatus*). Where groundcover is required quickly, it has been found effective to sow a nurse crop with the herbs. The nurse, such as Westerwold's rye-grass (*Lolium multiflorum*), generally behaves as an annual, germinating quickly and then dying back. If it is cut, no seed is produced and the species that is wanted can take over.

This research has produced lists of recommended species that are suitable for sowing on different soil types. Short and tall grassland mixes are also recommended, together with sowing rates. This information is summarized in Table 7.9.

On small areas seed can be sown by hand, but on larger areas it should be sown mechanically. The grass and wildflower seeds should be thoroughly mixed, although the great disparity in seed size can make this difficult. The seed bed should consist of a fine tilth, which can be achieved by repeated harrowing and rolling, though this should not be done too much if high moisture loss is likely. Following sowing, light raking or harrowing has been shown to improve germination by ensuring good contact between the seed and the soil. The seed should be sown in the spring.

Subsequent management, especially over the first eight to ten weeks, is crucial both to the establishment and to the final composition of the grassland. The sward should be cut with a rotary cutter at a height of 100 mm, six to eight weeks after sowing. This reduces weed competition, and even kills the taller grasses. The aim of subsequent management is to allow the small herbaceous species to develop alongside the sown grasses, without too much competition from the weeds or the nurse crop. This is best achieved by cutting at approximately two-month intervals, depending on growth, until late October (in southern England). In the second year cutting requirements will be less, and a cut in April and in October may be all that is required. It is always an advantage to take away the cuttings, as this will serve to steadily reduce the soil fertility. The use of grazing animals is also an option instead of manual cutting, though physical damage of the soil and sward would have to be carefully monitored in this case.

In recent years these techniques have been tested on many sites and especially by urban ecology groups trying to create species-rich grasslands in towns and cities (see Plate 7.9). Other appropriate sites include new roadside verges, country parks and land adjoining grassland nature reserves where the area of ecologically

PLATE 7.9 **Wildflower meadow established from seed, at the International Garden Festival, Liverpool, 1984.** (*Landlife*)

TABLE 7.9

**Lists of species recommended for creating species-rich grasslands on three soil types** (*From Wells* et al., *1981*)

| 1. Seed mixtures for sowing on heavy clay soils | Sowing rate (kg/ha) | | Sowing rate (kg/ha) |
|---|---|---|---|
| **(a) Grass and short herb mixture** | | **(b) Grass and tall herb mixtures** | |
| (i) *Alopecurus pratensis* | 5.0 | (i) *Alopecurus pratensis* | 5.0 |
| *Briza media* | 0.5 | *Briza media* | 0.5 |
| *Festuca rubra* 'Highlight' | 10.0 | *Cynosurus cristatus* | 5.0 |
| *F. rubra* 'Rapid' | 8.0 | *Festuca rubra* 'Cascade' | 10.0 |
| *Hordeum secalinum* | 1.0 | *F. rubra* 'Highlight' | 10.0 |
| *Trisetum flavescens* | 1.0 | *Hordeum secalinum* | 1.0 |
| *Anthyllis vulneraria* | 3.0 | *Trisetum flavescens* | 1.0 |
| *Chrysanthemum leucanthemum* | 0.2 | *Centaurea nigra* | 1.0 |
| *Galium verum* | 0.3 | *C. scabiosa* | 1.0 |
| *Leontodon hispidus* | 0.5 | *Chrysanthemum leucanthemum* | 0.5 |
| *Lotus corniculatus* | 1.0 | *Daucus carota* | 0.9 |
| *Medicago lupulina* | 2.0 | *Filipendula vulgaris* | 1.0 |
| *Plantago media* | 0.2 | *Geranium pratense* | 2.5 |
| *Primula veris* | 0.5 | *Hypochoeris radicata* | 0.3 |
| *Prunella vulgaris* | 0.5 | *Lotus corniculatus* | 1.0 |
| *Rhinanthus minor* | 2.0 | *Plantago lanceolata* | 2.0 |
| (ii) *Achillea millefolium, Anthoxanthum odoratum, Betonica officinalis, Lotus uliginosus, Ononis repens* | | *Poterium sanguisorba* | 0.3 |
| | | *Ranunculus acris* | 1.0 |
| | | *Silene alba* | 0.5 |
| | | (ii) *Agrimonia eupatoria, Knautia arvensis, Lathyrus pratensis, Ranunculus acris, Ononis spinosa, Rumex acetosa, Tragopogon pratensis, Vicia cracca, V. tetrasperma* | |

| 2. Seed mixtures for sowing on chalk and other limestone soils | Sowing rate (kg/ha) | | Sowing rate (kg/ha) |
|---|---|---|---|
| **(a) Grass and short herb mixture** | | **(b) Grass and tall herb mixture** | |
| (i) *Briza media* | 0.5 | (ii) *Bromus erectus* | 2.0 |
| *Cynosurus cristatus* | 5.0 | *Cynosurus cristatus* | 5.0 |
| *Festuca rubra* 'Highlight' | 10.0 | *Festuca longifolia* | 10.0 |
| *F. rubra* 'Rapid' | 8.0 | *F. ovina* | 4.0 |
| *Koeleria cristata* | 0.1 | *F. rubra* 'Highlight' | 10.0 |
| *Trisetum flavescens* | 1.0 | *F. rubra* 'Rapid' | 8.0 |
| *Anthyllis vulneraria* | 3.0 | *Centaurea nigra* | 1.0 |
| *Campanula glomerata* | 0.01 | *C. scabiosa* | 1.0 |
| *C. rotundifolia* | 0.01 | *Chrysanthemum leucanthemum* | 0.2 |
| *Chrysanthemum leucanthemum* | 0.2 | *Clinopodium vulgare* | 0.1 |
| *Galium verum* | 0.3 | *Daucus carota* | 0.5 |
| *Hippocrepis comosa* | 0.1 | *Galium verum* | 0.3 |
| *Medicago lupulina* | 2.0 | *Lotus corniculatus* | 1.0 |
| *Plantago media* | 0.2 | *Onobrychis viciifolia* | 3.0 |
| *Primula veris* | 0.5 | *Reseda lutea* | 0.03 |
| *Prunella vulgaris* | 0.5 | *R. luteola* | 0.01 |
| *Scabiosa columbaria* | 0.5 | *Scabiosa columbaria* | 0.5 |
| *Thymus drucei* or *T. pulegioides* | 0.1 | *Tragopogon pratensis* | 1.0 |
| *Veronica chamaedrys* | 0.1 | (ii) *Agrimonia eupatoria, Knautia arvensis Pimpinella saxifraga* | |
| (ii) *Cerastium holosteoides, Euphrasia nemorosa, Hieracium pilosella, Hippocrepis comosa, Linum catharticum, Ononis repens* | | | |

| 3. Seed mixtures for sowing on alluvial soils | Sowing rate (kg/ha) | | Sowing rate (kg/ha) |
|---|---|---|---|
| **(a) Grass and short herb mixture** | | **(b) Grass and tall herb mixture** | |
| (i) *Agrostis tenuis* | 1.0 | (i) *Agrostis tenuis* | 1.0 |
| *Alopecurus pratensis* | 5.0 | *Alopecurus pratensis* | 5.0 |
| *Briza media* | 0.5 | *Cynosurus cristatus* | 5.0 |
| *Cynosurus cristatus* | 5.0 | *Festuca rubra 'Dawson'* | 10.0 |
| *Festuca rubra 'Dawson'* | 10.0 | *F. rubra 'Cascade'* | 10.0 |
| *F. rubra 'Cascade'* | 10.0 | *Poa pratensis 'Baron'* | 3.0 |
| *Poa pratensis 'Baron'* | 3.0 | *Chrysanthemum leucanthemum* | 0.2 |
| *Chrysanthemum leucanthemum* | 0.2 | *Daucus carota* | 0.9 |
| *Conopodium majus* | 1.0 | *Lotus corniculatus* | 1.0 |
| *Daucus carota* | 0.9 | *Lychnis flos-cuculi* | 0.005 |
| *Galium verum* | 0.3 | *Plantago lanceolata* | 2.0 |
| *Hypochoeris radicata* | 0.3 | *Poterium sanguisorba* | 0.3 |
| *Lychnis flos-cuculi* | 0.005 | *Primula veris* | 0.5 |
| *Medicago lupulina* | 2.0 | *Rhinanthus minor* | 2.0 |
| *Plantago media* | 0.2 | *Sanguisorba officinalis* | 0.5 |
| *Poterium sanguisorba* | 0.3 | *Silaum silaus* | 1.0 |
| *Primula veris* | 0.5 | *Silene alba* | 0.5 |
| *Prunella vulgaris* | 0.5 | (ii) *Bromus commutatus, Ranunculus acris, Rumex acetosa. Tragopogon pratensis* | |
| *Rhinanthus minor* | 2.0 | | |
| (ii) *Anthoxanthum odoratum, Cerastium holosteoides, Hordeum secalinum, Poa trivialis, Taraxacum officinale* | | | |

*Notes*:

(i) Tested in field trials.
(ii) Untested in field trials, but probably suitable.

valuable habitat can be extended. Artificial meadows also have a valuable educational function, and the techniques have met with a lot of interest from schools.

## 7.4 SOURCES OF PLANT MATERIAL AND GRANT AID

### Obtaining native plant material

For advice on obtaining native plant material, contact any one of the following: the local authority, local naturalists' groups, urban wildlife groups, the Nature Conservancy Council regional office, the Forestry Commission (for trees) or any other organization with an interest in ecology and the environment. Listings of commercial suppliers can be obtained from journals such as *Horticulture Week* or, more locally, British Telecom *Yellow Pages*.

Several charitable trusts have developed their own nurseries, specializing particularly in wild herbs and grasses for their own use. They offer advice and plant material for sale. At the time of writing three such nurseries are known. These are run by:

(a) Landlife (formerly the Rural Preservation Association), The Old Police Station, Lark Lane, Liverpool L17 8UU. Tel: (051) 728 7011. See Plates 7.10 and 7.11.
(b) Tower Hamlets Environment Trust (THET), Brady Centre, 192/6 Hanbury Street, London E1. Tel: (01) 247 6265.
(c) Urban Wildlife Group, 11 Albert Square, Birmingham B4 7UA. Tel: (021) 236 3626.

A number of grass seed houses now supply wildflower mixes as standard including particular mixes for different situations, such as reclamation mix or steep embankment mix. Before using such seed it is worth investigating its origin, since it may have been imported from abroad and include non-native species.

Alternatively, it may be appropriate to consider obtaining material from a local site, either as individual plants, cuttings or seed. Permission from the landowner

PLATE 7.10 **Derelict inner city site in Liverpool, 1984.** *(Landlife)*

PLATE 7.11 **The same site as in Plate 7.10 after restoration in 1985.** *(Landlife)*

PLATE 7.12 **The native daffodil,** *Narcissus pseudonarcissus,* **can be used as effectively as any of the cultivated species and varieties of daffodil.** *(Dick Hoyle)*

must be obtained before removing anything, but such a source will have the advantage that the material will be adapted to local conditions. In the case of aquatic plants, importing plants from a local source will also mean the importation of local mud probably containing animals and seed to inoculate the new water body, giving a head start to its development.

Examples of native species are shown in Plates 7.12 to 7.17.

## Grant aid

Grant aid for the planting of native plant material is available from several sources. Charitable trusts are one such source, and their aim is to give aid principally to voluntary groups. For the availability of grants, refer to two publications. The first is entitled *Grants to Voluntary Organisations*, available free from the Department of the Environment (Room P2/102, 2 Marsham Street, London SW1 3EB). The other, *Directory of*

*Grant Making Trusts*, is produced annually by the Charities Aid Foundation, 48 Pembury Road, Tonbridge, Kent TN9 2JD, and lists over 2400 charitable trusts.

Statutory authorities also provide grant aid. The main grant aiding bodies are:

(a) Nature Conservancy Council (NCC) − The NCC awards discretionary grants for up to 50 per cent of cost for work in which the primary objective is to enhance wildlife habitats or species. For further details contact The Grants Officer, NCC Head Office, Northminster House, Peterborough, Tel: 0733 40345.

(b) Countryside Commission (CC) − The Countryside Commission awards grants up to a 50 per cent maximum on tree planting, conserving existing trees and other landscape features, such as stone walls or hedges. The schemes are administered by the local authority acting as agent for the Commission. For further details contact one

PLATE 7.13 **The distinctive heads of** *Dipsascus sylvestris*, **the wild teasel, shown to effect against a dark background.** *(M. Nimmo)*

of the regional offices of the Commission or alternatively the local county council offices. The Commission's Head Office is at John Dower House, Crescent Place, Cheltenham, Glos GL50 3RA. Scotland has a separate Countryside Commission for Scotland; the Head Office is at Battleby, Redgorten, Perth, Tel: 0738 27921.

(c) Forestry Commission (FC) – Until recently the Forestry Commission only awarded grants where the principal objective was softwood timber production, but in 1985 the Commission introduced the Broadleaved Woodland Grant Scheme to 'encourage the rehabilitation of existing broad-leaved woodlands, by natural regeneration and planting, and the establishment of new ones'. To be eligible for any grant from the Forestry Commission, the site in question must be 0.25 ha or larger. Contact either the local authority forester or the Private Woodlands Officer at one of the Forestry Commission's regional offices. The Head Office of the Forestry Commission is at 231 Corstorphine Road, Edinburgh EH12 7AT, Tel: (031) 334 0303.

(d) Ministry of Agriculture, Fisheries and Foods (MAFF) – The objectives of MAFF in awarding grants are principally to encourage agricultural production, though recent concern about agricultural overproduction, loss of hedgerows etc. has resulted in a shift in grant policy and grants are currently available for conservation work. Con-

PLATE 7.14 *Tussilago farfara*, **the coltsfoot, is valuable for its early flowering (from February onwards) and later as groundcover.** *(M. Nimmo)*

PLATE 7.15 **Wild garlic** *(Allium ursinium)* **suited to heavy clay soils in shade.** *(David Parker)*

PLATE 7.16 *Iris foetidissima,* **or gladdon, showing its graceful tapering foliage and orange-red seeds.** *(Dick Hoyle)*

127

PLATE 7.17 *Helleborus foetidus*, **or stinking hellebore, with its distinctive winter flowers.** *(Dick Hoyle)*

tact the ministry on (01) 233 3000 for the addresses and telephone numbers of local divisional offices.

## 7.5 RECENT DEVELOPMENTS AND LIKELY FUTURE TRENDS

The 1980s have seen great changes in the public's perception of nature conservation and landscape design and management. There has been an increasing expectation that certain types of designed landscape should take more account of ecological considerations and especially of the use of native plant species. Publications in this period have reflected this trend together with, for example, an enthusiastic development of urban ecology units. Linked to this, landscape architects are increasingly expected to prepare schemes in both urban and rural situations that require a substantial knowledge of ecological principles and natural history. For example, with the extractive mineral industries, planning permission for new work has increasingly required not simply 'restoration' but a carefully planned restoration and creation of plant communities that will

develop ecological interest. Where land of high nature conservation interest is concerned, the stipulation will now be for the replacement, as far as can be achieved, of the former vegetation of the site.

There has been a considerable development in urban ecology, with the establishment of active groups in most of the major conurbations in the UK. The most active groups are in Liverpool, Birmingham and London. For example, Liverpool hosts the national charity, Landlife, which aims to protect and conserve British wildlife through practical projects. Landlife became aware that in order to achieve these aims it was vital that work could be initially undertaken in urban areas, so that the people who lived there could come to understand and appreciate their environment. Numerous practical projects have been undertaken, together with educational programmes, which have relied on conserving and creating sites of ecological interest within urban areas, using native species, and creating wildlife habitats. This has tied in with policies for inner-city regeneration and the need for the reclamation and re-use of derelict land.

In the urban fringe the Countryside Commission, in association with local authorities, has created several Groundwork Trusts. These were created to assist in the environmental improvement of urban areas that had a legacy of degraded and derelict land from industrial activity in the past. The first Operation Groundwork was in St Helens, Merseyside, and a great deal has been achieved in land reclamation and amenity creation and in the involvement of local industries and people in many projects. The use of sound ecological principles and native species forms an essential part of their project design.

In more rural areas land reclamation is also a pressing need, and increasingly these projects now take account of the existing vegetation of the area, much of which often consists of native species. As has been discussed above, new developments, such as mineral extraction and the laying of pipelines, now often require planning permissions which stipulate the restoration of specific types of vegetation following the completion of on-site operations. Rural areas are also subject to increasing pressures of urbanization, especially in south-east England. Should these developments proceed, then opportunities are opened up for the conservation and creation of rural features in more urban settings. Native vegetation would form an important part of these projects.

We are now witnessing the start of an extensive change in the management of the countryside of the UK. There is pressure for a deintensification of agriculture, resulting in different crops and management practices and in marginal land coming out of agricultural use altogether. There is thus a considerable challenge developing for landscape designers, managers and scientists, to help to guide the restructuring of the rural landscape. This impinges on an older debate about forestry policy, for example the planting of extensive conifer plantations on uplands. Much semi-upland and lowland farmland currently used for pastoral agriculture or marginal arable production would be very suitable for afforestation. The soils of these areas are better than those of the uplands, and the growing of trees becomes an attractive option on these areas. There is considerable pressure for this afforestation to include a significant proportion of native deciduous trees but purely short-term economic considerations dictate fast-growing, non-native coniferous species. The debate on the future of much of the rural landscape, including the possible replacement of native vegetation lost in the extension of intensive agricultural production, has only just begun.

## 7.6 SUMMARY OF GENERAL GUIDELINES

1. Planting and management for wildlife conservation must be based upon sound ecological principles. Unless there is a particularly important species or habitat to be conserved, the aim should be to create and maintain a variety of habitats and of species. This is best achieved by encouraging structural diversity of plant form, a variety of plant species, and a varied age structure. Wherever possible, marginal habitats should be increased by producing an indented boundary.

2. Planting schemes should use only native species unless an introduced species has a particular advantage for wildlife. They should be designed to increase plant and structural diversity.

3. Sudden, drastic changes in regime which are either natural (such as periodic inundation of lake margins or alternation between saltwater and freshwater) or man-made (for instance, sudden cessation of a management regime or sudden enrichment by fertilizer application) will tend to decrease species diversity. If changes in management regime are necessary, they should be as small and as gradual as possible.

4. Management operations, and the reasons behind them should be clearly set out in a management plan. This is particularly important in the case of woodland, where the management cycle may span decades or even centuries.

5. Removal of dead plant material and general tidying-up should be minimal and in any event only as much as is necessary to prevent accidents, fire or unsightly appearance.

6. The landscape architect would be well advised to seek advice from the landscape scientist and manager at both planting design and management plan stages. The landscape scientist, in particular, should be consulted at an early stage about what is possible and advisable for the site and about plant selection.

## ACKNOWLEDGEMENTS

The authors would like to thank the following for their assistance in the production of this chapter: Duncan Moffatt of Warrington and Runcorn Development Corporation; Gerald Dawe of the Centre for Urban Ecology, Birmingham; Grant Luscombe, Director of Landlife, Liverpool; Terry Wells of the Institute of Terrestrial Ecology, Monks Wood; and Mike Hendy for his drawings.

## FURTHER READING

ADAS *Wildlife Conservation in Semi-natural Habitats on Farms* (Ministry of Agriculture, Fisheries and Food, London: HMSO 1976)

Bornkamm, R., Lee, J. A. and Seaward, M. R. D. (eds) *Urban Ecology (Second European Ecological Symposium)* (Oxford: Blackwells 1982)

Baines, C. *How To Make a Wildlife Garden* (London: Elm Tree Books/Hamish Hamilton 1985)

Baines, C. and Smart, J. *A Guide To Habitat Creation* (Greater London Council 1984)

Beckett, K. and Beckett, G. *Planting Native Trees and Shrubs* (Norwich: Jarrold 1979)

Bradshaw, A. D., Thorp, E. and Goode, D. A. (eds) *Ecology and Design in Landscape* (Oxford: Blackwell Scientific 1986)

Briggs, S. A. (ed.) *Landscaping for Birds*, Audubon Naturalist Society of the Central Atlantic States Inc., (Washington 1973)

British Trust for Conservation Volunteers Handbooks:

Agate, E. *Waterways and Wetlands – A Practical Conservation Handbook* 1981

Agate, E. *Footpaths – A Practical Handbook* 1983

Brooks, A. *Coastlands – A Practical Conservation Handbook 1979*

Brooks, A. *Dry Stone Walling – A Practical Conservation Handbook 1983*

Roper, A. *Hedging – A Practical Handbook 1975*

Roper, A. *Woodlands – A Practical Handbook 1980*

Centre for Urban Ecology/West Midlands Think Green Network *Resource Centre, Library Reading List No 7* (an excellent bibliography of environmental publications 1987)

Coppin, N. J. and Bradshaw, A. D. *A Guide to Quarry Reclamation: A brief Account of Methods of Establishment of Vegetation in Quarries and Non-metal Open Pits* (London: Mining Journal Books 1982)

Corder, M. and Brooker, R. *Natural Economy – An Ecological Approach to Planting and Management Techniques in Urban Areas* (Huddersfield: Kirklees Metropolitan Council 1981)

Countryside Commission *Advisory Series, No 13, Grassland Establishment for Countryside Recreation* (Cheltenham: Countryside Commission 1980)

Countryside Commission for Scotland *Lochshore Management* (Perth 1986)

Davis, B. N. K. *Ecology of Quarries – The Importance of Natural Vegetation*, ITE Symposium No 11, ITE, Monks Wood Experimental Station 1982

Dowdeswell, W. H. *Hedgerows and Verges* (London: Allen and Unwin 1987)

Duffy, E. *et al. Grassland Ecology and Wildlife Management* (London: Chapman & Hall 1976)

Dutton, R. A. and Bradshaw, A. D. *Land Reclamation in Cities – A Guide to Methods of Establishment of Vegetation on Urban Waste Land* (London: HMSO 1982)

Ecological Parks Trust *The William Curtis Ecological Park, Reports 1 to 4* (London: Ecological Parks Trust 1978–81)

Edlin, H. L. *Trees, Woods and Man* (London: New Collins Naturalist Series 1970)

Emery, M. *Promoting Nature in Cities and Towns: A Practical Guide*, Ecological Parks Trust 1986

Fairbrother, N. *New Lives, New Landscapes* (London: Architectural Press 1970)

Gimingham, C. H. *Ecology of Heathlands*, (London: Chapman & Hall 1972)

Green, B. *Countryside Conservation 2nd Edition: The Protection and Management of Amenity Ecosystems* (London: Allen & Unwin 1985)

Haslam, S. M. and Wolseley, P. A. *River Vegetation: Its Identification, Assessment and Management* (Cambridge University Press 1981)

Haywood, S. M. *Quarries and the Landscape* (London: The British Quarrying and Slag Federation 1974)

Humphries, R. N. and Elkington, T. T. *Reclaiming Limestone and Fluorspar Workings for Wildlife* (Pergamon Press 1981)

Lewis, G. and Williams, G. *Rivers and Wildlife Handbook: A Guide to Practices Which Further the Conservation of Wildlife on Rivers*, RSPB, Sandy and RSNC, Lincoln 1984

Lowday, J. E. and Wells, T. C. E. 'The Management of Grassland and Heathland in Country Parks', *CCP* **105** (Cheltenham: Countryside Commission 1977)

Macan, T. T. and Worthington, E. B. *Life in Lakes and Rivers* (London: Collins New Naturalist Series 1974)

Moffatt, D. *The Natural Approach to Structural Open Space At Warrington New Town*, Warrington and Runcorn Development Corporation 1984

Moore, I. *Grass and Grasslands* (London: Collins New Naturalist Series 1966)

Mellanby, K. *Farming and Wildlife* (London: Collins New Naturalist Series 1981)

Nature Conservancy Council (1984). *Nature Conservation in Great Britain* (Peterborough)

Nature Conservancy Council *Forestry Operations and Broadleaved Woodland Conservation* (Peterborough 1984)

Nature Conservancy Council *Sand Dunes and Their Management* (Peterborough 1985)

Nature Conservancy Council *Wild Flower Grasslands From Crop-grown Seeds and Hay Bales* (Peterborough 1986)

NCB Opencast Executive *Hedges and Trees* (National Coal Board Opencast Executive 1979)

Newbould, C., Purseglove, J. and Holmes, N. T. *Nature Conservation and River Engineering* (Peterborough: NCC 1983)

Pollard, E., Hooper, M. D. and Moore, N. W. *Hedges* (London: Collins New Naturalist Series 1974)

Perring, F. H. and Walters, S. M. *Atlas of the British Flora* (E P Publishing Ltd 1976)

Peterken, G. *Woodland Conservation and Management* (London: Chapman & Hall 1981)

Rackham, O. *The History of the Countryside* (London: J. M. Dent & Sons Ltd 1986)

Roberts, R. D. and Roberts, T. M. *Planning and Ecology* (London: Chapman & Hall 1984)

Salisbury, Sir E. *Weeds and Aliens* (London: Collins New Naturalist Series 1969)

Sargent, C. *Britain's Railway Vegetation* (Cambridge: Institute of Terrestrial Ecology 1984)

Sheail, J. *Historical Ecology: The Documentary Evidence* (Cambridge: Institute of Terrestrial Ecology 1980)

Tansley, A. G. (Ed. M. C. F. Proctor) *Britain's Green Mantle* (London: Allen & Unwin Ltd 1968)

Tansley, A. G. *British Islands and Their Vegetation*, Vols 1 and 2 (Cambridge University Press 1939)

Teagle, W. G. *The Endless Village – The Wildlife of Birmingham, Dudley, Sandwell, Walsall and Wolverhampton* (Peterborough: NCC 1978)

Webb, N. *Heathlands* (London: Collins New Naturalist Series 1986)

Wells, T., Bell, S. and Frost, A. *Creating Attractive Grasslands Using Native Plant Species* (Shrewsbury: NCC 1981)

Williamson, N. A., Johnson, M. S. and Bradshaw, A. D. *Mine Wastes Reclamation – The Establishment of Vegetation on Metal Mine Wastes* (London: Mineral Industry Research Organisation, Mining Journal Books 1982)

# Chapter 8

# Urban Landscape and Roof Gardens

## STEPHEN SCRIVENS

## 8.1 INTRODUCTION

The prevalence of hard surfaces in our towns and cities has meant that plants can only survive if their needs are supplied artificially. As this chapter shows, plants can be successfully grown under artificial conditions in pits in paved areas, in plant containers, on balconies, in building courtyards and on roof gardens. The first part of this chapter tackles particular problems that landscape architects should keep firmly in mind when they are preparing a site specification for planting in urban conditions, and consists of sections covering general problems, environmental conditions, materials and construction, the substrate and irrigation. The emphasis and most of the examples are from roof gardens, but it is obvious that most of what is referred to is equally relevant to other urban landscape situations, such as pits, paved areas, balconies or building courtyards.

The final section attempts to place the rest of the chapter in context by looking at the specific case of the roof gardens on the former Wiggins Teape building, Gateway House in Basingstoke. It explains what factors were taken into consideration when the garden was designed, and also uses hindsight to describe the problems that had arisen by 1987, ten years after the original planting, as a warning to future designers of landscapes in urban conditions. It draws special attention to the need for long-term management plans in landscape design, and the particularly heavy maintenance demands for planting in urban conditions.

As will be shown in the rest of the chapter, the design of urban spaces is a very demanding branch of landscape architecture. Owing to the value that is placed on spaces within inner city areas by people, there is a considerable demand for plants to be grown in these areas. However, many pressures are placed on the plants used in such areas that are not commonly encountered in landscape design, and these have to be carefully overcome for successful planting.

The advantages of urban planting need not be limited to human visual enjoyment. For example, roof gardens can be used to provide additional insulation to buildings and, more importantly, to buffer the roof membrane against climatic variations. It is common to find that flat roofs require major renovation after as little as ten years, owing to the extreme environmental conditions to which they are exposed, including the effects of solar radiation and temperature extremes. Under a layer of moist soil the waterproofing is protected against these destructive influences and will remain in good condition for far longer than will an exposed counterpart. Urban landscape can also be used to provide a level of much appreciated shelter from the effect of the sun, as in a plaza that includes or is surrounded by trees. Plants can also act as a visual screen to improve vistas.

In the urban context plants may be used in semi-natural conditions within a short distance of buildings, so that they are rooting into an almost natural matrix, as is shown in Plate 8.1. However, close to the foundations of buildings or in areas of redevelopment the plants often finish up growing over areas of heavy compaction where the subsoil, if it still exists, is almost as structureless as a slab of concrete. In such cases it is of academic interest that the planting is at ground level, as the plants have little chance of penetrating downwards or sideways. For this reason, ground level plantings can be as unnatural as a roof garden and must be treated with the same degree of technical consideration. Plants can also be associated with the buildings, both on terraces, as is shown in Plate 8.2, and ultimately as roof gardens themselves.

It can therefore be seen that, although it might seem logical to regard a tree which is grown outside a downtown development as having an almost natural rooting environment, it is as artificial as any tub, elevated planter or roof garden. In fact a plant which is grown at ground level may be in a less desirable position than one on the top of a building as it will be subjected to

PLATE 8.1 **The Kantonsspital at Basle. Even in these artificial conditions the trees and shrubs are thriving; the growing conditions are not dissimilar to a natural matrix.** (Photograph: *Stephen Scrivens*)

PLATE 8.2 **At this retail complex in San Francisco trailing plants have been used to soften the angular lines of the building.** (Photograph: *Stephen Scrivens*)

more pollution and variable light levels owing to the shadows of adjacent buildings. For these reasons, the problems which are associated with any plant which is to be grown in an inner city area are many and complex and must be addressed with care if urban landscape designs are to be successful.

Roof gardens are attracting greater public interest as cities become larger and more congested. Such interest has accelerated as a result of increasing awareness of the quality of life. Gone are the days when a building was a basic structure in which mundane activities took place. Today it must be an attractive and stimulating environment in which the individual can take a personal interest. This requirement means almost by definition that there must be areas for passive recreation where there are opportunities to relax in the open air. The problem is that to create areas of open parkland in the middle of a city is very expensive. However, cities do contain many square miles of roofs which are generally unused and often an eyesore. With careful design, a useful green oasis can be created on a roof in the heart of a city.

The first structure specifically to carry plants was the great ziggurat of the Sumerian city of Ur, which was built about 500 BC, at the same time that King Nebuchanezzar was building the Hanging Gardens of Babylon. This was one of the Seven Wonders of the World, and one of the few stone structures in the Kingdom of Mesopotamia. It was built over barrel vaults and had its own irrigation system, which was fed from its own well, probably by the use of an endless belt.

Roof gardens have historically had more mundane roles to fulfil, however. In North Africa water cisterns are still covered with domed shell roofs, which are waterproofed with bitumen and covered with soil and gravel that in turn support coarse grasses to provide thermal insulation. This system of construction is a traditional technique, developed during the time of the Roman occupation. For similar reasons it has been common practice for centuries in Scandinavia and North America to use earth sods to protect the waterproof membrane of tree bark and to provide a degree of thermal insulation.

There is a cost penalty in building roof gardens, but it need not be great, as it is not necessary to have vast depths of soil to grow plants in. It is possible to create a very pleasant effect with as little as 60 cm of soil, and this could include trees up to 5 m tall, if the soil depth can be increased locally.

The skill of designing in urban areas is to determine whether there can be open vistas across the surrounding city or whether the landscape can better be turned in on itself and so provide a sense of enclosure. In view of the blustery nature of many urban environments, a combination of the two philosophies might be desirable. Some areas might be left open, around the edges of a development, say, but further in a number of enclosed spaces can be formed. Given sufficient space, it may well be expedient to emulate the well known diversity of the roof garden on the original 'Derry and Toms' building in London, with its range of gardens, each with its own theme. In this case the design concept might be unifying, but the sub-areas can be used to express certain themes.

## 8.2 GENERAL PROBLEMS RELATING TO ROOF GARDENS

### Roof loadings

The production of roof gardens is often regarded with apprehension because of the considerable weight which they add to the roof. Traditionally a soil profile of 1 m or more thickness has been used. It is then assumed that this will enable the plants to develop without undue moisture stress and so produce a durable landscape.

However, this simple approach produces a tremendous weight penalty of 2 or more tonnes per square metre. For example, at Arundel Great Court the soil profile is 2 m deep in some areas. Supporting these loads is usually prohibitively expensive and so renders many schemes unacceptable. In engineering terms such a load would be in excess of 30 kN. This contrasts with a normal office floor, which will be designed to take a total load of 6 kN. Yet experience with schemes like Gateway House indicates that much can be done with only 300 mm of topsoil overlying a 50 mm thick drainage layer to give a saturated density of only 650 kg per square metre. However, this type of construction does require a comprehensive irrigation system.

Unfortunately, sufficient consideration is seldom given to matters of landscape until the design is well advanced and the most important engineering factors have been fixed. Frequently, requests for extra soil depth are met with a rebuff, owing to problems of loading. Similarly, requests for the provision of irrigation water storage are ignored, because of the engineering difficulties of providing it. Design therefore calls for the integration of two factors: firstly, the organic requirements of living plants and, secondly, the integration of these requirements into the total architectural concept.

### Human design factors

Where there are changes of level of more than 300 or 400 mm, it is necessary to make provisions for safety in the form of a perimeter barrier. On many European projects a single-strand wire fence is common, but in Britain a more substantial steel barrier is usually considered necessary. Solid balustrades of reinforced concrete faced with brick are also frequently used,

PLATE 8.3 **On the roof of the Willis Faber Dumas Building in Ipswich a simple laurel hedge hides the parapet fencing and provides a visual barrier at the edge of the roof.** (Architects: *Norman Foster Associates*; Photograph: *Stephen Scrivens*)

although careful detailing is required if separation is not to occur.

Unfortunately, almost any fence is obvious if it is silhouetted against the sky, but the impact of such features can be reduced by drawing them back from the parapet and allowing the planting to run under it. There are difficulties with such a proposal, as any balustrades have to connect with the underlying structure, which usually means penetrating the membrane. The other difficulty is that maintenance staff working outside such barriers have to wear safety harnesses and this is often resented. Another possibility is to end the garden before the parapet, and place a hedge or some other planting in front of the parapet, as is shown in Plate 8.3.

Vertigo is a problem that is often raised, but little is known about it. A broad perimeter planting or heavy balustrade may reassure vertigo sufferers by keeping them away from the edge and so preventing the eye from seeing an empty foreground.

Another serious problem with any exposed project is that of children dropping objects over the edge. There have been cases where roof gardens have had to be closed because of this. If children are to remain un-

supervised on an elevated area, there may well be a good case for erecting a close-mesh fence. If ball games are contemplated, then a totally enclosing cage is probably essential, if somewhat unsightly. A similar problem which can also be serious is that debris, such as cans, can roll off the edge of the roof, so there should be some form of low parapet wherever paving abuts the roof edge.

## 8.3 ENVIRONMENTAL CONDITIONS THAT AFFECT URBAN LANDSCAPES

### Wind

One of the most serious problems of growing plants on and around urban structures is the high degree of exposure. At roof level it is common for wind speeds to be more than double those experienced at ground level. If it is not necessary to have a view in all directions, then the structure itself can have a configuration which imparts at least some degree of protection. The plants will still almost always experience a less than satisfactory aerial environment, however.

134

## Light and temperature

Probably the most important factor for any plant is light, as the whole of its existence revolves about its ability to produce carbohydrates. It is interesting to note that in many urban situations plants tend to grow rapidly. This is to be expected, for in what other landscape situation are plants provided with 300 mm to 1000 mm of good quality improved top soil, regular irrigation, high root temperatures and a high level of general maintenance? (The effects of microclimate and light are illustrated in Figures 8.1 and 8.2, and Plate 8.4.)

As a general rule, growth rates accelerate as root temperature rises. Some preliminary studies indicate that it is common in winter for the soil of a roof garden to be at least 3 °C if not 5 °C higher than in the surrounding landscape. This increase in root temperature has a considerable effect on the vigour of the plants, as they start to grow earlier in the spring and their growth is sustained longer into the autumn.

## Roots

The selection of plant material for urban landscapes is surrounded by myth. Some plants are even condemned because they have tap roots. This is strange because, although logic might indicate that plants would appreciate and exploit a deep soil, this is not usually found to be the case. Often they exploit distinct zones within the available plant profile and do not spread out. This could point to some ecological factor which is based on an interaction between drainage and irrigation, and reinforces the findings of ecological studies on root systems in natural plant communities, which indicate that individual species tend to occupy specific zones within a soil profile.

It is true that many plants have tap roots when they are small but it is doubtful whether they have any effect after the first few years. It should also be remembered that the modern nursery practice is to undercut young trees so as to encourage the formation of a fibrous root system.

Most roots develop in a horizontal manner. This is to be expected, as in natural situations the topsoil is not more than 300 mm to 400 mm thick and is frequently much shallower, and it is in this layer that most nutrients are to be found. Some roots do penetrate to a considerable depth: for example, depths of more than 6 m are reported for occasional tomato plant roots. However, these are not major root formations and are usually no more than rogue developments.

In the case of large trees growing on deep soils, a large hemispherical mass can develop with a radius of more than 3 m. However, even this is insignificant when the total rooting area is considered i.e. the roots can extend for a distance in excess of the height of the tree. As a result, it may be concluded that although

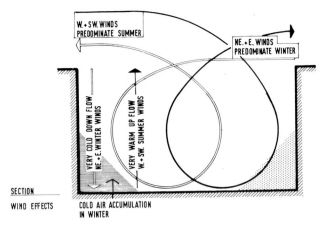

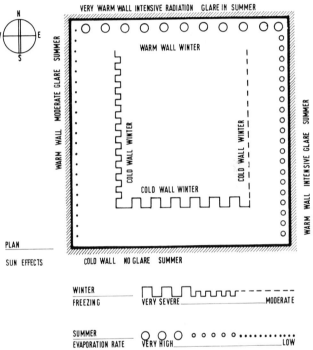

FIGURE 8.1 **Typical microclimate conditions in a courtyard.**

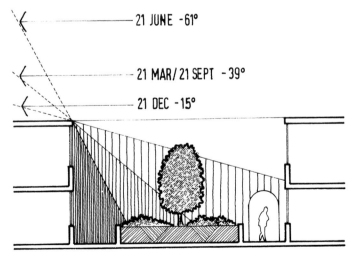

FIGURE 8.2 **Effect of surrounding buildings on distribution of sunlight throughout the year.** *(Richard Baker)*

135

PLATE 8.4 **The limited light source in this deep courtyard is used to create dramatic contrasts of light and shade. Arcadia Garden Condominium, Singapore.** (Landscape Architect: *Brian Clouston & Partners*)

PLATE 8.5 **As little as 1 cu. m of soil can allow a 20-foot tree to grow. These planting pits are above an underground car park. Highgate New Town, London.** (Landscape Architects: *Brian Clouston & Partners*)

most plants will appreciate and exploit deep soil, it is not necessary for most species in terms of their evolutionary development (Plate 8.5).

## Root penetration

There is often considerable apprehension when growing plants over a waterproof membrane that it will be penetrated by the plants' roots. Roots will penetrate a membrane that has been fractured but they will not drive their way through a continuous layer. A single sheet of polythene buried in the soil is impervious to normal root activity, so a roofing membrane backed by a concrete slab should be infallible. If a membrane does fail, then roots might well penetrate, but complaints about leaks will be received long before this occurs.

## 8.4 MATERIALS AND CONSTRUCTION

## Tanking materials

Although many tanking systems are available for use in planters and on roof gardens, mastic asphalt is the most widely used. However, in the case of Arundel Great Court, reinforced elastometric bitumen was used, and in Switzerland polyvinyl chloride sheet is used over small areas. Examples of butyl rubber or ethylene propylene diene monomer (EPDM) are not found in Europe, although they are used in North America. This lack of diversity probably reflects a conservatism among European architects rather than any problems that are experienced with these systems.

Whichever tanking system is selected, it must be carefully detailed and installed because repairs are hard to effect once plants are in place. If a roof garden is planned, then the tanking should be tested much more stringently than is usual for a flat roof before the garden is constructed. Such testing would include a flood test lasting several days.

## Thermal insulation

It is often assumed that the presence of soil over a building contributes to the thermal insulation of the structure (Plate 8.6). This is not altogether accurate, as the thermal value of wet soil is very low. However, it is certain that a roof garden does buffer the roof membrane against extremes of climate and so extends the life of any membrane. A good example of this is the roof garden of the original 'Derry and Toms' building mentioned earlier, where the mastic asphalt layer is in almost perfect condition after fifty years.

PLATE 8.6 **Roof planting can provide insulation and a more interesting roofscape without the necessity for any structural reinforcement if no foot traffic is anticipated. Kantonsspital, Basle.** (Photograph: *Stephen Scrivens*)

Analysis of the construction at Gateway House shows that the uncovered portion of the roof has a U-value of 0.93 W/m² °C, whereas those areas covered by garden have a U-value of only 0.585 W/m² °C. Obviously this building does not have the level of insulation that would be required today, but here the roof garden does increase the building's thermal efficiency. Whether or not this is particularly cost-effective is hard to determine, since the initial cost of producing a garden is considerably more than that of other insulation materials, and maintenance costs are not easily compared.

## Digging

No roof membrane can be relied upon to withstand the impact of forks or other sharp garden tools, so it is advisable to provide a protective layer on top of the membrane. In the UK the Mastic Asphalt Council and Employers' Federation recommend paving slabs laid to BS:CP144 Parts 3 and 4. While these are adequate to protect against mechanical damage, it could be possible for roots to find their way between the slabs; so they should only be used when the planting has a shallow root system, for example with grass. Alternatively, the membrane can be covered with a protective screed, which will be more impervious to roots.

The best solution is a 50 mm thick screed of 1:3 cement and zone 6 sand. The only problem with such a screed is that the lime that it contains can be picked up in the drainage water. It can then be precipitated when it comes into contact with the air at the drainage point. As a result, a sealing paint should be applied to the surface of the screed.

There may be a temptation to use insulation slabs on top of the membrane for protection, instead of paving slabs or a screed. Most insulation materials are too soft, but foamed glass can provide both protection and thermal insulation. A new material which has been developed for use with upside-down roofs is GRC-faced extruded polystyrene board which provides insulation at the same time as protection.

Protection of the membrane is not only required on the horizontal plane, but is equally important for upstands. This is likely to be particularly significant with asphalt and other materials that are bonded to the structural upstand and are softened by heat. Upstands on south-facing walls that are above soil levels are most vulnerable and should at least be treated with solar reflecting coating.

## 8.5 DRAINAGE

## Drainage points

Many different ways are found for detailing drainage points. They range from the indiscrete manhole covers to be found on the Willis, Faber & Dumas building, shown in Plate 8.5, through to the small lids at Gateway House. The latter, however, are often susceptible to blockage by limescale, owing to the narrow gap through which the water drains.

The alternative to visible drainage points is to have them totally hidden below the soil, as at Arundel Great Court. This may have certain aesthetic advantages, but can pose problems, as they are difficult to inspect. It is important to ensure that drainage points can be inspected from above and below, since they will require cleaning either after construction or to remove limescale.

## Drainage layers

There are three main approaches that can be adopted with a drainage layer.

1. The traditional approach with the roof laid to a gentle fall to encourage a run-off through granular base material.
2. The half hydroculture or 'Optima' type system shown in Plate 8.7, which has a flooded drainage layer and functions well on a flat roof, although a slight fall should still be incorporated to facilitate drainage if repairs become necessary.
3. The roof is sloped to drain the compost without the need for a drainage layer. The exact slope that is necessary varies, but lies between 10° and 15°. This third approach has certain advantages, but requires careful design to be successful.

## Flooded drainage layer irrigation

In most situations the only practical way of applying water to an urban landscape is by means of conventional drip or sprinkler irrigation techniques. However, when there is a level, waterproof base layer, it is quite reasonable to use a flooded drainage layer. In this technique a layer of gravel or low density aggregate is placed over the area to a depth of between 75 mm and 150 mm. This is then flooded by water so that at its maximum level there is an air gap between the surface of the water and the soil separating membrane of no more than 20 mm.

Such a technique obviously demands that the gravel or aggregate is very level. If the surface is not level, then there will be areas of drought and other areas of waterlogging within the landscape.

This half hydroculture system is sold in Europe under the trade name of 'Optima'. The system works well and has much to commend it, although the number of species that appear to be truly successful in it is limited. Plants like cotoneaster, juniper and pines do well; grasses and other surface rooting plants do not. Half hydroculture considerably reduces the irrigation requirements by retaining rainwater over the main body of the roof. Of course, this extra weight has to be carried by the structure, but it does provide the plants with water for at least six weeks in a dry summer.

There are thus only two tried and tested methods of construction. The first is to have a free-draining roof, which has a low weight penalty because surplus water is removed. The second is to retain water on the roof, which has an additional weight penalty of up to 150 kg/m$^2$. On thicker roof profiles this becomes a less significant part of the total roof weight than on thin ones.

The main reason for the success of the water-retaining system is that the water is introduced to the base of the soil profile. Water is lost from both the plants and the soil, but water which is lost from the soil comes only from the upper 300 mm or so. Water loss from below this level is almost totally dependent on the activity of the plants. The basic concept behind subterranean irrigation is that the standing water in the drainage layer must first pass round the surface of the drainage layer and into the soil separator. From this point it moves into the main body of the substrate and is then lifted by surface tension upwards through the soil. This process is assisted by the saturated vapour between the particles which form the drainage layer. (A control assembly is shown in Plate 8.7.)

As the distance between the rising water and the surface from which it originates increases, so the tension within the system increases until the point is reached where the surface tension exerted by the substrate is insufficient to raise the available water any further. This cut-off point is a clearly defined line, and it is possible to excavate to this level in an established system. The important detail to remember is that the depth of capillary lift is dependent on a number of conditions, and in particular on the detailed composition of the substrate. However, the most powerful regulating force is the drainage layer itself, owing to the large size of its component elements. As has been stated above, the ideal separation distance at the upper level of water is usually of the order of 20 mm below the soil separating membrane. However, this distance can be increased to 75 mm and still leave an adequate layer of moist earth to sustain plant growth. This is a good starting point for calibrating any system, although careful adjustment of the water level to the highly variable nature of any system will always be necessary on site, because of the specific characteristics of the system's components. The need for careful adjustment of the water level means that the roof drains must be able to be adjusted upwards and downwards with the seasons.

## Water retention and weight penalties

In many ways it is easier to have a saturated substrate than one with the correct moisture content. An example of this is the roof garden on Harvey's store in

PLATE 8.7 **Flooded drainage layer irrigation control assembly, using a ballcock with a flat float — note the nose pipe coupling on the side of the feed and the adjustable spillway.**

Guildford, which relies on the water in the pools percolating through openings in the walls of the planter and so into the soil. The substrate is permanently wet, but such conditions are conducive to the growth of moisture-loving plants. However, in most situations the substrate must be maintained at a lower moisture level if it is to be suitable for normal shrubs.

## Drainage materials

Materials that are suitable for drainage layers include 'Leca', 'Lytag' and pea gravel. Lightweight aggregates are usually favoured, but pea gravel is slightly more water retentive than 'Leca'. 'Lytag' has the advantage that it can absorb more than 15 per cent of its own

139

PLATE 8.8 **Roof garden techniques were used in this courtyard at Guildford Crown Court as the building was constructed on an old gaswork site.** (Landscape Architects: *Brian Clouston & Partners*; Photograph: *Peter Lake*)

PLATE 8.9 **A roofscape can minimize the visual intrusion of a building in the landscape. The Scottish Widows Headquarters, Edinburgh.** (Landscape Architect: *Dame Sylvia Crowe*; Photograph: *Margaret Turner*)

weight in water, and so acts as a reservoir. Unfortunately, it is difficult to free the latter product from the dust associated with the manufacturing process, and it can degenerate slightly with time. 'Lytag' also has a very high pH of about 8.0 to 9.0, which is acceptable to some plants but not to acid-loving species. This alkalinity makes it unacceptable for use with a flooded drainage layer and supplements the action of a cement sand screed in producing an unwanted calcareous deposit in the drains.

'Leca' on the other hand is strong, inert and is admirable as a granular drainage material. On balance, it would seem that non-calcareous pea gravel is to be preferred with thin substrate profiles, while 'Leca' is to be recommended for most deeper ones. The drainage layer only needs to be deep enough to remove excess soil moisture. From inspection of roof gardens, a drainage layer of as little as 50 mm is often adequate. If the drainage layer is to be used as a reservoir, 150 mm is the recommended minimum depth.

Drainage materials do not appear to offer any real resistance to the lateral movement of water. It appears reasonable to rely on a 1:50 fall to carry water to the drainage points. These points should be located at not more than 40 m intervals, so that the maximum lateral movement to the point of discharge does not exceed 20 m. There should also be no fewer than two drains in any area, in view of possible blockage.

## Plastic drainage foam

In recent years there has been a renewed interest in the use of urea formaldehyde foam in roof garden construction. The original development was taken up in the late 1960s and several schemes were built in Western Europe using this technique. Unfortunately, early experiences with such systems were disappointing. There were technical problems with producing foams that had uniform properties over the whole area of a roof, and several schemes failed because the foam collapsed. However, new developments have meant that it is now possible to produce a strong foam which will hold up to 80 per cent of its volume in water and has a life span of at least twenty-five years. Such foams are widely used in Holland and Belgium and appear to be most successful.

## Filter layers

It is usual to separate the growing medium from the drainage layer by the use of a filter layer, but its effectiveness is questionable where the growing medium is not disturbed after construction. At the Scottish Widows building (Plate 8.9) a separation layer of hessian sacking was used between the topsoil and the 'Lytag' layer. This decomposed gently so that the stability of

the substrate was maintained and mixing has never occurred.

Traditionally, the separating layer consisted of a glass fibre mat up to 50 mm thick. This was compressed by the weight of the growing medium to a layer only 5 mm thick. It was easily torn and this caused considerable problems during the construction stage. In contrast, the new generation of polypropylene and polyethylene fibre mattings are proving to be admirable filter layers, because they combine considerable strength with efficient filter properties.

It was once common to cover the filter membrane with a layer of peat about 50 mm thick. Many properties have been attributed to this layer, including improved filtering and storage of moisture. There does appear to be increased root activity in this zone, which supports the latter assertion. However, when this layer is compressed by the overlaying substrate and oxidized for a few years, it is soon reduced to a layer only a few millimetres thick. One reason for having this layer may have been a historic concern for protecting the glass fibre mat during construction, but with the introduction of synthetic fabrics this is no longer necessary.

## 8.6 THE SUBSTRATE

### Substrate stability

With exposed sites there may be some apprehension about the stability of the substrate. If it is very sandy or peaty and it is allowed to become dry, then wind erosion may occur. It is possible to stabilize a substrate with a surface layer of finely woven, ultraviolet-resistant polypropylene mesh, although it is necessary to anchor this at regular intervals if it is to perform properly. However, observation would seem to indicate that movement of substrates by both wind and rain is considerably less than might be expected. The rapid development of ground cover vegetation gives the best defence against any possibility of erosion.

### Earth moulding

Wherever trees are planted, it may be considered beneficial to increase the soil depth in their immediate area, as has been done at Gateway House and Derry and Toms, and as is shown in Plate 8.10. However, this must be done gradually and not in the form of a mound, since the roots will tend to surface around the edge of the mound as the tree gets older, and this is not conducive to the long-term health of the tree.

### Substrate formulation

The traditional substrate for a roof garden has always been improved topsoil. Materials that can be used to improve the topsoil include expanded polystyrene,

141

PLATE 8.10 **Greater loads can be placed over the column points of a building.** (Photograph: *Stephen Scrivens*)

perlite and bark, but the most commonly used is peat. All of these tend to produce a more open texture with improved drainage properties. However, organic materials, such as peat and bark, do degrade, over a period of time. Peat, for example, oxidizes at a rate of 15 to 20 per cent per annum. Coarse bark is less susceptible to degradation, and some new brands of composted horticultural bark are just coming on to the market. It is always advisable to purchase bark from a specialist dealer, as it must be fully composted before use.

Totally inert materials, such as expanded polystyrene and 'Leca', reduce the mass of the substrate, but also reduce its other physical properties such as water retention and anchorage. Some materials, such as vermiculite and coarse grades of perlite, do improve soil structure while slightly increasing moisture retention and anchorage. However, vermiculite tends to collapse after a year or so, and coarse perlite seems to be adversely effected by cultivation. The fact that these materials have an open pore structure also means that when they are saturated their density is not dissimilar to that of the soil that they are trying to lighten. The effect is therefore only to increase the apparent depth of the substrate. They should be regarded as a way of improving structure, not of reducing substrate density, which in itself would be a pointless operation. In other words, a soil is

intended to hold water and nutrients and to provide anchorage. A light, open material will not fulfil any of these functions.

The mixing operation associated with improving soils frequently does far more harm than good to the structure. Any natural structure that the soil originally had is effectively beaten out of it by the mixing and the installation process. Peat compost will generally accept brutal mixing, but loam soils will not. It would almost certainly be better to bring the soil on site with minimum disturbance and then to fold the peat in in distinct bands which are then slowly incorporated into the profile by natural weathering processes.

## 8.7 IRRIGATION

Any major reduction in the soil moisture level below its theoretical maximum will prevent a plant from absorbing water at its optimum rate. However, slight water stress can be desirable as it prevents excessively soft growth from developing.

All actively growing plants require continuous supplies of water if they are to develop their full potential. Probably the most important function of water is that of cell enlargement. The walls of young cells are stretched by internal osmotic pressure and the increase in size is made permanent by the incorporation of new material. Any shortage of water will reduce this ability to expand so that the benefit of new tissue generation is not fully realized and potential plant growth is lost.

Irrigation is vital in urban landscape because of the high degree of exposure and the limited soil depths. The only source of water that is generally considered by designers is the municipal water supply. Unfortunately, in many countries access to municipal supplies is not unlimited. In Britain there is some restriction on the use of the mains system in most years. This is a serious shortcoming because an urban landscape only needs to be dried out once for many of the more common landscape plants to die. In some cases the water supply may come from boreholes, which are not subject to the same restrictions as municipal supplies. However, the only certain way of guaranteeing a supply is to plan for water storage capacity within the building itself.

During the average summer there is a period of several months when the water lost from the soil is greater than that which is added in the form of precipitation. This imbalance between precipitation and water loss usually begins in May and continues until it starts to rain in the autumn. In conventional landscapes the soil contains a reserve of moisture which is sufficient for most plants to survive, but not to prosper, through this period. However, in the highly contrived situation which exists in an urban landscape there is seldom a sufficient depth of soil, so it is always necessary to consider a comprehensive irrigation system for the summer months.

# Water loss

Water is lost from an area of landscape by one of three processes:

drainage to waste;
evaporation from the substrate;
transpiration by the plants.

The loss of water from the surface of the soil may often equal that from the vegetation if the soil is not completely covered. The loss of water from the surface of a soil usually occurs from the upper 300 mm of the soil profile. The loss of moisture from below this layer is almost entirely due to the activity of plants.

Transpiration is most intense in conditions of high light levels, high temperature, low humidity and rapid air movement. Should it exceed the rate of water uptake, the plant will wilt.

The rate of water loss from an area of landscape is often in excess of 3 mm per day in dry weather. In fact in warm, exposed locations, it would not be unreasonable to expect a rate of water loss of 5 mm per day. This means that the rate of water loss is in excess of 25 mm per week, and could be in excess of 35 mm per week in the most extreme conditions. As it is common to find that the rate of evapo-transpiration is far in excess of

precipitation for several months each year, it is necessary to make an allowance for these volumes of water when considering any landscape design proposal. Obviously, it is necessary to have some awareness of what levels of water deficit are normal in the area in question. There is very seldom data available of direct relevance, but either the meteorological or agricultural authorities prepare tables and maps of soil moisture deficits to assist farmers. These have to be treated with caution, as they relate to the open country and not to the dry, turbulent air of cities. For this reason, it is not unreasonable to allow an additional 50 per cent to any figures to compensate for these factors.

## Estimation of water loss

The loss of water from both soil and plants will depend upon the difference in temperature between the soil and plant system and the air, the relative humidity of the air and the ability of the system to donate water. In Britain, during bright sunlight, the rate of water loss from an area of complete vegetation cover is almost equal to that from an open water surface. However, the main source of water loss from a plant is transpiration due to warming by radiant energy. The absence of such heating at night and variations in seasonal day length mean that this simple theoretical relationship must be modified. The following modification factors are suitable for plants which are grown outside in temperatures similar to those of a sub-tropical climate (northern hemisphere), and give a rate of loss due to transpiration expressed as a percentage of the loss from an open water surface.

May to August – 80 %
September to October – 70 %
March to April – 70 %
November to March – 60 %

Unfortunately, the loss of water from plants in an urban environment is more complex, and it is exceedingly difficult to predict.

In eighteen years out of twenty there will be a period when plant growth will be checked by a lack of water. The total volume of water required to ensure that such a check does not occur in the driest five years in twenty will exceed 300 mm in many urban locations.

The objective of an irrigation system is to ensure that the growth of any plant is not restricted by a shortage of water. To achieve this, no plant should experience a soil moisture deficit in excess of 50 mm. The total volume of irrigation water which is required can then be obtained from the appropriate tables by finding the irrigation figure which ensures that a maximum soil deficit of 50 mm is not exceeded during the months of risk, say from May to September inclusive. This figure will be expressed as a depth, and all that is required is to multiply this by the area of the planting in question to obtain the volume of water which will be required.

It should be remembered that many urban landscapes, and particularly roof gardens, are exposed to strong turbulent winds, so evapo-transpiration losses may be higher than anticipated by simple calculation. Also, these figures assume that no water is lost either by missing the soil and running to waste or by excessive irrigation water draining straight through the soil. Foliage will also often cover many times the area of the planter, and so consume the water many times faster than would otherwise be the case. Water should also be conserved by irrigating in the early morning when the air is cool, and at well spaced time intervals, that is over several days. This allows the rate of evaporation from the surface of the soil to fall off after a few days and then to stay low, as opposed to regular irrigation, where surface evaporation rate remains permanently high.

## The behaviour of water in a soil

In a soil, the irregularly-shaped inorganic particles do not fit together closely and there are often voids or interstices present. The organic material which is also present in most soils has a natural sponginess which ensures the presence of pores. A film of water is attached to the constituents of the soil by molecular attraction, and as the water is lost, it is replaced by air. As a saturated substrate drains, the film of water around each particle is reduced in thickness and the attraction between the remaining water and the compost is increased. Ultimately, an equilibrium is reached where the water ceases to move and the soil is said to be at field capacity, that is, retaining the maximum amount of water that it can. A plant in a soil at field capacity can absorb water with little effort, but as the water content falls, so the water bond with the soil increases and the water uptake becomes more difficult. Eventually a point is reached where the attraction of the soil to the water is so great that uptake ceases, with the result that the foliage wilts. The point at which this occurs is called the permanent wilting point, and a plant taken beyond this point will not recover even when placed in a humid environment. From the argument above it follows that between field capacity and the permanent wilting point there is water in the soil which the plants can abstract. The actual amount of water which is available will depend on the nature of the soil, and is very variable. From this it can be seen, for example, that sand has a lower maximum water content than clay, although it tends to be held with less tenacity. This means that the sand contains a smaller volume of water which is more readily available but also more quickly exhausted. A similar situation is true with organic materials, which usually have a high moisture retention capacity. It has been found that the fastest growth is achieved with an open soil, provided that the water is frequently restored.

Water may be applied to a compost from above or below. Entry from below is often referred to incorrectly as a capillary process and occurs as a result of surface tension lifting water around the surface of the various substrate components. Entry from above is governed by the rate of infiltration, and should water be applied faster than this rate, then run-off will occur.

PLATE 8.11 **Groundcover on the Central Station Roof Garden, Berne.** (Photograph: *Ian Laurie*)

When water is applied to the surface of a substrate, it will bring each successive layer to saturation before further downward movement occurs, as gravity draws the water downwards and the surface tension of the components of the substrate attracts it. The lower, drier layers still exert a suction on the upper layers, but further downward movement cannot occur if there is no free water available. As a result, any attempt to moisten a soil lightly will result in only a limited depth of penetration. Surface irrigation can only take the form of flooding all the voids in the substrate and then allowing gravity to draw the surplus through.

## Integrated system design

When large-scale planting or planting in inaccessible localities is proposed, consideration should be given to the installation of a comprehensive irrigation system. Fully automatic irrigation systems often meet resistance, despite the technology and expertise which are now available, but manually activated systems offer considerable reduction in labour input.

## Hand watering

It is almost inevitable that when plants are used in urban situations there will be a need for some degree of hand watering. This is normally a labour-intensive operation but it can be greatly reduced by the provision of certain facilities.

It is important to remember that watering a landscape is not the same as watering a domestic garden, and so the provision should be for large bore, heavy duty industrial hoses. Certainly such pipes should have an inside diameter of not less than 1.8 cm (3/4 inch) and preferably 2.5 cm (1 inch).

The source of the water for a hosepipe is obviously dependent on the location of the services within the development. It is always advisable to make a provision on the irrigation system for quick-fit hosepipe connectors. These can also be used for washing down surfaces and for general building maintenance such as cleaning windows.

Where taps are provided, it is important to ensure that there is a drain placed directly beneath them. Often it is preferable to secrete the whole assembly within a pit in the landscape, and often this becomes a storage place for the hosepipe.

Where hand watering is necessary, suitable supply points should be spaced so as to reduce the length of hose which is required, which should never be more than 30 m. In certain situations, permanently mounted hose reels can offer a neat storage solution.

## 8.8 CASE STUDY: GATEWAY HOUSE

The Gateway House site at Basingstoke was built by Wiggins Teape in 1976, and integral to the design were extensive roof gardens over the five levels of the building, as is shown in Plate 8.12. Gateway House was built on a site sloping southwards to provide an extended view over the gardens and to shield the occupants from a busy dual carriageway road running to the north of the building.

As can be seen from Figure 8.3, the design of the building is complex. We consider here the roof garden design aspects of the site, what had been learnt ten years after the original planting, and the effect on the building of its being left empty for three years between Wiggins Teape moving out in 1983 and IBM purchasing it in 1986.

## Garden construction

At each level, the roof comprises a concrete slab without falls, covered by a 50 mm thick layer of cellular glass insulation. Over this is a three-coat layer of mastic asphalt protected by a cement and sand screed laid to falls of maximum thickness 100 mm and minimum thickness 25 mm (Figure 8.4). The fall to which the screed was laid ensures that the water is carried through the 50 mm Leca layer to the drainage points. In order to test the surface, the roofs were originally flooded for two weeks. The surface was initially successful, but over the years there were problems with the small voids between the screed and the drainage point collars, which tended to get blocked. There were also problems with the Leca layer, which became congested with fine root growth, which suggests that the topsoil had been poorly irrigated, and the roots had grown down looking for available water. This was probably due to poor irrigation over the three years when the building was empty.

Another problem was caused by the glass fibre soil separator being compressed from 50 mm to only a few millimetres thick. At the time of writing it is still intact, but is seriously worn and a layer of silt is building up between the Leca particles and is getting trapped by the roots. It seems strange that an obsolete material like glass fibre was used at all, when synthetic fibre matting was readily available in 1976, and would not have been prone to compression.

A final problem was with the drains becoming blocked with calcium deposits, as a result of calcium passing into solution from the sand and cement screed. This deposition is still taking place, and the drains need regular maintenance.

## Soil condition

The soil consisted of silt topsoil removed from around Heathrow Airport. This was laid to a minimum depth of 225 mm, and was mounded around areas of tree planting to 900 mm depth. Over the years a number of

PLATE 8.12 **Gateway House, Basingstoke.** (Architects, Engineers and Quantity Surveyors: *Arup Associates*; Photograph: *Martin Charles*)

these mounds have had to be extended to allow for root growth.

Although a peat mulch was used throughout the scrub area, the mulch has now been completely mixed into the soil matrix. Because of this, and the fact that the topsoil was severely compacted during its initial transportation, much of it is still extremely hard, and digging through it is difficult. This could have been avoided if the topsoil had been enriched with organic material throughout its profile before it was laid down on the roof. Since little organic material seems to have been added to the original, the topsoil is now lacking in organic material.

Analysis of the site has shown that there is a severe nutrient imbalance that needs urgent attention if growth is not to be further retarded. However, this state of affairs is not unusual in amenity sites in Great Britain, as few people appear to appreciate the need to maintain the correct balance of nutrients over time. Although a great deal of effort is generally put into testing a soil at

installation the nutrient balance is rarely checked thereafter. This points to the need for regular maintenance if growth is to be optimized and the original investment is not to be wasted.

## Irrigation

The irrigation system is fed on rainwater, which is stored in the basement of the building in a 144 m$^3$ galvanized steel tank. Surplus rainwater overflows into the local surface sewer. It seems that this storage capacity is adequate, since it provided the only source of water during the hot summer of 1976, when the mains supply was cut off.

The water is pumped to the garden areas by a 17.5 hp 3-phase electric pump. Originally there was difficulty in maintaining the pressure to the higher levels, but this has since been solved.

The main problems with the irrigation system are due to the choice of spray nozzles. The water is distributed

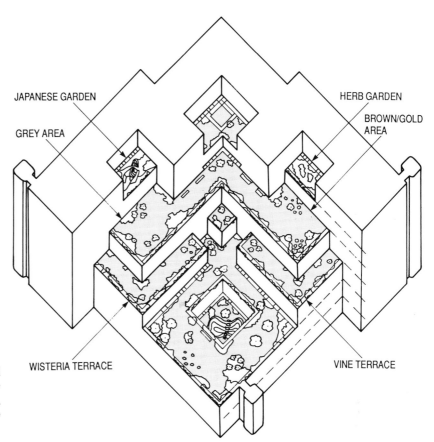

JAPANESE GARDEN

GREY AREA

HERB GARDEN

BROWN/GOLD AREA

WISTERIA TERRACE

VINE TERRACE

FIGURE 8.3 **A picture of the spatial logic and symmetry not immediately apparent beneath the foliage at Gateway House.** *(Courtesy of the Architects' Journal)*

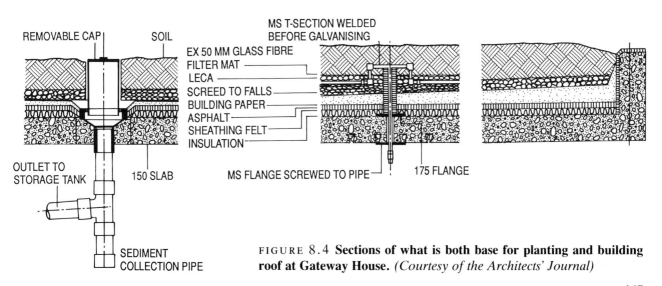

REMOVABLE CAP

SOIL

MS T-SECTION WELDED BEFORE GALVANISING

EX 50 MM GLASS FIBRE
FILTER MAT
LECA
SCREED TO FALLS
BUILDING PAPER
ASPHALT
SHEATHING FELT
INSULATION

OUTLET TO STORAGE TANK

150 SLAB

MS FLANGE SCREWED TO PIPE

175 FLANGE

SEDIMENT COLLECTION PIPE

FIGURE 8.4 **Sections of what is both base for planting and building roof at Gateway House.** *(Courtesy of the Architects' Journal)*

PLATE 8.13(a)−(b) **Gateway House in 1977 just after planting and in 1986. Many of the shrubs have been very successful despite apparently adverse conditions and have now reached maturity.** (Architects, Engineers and Quantity Surveyors: *Arup Associates*; Photograph (a): *Richard Bryant*; Photograph (b): *Martin Charles*)

by 25 mm uPVC pipes which supply 12 mm risers to the individual pop-up nozzles. An early problem was that the nozzles spray in a full circle, so the windows close to them had to be cleaned after each watering. More serious have been problems due to the construction of the nozzles. They are protected only by a PVC collar and have been continuously damaged by mowing machines. This problem would have been far less serious

if the risers had been made out of metal and had been articulated, or if sport field nozzles had been used. The other problem was due to the nozzles being positioned in areas of shrubs and trees. This has meant that as the vegetation has grown denser, so areas of planting have been shielded from the nozzles and have not been adequately irrigated.

A final problem occurred when the building was

148

unoccupied. The irrigation sprinklers are controlled by a timer which is manually activated. This meant that there were long periods without irrigation, and the plants have suffered as a result. Owing to the 225 mm depth of soil, there is only a maximum of 50 mm to 75 mm of available water. Evapo-transpiration reaches 25 mm per week at times, and so a period of only three weeks without irrigation would lead to plant stress. Since there are well established methods for automatic-

ally controlling irrigation systems, it would have been sensible to install an automatically operated system in the first place.

## Ornamental pools

The pools were produced by forming rings of no-fines Leca concrete. Each pool is covered by a butyl rubber

149

sheet which is hidden by a layer of cobbles. Unfortunately, the slope of the butyl rubber is too steep, and the cobbles have tended to roll into the pools to expose the rubber sheet.

On the plus side, however, the pools still contain plant life and fish, revealing that a balance has been established. The pools are very 'organic', and have some soil and algae in them. The idea of the pools has worked well.

## Plant selection and growth

Originally, a wide range of plants was used to try to produce a garden-like look. It was hoped that they would demonstrate the potential of a shallow substrate when it was well irrigated. Many of these plants have done well, particularly *Eleagnus pungens*, *Eucalyptus gunnii*, *Cotoneaster* spp, *Spiraea* spp, *Viburnum tinus*, *Mahonia japonica* and *Berberis darwinii* 'Atropurpurea'. However, in general the planting is showing signs of overmaturity. This is often the case after ten years, and it is generally necessary to replace, or at least to reinvigorate, many shrubs after this period.

However, the major problems with the plants are due to the overelaborate choice of species, and a failure of the designers to anticipate what the gardens would look like after the plants had reached maturity. While it may look good to have ten different species along one elevation when they are small, the same is not true when each plant covers 4 m². The effect is not then one of unity, but merely of a mixed collection of plants. How the plants have grown is shown in Plate 8.13 (a) and (b).

In some places the plants have grown so large that they actually obscure the view from offices. This points to the fact that landscape architects must always give the particular problems of a site high priority in a design. The comfort of the people that will use the amenity must come before the aesthetics of the planting.

In general, all the plants seem to be suffering from a lack of fertilizer balance, and some plants, such as the hydrangeas, heathers and rhododendrons, have been particularly unsuccessful, since no attempt was made to provide them with their particular rooting requirements of low acidity and high moisture. Many of these problems are due to the lack of maintenance while the building was uninhabited. However, they do point to the need for constant maintenance, and also for the initial design to take the likely level of future maintenance into account.

As well as the ground plants, a large number of climbers were planted. These have, on the whole, been unsuccessful, since no adequate support structure was provided for their growth. Black plastic mesh was provided, but it would have been better if a coarser, heavier duty mesh had been used.

## Theme gardens

The smaller, high level theme gardens have been unsuccessful. The Japanese garden has turned into a thicket. The herb garden is still disappointing and the fruit trees have never developed and are suffering from acute drought and exposure. The trouble with theme gardens is that they require very careful attention, above and beyond normal maintenance. For this reason, they should only have been included in a design if extra attention could have been guaranteed.

## Landscape maintenance

Maintenance was initially not seen as a problem, and little thought seems to have been given to it. This is shown by the fact that there was no provision for either storing equipment or disposing of waste on the roofs. Equipment therefore has always had to be carried through the building, and rubbish has had to be carried away in maintenance personnel's vehicles. It is obvious that a great deal of effort could have been saved by providing storage space and a means of waste disposal on the roof.

## Building maintenance

The gardens seem to have had little adverse effect on the building. As they have matured, the original problems of irrigation water and rain splash against the windows have become much less important. Vegetation moving against the building surface over the years has not damaged the anodizing, as was originally feared. However, the plants do attract a great number of birds, and this causes a problem of bird droppings. This means that the building needs regular cleaning. The importance of this has become apparent, as the building was neither cleaned nor waxed for several years.

## Summary

Although the planting has been successful, in that most of the plants are still alive and have shown growth, numerous problems have been highlighted over the years.

The garden-like planting design has been partially successful, but the gardens only look attractive now in areas where large numbers of the same species have been used. It is obvious that any project of this scale will need a large and continuous maintenance operation, and that this must be planned and budgeted for in the original design specification. Without it, much of the original work will be worthless after only a few years.

## 8.9 CONCLUSION

This chapter has pointed to many of the problems that must be considered when designing for urban conditions. These problems have been discussed both in general terms, and in relation to Gateway House. From the case study it is obvious that many of the points discussed in the early parts of the chapter will be applicable to all urban landscapes. There are also likely to be site-specific requirements and potential problems in any design, and a great deal of thought and analysis should go into pre-planning. It is also obvious that no matter how great the temptation to produce a spectacular design, the limitations of the site and the requirements of the inhabitants or users of the site must always take an important place in the design.

Finally, the chapter points to the extremely high importance that must be placed on catering for, planning and budgeting an adequate and continuous maintenance programme. Without this all a designer's good work can be undone in a few years.

## ACKNOWLEDGEMENT

The case study of Gateway House was previously published in the *Architects' Journal* (details below).

## FURTHER READING

*Architects' Journal* 'Roof Gardens: Construction', 27 February, p.447 (1980)

*Architects' Journal* 'Gateway House, Basingstoke: Roof Gardens', 26 March, p.631 (1980)

*Architects' Journal* 'Arundel Great Court: Roof Gardens', 9 April, p.733 (1980)

*Architects' Journal* 'Scottish Widows: Roof Gardens', 24 September, p.611 (1980)

Ashberry, A. *Gardens on a Higher Level: for Windows, Balconies and Courtyards* (London: Hodder and Stoughton 1969)

Guccione, B. 'A Roof Garden by Sylvia Crowe at Edinburgh' (Scottish Widows), article in Italian, *L'Architettura Cronache e Storia*, June, p.452 (1985)

Scrivens, S. and Cooper, P. 'Roof Gardens: Irrigation', *Architects' Journal*, 12 March, p.537, and 19 March, p.583 (1980)

Scrivens, S. 'Roof Gardens: Suffolk Hospital', *Architects' Journal*, 16 April, p.781 (1980)

Scrivens, S. 'Roof Gardens: Willis Faber and Dumas', *Architects' Journal*, 17 September, p.569 (1980)

Scrivens, S. 'Roof Gardens: Derry and Toms', *Architects' Journal*, 15 October, p.759 (1980)

Scrivens, S. 'Roof Gardens: Uetlihof, Zurich – Credit Suisse Administration centre', *Architects' Journal*, 10 February, p.63 (1982)

Scrivens, S. 'Roof gardens: Kantonsspital, Basle', *Architects' Journal*, 17 February, p.65 (1982)

Scrivens, S. 'Roof Gardens: Harvey's Store, Guildford', *Architects' Journal*, 24 February, p.85 (1982)

Scrivens, S. 'Roof Gardens: Kingston Hospital, Kingston-upon-Thames', *Architects' Journal*, 24 February, p.89 (1982)

Scrivens, S. 'Roof Gardens: Design Guide', *Architects' Journal*, 17 March, p.73 (1982)

Scrivens, S. 'Growth Industry: Roof Gardens', *Building*, 27 January, p.26 (1984)

Scrivens, S. 'Landscape Revisit: Gateway House, Basingstoke', *Architects' Journal*, 11 December, p.41 (1985)

# CHAPTER 9

# Transplanting Semi-Mature Trees

## R. L. HEBBLETHWAITE

## 9.1 INTRODUCTION

The British Standards Institution pamphlet *Transplanting Semi-Mature Trees* (BS 4043) gives the following definition: 'A semi-mature tree is a tree or shrub at an advanced stage of growth which is to be transplanted with a rootball, or in certain cases, bare roots, and is of such combined size and weight that special equipment is needed to carry out the operation. Such trees will generally be between 6–15 m in height and will weigh between 250 kg (5 cwt) and 10 tonnes (approx. 10 tons); they also include certain shorter trees and shrubs which weigh over 250 kg (5 cwt) and need special lifting equipment because of their spread and weight.'[1]

## 9.2 THE USE OF SEMI-MATURE TREES

There is a psychological requirement for new works of man — new buildings, recreational areas, industrial installations — to appear to have been set in well conserved landscape. If there were no large trees on site the scale of the semi-mature tree or a group of them gives an 'established' atmosphere. The scale in relation to the size of the new structure or space gives balance. Man relates the age and size of the tree to previous experience and is reassured in a newly created environment by the maturity and sense of security of the trees' visual impact.

No matter how attractive and aesthetically pleasing an architect's design for a building is, a new building gives a bare unameliorated impression unless it stands adjacent to conserved trees. It is most unlikely that a building is so badly designed and of such poor material that it has to be entirely screened. If partial screening is required to allow acceptance into the landscape, the scale of the semi-mature tree supported by younger trees and shrubs is of great benefit. Many buildings, attractive to their own right, are framed immediately by the use of these larger trees.

If it is necessary in the interests of the community to build a large construction, hundreds of feet in height, placing semi-mature trees adjacent to it is useless to the long-distance viewer. However, judiciously selected sites adjacent to sensitive viewpoints can be used to plant large trees and/or shrubs which can partially or completely screen the construction from the viewpoint. The exact height of the tree or trees required can be worked out by the Zone of Visual Influence Method taking into account the curvature of the earth and refraction of light.[2]

There are good reasons for choosing the majority of trees for planting in a new development of the same genus and species as those found locally to give a sense of continuity and integration. It is difficult for those not experienced in arboriculture, horticulture, or silviculture to recognize the connection between young newly planted nursery stock of the same genus and species as those in the adjacent countryside. Semi-mature trees give an immediate visual continuity in size, form, scale and texture.

Vandalism of young newly planted stock is not unknown. It is probably true that the use of semi-mature trees or advanced nursery stock reduces the incidence of vandalism on newly planted stock. With very small stock the main stem may be broken and any penknife attack is almost fatal to the shape or existence of the tree. With semi-mature trees, providing that they are reasonably safeguarded by adequate fencing, a single penknife attack does little proportionate damage.

It has been estimated that a 25-year-old semi-mature beech in a deep loam has a leaf area of fourteen times the area over which the canopy extends on the ground. All the leaf area is capable, by transpiration and evaporation, of adding water vapour to the atmosphere thereby creating higher humidity. It has been estimated that a single 15 m (50 ft) silver maple may transpire as much as 268 litres (58 gallons) per hour.[3] The use of semi-mature trees may therefore be responsible for small localized increases in relative humidity which may be beneficial to the establishment of young stock in the area. This assumes that the semi-mature tree has been moved properly and comes out into reasonable leaf.

The use of semi-mature trees with larger leaf area may help to control the air pollution of the environment in larger measure than if small nursery stock is used in the same positions. This is particularly true in the enclosed areas of towns. The advisability of starting with a large tree to help control pollution and 'sweeten' the air is recommended, for example lead, zinc and other heavy metals can be adsorbed and absorbed by leaves.

A semi-mature tree will already have started to show the characteristics of a mature specimen of the species in its bark texture: in many cases this can be aesthetically attractive to its immediate environment. For example, if a semi-mature *Acer rufinerve* (snakebark maple) is used the 'snakebark' effect is very pleasing: the reddish brown bark of the semi-mature *Arbutus unedo* (strawberry tree) is also attractive in the area from which it is seen.

The framework of branches is already formed in a semi-mature tree so that it can be chosen with a very good idea of its mature appearance. Smaller trees may need expert directional pruning to form them into a shape typical of the type. Semi-mature trees provide all the joys associated with well established trees – the movement of the shadow of leaves on the ground, the sound of wind among leaves, and drifts of leaves from the autumn fall from deciduous trees.

The importance of trees in a continental climate, where summer temperatures rise into the 30s Centigrade (90s Fahrenheit) and above, is enhanced by their shade value. In some of these countries trees which in maturity reach heights of over 21–27 m (70–90 ft) are known as 'shade trees'. The importance of shade for protection from the heat of the sun in Great Britain is perhaps not so great: however the cool shade of trees is appreciated on hot days.

Although semi-mature trees give an immediate effect, the planting of advanced nursery stock trees 3–5 m in height in advance of new building may be preferable to planting semi-mature trees after completion. Trees planted prior to or during construction must be protected from damage by post and rail fencing and their routine maintenance must not be neglected. There are also restraints on the site if an early planting of smaller trees is made; these are:

(i) supervision of maintenance required throughout the contract;
(ii) restriction of usable building space;
(iii) possible interference with options of access;
(iv) restriction of options for services.

Before deciding to incur the larger initial cost and involve site staff in maintenance responsibility the

PLATE 9.1 **Semi-mature trees planted near a nuclear power station.** *(R. L. Hebblethwaite)*

benefit of using semi-mature trees must be carefully analysed. All transplanted trees suffer a check in growth. The growth of well-prepared and carefully selected advanced nursery stock may overtake larger semi-mature trees after a period of seven to ten years unless selection, moving methods, conditions on site and after-care are particularly good for the semi-mature stock. Extensive plantings of semi-mature trees should always be supported with advanced nursery stock and possibly smaller trees.

153

PLATE 9.2 **Semi-mature Scots pines planted round a lake at Solent Business Park.** (Landscape Architects: *Brian Clouston & Partners*; Photographer: *Alistair Hunter*)

## 9.3 RESTRAINTS ON USE

Before the decision is made to plant semi-mature trees, considerable thought must be given to the physiological requirements, species, preparation, siting and moving and maintenance. Even though the requirements of the site demand a semi-mature tree, it may not be possible to move and plant such a tree on the site under consideration. A short check list is suggested which may help the decision.

A semi-mature tree and root ball may weigh on average between 5 and 10 tonnes; trees have been moved up to 20 tonnes:

(i) Can a truck and the tree and ball be brought over or under services into the site?
(ii) Are there any services under the tree area that cannot stand the weight plus another ton or two of water?

A semi-mature tree often has a spread, even when being moved, of 5−7 m:

(i) Is there adequate head and spread room for tree and truck to be manoeuvred close to the planting area?
(ii) Will it be necessary to remove telephone or electric overhead cable to bring the tree into the site and can this be done?
(iii) Will there be room for the natural spread of branches when planted and when mature?

If some of these difficulties are insuperable it may be better to use lighter, advanced nursery stock, and if there is inadequacy in skilled maintenance staff one has less capital at stake.

## 9.4 PHYSIOLOGY: BASIC KNOWLEDGE FOR TREE MOVING

A good knowledge of physiology is necessary to move semi-mature trees successfully. The main problems are discussed below.

154

Trees absorb water most quickly through the growing roots just behind the meristematic region of the root cap, and through the root hairs produced from the cortex, a short distance back from the growing root tip. For successful moving, *it is essential to keep a mass of young roots intact, in contact with the soil, and without disturbance.*

## Soil conditions

Protoplasm is less permeable and water more viscous at low temperatures; both factors reduce water absorption. Trees should therefore be moved when there is warmth in the ground in early autumn or spring; autumn is preferred. This point is most important with evergreens.

Intake of water by osmosis occurs when the soil solution concentration is less than the solution in the plant root cells. If the situation is reversed, water will be drawn out of the root cells (plasmolysis). It is therefore essential to use organic, slowly available fertilizers around the newly transplanted rootball according to the soil analysis requirement.

The fertilizer should be well mixed with backfill material before the operation, not thrown in with a bucket or spade as backfilling progresses. Very weak liquid feeds may be given every three or four weeks during spring and early summer growth periods for the first three years after transplanting.

*Soil oxygen and carbon dioxide – relation to backfilling*
  (i)   Heavy tamping of backfill should be avoided, particularly of heavy and clay soils, to prevent exclusion of oxygen and build up of carbon dioxide.
  (ii)  Insufficient oxygen restricts respiration of the root and slows metabolism and thereby absorption of salts, which lowers the Diffusion Pressure Deficit (DPD), slowing down the intake of water by osmosis.
  (iii) Accumulation of carbon dioxide increases protoplasm viscosity and decreases permeability slowing down the intake of water.[4]

A badly-drained planting pit will have the same results as above, with lowered oxygen and increased carbon dioxide. Field drains may be placed from the base of the pit to storm drainage or a sump, if water levels allow the latter. Cracking of a heavy soil can be accomplished before planting with a 'pop-shot' of 115 g (4 oz) gelignite charge, drilled in the hole from the base of a 'back hoe excavated pit' (*see Specification 1975*).[5] Permission must be obtained from the engineers and/or the architects for the site for explosives employed.

## Water availability and requirements

Fine soils such as clays adsorb more water than sands. Each particle resists the pull on its adsorbed water by osmotic pressure with gravitation, adsorptive and hydrostatic forces. The adsorptive capacity of a fine clay has to be satisfied before water is freely available to a plant root. Clays above field capacity need watering less frequently than sandy soils.

## Desiccation

The most difficult problem is desiccation as a result of loss of water by the tree or shrub in excess of the amount entering the plant, causing wilting, and if continued, ultimately death. 90 per cent of water taken in by the tree is lost by evaporation through the leaves (assuming transpiration to be a controlled water loss).

PLATE 9.3 **A Japanese maple** *(Acer palmatum)* **during autumn after spring planting, New Jersey, USA.** *(R. L. Hebblethwaite)*

PLATE 9.4 **Tuberous roots on an alginate treated aquilegia.** *(R. L. Hebblethwaite)*

PLATE 9.5 **Field-dug *Viburnum tinus* in mid-June. Alginate treated and turgid.** *(R. L. Hebblethwaite)*

# The root system

The root system is of prime importance in successful tree removal. Throughout the root system the newly formed young roots are the most important; root tips and root hairs absorb the major portion of the tree's moisture and solutes. Trees with a good fibrous root system can be moved successfully without preparation. Otherwise they should be prepared three or four years in advance of transplanting, to encourage fibrous roots to develop within the size of a movable rootball.

A root-balled semi-mature tree has a very limited root area on transplanting; the surface area is usually within 25 m² for watering (approx. $\frac{1}{400}$ ha). The volume of water of 25 mm (1 in.) rainfall on a hectare is approximately 254 255 litres (56 000 gal). The same amount of rainfall on 25 m² equals 636 litres (140 gal). A reasonable amount of water per month during May to September for transplanted semi-mature trees would be 25 mm. If the rainfall is expected to be low, e.g. 8 mm, $\frac{2}{3} \times 636$ litres will be necessary to make up the 25 mm required on the semi-mature tree's watershed area; i.e. 424 litres (94 gal) to each tree, applied in two soakings of 212 litres each, one week apart. (The two soakings are only for *this* application of 424 litres, to avoid excess run off.)

## Aids to transplanting

*Use of root-inducing hormones.* A concentration of 10 ppm IAA (indole − 3 − acetic acid) will stimulate root growth. Higher concentrations inhibit root elongation and cause branching of roots. A very light dusting, so that the white coating can barely be seen (about 7 g (¼ oz) per m²) on the outside of the rootball, is sufficient.[6]

*Use of alginates to induce water intake.* Water dispersed alginate concentrates form complex polyuronide hemi-cellulose substances. When roots are coated with these substances, the induction of water is enhanced. This is shown in practice in the following three examples.

(i) After washing soil off the roots of *Aquilegia*, those soaked in alginates survived without wilting although in full flower and leaf. Roots of treated plants showed tuberous swellings (*see* Plate 9.4).

(ii) For the landscape plan of the new headquarters of the Central Electricity Generating Board's Generation Development and Construction Division, a semi-mature tree (*Arbutus unedo*) was moved. It was prewatered with alginate before digging, and granular alginate was used in the backfill. The tree, with a 5 ton ball, never flagged and has continued to grow, making 450 mm of new growth on some branches the following year. The total absence of wilting and the success of planting this subject, which is generally regarded as difficult to move, were significant.

(iii) *Viburnum tinus* were field dug in June after prewatering with alginate. Roots were roughly balled, tops reduced, and the rest of the leaves sprayed with an anti-desiccant. Granular alginate was used in the backfill. The plants moved with negligible flagging, and in mid-June this is significant.

Although no confirmed theories are available on the action of alginates, they may act in the three following ways.

(i) Polyuronide hemi-cellulose materials can absorb calcium, potassium and some other metals. In so doing they reduce the viscosity of the soil solution which would induce more water to flow into the root hairs by osmosis.

(ii) A polyuronide structure is capable of tremendous expansion by induction of water in and onto its structure. The expansion pressures may well overcome the viscosity of the liquid inside the root and force water into the plant.

(iii) Although it is not fully understood, the action of the alginate may overcome the balance of ions defined in the Donnen equilibrium and concentration pressure gradients.

## Summary of steps to take to ensure necessary root action and prevent desiccation

(i) Move the tree with an adequate sized ball which must not be broken after digging and balling to ensure conserving maximum fine roots.

(ii) Always dig at right angles to the edge of the ball to prevent 'lever' breakage of the ball (*see* Figure 9.1).

(iii) Trees with a normally poor root system must be prepared three years in advance of removal.

(iv) Move when ground temperatures are warm, during early autumn or spring.

(v) Use fertilizer sparingly; treat new roots like those of a seedling.

(vi) Backfill with an 'open' mix of seven parts loam, three parts sphagnum peat, and two parts sharp sand. Do not over- or under-consolidate.

(vii) Water well when planting and then as limited rainfall makes it necessary.

(viii) Use root-inducing hormone on ball surface.

(ix) Use alginates before moving and during backfill operations.

## The stem, or trunk and branches

The aerial part of a semi-mature tree may be pruned to alleviate the imbalance of 'head' to root when trans-

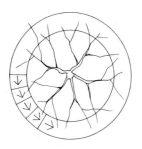

FIGURE 9.1 **Always dig at right-angles to the root ball to prevent 'level' breakage of the ball. Arrows indicate direction of spade leverage.**

planting. Judiciously retaining the form, it is better to reduce the head by removing two or three main branches, the cut ends of which can easily be painted with tree wound dressing. Many small cuts require far more cambium growth to cover them, causing a strain on the tree resources, and to paint all cut surfaces is wasteful of labour. Removal of large branches should be in accordance with BS 3998.

The bark of a semi-mature tree in a position exposed to full summer sun should be wrapped. The wrapping insulates the xylem tissue and may reduce the temperature of the leaf by one or two degrees, which will reduce transpiration loss.

Damage to the trunk or main stem should be avoided. Both parasitic and saprophytic fungi may enter through broken bark, the latter in some cases becoming parasitic. Insects obtain easier access to soft tissue for egg laying and food supplying through broken bark, and may carry pathogens on their feet.

Deep damage to the xylem will prevent some water and solutes from reaching the leaves. Shallow damage through the cuticle and cortex into the phloem will limit the flow of elaborated materials to the root system.

157

PLATE 9.6 **Pin oak** *(Quercus palustris)* **transplanted two months previously. Note bark wrapping.** *(R. L. Hebblethwaite)*

If the tree suffers damage in the transplanting process, this will further strain the tree's ability to survive the move.

Damage to the stem inhibits the natural rhythm of diurnal expansion and its possible role in the movement of water to the top of a tree. According to the transpiration cohesion-tension theory, the sun evaporates water from the leaves and the xylem becomes a passive pipeline through which columns of solutes are pulled under tension. Measurements of the tensile strength of water have exceeded 300 atmospheres.[7]

To raise water to the top of a 120 m (400 ft) tree would require a difference of only 13 atmospheres. Although friction and adhesion forces and gravity oppose the movement of water upwards, it is thought that sufficient tensile strength is present to overcome them. Values of root pressure have been measured up to 6 atmospheres, but 2 atmospheres is nearer normal. The difference between the two pressures causes tension and narrowing of the diameter of the xylem cells, starting at the bottom of the tree and measurable on a dendograph. The minutely lessened perimeter gradually works its way up the tree having a squeezing effect on the solutes in xylem above it, thereby aiding the movement of xylem solutes and phloem materials along

extended branches and to the top of the tree. At night with transpiration lessened and stomata enclosed, xylem tissues gradually fill out with a second wave of movement expanding the perimeter. If tissues are broken, both the continuous tube system and the xylem reduction effects are broken for the area of damage.

## The leaves

Water may be taken into a tree through the leaves during rain or overhead spraying through channels of pectinaceous material in the upper epidermis. These form a continuous passage for water from the surface to vascular bundles. The channels are few in number, and normally the cutinous layer only absorbs water to a small extent, dependent on the DPD of the epidermal cells.

The main aid to a moved tree is to prevent moisture loss from any part of the plant until the root system can reestablish in the new root-environment. Only after new root hairs are made and water absorbed through them can a water balance be achieved between transpiration and evaporation and water induction.

Water from the root system moves into the leaf cells from the vascular bundles of veins, is transpired into

158

the intercellular spaces between the mesophyll cells and moves through the stomates (when open) as water vapour. The movement of water into the intercellular spaces depends on the difference in water vapour pressure between the atmosphere if the stomates are open and the vapour pressure inside the leaf. The atmosphere inside the leaf is generally assumed to be near saturation and of high water-vapour pressure; that of the atmosphere outside the leaf unsaturated and of less water vapour pressure. Water vapour will therefore move from high to low vapour pressure and diffuse through the stomata. This movement has to be restricted, which can be accomplished in several ways.

The stomata through which 90 per cent of moisture vapour loss occurs, become closed during darkness, the intercellular spaces become saturated and water movement stops from the mesophyll cells as pressures inside the leaf equalize.

Digging and transportation between sites can be restricted to a period of dull days. The road transport period can be carried out, if the tree is evergreen or in leaf, during the evening. Medium sized trees or shrubs can have a canopy supported over them during transportation and for a week after transplanting. The canopy should not be such as to trap the heat of the sun e.g. not black or clear polythene – but rather tight hessian which can be wetted.

A leaf will heat up in the sun between 2° and 10°C higher than the surrounding atmosphere. Wrapping the bark reduces the temperature of solutes reaching the leaf by its insulating effect. An overhead spray will cool the leaf both on contact and during evaporation. Increased temperature in the leaf increases vapour pressure, increasing the DPD resulting in even greater transpiration and water loss on evaporation. Wrapping or overhead spraying helps the tree to overcome the transplanting physiological condition.

A vaporizing nozzle fixed at the top of the tree to a 12 mm water hose can be turned on during dry or windy days. The air humidity caused will reduce the DPD, thus reducing transpiration, and the moisture will also cool.

Modified polyvinyl resins are used to form a membrane over the leaf almost impervious to water, but allowing the passage of gases. The membrane decreases transpiration and thereby evaporation. The leaves of evergreen trees should be sprayed before moving. Bare root trees benefit from a cover spray over their roots. Oedema of the leaves can be caused by anti-desiccants applied during periods of excessive transpiration.

Anti-desiccant is best put on in early morning or early evening or in dull humid weather.

## Flowers and fruit

Flowers and fruit take energy and moisture from the tree or shrub. During the period of establishment, for two or three years, within reasonable labour cost, removal of flowers and fruit is beneficial to successful transplanting.

## 9.5 THE PRACTICE OF TREE MOVING RELATED TO PHYSIOLOGY

Trees should be chosen not only for their shape and size relative to the site, but also for their ability to tolerate the indigenous ground and air conditions (*see* Table 9.1). Appendix A of BS 4043 contains a list of trees suitable for transplanting when semi-mature.[8] The species listed below have been successfully transplanted and could usefully be added to the list:

| | |
|---|---|
| *Arbutus unedo* | – strawberry tree |
| *Magnolia grandiflora* | – evergreen magnolia |
| *Pinus strobus* | – white pine |
| *Quercus palustris* | – pin oak |
| *Tsuga caroliniana* | – Carolina hemlock |

## Preparation

The tree pit should be dug before the tree is moved. Good drainage is essential. A 150 mm (6 in) gravel layer at the bottom of the hole covered with turf upside down and linked to a sump or main drain is necessary in heavy clay soils. Providing the water table is at the bottom of the hole or below it, light soils do not usually need additional drainage.

TABLE 9.1

**Deciduous tree species commonly used in landscape schemes, suitable for semi-mature planting**

| Easily established | More difficult |
|---|---|
| *Acer platanoides* | *Betula alba* |
| *Acer pseudoplatanus* | *Carpinus betulus* |
| *Aesculus hippocastanum* | *Castanea sativa* |
| *Alnus glutinosa* | *Crataegus* spp. |
| *Arbutus unedo* | *Fagus sylvatica* |
| *Betula verrucosa* | *Fraxinus excelsior* |
| *Cedrus deodar* | *Ilex aquifolium* |
| *Chamaecyparis* sp. | *Larix* sp. |
| *Cornus florida* | *Prunus* spp. |
| *Cupressocyparis* sp. | *Quercus* spp. |
| *Malus* sp. | *Robinia pseudoacacia* |
| *Platanus hybrida* (x *acerfolia*) | *Salix* spp. |
| *Poplar* sp. | *Sorbus* spp. |
| *Quercus cerris* | |
| *Salix babylonica* | |
| *Tilia x euchloria* | |
| *Tilia platyphyllos* | |
| *Tsuga heterophylla* | |
| *Ulmus* spp. (only use where trees isolated from diseased elms) | |

In heavy clay or other compacted soil it is beneficial to crack the area around the pit and the sub-soil below the hole with a 115 g (4 oz) stick of 20 per cent gelignite as follows:

(i)   Permission must be obtained in writing to carry out blasting from any authority with underground services within 20 m laterally from the tree pit site. Obviously one would not be blasting over the tops of services.

(ii)  Employ an operator with a licence to carry out gelignite blasting — e.g. operators who blast ditches for farm dams.

(iii) Make a hole with a soil auger or steel pointed rod at the tree pit site, about 450–600 mm (18–24 in) deep. The 115 g charge is fitted with an electric detonator and placed at the bottom of the hole. The hole is back tamped gently with sand or fine soil. A number of holes can be blown at once using a 12 volt car battery.

(iv)  After the pit has been excavated by hand or back hoe (workers should keep clear of smoke which may cause bad headaches if inhaled), a further charge can be placed 450–600 mm deeper than the bottom of the pit to crack the sub-layer, creating fissures for drainage and root expansion. Sharp sand can be beneficial if washed into the fissures to prevent them from closing up or being clogged with clay particles.

(v)   The sides of the pit should be roughened with a fork or pick to ensure a good bond with the backfill.

(vi)  The hole should be 450 mm wider all around than the width of the ball and 150 mm deeper to allow for 250 mm of good backfill mix, tamped firm to 150 mm.

## Backfill mix

A satisfactory mix consists of seven parts friable loam, three parts sphagnum peat and two parts sharp sand. 10:10:10 N:P:K fertilizer should be added to the backfill and thoroughly mixed before use at the rate of ½ kg (roughly 1 lb) per m³. The backfill mix should be ready at the hole before the tree is moved. Specifications for tamping vary according to the amount of clay particles in the loam: medium tamping for a heavy loam, heavier tamping for light loams. The heavy end of a pick-axe handle has a 'sheep's foot' effect as a tamper, in finding voids and pushing soil in and around the ball of the tree. Good results are generally obtained if a medium firm tamping is given to backfill every 150–200 mm, and when half full, the backfill is flooded for further settlement. After excess water has disappeared (which proves reasonable drainage), further soil is added, tamped, and a final watering given just before the final 75 mm of backfill is added.

160

## Digging the tree

Preparation for moving non-fibrous rooted trees should start three years before moving.[9] This allows trenches to become tight with fibrous roots, and eventually makes it possible to move the tree. Less time is insufficient since much of the soil and new root will be too soft to obtain a hard ball periphery.

Normally the rootball would be 300 mm (1 ft) diameter per 25 mm (1 in) diameter of trunk of stem measured at 720 mm (2 ft 6 in) above ground level. Below a stem diameter of 100 mm (4 in) the diameter of the ball should be increased, and above a stem diameter of 200 mm (8 in) it should be reduced. For example a 50 mm (2 in) diameter tree would need a 700 mm (3 ft) diameter ball, and a 250 mm (10 in) diameter tree would need only an 1800 mm (6 ft) diameter ball.

*Sequence for digging a root ball*

The sequence of operation is as follows (*see* Figure 9.2):

1.  Three days before lifting, soak the ball in alginate solution.
2.  One day before lifting, spray bark and leaves, if present, with an anti-desiccant.
3.  Immediately before lifting judiciously remove some branches to balance the head and root, and paint cuts with an asphaltum or tree wound paint.
4.  Tie up the lower branches to the centre of the tree, being careful to prevent chafing the bark. (Use an air hose with wire threaded through it, or strong hessian or cloth loops with string attached.)
5.  Measure off the radius from the bole of the tree for the ball.
6.  Make a cut with a sharp spade all round the circumference of the ball, a few inches wider than the final ball width.
7.  Mark the outer circumference of the trench about 750 mm (2 ft 6 in) wide, and cut this vertically with a spade.
8.  Dig out the trench, facing ninety degrees away from the tree. Never dig towards the tree as this will break the edge of the ball.
9.  Topsoil and subsoil should be kept separate.
10. When the tree has been 'cored' to a depth of about 900 mm (3 ft) undercutting can take place so as to leave the tree on a neck or pedestal of subsoil. The edge of the ball can now be combed with a hand fork to the correct width, heavy roots being cut back, and light ones retained.
11. Dust the ball with root-inducing hormone at 10 ppm strength.
12. Arrange strong hessian around the ball and use 'pinning nails' to secure it. These are specially long-pointed hardened nails, about 75 mm (3 in) long.

PLATE 9.7 **Ball of strawberry tree** *(Arbutus unedo)* **dug and ready for hessian rope binding.** *(R. L. Hebblethwaite)*

13. Arrange a wire or rope concertina around the whole tree, a circle of wire or rope being fixed as far under the ball as possible, into the undercut. Make another circle of wire or rope on top of the ball and thread through the top loop of the 'concertina'. As the loops are pulled tight, the smaller loop of wire under the ball resists the pull of the upper circle. Cross ties across the circle make the ball even tighter. If wire is used a meat hook can be twisted through it to form a loop, the more twists, the tighter the ball. Experience teaches the breaking point of the wire.

14. Dig a ramp on the side from which the tree is to be removed. A very strong board, flat on top, is used for mounting the tree or shrub. A high hitch, well-padded, is attached two thirds of the way up the tree to lean it away from the ramp. Usually the ball breaks off the pedestal of soil and sometimes a tap root has to be sawn.

15. The board is placed under the ball, and the tree released back on the board. The ball is twisted with tyre chains or hessian until centrally placed on the board.

16. The ball is securely lashed to the board by means of a strong wire loop, or eye bolts at each corner. *From this time on, the ball is not touched.*

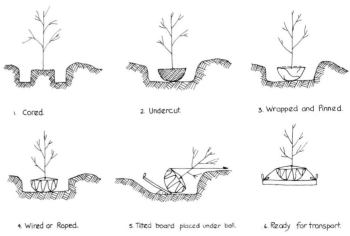

1. Cored.     2. Undercut.     3. Wrapped and Pinned.
4. Wired or Roped.     5. Tilted board placed under ball.     6. Ready for transport.

FIGURE 9.2 **Sequence of digging a semi-mature tree.**

161

PLATE 9.8 **Balled semi-mature hornbeam** *(Carpinus betulus)* **moved in New York State. Note board and size of picks.** *(R. L. Hebblethwaite)*

PLATE 9.9 **Semi-mature yew** *(Taxus baccata)* **in USA moved on a steel sled. Note tyre chain.** *(R. L. Hebblethwaite)*

PLATE 9.10 **Semi-mature juniper** *(Juniperus virginia)* **moved on a wooden sled.** *(R. L. Hebblethwaite)*

17. The board may be winched on planks and rollers, or lifted by slings and crane, onto a low loader trailer.

18. The process is reversed to get the ball into the tree pit on site. A further anti-desiccant may be sprayed. Backfilling and watering should be carried out as described above.

*Bare-root moving (dormant deciduous trees only)*

If a semi-mature tree is taken from a light sandy loam and it is not possible to obtain a firm ball of soil and roots, it may be moved bare root with special precautions to prevent the roots drying out. A medium sized semi-mature tree can be lifted with a front-end-loader caterpillar tractor and a good operator. A trench is dug on three sides of the tree about 3.5 m away from the trunk. With the bucket on the fourth side about 750 mm deep the tree can be lifted and teased out of the soil by skilful manipulation. This type of operation is most successful with very fibrous, surface rooting trees such as maple and birch.

## Transportation and planting

Transport should take place in the evening if possible, or in the case of a large shrub or small tree, under light sheeting. The vehicle should move slowly, at not more than 10 mph. Windy weather should be avoided. The hessian, leaves and bark should be soaked to create a humid atmosphere around the ball. The tree and board should be securely tied to the trailer to prevent movement during transit, always remembering to protect bark with expanded polystyrene cushions or wire rope covered with rubber hose.

Generally speaking it is best to place a tree in the same direction it faced before being moved. Planting mix and backfill procedure should be carried out as we have previously said (9.4). Staking should be secure and adequate for the size and weight of the tree when full of moisture and under heavy wind pressure.[10]

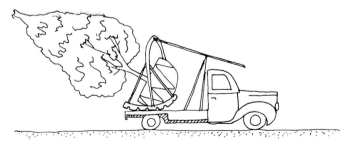

FIGURE 9.3 **Semi-mature tree in transport.**

163

PLATE 9.11 **A Newman Major trailer being loaded using a truck winch to lever the trailer and tree through 90°
from vertical to horizontal.** *(By permission of Newman)*

## After care

The tree should never be short of 'available' water,
particularly for the first two years after planting. This
must take into account the adsorption, adhesion, and
the cohesive nature of very fine soil particles. With the
7:3:2 mix, water should be available to the roots under
normal osmotic pressure.

BS 4043 shows turnbuckles in the staking wires.[11]
These should be inspected every week and after heavy
winds, and tightened as necessary in the first few months
after planting when some stretching of the wire rope
may occur. After four months, monthly inspections are
enough.

A watch should be kept for disease. Most fungicides
are preventative, not curative. If the species is known
to be susceptible to disease, routine sprays should be
applied.

Pests are usually noticed by the layman only after
damage to the plant makes it obvious that the pest is
present. A well trained arboriculturalist will look out
for pests before they have had a chance to ruin the
appearance and recuperative efficiency of the tree.
Such pests as aphis, red spider, thrip, capsid and leaf
hoppers can cause a great loss of liquids and leaf
surface essential to the recovery of the tree, if left
untreated.

A watch should be kept for mineral deficiencies

164

PLATE 9.12 **Extension segments being added to a Newman frame to allow it to hold a root ball of 2.4 m diameter.** *(By permission of Newman)*

particularly magnesium, nitrogen, potash, phosphate and lime-induced iron deficiency. Expert advice should be sought with regard to the amount of corrective mineral to apply and its form.

## 9.6 CONCLUSION

The basic physiology regarding tree moving should be understood at least by the foreman of the moving crew, if not the crew themselves. Necessary specifications should include those based on physiology. The confidence of the general public and local authorities in planting semi-mature trees can only stem from a high success rate, and the latter is only achieved by giving due regard to relevant plant physiology in tree moving and after care.

## FURTHER READING

Cutler, D. F. and Richardson, I. B. K. *Tree Roots and Building* (Harlow: Construction Press 1981)

Fox, D. G. 'Carbon Dioxide Narcosis' *J. Cell Comp Physiol*, Vol. 3, p.75 (1933)

Hartt, C. E. 'The Effect of Temperature upon Translocation of C14 in Sugarcane', *Plant Physiology*, vol. 41, p.309

PLATE 9.13 **The Newman treeporter can dig seven sizes of root ball, from 0.8 to 2.0 m diameter.** *(By permission of Newman)*

Kramer, P. J. 'The Relation between Rate of Transpiration and Rate of Absorption of Water in Plants', *Am. Jnl. Botany*, Vol. 24, p.10 (1937)

Landscape Institute/JCLI *Frost Damage to Trees and Shrubs – Report* (June 1985)

NHCB *Building Near Trees*, Practice Note No. 3 and Supplement *A Quick Way to Find the Right Depth of Foundations on Clay Soils* (1985)

Patch, D. 'Advances in Practical Arboriculture', *Forestry Commission Bulletin* 65 (1985)

Powell, C. C. 'Tree Health from Top to Bottom', *Journal of Arboriculture*, vol. II No. 5 (May 1985)

Reynolds, E. R. C. *A Report on Tree Roots and Built Development* (London: Department of the Environment 1979)

Roberts, E. A., Southwick, M. D. and Palmer, D. H. 'A Microchemical Examination of McIntosh Apple Leaves showing Relationship of Cell Wall Constituents to Penetration Spray Solutions', *Plant Physiology*, Vol. 23, p.557 (1948)

Tree Council/RIBA *Trees and Buildings: Complement or Conflict* (1979)

Wager, J. A. 'Reducing Surface Rooting of Trees', *Journal of Arboriculture*, vol. II No. 6 (June 1985)

## REFERENCES

1. 'Transplanting Semi-Mature Trees' *British Standards Institution* BS 4043 (1966)
2. Lovejoy, D. (ed.) *Land Use and Landscape Planning* (Aylesbury: Leonard Hill, International Textbook Co.) Chapter 2, pp.45–7 (1973)
3. Cummings, W. H. A. 'A Method of sampling the Foliage of a Silver Maple Tree', *J. Forestry*, Vol. 39, p.382 1941)
4. Bonner, J. and Galston, A. W. *Principles of Plant Physiology* San Francisco: W. H. Freeman & Company (1952)
5. *Specification 1975*, 76th edition, Architectural Press, pp.1 and 51–2. 'Backhoe', under 'Contractors Equipment is shown as a back-acting mechanical digger'
6. Devlin, R. M. *Plant Physiology* (New York: Van Nostrand Reinhold), 2nd edition p.316 (1969)
7. Meyer, B. S. and Andersen, D. B. *Plant Physiology*, (Princeton, New Jersey: D. van Nostrand Reinhold) (1952)
8. B.S. 4043, op. cit.
9. Ibid.
10. Ibid. Appendix C. p.111
11. Ibid. p.25

PLATE 9.14 **Semi-mature willows — University of York.** *(Maurice Lee)*

# CHAPTER 10

# Reclamation and Planting of Industrial and Urban Wasteland

## DR R. P. GEMMELL

## 10.1 INTRODUCTION

It is often difficult to establish vegetation on wasteland because of chemical toxicity, infertility, adverse physical structure for root growth, shortage of moisture and other factors. Nature herself is sometimes able to overcome these problems, but only very slowly. Fortunately for the landscape architect, scientists have devised special treatments to overcome these growth problems so that planting can be successfully carried out on wasteland. However, sites vary so much in type and in the extent of the problems related to them that there is no universally applicable treatment to make wasteland suitable for planting. Successful planting depends on carrying out ecological surveys, soil analyses, consideration of suitable treatments, special cultivations and a suitable choice of species for each individual site.

The ecologist or landscape scientist has an important advisory role when planting is to be carried out on difficult sites. It is vital that the relevant experts are consulted at the outset, before schemes are planned and designed. The experts should be asked:

(a) To advise on the feasibility of planting different types of vegetation.
(b) To specify soil analyses and provide interpretation of the results.
(c) To carry out ecological surveys to identify any wildlife habitats that are worth protecting.
(d) To devise soil amelioration and cultivation treatments.
(e) To select suitable species and varieties of plants for toxic sites.
(f) To supervise specialized amendment, cultivation and planting methods.
(g) To monitor soil conditions and plant growth to give advice on how to manage the site after planting is completed.

## 10.2 FACTORS INHIBITING PLANT GROWTH

Wasteland, including urban sites, often has no topsoil. The ground may consist of industrial waste, demolition rubble, subsoil or other materials. Table 10.1 lists the main problems affecting plant growth and indicates where they are likely to occur.

## 10.3 TECHNIQUES FOR SPECIFIC SITES

The following types of wasteland or disturbed ground are considered in detail:

1. Colliery spoil from deep mines.
2. Ironworks and steelworks wastes, blast furnace slag.
3. Pulverized fuel ash (PFA) from power stations.
4. Metalliferous wastes and sewage sludge.
5. Alkali wastes.
6. Chemical wastes, gas-works sites and contaminated ground.
7. Quarries, pits and their spoil heaps.
8. Urban and industrial sites, including railways, canals and reservoirs.

For each of these types of site the main problems are described, soil analyses and ecological surveys are recommended, and suitable treatments are advised. Where necessary, advice is given on after-management.

## Colliery spoil from deep mines

### Problems

Acidity or low pH of the soil is the commonest problem in trying to reclaim wasteland. Many tips are extremely acidic, with pH values in the range 2.5 to 4.0. There is also a great variation in the pH values of the spoil, and while some spoils have pH values down to about 1.5,

TABLE 10.1
**Problems affecting plant growth on wasteland**

| Problem | Occurrence |
| --- | --- |
| Acidity (low pH) | Colliery spoil, oil shale, metal mine spoils, gas-works waste, china clay waste, gritstone quarries and spoil heaps |
| Potential acidity (acid regeneration) | Colliery spoil, gas-works waste |
| Metal toxicity (zinc, copper, lead, etc) | Metal mine spoils, metal smelter wastes, sewage sludge, chemical wastes, fluorspar tailings, soils near metal refineries |
| Alkalinity (high pH) | Blast furnace slag, ironworks and steelworks wastes, alkali wastes, pulverized fuel ash |
| Chemical toxicity (chromates, borates, complex cyanides etc.) | Chemical wastes, chromate smelter waste, pulverized fuel ash, gas-works waste, paper wastes, chemical works sites |
| Salt toxicity (salinity) | Oil shale, chemical wastes, alkali wastes, pulverized fuel ash, some colliery spoils, chemical works sites |
| Nitrogen deficiency | Most sites and wastes except sewage sludge and domestic refuse |
| Phosphate deficiency | Most sites and wastes except sewage sludge and domestic refuse |
| Phosphate fixation (immobilization of phosphorus) | Colliery spoil, gas-works waste, blast furnace slag |
| Toxic gas emission (methane, ethylene) | Domestic refuse, gas-works waste |
| Consolidation (high density) | Colliery spoil |
| Concretion and cementation | Blast furnace slag, pulverized fuel ash, some alkali and chemical wastes |
| High porosity | Brick rubble, blast furnace slag, china clay waste, boiler ash, quarry and gravel pit spoils |
| Low moisture-holding capacity | Most wastes except sewage sludge and pulverized fuel ash |

others are neutral (pH 5.0 to 7.0) and a few are even alkaline (pH 7.0 to 8.5). Low pH values, below about 4.0, are directly harmful to plant roots and result in metal toxicities. Acidity also damages the soil structure by deflocculating the clay colloids, causing poor drainage and oxygen starvation of plant roots.

Acidity is caused by the reaction of oxygen and water on iron pyrites in the spoil to produce sulphuric acid as follows:

$$2FeS_2 + 2H_2O + 7O_2 = 2FeSO_4 + 2H_2SO_4$$
$$4FeSO_4 + 10H_2O + O_2 = 4Fe(OH)_3 + 4H_2SO_4$$

Because acidification depends on atmospheric oxygen and soil moisture, it occurs only at the surface of spoil heaps, or when they are regraded. Most freshly mined or recently regraded spoil is neutral or alkaline. The acidity may take days, weeks, months or even years to develop, depending on the chemical composition of the spoil.

The production of sulphuric acid, a process called acid regeneration, may last for many years. The quantity of acid produced depends on the amount of iron pyrites in the spoil. For every 1 per cent of pyrite, roughly 40 tonnes of sulphuric acid per hectare can be generated in the surface 15 cm layer of the spoil. Many spoils contain 1 or 2 per cent of pyrite, and some contain up to 5 per cent, so enormous quantities of acid can be produced. However, the actual quantity of acid that is released is complicated by the fact that most spoils also contain calcium carbonate and other minerals which neutralize some or all of the acid. For practical purposes, 1 per cent of pyrite in spoil gives rise to a lime requirement of 40 tonnes per hectare to 15 cm depth, and 1 per cent of calcium carbonate content is equivalent to 23 tonnes per hectare of limestone applied. Obviously, spoils with 1 per cent pyrite content and 2 per cent calcium carbonate content do not need liming. In addition, some spoils are saline because of high concentrations of soluble salts. However, this problem is rather unusual.

All spoils are very infertile because they contain virtually no nitrogen or phosphates. Moreover, many spoils exhibit phosphate fixation, which is the immobilization of phosphate fertilizer by amorphous ferric hydroxides on the spoil mineral particles. However, potassium is usually present in abundance, being released from clay minerals. Trace nutrients are also present in sufficient quantities in the spoil to provide plants with most of the food that they need.

Physical problems of growing plants on colliery spoil include compaction, consolidation and a high stone content in the spoil.

## Ecological survey

Detailed wildlife and habitat surveys should be carried out because many sites will have been colonized naturally by valuable flora and fauna. For example, in Britain some old spoil heaps support birch and oak woodlands. Many tips support scrub of gorse, bramble, hawthorn and willows. On acidic spoils heathland often develops, whereas on neutral or calcareous spoils there may be species-rich grasslands with many interesting wild flowers and orchids. Washery waste and coal slurry are often colonized quite rapidly by interesting plant communities. Such wildlife features and natural vegetation should be retained if possible, to capitalize on what nature has achieved.

A preliminary ecological survey is useful in other ways. The type of vegetation, however sparse, is often indicative of spoil chemical conditions. For example, wavy hair-grass is indicative of moderate spoil acidity, whereas red fescue and cocksfoot grasses indicate neutral or only slightly acidic conditions. If the spoil is bare, it is likely to be very acidic. A pH survey should then be undertaken to give a more detailed analysis of the spoil conditions.

## Soil analysis

Samples of unweathered spoil should be taken from boreholes before regrading, or from the surface after regrading the spoil. Each surface sample should be a composite of ten or more sub-samples, collected at random from within a 25 m radius of the main sampling point. The sub-samples should be added together or bulked, and mixed well. At least six composite samples should be taken from each type of spoil, but preferably more if time and money are available. Ideally six to twenty samples should be taken, depending on the size of the area to be treated. The site should be compartmentalized for sampling purposes, according to spoil type or origin. This is important because different spoil heaps on the same site often vary markedly in chemical composition and acidity.

The pH of the spoil should be determined by mixing the samples with water to form a slurry which can then be analysed by means of a pH meter fitted with a glass electrode. The lime requirement, if the pH is below 6.0, should be measured by a buffer solution (such as Shoemaker or Woodruff), but three modifications are necessary when analysing spoil. First, the period of incubation should be extended from 30 minutes to 24

PLATE 10.1 **Experimental grass plots on colliery soil. The trials investigated the effects of fertilizer and cutting treatments on grass seeded directly into the spoil.**

PLATE 10.2 **Dieback of grass on colliery spoil caused by sulphuric acid released by iron pyrite oxidation. The pH of the spoil fell from 7.0 to 3.0 in 12 months.**

PLATE 10.3 **The effect of nitrogen deficiency on the growth of grass on colliery spoil. Note the dense growth in the plots treated with nitrogen fertilizer.**

hours with constant shaking. Second, if the final spoil and buffer solution pH is less than 5.5, the test should be repeated, using half the initial quantity of spoil or twice the amount of buffer solution. For very acidic spoils, the amount of buffer solution should be increased fourfold. Third, if the spoil pH is less than 3.5, the result of the lime requirement test should be doubled.

Potential acidity can be estimated by chemical analysis of the amount of iron pyrite ($FeS_2$) present, using the differential iron method (or a similar method). Allowance should be made for the carbonate content of the spoil, which is measured by treatment with hydrochloric acid and back titration with alkali to determine the amount of acid that has been neutralized. The results should be interpreted as described earlier. In practice, it should be assumed that cultivation is to be to 30 or even 45 cm depth, so the lime requirement based on only 15 cm depth should be doubled or tripled as is appropriate.

Salinity should be determined by measuring the electrical conductivity of a saturated paste extract, 6–10 mmhos being considered to be moderately toxic to plants and over 10 mmhos highly toxic.

Phosphate is usually determined by extracting the spoil with 0.5 N sodium bicarbonate solution at pH 8.5 and colorimetrically determining its concentration. Phosphorus concentrations below 20 ppm indicate that fertilizer is needed. Values of 5–10 ppm of phosphorus show that a moderately high rate of phosphate should be added and 0–5 ppm P show that a very high application rate is needed. Phosphate fixation capacity can be estimated by shaking the spoil with calcium tetrahydrogen diorthophosphate for 24 hours and analysing the amount of phosphate absorbed. There is little point in measuring potassium status, as this is usually adequate. However, for guidance, 100 ppm K or more is sufficient for plant growth, 50–100 ppm indicates a moderate deficiency and 0–50 ppm K a high deficiency. Nitrogen can always be assumed to be nil, so this fertilizer is certainly required.

## Planting of grassland and trees

Table 10.2 summarizes the cultivation and planting techniques for colliery spoil.

The application of ground calcitic limestone is crucial for successful planting on acidic spoils. Magnesian limestone is not recommended, because it can result in excessive levels of soluble magnesium sulphate developing in very acidic spoils. The rate of limestone application should be based on the potential acidity of the spoil, so that acid regeneration and dieback do not occur. Most acidic spoils require at least 30–50 tonnes per hectare of limestone but very acidic sites may require around 100 tonnes per hectare or more for permanent control of acidity. In exceptionally acidic spoils up to 400 tonnes per hectare of limestone have been necessary. Experience has shown that this does

TABLE 10.2
**Cultivation and planting of colliery spoil**

1. Landscape modelling and grading
2. Ground calcitic limestone application
3. Ripping to 50 cm depth at 40 cm centres with a tracked machine
4. Allow several months for salts to be washed out (saline sites only)
5. Chisel ploughing, disc harrowing, tine harrowing etc.
6. Grading and levelling
7. Spread topsoil, subsoil or sewage sludge (if available)
8. Apply phosphate fertilizer (triple superphosphate etc.)
9. Fixed-tine cultivation and disc harrowing
10. Stone picking
11. Chain harrowing
12. NPK fertilization
13. Grass and clover seeding
14. Seed harrowing and rolling (not for small seeds)

not result in trace-element deficiencies or other over-liming problems. Agricultural ground limestone should normally be used (40 per cent passing a No. 100 BS sieve), but for rates above 100 tonnes per hectare, coarsely ground limestone, such as 3 mm to dust material, is better and cheaper.

The ground limestone should be thoroughly incorporated into the spoil by ripping and deep cultivations. Ripping relieves compaction as well as facilitating chisel ploughing, tining and harrowing. If soil cover is available, it should be spread after liming and lime incorporation.

Most sites require at least 1 tonne per hectare of triple superphosphate (45 per cent $P_2O_5$) or 2.5 tonnes per hectare of superphosphate (18 per cent $P_2O_5$) because of phosphate fixation. If phosphate fixation capacity is high, as is often the case on very pyritic spoils which need high liming, the phosphate application rates should be doubled. After integrating the phosphate, a general compound fertilizer, such as NPK 20:10:10, should be applied at about 500–625 kilograms per hectare for agricultural land or 325–500 kilograms per hectare for amenity grassland. To provide organic matter and additional nutrients, sewage sludge may be applied, but this is not essential.

Grass seeding techniques are similar to those used on normal soils, but seeding rates should be increased by 50 per cent or so because of the poor seedbed conditions. The inclusion of a high percentage of clover seed is very important as an additional and long-term source of nitrogen fertility. For amenity grassland, the persistent and low-growing wild white varieties should be sown. Small seeds of bents and fine-leaved fescues should not be harrowed into the spoil, because this will reduce germination.

Sites to be planted with trees should be cultivated, fertilized and grassed in the same way, in order to provide a green cover and stabilize the spoil. Fine-leaved fescues and wild white clover are best. Trees and shrubs should be planted a year or so later, after loosening the spoil by single-tine ripping to 60 cm depth. Deep ripping has several advantages: it makes planting easier, quicker and cheaper, increases survival rates and improves subsequent growth. The trees should be planted along the rips, or at their intersections if the ground is cross-ripped. The grass and clover around each tree should then be killed with a suitable herbicide, otherwise they will dry out the spoil, resulting in poor tree survival and growth.

Alder and birch are excellent species, but a wide range of other trees and shrubs, including oak, should be planted at the outset.

### After-management of the site

Reclaimed land should be monitored and carefully managed for at least five years after treatment in case dieback and regression of the vegetation occurs. Soil analyses should be carried out annually for pH, lime requirement and phosphate and potassium levels on all colliery spoil sites.

Regeneration of acidity is the commonest problem. The first signs are usually localized bare patches, but annual pH checks will detect acidification at an early stage. The best method is to take 50 to 100 individual surface spoil samples (not composites) per field for pH analysis. The presence of a few highly acidic samples or a low average pH value indicates serious acidification. This is an early warning system which enables acidification to be controlled by surface dressings of ground limestone at 20−50 tonnes per hectare. Individual areas of dieback, if present, should be given 100−200 tonnes per hectare of ground limestone.

The maintenance of phosphate fertility is the second most important problem. Again, annual phosphate monitoring tests should pick this up at an early stage. The deficiency can be corrected by top-dressings of around 500 kilograms per hectare of superphosphate, or of triple superphosphate if the deficiency is extreme. A satisfactory phosphate level is essential for maintaining clover growth and nitrogen fixation.

Nitrogen deficiency is indicated by yellowing of the grass, poor growth, and the spread of clovers. It can be remedied by top-dressings of nitrogen fertilizer such as ammonium nitrate, or by applying sewage sludge or farmyard manure. However, it is better to rely partly on nitrogen fixation by clovers.

The third major problem in managing colliery spoil after it has been reclaimed is consolidation. This results from the natural collapse of the spoil because of its poor soil structure. The bulk density increases to about 2 grams/cm$^3$ after planting, which dramatically reduces the oxygen content of the spoil, its moisture-holding capacity and its porosity. Consequently the spoil dries out in summer and becomes waterlogged in winter. The growth of grassland may be reduced by up to 80 per cent as a result, which severely limits the cropping capacity of the land. Little if anything can be done to remedy this problem, although it is not a serious constraint if the land has been reclaimed for public open space, woodland or wildlife habitats.

# Ironworks and steelworks wastes (blast furnace slag)

### Problems

The waste produced by ironworks and steelworks is highly calcareous and always alkaline. Its pH varies from 7.0 to 12.5, most unweathered slags having a pH of about 10.5. The alkalinity is due to the presence of calcium hydroxide and the hydrolysis of calcium silicates in the slag. Freshly tipped or regraded wastes are strongly alkaline (pH 10.5 or above) but old tips are generally less alkaline (around pH 7.0) because the free lime is washed out of the surface by rain.

The slag is extremely deficient in phosphate and contains practically no nitrogen available for plants. Its high lime content also causes phosphate fixation or immobilization. A major problem is the physical structure of the waste, especially the presence of lumps of fused slag, which will obviously provide resistance to root growth.

### Ecological survey

Many old blast furnace slag tips have been colonized naturally by limestone flora and should be examined for possible wildlife value before landscaping plans are drawn up. There are several documented sites throughout Britain which have developed species-rich communities of wild flowers, scrub and developing woodland. Tips near Wigan, for example, provide a habitat for colonies of wild orchid and unusual lime-loving plants which are rare in other parts of the region. Such species-rich vegetation attracts numerous butterflies, moths, insects and birds. Tips which have become attractive and important wildlife assets should be protected and managed for nature conservation, and this in itself is not an easy task.

### Soil analysis

It is vital to carry out pH surveys because of the risk of high alkalinity in the slag. Surface samples should be taken immediately after regrading; if done later, sub-surface samples at 10 cm depth should also be obtained, because strong alkalinity can persist in the rooting zone. There is little point in analysing for phosphate and potassium levels, since these can be assumed to be very low or nil.

PLATE 10.4 **Blast furnace slag tips from the smelting of iron ore. The high pH and low fertility prevented grass growth.** *(R. P. Gemmell)*

PLATE 10.5 **Grass trials on blast furnace slag. The waste was treated with nitrogen and phosphate fertilizers. Red fescue was the most tolerant type of grass.** *(R. P. Gemmell)*

### Planting of grassland and trees

Alkalinity in the slag cannot be treated chemically, so there is no artificial method of reducing the high pH. The only options available are to cover the slag with soil or other material, or to allow natural leaching by rainfall to wash out the free lime after regrading. A period of twelve to eighteen months is normally sufficient to lower the pH to about 8.0 at the surface.

Phosphate fertility can be improved by adding triple superphosphate or superphosphate at rates up to 1 tonne and 2.5 tonnes per hectare respectively, depending on the pH of the slag. On well weathered or old slag, if the pH is around 7.0, half these rates should suffice, since phosphate fixation is much greater at high pH.

Nitrogen fertilization is extremely important, 625 kilograms per hectare of a 20:10:10 fertilizer being suitable for grassland. Because the fertilizer is readily leached, a slow-release source of nitrogen such as sewage sludge, broiler manure or sulphur-coated nitrogen fertilizer is most effective. Alternatively, a second dose of NPK 20:10:10 fertilizer at 500 kilograms per hectare should be applied after about two to three months.

Only species tolerant of highly calcareous soils should be planted in the slag. The most tolerant amenity grasses are red fescue, sheep's fescue and similar fine-leaved fescues. Ryegrasses are unsuitable and bent grasses are intolerant of the alkalinity in the waste. The best legume for nitrogen fixation is common birdsfoot trefoil, because it is fairly tolerant of high pH, but wild white clover is excellent if the pH is below 7.5. Suitable trees and shrubs are those characteristic of chalk and limestone habitats, such as birch, ash, hawthorn, blackthorn, goat willow, rowan and bramble. Other species with appreciable tolerance are alder, black locust, gorse, tree lupin, buddleia, sea buckthorn and privet.

### After-management

Maintenance of nitrogen and phosphate fertilities are the main problems to be overcome. The best approach is to apply plenty of phosphate to stimulate clover growth and nitrogen fixation, thereby promoting a self-maintaining grass cover.

## Pulverized fuel ash (PFA)

### Problems

Pulverized fuel ash is the ash derived from the burning of pulverized coal in power stations. It has been produced in Britain since the 1950s. Although considerable quantities are used for road construction and other purposes, large deposits are tipped as waste.

The ash (PFA) is often toxic to plants because of its high borate concentrations, high levels of soluble sodium and potassium salts and high pH (alkalinity) which may approach 12.0. Not all PFA is toxic to plants, since some ashes contain low levels of toxins.

However PFA is always deficient in nitrogen and usually in phosphate as well.

A physical problem to plant growth on some types of PFA is pozzolanic cementation, which causes concretions. These can seriously obstruct root growth.

### Ecological survey

PFA tips can become valuable wildlife habitats through natural colonization. Important features that have been noted on PFA tips are large colonies of wild orchids, particularly marsh orchids and marsh helleborine. The colonies are often extremely dense, with swarms of very vigorous hybrids. Colonies containing more than 100 orchids per square metre have been reported. Several unusual and uncommon plants can also grow on the ash, notable examples being yellow birdsnest and stagshorn clubmoss.

One PFA site at Wigan is of regional wildlife importance for its exceptional plant communities and species diversity. The ash deposit areas contain open water, reedbeds, marsh, willow carr, species-rich grasslands, tall herb communities and developing woodland. Small patches of acidic grassland, heath and sphagnum moss hummocks also occur. The ash vegetation supports a wide range of animal life, including butterflies, moths, many insects and birds.

### Soil analysis

Natural leaching by rainfall eventually washes out the toxic constituents of PFA. Therefore, soil tests should be conducted on samples from boreholes, pits, or surface material immediately after regrading. As has been described for colliery spoil, a compartmental method of sampling should be adopted if different types of ash are present. Tips often consist of ash from more than one power station, so the content of the ash will not be homogeneous. The toxicity of PFA is also influenced by the type of coal burnt, its combustion temperature and whether the ash is lagooned or not.

Ash pH should be measured, but lime requirement tests are unnecessary because PFA is invariably alkaline. Salinity or soluble salt content should be determined and assessed as for colliery spoil. The analysis should include water-soluble boron, 10-30 ppm being interpreted as moderately toxic and over 30 ppm as highly toxic. A further useful measurement is calcium carbonate content, since some types of ash are highly calcareous. Available phosphate and potassium levels should be analysed so that fertilizer requirements can be estimated.

### Planting of grassland and trees

Herbaceous and woody plants can be grown directly in PFA if the salt and borate levels are low or if the ash is well weathered. Toxic ashes should be covered with 10 cm of soil or subsoil for amenity grassland and 30 cm of topsoil for arable crops. An alternative approach is to incorporate organic materials such as sewage sludge or peat in the ash. If cementation occurs, the ash should

175

**TABLE 10.3**
**Species tolerant of pulverized fuel ash (PFA)**

| Tolerance | Grasses | Legumes | Trees and shrubs |
|---|---|---|---|
| High | Red fescue | Common melilot<br>White melilot | Alder<br>Sea buckthorn<br>Poplars<br>Willows |
| Medium | Cocksfoot<br>Perennial ryegrass<br>Common bent-grass | White clover<br>Red clover<br>Alsike clover | Birch<br>Sycamore<br>Black locust<br>Hawthorn<br>Gorse |

be subsoiled to break up the concretions. High fertilizer rates are needed, particularly of nitrogen and phosphates.

Selection of species is important because certain grasses, legumes, trees and shrubs are tolerant of PFA, and particularly of its boron content. Table 10.3 shows which plant species have significant tolerance of PFA.

### After-management
Phosphate levels should be monitored, since phosphate deficiency can restrict plant growth. Shortage of nitrogen is the most likely problem. This can be remedied by fertilization, but the establishment of nitrogen fixers such as clovers is the preferable solution.

## Metalliferous wastes and sewage sludge
### Problems
Most metalliferous wastes occur in the countryside, especially in the tips of mine spoil from ancient zinc, copper and lead workings. Many of the tips have remained bare or sparsely vegetated for hundreds of years because of their toxic metal contents. Some still cause water pollution, destroying the fish and aquatic invertebrate life of streams and rivers whose catchment areas contain the tips.

The waste from the smelting of metal ores is considerably more toxic than the spoil heaps. This is because smelting increases the solubility of the metals. The Lower Swansea Valley (Plate 10.6) was once a world centre for non-ferrous metal smelting, but most of the derelict land has now been reclaimed.

Metalliferous wastes of recent origin are the tailings from fluorspar extraction. Sewage sludges, particularly those contaminated with industrial effluents, often contain toxic amounts of zinc, copper, cadmium, chromium and other metals. Soils may also be polluted by metals from copper refineries. Zinc contamination of soil is a problem under electricity pylons, particularly on acidic soils and moorlands.

Acidity may occur, particularly in copper mine spoils. All mine spoils and smelter wastes are deficient in the major nutrients nitrogen and phosphate. Sewage sludge is one of the few wastes which has a high fertility.

### Ecological survey
Many of the old metal mine spoils have a very sparse grass cover. The plants are tolerant of the metals in the wastes. Only a few grass species have metal-tolerant strains, notably red fescue, common bentgrass and sweet vernal grass. The tolerance of these plants is usually very specific to the metals concerned but they are also adapted to low fertility and drought.

The metal-tolerant vegetation of tips should be retained if possible for several reasons. First, it stabilizes the tips against water and wind erosion, which can cause serious pollution of adjacent land and watercourses. Second, the flora may be of scientific interest for its communities of sea pink, harebell, calamine pansy, alpine penny-cress, spring sandwort and sea campion. Third, some tips are of nature conservation value for their rare plants, such as dark red helleborine, frog orchid, grass of Parnassus, maiden pink and the forked spleenwort fern.

In contrast to metal mine spoil, sewage sludge is usually densely colonized by tall herbage, marsh, reed-bed and willow carr. This vegetation supports a rich insect fauna and birdlife. However, if metal levels are very high there may be no vegetation.

### Soil analysis
Toxicity should be assessed by determining the plant-available levels of metals in the wastes. Samples should be extracted with ammonium acetate or acetic acid solutions. Table 10.4 indicates the concentration ranges which are likely to be toxic in different wastes.

The term 'zinc equivalent' is often used to determine the toxicity of sewage sludge or the land to which it has been added as a fertilizer. Many industrial sludges are extremely toxic because of their high concentrations of metals. About 250 ppm of total zinc is the maximum

PLATE 10.6 **Zinc smelter waste in the Lower Swansea Valley. Only zinc-tolerant grasses can grow directly in the waste.** *(R. P. Gemmell)*

TABLE 10.4

**Concentrations of metals causing toxicity in metalliferous wastes**

| Waste | Analysis | Metal toxicity range |
|---|---|---|
| Zinc smelter waste or zinc mine spoil | Acetic acid extraction | 10 000−20 000 ppm zinc |
| Copper smelter waste or copper mine spoil | EDTA extraction | 1 000−3 000 ppm copper |
| Sewage sludge | Total metal determination | 0.5−5.0% zinc<br>0.2−1.2% copper<br>0.03−0.4% nickel<br>0.03−1.0% chromium |
| | Acetic acid extraction | 1 700−3 500 ppm zinc<br>100−3 000 ppm copper<br>120−2 000 ppm nickel<br>20−100　ppm chromium |

concentration that can be added over a long period without causing toxicity. Not more than 560 kilograms of zinc should be added to 1 hectare over 30 years, equivalent to 19 kilograms annually. Copper is about twice as toxic as zinc and nickel eight times so. The 'zinc equivalent' value enables all the metal concentrations to be expressed in terms of zinc after allowing for their different toxicities. Thus the maximum amount of all metals that can be added safely is 560 kilograms zinc equivalent per hectare over 30 years, or 19 kilograms per annum.

### Establishment of grassland and trees

Organic matter can be applied to complex or make insoluble the metals in the wastes. Sewage sludge from the activated sludge process is usually the best organic matter source, but it must have a low metal content. For metal mine spoils, 5–10 cm of sludge should suffice, but the more toxic smelter wastes require 10–15 cm of organic material. If the waste is acidic, lime should also be applied.

Another method of producing an environment suitable for tree or grass planting is to provide a metal-free rooting medium by covering the wastes with topsoil, subsoil, neutral colliery spoil or similar materials. The minimum thickness of cover for grass is 10 cm, but 20–30 cm is preferable. Up to 2 m of cover may be needed for trees.

The problem with organic matter treatment is that the sewage sludge can become saturated with metal ions, or it may degrade and disappear altogether, leading to renewed toxicity. Even soil coverings may become toxic, because of the upward movement of metal ions, particularly if finely grained materials such as sand or PFA are used. The only permanent treatment is to plant metal-tolerant grasses, varieties of which are now commercially available.

### After-management

Metalliferous wastes, apart from sewage sludge, are extremely infertile. Although metal-tolerant grasses are adapted to low fertility, regular fertilization is essential to maintain growth and build up a reasonable and stable humus layer.

# Alkali wastes

### Problems

Alkali wastes from the manufacture of soda ash (sodium carbonate) contain large amounts of calcium hydroxide or free lime, resulting in pH values of around 12.7. High concentrations of soluble salts such as sodium sulphate are also present.

Most alkali tips are of considerable age, particularly the Leblanc tips, which were dumped about 100 years ago. Rainfall has gradually washed out the salts and

alkalinity from the surface, leaving a light-textured material with a high calcium carbonate content.

### Ecological survey

Many of the remaining alkali waste tips support a very unusual and species-rich flora of lime-loving plants. One site near Bolton in Lancashire, recently scheduled as a Site of Special Scientific Interest, is noted for its huge colonies of fragrant orchids and several species of marsh orchid. Other plants of importance are blue fleabane, purging flax, centaury, carline thistle and blue-eyed grass. The flora resembles that of a calcareous dune slack or species-rich limestone vegetation. There are important lime beds in Cheshire too, from the Solvay or ammonia soda process which replaced the Leblanc process.

All alkali waste sites should be carefully surveyed, because of their likely ecological value. The same applies to other types of lime waste, such as lime-kiln residues, limestone tailings, calcareous sands and gas lime tips.

### Soil analysis

Site materials suspected to be alkali or lime wastes should be investigated by measuring pH and calcium carbonate content (per cent) as described for colliery spoil. Any material with a pH over 7.0 and a calcium carbonate content of over 20 per cent or so is likely to be lime waste. Samples should be taken at 5–10 cm depth and at 1–2 m depth, since only deep samples will reveal the nature of the majority of the waste, which is often strongly alkaline and toxic if brought to the surface.

### Reclamation and conservation

Alkali wastes can be used as liming agents for treating acidic colliery spoil if conveniently located in coalfield areas. However, most sites should be left undisturbed because of their wildlife conservation value and potential. If regrading has to be done, the redistributed waste should be allowed to weather and colonize naturally. Vegetation establishment can be speeded up by applying about 5 cm of organic material, such as peat or sewage sludge, followed by seeding with red fescue and lime-tolerant wildflower seed mixtures.

Tips with a sparse vegetation can be made attractive and colourful by planting wildflower seed mixtures suitable for calcareous grasslands. Wildflowers which have been shown to spread rapidly include kidney vetch, yellow wort, yellow rattle, wild thyme, ox-eye daisy and salad burnet. It may be necessary to apply a little fertilizer, such as NPK 17:17:17 at no more than 250 kilograms per hectare. This should raise the fertility sufficiently to improve the growth of colourful flowers without destroying the species richness of the flora. Thereafter fertilizer should not be applied, otherwise dense grass growth will swamp the attractive wildflowers.

PLATE 10.7 **A chemical waste tip. The dark areas are iron pyrite, which is producing run-off containing sulphuric acid.**

PLATE 10.8 **The sulphuric acid run-off from chemical waste. The acid run-off killed the grass adjacent to the site. The release of acid from pyrite depends on its reaction with oxygen. Covering the pyrite with about 2 m of soil or subsoil would have stopped the acid production.**

# Chemical wastes, gas-works waste and contaminated land

## Problems

Sites contaminated by chemical wastes, gas-works residues and soluble industrial materials pose the greatest planting problems. Examples are chromate smelter waste, which contains high levels of toxic chromates, and gas-works waste, which contains sulphuric acid and complex cyanides. Often pH values as high as 12.7 occur in chromate waste, whereas gas-works spent oxide is intensely acidic, with pH values as low as 0.6. Other common contaminants of industrial land are toxic metals, soluble salts, phenols and oils.

## Ecological survey

Land contaminated by the type of chemical described above is usually barren. Adjacent areas may be affected by the pollution, wetlands being particularly vulnerable. However, reedbeds often absorb pollutants: it has been found that reed (*Phragmites*) and branched bur-reed (*Sparganium*) can absorb large quantities of acid, iron salts and complex cyanides released from gas-works waste. Such vegetation should be carefully protected and used for pollution control.

## Soil analysis

Comprehensive chemical analysis of site materials is essential to identify hazardous substances as well as those toxic to vegetation. Historical records of site usage and tipping may give important leads as to the nature and location of contaminants. A comprehensive trial pit and borehole survey should be undertaken, and the samples analysed for all possible toxic metals, soluble salts, acids, alkalis, phenols, oils and other suspected organic substances.

## Establishment of vegetation

For heavily contaminated sites, suitable soil cover material is essential, so that the roots of plants are isolated from the underlying toxins. For grassland the cover should be at least 20–30 cm thick, and for trees up to 2 m is advisable.

In some situations a capillary break should be constructed to prevent soluble contaminants from rising to the surface in dry weather. Granular materials, such as coarse gravel or demolition rubble, provide good capillary breaks. They should be covered with a layer of soil or other growing medium. Alternatively, a primary cover of clay can be spread to create an impermeable layer over which topsoil or subsoil is spread, as is done in refuse tip or landfill site restoration. Capillary breaks should be up to 50 cm thick, depending on the nature and extent of site contamination. The secondary cover or growing medium should provide a rooting depth of 30 cm or more, depending on the type of vegetation to be planted.

## After-management

Site monitoring by inspection and soil analysis is recommended, because local seepages and unforeseen contamination can easily occur after treatment. Lateral seepage of contaminated water can occur after heavy rainfall, especially on sloping ground. Exact water table changes within reclaimed sites can be very difficult to predict, leading to uncertainties about the mobility and behaviour of contaminants. Further drainage work and treatment of locally contaminated surface areas may be necessary to prevent the local water table from rising too high.

# Quarries, pits and their spoil heaps

## Problems and opportunities

Hard rock quarries, clay pits, sand and gravel workings and their associated spoil heaps do not pose chemical toxicity problems to replanting. Because environments similar to them occur naturally, many plants are well adapted to these sites, and will either colonize them or can be planted easily.

Having said this, natural rock or overburden acidity, low fertility and physical factors such as bare rock or unstable mineral particles can restrict plant growth in quarry workings. However, many sites are extremely conducive to plant colonization, particularly where there is a stable, damp and base-rich mineral substrate, good moisture retention, shelter and freedom from disturbance.

## Hard rock quarries

Abandoned limestone quarries and chalk pits can be colonized naturally in species-rich grasslands, scrub and woodland in their dry parts. Wet areas will be readily colonized by rich aquatic plant communities, reedbeds, marsh and damp grassland. Numerous limestone and chalk workings have become wilderness areas of great natural beauty, some being protected as nature reserves and SSSIs. They can be habitats for rare and unusual plants such as bee orchid, fly orchid, dark red helleborine and man orchid. The diverse vegetation attracts an abundance of insect and invertebrate life.

Gritstone, sandstone and slate quarries are colonized slowly because of their acidic conditions, which favour heath and acidic grassland plants. Nevertheless, many old quarries have a complete cover of heather and moorland species as well as bog and marsh plants where drainage is impeded. In the absence of grazing, scrub and birch or oak woodland can develop.

## Clay pits, sand and gravel workings

Clay pits are the most favoured mineral extraction sites for natural colonization. They contain open water with various types of aquatic vegetation, reedbeds, marsh, willow carr and damp grassland. Damp, base-rich clay substrates are ideal for the establishment of species-rich communities of marsh and damp grassland plants.

Where acidic clays and sands occur, acid grassland and heath can develop. The varied topographies of clay pits, with their wide range of physical and chemical soil conditions, provide opportunities for a wide range of vegetation types and wild plant species to establish themselves.

### Conservation, reclamation and planting

Reclamation and planting are unnecessary where attractive natural colonization has already occurred. Nevertheless, active management should be planned because natural successional changes can destroy the richness of species and wildlife diversity. Woodland and scrub invasion should be controlled to protect heath, grassland and marsh. Wetlands should be maintained by clearing excessive reedbed development. Invasive plants, such as Himalayan balsam and bracken, should be checked or eliminated.

The reclamation of proposed, active and recently abandoned mineral workings should be planned very carefully. It is vital to leave the sites with a varied topography and with a wide range of suitable surfaces for planting different vegetation types and species, as is indicated in Table 10.5. It is no longer necessary to rely on natural colonization, which is slow and unpredictable. It is now possible to speed up vegetation establishment by fertilization, liming and other techniques, followed by the planting or seeding of wild species. The commercial availability of wildflower seed mixtures and transplants has given a new dimension to planting areas like these for wildlife and amenity. Herbaceous vegetation types can now be designed and planted almost as easily as woodland and scrub. A wide range of wildflower seed mixtures is being marketed, many of them specially designed for calcareous grasslands, acidic grasslands, marsh communities and many other types of environment.

## Urban sites

Major efforts are being made to reclaim urban wasteland sites. There is a strong movement to encourage wildlife into urban areas, by planting trees, shrubs and wild vegetation wherever possible. Urban wasteland and derelict sites present extremely good opportunities

PLATE 10.9 **An attractive parkland landscape established on a former refuse tip on the outskirts of London, at Willow Tree Lane Hillingdon.** (Landscape Architects: *Brian Clouston & Partners;* Photographer: *Peter Lake*)

to do this, and to try to speed up the revegetation of urban areas.

Urban clearance sites are the commonest and most obvious form of wasteland in towns and cities. These usually consist of brick rubble, concrete, stone, mortar, boiler ash and subsoil, where mills and slums have been demolished. The ground is nearly always infertile, owing to deficiencies of nitrogen and phosphate, but is rarely acidic or toxic. Most building rubble contains plenty of lime and calcium, so the pH is usually high, except where boiler ash, which tends to be slightly acidic, is present resulting in pH values around 4.0 or 5.0. A few sites pose serious toxicity problems where the ground has been contaminated by gas-works, chemical factories and oil spillage, but these problems are relatively uncommon.

Left to nature, cleared urban sites will be colonized by a wide range of weed species, such as rosebay willowherb, coltsfoot and common grasses such as Yorkshire fog. Colonization by clovers raises the nitrogen fertility, and eventually a coarse grass cover may develop. The next stage is scrub invasion, usually by willows, which can root into the consolidated ground. However, the whole process can be dramatically speeded up by applying fertilizer to increase the nitrogen and phosphate levels. The application of NPK 17:17:17 fertilizer, or anything similar, at about 500 kilograms per hectare is all that is usually necessary to establish a

PLATES 10.10 & 10.11 **The site of the Liverpool International Garden Festival before and after reclamation, showing the transformation of a previously derelict docklands site used for oil storage and rubbish dumping into a horticultural festival parkland.** (Landscape Architects for Landfill: *Brian Clouston & Partners*)

cover of red fescue and wild white clover or birdsfoot trefoil. A second addition of fertilizer may be needed to boost nitrogen fertility until nitrogen fixation by the clover occurs; thereafter the grass and clover should provide an attractive and self-sustaining cover until the land is redeveloped. If permanent vegetation is needed, the planting can be diversified by sowing wildflower seed mixtures into local areas of turf treated with herbicide. Trees and shrubs can be planted too, using a wide range of species, but especially pioneers such as willows, poplars, hawthorn, birch and alder.

Domestic and commercial refuse is often tipped in urban areas and blinded with clay or subsoil. In some cases the refuse emits methane and other gases which are toxic to plant roots. Anaerobic conditions can develop in the refuse and soil cover because of water-logging or gas emission. Where landfill gas is a problem, the waste should be capped with clay and vents provided to allow gas to seep into the air instead of throughout the soil cover layer. Planting methods similar to those used on urban clearance sites are applicable. Hawthorn is a good pioneer, but where anaerobic conditions occur species tolerant of waterlogging, such as willows, sallows, poplars, alder and birch, should be chosen. Numerous refuse tips have been colonized naturally to grassland, marsh, tall herbage, scrub and woodland, providing wilderness for wildlife in urban areas where such habitats are otherwise scarce. These

183

TABLE 10.5
**Methods of creating and improving habitats for different types of vegetation**

| Treatment | Habitats and vegetation types |
| --- | --- |
| Topographical variations: hollows, mounds, cliffs, ledges, rock piles etc. | Ponds, reedbeds, marsh, bog, damp grasslands, scrub and wet woodland in hollows and low-lying areas. Dry grassland, scrub, heath and woodland on dry areas. Cliff flora on rock faces and ledges |
| Placement of clay | Ponds, reedbeds and marsh. Acid clay and peat for bog, lime-rich clay and peat for fen |
| Placement of sand, gravel, subsoil or peat | Various species-rich grasslands and heath, the low fertility promoting a rich flora, preventing dense grassland and weed establishment |
| Placement of topsoil, silt and fertile materials | Dense grassland and tall herb vegetation, hay meadow and dense scrub or woodland |
| Lime application or lime wastes | Calcareous, species-rich grasslands, marsh, fen and calcicolous scrub |
| Damming and diversion of streams | Ponds, reedbeds, marsh, fen, willow carr, wet woodland and streamside habitats |
| NPK fertilization | Low fertility for species-rich grassland, high fertility for dense grass and tall herb cover, P and K for clover growth |
| Fencing to control grazing | Promotion of woodland, scrub, tall grassland |
| Grass cutting and grazing at selected times | Development of species-rich grassland, hay meadows |
| Coppicing, thinning and local felling | Woodland and scrub management, coppice with standards, woodland glades, control of invasive species |
| Desilting, dredging and reed clearance | Creation and maintenance of open water habitats |
| Introduction of plants by seeding, transplants, turf, litter and topsoil spreading | Creation of species-rich calcareous and neutral grasslands, acid grasslands, heath, marsh, reedbed, aquatic vegetation, scrub and woodland |
| Soil stripping over clay | Recolonization to damp, species-rich grassland and marsh |
| Herbicide application (selective and total) | Removal of undesirable plants such as bracken and invasive weeds, killing of grasses prior to seeding with wildflower seed mixtures |

habitats should be retained and managed positively, to improve their diversity and richness of species. The wildlife in such areas can often be enhanced by thinning of trees and shrubs, coppicing, interplanting with further species and seeding to wildflower mixtures.

Part of Liverpool's docklands were reclaimed for the Liverpool International Garden Festival. See Plates 10.10 and 10.11.

Other urban sites offering major reclamation and planting possibilities are disused railways, railway sidings, canals, reservoirs and mill ponds. Railway lines and canals often penetrate to the heart of towns and cities of all sizes, including the great conurbations. They provide important corridors for wildlife and footpaths if managed correctly.

Railway vegetation is often extremely diverse and species-rich. Lime-loving plants are often found on the calcareous ballast used for the track bed. Streams, pools, marshy areas and reedbeds are found in cuttings. A wide range of vegetation types occurs on the slopes of cuttings and embankments, notably different types of grassland, ericaceous heath, bracken, bramble patches, tall herb vegetation, thicket scrub and woodland. Also rock plants and ferns grow on rock faces and bridges. Unfortunately, however, disused railways suffer from a serious lack of management, which allows successional vegetation such as dense woodland; scrub and rank grassland to destroy the diversity of any previous wildlife habitat. Therefore reclamation and planting should seek to reduce woodland and tall shrub invasion by removal of sycamore, birch, goat willow and common sallow, especially along the trackway and lower slopes of cuttings. Low-growing thicket scrub of bramble, blackthorn, gorse, wild rose and holly should be actively promoted. The grasslands should be managed for species richness by cutting and liming, with seeding to wildflower mixtures wherever appropriate. Wetland vegetation and heath should be cleared of over-growing trees and shrubs so that lower levels of vegetation are not shaded out. The selective use of herbicides may be necessary to achieve these aims where the successional vegetation has reached an advanced stage. The general aim should be to maximize the habitat diversity. This should include tree and shrub planting of native species where woodland and scrub are absent or scarce.

Like the railways, many of the disused canals are losing much of their former wildlife interest. Great water-grass (*Glyceria maxima*) has completely choked extensive lengths of open water habitat. The only effective reclamation treatment is the dredging of a deep, central water channel, the clearance of much of the reedbed, and the development of a zoned, marginal vegetation. Ideally the central channel should be bordered by a zone of submerged vegetation rooted in deep water. The latter should be bordered by a zone of floating-leaved aquatic plants growing in water of medium depth. The canal sides should be edged with reeds or other emergent plants in places, but with plenty of bays left clear. Rupestral or stonework plants should be retained, but trees and shrubs should be removed. Natural colonization should be allowed to occur after dredging and reed clearance, but if this is slow, native aquatic plants can be reintroduced. Similar principles of reedbed clearance and aquatic habitat restoration are applicable to derelict reservoirs and mill ponds.

## FURTHER READING

Bornkamm, R., Lee, J. A. and Seaward, M. R. D. *Urban Ecology* (Oxford: Blackwell 1982)

Bradshaw, A. D. and Chadwick, M. J. *The Restoration of Land* (Oxford: Blackwell 1980)

Bradshaw, A. D., Goode, D. A. and Thorp, E. *Ecology and Design in Landscape* (Oxford: Blackwell 1986)

Chadwick, M. J. and Goodman, G. T. *The Ecology of Resource Degradation and Renewal* (Oxford: Blackwell 1975)

Gemmell, R. P. and Connell, R. K. 'Conservation and creation of wildlife habitats on industrial land in Greater Manchester', *Landscape Planning* **11**, pp.175–86 (1984)

Goodman, G. T. and Chadwick, M. J. *Environmental Management of Mineral Wastes* (The Netherlands: Sijthoff and Noordhoff 1978)

Hackett, B. *Landscape Reclamation Practice* (London: IPC Science and Technology 1978)

Hutnik, R. J. and Davis, G. *Ecology and Reclamation of Devastated Land* Vols. 1 and 2, (London: Gordon and Breach 1973)

Smith, M. A. *Contaminated Land – Reclamation and Treatment* (New York: Plenum Press 1985)

PLATE 10.12 **Land reclaimed for a golf course**. (Landscape Architects: *Brian Clouston & Partners*. Photograph: *Judy Snaith*)

CHAPTER 11

# The Landscaping of Reservoir Margins

## A. D. BRADSHAW AND C. J. GILL

## 11.1 INTRODUCTION

In a country such as Great Britain with one of the densest populations in the world, the wholesale use of land for storage of water causes serious problems, not only because of the destruction of agricultural land, but also because of loss of public amenities. The loss to the public has been realized, and now, in contrast to past practice, the public are being allowed extensive access to every new reservoir being built.

In fact reservoirs are of great amenity value. The public, once allowed access, will be able to view the whole reservoir at close range and will hope to find not only sporting and recreational facilities, but also considerable aesthetic enjoyment. It is here that the problem lies, for reservoir levels fluctuate more than those in natural lakes (Figure 11.1). The low water levels which usually occur in the summer when recreational use is at its peak, expose bleak margins which are open to a great deal of criticism (see Plate 11.1) Landscape architects have long been concerned about the best treatment for reservoir margins but a satisfactory solution has yet to be found.[1]

Where trees have been used as a landscape feature in the past, the margins have been scrupulously avoided and other vegetation has not been consciously planted (e.g. Treweryn, Clywedog, Derwent).

A general aim of landscape design is to create a harmonious landscape in sympathy with its surroundings. In a rural area the landscaping should be as natural as possible and plants should be used which resemble closely in layout and species those that can be found locally. The main characteristic of natural water bodies is the lack of a bleak margin because adapted vegetation has colonized down to the average water level. If the margins of new reservoirs could be similarly covered with plants, they would resemble natural margins much more closely and be much more acceptable.

To provide a natural groundcover for the margin, the first step is to find suitable flood-tolerant plant species. Then the ecological difficulties set by the habitat must be overcome, and the quality of the water must not be endangered.

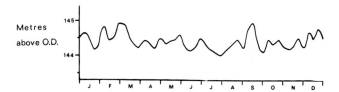

(a) ULLSWATER LEVELS (1966)—A NATURAL REGIME

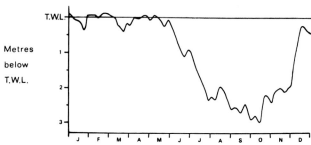

(b) VYRNWY LEVELS (1966)—A DIRECT SUPPLY REGIME

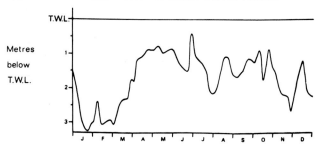

(c) TRYWERYN LEVELS (1966)—A REGULATORY REGIME

FIGURE 11.1 **Typical annual cycle in water level fluctuations in three water bodies.** *(C. J. Gill: Courtesy of a) North West Water Authority; b)c) Severn-Trent Water Authority)*

186

## 11.2 FLOOD-TOLERANT PLANTS

The different categories of plant material available are:

(a) annuals replacing themselves by seed every year;
(b) herbaceous perennials spreading vegetatively into the bare zone as it becomes exposed every year;
(c) herbaceous perennials permanently rooted in the margin able to tolerate submergence and exposure;
(d) floating vegetative mats which rise and fall with water level;
(e) perennial trees able to grow at and just below top water level with their bases in the water.

Annuals and vegetatively spreading perennials already grow in limited areas of the margins of most upland and lowland reservoirs.

Permanently rooted perennials are rarer, although there are good examples at Treweryn reservoir (Gwynedd), which was flooded in 1965. There small patches of pasture vegetation containing species such as *Ranunculus flammula* (spearwort) still become green and resume photosynthetic activity when unflooded. In the alluvial deltas of Lake Vyrnwy (Powys) and Thirlmere (Cumbria), permanently rooted species such as *Phalaris arundinacea* (reedgrass), *Equisetum*

*fluviatile* (water horsetail) and *Littorella uniflora* (shore-weed) thrive down to about 1, 1.5 and 2 m respectively below top water level.

The plant material of the first three groups is hardly of sufficient size to contribute much to the landscape. At best it will provide the reservoir with a green instead of a grey rim, which will not greatly alleviate the main aesthetic problem. In addition all three types of plant demand the presence of a hospitable soil surface relatively unexposed to erosion by waves. It may be possible to hasten what natural colonization will occur by introducing *Littorella*, *Ranunculus*, *Phalaris*, etc. on the appropriately sheltered margins of newly-filled reservoirs in which the species do not already exist.

Floating mats of vegetation are a common tropical phenomenon, but in existing natural and artificial areas of water in Britain they are almost completely absent because of the effects of wind, rather than total lack of appropriate species; this suggests that they are unlikely to succeed in Britain.

The common natural occurrence of trees on the margins of lakes and some reservoirs, and the success of tree planting for margin stabilization along Eastern European reservoirs, make the last category promising.[2] Trees are more likely to grow successfully and they provide a type of vegetation in scale with the landscape of a reservoir. Plate 11.2 shows by montage how groups

PLATE 11.1 **Natural colonization of drawdown zone at Lake Vyrnwy Reservoir.** *(C. J. Gill: Courtesy of Severn-Trent Water Authority)*

FIGURE 11.2 **Artist's impression of reservoir planting and recreation.** *(Andrew Donaldson)*

PLATE 11.2 **Montage demonstrating the visual effects of tree planting at and below TWL, at Treweryn (Llyn Celyn) Reservoir.** *(C. J. Gill: Courtesy of Welsh National Water Development Authority)*

of trees, judiciously planted, can break up the stark horizontal top water line and could greatly improve the appearance of the margin at times of drawdown. Trees have the added advantage that they are less likely to upset the quality of the water.

## 11.3 TREES

### Tree growth in flooded conditions

It is no use planting trees on margins unless the ecological problem is understood. The subject has been discussed thoroughly elsewhere,[3] but the key points are:

(i) Tree growth in waterlogged conditions is dependent on satisfactory root growth.

(ii) Oxygen is necessary for root growth, for aerobic root respiration. In a soil at or below field capacity, sufficient oxygen can diffuse from the soil atmosphere to permit tree growth. Moisture levels above field capacity, as in a waterlogged of submerged soil, affect tree growth adversely by retarding oxygen diffusion.

(iii) The amount of oxygen that can diffuse into a root in submerged soil is increased in soils of large particle size, and by well aerated water, i.e. where the water is shallow or moving.

(iv) Because root growth is greater in spring and summer than in winter, respiration rates and therefore oxygen needs are also greater in spring and summer. Spring and summer flooding is thus more prohibitive to tree growth than winter flooding, not only because of heavier oxygen demand, but also because of a relative oxygen shortage owing to high microbial respiration rates and to lack of wind-mixing.

(v) Most tree species can survive short periods of flooding, especially in winter. Adapted species can withstand spring and summer flooding to a varying extent.

### Tolerance of different species

Although there are general responses to flooding, tree species differ markedly in flooding tolerance. Evidence is emerging that flood-tolerant species owe their success to an ability to produce new roots very rapidly from the upper, older parts of the root system, in response to mortality of the deeper roots.[4] Floor-intolerant species lack this ability and cannot quickly replace drowned roots. The new roots are usually confined to the top soil horizons which are better aerated, although only relatively so. These roots may also possess anatomical and/or metabolic adaptations enabling them to grow better in these conditions. (This behaviour has a bearing on the last part of this chapter.) To the landscape architect the important point is that certain species are much more tolerant of long periods of flooding than others. Table 11.1 has been compiled from various sources and indicates species which are likely to show considerable tolerance under British conditions. For further information more extensive lists are available.[5]

These tolerant species differ in the amount of flooding

189

## TABLE 11.1
### Some of the more flood-tolerant species

| Very tolerant | Tolerant |
|---|---|
| *Alnus glutinosa* (common alder) | *Betula pendula* (silver birch) |
| *Alnus incana* (grey alder) | *Cornus stolonifera* (red osier/dogwood) |
| *Populus* × *euramericana* – 'Robusta' 'Heidemij' 1–214, 'Serotina', 'Regenerata', 'Marilandica' (hybrid black poplars) | *Populus nigra* (black poplar) |
| | *Populus trichocarpa* (black cottonwood) |
| *Salix alba* (white willow) | *Salix caprea* (goat willow) |
| *Salix cinerea* (common sallow) | *Salix fragilis* (crack willow) |
| *\*Salix hookeri* (Hooker's willow) | *Salix phylicifolia* (tea-leaved willow) |
| *\*Salix lasiandra* (pacific willow) | *Salix purpurea* (purple osier) |
| *Salix triandra* (almond willow) | |
| *Salix viminalis* (common osier) | |
| *Taxodium distichum* (swamp cypress) | |

\* Recently introduced from Oregon and tested in the UK with some success.

they will stand, and those particularly tolerant are singled out. In general adapted trees can probably survive prolonged periods of partial inundation, provided that on average they are unflooded for at least 50% of the growing season.

## Natural tree growth on reservoir margins

Reservoirs and lakes differ in the amount of natural tree growth on their margins. In the Lake District and Wales some of the lakes and reservoirs which have been in existence for a long time have margins well colonized by trees (e.g. Ullswater, Windermere and Vyrnwy — *see* Plate 11.3). There are other reservoirs which are too young yet to have been colonized by trees. Some much older lakes and reservoirs still have

no trees growing on their margins, which are often harsh and strongly eroded. The reasons could be either that the environment is too extreme, or that suitable trees do not grow nearby. It may be that natural colonization is rendered difficult by local conditions, but not growth, so that if trees were established by artificial means, they would flourish.

## 11.4 ENVIRONMENTAL VARIABLES DETERMINING PLANT GROWTH

There are four environmental variables operative in the drawdown zone environment obviously capable of determining the presence or absence of vegetation and its type:

1. Water manipulation patterns
2. Exposure to wave action
3. Soil type
4. Grazing

If these four variables are compared between a number of reservoirs (some colonized, others not), the possibility of tree growth under certain circumstances can be assessed, and the way prepared for a biotechnical solution to the aesthetic problems of new reservoirs.

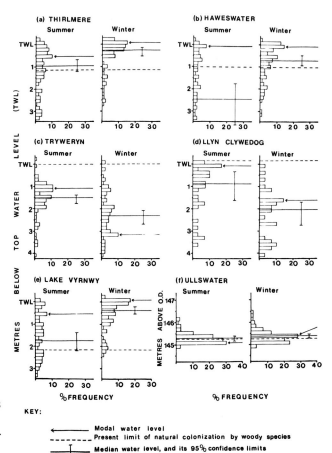

FIGURE 11.3 **Water level frequencies for five reservoirs and one natural lake.** *(C. J. Gill: Courtesy of a)b)f) North West Water Authority; c)d)e) Severn-Trent Water Authority)*

190

PLATE 11.3 **Summer drawdown in a quiet corner of the Elan Valley Reservoir.** *(C. J. Gill: Courtesy of Welsh Water Development Authority)*

## Water manipulation patterns

These are important because they determine the frequency, duration and extent of flooding to which margin vegetation is subjected. Weekly water levels over certain years for several reservoirs are plotted as histograms showing percentage frequency of different levels for (*a*) the six months May-October and (*b*) the six months November-April (*see* Figure 11.3). From an ecological standpoint this diversion is more meaningful than that of second and third quarters versus first and last quarters because the period May-October approximates more closely to the growing season of woody species. On the histograms are marked:

(i)   top water level (TWL) − dam level;
(ii)  the point estimate of the median water level, the average during the years studied. The zone above this level would, on average, be unflooded for 50% of the period;

(iii) the 95% confidence limits of the median indicative of the range of fluctuation;
(iv)  the modal water level, the most commonly prevailing level and therefore that at which wave action ought to have been most severe;
(v)   the lowest limit of natural growth of semi-mature or mature trees at present.

When predictions are being made for the future, allowance for change in variables such as management must be made.

In the reservoirs shown the main points to notice are that Thirlmere, Haweswater and Lake Vyrnwy were all supply reservoirs at the time of analysis and have a significantly lower median level in summer than in winter, whereas Tryweryn and Llyn Glywedog were both regulatory reservoirs operating with a system of retention levels which resulted in their winter median level being lower than the summer one. Lake Vyrnwy has the lowest and most widespread natural colon-

191

ization. Only Thirlmere has a summer median level significantly higher than that of Lake Vyrnwy, and this suggests that flooding itself is not prohibiting tree colonization in the other reservoirs (Haweswater, Tryweryn and Llyn Clywedog). It is interesting to compare the reservoir histograms with those for Ullswater (a natural lake at the time of analysis). The frequency distribution is approximately normal and tree colonization coincides with the median water level, which is the same in summer and winter.

Taken as a whole it is important to realize how far down the flooded margins trees can grow successfully. Observations on other lakes confirm this. The crucial point is that it is the summer median water level which is critical; in no case can tree growth be found much below this.[6]

## Exposure and wave action

The effect of this on plant life is most difficult to assess or predict. But wave action particularly can be more important than flooding in prohibiting colonization because it causes erosion and damage to plants.[7]

Changes in water level extend the zone subjected to erosion, the effects of which depend on the nature of the bank surface and its profile, the size of the waves, and the degree of exposure to them. These in turn are determined by the size and shape of the reservoir and its orientation and exposure in relation to the prevailing wind. In a natural lake where the level does not commonly fluctuate more than 2 m (6 ft), the effect of waves is to cut a terrace round the shore some 1−2 m below the mean water level. In terms of colonization this is extremely important because this terrace protects the shore above by causing waves to break, so that erosion is slowed down and something approaching equilibrium is gradually attained. Greater changes in levels disturb this quasi-equilibrium and cause renewed erosion in exposed areas.

Reservoir differ in their exposure. Vyrnwy and Clywedog are certainly less exposed than Thirlmere, Haweswater and Tryweryn. At Haweswater the steady erosion of the afforested bank above TWL on the north shore (trees notwithstanding) bears witness to the potency of this factor, but at the south-western end there are a few sheltered areas, where tree growth should be possible.

At Tryweryn the strong erratic winds which prevented the establishment of a sailing club have a large reach over the lake surface, and erosion can already be seen along most of the margin. Only time will show the extent and severity of wave action in this reservoir and in Clywedog, although it will certainly be less severe in the latter, whose narrow ramifying shape precludes any great reach of wind over water.

At Ullswater erosion has resulted in the formation of a very gently shelving terrace typical of natural lakes

and the equilibrium described above has been attained; this equilibrium has allowed vegetation to colonize strongly down to median water level despite the erosion.

Species differ in their tolerance to erosion as well as in their tolerance to flooding. There is little critical evidence but species which have been recorded as particularly satisfactory, usually because of their ramifying root system and ability to regenerate from exposed roots, are listed in Table 11.2

The effect of wind is not only to cause erosion by waves, but also to cause direct damage to plants themselves. In upland regions wind speeds are usually higher than in the lowlands, and may be further increased by the contours of the surrounding hills. It would be quite wrong to expect standard or half standard trees to survive even with staking. Even large bush trees will blow over or twist themselves off their roots. Planting material will usually have to be less than 60 cm tall.

At the same time such exposure may preclude the use of tall fast-growing material such as poplars or willows. In very exposed sites bush material such as the sallows (*Salix cinerea*, *S. caprea*), found naturally in very exposed habitats, may be the most satisfactory.

## Soil type

The first attribute of soil type is its physical structure, whether composed of clay, silt, sand or rock. This depends mainly on the original parental material but it also depends on the amount of soil erosion which removes the finer particles. Margins made of clays and silts usually indicate lack of erosion and therfore sites suitable for tree planting. However, the fine particle size of these soils restricts air movements especially when they are waterlogged, and drainage is slow, thus

TABLE 11.2

**Species noted for their relative resistance to wave action and undermining, grouped in order of decreasing resistance**

| | |
|---|---|
| *Salix acutifolia* | Most resistant |
| *Populus deltoides* | |
| *Populus trichocarpa* | |
| *Populus × euramericana* | |
| *Salix alba* | |
| *Salix cinerea* | |
| *Salix triandra* | |
| *Taxodium distichum* | |
| *Alnus glutinosa* | |
| *Salix caprea* | |
| *Cornus sanguinea* | |
| *Ulmus pumila* | |
| *Acer negundo* | least resistant |

PLATE 11.4 **General view of Llyn Briane Reservoir, Dyfed, Wales, showing tree planting close to the water's edge.** *(K. Stansfield)*

it is possible that trees will suffer from waterlogging more on these soils than on more freely draining coarser materials. The second attribute is pH (acidity) and nutrient status. Reservoir soils can be divided into those which are oligotrophic (lacking in nutrients and with a pH below 5), and those which are eutropic (with adequate nutrients and a pH above 5). Very few plants can grow in extremely oligotrophic conditions. Mostly upland reservoirs tend to be ligotrophic but it is unlikely that tree growth will be totally prevented by low soil nutrient status on any reservoir margin. But some species such as goat willow (*Salix caprea*), common sallow (*Salix cinerea*) and alder (*Alnus glutinosa*) are more tolerant of low nutrient conditions than others, such as willow (*Salix alba* and *S. fragilis*) and osier (*Salix viminalis*), and should be chosen for areas where soil analyses show poor conditions.

There is enormous variation in soil type from one part of any reservoir to another, due to geological accident and local drainage conditions. The consequences of this are particularly visible in lakes and old reservoirs in which there is good tree colonization, and a variety of species. In planting programmes on new margins different planting material may have to be chosen for different parts of the same reservoir. This necessity may have aesthetic virtues.

## Grazing

This is a factor which can drastically modify colonization patterns on reservoir margins, because sheep frequently have extensive access to them especially in upland regions. Rabbit grazing may also be important locally. Tree seedlings on the Vyrnwy margin are grazed by hares and occasionally by trespassing sheep but of the five reservoirs considered here, Vyrnwy undoubtedly suffers the lightest grazing. The presence of sallow saplings on the islands of Thirlmere and Haweswater in contrast to the barren margins indicates that grazing by sheep may well be a critical factor in these two reservoirs. On the other hand the lack of tree regeneration within fenced field plots at Tryweryn suggests that grazing is possibly not so important there. Its significance at Llyn Clywedog is difficult to assess, there being no islands or sheep enclosures in this reservoir.

## 11.5 PLANTING PRINCIPLES

From both the landscape and ecological viewpoints, trees seem to be the most promising vegetation to use to combat the aesthetic problem of reservoirs. So far as flooding is concerned there are native species available which are sufficiently tolerant to be planted successfully

193

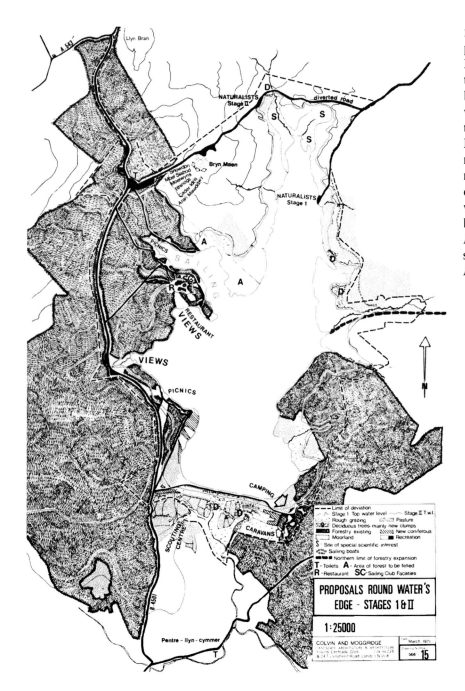

FIGURE 11.4 **Plan showing proposed margin development at Brenig Reservoir. Heavy afforestation of surrounding hills and broken contours forming the rim were expected to help to alleviate the problems of exposed shoreline. It was hoped that extensive exposed marshy and peaty land in the north of the lake would regenerate quickly as the water receded, and would prove to be attractive to birds.** *(Welsh National Water Development Authority.* Landscape Architects: *Colvin and Moggridge.)*

down to about 2 m below TWL in many reservoirs, the exact limit of growth depending on the regime. This would allow plantings which would substantially break up the drawdown effect since plantings of woodland could be brought right down to the water instead of stopping at just that point where the rim is emphasized and made even more artificial. See Plate 11.4.

One of the best examples of what can be achieved is provided by Lake Vyrnwy where natural colonization at the east end has completely transformed the bare margin. A great deal of planting has been done in reservoir drawdown zones in the USSR, Rumania and Czechoslovakia and although the aim was margin stabilization rather than aesthetic improvement, we could learn much from the sophisticated techniques used there.

Wave action, especially when it interacts with pedo-geological factors to produce highly-eroded substrates, must be recognized as the most powerful factor in limiting the sites on which planting would be practicable. Although some species are relatively resistant to wave action and undermining, very exposed shores would be best avoided in all planting schemes.

The wave action operating in a particular site can be easily assessed by an inspection of the soil structure. Sometimes the interaction produces a thin layer of stones or small rocks on the shore surface which are too large or too firmly embedded to be moved and hurled by the waves against any trees present. This layer acts as a wave shock absorber and often overlies an ideal planting medium consisting of a stable clayey soil (as at Vyrnwy) or even a truncated brown earth (as at Thirlmere).

In all but the most exposed reservoirs there are large parts of the margin in which planting could be attempted with a reasonable chance of successful establishment, given protection from grazing influences. There are a few other problems, but attention must be paid to ecological factors such as soil nutrient status, exposure, etc. Successful long-term growth will depend on finding trees whose ecological requirements are best suited or most adaptable to the environment in which they are to be planted.

## 11.6 PRE-PLANTING OF NEW RESERVOIRS

If the Water Authority gives careful consideration to planting the margins of new reservoirs at the design stage, rather than later in the process, the site can be pre-planted. There is every likelihood that the scheme will be more successful as a result since observation of mature trees under flood indicates that pre-planting of the future shore-lines as soon as the TWL can be predicted gives a better chance of survival than later planting. There are several reasons for this:

(a) Flood damage increases with the proportion of the shoot flooded.[8] A pre-planted tree, when eventually flooded, will be relatively tall and a smaller proportion of the aerial parts will be inundated.

(b) The foliage will be well developed and better able to provide photosynthate for production of new surface roots when necessary.

(c) The larger root system, although vulnerable to flooding, can provide firm anchorage against wave action.

(d) From the landscape architect's view-point, pre-planting is also advantageous because the planting operation is unhindered by inundations, and because the trees will exert their visual and stabilizing effects immediately the reservoir is filled.

Selection of species suitable for preplanting is not difficult. The natural distribution of tree species is largely determined by the seed and seedling ecology of the species concerned. It is well known that a given species can be artificially established in sites which could not be colonized naturally by that species. For example, *Alnus glutinosa* grows naturally on wet sites because its seed is dispersed by water and will germinate only under conditions of a high watertable.[9] Once

established, although noted for its flood tolerance, it grows best in rather drier conditions and has been extensively used on well-drained motorway embankments in this country. Thus whilst it is unlikely that species noted for their flood tolerance will be found growing naturally on the upper slopes of a valley scheduled for reservoir construction, there is no reason why such trees should not be planted on the future shore-line long before the reservoir is filled.

## Evaluation of margins before planting

When developing the landscape plan for a new reservoir, the architect and engineer between them usually have no difficulty in identifying those parts of the margin likely to present aesthetic or erosion difficulties which might benefit from planting. The ecologist can help to evaluate the suitability of these areas for planting.

### a) *Horizontal limits*
Soil type and profile must be inspected carefully. Areas covered with deep peat should be avoided because although various species can grow successfully on drained peat, the same peat when flooded is often a poor substrate for tree growth owing to toxicity factors or to unavailability of mineral nutrients.

The profile of lighter mineral soils can become drastically changed under the influence of wave action. The smaller particles tend to be exported and the larger particles and pieces of parent material are left overlying the lower horizons of the truncated profile. When these soils occur in areas likely to be exposed to wave action, some erosion can be anticipated. But such soils are well-suited to planting and may gradually become stabilized against moderate wave action. It must be emphasized that erosion caused by large waves (more than 1 m observed on some reservoirs) cannot be combated by tree planting. The power of wave action will be determined by the prevailing winds and the reach of wind over water.

Heavy clay soils, common on many reservoir sites, are also well-suited to planting and are less susceptible to erosion after reservoir filling.

### b) *Vertical limits*
How is one to determine the contour down to which planting is likely to be successful? The significance of flooding in the growing season has already been stressed. If one can characterize the average growing season at the reservoir site, and if one can predict the average annual pattern of drawdown, it is possible to determine the lowest contour which will, on average, be unflooded for at least 50% of the growing season. This contour is termed the 'summer median water level'.

This exercise was carried out for the Brenig Reservoir in Clwyd and for the Rutland Walter pumped storage scheme in what was formerly Rutland, now Leicestershire. These are worth considering in detail.

*Brenig reservoir* (Figure 11.4)

Vegetation in Britain generally begins to grow when the daily mean air temperature exceeds 4.4°C (40°F). The mean daily range between minimum and maximum air temperature is 8.8°C and cambial activity can therefore be assumed to begin when the daily minimum air temperature exceeds 0°C (32°F).[10] The cessation of growth is dependent on several factors but cambial activity is generally assumed to have ceased by 1 October.

The nearest meteorological recording station to Brenig was at the Alwen Reservoir, where a study of five years of temperature records, corrected for the difference in altitude, showed that at Brenig the start of the growing season varied between 18 March and 22 April. Drawdown patterns that would have occurred during the years 1959–69, had Brenig then been operating in accordance with the 'optimum' working rules, were analysed. These analyses were combined to show the proportion of the growing season for which the roots of trees, growing at a range of levels below TWL, would have been inundated on average over the 1959–69 period (Table 11.3). Two lengths of growing season have been considered, a 'long' one from 18 March to 1 October, and a 'short' one from 22 April to 1 October. From Table 11.3, it appeared that the vertical limit for pre-planting lies between 0.7 m and 1.0 m below TWL depending on the date adopted as the start of the growing season. In the case of Brenig, this rather shallow limit was not surprising because

TABLE 11.3

**Amounts of inundation experienced by different contours below TWL at Brenig 1959–69**

| Level (m below TWL) | Long growing seasons (2 167 days) | | Short growing season (1 782 days) | |
|---|---|---|---|---|
| | No. of days of inundation | % inundation | No. of days of inundation | % inundation |
| 0 | 0 | 0 | 0 | 0 |
| 0.2 | 503 | 23.2 | 294 | 16.5 |
| 0.4 | 608 | 28.1 | 358 | 20.1 |
| 0.6 | 860 | 39.7 | 558 | 31.3 |
| 0.8 | 1 122 | 51.8 | 753 | 42.3 |
| 1.0 | 1 322 | 61.0 | 937 | 52.6 |
| 1.2 | 1 488 | 68.7 | 1 103 | 61.9 |
| 1.4 | 1 680 | 77.8 | 1 301 | 73.0 |
| 1.6 | 1 820 | 84.0 | 1 435 | 80.5 |
| 1.8 | 1 942 | 89.6 | 1 557 | 87.4 |
| 2.0 | 2 005 | 92.5 | 1 620 | 90.9 |

proposed summer retention level was coincident with TWL and because the role of the reservoir in the regulation of the Dee was to provide water for substantial use only in reinforcing the releases from storage elsewhere in the system during severe droughts.

*Rutland Water pumped storage scheme*

The success of the method is dependent on reasonably accurate prediction of the drawdown patterns of the future reservoir. This may be particularly complicated for pumped storage schemes, when rates of filling and of emptying are governed by a complicated and interacting set of factors. Even if the patterns can be predicted, levels in the first few years after filling may tend to be very high, with obvious complications for trees pre-planted to levels based on the expected drawdowns of subsequent years.

The margins of the Rutland Water pumped storage scheme were pre-planted with appropriate tree species, but the limit of 1·2 m below TWL represented a compromise between the drawdowns eventually anticipated and the sustained high water levels initially expected. In this case, the trees had four years to establish before being flooded and some of them were mound-planted to aid survival in the first years of flooding. Another treatment tested, albeit only on a field-plot scale, was the use of a mulch designed to encourage the development of a strong lateral root system despite the initial free drainage.

Plates 11.5–11.7 show aspects of this exercise at two points in time. In the event, mulching proved to be highly important to the survival of almost all species during the summers prior to reservoir filling. Once flooding commenced, the herbaceous sward quickly died, but the preplanted species of *alnus*, *salix* and *populus* showed good survival and growth at and below TWL during the years of monitoring.

## 11.7 CONCLUSION

Landscape architects have always been pioneers coping with novel situations. The richness of tree growth in city parks and country estates is witness to their tenacity and success in testing new species. Reservoirs are a very real problem which can benefit from their skills and energy, and this chapter has set out some guidelines for tackling one aspect of design that has traditionally caused difficulties.

### ACKNOWLEDGEMENTS

This work was supported by grants from the Natural Environment Research Council and the Water Resources Board. Water level data and photographs are used by kind permission of the City of Birmingham Water Department, Liverpool Corporation Waterworks, Manchester Corporation Waterworks, the

PLATE 11.5 **Mowing and mulching at the Rutland Water site two years before flooding. Mulched plots are to the left and one of the two unmulched plots is to the right.** *(C. J. Gill)*

PLATE 11.6 **The Rutland Water trial planting two years after reservoir filling. The water level was 0.5 m below TWL when this photograph was taken.** *(C. J. Gill)*

PLATE 11.7 **Detail of inundated trees at Rutland Water, two years after reservoir filling.** *(C. J. Gill)*

Clywedog Reservoir Joint Authority, the Cumberland River Authority, the Dee and Clwyd River Authority and the Welland and Nene River Authority. The authors are grateful to Mr. A. Tollitt for the plates.

REFERENCES

1. Gibberd, F. 'Landscape of Reservoirs', *J. Inst. W. Eng.*, 15, 88 (1961)
2. Gill, C. J. 'The Flooding Tolerance of Woody Species – a review', *Forestry Abstracts*, 31 (4), 671 (1970)
3. Op. cit.
4. Braun, H. J. 'The growth of poplars under conditions of an alternating or constant high water table'. *Allg. Forst-u Jagdztg.*, 114, 89 (1973)
5. Gill, op. cit.
6. Hall, T. F. and Smith, G. E. 'Effects of flooding on woody plants, West Sandy dewatering project, Kentucky reservoir', *J. For.*, 53 (4), 281 (1955)
7. Gill, C. J. 'Studies of radial stem growth in *Salix cinerea* L., on a reservoir margin'. *J. Appl. Ecol.*, 1974, 11 (1), 215 (1974)
8. Gill, op. cit. 1970
9. McVean, D. N. 'Ecology of *Alnus glutinosa*: II, Seed distribution and germination', *J. Ecol.*, 43, 61 1955 and McVean, D. N. 'Ecology of *Alnus glutinosa*: III Seedling establishment', *J. Ecol.*, 44, 195 (1956)
10. Manley, C. *Climate and the British Scene* (London: Collins 1952)

A paper on the same subject by the authors of this article appeared in the *Journal of the Institute of Water Engineers*, 1971, Vol. 25, No. 3, p. 165 entitled 'Some aspects of the colonization of upland reservoir margins'.

# Plants and Air Pollution

## DR J. L. INNES

The author would like to acknowledge his debt to Dr P. J. W. Saunders and C. M. Wood, the authors of this chapter in the first edition of *Landscape Design with Plants*. Their writing provided the basis for this new and updated chapter.

## 12.1 INTRODUCTION

Air pollution may be defined as the disposal by man of any waste matter or energy into the atmosphere which produces adverse effects upon the environment. This chapter describes the adverse effects of pollution upon plants and the ways in which planning and appropriate planting can reduce the impacts of air pollution.

## 12.2 SIGNIFICANCE OF AIR POLLUTION IN PLANTING SUCCESS

Air pollution is only one of a number of factors affecting the success of planting schemes and, in the majority of situations, it is relatively insignificant. Other problems, such as compacted and contaminated soils, are likely to be much more significant, especially when planting on derelict industrial sites and spoil tips. In severe cases it may be necessary to recontour the land and to install land drains to improve the site, and to import clean topsoil to overcome toxicity problems. Most schemes call for the application of organic material (for instance, peat, sewage sludge and manure) and fertilizer (by broadcast spraying, for example) or specific techniques, such as bedding for tree roots. Ameliorants may also be added to counter specific problems. The use of extra lime to neutralize high acidity is an example of this.

All of the factors mentioned above interact to produce growing conditions unique to each site, and careful site preparation and species selection are therefore essential to reduce any difficulties of establishment. Planning to limit the effects of air pollution is most important on sites close to busy roadways, older high density housing, urban commercial centres and various heavy industries,

and generally in areas where the local topography promotes the concentration of atmospheric pollutants.

## 12.3 TRENDS IN POLLUTION AND PLANTING

Monitoring of air pollution is essential to discover local levels of the various pollutants. In Britain most monitoring is conducted by the Warren Spring Laboratory (part of the Department of Trade and Industry). The co-ordination and planning of routine monitoring programmes are the responsibility of the Air and Noise Division of the Department of the Environment, which collates, interprets and publishes the results of air-pollution monitoring in the UK. Results are published annually in the *Digest of Environmental Protection and Water Statistics,* available from HMSO.

Despite the popular belief that pollution is getting worse, the available information indicates that trends vary greatly between individual pollutants. In general, acute local pollution has become very rare, whereas widespread low-level pollution has been increasingly recognized as a problem.

Reductions in pollution have occurred as a result of both active and passive measures. In the latter case, the general decline of heavy industry in the UK over the last twenty years has resulted in lower emissions of certain pollutants. However, much of the reduction can be attributed to specific, active moves to reduce air pollution. These have been undertaken both within the UK (for instance the Clean Air Acts) and as part of international legislation. For example, the European Community (EC) issued a directive in July 1980 setting sulphur dioxide and smoke standards. The limits are shown in Table 12.1. The guidelines recommended by

PLATE 12.1 *Tulipa gesnerana*. **Tulips are in general susceptible to damage by air pollutants, particularly fluorides. The photograph shows necrosis (tip burn) at the leaf tips and margins. This is a characteristic symptom of acute fluoride damage.** *(Courtesy of Rothamsted Experimental Station, Harpenden, Herts)*

the EC fall well below these maximum permitted values. Values in the UK are normally well within the limits set by the EC, with exceptions being largely restricted to the immediate vicinities of known point sources. Values for specific areas can be obtained from the annual reports entitled *UK Smoke and Sulphur Dioxide Monitoring Networks*, published by the Warren Spring Laboratory.

TABLE 12.1
**Limits set by EC for smoke and sulphur dioxide ($\mu g/m^3$)**

| Reference period | Smoke | Sulphur dioxide |
|---|---|---|
| Year (median of daily values) | 68 | If smoke < 34 : 120<br>If smoke > 34 :  80 |
| Winter (median of daily values October−March) | 111 | If smoke < 51 : 180<br>If smoke > 51 : 130 |
| Year (peak) (98 percentile of daily values) | 213 | If smoke < 128 : 350<br>If smoke > 128 : 250 |

In Britain, concentrations of smoke and sulphur dioxide in the atmosphere have been decreasing, and this trend is expected to continue. For example, average ground level concentrations of sulphur dioxide in urban areas have fallen by about 76 per cent since 1960. The content of sulphate in rainfall is expected to decrease as a result of reduced sulphur emissions, and evidence for a decrease in the frequency of particularly acidic rainfall is available from Pitlochry in Scotland. Trends in dust, grit and industrial pollutants (for instance, fluorides and metals) are generally uncertain, although emissions of lead from petrol-engined vehicles are known to be decreasing (25 per cent reduction between 1973 and 1985), and this trend should accelerate as a result of the introduction of lead-free petrol. Levels of zinc, arsenic, selenium and vanadium are also known to be decreasing.

Gaseous emissions from motor vehicles are increasing, thus raising local concentrations of ozone, oxides of nitrogen, peroxyacetyl nitrate and so on. The trend in ozone concentrations is uncertain, although it is generally believed to be increasing, and this is certainly the case for its precursors, hydrocarbons. As ozone requires sunlight to form, its concentration is strongly controlled by the weather. In the UK problems from ozone are most likely to occur in the south-east.

## 12.4 PLANTS AND ACID RAIN

Recently there has been great concern that acid rain could be affecting plant health. Acid rain occurs largely as the result of the burning of fossil fuels, and a variety of definitions of acid rain exist, although usually it is taken to be any rainfall that is more acidic than about pH 5.0 (distilled water at 20°C and in equilibrium with atmospheric carbon dioxide has a pH of 5.6). Its two most important anthropogenic components are sulphuric acid and nitric acid. In the UK these are normally in the proportion of 2:1, although as sulphate concentrations are decreasing and nitrate concentrations are stable or increasing, this ratio may well change over time. Direct effects of acid rain on water bodies and building materials have been observed, but the effects on plants are much less certain.

Although many experiments have been conducted, most of these used much more acidic solutions than are normally encountered in reality. There is considerable difficulty in interpreting the results of such studies, as the responses of plants to acid rain are often non-linear, so results from these studies cannot be extrapolated to plants grown under normal conditions.

In the present context, the most important aspect of the debate is the possible effects of acid rain on trees. A widespread and severe forest decline has been identified at a number of sites in Central Europe, and there are fears that the decline could be present over much wider areas of Europe than have been observed. There is no doubt that tree mortality has occurred, although in most cases the causes remain uncertain. Surveys have been undertaken in most European countries, and all of them have revealed results that point to possible damage as a result of acid rain. However, the surveys use non-specific symptoms (crown thinness and discolouration), and it is not possible to determine from the survey data alone the extent of damage by pollution.

In Eastern Europe and some of the eastern-most parts of West Germany the decline in trees is associated with very high levels of sulphur dioxide. The concentrations that occur at a regional level are similar to those that were once encountered in urban areas in the UK. In the Netherlands the damage has been linked to very high environmental levels of ammonia, which are thought to interfere with the trees' metabolism. Elsewhere the situation is much more uncertain. Most scientists believe that air pollution is in some way the cause, but the mechanisms have yet to be determined. Most theories revolve around the interaction of pollution with other stress factors. One particularly favoured hypothesis is that ozone, acid rain and frost interact on nutrient-poor soils, resulting in reduced vigour and the development of nutrient deficiencies, eventually leading to death.

Within the UK the levels of acidity that are normally encountered in rainfall are insufficient to cause direct damage to most plants. Research has indicated that a pH of < 3.0 for conifers and 3.0–3.3 for broadleaved trees is required to induce visible damage. While precipitation at this level of acidity has been encountered, it has not been of sufficient duration to induce damage. It is more likely that any adverse effects of acid rain occur indirectly through the soil or as a result of interactions with gaseous pollutants.

Surveys of tree health in the UK have been undertaken by the Forestry Commission since 1984, and although thin crowns appear to be widespread, there is no indication that pollution is the reason. On the other hand, it is impossible to rule out pollution, because of the many interactions that are known to occur between pollution and other stresses that have adverse effects on plants.

PLATE 12.2 *Gladiolus* or 'Snow Princess'. Like the tulip in Plate 12.1, necrosis has occurred initially at the tip of the leaves, presumably as a result of prolonged exposure to air pollutants, probably sulphur dioxide and/or fluorides.

PLATE 12.3 **Damaged Norway spruce and beech forest in the Ore Mountains of Czechoslovakia. The Norway spruce are mostly dead, whereas the beech have survived to date. Damage can be attributed to very high sulphur dioxide levels.** *(J. Innes)*

PLATE 12.4 **Tall trees adjacent to an industrial site in North Lancashire appear to have been affected by air pollutants (mainly sulphur dioxide, nitrogen dioxide and ammonia). Close to the points of emission, shorter trees and hedgerows are less affected, probably because the concentrations of pollutants are lower, near ground level.** *(K. Oates; Reproduced courtesy of Department of Biological Sciences, University of Lancaster)*

## 12.5 EFFECTS OF POLLUTION ON PLANTS

The symptoms of damage to plants due to pollution vary greatly. Factors that influence how the plants are affected include the following:

(i)   The species or cultivar exposed.
(ii)  The pollutant and the conditions of exposure.
(iii) The health and maturity of the plant.
(iv)  Other environmental stresses, such as temperature, soil moisture and level of competition.

It must also be remembered that plants are exposed to a whole range of pollutants and that air pollution often coincides with and contributes to other forms of pollution (such as soil contamination). This is especially true in industrial areas, where plants may be exposed to the whole range of anthropogenic stresses. As in the surveys of forest health, it is very difficult to discriminate between the direct and indirect effects of pollution and the diverse effects of natural disease, nutrient deficiency and abiotic damage (for instance, the result of frost or wind) on amenity plants.

For convenience, the effects of air pollution can be described in relation to three general types of exposure:

1. Acute exposure to high levels of pollution over relatively short periods of time (for instance, 750 µg of sulphur dioxide per $m^3$ of air for 6 to 24 hours) results in marginal and tip necrosis of leaves and causes new shoots to die back. The affected leaves will change colour according to the pollutant they are exposed to, but often they will be bleached white and may also be blackened with soot and grime. These high concentrations are no longer encountered in the UK.

2. Chronic exposure to lower levels of pollution over relatively longer periods of time (e.g. 300–600 µg $SO_2/m^3$ for several days) results in vague marginal and interveinal chlorosis (yellowing) of leaves which may be associated with early leaf fall and advanced senescence. Concentrations at this level are now rare within the UK.

3. Invisible injury due to exposure to low concentrations of pollutants over long periods of time (for instance, <100 µg $SO_2/m^3$ for many weeks or months) is probably more typical of general UK conditions in urban areas. (Annual concentrations of $SO_2$ in the mid-1980s have generally been less than 20 µg $m^{-3}$.) The effect of these levels of pollutant can be more insidious, because the injury is not visible. Advanced senescence and leaf fall may occur, together with reductions in growth. Inert dusts can produce the same results by blocking stomata and reducing the amount of light available to the leaf for photosynthesis. Modifications of soil conditions by pollutants can also

reduce growth rates. Invisible injury is not usually of immediate concern to the landscape architect attempting to revegetate severely polluted areas. However, its long-term consequences should be considered, because they can be ameliorated by proper selection of species and good soil conditions.

The total effect of pollution is rarely confined to one of the three categories described above. In practice, plants may be exposed to fluctuating levels of pollution, thus suffering two or more types of exposure over the growing seasons or years. Wide variations in exposure conditions can occur with pollutants such as ozone over much shorter periods of time, e.g. hours or days. The total effect of pollution is thus rarely discrete but more a matter of degree and type of exposure. This is especially true of perennial herbs, shrubs and trees, which, when exposed to chronic long-term pollution, may develop slowly, with poor flowering and fruiting characteristics and early senescence. The addition of a pollution-related stress can have fatal results in environments where plants are already under stress.

Trees exhibit a range of responses to pollution. Stunted top growth may occur, and this is often compensated by the development of adventitious shoots from the stem base. Adventitious shoots may also develop on the upper surfaces of branches of conifers where needle loss has occurred. However, the presence of such shoots must not be taken as an indicator of pollution stress, as they can form as a result of many different factors.

Some responses to pollution may be determined at least partly by the structure of the plant community. Thus, poor top growth may occur in the upper, more exposed region of the canopy. This will screen out some pollution and so permit smaller and more sensitive plants to survive below. Contaminants caught in the upper foliage may be transported to the soil in droplets falling from leaves and in water flowing downwards over the stem during periods of rain and mist. Further changes in the chemical composition of the water may occur as a result of ion exchange between water on and within the leaves or needles. The result is that concentrations of some ions may be much greater in throughfall and stem flow than in free precipitation.

## 12.6 SENSITIVITY OF PLANTS

More precise information on the sensitivity of different plants to air pollution has been obtained by experimental fumigation and controlled observation in a variety of countries. Although efforts have been concentrated on species of economic importance, there is an increasing amount of information related to trees and shrubs used in amenity schemes. Tables 12.2, 12.3, 12.4 and 12.5 summarise the results of fumigation trials conducted mainly by the US Environmental Protection Agency by grouping plants into three arbitrary categories of sensitivity. It is emphasized that these lists are by no means comprehensive, and that other trees and shrubs not included may well be sensitive to these elements to some degree. The lists only cover plants and shrubs although similar lists for ornamental plants and for other pollutants are available in some of the publications listed in Further reading, for instance, Taylor *et al* (1987).

It must be emphasized that these lists provide only a general indication of a particular species' resistance to pollution. A large number of such lists exist and they often provide conflicting evidence. For example, European ash is considered by some to be sensitive to ozone and by others to be insensitive to it. In several of the tables the same species is listed as falling into more than one sensitivity category. This is because there are differences in the recorded sensitivities of some individual species. These can be attributed to the following factors:

(i) Variations in the levels and durations of exposure to pollution.
(ii) Variations in environmental conditions during exposure to pollution, particularly light intensity, temperature and soil moisture.
(iii) Genetic differences within genotypes or between cultivars in their resistance to pollution.
(iv) Variations in the stage of development of the plant at the time of the test.
(v) Variations in pre- and post-fumigation conditions.

As an example of how differences in environmental conditions can affect the influence of pollutants on plants, the average concentration of sulphur dioxide required to injure the leaves of a plant after 24-hour exposure can be halved under warm, moist conditions but more than doubled under dry, cold conditions. Wind speed is another critical factor; plants exposed to high winds suffer far more damage in polluted areas than do those growing in sheltered sites.

Although conifers and other evergreens are generally more sensitive to most air pollutants than are deciduous plants, the relative order of sensitivity of plants to sulphur dioxide is almost the reciprocal of that for fluorine and fluorides. More information about the relative sensitivities of cultivars to combinations of pollutants would be extremely useful to landscape designers. In particular, it would extend the range of options for planting around specific industrial sites. However, any information of this type must be used in conjunction with practical experience of planting in polluted environments.

It has been shown that air pollution can affect plant pathogens, including fungi and arthropod pests. This can be turned to the plant's advantage in cases where the pathogen or pest (for instance, blackspot of roses, maple leaf tar spot or certain aphids) is inhibited by pollution. In others, however, pollution may assist the establishment of pathogenic organisms by predisposing the plant to infection (for instance, mould fungi on damaged wood or certain mites), or by inhibiting competitive species which previously limited the activities of the pathogen.

These subtle effects of pollution are not of immediate interest to landscape designers, but the results of current research into such problems may eventually provide better techniques and guidelines for successful planting in polluted areas. Generally, there is insufficient data to specify the precise pollution limits or even the relative sensitivities of many indigenous and ornamental plants used in the UK. Local, specific problems still arise with less common pollutants around industrial sites (for instance, cement dust and ethylene). Busy roads appear to be creating new problems as the impact of sulphur dioxide and smoke declines. For instance, some plants are adversely affected by dust and fumes (e.g. *Potentilla* sp.) and by road salt sprays (e.g. beech, cherry and privet). Increasing attention is now being paid to the sensitivity of indigenous plants to ozone, peroxyacetyl nitrate, oxides of nitrogen, ethylene and dusts when landscaping roadways.

## 12.7 CONTROL OF POLLUTION IMPACT BY PLANNING AND PLANTING

It is not widely appreciated that local planning authorities can exercise considerable control over air pollution by determining the location and design of activities that cause pollution. They can also reduce the effects of air pollution by ensuring that sensitive receptors, including plants, are not located in areas where concentrations of pollutants are high. There are in fact a large number of techniques for controlling pollution available to planning authorities. For example, conditions may be attached to planning permission related to the development of both emitters and receptors to mitigate pollution damage.

Some authorities are recognizing the contribution of planning to pollution control in the preparation of their long-term plans, and there are signs that better use of planning powers in controlling development is being made. Furthermore, suitable planting and design techniques, such as contouring, can help to reduce the impact of pollution on the area surrounding each source. The landscape architect can thus assist local planning authorities and industry by stipulating landscaping schemes around industrial and residential sites that will help to ameliorate the level of air pollutants.

Open spaces planted with trees, shrubs and herbaceous species, especially grass, alter the local climate, and can thus alter the dispersion of pollutants. Grass

## TABLE 12.2
## Relative sensitivity of trees and shrubs to fluorides

| Sensitive | Intermediate | Least sensitive |
|---|---|---|
| *Abies alba* | *Abies balsamea* | *Ailanthus altissima* |
| *Acer negundo* | *Abies grandis* | *Alnus glutinosa* |
| *Berberis vulgaris* | *Acer campestre* | *Berberis thunbergii* |
| *Carpinus betulus* | *Acer platanoides* | *Betula nigra* |
| *Fraxinus excelsior* | *Acer rubrum* | *Betula papyrifera* |
| *Ginkgo biloba* | *Acer saccharinum* | *Betula pendula* |
| *Larix occidentalis* | *Acer saccharum* | *Chamaecyparis* sp. |
| *Picea* sp. | *Berberis julianae* | *Coffea arabica* |
| *Pinus contorta* | *Berberis verruculosa* | *Cornus florida* |
| *Pinus mugo* | *Buxus sempervirens* | *Cornus stolonifera* |
| *Pinus ponderosa* | *Citrus limon* | *Cotoneaster* sp. |
| *Pinus strobus* | *Citrus paradisi* | *Eleagnus angustifolia* |
| *Pinus sylvestris* | *Citrus reticulata* | *Eunonymus alatus* |
| *Pinus taeda* | *Citrus sinensis* | *Eunonymus fortunei radicans* |
| *Populus tremula* | *Crataegus monogyna* | *Fagus sylvatica* |
| *Prunus domestica* | *Forsythia* sp. | *Gleditsia triacanthos inermis* |
| *Pseudotsuga menziesii* | *Fraxinus pennsylvanica* | *Juniperus chinensis* − Pfitzerana |
| *Quercus robur* | *Ginkgo biloba* | *Juniperus communis* |
| *Syringa vulgaris* | *Juglans regia* | *Juniperus horizontalis* − Plumosa |
| *Vaccinium* sp. | *Larix* sp. | *Juniperus virginiana* |
| *Vitis vinifera* | *Lonicera periclymenum* | *Ligustrum* sp. |
| | *Morus* sp. | *Liquidambar styraciflua* |
| | *Picea pungens* | *Liriodendron tulipifera* |
| | *Pinus banksiana* | *Magnolia* sp. |
| | *Pinus monticola* | *Parthenocissus quinquefolia* |
| | *Pinus nigra* | *Picea engelmannii* |
| | *Populus tremuloides* | *Picea glauca* |
| | *Prunus avium* | *Picea mariana* |
| | *Prunus cerasifera* | *Picea nidiformis* |
| | *Prunus persica* | *Platanus acerifolia* |
| | *Prunus serrulata* | *Platanus occidentalis* |
| | *Prunus virginiana* | *Platanus hispanica* |
| | *Pyrus malus* | *Populus alba* |
| | *Rhododendron ponticum* | *Populus balsamifera* |
| | *Sorbus aucuparia* | *Populus canadensis* |
| | *Syringa vulgaris* | *Populus nigra* |
| | *Taxus baccata* | *Populus trichocarpa* |
| | *Tilia americana* | *Pyracantha* sp. |
| | *Tilia cordata* | *Prunus armeniaca* |
| | *Vitis babruscana* | *Pyrus communis* |
| | | *Quercus* sp. |
| | | *Ribes* sp. |
| | | *Robinia pseudoacacia* |
| | | *Rubus* sp. |
| | | *Salix babylonica* |
| | | *Salix caprea* |
| | | *Salix pentandra* |
| | | *Sambucus nigra* |
| | | *Symphoricarpos rivularis* |
| | | *Thuja plicata* |
| | | *Ulmus americana* |
| | | *Ulmus parvifolia* |
| | | *Ulmus pumila* |
| | | *Viburnum dentatum* |
| | | *Viburnum prunifolium* |

TABLE 12.3
**Relative sensitivity of trees and shrubs to ozone**

| Sensitive | Intermediate | Least sensitive |
| --- | --- | --- |
| Ailanthus altissima | Acer negundo | Abies balsamea |
| Amelanchier alnifolia | Calocedrus decurrens | Abies concolor |
| Cotoneaster divaricata | Cercis canadensis | Acer grandidentatum |
| Cotoneaster horizontalis | Forsythia intermedia spectabilis − | Acer platanoides |
| Fraxinus americana | Lynwood Gold | Acer rubrum |
| Fraxinus pennsylvanica | Larix leptolepis | Acer saccharum |
| Gleditsia triacanthos | Libocedrus decurrens | Betula pendula |
| Juglans nigra | Ligustrum vulgare | Buxus sempervirens |
| Juglans regia | Liquidambar styraciflua | Cornus florida |
| Larix decidua | Philadelphus coronarius | Cornus racemosa |
| Ligustrum vulgare var. pyramidale | Pinus attenuata | Euonymus alatus compactus |
| Liriodendron tulipifera | Pinus contorta | Fagus sylvatica |
| Pinus banksiana | Pinus echinata | Ilex aquifolium |
| Pinus coulteri | Pinus elliottii | Ilex crenata |
| Pinus jeffreyi | Pinus lambertiana | Ilex opaca |
| Pinus nigra | Pinus rigida | Juglans nigra |
| Pinus ponderosa | Pinus strobus | Juniperus occidentalis |
| Pinus radiata | Pinus sylvestris | Kalmia latifolia |
| Pinus taeda | Pinus torreyana | Ligustrum amurense |
| Pinus virginiana | Prunus armeniaca var. Chinese | Mahonia repens |
| Platanus occidentallis | Prunus avium var. Lambert | Nyssa sylvatica |
| Populus maximowiczii, | Quercus coccinea | Paxistima myrsinites |
| Populus trichocarpa | Quercus palustris | Persea americana |
| Populus tremulides | Quercus velutina | Picea abies |
| Prunus avium var. Bing | Rhododendron catawbiense album | Picea glauca |
| Quercus alba | Rhododendron nova zernbla | Picea glauca var. densata |
| Quercus gambelii | Rhododendron roseum elegans | Picea pungens |
| Rhododendron kaempferi | Ribes hudsonianum | Pieris japonica |
| Rhododendron kurume | Sambucus melanocarpa | Pinus monophylla |
| Rhododendron obtusum | Synphoricarpos vaccinioides | Pinus resinosa |
| Rhododendron poukhanensis | Syringa vulgaris | Pinus sabiniana |
| Rhus aromatica | Tsuga canadensis | Prunus aremeniaca |
| Sorbus aucuparia | Ulmus parviflora | Prunus persica |
| Spirea vanhoutii | Viburnum dilatatum | Pseudotsuga menzies |
| Symphoricarpos alba | Viburnum setigerum | Pyracantha coccinea − Laland |
| Syringa chinensis | | Pyrus communis |
| Vitis vinifera var. Concord | | Quercus imbricaria |
| | | Quercus macrocarpa |
| | | Quercus robur |
| | | Quercus rubra |
| | | Rhododendron carolinianum |
| | | Rhododendron mollis |
| | | Robinia pseudoacacia |
| | | Rosa woodsii |
| | | Sequoia gigantea |
| | | Sequoia sempervirens |
| | | Sequoiadendron giganteum |
| | | Sophora japonica |
| | | Taxus densiformis |
| | | Taxus media hatfieldi |
| | | Thuja occidentalis |
| | | Tilia americana |
| | | Tilia cordata |
| | | Tsuga canadensis |
| | | Viburnum burkwoodii |
| | | Viburnum carlesi |

**Relative sensitivity of plants to PAN**, from EPA (1976)

| Sensitive species | Less sensitive |
|---|---|
| *Aster* sp. | *Abies balsamea* |
| *Dahlia* sp. | *Abies concolor* |
| *Fuchsia* sp. | *Acer platanoides* |
| *Mimulus* sp. | *Acer saccharinum* |
| *Mentha* sp. | *Acer saccharum* |
| *Ocimum basilicum* | *Begonia* sp. |
| *Petunia* sp. | *Betula pendula* |
| *Primula* sp. | *Cactaceae* |
| *Ranunculus* sp. | *Calendula* sp. |
| | *Camellia* sp. |
| | *Chrysanthemum* sp. |
| | *Coleus* sp. |
| | *Cyclamen* sp. |
| | *Cornus florida* |
| | *Dianthus caryophyllus* |
| | *Fraxinus americana* |
| | *Fraxinus pennslyvanica* |
| | *Gleditsia triacanthos* |
| | *Hedera* sp. |
| | *Larix decidua* |
| | *Larix leptolepis* |
| | *Lilium* sp. |
| | *Liquidambar styraciflua* |
| | *Liriodendron tulipifera* |
| | *Malus sylvestris* |
| | *Narcissus* sp. |
| | *Orchidaceae* |
| | *Picea abies* |
| | *Picea glauca* |
| | *Picea glauca densata* |
| | *Picea pungens* |
| | *Pinus nigra* |
| | *Pinus resinosa* |
| | *Pinus strobus* |
| | *Pinus sylvestris* |
| | *Populus maximowiezii* |
| | *Populus trichocarpa* |
| | *Pseudotsuga menziesii* |
| | *Quercus alba* |
| | *Quercus palustris* |
| | *Quercus robur* |
| | *Quercus rubra* |
| | *Rhododendron* sp. |
| | *Sorbus americana* |
| | *Syringa vulgaris* |
| | *Thuja orientalis* |
| | *Tilia americana* |
| | *Tsuga canadensis* |
| | *Vinca minor* |

swards absorb twice as much of some pollutants as does bare soil. This scavenging effect increases with the inclusion of shrubs and trees. Thus the average concentration of a pollutant in the atmosphere declines with increasing proportions of well planted open space in industrial and urban areas.

The air beneath a tree canopy contains only a fraction of the pollution found above and around the wooded area. The vegetation acts as a filter, the rate of pollutant removal being controlled by its physicochemical nature, the species and the height of the vegetation, and by the prevailing weather conditions (especially wind speed and air humidity). Generally, dusts and aerosols are filtered out the most rapidly, with gaseous pollutants, sulphur dioxide, hydrogen fluoride and nitrogen dioxide being removed less efficiently but more quickly than nitric oxide and carbon monoxide.

Tree barriers between industrial and residential areas can also reduce air pollution considerably. A plantation of 30 m depth gives almost complete dust interception and significant reductions in gaseous pollutant concentrations. Even a single row of trees can reduce pollution levels markedly if it is planted on green verges with or without an underlay of shrubs. One row can lead to 25 per cent reduction in dust concentrations observed in tree-lined streets. Free circulation of air within the canopy of a tree barrier also helps to promote the filtering of pollutants.

Successful planting of trees in shelter belts in polluted areas demands the consideration of several important factors:

1. The location of the planting site in relation to the source of pollution affects the degree of exposure of plants to the pollutants. Expert advice should be sought on the likely dispersion of pollutants from a particular source. As a rule of thumb, the maximum ground level concentration of pollution will usually occur fourteen chimney lengths downwind of the source. In valleys subject to frequent temperature inversions, however, abnormally high and prolonged exposure may occur.

2. Recontouring of land may be carried out to improve the appearance of the site, to promote drainage and to minimize erosion. It may also provide some shelter for plants during the early stages of establishment. Adequate topsoil should be provided to a depth of about 15 cm, although greater depths may be required for the planting of larger trees and shrubs. If the original soil is contaminated (for instance, with metals) it will be necessary to import sufficient quantities of clean topsoil. Soil compaction should be avoided at all costs, since good drainage is essential for early and subsequent growth.

3. Organic material (such as manure, sewage sludge and peat) and compound fertilizers are

TABLE 12.5
**Relative sensitivity to sulphur dioxide**

| Sensitive | Intermediate | Least sensitive |
|---|---|---|
| *Acer negundo* var. *interius* | *Abies balsamea* | *Abies amabilis* |
| *Ameliancher alnifolia* | *Abies grandis* | *Abies concolor* |
| *Betula alleghaniensis* | *Acer campestre* | *Acer negundo* |
| *Betula papyrifera* | *Acer glabrum* | *Acer platanoides* |
| *Betula pendula* | *Acer negundo* | *Acer saccharum* |
| *Betula populifolia* | *Acer platanoides* | *Buxus sempervirens* |
| *Cedrus atlantica* | *Acer pseudoplatanus* | *Carpinus betulus* |
| *Crataegus oxycanthoides* | *Acer rubrum* | *Chamaecyparis lawsoniana* |
| *Fraxinus pennsylvanica* | *Aesculus hippocastanum* | *Crataegus douglasii* |
| *Larix decidua* | *Alnus glutinosa* | *Forsythia* sp. |
| *Larix occidentalis* | *Alnus incana* | *Ginkgo biloba* |
| *Picea abies* | *Alnus tenuifolia* | *Ilex aquifolium* |
| *Pinus banksiana* | *Betula occidentalis* | *Juniperus occidentalis* |
| *Pinus resinosa* | *Betula pendula* | *Juniperus osteosperma* |
| *Pinus strobus* | *Carpinus betulus* | *Juniperus scopulorum* |
| *Pinus sylvestris* | *Castanea sativa* | *Ligustrum vulgare* |
| *Populus grandidentata* | *Corylus avellana* | *Picea pungens* |
| *Populus nigra italica* | *Crataegus monogyna* | *Pinus edulis* |
| *Populus tremuloides* | *Eunonymus europaeus* | *Pinus flexilis* |
| *Quercus ilex* | *Fagus sylvatica* | *Platanus acerifolia* |
| *Rhus typhina* | *Fraxinus excelsior* | *Platanus hispanica* |
| *Salix nigra* | *Juglans regia* | *Prunus laurocerasus* |
| *Sequoia sempervirens* | *Juniperus communis* | *Populus canadensis* |
| *Sorbus sitchensis* | *Laburnum anagyroides* | *Quercus gambelii* |
| *Ulmus parvifolia* | *Larix kaempferi* | *Quercus palustris* |
| | *Picea engelmannii* | *Quercus petraea* |
| | *Picea glauca* | *Quercus robur* |
| | *Picea sitchensis* | *Quercus rubra* |
| | *Pinus contorta* | *Rhus glabra* |
| | *Pinus monticola* | *Thuja occidentalis* |
| | *Pinus nigra* | *Thuja plicata* |
| | *Pinus nigra maritima* | *Tilia cordata* |
| | *Pinus nigra nigra* | *Wisteria sinensis* |
| | *Pinus ponderosa* | |
| | *Populus alba* | |
| | *Populus angustifolia* | |
| | *Populus balsamifera* | |
| | *Populus deltoides* | |
| | *Populus tremula* | |
| | *Populus trichocarpa* | |
| | *Prunus armeniaca* | |
| | *Prunus avium* | |
| | *Prunus padus* | |
| | *Prunus virginiana* | |
| | *Pseudotsuga menziesii* | |
| | *Quercus alba* | |
| | *Robinia pseudoacacia* | |
| | *Salix caprea* | |
| | *Salix fragilis* | |
| | *Salix viminalis* | |
| | *Sambucus nigra* | |

TABLE 12.5
Relative sensitivity to sulphur dioxide

| Sensitive | Intermediate | Least sensitive |
| --- | --- | --- |
| | *Sorbus aucuparia* | |
| | *Syringa vulgaris* | |
| | *Taxus baccata* | |
| | *Tilia americana* | |
| | *Tilia cordata* | |
| | *Tilia platyphyllos* | |
| | *Tsuga heterophylla* | |
| | *Ulmus americana* | |
| | *Viburnum opulus* | |

usually applied to the soil by broadcast techniques followed by ploughing into the topsoil layer. This will help the early growth of shrubs and herbs. Spraying techniques may be used to apply grass and clover seed in a slurry with organic material and fertilizers. Trees and larger shrubs are usually planted in deep furrows or individual pits packed with organic material, and with ample room for early root growth. The organic material helps to conserve water in dry, rocky soils. On some sites it may be necessary to apply special ameliorants to deal with specific problems of nutrient deficiency (for instance, additional nitrogen) and toxicity (by adding lime to counteract acidity).

PLATE 12.5 **The damage illustrated in the photograph, probably from sulphur dioxide and/or fluorides, is relatively slight, occurring on only a few leaves. This may be a reflection of the age of the leaves, as they are generally more susceptible at certain stages than at others. In addition, exposure may have been restricted by shading from other leaves. The leaves in the foreground show the characteristic necrosis at the tips and on the edges of the leaves.** *(Courtesy of Rothamsted Experimental Station, Harpenden, Herts)*

PLATE 12.6 *Mahonia aquifolium*. **As in the other photographs, the damaged areas are the tips and the margins of the leaves, probably from sulphur dioxide and/or fluorides.** (*Courtesy of Rothamsted Experimental Station, Harpenden, Herts*)

4. Careful selection of plants is essential to ensure establishment in severely polluted areas. Obviously, insensitive plants must be used close to sources of pollution. In the initial phases of establishment, dense tree barriers may be planted. Density can be increased by the pruning of young trees to promote adventitious growth from the stem base. Later, however, a more open plantation may be created to give a better appearance, while also promoting air circulation within a canopy. Mixed plantations may be established, provided that the outer and upper limits of the community are composed of insensitive species which will shelter the more sensitive plants.

5. It is important to ensure that weeds are suppressed in the immediate vicinity of newly planted trees and shrubs. In addition, various grasses planted as part of a landscaping scheme may compete with young trees. Generally, an area of at least 1.0 m diameter around transplants and 1.5 m diameter around standards should be kept free of weeds. The first spring and summer is the most important period for newly planted trees, as in later years they are much more capable of withstanding competitive pressure. The length of time that weeding needs to be continued depends on the degree of soil preparation, the species and quality of the plants, their suitability to the site and the amount of stress to which they are exposed.

Most of these considerations are familiar to the landscape designer who is concerned with giving young plants the best possible chance of establishment on polluted sites. However, if the conditions are particularly adverse, it may be necessary to consult a specialist.

In some cases, the application of certain chemicals can be used to alleviate pollution stress in plants. This tends to be very expensive and is generally impractical, but in some situations it may be feasible. Oxidant injury can be reduced in several species by the application of the fungicides benomyl (methyl 1-butyl-carbonyl-2-benzimidazole carbamate) and carboxin. EDU (N-[2-(2-oxo-1-imidazolidinyl) ethyl]-N-phenylurea) has also shown potential for reducing ozone injury in a number of woody species, including *Acer rubrum*, *Betula papyrifera*, *Fraxinus americana*,

*Gleditsia triacanthos*, *Koelreuteria paniculata*, *Platanus acerifolia*, *Syringa vulgaris* and *Tilia cordata*. Application of a polymeric coating (spodnam) has been found to reduce acute pollution injury to three spruce species.

As an additional benefit, noise is significantly reduced by tree barriers of less than 30 m depth, and the cosmetic and psychological benefits of planting are considerable. Soft surfaces do not, in any event, reflect sound to the same extent as hard surfaces and are thus preferred on noise abatement grounds.

To summarize what has been said, risks of planting failure in polluted areas can be minimized by obtaining all the available information and by testing the site conditions thoroughly. Similarly, the control of air pollution can be maximized by employing the most suitable plants and planting techniques at the particular site in an effective manner to best reduce the particular problems of pollution in an area.

## FURTHER READING

Anon. *Diagnosing Injury to Eastern Forest Trees* (United States Department of Agriculture, Forest Service 1987)

Davies, D. D. and Gerhold, H. D. 'Selection of trees for tolerance of air pollutants' *Better Trees for Metropolitan Landscapes* (edited by Santamour, F. S., Gerhold, H. D. and Little, S.), General Technical Report, Northeastern Forest Experiment Station, USDA Forest Service No. NE-22, pp. 61–6 (1976)

Davies. R. J. 'Trees and weeds – Weed control for successful tree establishment', *Forestry Commission Handbook* 2 (1987).

EPA (US Environmental Protection Agency), 'The photochemical oxidants', in *Diagnosing Vegetation Injury Caused by Air Pollution*. Applied Science Associates Inc., EPA Contract 68–02–1344

Freer-Smith, P. H. 'The responses of six broadleaved trees during long-term exposure to $SO_2$ and $NO_2$', *New Phytologist*, **97**, pp. 49–61 (1987).

Freer-Smith, P. H. and Lucas, P. W. 'Application of a polymeric coating can protect coniferous trees from acute pollution injury', *Forest Ecology and Management*, **17**, pp. 289–301 (1986)

Gilbert, M. D., Elfving. D. C. and Lisk, D. J. 'Protection of plants against ozone injury using antiozonant N-1(1.3-dimethylbutyl)-N-phenyl-p-phenylenediamine', *Bulletin of Environmental Contamination and Toxicology*, **18**, pp. 783–6 (1977)

Greszta, J., Braniewski, S. and Nosek, A. The effect of dusts from different emitters on the height increment of the seedlings of selected tree species', *Fragmenta Floristica et Geobotanica*, **28** pp. 67–75 (1982)

Hibberd, B. G. (ed.) 'Forestry practice', *Forestry Commission Bulletin*, **14**, 10th edition (1986)

Huttunen, S. 'Interactions of disease and other stress factors with atmospheric pollution', in *Air Pollution and Plant Life* (edited by Treshow, M.), Chichester: J. Wiley, pp. 321–56 (1984)

Innes, J. L. 'Air pollution and forestry', *Forestry Commission Bulletin*, **70** (1987)

Karnosky, D. F. 'Chamber and field evaluations of air pollution tolerance to urban trees', *Journal of Arboriculture*, **7**, pp. 99–105 (1981)

Kozlowski, T. T. 'Susceptibility of young tree seedlings to environmental stresses', *American Nurseryman*, **144**, pp. 12–13 (1980)

Kozlowski, T. T. 'Responses of shade trees to pollution', *Journal of Arboriculture*, **6** pp. 29–41 (1980)

Kozlowski, T. T. and Constantinidou, H. A. 'Responses of woody plants to environmental pollution. Part I – Sources and types of pollutants and plant responses', *Forestry Abstracts*, **47**, pp. 5–51 (1986)

Kozlowski, T. T. and Constantinidou, H. A. 'Environmental pollution and tree growth. Part II – Factors affecting responses to pollution and alleviation of pollution effects', *Forestry Abstracts*, **47**, pp. 105–32 (1986)

Kress, L. W., 'Effect of O and O + NO on growth of tree seedlings', in *Proceedings of the Symposium on Effects of Air Pollutants on Mediterranean and Temperate Forest Systems*, General Technical Report, Pacific Southwest Forest and Range Experiment Station, USDA Forest Service No. PSW-43, 239

McClenahen, J. R. 'Effects of ethylene diurea and ozone on the growth of tree seedlings', *Plant Disease Reporter*, **63**, pp. 320–3 (1979)

Morrison, I. K. 'Acid rain: A review of the literature on acid deposition effects in forest ecosystems', *Forestry Abstracts*, **45**, pp. 483–506 (1984)

Moyer, J. W., Cole, H. and Lacasse, N. L. 'Suppression of naturally occurring oxidant injury on *Azalea* plants by drench or foliar spray treatment with benzimidazole or oxathiin compounds', *Plant Disease Reporter*, **58**, pp. 136–8 (1974)

Ormrod, D. P. and Adedipe, N. O. 'Protecting horticultural plants from atmospheric pollutants', *Hort.Science*, **9**, pp. 108–11 (1974)

Patch, D. (ed.) 'Advances in practical arboriculture', *Forestry Commission Bulletin*, **65** (1985)

Steiner, K. C. and Davis, D. D. 'Variation among *Fraxinus* families in foliar response to ozone', *Canadian Journal of Forest Research*, **9**, pp. 106–9 (1979)

Taylor, H. J., Ashmore, M. R. and Bell, J. N. B. *Air Pollution Injury to Vegetation* (London: IEHO 1987)

Weinstein, L. H. 'Fluoride and plant life', *Journal of Occupational Medicine*, **19**, pp. 49–78 (1977)

Wilson, K. 'A guide to the reclamation of mineral workings for forestry', *Forestry Commission Research and Development Paper No. 141* (1986)

# CHAPTER 13

# The Use of Vegetation in Slope Stabilization

## NICK COPPIN AND RICHARD STILES

## 13.1 INTRODUCTION

Landscape design with plants depends on one understanding and utilizing the functional qualities of vegetation as well as its aesthetic and ecological attributes. Prominent among these functional qualities is its ability to protect and bind together the thin mantle of soil over the earth's surface.

The vital role that vegetation plays in stabilizing slopes and preventing erosion is clearly of considerable importance, and yet the positive exploitation of this role and its development in terms of landscape techniques has not been exploited to any great extent in the UK. With the advent of modern engineering materials and techniques, such as the use of steel and reinforced concrete, the potential of natural materials, and of vegetation in particular, has been largely neglected. The more recent introduction of geotextiles and geo-membranes has again focused attention on the potential of an approach to slope stabilization and erosion control which does not rely on the rigid artificial materials that have been used nearly universally up to now.

Essential to the creation of reinforced soil structures using geotextiles is the use of vegetation as a secondary component, though with a limited function. Developments in geotextiles have led to a renewed interest in the potential of vegetation as a primary stabilizing factor. The difficulties of taking the contribution of a variable biological material into account in engineering design has, not surprisingly, led to a cautious approach on the part of civil engineers. In terms of the large scale use of vegetation for slope stabilization, such efforts as have been made in the past have been aimed at investigating only the theoretical possibilities and conceptual background of vegetation use as a slope-stabilizing agent. However, efforts are now being made to encourage a wider acceptance of the practical possibilities of the applications of vegetation (CIRIA, forthcoming).

Literature and examples of the use of vegetation that we are aware of in the UK tend to be secondhand, coming almost exclusively from North America. Much of this work is, however, based on experience originating in the mainland of Europe, most of which we have long remained unaware of for reasons of language. The age-old tradition of using vegetation to prevent and repair the natural processes of erosion and mass wasting resulting from the instability of the ground surface has been kept alive on the Continent, in particular in the alpine regions of Europe. Here it has been developed and refined to an extent such that the rest of the world now looks towards the alpine countries, and to Austria in particular, as, in the wake of the environmental revolution, it begins to rediscover the potential of more natural approaches to solving landscape engineering problems (Stiles, forthcoming).

This chapter attempts to review the approaches and principles behind the use of vegetation for the stabilization of steep slopes. Its sets out first to summarize the mechanisms governing slope degradation and erosion as a basis for defining what functions vegetations has to perform in preventing them. Techniques for achieving the desired vegetation cover are outlined and the experience gained on the continent is described. The principles and procedures set out in this chapter can be applied to solving slope stabilization problems in all situations and at a wide range of scales, from small landscape schemes to large scale civil engineering and erosion control works.

## 13.2 SLOPE EROSION PROBLEMS

### Types of instability

Steep slopes present obvious problems of potential instability and two major types can be defined:

1. Deep-seated instability inherent in a slope, usually manifested as a rapid slope failure occurring somewhat unpredictably.
2. Surface instability caused by many natural degradation processes which occur slowly but more or less continuously over long periods of time. The principal agents are gravity and water, which between them cause soil creep and erosion.

The analysis of slope instability, especially deeply seated instability, is a complex process involving geotechnics and soil engineering. However, a very brief summary of how these types of instability can occur is given below.

## Deeply seated instability

Slopes whose gradients are steeper than those which can be supported by the inherent strength of the material of which they are composed are unstable and will fail. Failure can take several forms, most of which are intermediate between:

1. Deep-seated rotational failures or landslips.
2. Shallower planar slips or landslides.

In both cases the critical property is the soil strength, and more particularly its shear strength acting on the plane parallel to the slope surface. If the weight of the soil being supported is greater than the shear strength of the critical plane, then failure will inevitably occur.

Soil shear strength is determined by:

(a) soil density;
(b) clay content;
(c) water content or pore water pressure.

Instability problems are normally associated with cohesive (silty or clay rich) soils with poor drainage. It is possible to analyse the stability of a slope to estimate a factor of safety (*cf.* BS 6031:1981, *Code of Practice for Earthworks*).

When placed in a mound, soil will 'flow' until it reaches a characteristic angle of repose. In geotechnical terms this process is equivalent to the failure of the slope, whereby slumping continues until the inherent soil strength can support the weight of the remaining soil mass. The natural angle of repose of loose, tipped soil is usually much shallower than can be achieved using heavy engineering machinery and compaction of the soil under optimum conditions.

There are many situations where a weakness in the soil profile can become a failure plane and lead to slope failure as a planar slip. A loose or permeable soil layer overlying rock or a very dense compacted stratum can give rise to these conditions. Placing topsoil on embank-

PLATE 13.1 **Slumping occurring on a highway embankment where the topsoil has not been 'keyed into' the subsoil beneath.** *(Pam Hoyle)*

PLATE 13.2 **Wasting on a road cutting due to creep, slides and water erosion.** *(N. Coppin)*

ments without due regard to the continuity of the soil profile or the behaviour of percolating water creates just these sorts of conditions, and is unfortunately an all too common occurrence (see Plate 13.1).

## Soil creep

This is a natural process on steep slopes where the surface soil moves gradually downhill under the influence of gravity. Usually some other agent, such as water, animal trampling or surface weathering, is responsible for disturbing the soil. Freeze–thaw cycles and surface weathering will also produce loose soil material which then moves under the influence of gravity.

The whole process of gradual soil movement by creep, slides and slope movement can be considered as mass wasting. It occurs even on slopes which would be considered stable according to geotechnical criteria, but which continually move as weathering and gravity act upon them (see Plate 13.2).

214

## Water erosion

Scour and erosion of a slope surface during and after heavy rainfall can be dramatic. Apart from the soil loss itself there are considerable problems downstream, caused by the additional erosive effect of waterborne material, from the effects of sediment in streams and rivers and from siltation. The mechanics of rainfall erosion work in three stages:

1. Raindrop impact, which breaks down the soil aggregate and detaches soil particles (which can themselves bounce several centimetres).
2. Sheet erosion by overland flow of water which transports the detached soil and can also scour more soil from the surface itself.
3. Rill and gully erosion occurs as the overland flow concentrates into channels, thereby focusing the erosive forces and kinetic energy associated with sheet flow.

The first two stages of erosion due to rainfall have

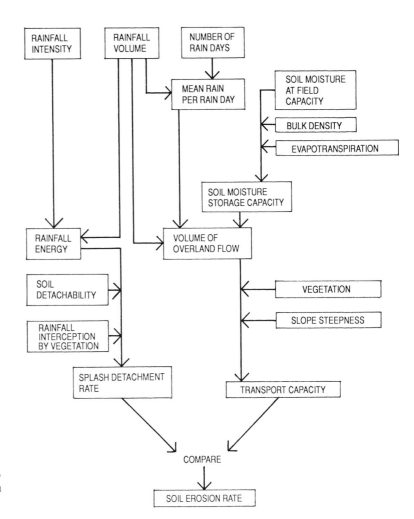

FIGURE 13.1 **Flow chart for the Morgan, Morgan and Finney model of soil erosion by rainfall.** *(After Morgan, 1986)*

been extensively modelled. The Morgan, Morgan and Finney model (Morgan, 1986) has been developed for predicting soil loss in temperate climates such as the UK (see Figure 13.2). More widely used throughout the world, especially in tropical climates, is the Universal Soil Loss Equation (USLE) developed in the USA (Wischmeier and Smith, 1978). The USLE states that:

$$\text{Soil loss} = R \times K \times L \times S \times C \times P$$

where R is the rainfall erosivity based on its duration and intensity; K is the erodibility of the soil, which depends on its texture, permeability and organic matter content; L and S are factors based on the length and gradient of the slope; and C and P are factors based on the vegetation cover and soil conservation practices employed.

The widest application of these models is not in evaluating actual soil loss, but in determining the risk or likely extent of erosion of a slope (CIRIA, in preparation). As risk assessment techniques, the models become useful design aids, where they can be changed to alter the factors in the equation until the slope is theoretically resistant to erosion. Factors that account for the erosion protection of different vegetation systems can be included in this process.

## 13.3 THE ROLE OF VEGETATION

### Soil reinforcement

The mechanical effect of plant roots on soil is widely accepted, but is very difficult to quantify. It is therefore unusual to include a factor for enhanced soil shear strength due to the presence of roots in slope stability analysis. However, procedures do exist and are being developed further (Gray and Leiser, 1982; CIRIA, in preparation), though basic data on the shear strength of root reinforced soil masses are sparse.

The effects of vegetation on the mechanical behaviour of soils can be summarized as follows:

| **Beneficial effects** | **Adverse effects** |
|---|---|
| 1. Reinforcement of soil, increasing shear strength | 1. Large, heavy areas will surcharge the slope adding weight |
| 2. Deep roots anchor unstable strata into stable strata or bedrock | 2. Trees exposed to wind transmit dynamic forces into the slope (windthrow) |
| 3. Deep roots support the unstable soil mantle through buttressing and arching | 3. Root wedging of near surface rocks and boulders |
| 4. A network of surface roots creates a reinforcing membrane retaining the underlying strata | |

Vegetation will also substantially affect slope stability through hydrological effects.

Much is sometimes made of the depth which plant roots can reach, but the root systems of most plant species tend to be concentrated within the upper soil layers. The effect that vegetation can have on deep-seated instability below 1.5 m, such as rotational slides, is therefore very limited. However, the potential effects on the more common, shallower slopes can be substantial if the right vegetation is used. Deep rooting with a mixture of deep tap roots, well branched lateral roots and dense fibrous roots is ideal. Deep roots are most likely to be provided by trees and shrubs, though care should be taken with the larger tree species, whose root systems may be so extensive as to have adverse effects on slope stability.

# Surface effects

Surface vegetation has a considerable influence on sheet and gully erosion, acting in a number of ways; including the following:

(a) Roots bind soil particles at the ground surface, restraining soil movement and reducing soil erodibility.
(b) Stems, leaves and litter reduce the velocity of surface water run off and thus its scouring effect.
(c) Soil permeability is increased, thus reducing the volume of surface water run off by increasing infiltration.
(d) The vegetation canopy intercepts rainfall and reduces erosivity.

Grass and herbaceous vegetation produces very good surface effects and is very effective at controlling erosion. Deeper rooting than is provided by herbaceous vegetation is unnecessary and may even be undesirable. However, tussocky or clumped vegetation may concen-trate overland water flow, leading to a localized increase in water erosion.

# Soil moisture balance

Hydrological effects are relevant to both soil stability and surface protection. The water content of the soil is fundamental to its strength, and so the amount of water entering and leaving the soil via the surface is very important. The volume of overland water flow relative to infiltration is significant to both deeper rooted and surface effects.

The effects of vegetation on increasing and decreasing soil moisture are:

| **Increase** | **Decrease** |
|---|---|
| 1. Roots open up the soil and allow higher rates of infiltration | 1. Foliage intercepts rainfall, some of which evaporates directly without entering the soil |
| 2. An initial depletion of soil moisture may accentuate desiccation cracks resulting in higher infiltration capacity | 2. Roots extract moisture from the soil, which is transpired via the leaves, leading to lower pore water pressures and higher soil suction |

The effects of vegetation on the soil water hydrological cycle are illustrated in Figure 13.2. Reducing soil pore water pressure (moisture content) increases slope stability by increasing the strength of the soil. High pore water pressure decreases soil strength by decreasing the friction between soil particles. Procedures for estimating soil moisture balance over time using rainfall data and calculated potential evapo-transpiration rates are well established (Smith, 1976; Doorenbos and Pruit, 1975). The effects of different types of vegetation, especially trees, are not so easy to predict, but measurements made on two species, pine and oak, are illustrated in Figure 13.3.

# Reconciling beneficial and undesirable effects

For any particular slope in question there will be a number of potential stability factors to consider. The particular function that vegetation has to perform will vary, and plant species with appropriate properties will need to be selected for each situation. However, there are a number of potential conflicts which need to be borne in mind.

Water exerts a fundamental influence on slope stability. Slopes are usually constructed so as to reduce infiltration and shed as much water as possible. This shedding of water can create severe erosion problems,

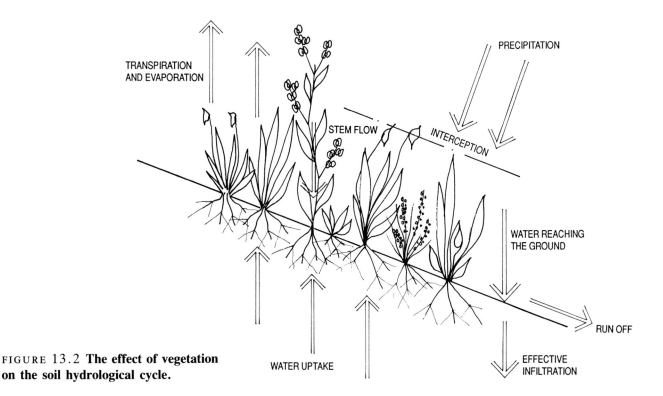

FIGURE 13.2 **The effect of vegetation on the soil hydrological cycle.**

Labels in figure:
TRANSPIRATION AND EVAPORATION
PRECIPITATION
STEM FLOW
INTERCEPTION
WATER REACHING THE GROUND
RUN OFF
WATER UPTAKE
EFFECTIVE INFILTRATION

so vegetation is necessary to protect the surface. However, vegetation exerts its own influence on the soil moisture status. Not only does its presence increase infiltration to some extent, but plants need a reasonable depth of permeable soil in which to root, and they need a soil which will provide sufficient soil moisture storage so that they can survive extended dry periods.

The conflict described above will only be resolved if a proper examination is made of each case of the potential benefits of vegetation through root reinforcement and erosion control against the potential adverse effects of soil moisture retention. Perhaps a slightly more open-minded approach to slope design, including vegetation as a fundamental part of the process and not just the surface finishing, is needed.

## 13.4 ENVIRONMENT AND SOIL

### Site assessment

The procedures normally adopted for assessing a site for its potential for vegetation growth are still applicable, perhaps more so when the plants are being used actively to improve slope stability, as the performance of the plants is crucial to their function. Firstly, the site assessment is applied to the selection of suitable plant species and to their potential performance under the prevailing conditions. Secondly, the assessment is used as the basis for determining the extent of erosion and/or slope instability and the functional qualities that will be required (see Table 13.1).

The assessment will also indicate which method of establishment should be adopted and the need for any short-term protection measures during the time that the plants are becoming established and fully functional.

### Soils

Once again, consideration of the soil environment should only be an extension of what is normal good practice. However, it is frequently the case when dealing with slopes that the topsoil is absent or only very sparse. It is therefore necessary to pay particular attention to the selection, construction or preparation of the soil profile.

For adequate growth of plants the soil profile should fulfil two basic requirements:

1. **Root permeability** Roots are unable to penetrate compacted soil and cannot exploit a sufficiently large volume of soil to obtain the required water and nutrients. The most useful criterion for measuring this is the packing density (Jarvis and Mackney, 1979). Packing density is defined as:

   Packing density = Bulk density + (0.009 × % clay) g/cm$^3$

   A packing density of less than 1.4 is low, 1.4 to 1.75 is medium, and greater than 1.75 is high and restricts root growth.

2. **Profile available water** The soil profile down to about 1 metre depth or to an impermeable layer, whichever is the shallower, provides the available

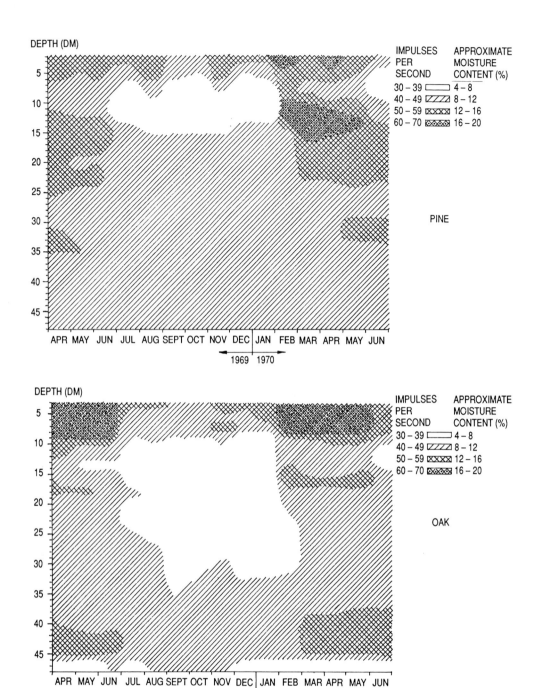

FIGURE 13.3 **Changes in soil moisture content beneath young stands of pine and oak woodland on unconsolidated, lowland, sedimentary soils over the period May 1969 – June 1970 in the Forest Hydrological Research Area, Frankfurt, West Germany.** *(From Brechtel, H-M. and Hammes, W., 1985)*

soil moisture storage. The available water for each layer is summed to give the total water availability for the soil profile. Less than 100 mm of profile available water (PAW) would represent a droughty soil, and less than 150 mm slightly droughty (Jarvis and Mackney, 1979).

Both of these parameters are functions of soil texture, soil density and soil structure. Soil fertility is also important, but in a different way. Fertility can to some extent be supplied artificially, and does not limit the long-term soil potential. The soil physical properties on the other hand are not easy to modify, and certainly not in the short term. It is therefore more important to get the soil profile right than to worry about soil fertility. The design or selection of soil materials should bear this point firmly in mind, rather than rigidly adhering to the idea of importing topsoil.

## TABLE 13.1
**Parameters for slope stabilization**

| | Plant growth | Stabilizing function |
|---|:---:|:---:|
| **Climatic** | | |
| (a) Rainfall | | |
|     Quantity | × | × |
|     Intensity | | × |
|     Seasonality | × | × |
| (b) Temperature | | |
|     Growing season | × | |
|     Extremes | × | × |
|     Exposure | × | |
|     Evapo-transpiration | × | × |
| **Soil physical** | | |
| Texture | × | × |
| Available water | × | |
| Strength | | × |
| Erosion risk | | × |
| Permeability | | × |
| Rootability | × | |
| **Soil chemical** | | |
| pH | × | |
| Fertility (NPK) | × | |
| Cation exchange | | |
| Capacity | × | |

Topsoil has many advantages of course, but it also has some disadvantages. It is usually expensive to import, is sometimes of dubious quality, contains weed fragments and seeds, structure is often destroyed during handling and it may be too fertile for the purpose if a low maintenance sward is desired.

Whether topsoil is used or not, proper attention to the whole soil profile is important, especially the selection of suitable materials, their handling and the continuity between the soil layers. Normally the soil profile down to 0.75 m or even 1 m should be considered in this context, not just the 300 mm or so depth of surface soil that is spread last of all. However, on slopes this is not always practicable.

Soils on steep slopes often have to be compacted to exclude water and increase soil strength. The depth of the soil profile is then only 300–400 mm at best, and usually less. However, an understanding of the soil profile will at least mean that the limitations of this situation are fully appreciated. When spreading soil as a surface covering (whether topsoil or selected soil), it is important to establish proper continuity between this layer and the underlying compacted soil. This means some cross-slope scarification and the elimination of the regular vertically striated surface finish, which is usually achieved with excavation machinery.

## Cultivation and preparation

Once a steep slope is finished and formed, the ability to carry out any further cultivation depends on the slope gradient:

| | |
|---|---|
| Up to 1 in 3 (18°) | – normal agricultural machinery. |
| Up to 1 in 2.5 (22°) | – normal agricultural machinery working up and down slope, or with wide wheels. |
| Up to 1 in 1.75 (30°) | – special machinery with tracks or very wide wheel base. |
| More than 1 in 1.75 | – working from top and bottom of slope only. |

Although vegetation itself is the principal factor controlling erosion and surface instability, there are certain soil conservation measures which should be adopted to reduce the erosion risk. These include:

1. Limiting the length of slope by interrupting long slopes with ditches, ledges or narrow berms to intercept overland flow of water and divert it from the slope. Preventing water flowing on to a slope from higher ground by installing a cut-off drain at the top.

2. Ridging, grooving or scarifying across the slope to increase surface roughness and thereby reduce surface water flow. This will also increase infiltration, which is better for plant growth (by increasing soil water storage), but may be undesirable for slope stability if the effects of increased pore water pressure are not counteracted by improved plant growth.

3. Stair-step grading, forming a series of ledges with not less than 1.5 m horizontal ledge to 1 m vertical face. Soil sloughing off the faces catches on the ledges and forms an ideal growing medium for plants. When seeded, the profile of the slope is soon disguised (Schaller and Sutton 1978).

Soil conservation techniques are fully described in Hudson (1971). Their application has to balance the need to increase surface roughness to reduce water run-off with the need to shed water for slope stability. This can be achieved, for example, by cross-slope grading or finishing carried out at an angle to the contours to encourage slope drainage during periods of heavy rainfall.

Special implements have to be used to carry out grading and cultivation on steep slopes, where the tractor is operating from either the top or bottom of the slope. Ridging or grooving implements with notches or serrations at 300–400 mm intervals on a blade can be mounted on hydraulic arms for cross-slope cultivation.

## Fertilizers

The use of fertilizers on slopes is similar to their use in any other situation, bearing in mind that repeated

219

maintenance visits are difficult and the soils are often very poor. Slow release fertilizers and organic manures usually give the best long-term results. Fertilizer requirements should be based on the existing soil fertility, the cation exchange capacity of the soil and the vigour of vegetation growth that is required.

A vulnerable area on all slopes is the upper part and the crest. Particular attention should be paid to fertilizing these areas, as they are the most susceptible to leaching and exposure.

Deep placement of fertilizers has been used to encourage deeper rooting, with varying degrees of success. The effects of this are not sufficiently well understood for recommendations to be made, but elements such as calcium and phosphorus, which are relatively immobile in the soil compared to nitrogen, are likely to have some beneficial effect by deep placement. Phosporus is an essential element for root growth.

## 13.5 USE OF GRASSES AND HERBACEOUS PLANTS

### Stabilization qualities

Grasses and herbs are very cheap and versatile materials, and are therefore widely used for slope protection and erosion control. Grasses have very dense but shallow root systems concentrated towards the surface, with 40–60 per cent in the top 25 mm and 60–80 per cent in the top 50 mm of the soil. Even though rooting depths of up to 1 m are quoted for grasses, the root density below the upper soil layers is very low (Garwood, 1967; Parr *et al.*, 1985).

Regular cutting of grass swards substantially reduces root growth. For any given species or cultivar the ratio between the levels of root and shoot growth tends to remain constant, and experiments have shown that cutting the sward to 40 mm reduces the root biomass below 15 cm depth and cutting it to 20 mm reduces the biomass by 35 per cent at all depths (Parr *et al.*, 1985)

Grasses are therefore most useful in surface protection and reinforcement, having little effect below 100 mm or so. Individual species should be selected on the basis of their specific characteristics and ability to bind the soil. Those which have a creeping habit will be the most useful, spreading either by rhizomes (tough underground stems) or stolons (overground runners or stems which root from nodes and can produce a very compact dense sward). Tussocky grasses which do not spread in this way have more limited application and may even be undesirable.

Many other herbaceous species are deeply rooting and have a wide application for slope planting. The recent interest in wildflowers for inclusion in grass mixtures means that a wide range of species is available. Legumes such as clovers, trefoils and vetches have large root systems, some with deep tap roots. For slope protection and soil reinforcement a sward should contain a much higher proportion of legumes and herbs, with more extensive root systems than can be achieved with grass-dominated swards.

A list of species with good stabilization properties is given in Table 13.2. Selection for a particular site should include other factors, such as soil type and climate, in the same way as for selecting species for any other situation.

Quick establishment from seed is usually a prime requirement for slope seeding. Temporary protection provided by a mulch or soil binder will last only a few weeks. Unless the sward is established in this time, a period of high erosion could cause extensive damage. Unfortunately, species which tolerate the hostile conditions common on slopes and which are 'low maintenance' are slow growing and slow to establish themselves. It is therefore usual to include a quick growing 'nurse' species in the seed mixture which will provide some initial cover while slower growing species establish themselves but, which will die out in a year or so. Italian Ryegrass (cultivars Westerworlds or Weldra are suitable) or cereals such as barley are widely used nurse species. The proportion of nurse species in the seed mixture should be kept quite low, so that they do not crowd out the slower growing species.

Low maintenance is another important criterion. Infrequent cutting is desirable anyway to maximize root development, but cutting or mowing of swards on steep slopes is usually difficult or impractical. For cultivated low maintenance, cultivars which produce shorter, denser growth can be selected. However, the likelihood is that these species will also have feebler root systems.

### Hydroseeding

Hydroseeding or hydraulic seeding is a technique used for applying seed, fertilizer and any other soil ameliorants to steep or inaccessible places. The seed is only applied to the surface, so a good mulch is essential and the texture of the soil surface is also an important factor in the success of the seeding. Conventional seeding with drilling or broadcasting machinery, followed by harrowing or rolling, will usually give better results, whatever the soil type, because the seedbed can be properly prepared and the seed placed at the right depth and in good contact with the soil. It is more difficult, and usually more expensive, to get good consistent results with hydroseeding. Nevertheless, it is a widely used technique and it is often the only practicable method of applying seed to steep slopes.

Unfortunately, hydroseeding tends to be treated as a magic wand technique, without regard to its limitations. It is often promoted as an alternative to topsoil or the technique to be used if topsoil is not available. This is, however, not so, and proper soil preparation and

220

TABLE 13.2
**Species with good soil stabilization qualities for use in Britain**

| Species | Comments |
| --- | --- |
| **Grasses** | |
| *Agrostis tenuis* (Common bent) | Tufted perennial spreading by short, stout rhizomes and stolons. Wide soil tolerance. Especially likes dry, acid soils. |
| *Agrostis stolonifera* (Creeping bent) | Spreads by leafy stolons to form a close turf. Wide tolerance but prefers damp soils. |
| *Agrostis canina*, Subsp. *montana* (Brown bent) | Densely tufted rhizomatous perennial. Wide tolerance of soils, including those in drought conditions. |
| *Agropyron repens* (Couch or twitch) | Aggressive spreading species with vigorous rhizome system. Prefers deep, fertile soils. |
| *Arrhenatherum elatius* (Tall oatgrass) | Tall perennial with deep, strong roots and occasional rhizomes. It is tussocky with a wide tolerance of soils. Common coloniser of steep slopes. |
| *Poa pratensis* (Smooth meadow grass) | Densely spreading perennial with tough, short rhizomes. Wide tolerance of soil conditions. Many low maintenance cultivars. |
| *Festuca rubra rubra* (Creeping red fescue) | Densely spreading perennial with tough, stout rhizomes. Very wide tolerance of soil conditions, especially acidic and salty (slender types). |
| *Bromus inermis* (Smooth brome) | Rhizomatous perennial with extensive roots. Wide tolerance but prefers fertile soil. |
| **Legumes** | |
| *Trifolium hybridium* (Alsike clover) | Tufted perennial, deep taproot. Not tolerant of acid or infertile soils. |
| *Lotus corniculatus* (Bird's foot trefoil) | Perennial herb with prostrate or ascending shoots, has deep taproot. Native types have wide tolerance of site and soils but imported european cultivars are not so good. Many USA cultivars. |
| *Coronilla varia* (Crown vetch) | Bushy perennial, very deep rooting, Wide tolerance of site and soils but prefers neutral−alkaline. Slow to establish (2 years). |
| **Forbs** | |
| *Achillea millefolium* (Yarrow) | Rhizomatous perennial herb, deep rooting with strong horizontal rootstock. Wide tolerance of soils. |
| *Chrysanthemum leucanthemum* (Ox-eye Daisy) | Deep rooting perennial. Tolerates infertile and dry soils, but avoids wet ones. |
| *Sanguisorba minor* (Salad burnet) | Deep rooting perennial, very drought tolerant but prefers alkaline soils. |
| *Stachys officinalis* (Betony) | Rhizomatous perennial, tolerates many soil types. |

amelioration are as important when using hydroseeding as at any other time. The association with lack of topsoil arises from its use on steep or inaccessible areas where spreading topsoil or proper soil preparation is difficult or impossible, but this does not mean that it is unnecessary or should be omitted as a matter of course.

The important factors and components in the hydroseeding process are given below.

## Soil surface
A loose rough surface will give the best results, allowing the seed to fall into the crevices and hollows where the microclimate is more favourable. A smooth, clean soil surface will leave the seeds exposed and is very inhospitable.

## Seed mixture
Species suitable for the soil, climate maintenance regime and function should be carefully selected and mixed. Seed rates should be increased to allow for losses on unprotected slopes, and about 10 $g/m^2$ is usually appropriate.

## Fertilizers
If these are applied along with the seed, then the concentration of harmful salts at the soil surface may

221

affect the germinating seeds. Either slow release fertilizers should be used or the application of soluble fertilizers split, with up to 20 g/m$^2$ being applied at the time of seeding and any remaining fertilizers delayed until after germination. Coated slow-release fertilizers, which work by having a soluble fertilizer contained within an insoluble coating, should not be used as the coating breaks down when it goes through the hydroseeding pump.

### Mulches

Surface sown seed is very vulnerable to drought; even short, dry periods of only a few hours can decimate germinating seeds. A protective mulch cover is therefore essential − a minimum of 1.5 tonnes per hectare if the soil has a good surface and the season is moist, and up to 3 tonnes per hectare if the soil surface is smooth or drought is likely. Suitable mulch materials include:

  chopped hay or straw;
  ground wood fibre (unbleached);
  peat (fibrous);
  cotton or cellulose fibre (proprietary products);
  shredded paper;
  fibreglass rovings.

Long-fibred materials will also stabilize the soil surface and provide some erosion control, especially if tacked down with a binder.

### Binder

Soil stabilizers or binders are usually added to the hydroseeding mixture in order to:

  improve aggregate stability of the soil, making it less susceptible to raindrop impact;
  glue down the other constituents, especially the mulch;
  reduce the erodibility of the soil surface itself, by restraining soil particles.

Several types of soil stabilizer are available:

  Starch polymer (gel type) − not now normally used.
  Fat/lignin latex (membrane type) − can be toxic to young seedlings, reduces water infiltration.
  Alginurate (gel type) − good water holding properties, widely used.
  Polyvinyl acetates acrylic co-polymers (crust type) − widely used.
  Butadiene oils (crust type) − not very feasible, some are toxic to young seedlings.
  Styrene butadiene (crust type) − most are very effective with a strong flexible crust.
  Resins (crust type) − not widely used.
  Rubber polymers (crust type) − can be toxic to young seedlings, reduce water infiltration.
  Bitumen (membrane type) − reduces water infiltration, good mulch binder but can be toxic to young seedlings.

### Application

The constituents are all mixed up into a slurry with water, usually to give a liquid application rate of about 2 litres/m$^2$. With lower rates it is difficult to get an even application, and higher rates would be used on very variable areas. Variability in application rates is quite normal when hydroseeding, though an experienced operator should keep this within ± 20 per cent.

## Mulch seeding

This technique is a variation on hydroseeding, but where a large quantity of mulch is applied. It is used in situations where the climate or erosion is very hostile and it is necessary to give the seeds and the soil surface a much greater degree of protection.

After preparation of the soil surface and applying fertilizers, a heavy mulch of straw (up to 4 tonnes/ha) is applied and tacked down with a binder. Special machinery which blows on the mulch and applies the binder at the same time (see Plate 13.3) is usual. Alternatively, it can be spread by hand, with the binder (and other materials) being applied using the hydroseeder. The seed is usually broadcast (or hydroseeded) on top of the mulch so that it falls down into it.

As an alternative to straw, fibreglass rovings can blown on pneumatically. This is very expensive but gives a high degree of surface protection. Bitumen is the usual binder applied.

## Seed mats and netting

In extremely unstable conditions the slope can be protected with netting or mesh pegged into the soil surface. Three basic types of net are available.

1. Biodegradable jute netting with a coarse mesh (10 to 15 mm mesh). This has a fairly short-term effect (1−3 years) but is very effective for erosion control and conforms well to the soil surface.
2. Three-dimensional polypropylene netting. This has considerable tensile strength and gives permanent reinforcement to the soil surface. The spun mesh is filled with soil, so it is effectively buried.
3. Mats of straw and/or coir fibres sewn between two light polypropylene woven meshes. This is essentially a straw mulch with some minimal reinforcement, and is very effective for short-term erosion control. It can be supplied and installed with a seed mixture already embedded into it.

For all these types of netting it is critical to get a good contact between the material and the soil surface. This means preparing a loose stone-free surface with no major undulations. The netting is pegged down firmly to the soil with 300 mm or so steel pins or staples usually placed 0.5 m apart. Edges are overlapped as

PLATE 13.3 **Mulch-seeding application of chopped straw with a dry mulch blower.** *(N. Coppin)*

appropriate, and most mat manufacturers provide installation details and specifications.

## Turfing

If an instant sward is required, then turf is the only option. Normal turf can either be produced as for lawns or can be specifically grown from the desired seed mix. Turf can also be used as a pre-grown mat containing a proprietary three-dimensional netting. This material is lighter and can be handled more cost effectively if the right machinery is available.

Turf can be placed either as a continuous cover, which is very expensive, or in rows or lattice arrangements across the slope. The row or lattice formation gives some immediate slope protection at lower cost, though the interstices should be seeded as usual (or planted, as is described in Section 13.6).

## Management

For most slopes management will be minimal. Certainly mowing will be impracticable. Some initial aftercare

with fertilizers and other materials will be necessary in order to establish the sward properly and an aftercare programme of five years or so should be considered with regular monitoring of progress. On infertile subsoils the development of soil fertility is important. If the early aftercare maintains the fertility at too high a level, then the low maintenance species will not establish themselves properly, and when fertility ceases, there will be an inevitable regression of the sward. Achieving the right balance between species and soil fertility is a difficult process.

Legumes, which fix atmospheric nitrogen and return it to the soil, will be an essential part of any low maintenance sward. They provide the only practicable long-term method of building up soil fertility. However, it should be remembered that the widely used forage legumes, such as clover, require high levels of other nutrients, mainly phosphate and lime, in order to continue growing and fixing nitrogen.

In the absence of any regular mowing or grazing, succession will usually begin fairly quickly, and the sward will be invaded by taller and more competitive herbaceous species, shrubs such as willow and bramble

223

and eventually by trees. The direction of the succession is determined mainly by climate, and in the absence of any interference will eventually reach the potential natural vegetation.

The succession may or may not be desirable in relation to the function that the vegetation is meant to perform. If it is not desirable, then some positive management is necessary in order to influence the succession or to maintain it at a pre-determined level. Management options include:

(a) Occasional defoliation by cutting, grazing or fire to remove developing scrub.
(b) Selective removal of invading species.
(c) Maintaining a low soil fertility by omitting legumes from the seed mix and the regular removal of biomass.

## 13.6 USE OF WOODY PLANTS

Vegetation dominated by woody species represents the natural long-term plant cover over large parts of the earth's land surface. The natural climax vegetation of the majority of habitat types of most of north west Europe, including steeply sloping ground in the British Isles, is deciduous woodland. In many situations therefore long-term slope stabilization may best be achieved by establishing a stable cover of woody vegetation.

## Stabilization qualities

The ways in which woody vegetation is effective in stabilizing slopes are essentially similar to the way in which herbaceous species function. Nevertheless, the scale and structure of the majority of woody plants means that their functions vary in their degree of effectiveness as compared to herbaceous plants in the following ways:

1. Interception of precipitation by the canopy occurs on a much greater scale, owing to the much larger leaf area and its layered arrangement above the ground. This effect is particularly important where precipitation on slopes can be in the form of snow, and where erosion risk also takes the form of avalanche hazard.
2. Maximization of infiltration and prevention of surface water run-off developing into sheet flow is likely to be less effective. This is because the density of shoots penetrating the soil surface is usually lower. However, greater interception will to some extent compensate for the lower effectiveness in combating surface erosion.
3. The effectiveness of binding soil particles will vary with the root morphology. The effect of reinforcing the soil profile will generally be more significant simply because woody species have more extensive root systems.

There is still relatively little detailed or reliable information about patterns of root growth. Although the popular conception that the biomass that is visible above ground is mirrored in form and scale beneath the ground surface is certainly an over-simplification, it is clear that the correlation between root and shoot growth is relevant in time as well as space.

The majority of the parts of woody vegetation below ground are perennial, and this suggests that the effectiveness of trees and shrub roots in binding and reinforcing the soil will be only minimally diminished during the winter months and will gradually increase over time as the size of the plant increases. This is in clear contrast to the annual periodicity of herbaceous vegetation.

Information on root form within the soil profile is sparse and even excavation will give only a partial picture of the root architecture, with little indication of the dynamics of the 'underground forest'. Rooting depth of woody species is assumed to be greater than that for herbaceous vegetation and thus the potential for deeper seated stabilization is increased. There will also be variation between species and vegetation types. The conventional classification of woody plants into fibrous and tap-rooting species is not sufficient on its own for the purposes of considering vegetation for slope stabilization. Schiechtl (1973) recommends a categorisation into 'extensive' (widespread or deep rooting species) and 'intensive' rooting species (which root densely within a relatively small volume).

It is to be expected that the tensile and shear strength of the roots of woody plants would generally be greater than those of herbaceous species. Measurements made during the first year of root growth indicate no significant differences (Schiechtl, 1973), but only in woody species do root diameters increase from year to year. The relationship between root diameter and root strength is, however, not a linear one. Strength is also not the only important parameter; the quantity of root growth, orientation, diameter and density are all significant factors in considering the stabilization qualities of woody plants, although these will be affected by soil conditions.

Figures quoted by Gray and Leiser (1982) also show considerable differences between different tree species, as well as a relative decrease in strength per unit cross-sectional area as roots grow in diameter. Nevertheless, the forces which thicker roots (as are to be found only in woody species) are able to withstand are considerably greater. Loss of root strength with age appears to markedly accelerate in some species after felling of the tree, implying that the strength of the dead, lignified root tissue contributes only a part, though 50 per cent or more, of the root strength.

The cumulative impact of these differences in the degree of effectiveness in slope stabilization means that while herbaceous vegetation is arguably most effective in minimizing the impact of surface erosion, woody species have the potential to enhance the stability of slopes which have deeper seated problems and which could otherwise lead to mass movement.

## Suitable species

There are a number of criteria which should be considered in selecting woody species for slope stabilization purposes (Schiechtl, 1973). These include:

(a) (aut) ecological criteria;
(b) phytosociological criteria;
(c) availability/ease of propagation criteria;
(d) biotechnical criteria.

The first three of these are equally applicable to the selection of species for any use in any planting scheme, and can be dealt with very briefly. The adaptation of the species used to the soil and climatic conditions in which it will have to grow is of particular importance as far as the success of the plant is concerned. However, selection of an appropriate species is not sufficient in itself. It is also important to make use of actual material that is used to growing in conditions as similar as possible to those in which it will be expected to perform.

Apart from the initial objective of slope stabilization, one of the most important objectives of using plant material is to achieve a vegetation cover which is stable and will require a minimum of management. Plant sociological approaches regard vegetation as a series of recognizable plant communities (Braun-Blanquet, 1965; Müller-Dombois and Ellenberg, 1974; and the forthcoming UK National Vegetation Classification). On this basis the selection of species will not take place on an individual basis, but through determining the plant community likely to be naturally indigenous to the site in question, and with regard to its likely successional development.

Clearly, species which are not available, either commercially or through lack of accessibility close to the site of use, are unsuitable for application in large scale stabilization work. Material which can be easily gathered and propagated has the advantage of being far more economic to use, but ease of vegetative propagation can also be equated with ease and reliability of the establishment of non-rooted woody material.

Biotechnical criteria for species selection are based on a number of species specific, i.e. genetically determined, physical and physiological characteristics of plant growth. Relatively little information is available with regard to these plant attributes, although a limited amount of work has been done for a few species. The main biotechnical criteria are as follows:

(a) rooting form, especially in relation to slope;
(b) shear and tensile strength of roots;
(c) formation of large root biomass;
(d) rapid growth of roots and shoots;
(e) ability to regenerate or spread vegetatively;
(f) resistance to mechanical stress;
(g) survival of shoot burial and root exposure.

Trees and shrubs which tend to fulfil the majority of these criteria are woody ruderals characteristic of disturbed habitats, such as willows, alders and poplars. All have wide ecological amplitudes, tend to form adventitious roots easily and produce large quantities of small seed.

## Conventional horticultural approaches

'Horticultural' approaches to plant establishment, that is the planting of individual rooted plants into a topsoil substrate, have generally been the subject of critical scrutiny during the last decade, in particular with regard to the creation of areas of native vegetation within a large scale landscape context. The principles involving the use of small material, working without topsoil and so on obviously apply to planting on slopes in the same way as elsewhere.

Large container-grown material and species which spread vegetatively to give a quick cover without necessarily rooting may appear to give a relatively rapid soil cover to minimize erosion caused by surface run-off. However, the tendency for root development to remain limited to within the rootball for a long period after planting will mean that the soil mass will remain unreinforced by root growth. Similarly, on topsoiled slopes the tendency for root activity to remain within the discrete topsoil layer, and not to bind the slope as a whole, is part of the whole question of the pros and cons of topsoil already discussed.

Plant spacing is more critical on a slope, where one of the main reasons for planting is to achieve a rapid soil cover. On slopes the use of mulches between plants serves to protect the soil surface from the effects of rainfall and run-off as much as to retain soil moisture and suppress weed growth. Consideration should be given to the preparation of the slope surface before planting to minimize the impact of run-off. Planting in furrows or on terraces cut at a shallow angle to the horizontal will help both the control and the capture of surface water. Planting of transplants in this manner is often combined with various of the continental bioengineering techniques described below.

## Bioengineering approaches

Construction techniques using plant material have long been part of accepted landscape practice, both in the stabilization of steep slopes and of the banks of water courses in the German speaking countries of central Europe. The term *Ingenieurbiologie* − literally 'engineering biology' − was coined in the late 1930s (Pflug,

225

PLATE 13.4 **Slope fascines arranged in a diamond pattern, stabilizing a new road cutting through a water-bearing soil stratum in Upper Bavaria, one season after construction.** *(R. Stiles)*

the application of bioengineering techniques in the fields of river bank and coastal protection (DIN 19, 657), torrent control (DIN 19, 663) and general landscape construction (DIN 18, 918). The specification of the 'standard' bioengineering techniques is included in the computerized national construction specification documents (Deutsches Institut für Normung, 1976).

In addition to these and other official publications there is an extensive literature of standard textbooks and journal publications, few of which are available in English. In 1979 Die Gesellschaft für Ingenieurbiologie (The Society for Bioengineering) was founded to further the discipline. Although based in West Germany, its membership is taken from several countries.

The essential difference between the majority of the continental bioengineering techniques and those described above as conventional horticultural techniques concerns the predominant use of live but non-rooted plant material. Various forms and sizes of material are used, ranging from thin flexible wands, through thicker pegs and poles to whole branches several metres long.

The use of woody material from which to establish vegetation has one important advantage for slope stabilization above and beyond the practical and economic considerations of cost, convenience and effectiveness. Inserting relatively large masses of woody material into the soil causes an immediate stabilizing effect, even before any root or shoot development has taken place.

A selection of the techniques concerning the use of woody plants covered by DIN 18,918 is outlined below. Forms of construction exclusively using woody plants are covered, as are combined methods using both plants and non-living material. The techniques can be used in the stabilization of newly created slopes as well as in the repair of erosion damage or partial failure of existing areas.

## Slope fascines

This technique is used primarily to prevent erosion of and to stabilize topsoiled or wet cut slopes on relatively deep soils. Fascines are made from long, straight branches of living woody material of at least 10 mm in diameter, bound together with wire in bundles so that the cross-section at any point contains at least five branches. They can either take the form of discrete lengths of up to 5 m or of continuous bundles intended to run without a break for the whole length of the slope that is to be stabilized (see Plate 13.4).

Parallel ditches are dug in the slope, usually at intervals of several metres, either horizontally with gaps to allow for drainage or continuously at an inclination of up to 30° to aid and control surface water run-

1980) at the end of a period when a long standing collection of practical techniques had begun to emerge as a discipline in their own right.

Much of the pre-war activity in this field had been stimulated by the construction of the new autobahns. This in turn employed techniques developed for slope stabilization in the more extreme conditions of the Alps. The codification of this experience in the form of official publications, guidelines and standards gives some indication of the importance and growth of the subject, as well as the areas of application. A few examples are quoted below.

In 1962 the German Road Research Institution published a research paper on 'Green construction in highway engineering' and this has been regularly updated. It now takes the form of official recommendations for good practice in the treatment of highway embankments. The most recent edition of it was published in 1983 (Forschungsgesellschaft für Strassen und Verkehrswesen, 1983). There are at present three different German Standards (DIN Normen) dealing with

PLATE 13.5 **Forestry transplants planted between slope fascines to provide for long-term stability of the slope to take over from the willow pioneer vegetation, one season after construction.** *(R. Stiles)*

off. Slope fascines can also be laid in a diamond shape. The prefabricated fascine bundles are laid in the ditches and staked at regular intervals. The ditches are then filled to the surface, completely covering the fascines, with earth dug from the next up slope ditch, construction taking place from the bottom to the top of the slope.

The method is easy and quick to implement, requiring relatively little movement of earth. It can be used over quite large areas. However, it gives only short-term and relatively shallow protection, as the fascines are laid directly on or below the slope surface. For this reason it is recommended that planting of a long-term community should be carried out between the fascines as soon as possible (see Plate 13.5).

### Branch layers

Branch layers are used for the stabilization of steep labile slopes in either cut or fill material, as well as for hindering surface erosion. They are most effective, though, for stabilizing fill material, and this application is described here.

Branches of up to 7 m long, although 2 m is more common, are placed in a criss-cross fashion in horizontal courses and then covered with layers of fill material so that only their ends protrude from the face of the slope. The branches are placed with their lower ends facing into the slope and pointing down at an angle of about 10°. Not more than between one quarter and one fifth of each branch should protrude from the face of the slope. The protruding branch ends help to control surface run-off and to prevent erosion (see Plate 13.6).

The placing of fill material on top of each branch layer can be done by machine, although attention must be given to ensuring that a sufficiently fine substrate is provided and carefully compacted to prevent any voids around the branches.

Branch layering has the most deep seated effect of any biological slope stabilizing method. The soil is reinforced immediately by the branch layers, and their rooting and development considerably enhances this effect, while also rendering it more or less permanent. There is no need to select the plant material carefully;

227

PLATE 13.6 **Fill slope of material excavated from a Swiss alpine tunnel, tipped and consolidated in layers with horizontal willow branch layers inserted between in finer material. The illustration shows the condition after 4–5 years' growth. The slope is subject to frequent avalanche damage, and the varying degree of shoot growth reflects this.** (*R. Stiles*)

whole branches of more or less any form together with all their side shoots can be used.

Including rooted plant material with the branch layers makes it possible to add what should develop into the final vegetation community for the habitat concerned, such that initial stabilization and the long-term vegetation cover can be provided in a single process. This variant is described as hedge branch layering.

### Hardwood cuttings and joint planting

The aim of this method is to provide a rapid and simple method of stabilizing slopes, and in particular those slopes subject to problems of a high soil moisture content. In combination with stone pitching, cuttings considerably strengthen the structure of the slope.

Cuttings of between 250 and 400 mm long are taken from straight branches which are several years old, having a diameter of between 10 and 50 mm. The cutting length will depend on the soil type to be stabilized; with heavy clay soils they could be cut as short as 150 mm and with light, sandy or stony soils they will need to be 600 mm or more. They should be placed into the slope surface as irregularly as is possible. Recommendations regarding the planting density range from between two and five to between ten and twenty cuttings per square metre.

Should the ground surface be too hard, holes can be driven in using metal stakes, although if this is done, care must be taken to ensure that they are refilled after planting to prevent voids around the cuttings and prevent them from drying out and dying. Otherwise the cuttings are placed directly into the ground so that not more than one quarter of their length protrudes. Some authorities even suggest that they are completely buried.

Where cuttings are used for joint planting, their length should be such that they are able to pass through the depth of the stone facing and into the earth below the required depth. The joints should subsequently be filled with suitable soil material to prevent the cuttings from drying out. This can be done by spreading and brushing in dry soil or by using water to wash it into the joints. With joint planting, the density of the cuttings per square metre will be a function of the size of the stones used for pitching the surface of the slope (see Plate 13.7).

## Slope grids

This technique aims to provide both immediate and long-term stabilization to localized areas of instability or failure within an existing or newly formed cut slope.

Timber of appropriate type and dimensions is used to construct a grid with cells of about 2 m square, the exact size and form of construction depending on the nature of the stabilization problem. Because of the need to anchor the structure to the ground, grids are used at the base of a slope to allow a simple footing to be constructed on level ground.

The recommended maximum height for a slope grid is 10–20 m. Drainage between the face of the slope and the slope grid construction must be ensured. For stabilization of surface failures a single grid is likely to be sufficient, while if there is a relatively deep seated problem to be repaired, a double grid will be required; its depth will be a function of the depth of the failure.

Horizontal and vertical members are joined, usually by nailing, and the whole structure is anchored to the slope by means of steel reinforcing bars or any similar and appropriate anchor. It is sometimes also possible to use live timber pegs to help with securing the grid, in which case, when these develop roots, the linkage between grid and slope will be considerably enhanced.

The open squares within the grid are backfilled with local soil and can be planted using a number of techniques, including using woody cuttings, branch layering and rooted plant material (see Plate 13.8). Alternatively, the squares may be seeded, although this will not provide the long-term deep binding of the slope resulting from woody material.

The function of a slope grid is that it is able to stabilize the whole of the slope, not just the area that it occupies but the area above it as well. Because it is a rigid structure, it is immediately effective. Depending on the nature of the planting in the grid squares this will gradually take over the function of stabilizing the ground as it develops.

The combination of immediate stabilization by means of a rigid structure with a long-term planting which will increase in effectiveness over time makes this a valuable technique. The opportunity to combine it with a number of different planting techniques means that it can be easily adapted to specific situations.

PLATE 13.7 **Joint planting with willow on a stone-faced river bank. The stone is only visible in areas that are used to gain access to the river bed. Elsewhere growth of the willows has completely covered the stone-work.** *(R. Stiles)*

## Live crib walls

This technique is intended to provide immediate stabilization and a long-term fixed point around which other bioengineering solutions can be applied. Planted crib walls are usually constructed as discrete structures to perform the same function as gravity retaining walls. They may be situated at the base of a slope or at intervals up its side, either 'leaning back' against the slope or tied into it by the headers or with steel anchors.

Crib walls consist of long header beams which are laid horizontal and parallel to the face of the slope, and shorter stretchers which run between them at right-angles back into the slope at an angle of at least 10° to the vertical. The materials used can either be timber, roundwood or sawn, or specially shaped, precast concrete elements.

A timber crib wall can have single or double rows of stretchers, while most precast concrete systems are double. With a timber system, Begemann and Schiechtl (1986) recommend that at least half the length of the header is driven back into the undisturbed slope (see Plate 13.9). Alternate rows of headers and stretchers are built up and fixed at every point where they overlap. The resulting void behind them is successively filled

PLATE 13.8 (a) **Road embankment in a cutting stabilized with a slope grid and willow branch layers.** *(R. Stiles)*

PLATE 13.8 (b) **Detail of Plate 13.8(a).** *(R. Stiles)*

with substrate, and between each course rows of branches are laid at a rate of at least ten per metre and then covered with the fill material, which should contain as much fine material as possible. Ideally the bases of the branches should reach into the undisturbed material of the existing slope (see Plate 13.10).

## Management

The management of woody vegetation is of considerable importance in maintaining its function for slope stabiliz-

PLATE 13.9 **Detail of timber crib wall, showing freshly-placed willow branches directly above the stretcher beams.** *(R. Stiles)*

PLATE 13.10 **Live timber crib walls in the Swiss Alps, showing two stages of development of willow cuttings. The wall in the background is one season old, while that in the foreground has just been completed.** *(R. Stiles)*

ation. Given the phytosociological criteria referred to previously, depending on which woody species are selected on the basis that they form part of the potential natural vegetation of the area, management needs to be conceived and carried out with the aim of establishing this vegetation type as rapidly as possible by short-cutting the succession process and with the aim of creating a stable climax woodland community. This may call both for the suppression of competition and the stimulation of growth with fertilizers.

In the case of both conventional horticultural and bioengineering approaches to the use of plant material, normal establishment maintenance is vital to ensure that planting takes properly and that dead material is removed and replaced. The instability of the slope environment may mean that plants will become buried or, conversely, that they will have their roots exposed. Such problems need to be rectified until plants are properly established. Similarly bioengineering constructions, with fascines or brush layers for example, need to be monitored and repaired as soon as any damage occurs.

If the species have been chosen correctly and the site has been properly prepared, intensive maintenance should no longer be necessary reasonably soon after the initial establishment of a long-term vegetation community has been ensured.

Where for reasons of the wider environmental or more specific slope conditions it is desirable to maintain a pioneer vegetation of willows, for example, it may be necessary to arrest the natural succession process by removing colonizing trees, which would otherwise rapidly shade out the pioneer species. The ability of such species to carry out stabilization functions is, as has been discussed above, dependent on vigorous young root growth. Regular coppicing of the vegetation will have a rejuvenating effect on root as well as shoot growth. The harvesting of vegetative material for propagation or directly for new construction work can frequently be combined with this sort of management operation. It may also be beneficial to remove larger trees in order to reduce the load on the slope and to minimize the risk of damage by wind.

## 13.7 CHOOSING THE RIGHT METHOD

It is not possible, or appropriate, to lay down rules or prescriptions for which technique should be used in any given situation. The designer will have to take into account a number of factors, including:

(a) the nature of the site;
(b) the nature and extent of the problem;
(c) available materials and plants;
(d) accessibility and machinery available;
(e) costs;
(f) reliability and consequences of failure;
(g) maintenance requirements.

He will also have his own preferences, or those of his client, to take into account.

The selection of suitable species will depend on:

(a) The method and ease of propagation of seed, plants and cuttings.
(b) Stabilization qualities, including root architecture and depth and form of top growth.
(c) Site criteria, such as climate, soil conditions and fertility.
(d) Resistance to damage by mechanical forces, root exposure and the ability to self-repair.

231

TABLE 13.3
**Approaches to slope protection and erosion control (After Gray and Leiser, 1982)**

| Category | Examples | Appropriate uses | Function or role of vegetation |
|---|---|---|---|
| **1. Live construction** | | | |
| 1.1 Conventional plantings | Seeding grasses and Herbs, planting shrubs. | Control of surface rainfall and wind erosion. To reduce surface weathering by frost. | Bind and retrain soil particles. Filter soil particles from run-off. Intercept raindrops, Maintain infiltration, Change thermal character of ground surface. Insulation. |
| 1.2 Woody plants used as reinforcement and barriers to soil movement | Planting trees and shrubs. Live staking/cuttings. Contour wattles/fascines. Brush and hedge layering. | Control of surface rainfall erosion (rolling and gullying). Control of shallow translational mass movement. | Same as above, but also to reinforce soil and resist downslope movement of soil masses by buttressing. Increase soil tensile strength by root reinforcement and removal of moisture. |
| **2. Mixed construction** | | | |
| 2.1 Woody plants grown in interstices of low porous structures or benches of tiered structures | Vegetated revetments (rip-rap, grids, gabions, blocks, netting). Vegetated retaining walls (cribs, gabions and so on.) | Control of shallow mass movements and resistance to earth forces. Improvement of appearance and performance of structures. | Reinforcement of soil and fill behind structure into a monolithic mass. Remove moisture from soil or fill behind structure. |
| 2.2 Toe walls at foot of slope used in conjunction with planting on the face | Lowbreast walls of stone and masonry with vegetated slope above. | Control of erosion on cut and fill slopes subject to undermining at the toe. Reduction in slope angle and/or length. | Reduce or prevent erosion on the slope face above retaining wall. |
| 2.3 Geotextile reinforcement of soil surface | Surface protection and reinforcement with polypropylene mat. | Bank and slope protection from severe erosive forces or surface instability. | Anchoring of reinforcement to soil surface. Reduce or prevent initial surface erosion which will expose geotextile. |
| **3. Inert construction** | | | |
| 3.1 Conventional structures | Gravity walls, cantilever walls and pile walls. | Control of deep-seated mass movements and restraint of large lateral earth forces. Retention of toxic or aggressive fills and soils. | Mainly cosmetic. |

(e) Plant sociological criteria, such as the ability of mixtures of species to combine into a suitable plant community.

Plant species have their own strategies for survival. Grime (1979) describes three basic strategies according to which plants can be classified: competitors – plants characteristic of highly fertile, low stress environments; stress tolerators – plants able to survive in stressed environments; and ruderals – opportunist species which can quickly colonize bare ground. In selecting species for slope stabilization it is useful to bear in mind that species normally selected for initial planting tend to exhibit a ruderal or ruderal-stress tolerant strategy. The succession will then proceed in the direction of com-petitors under fertile conditions and stress tolerators in infertile environments.

Plants can be used in a number of ways, and approaches varying from pure 'live construction', with vegetation providing all the protection, to 'hybrid' techniques using a combination of plants with inert materials. These approaches are summarized in Table 13.3.

Seeding techniques vary across a spectrum from simple broadcast sowing to heavy mulch seeding, with many possible combinations of mulch, fertilizer and binder. The choice depends on a combination of site conditions, climate and erosion and slide risk. Table 13.4 summarizes the applications of the various methods.

TABLE 13.4

**Application of various seeding methods to different situations.** *(Schiechtl, 1980)*

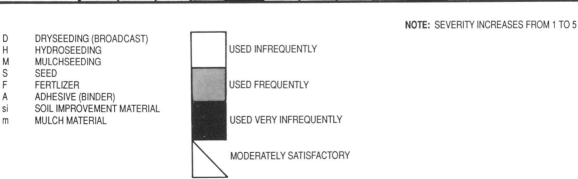

| | METHOD | SOIL CONDITION | | | | | CLIMATE | | | | | EROSION AND SLIDE DANGER | | | | |
|---|---|---|---|---|---|---|---|---|---|---|---|---|---|---|---|---|
| | | 1 | 2 | 3 | 4 | 5 | 1 | 2 | 3 | 4 | 5 | 1 | 2 | 3 | 4 | 5 |
| 1 | D H/sf | | | | | | | | | | | | | | | |
| 2 | D H/sfa | | | | | | | | | | | | | | | |
| 3 | DH/sfsi | | | | | | | | | | | | | | | |
| 4 | M/sfm | | | | | | | | | | | | | | | |
| 5 | D H/sfasi | | | | | | | | | | | | | | | |
| 6 | M/sfsim | | | | | | | | | | | | | | | |
| 7 | M/fsam | | | | | | | | | | | | | | | |
| 8 | M/sfasim | | | | | | | | | | | | | | | |

NOTE: SEVERITY INCREASES FROM 1 TO 5

D   DRYSEEDING (BROADCAST)
H   HYDROSEEDING
M   MULCHSEEDING
S   SEED
F   FERTLIZER
A   ADHESIVE (BINDER)
si  SOIL IMPROVEMENT MATERIAL
m   MULCH MATERIAL

USED INFREQUENTLY

USED FREQUENTLY

USED VERY INFREQUENTLY

MODERATELY SATISFACTORY

233

# REFERENCES

Brechtel, H. M. and Hammes, W. (in Pflug, W. (ed.) *Wurzelwerk und Standsicherheit von Boeschungen und Haengen, Jahrbuch 2 des Gesellschaft für ingenie-biologie* (Aachen: Sepia Verlag 1985)

BS 6031: 1981, *Code of Practice for Earthworks* British Standards Institution

Braun-Blanquet, J. *Plant sociology: The Study of Plant Communities*, (transl., rev. and ed. by C. D. Fuller and H. S. Conrad), (London: Hafner 1965)

CIRIA – Construction Industry Research and Information Association (forthcoming) *The Use of Vegetation in Civil Engineering*

Coppin, N. J. and Bradshaw, A. D. *Quarry Reclamation* (Mining Journal Books 1982)

Deutsches Institut für Normung *Standard-leistungsbuch für das Bauwesen – Leistungsbereich 003 Landschaftsbauarbeiten* (Berlin: Beuth Verlag 1976)

Doorenbos, J. and Pruitt, W. O. *Guidelines for predicting crop water requirements*, Irrigation and Drainage Paper No. 24 (Rome: FAO 1975)

Forschungsgesellschaft für Strassen und Verkehrswesen, Arbeitsgruppe Strassenentwurf *Richtlinien für die Anlage von Strassen (RAS), Teil Landschaftsgestaltung (RAS-LG), Abschnitt 3: Lebenverbau RAS-LG 3* Cologne (1983)

Garwood, E. A. 'Studies on the roots of grasses, *Annual Report of Grassland Research Institute*, **166**, pp. 72–79 (1967)

Gray, D. H. and Leiser, A. T. *Biotechnical Slope Protection and Erosion Control* (New York: Van Nostrand Reinhold 1982)

Grime, P. *Plant Strategies and Vegetation Processes* (London: John Wiley 1979)

Hudson, N. *Soil Conservation* (B. T. Batsford 1971)

Jarvis, M. G. and Mackney, D. *Soil Survey Applications*, Technical Monograph No. 13, (Harpenden: Soil Survey of England and Wales 1979).

Morgan, R. P. C. *Soil Erosion and Conservation*, (Longman 1986)

Müller-Dombois, D. and Ellenberg, H. *Aims and Methods of Vegetation Ecology* (New York: John Wiley 1974).

Parr, T. W. Cox, R. and Plant, R. A. 'The éffects of cutting height on root distribution and water use of ryegrass (S23) turf', *Journal of Sports Turf Research Institute* **60**, pp. 45–53 (1985)

Pflug, W. *Zur Gründung der Gesellschaft für Ingenieurbiologie in Jahrbuch der Gesellschaft für Ingenieurbiologie* (1980)

Schaller, F. W. and Sutton, P. (eds) 'Reclamation of drastically disturbed land, *Procedures Symposium of American Society of Agronomists*, Madison, Wisc. (1983)

Schiechtl, H. M. *Sicherungsarbeiten im Landschaftsbau* (Munich: Callwey Verlag 1973)

Schiechtl, H. M. *Bioengineering for Land Reclamation and Conservation* (Edmonton: The University of Alberta Press 1980)

Smith, L. P. *The Agricultural Climate of England–Wales*, Technical Bulletin 35, Ministry of Agriculture, Fisheries and Food (London: HMSO 1976)

Stiles, R. (forthcoming) *Biological Construction Techniques in Central Europe* (Stuttgart: Karl Krauner Verlag)

Wischmeier, W. H. and Smith, D. D. *Predicting Rainfall Erosion Losses – A Guide to Conservation Planning*, US Department of Agriculture, Agriculture Handbook No. 537 (1978)

Young, A. *Slopes*, Geomorphology Texts No. 3 (Longman 1972)

# Planting in Tropical Lowland Areas

## HENRY STEED

The author would like to acknowledge his debt to W. Bowen, B. T. Siedlecki and Dr T. G. Walker, the authors of this chapter in the first edition of *Landscape Design with Plants*. Their writing provided the basis for this new and updated chapter.

## 14.1 THE TROPICS

The tropics are the areas of land between latitudes 23.5°C north and south of the equator, and literally represent the extremes of the sun's noon vertical position at times of the summer and winter solstices However, although circles of Cancer and Capricorn represent constant hours of daylight, plants do not follow this criterion alone. Variations in temperature, humidity, rainfall, soils and exposure cause the limits of the tropical ecological zones to vary, generally extending them well north or south of their respective tropic lines. Mild climates, where frosts are absent, are known as the sub-tropics. These include the Mediterranean type of climate experienced in South Australia, South Africa, California and the Mediterranean itself. For plant types there is no clear distinction between sub-tropic, tropic and equatorial, but this general guide can apply:

1. Sub-Tropical — absence of frost, but distinctive cool season.
2. Tropical — year-round minimum temperature of 18°C. Noticeable seasons, usually wet and hot in summer and dry and cool in winter.
3. Equatorial — minimal seasonal difference, wet or dry variation only

Figure 14.1 shows the general limits of the sub-tropical region in relation to the tropics themselves. Plants are usually tolerant of a wide range of conditions and will pass through these regional differences if their main requirements are met. Hence equatorial plants can be grown in desert areas with suitable humidity and watering, and temperate plants can be grown in the cooler temperatures and less heavy rainfall of equatorial highland regions.

The main continental land areas of the tropics are distinctly separated from each other by the oceans, and in most cases contain their own type of flora and ecology. The original forests of these regions are quite different from each other: the Amazon basin, Central Africa and South East Asia all have their own type of rainforest and associated sub-flora. Thus, a designer operating in one region would find it hard to draw on information from another region and be able to prepare sensible designs. There is available a wide range of 'Pan-tropic' species, now found in most tropical countries as commercially grown plants, but use of these alone is unlikely to be interesting or well received by clients and informed local people. In all areas, without exception, local knowledge has to be obtained in order to prepare interesting and appropriate plant designs.

This chapter by necessity, however, takes on a slightly 'Pan-tropic' form, in that each region is not described separately and detailed descriptions of local plant types are not covered. The detailed descriptions relate mainly to South East Asian regions since this is the area most familiar to the author. The aim is to provide design criteria suitable for use in any tropical region, except for arid areas (information on which you should refer to Chapter 15) the sub-tropics, and uplands above 3000 feet [900 m]. Designers, whether designing for schemes in their own countries or foreign designers working abroad, may find these criteria a useful check-list to apply to local conditions.

## 14.2 TROPICAL REGIONS AND THEIR CHARACTERISTICS

While preparing detail designs or design briefings, it is wise to determine the regional characteristics of the area in which the design is to take place. The macro-climatic influences on different areas will combine with geographic factors to create the individual character of a region. The map in Figure 14.1 indicates these broad characteristics. The areas of the tropics can be divided into:

1. Wet tropics – very high rainfall (300–500 cm); temperature 20–34°C.
2. Humid tropics – high rainfall (200–300 cm); temperature 18–36°C.
3. Sub-humid tropics – rainfall (100–200 cm); temperatures 10–40°C.
4. Semi-arid tropics – low rainfall (50–100 cm); temperature 2–40°C.
5. Arid tropics – very low rainfall (5–50 cm); temperature 2–45°C.

Sub-tropical regions will display these same characteristics, but tend to have lower minimum temperatures over a longer season. They are still likely to have extremely hot maximum temperatures. It is noticeable that lower rainfall and wider temperature ranges are characteristics of an arid or semi-arid climate. Humidity may, however, be ralatively high even in dry zones, especially in those close to warm sea bodies, such as the Indian Ocean and the Persian Gulf. Conversely, humidity can be very low in desert fringe or rain shadow areas, due to low ambient moisture levels. Beyond the macroclimatic zones all areas are influenced by more specific patterns which strongly affect landscape types. Some important influencing factors are given here:

1. Monsoon seasons and prevailing wind directions.
2. Winds peculiar to a particular area.
3. Humidity patterns and fire-prone seasons.
4. Typhoons or winds of destructive force.
5. Altitude: variations in rainfall, cloud layer and temperature.
6. Hours of sunlight and presence of cloud layer.

These elements are general influences on regional character. Local and microgeographic elements also need to be studied to interpret and understand the existing landscape of an area. Thus, tropical islands will have quite a different character from large land masses, and ocean currents will affect temperature and humidity. There may be only small seasonal temperature ranges in warm sea areas but these may be coupled with intensely high light levels and only minimal rainfall. Fresh water from coral deposits may exist, but may also be brackish and water catchment capacity may be quite limited.

Coastal landscapes generally are influenced by prevailing wind, currents and rain, but more noticeably by their relative shelter and the depth of the sea around them. Oceanic coastlines are usually deep and clear, with sand or rock fringes, and are often forested, owing to man's less frequent activities along inhospitable seaboards. More enclosed seas (such as the Caribbean and the South China) are shallower, and coastlines are more silted, once outflow from rivers is deposited, not drifted away. Mangroves and swampy coasts are prevalent. Cultivation on flat ground and ease of access for boats mean greater concentration of settlements. On the other hand, arid coastlines are influenced predominantly by the desert on the land side rather than the sea, and occupy large stretches of what would otherwise be lush coastline if sufficient moisture was present.

Lowland regions and foothills are commonly the most populated and cultivated areas. Natural vegetation is likely to be minimal in developed areas, and impenetrable where undeveloped as secondary or scrub forest. Lowlands are the zones of the greatest exploitation and removal of rainforest or indigenous woodland, since they are the most accessible, and demands for development of these areas is the greatest. Past forest removal has usually resulted in plantation and agricultural landscapes. Modern forest removal is often for townships, industrial development and transport services, and is usually on a massive scale, with consequent loss of vegetation, soil erosion and water shortage. It is here, in the tropical islands and lowlands, between the coastline and land up to 3000 ft (900 m), where maximum development activity is likely to occur, and the landscape designer is most likely to find himself in demand. This applies in all the tropical regions – wet, humid and arid.

Upland areas above 3000 ft (900 m) will be cooler and have different rainfall patterns to the lowlands, and this will result in changes of flora up to 18 000 ft (5500 m), where frost is permanent and settlements are almost nonexistent. Ocean currents, proximity of deserts and major weather patterns play a distinct role in the wetness or dryness of mountain ranges, and familiarity with the peculiar climate and geography of uplands will be essential to any designer working in these areas.

Having taken a brief look at the nature and character of the tropics, and broadly determined the elements that the designer needs to study, we now describe the local and site-specific factors that need to be included or considered in the design and design brief.

## 14.3 FACTORS AFFECTING PLANTING IN TROPICAL REGIONS

## Climate and weather

Detailed familiarity with local climate and microclimatic conditions is essential. Seasonal variations may be minute, but knowledge of the different seasonal patterns is critical in planning planting operations. The sun plays a far greater part in the pattern of life in tropical regions than it does in temperate or even warm temperate areas. Intense heat, humidity and light, vital to tropical plant growth, are enervating to man. It is, however, a mistake to believe that plant growth is guaranteed under such lush conditions.

Soil temperatures at the surface may vary by as much as 28°C (50°F) between 7 o'clock in the morning and 3 in the afternoon as a result of the fierce sun. At a depth of 5 cm this variation drops by 17°C (30°F), while at

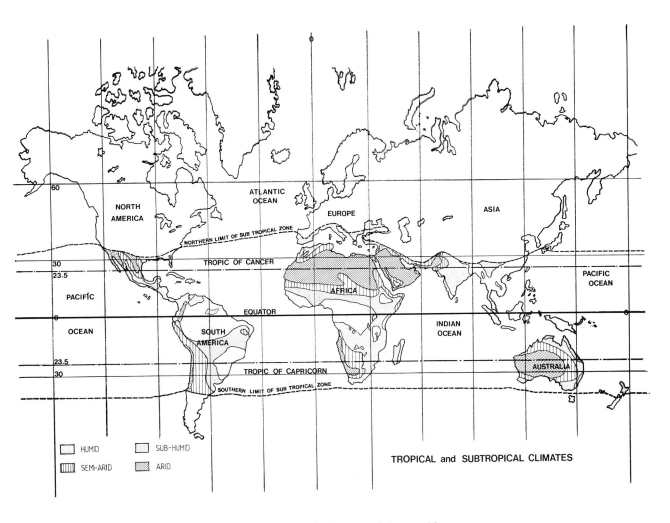

FIGURE 14.1 **Map showing the tropical and subtropical areas of the world.**

1.2 m it is only 1°C (2°F). Such temperature variations can play havoc with shallow-rooted plants which are not given adequate protection against the sun or adequate water during establishment periods.

Temperature statistics can be misleading if humidity is not considered alongside them. Humidity can vary tremendously within a few hours, especially after rain. In dry seasons, the humidity will be low and the air may be laden with microscopic dust particles which penetrate and clog the leaves of the vegetation, as well as machinery and instruments. In wet seasons, humidity levels can reach close to 100 per cent and, apart from stimulating rapid plant growth, fungus, algae and pests will proliferate.

Rainfall varies in amount in different areas from virtually zero in dry seasons to hundreds of centimetres in the wet season. Rainfall can vary distinctly between one area and another quite close to it. Islands, in particular, often have very different amounts of rainfall on different sides.

Where rainfall is permanently or seasonally low, irrigation will be required. How much irrigation can be used will depend on the availability and legality of using water for such purposes. Maintaining irrigation prompts

a review of which parts of the landscaped area will need regular irrigation and which will need it only periodically or not at all. (Irrigation is considered in detail in Chapter 15.)

Tropical rain is frequently of great physical force and volume; 5 cm (2 in) of heavy, pounding rain may fall in an hour, and often more than 30 cm will fall during a day. Consequently, exposed ground is unable to absorb these large amounts of water and severe erosion can occur, with the topsoil being partially or totally stripped off. In regions where very heavy rainfall occurs, special care should be taken when planting on sloping sites to counter these effects.

The siting of paths or level berms along contours may provide barriers to erosion, and in areas of heavy rainfall large open drainage channels (or scuppers) can be dug to run alongside them. Many buildings have no rain gutters, and water either cascades over the whole length of the roof or is discharged through protruding gargoyles. The area where the water hits the ground must be suitably treated by gravel strips or loose cobbles to prevent erosion and splash stains, or by apron or scupper drains.

In parks or other public open spaces, the provision of

237

covered walkways or shelters against the hot sun and torrential tropical downpours is essential. Lack of air movement in still weather can cause sheltered areas to be stifling and hot, and all means of creating ventilation and breezes that are available to the designer should be used.

Wind is a problem in many areas, bringing both discomfort to the individual and damage to the plants, especially if it is salt- or sand-laden. The provision of windbreaks in these areas is desirable. Suitable trees, such as *Casuarina* spp., are adaptable in almost all regions; their very flexible branches and twigs are more likely to break the force of the wind and diffuse it rather than create an impenetrable barrier, which can lead to wind turbulence damage. Windbreaks for coastal areas using screw pine (*Pandanus*), the sea-grape (*Coccoloba uvifera*), and mahoe (*Thespesia populnea*) can make a useful secondary storey to the taller *Casuarina*.

In some areas, hurricanes, cyclones or typhoons may be encountered. There is little that can be done to resist their effect except to avoid the use of materials which can be easily whipped away and turned into lethal objects, such as galvanized sheeting. The planting of small, sturdy trees in exposed areas can reduce damage and ensure that some vegetation is left in the wake of the storm. Local knowledge of how these storms behave is vital.

## Soils

Tropical soils are as varied and complex as temperate soils. Humus-rich forest soils are, however, an extremely fragile medium, rarely recoverable during forest removal. The intense integration of root mass and humus means that on removal of trees and root systems at site clearance virtually nothing is left, and machinery trying to gather the remains up will invariably grind it into the poor subsoil beneath.

Soils in exposed areas usually have a minimal humus layer, but have a great depth of soft to medium-hard weathered rock. Laterites, volcanic rocks and granites are commonly sub-aerially decomposed to depths of 20 m. These are mostly the 'soils' that are excavated for landscape projects. Nutrient-rich, often highly acidic, garish yellow or red in colour and usually with a poor texture, these sub-soils support remarkably rapid plant growth, especially of native indigenous species. However, for long-term and rich growth, amelioration is essential, and the addition of neutral organic composts and salt-free sand will provide nutrient and texture. Surface mulching and the addition of composts and fertilizers will be necessary to promote flowering and rich green foliage. High quality loam soils are sometimes obtainable where agriculture holdings are being cleared, but frequently the cost of transport and the difficulty of storage means that these soils are unavailable when

projects are under way. Soils stored over more than one month should be provided with base drainage and kept in low mounds planted with short-lived legumes such as *Medicago*.

Alluvial soils, forest peats and volcanic ash soils can be rich in nutrients but are often easily eroded. Fibrous ameliorants, such as coconut peat or rice straw, may be needed to bind such soils, or alternatively, surface matting or netting can be used to cover and protect the surface. However, note that it is important to test all ameliorants for soluble salt levels before use, since few tropical species are tolerant of salt.

The rapid decomposition of vegetable matter in soil is soon exhausted and either leached into deeper layers of the soil, oxidized by exposure to sunshine or washed away by rains, unless it is replenished constantly by fresh leaf fall. This rapid exhaustion is exemplified by the type of agriculture known as 'slash and burn'. In this system, shallow-rooted agricultural crops exhaust the upper strata of the soil within a few years, with no amelioration or cultivation techniques used, and farming has to move into a new area, leaving the old area to be colonized by scrub and slowly rejuvenate itself. With their deep roots, scrub species will reach the nutrients and moisture which are often as much as 15 m or more below the ground. Forest species may never recolonize such poor soils unless secondary woodland species provide sufficient humus layer.

The cultivation of soil in horticultural practice is surprisingly little understood. The breaking up of soil for agriculture is certainly done, but generally techniques for efficient production and conservation of friable loams are not used, and in many areas the tools for achieving these, such as forks and rakes, are not available. However, very fine-textured cultivated soils pack down to a solid mass in heavy rain and then bake hard in the sun. A slightly coarse texture with plenty of fibrous content is ideal. Adequate provision needs to be made for the settlement of cultivated soil, and for reworking the surface in the establishment months after planting.

Subsoil drainage is also a much misunderstood element in tropical landscapes. The huge volumes of water entering the soil cannot be guaranteed to soak away. In wet seasons, slow percolation of water can result in algal growth and fungal attack of the topsoil. Lawns can become boggy and the growth of roots in trees and shrubs can be choked by lack of oxygen. Subsurface, porous drainage is essential and filter-wrapped French drains or perforated pipes should be included in every scheme along the sides of paths, on areas of lawns, at the foot of slopes and alongside any impervious barriers such as walls or concrete drainage channels. Equally, tree pits dug into hard ground can be the cause of waterlogging, and outlet drains should be included wherever heavy soils are suspected. For trees in paved areas, outlet drains are essential.

Equally important, soil oxygenation and maintenance of soil porosity must be attended to, especially in areas where root growth may be restricted. The introduction of porous soakaways at soil level, penetrating down to mid-root level (500–750 mm) between trees, will ensure adequate aeration. Hard impervious surfaces around trees should be kept as far away as possible, and open textured blocks or grass and concrete slabs in a wide area around the tree will promote deep rooting. This is especially important where large shade trees are used near paved areas and shallow rooting must be minimized. Surface roots can cause costly breaking up of surfaces, kerbs and drains. Naturally, trees with known destructive root habits should be avoided in such situations.

When a landscape scheme is planned, a soil analysis should be made to find out what nutrient supplement is required and whether soluble salts are present. Maximum use should be made of natural manures and compost, as they not only provide some nutrients but also improve the soil texture and its properties of water retention. Care must be taken in using manures to avoid plagues of flies and cockroaches, and insecticide treatment must be specified.

When planting trees and shrubs, extra large planting holes should be prepared in advance and the soil to be placed in them should be enriched with compost, sand and fertilizer. Fresh soil should be imported for back filling of tree pits and shrub areas.

## Water

Before initial proposals are drafted, it is essential to establish the source of local water supplies. In hot and even wet climates some watering of plants will almost certainly be necessary. The designer must ascertain whether the public water supply is subject to periodic restrictions (normally at times when the plants need water), and if suitable water for plants is available from reliable independent sources. Most young plants will require initial watering before they become established, and this can be helped by judicious positioning of soakaways that will take water from roofs, car parks and roads. Even silt chambers and manholes can be modified to act as soakaways. If they are constructed of honeycomb brickwork without a solid base and are filled with gravel or crushed stone up to the outlet level, they will supplement soil moisture while avoiding becoming mosquito breeding grounds.

Irrigation may also be required, even in the wet tropics. The intense heat will dry the soil in a matter of hours, leaving shallow-rooted plants parched by late afternoon. These conditions without rain for even a few days can result in plant death or severe stunting. Whether irrigation is by manual hosepipe watering, by drip irrigation or by sprinkler, either manually operated or automatic, provision needs to be made both for the permanent supply, the necessary pressure and the management to operate and maintain the system. Planting in drought-prone areas such as roof gardens and plant containers requires ample water, and early provision of pipework and taps at the construction stage is vital. Adequate drainage is also essential to prevent waterlogging and, when heavy rain does come, flooding and overflowing.

Water as a feature of the design has been a traditional ingredient in the tropical or arid region garden. The inclusion of water features should be considered wherever possible. Algal growth is probably the biggest single plague of tropical water features, especially in full-sun locations. Where water plants and fish are not present, chlorination should be used. Where natural water is needed, aeration and oxygenation and circulation and filtration are necessary. The use of aquatic plants is dealt with in this chapter. Water also brings problems of mosquito breeding, snakes, scorpions and noise and spawn from frogs, all of which must be appreciated and countered.

## The human factor

Both social and political attitudes have a tremendous bearing on the landscape of different tropical areas. The evocative beauty of the island of Bali in Indonesia is a product of the local people's attitude to their environment, their dedication to agricultural labour and the rich traditions of social custom and religion. Many areas do not have such historic coherence or conservatism. The inflexibility of government planning systems and the severeness of modern engineering have seen many beautiful tropical environments disappear under the axe of modern (usually western style) development. It is, however, in the very areas of apparently brutal change that the landscape designer is most likely to be employed. Environmental conservation and landscape aesthetics are certain to be minority items in planning and cost priorities, and the landscape designer will have to be thoroughly convincing to ensure that any special needs are covered and that the budget is provided.

Rarely will the landscape designer be working alone. Multi-discipline projects are the norm nowadays, and the landscape designer will need to be familiar with local professional standards, methods of contract, government submission requirements and regulations. For foreign consultants working in a new location, a rapid familiarization stage is important if embarrassing or costly mistakes are to be avoided.

Local customs, lifestyle and the local labour force are likely to affect the implementation of landscape designs in tropical areas. Local customs can only be ascertained by first-hand experience of an area on the part of the designer. Behaviour that is regarded as standard throughout temperate regions is unlikely to have any parallels in the areas under discussion. Where there are strong local traditions, these may often profitably be used as the basis for designs. In multi-racial societies it is important to be careful to avoid offending people of particular cultures, religions or backgrounds, in following the traditions of other sectors of the community.

In the tropics, as elsewhere, the long term success of any landscape design is in the hands of the maintenance staff. Even in areas where landscape design is reasonably well established, the labour that is available for maintenance may have limited training and limited exposure to modern techniques. Tools may be of local origin or made by the maintenance staff themselves and machinery, if installed, may last only a short time and once broken may not be repaired. Existing trees on the site may be used by workmen for fuel or as shelter and thus must be protected.

The attitude towards maintenance will be influenced by the designer's insistence that the long-term survival of a landscape, including drainage and irrigation, depends on a proper long-term maintenance plan. Ideally, whether the owner is going to maintain a site with his own staff, or by contract, the designer will have to prepare a detailed maintenance specification and do everything he can to ensure it is implemented.

The designer's efforts will only survive if he gives high priority to the simplicity of any maintenance that will be required. Many schemes fail, even in countries where skilled staff are available, because the maintenance is too complex, too much equipment is needed and the equipment is too expensive and too time-consuming. Advanced preparation, with research into methods, staffing and resources, adequate budget provision and early agreement of future management arrangements with the client is essential.

Vandalism has traditionally not been a problem in most tropical countries. Religious principles and strong family discipline have kept the problem very low. However, the influx of western style development, education and economics in most areas has brought with it a spate of western social problems. Industrial economics, unemployment and competitive education systems have generated the hitherto unknown problem of vandalism. How far this will spread and if it can be controlled remain to be seen. Designers should, however, be aware of the possible damage to schemes by disgruntled persons, and the possibility of certain fruits and leaves being taken for cooking.

Many countries impose severe import restrictions on plants, some excluding certain species and genera only while others have a more or less blanket embargo. Most countries require import licences, and health inspection procedures must be followed. Certain types of propagules, such as seeds, may be exempt from

PLATE 14.1 **A magnificent specimen of** *Enterlobium saman (Samanea saman),* **the rain tree, in the gardens of the British Embassy, Bangkok.** *(Maurice Lee)*

PLATE 14.2 **Shade planting in the car park of the Singapore World Trade Centre, showing** *Pterocarpus indicus* **taken at 11.30 am.** *(Henry Steed)*

restrictions. The practitioner has a clear moral duty to be careful what new plants are introduced, even if few legal restrictions exist in a particular country. There are a number of cautionary examples of uncontrolled invasion on a spectacular scale following the introduction of alien plants, such as the prickly pear and *Lantana* in Australia and privet (*Ligustrum*) in Mauritius. This is especially true of floating aquatic plants, which have caused considerable difficulties on rivers and lakes in the past, examples including *Eichhornea* and *Salvinia*. Their introduction into a number of countries has carried severe penalties. Care should also be taken that a request for plants does not result in plants being stripped from the nearby forest rather than being raised in local nurseries.

Importation of plants may also be prohibited or restricted not only to avoid the introduction of pests and disease but also in the interests of the conservation of rare species. Implementation of the terms of the Washington Convention on Trade in Endangered Species of Wild Fauna and Flora, held in March 1973, introduced new restrictions of which landscape architects should be aware.

## 14.4 FACTORS AFFECTING PLANTING DESIGN IN TROPICAL REGIONS

### Heat, light and shade

The provision of shade to allow people to escape the sunlight and heat has been the main consideration factor in planting in tropical and arid regions for many centuries. It is difficult for temperate region dwellers without experience of hot climates to appreciate the blessing of adequate shade. Shade provided by plants can be as important in the tropics as a sound roof is in more temperate regions, reducing the glare and heat reflection from hard surfaces, cooling the surroundings and providing the psychological benefit of greenness and seclusion (see Plate 14.1). In tropical and equatorial regions the sun rises fast, heating surfaces within an hour or so. From mid-morning onwards the sun will beat down almost vertically, reducing shadows to a minimum, glaring at light levels of up 120 000 lux and raising temperatures at midday to well over 40°C (104°F).

The size and types of plant used to provide shade are

determined by the purpose for which the shade is required. For instance, shade trees for car parking may be different from those provided for walking or sitting areas. However, shade plants should always be evergreen or be without leaves for only a very short, cool period in the year.

The use of trees to provide shade for cars to be parked in (Plate 14.2) is very important, as the metalwork and car seats can become blisteringly hot when parked in the open, even on an overcast day. For large car parks, spacing broad canopy trees at one tree per 3–4 cars (7.5–10 m spacings) will provide good coverage. Although carports may be an integral part of residential design, it is advisable to provide additional shade trees bordering the driveway to cope with visitors' cars. Scale must be taken into account and care must be taken not to plant trees which grow too large in restricted areas. One of the most impressive large shade trees for big open areas is the rain tree, *Samanea saman*. This has a short trunk and produces a broad umbrella-shaped canopy. The crowns of some specimens may reach a diameter of almost 60 m (200 ft) under good conditions; thus it needs careful siting in places where there is plenty of space, especially as its roots are wide spreading. The grass under its shade usually remains green, even though it may be brown and parched a few yards away, and when light levels drop, for instance before rain, the leaves close up, allowing abundant rainwater to fall around the roots of the tree. Small evergreens which may be used in drives, courtyards and smaller spaces, such as *Cordia*, *Bauhinia* and *Lagerstroemia*, have the advantage that they produce clusters of conspicuous flowers and can tolerate dry season conditions.

For the shading of roads and wide avenues it is desirable to achieve a quick cover, and it may be advisable to plant trees at about half the final planting distance and then remove alternate trees when their canopies meet. Trees which produce large or pulpy fruit should be avoided, as they are messy and constitute a hazard to safety. Very large-leaved palms should not be planted too close to road edges, as they might shed their very heavy leaves, thus causing damage or accidents. *Samanea saman* makes a very useful roadside shade tree, as does *Tamarindus indica* (tamarind), a very handsome tree with attractive feathery foliage. *Pterocarpus indicus*, the Burmese rosewood, is also a dense, fast-growing tree with a broad shade canopy, ideal for roadside and car park planting. Unlike the rain tree however, *Pterocarpus* supports little growth under its canopy, consuming all the water and nutrients that are available.

When designing large schemes such as golf courses, riding paddocks or sports fields, shade should be provided at fringe areas. It is always welcomed by spectators, maintenance staff and resting participants.

Shade provided by planting can be supplemented by shade structures in landscape areas. Covered walkways with solid canopies keeping out rain and heat are ideal where dry conditions are wanted. In garden areas, pergolas and covered arbours planted with climbing plants can be cool, ventilated and attractive. The spectacular range of exotic climbing plants available in the tropics is often overlooked, and these garden structures are ideal for displaying them. Caution should be used in residential areas, however, that dead leaves can be cleared out from under the growth of the climbers. Cockroaches, spiders and snakes can live in these layers, causing much upset to residents.

## Ventilation and breezes

Stifling heat and lack of air movement are characteristic of the tropical forest environment, and humidity, combined with high temperatures, is enervating. Conversely, hilltops and open coastal areas, where breezes prevail, can be cool and pleasant, even when the ambient day temperature is high. Night-time breezes are much sought after, as hot, humid and airless nights are

PLATE 14.3 **Light shade over a concrete walkway in the Singapore Botanical Gardens, provided by** *Roystonea* **spp. Note the perforated slabs for aeration of the soil below the trees.** *(Henry Steed)*

PLATE 14.4 **Formal urban planting over structure on the second level of Marina Square in Singapore, showing** *Bauhinia blakeana.* **The soil depth is 1.2 m over the roof structure. Note the angle of the afternoon sun two and a half hours before sunset.** *(Design by Henry Arnold;* Photograph: *Henry Steed)*

most unpleasant. Ventilation and the catching or instigation of breezes should be an early consideration in the design of planting. Solid barriers of vegetation or enclosures will invariably cause the trapping of warm air and high humidity. Open breezeways or funnels should be left through any landscape, especially where prevailing wind directions or convection can be used.

Avenues and groves of trees, particularly where perched up or set on slopes, will cause a funnel effect. Partly closed tree canopies high above roads or paths with the sides along avenues kept open will encourage convection air movements even on hot days, and this is illustrated in Plate 14.3. Valleys are also likely to form funnels, and should be left relatively open to allow free air passage. Locally, seats and benches should be sited in well ventilated and shady areas, and be close to ponds, waterfalls or the sea wherever possible. Moving water cools and channels air and creates surprisingly strong breezes. Garden structures, fences and park buildings should also be designed for maximum ventilation and to encourage air movement. In site planning work, at the early stages of a project, it is important to introduce landscape ventilation requirements to both the architect and the engineer. An example of a well-ventilated and shaded area is given in Plate 14.4.

## Orientation and light intensity

The sun's path from dawn to dusk is not a race to its overhead position and back. The sun, even in equatorial areas, takes up to 4 hours to reach vertical and 4 hours to set. The effect on plant material is very noticeable, especially with regard to flowering and sun or shade tolerance. Great care needs to be taken in selecting positions for flowering plants that need long hours of sunshine or for shade-tolerant plants that cannot take direct sun.

Little study has been done on this subject, so few references are available. Local horticulturalists are often empirical in their opinions. The conditions that are needed to ensure that orchids or bougainvilleas will produce prolific flowers are still hotly debated. It is clear, however, that most tropical flowering plants need the maximum full sunshine possible to flower, and it is the degree of flowering under fewer hours of sunlight that has to be determined. Many species will flower quite well under light shade and will produce more abundant leaf growth (for instance *Ixora*, *Tecomaria* and *Crossandra*). They will, however, require a distinct amount of morning or afternoon sun to flower, and the orientation of beds must be worked out to achieve at

243

PLATE 14.5 **Sunny but naturally ventilated garden at the Swiss Club, Singapore, with creation of open areas from existing forest to provide a broad sense of space.** (Landscape Architects: *BCP Asia*)

PLATE 14.6 **Light intensity and orientation are important factors in planning lush shady areas with the angle of the sun at 11 am the *Asplenium nidus* is in hot, bright sunshine and the *Philodendron selloum* in partial shade.** *(Henry Steed)*

PLATE 14.7 **Controlled urban planting from outside the Tat Lee Bank Building, with fern trees** *(Felicium decipiens)* **and bamboo palm** *(Chrysalidocarpus lutescens)* **over** *Sanchesia nobilis, Phyllanthus myrtifolius* **and** *Pandanus pygmaeus*. **The raised beds with sloping copes are to discourage sitting by pedestrians**. (Landscape Architects: *BCP Asia*)

least 4 hours of sunshine a day for most flowering plants.

More difficult to cater for are the shade-tolerant plants. Most of the lushest, exotic ground-level species will only grow in shaded conditions. Many will not tolerate any sunshine at all. It is vital to study the sun's path in any scheme to establish the positions of shade at different times of the day. There is nothing more annoying than to lay out a plant bed with shade-tolerant species under a canopy, for example, and then to find that the hot 9 o'clock morning sun shrivels up the carefully selected plants. Charts giving the sun's angle are widely used by architects and should be obtained to avoid this problem (Plate 14.6).

Morning sun will be hot, but air and soil temperatures may not rise until 10 or 11 o'clock. Many plants, such as shade-tolerant aroids, having settled down in the cool evening and night, cannot stand this rapid blast of direct heat and blinding light intensity of up to 120 000 lux. Some flowering plants, however, prefer the cooler light air and soil of the morning and flower well in the bright light. These same plants may not tolerate the more oppressive heat, humidity and warmer light of the afternoon sun, being exhausted by the end of the

hot, baking day. Conversely, many shade-tolerant plants, having warmed up gently over the day (in the shade) can often take several hours of afternoon sun without damage. Establishing the sunshine patterns is also useful in the positioning of sitting areas, pergolas and shelters and shade trees and buildings, since humans are equally affected by the direction of morning and afternoon sun. See Plate 14.5.

## Accessibility and barriers

While enclosure is not desirable for ventilation reasons, free accessibility into landscape areas may result in damage, wearing out or loss of a particular effect. The layout of planting and plant types for control of pedestrian movement or the need to erect barriers should be assessed at the design stage. The problems of design for the survival of planted areas against pedestrian onslaught is the same in tropical and temperate countries. In urban areas and parks, there are likely to be very large numbers of pedestrians, most of whom will seek the quickest route to their destination, and once a path across a bed is worn bare, nothing will grow in the compacted soil under the resultant constant trampling.

245

The use of spiny plants may be a deterrent, as long as they have the time to establish themselves. Although spiny plants such as bougainvillea and *Pandanus* are effective in blocking crossing of beds, they may be a nuisance to those walking along the paths by catching clothes or scratching arms and legs, and should therefore be kept back from path edges. *Agaves* and spiny palms can also be used but should be kept well away from paths, since their spines can be dangerous. It may be more effective, for pedestrian control, to create physical barriers, either temporary to allow plant establishment or permanent to ensure that crossing will not even be thought about. The use of raised planters to separate or infill between pedestrian routes can be used to protect plants as well as create shaded sitting areas, as is illustrated in Plate 14.7.

Low rails set along the edges of beds or higher fences concealed in the centre of plant masses can be used as suggestive or positive barriers.

Clipped hedges are easily developed, with many suitable tropical species available (see Plant Lists, Tables 14.1 to 14.12). Internal fences may be needed during the establishment of hedges to prevent people from crossing them. Some climbers can be trained up chain-link fences to form dense hedges, but care must be taken to avoid the later collapse of the fence under the weight of the plant. Adequate foundations, rust protection and cross bars need to be included in specifications. Clipping methods of hedges and fences with hedges need to be specified, especially if accurate forms or straight lines are required. Small-leaved species may be cut with mechanical trimmers (if available), but large-leaved or flowering plants need to be cut with shears or secateurs to avoid disfigurement. Flowering hedges need to be selectively pruned by hand to avoid removal of budding flower heads.

In designing hedges and tight enclosures of planting, ventilation, security and safety must be considered. Hedges should not block the flow of air into public spaces or trap afternoon heat from the sun. Solid hedges may not keep people out; in fact they may allow unwanted people to remain hidden from view. Solid hedges may also harbour monkeys, snakes and insects, all of which can be dangerous pests. Ideally, hedges should be broken up into part hedge and part fence, with gaps or arches allowing visibility and airflow. Such an arrangement is shown in Plate 14.8.

# Night time and lighting

The long tropical night can be a time of pleasant coolness and romantic atmosphere. There is little variation in the length of night throughout the year, and thus evenings become an integral part of the day's activities. Entertaining and eating almost always take place after sundown, and in many places out of doors. Exploitation of the delights of the tropical evening is sadly missed in many countries where air-conditioning has tempted people indoors, away from the possibility of insect attack and humidity. The cost of fuel bills and increasing awareness of sensory experiences is tempting many people back to outdoor night activity, and this move is providing the landscape designer with ample opportunity to create exciting and atmospheric effects.

Lighting equipment is so diverse that fixtures for almost any effect can be found. Large trees such as *Ficus* species, with curtains of trailing roots, or palms, with their striking architectural forms, are magnificent when lit by spot or floodlights. Plants with giant leaves, such as *Monstera* or Traveller's palm (*Ravenala*), create an exotic ambience when lit with front lighting from below, silhouette lighting from behind and 'moon-lighting' by cool light from above (Plate 14.9).

Illumination by small spotlights of individual specimens with striking forms or the lighting of statues and water or rock features will create focal interests as is shown by Plate 14.8. In order to allow special features to read well, pathway light levels should be kept as low as possible. Even in public open spaces, minimal illumination of paths, using directional down lights with just enough light to provide safety, should be used so as not to compete with individually illuminated focal features. To obtain contrast, the use of low energy, warm coloured, sodium type lights should be considered for paths, with brighter, cooler, mercury type lights used for plants and water features. Cool blue light enhances the green of foliage and the blue of water, whereas warm yellow light turns foliage brown and water green.

The concealment of cables and junction boxes should not be overlooked at the design stages, but, at the same time, access for maintenance must be available, especially as corrosion or leakage of junctions in torrential rain can cause the tripping of entire lighting systems. The main distribution boxes and control panels can be obtrusive elements and careful siting is necessary to provide access but at least partial concealment.

# Space and grass

The development of generous space is as necessary as the creation of shade and cool conditions. The contrast between brilliant light and deep shade can be used to great advantage in the layout of sites. In city environments, space is at a premium, and the designer needs to stretch or even create the illusion of volume, especially where high rise buildings dominate ground levels areas. The partly enclosed voids of tree groves and avenues with no side planting can provide delightful airy spaces with a roof-like canopy and colonnade effect of trunks. Combining this with outer stretches of paving or grass will provide the sense of space needed to combat the bulk of buildings.

The establishment of lawns and large grass areas is

PLATE 14.8 **Three-month-old** *Casuarina equisetifolia* **being trained into a 3 m arched hedge, with eight plants per block, on Sentosa Island, Singapore. The expected time to completed growth is eighteen months, and the grass on the terraces is** *Axonopus*. (Landscape Architects: *BCP Asia*)

simple in the wet tropics, but difficult in areas with long dry seasons or low annual rainfall. Before specifying the planting of lawns, the local techniques of grassing and the availability of materials will have to be evaluated. Most tropical countries do not have a grass seed production industry, and seeds of suitable fine-leaved species such as Bermuda grass, Zoyzia and Kikuyu grass will have to be imported from sub-tropical producer countries. On-site seeding is, however, quite difficult, and disturbance by heavy rain, fungal attack and desiccation at the soil surface mean that site seeding is little used.

Turf production may be locally practised, but if it is not, then turf farms will have to be set up to produce the required quantities of turf. Stoloniferous wet tropic grasses, such as *Axonopus* species, can be easily established from sprigs or cut sods laid over prepared soil and top-dressed with friable soil to prevent drying out. Hydroseeding is increasingly practised in tropical areas

PLATE 14.9 **Unusual fruit lit at night, showing** *Couropita guianensis*, **the cannonball tree, with its fruit attached to its stem.** *(Henry Steed)*

and should be considered where research and trials have been done or can be included in projects. All grass areas will require abundant watering, especially in the establishment period, and where dry seasons or dry soil conditions will cause the grass to turn brown, irrigation should be incorporated, using mobile or fixed pop-up sprinklers. Manual watering for small lawns is satisfactory, provided that thorough coverage is ensured.

In areas of extreme dry seasons, where water restrictions are regularly imposed, designs must take account of the fact that the grass will be brown and thus very vulnerable to wear and tear. Only drought-tolerant grasses, such as Bermuda grass, or easily replaceable grasses, such as *Axonopus*, should be used in these situations, and suitable pedestrian controls should be used to keep people away from grassy areas. Maintenance schedules should allow for annual part replacement at the start of the wet season.

Few grasses will grow well under trees or heavy shade, and, as with the orientation of shrubs and ground cover, grasses should be kept in full sun or have no more than 6 hours' shade in a day. Conversely, grasses compete with other plants for nutrients and should therefore be kept away from the bases of shrubs unless they are used for slope stability. Mulches can be used below shrubs to conserve moisture and keep invasive grasses away from root feeding areas.

Grass is the most efficient slope vegetation, provided that it can be established and kept properly maintained. Sprigging of individual shoots, close turfing and hydroseeding are all commonly practised. Spot turfing or strip turfing on slopes, where areas of soil are left between turfs is not recommended, as erosion is certain to take place in heavy rain, washing the whole surface down. Total immediate cover by close turfing or hydromulching, and watering and cutting regimes should be started immediately and continued indefinitely. Grass may be used as a temporary cover under shrubs or tree saplings on slopes, and if necessary the grass can be removed once the top cover is established. Care should be taken on steep slopes that labourers cutting grass do not damage the slope by walking on it. For this reason, the maximum slope gradient should be set at 1:2–1:2.5.

## Maintenance

The future of a landscape design rests with those who will maintain projects after they have been planted. It is the task of the designer to ensure that adequate provisions are brought to the client's attention and that everything possible is done to ensure that the maintenance system is set up. This may mean introducing new techniques or may require the importing of new equipment, but without these specialized operations cannot be done. Sophisticated cutting and grass maintenance equipment, found on golf courses worldwide, rarely penetrates to the horticultural industry. Equipment developed in western countries to be labour-saving is often ignored in tropical countries as being inappropriate for local conditions. It is often not until they get the chance to use them they workers discover the benefits of tools designed for people and not for particular localities.

It is not safe, however, to use temperate climate techniques for tropical maintenance work, even if tool technology can be transferred. Watering, grass cutting, fertilizing, pruning, soil cultivation, and insecticide, herbicide and fungicide treatments are all different and require good local knowledge before particular practices can be specified. All elements are likely to be needed for twelve months in the year. Only those places with distinct cool, dry seasons (mostly sub-tropic) will also require a winter style regime. Pruning in non-seasonal climates will be needed all the year round, and many shrubs will need regular control to prevent swamping of other areas. Pruning for flowers needs to be carefully done to avoid removal of new flowering shoots. Laborious selective pruning by hand to control the shape of flowering plants is the only solution. Once the techniques have been perfected by maintenance staff, spectacular flowering is possible.

Grass cutting also takes place throughout the year, and considerable resources are needed to keep up quality cutting over large areas. Different techniques of cutting will be needed for each grass type, and maintenance plans must allow for obtaining suitable cutting and grass management equipment and for staff and supervisor training. Maintenance of irrigation systems also requires training or hiring of maintenance contractors.

Attack by insects and fungi are a serious year-round problem in tropical areas. Spraying programmes, with the use of approved pesticides and fungicides, need to be set in motion immediately after planting. Designers must familiarize themselves with locally available and approved chemicals, locally practised techniques and the local availability of spraying equipment and training. The virulence and destructiveness of tropical pests must not be underestimated. Termites, stem borers, aphids, mealy bugs, red spiders, caterpillars and many fungi can all totally destroy plants if they are not checked. Snails especially will totally defoliate fleshy ground cover, and regular snail baiting should be undertaken.

Weeds are as much a problem in tropical climates as in temperate regions, only in the tropics they flower and seed all the year round. Weeding, mulching and soil cultivation programmes should thus be started immediately after planting. Fortunately, most fast-growing herbaceous weeds are weak and shallow-rooted, and can be readily pulled up. Woody and spiky weeds such as *Mimosa pudica*, and rhizomatrous grasses such as *Imperator*, are real pests and very hard to eradicate. Selective herbicides are unfortunately very difficult to use, as most tropical ornamentals will not tolerate them. Only spot weed-killing with contact herbicides or manual removal is reliable, and until thorough research is documented, this is the best method to follow.

Fertilizer use is essential in tropical landscape work, especially to sustain rich green foliage and abundant flowering. For maximum flowering of plants such as *Allamanda*, *Crossandra* and *Ixoras*, fertilizing every two weeks with low nitrogen, high phospate/potash granular fertilizers is required. Slow release fertilizers can be used, but these cannot be expected to last for more than about two months. High nitrogen fertilizer with some lime for grass areas will generate deep green grass. Care must be taken, however, not to stimulate algal growth in wet weather, and to avoid pollution of nearby watercourses with excessively rich discharge. In wet weather, only very light applications of fertilizer should be used. Organic composts are ideal for improving bulk and fibre in soil, with added nutrient value; however, composting is not as much used as it could be, and much valuable vegetable matter is wasted. Composts such as sewage sludge, plantation wastes and coconut peat may be available, but these should be checked for heavy metals and soluble salts before use.

A large amount of detail needs to be incorporated in maintenance plans. This description highlights just a few particular considerations, and designers need to carefully study the full spectrum of maintenance requirements for their particular scheme. These requirements will include staffing levels, supervision levels and training, equipment, equipment storage and maintenance, supplies, storage and safety of materials and chemicals, water supply and irrigation maintenance, annual budget provision and assistance to the client in setting up the long-term maintenance programmes.

## 14.5 PLANT MATERIAL AND ITS USE

## Diversity of plants

The range and scope of the tropical flora are far in excess of those found in temperate regions. This gives the landscape architect faced with the ubiquity of modern architecture the opportunity to use indigenous species to help to maintain the local character. There are widely grown pan-tropic species, such as *Delonix*, bougainvillea and *Hibiscus*, which will nearly always be available to the designer, but the work will retain a greater degree of individuality if as much use as possible is made of indigenous plants. Not only are the results aesthetically pleasing, they may in addition be well received locally. For instance, the oil palm (*Elaeis guineensis*) is looked upon with affection by the Ghanaians; thus the planting of an avenue of oil palms would receive the approbation (and protection) of the local populace. Care must also be taken to observe the opposite sensitivity, where plants are shunned for religious or traditional reasons. Liaison with local

botanists or horticulturalists will prove of great value in identifying indigenous plants, which can then be cross-checked in regional flora publications or encyclopaedias such as *Exotica* and *Tropica* by Alfred Graf.

Because of the wide range of climates and different floristic regions, the plants available in Mexico, Brazil, West Africa, India and the Far East are still, except for the pan-tropic species, quite distinct and used mostly within their own regions. The landscape architect should familiarize himself with the local flora and use it to maximum advantage. This, however, is not meant to deprecate the use of the many pan-tropic species which may be common to two or more continents. These, after all, are usually the adaptable species, and it is from many of these that numerous very valuable cultivars have been bred. It is important to keep abreast of the production of cultivars and selection of high performance varieties. The isolation of exceptional plants continues to increase, year by year. Plant introductions also take place, especially at botanic gardens, research institutions and government agricultural stations; and the contrasts in texture and form that can be achieved by use of a wide variety of plants are shown in Plates 14.10 and 14.11, from the Singapore Botanic Gardens. Information on successful new plants should also be obtained wherever possible.

## Plant behaviour

While there are many distinctly evergreen and deciduous trees in the tropics, in numerous species the distinction is blurred. Leaf fall may not occur simultaneously over the whole tree, but in waves that affect a branch or portion of a tree at a time, new leaves being produced on some parts while old ones are shed elsewhere. Some trees may show all growth stages at the same time. Thus, it is not unusual to see a mango tree which has old leaves on some branches, is dropping them on other parts, has new leaves on yet other branches and is also producing flowers and mature fruit.

In some species not all individuals act in concert, some being at a different stage than others, some perhaps producing new leaves while others are fruiting. This is often seen in the silk cotton tree (*Ceiba pentandra*), one specimen of which has even been observed showing different behaviour in the two vertical halves of the tree — one half in full leaf, the other bare and fruiting.

Other trees have well marked phases, such as a leafy period followed by leaf fall and bare branches, then flowering occurring on the bare branches and fruiting, followed by a flush of new leaves. Such trees can be made a feature, as they show a new and interesting aspect at different times of the year. By careful selection of trees and plants, one can give an impression of stability in some areas or exciting change in others.

A number of plants are monocarpic and will die

249

PLATE 14.10 **Space and grass with the dramatic forms of palms set in open lawns in the Singapore Botanical Gardens. Enclosure is provided by** *Heliconia* **on the left and** *Hymenocallis* **on the right.** *(Henry Steed)*

PLATE 14.11 *Baekia frutescens* **set in** *Ophiopogon jaburans* **(dark green and variegated grasslike lilies) with** *Areca* **spp. in the centre and bamboo at the back showing contrasts in texture and form, from the Singapore Botanical Gardens.** *(Henry Steed)*

after flowering, for instance agaves, some palms and bamboos. In a sense therefore such plants are temporary, even though it may be a decade or much longer before flowering and death. Some thought must therefore be given to their replacement, or initial planting can be planned to give a range of ages where this is possible. Particular care should be taken with some bamboos, especially those from the Indian region, as many have a fixed life cycle. All the plants will flower in the same year and die, so that having a group of plants of different ages in this case does not solve the problem.

## Growth rates

The designer used to making allowances for the time taken for temperate planting to mature will need to readjust to tropical growth rates, matching these to the design purpose. In trees, a growth rate of up to 2 m (6 ft) per year is commonplace, and in some bamboos, 8–10 m (25–32 ft) a year is not uncommon in areas of good soil and rainfall. Not all plants grow at such indulgent rates, and many are extremely slow. Some are only low growing and remain small even after years of growth. If this design adjustment to growth rates is not made, the designer may overplant or plant species may attain a size too great to be acceptable for the design purpose.

To determine growth rates of individual species, observation and research will be necessary to establish performance. One example is rarely enough, since two plants of the same species in different areas or soils are likely to perform differently. Soils, aspect, shade, shelter, atmospheric pollution, maintenance and wear and tear will all affect performance. Invariably, hard and compacted ground will stunt plants severely. Even massive tree species will remain dwarfed if adequate rooting conditions are not provided. Waterlogged plant pits will also cause stunting or death of plants, and adequate drainage of pits must be considered early on, especially to ensure connections under paving or roads.

There are two schools of thought on plant spacing with tropical species. The first calls for planting of individual plants in their final position at wide spacing with grass maintained between plants until the shrubs finally close up. Unfortunately, since real growth rates are so hard to predict, this type of planting area rarely does close up, and when they become straggly, the shrubs get pruned back, thus worsening the situation. The second method calls for the immediate effect of dense, close planting (Plate 14.12), as is practised in temperate landscapes. Generally, plants will totally cover the ground within 3 months, and remain closed permanently, needing clipping from time to time to keep them from getting too leggy. This technique is becoming increasingly used as the effect is so fast, and the plants seem to suffer little detriment from the close spacing. Most tropical plants are adapted to living with

PLATE 14.12 **A multitude of foliage shapes, with** *Osmoxylon geelvinkianum* **in the centre,** *Pandanus* **spp. to the left and** *Monstera deliciosa* **and** *Heliconia rubra* **to the right, showing different texture and form, from the Singapore Botanical Gardens.** *(Henry Steed)*

high root and shade competition and thrive when densely packed. For mass shrub planting to create three-dimensional sculptural effects, this close planting technique is essential. The general spacings for different size categories are set out below.

1. Grass sprigs or rhizome planting – 50–75 mm centres.
2. Rooted shoot, herbaceous ground cover – 50–75 mm centres.
3. Small, non-spreading ground cover – 100–200 mm centres.
4. Spreading and woody ground covers – 250–400 mm centres.
5. Small shrubs, clump forming herbaceous – 500–600 mm centres.
6. Medium size shrubs and herbaceous – 600–750 mm centres.
7. Large spreading shrubs, tall herbaceous – 750–1200 mm centres.
8. Cluster palms, sapling planting, small trees – 1200–2000 mm centres.
9. Small tress, palms, bamboo clumps – 3–5 m centres.
10. Medium sized tress – 5–8 m centres.
11. Large and spreading trees – 7–12 m centres.

Planting to these relatively close spacings will mean dense thicket growth early on. For some species rampant growth may begin to swamp surrounding areas within 2–3 months of planting. Advance knowledge of this is essential, and pruning of rampant shrubs must be included in the maintenance plans. For certain ornamental schemes, ground cover may be sacrificial, designed to last only during the first year or so while main blocks of shrubs are establishing themselves. Eventually the ground cover will all but disappear, leaving strongly formed blocks of taller shrubs to dominate the plant bed.

Thinning out is rarely necessary, as plants in dense masses either live in symbiosis with each other or the weak ones die out. It is better not to thin out, since more damage can be done during this operation than by leaving the plants to fend for themselves.

## 14.6 DESIGN OPPORTUNITIES AND CONSTRAINTS

Before looking at specific planting types, it is worth studying the opportunities and constraints that will influence the designer's approach to a project.

## Siting of trees

When planting trees near buildings, designers should consider their ultimate size and properties. Difficulties arise from placing too large a tree near a building, resulting in damage to the roof or foundations and blocking of the gutters or drains. It is common practice for telephone lines and power supplies to be carried by overhead cables, and care must be taken that trees do not encroach on them and have to be mutilated at frequent intervals. Trees do, however, provide cooling shade, especially to patios and driveways, so the need to plant tress near buildings may outweigh the strictly practical considerations. Smaller-growing trees, especially trees with less aggressive and non-surface rooting, should be selected. Cross sections should be drawn where plants appear to be close to buildings, showing the ultimate size and spread of the plants.

The abundance of underground services and septic tanks means that trees which have invasive roots, such as *Albizias* and *Spathodea*, should be treated with the same caution in their siting as are poplars in temperate regions, and planted well away from anything that may be damaged. *Spathodea*, a tree with beautiful red, tulip-like flowers, has the further disadvantage that if allowed to grow too large, it is susceptible to wind damage, as well as dropping its large flowers in messy heaps. These excellent plants should be used in parks and woodlands, where their flowers can be enjoyed from a distance.

## Planting for seasonal and diurnal effect

Imaginative planting can provide the feeling of change, which becomes even more important in a climate which is non-seasonal. While some plants are used because of their form, and therefore need to be more or less constant to fulfil their function, seasonal variety can be achieved by using flowering shrubs, climbers and herbaceous plants. Judicious selection of trees that show marked differences at different times of the year can help to give the impression of change in the environment. Many trees produce brightly coloured leaves (whether young or old), attractive foliage, conspicuous flowers and periodic leaf fall. *Hevea braziliensis*, the rubber tree, can display complete seasonal change over a large area of plantation, depending on weather conditions. Thus, one valley in a plantation area can be bare of leaves, the next valley flushing spring foliage and another valley in autumn colour.

Changes in appearance may occur not only from month to month but also between one part of the day and another: for example, flowers may open in the early morning and be finished by dusk, by which time a number of other night-blooming cacti may be opening their flowers. This diurnal effect is subtly underlined by scented plants, which tend to be more prominent in the evening and night-time.

## Planting for audible effect

Sound can give the psychological illusion of coolness. The slightest air movement makes *Casuarina* trees' feathery branches and twigs move and make the soughing sound of a refreshing strong breeze. This is particularly marked at night if a *Casuarina* is planted near a bedroom. Another tree that gives an enhanced impression of air movement is *Albizia lebbeck*, whose seeds are rustled in the pod by a light breeze. Not all sound, however, has the same evocative quality: for example, the rattling dry sound of dead palm leaves can be both irritating and an unwelcome reminder of great heat. Bamboos are particularly audible plants, and the rustling of the slender fine-leaved bamboos is cooling and relaxing. However, the giant bamboos creak and make the most eerie knocking noises.

## Planting for scent

No garden, no matter now beautiful and colourful it may be, is complete without scent, and this is especially true in the tropics, where scented plants help to mitigate the effects of the heat and dust. Careful thought should be given to the siting of the plants, especially where scent is required at night, so as not to get incompatible combinations in the same area. While scent is mainly produced by flowers, it should be remembered that leaves and fruit also smell.

One of the most beautifully scented trees, and one which is used extensively in the perfume industry, is the ylang-ylang, (*Cananga odorata*). It is in bloom for much of the year and the yellow flowers are particularly fragrant in the cool of the evening. *Michelia alba*, a fast-growing evergreen, is another highly scented tree

with creamy-yellow flowers. A single tree can be smelt up to 100 m away on a still warm night.

Many night-scented shrubs, such as *Cestrum nocturnum*, are available, as well as shrubs which produces a heavy scent in the cool of the evening, such as *Brunfelsia calycina*. The large, white flowers of *Gardenia jasminoides* provide a useful daytime supplement. The delicately perfumed frangipani, *Plumeria rubra*, has many virtues, bearing beautiful waxy cream, yellow or red flowers and still being striking when it is almost bare of leaves. In addition, it is very drought- and salt-tolerant and thrives in dry positions and by the sea.

The sweet scent of plants such as *Datura*, *Aglaia* and *Murraya* is particularly strong in the early evening and is believed by some people to ward off mosquitoes. Scent may be provided in a space-saving form by the use of climbers such as the climbing ylang-ylang (*Artabotrys odoratissimus*), various species of *Jasminum*, the white, waxy petalled *Stephanotis floribunda* and the yellow-flowered *Lonicera macrantha* (honeysuckle).

Among the herbs the ginger lily, *Hedychium coronarium*, with white flowers, is suitable for planting by a stream or pond, and *H. gardneranum*, with yellow and red flowers, for higher elevations. These are exceptionally heavily scented plants and should be used with discretion, for while the scent is delightful when wafted from a distance, it can prove to be overpowering and sickly at close quarters.

Effective use may also be made of plants whose scent

PLATE 14.13 **Dense screening provided by** *Ardisia elliptica* **about two years after planting.** *Excoecaria bicolor* **forms a low edge, obscuring the road behind.**

is released by something brushing against the foliage or by rubbing the leaves between the fingers. *Eucalyptus* species are especially refreshing, and many can also be pollarded or be kept as bushes. *Baeckia frutescens*, a small tree resembling a weeping willow, also has highly scented foliage. The bay rum tree (*Pimenta racemosa*) and the related pimento or allspice (*P. dioica*) have aromatic leaves when crushed. The clove (*Eugenia aromatica*) and citrus trees are equally fragrant. *Lippia citriodora* is a small shrub which will give off its scent when the leaves and stems are brushed in passing. Thought should be given to the strategic placing of plants near paths where they may be brushed against accidentally.

## Planting for flowering effect

The great joy of many tropical plants lies in their spectacular profusion of flowers and the vast range of colour, from the most flamboyant reds and yellows to subdued blues and violets. Most trees tend to flower when the branches are bare or have few leaves. This is often dependent on the seasonal temperature and humidity. Most of the best flowering trees grow in areas with distinctly cooler dry seasons, and flower less profusely in wet equatorial areas.

Flowering trees, shrubs, herbaceous plants, aquatics and climbers are so plentiful that Alfred Graf's splendid encyclopaedia of exotic tropical plants and trees, *Tropica*, contains 900 pages of colour photographs, mostly showing tropical flowering plants. This chapter can only touch on such a vast subject, and reference should be made to *Tropica* to get an idea of the huge variety of tropical flowering plants that are available.

Planning designs to achieve spectacular or subtle effects with flowers requires detailed knowledge of the flowering habits of local plants. Abundant flowering depends on many factors, and automatic profusion should not be expected. In fact, it should first be assumed that rich flowering effects will be difficult to achieve, and planning for layout and maintenance should prepare for unpredictable performance. The hours of sunlight will influence flowering more than anything else, and generally good flowering will occur when full sun is available. However, some plants prefer some shade, so care should be exercised. Humidity and soil moisture will also usually influence flowering. In equatorial areas it is during a dry spell that plants usually burst into blooms and in areas with a dry season flowering is often at the beginning or end of that season.

Fertilizing is also a key factor, and most plants will not bloom well in improverished soils. Free draining, rich soils with regular addition of organic compost or fertilizer will help to produce spectacular results. However, for some plants fertilizing will simply produce huge foliage growth and little flowering. The selection

of aspect, soil and plant type needs to be based on observations of local examples for successful flowering to be likely.

Pruning is also a key factor, especially with shrubs and ground cover. For most tropical plants, pruning to induce flowering is not possible; and the problem is more one of pruning to stop the foliage overpowering the flowers. Selective pruning to remove leaf growth, thus leaving the flowers exposed on the outside, is the only way of ensuring dramatic displays of the most showy plants. For trees, pruning for flowers is not generally necessary.

The use of annuals and bedding plants is of increasing interest in the tropics, and much research is being done to select strains of flowering annuals which can survive tropical conditions. For areas with known dry or cool periods, seasonal bedding is quite possible. Heavy rain, high humidity and attack by fungi are usually the most serious problems. Shelter, dry, free-draining soil and regular chemical treatments can help to overcome these problems.

## Planting for foliage effect

Selecting plants for foliage effects is perhaps the most exciting opportunity in tropical planting design. Every texture and colour imaginable are available in the tropics, from the huge leaves of palms and bananas down to tiny leaves on conifers, ferns and miniature herbaceous plants. Leaf colour ranges from dark, glossy greens to brilliant apple greens, variegations from near white to the rainbow colours of *crotons*.

Planning for foliage design to obtain balanced textures and colours in association with neighbouring plants requires the following considerations.

### (a) *Texture*

Leaf size and density of leaves covering the outer face of the plant or, in the case of herbaceous plants, the density of the mass of foliage must be considered, Habit of leafing (whether drooping, horizontal or upright), form of leaf (whether rounded, crinkly, spiky or elongated), texture of leaf (whether soft, rough, smooth, hairy or glossy) and thickness of leaf (whether thin and light, papery, thick or succulent) and how to combine these various combinations is a first consideration in layouts.

### (b) *Density*

For trees, the density of foliage will determine the amount of light passing through, ranging from very dense and almost totally dark, to light and feathery with hardly any shade. For shrubs, density relates to whether shrubs form a dense screen or can be seen through, for ground cover, whether they form a dense mat or partial cover. For open shrubs, underplanting with further ground cover or grass may be necessary.

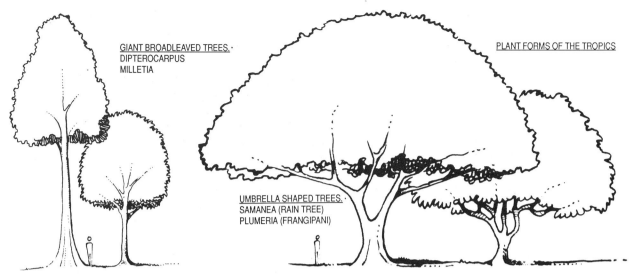

GIANT BROADLEAVED TREES.
DIPTEROCARPUS
MILLETIA

UMBRELLA SHAPED TREES.
SAMANEA (RAIN TREE)
PLUMERIA (FRANGIPANI)

FIGURE 14.2 **Giant broadleaved trees** *(Dipterocarpus* **and** *Milletia).*

FIGURE 14.3 **Umbrella-shaped trees** *(Samanea* **rain tree) and** *Plumeria* **(frangipani).**

### (c) *Colour (greens)*

Greens of every hue and tone are available. The darker greens will generally provide a heavy, dense effect, the lighter greens an airy, cool effect. Most dark green leaves in tropical plants are glossy. The designer can select plants to obtain contrast, such as light coloured leaves against dark green plants. Some blue-green plants are available to provide relief from plainer greens.

### (d) *Colour (variegations)*

Totally variegated plants, such as *Crotons* or *Coleus*, or variegated varieties of normally green plants are widely available. Massed groupings of red-leaved plants are a matter of taste, but can be overpowering. Small accents or splashes of colour with these bright plants are advised. Variegated ground cover in masses can provide a striking contrast to darker plants. Variegated feature plants with spiky leaves provide good focal accents.

### (e) *Colour (flushing)*

The young leaves of many trees and shrubs are highly coloured and tend to hang down in soft limp bunches, ranging in colour from bright reds to blue, purple or white. From a distance plants appear to be in full flower. Seasonal occurrence may be unpredictable, but each species tends to flush at the same time. Large masses of one species can be spectacular.

### (f) *Colour (autumnal)*

Autumn type colours tend to be rare in the tropics, but there are many species which have a period of leaf fall (wintering) preceded by total or partial colouring of the leaves. Some trees have constant leaf drop and some have yellow or red leaves present all the year round. Selection should be based on the observed habits of these trees.

## Use and variety of plant forms

The tropical environment provides a spectacular range of plant forms and shapes that can be used to give exotic and exciting effects. Giant broadleaved columnar trees, umbrella-shaped trees of enormous width, plants with dramatically tiered branches, huge leaves of bananas, aroids and gingers, erect clumps of bamboo, giant climbers, a multitude of palms, tree ferns, spiky pandanus and dramatic epiphytes are available to create lush landscapes.

The plant lists in Tables 14.1 to 14.12 explain briefly the different forms of the main plant types. Form is categorized as:

(i) overall silhouette or shape (rounded or columnar);
(ii) relative height and spread (tall or broad);
(iii) density of foliage (dense or sparse);
(iv) branching habit (upright or spreading);
(v) special character (twisted or prostrate).

Familiarity with the habit of plants from youth to maturity is important. The ultimate height, spread and density of trees cannot be predicted when they are young. Bushy shrubs may become open and sparse when older. Climbers may have large leaves when climbing, but small leaves when trailing. Cycads start as prostrate rosettes of stiff palm-like leaves, and grow on short trunks when older to resemble stocky palm trees.

The creation of interesting associations between the different forms is the key to the successful use of the huge range of plants available. It is easy to overdo planting texture and colour effects, and bold treatment in large masses is important to avoid bitty or overcrowded schemes.

FIGURE 14.4 **Tier-branched trees** *(Terminalia and Araucaria)*.

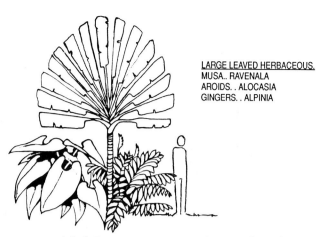

FIGURE 14.5 **Large-leaved trees** *(Ravenala, Alocasia and Alpinia)*.

# Establishment techniques

The establishment of tropical plant material is not well documented. Research and development of plant hybrids, planting methods and horticultural technology are well behind those of temperate countries. The creation of detailed and well researched specifications is essential if high quality and long lasting work are to be achieved. This section offers some guidelines in the approach to the successful specification of plant types.

## (a) *Advance growing of plants*
Transplanting risks are high in tropical areas because of the possibility of desiccation, termite attack, broken root ends, lack of subsequent watering and irreparable damage to tap roots. These factors can be avoided by container culture under advance nursery growing. Good nursery practice, the use of effective maintenance and

temporary shading or windbreaks should all be researched and specified wherever possible at least a year before planting. This also ensures that the correct species can be obtained.

## (b) *Plant sizes*
The use of heavy nursery stock or semi-mature trees is less valid in tropical than in temperate regions because the growth rates of normal size planting material are so rapid. Clients will, however, often require as instant an effect as possible. Several species are capable of being transplanted at a large size, with stem diameters of 300 mm and without lengthy preparation. The bulk of branches and roots can be cut and the tree transplanted virtually as a giant cutting. These instant trees are limited to a few very hardy species such as *Pterocarpus indicus*, *Peltophorum pterocarpum* the *Khayas* (see Plate 14.14) and *Samanea saman*. For large tree stock,

FIGURE 14.6 **Bamboo** *(Thyrsostachys and Bambusa)*.

FIGURE 14.7 **Giant climbers** *(Scindapsis, Thunbergia and Mucuna)*.

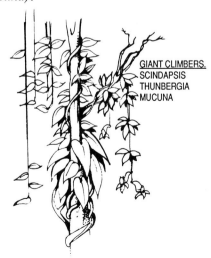

256

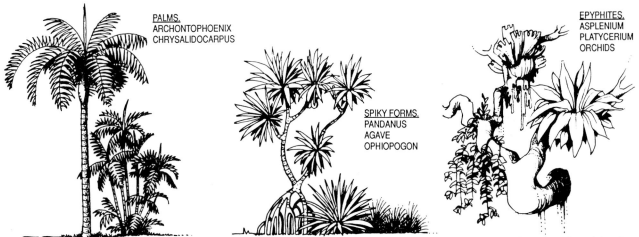

FIGURE 14.8 **Palms** (*Archontophoenix* **and** *Chrysolidocarpus*).

FIGURE 14.9 **Spiky forms** (*Pandanus, Agave* **and** *Ophiopogon*).

FIGURE 14.10 **Epyphites** (*Asplenium, Platycerium* **and** *orchids*).

aeration and drainage of tree pits is very important. Great care must be taken, however, to avoid using trees with severe bark damage or central rot. Pruning and insect and fungus prevention must be thorough and skilfully performed, or the tree's life will be very short. Beyond this limited but useful technique, large nursery grown stock will be invariably hard to find, and collection of trees for advance growing is imperative if plants of any size are required for quick effect. Saplings and feathered whips (1.0–1.8 m) are valuable for bulk planting. Often these trees will overtake larger specimens in a few years, and deep soil cultivation, organic manures and plant pit drainage are important for saplings.

## (c) *Planting methods*

Generally, tree pits should be at least 1 m³ (35 ft³) and average shrub pits 1/8 m³ with infilled topsoil. These should be finished to a slightly lower level than the surrounding area to facilitate watering and the retention of rain. Where the soil is wet and heavy, it is advisable to dig deeper holes and to put drainage stones or, in dense soils, subsoil drains in before filling the holes with soil compost. Stakes should be termite-proof, and of treated sawn timber, and tree ties should be of a durable synthetic material and light-coloured to avoid overheating. It is important to specify tree staking carefully, as many unsuitable techniques are practised. Tree ties should be shifted regularly to avoid problems with ants and fungi.

PLATE 14.14 *Khaya senegalensis* **only two years after planting as base-rooted trunks without branches known as Inotant Trees. Planted by the Public Works Department in Singapore.** (*Henry Steed*)

## (d) *Shrub, herbaceous and climber planting*

Ideally, shrubs should be planted in prepared beds of good quality soil, cultivated to a depth of at least 300 mm and ameliorated thoroughly to improve soil texture and drainage. Small stock sizes for shrubs are

better than large stock sizes, since large stock is hard to keep in nurseries and is generally etiolated and overgrown.

For individual or specimen shrubs, large, deep pits should be dug and backfilled with high-quality, rich soil mix. Drainage in heavy soils is essential.

### (e) *Grass*

In many tropical areas, establishing grass by seed is not practicable because of the variability of rainfall and fungal and insect problems. Grass can be planted by establishing nursery beds of a stoloniferous species such as *Cynodon dactylon* (Bermuda grass) and subsequently planting small clumps of stolons at 25 cm (10 in) distance at the very beginning of the rainy season. These clumps soon proliferate and a sward is rapidly formed, becoming well established by the following dry season. This spot turfing is useful over large, flat areas, but can allow serious erosion in wet weather in sloping landscapes. For slopes steeper than 1:15, close turfing is recommended to achieve total cover immediately. For very successful grasses, such as *Axonopus compressus*, rough clumps can be bedded down to form a cover, and this cover can be topdressed with a sand and soil mix to cover the grass leaves. The soil cover protects the grass from the sun and encourages fast cover and rooting. Cutting can be expected within 3 weeks of planting.

### (f) *Sourcing of materials*

The normal back-up services of good nurseries and skilled contractors are available in relatively few tropical or arid regions. Thus, it is of vital importance to discover any plant-growing organizations in the area. Local sources may include government nurseries, local authorities, existing private gardens, botanic gardens and educational establishments. As propagation from seed or by vegetative means is rapid, a project of any size or duration would be justified in setting up a small nursery of its own at an early stage, especially if plant material has to be brought from a distance. It is recommended that seed and plant material be purchased from sources within the climatic region concerned as much as is possible as a greater chance of success is likely when using acclimatized material. The seed of many tropical species loses its virtue in a very short time (a matter of weeks in some cases), and storage in reduced temperatures and humidities is necessary.

## 14.7 PLANTING TYPES

The plant lists in Tables 14.1 to 14.12 are intended to provide designers with a sample palette of tropical planting types that are most likely to be included in designs. The categories listed are typical of those likely to be used in a bill of quantities, and give subdivisions based on size and mass. Planting is a three-dimensional exercise and these categories are selected in accordance with the final three-dimensional effects of the design.

258

The plant lists are, however, extremely general. Coverage of usable lists in each tropical region would need a number of volumes of books of this length. To give an example of the extent of the choice of tropical plants available, there are around 8000 species of flowering plant in Malaysia alone, at least 2500 of which are trees. Horticulturally available plants will number hundreds of species in any one area, many of which could be quite different from those available in another nearby region.

The plant lists shown here are broadly based on a South East Asian palette. Of course, many pan-tropical and introduced species from other parts of the world are used in this area, so some cross-referencing is possible. The format of the lists will, however, be useful in providing the basis for expanded individual lists and plant reference files. A broad division of the types of plants that are available is given here.

1. Broadleaved trees — These cover almost all tropical trees including those with pinnate leaves as well as broader or glossy leaves. Broadleaved trees can be subdivided into large trees, of ultimate height 15 m and upwards; medium trees, of ultimate height 10–15 m; and small trees, of ultimate height 3–10 m. These all include monopodial (single leader), sympodial (branched), and multi-stem species.

2. Conifers — The range of conifers that can be used in the tropics is quite small. They are, however, very useful in creating a diverse effect, especially with their fine needles or small foliage and upright columnar habit. Many sub-tropical pines, podocarpus, thuja, cypress and junipers will tolerate even equatorial climates if given rich but dry, free draining soils, and elements of michorrhized fungus.

3. Palms — There are two principal forms of palm that will be used by the landscape designer: single stem palms having one trunk or one trunk emanating from one root system; and multi-stem palms having multiple suckers forming a clump. There are numerous sizes and shapes within these categories. Leaf shape varies from feather-form leaves (e.g. the coconut) to fan-form leaves (for instance *Livistona*). Palms range in size from giant 25 m palms to clusters at 4 m, down to delicate prostrate palms. All palms need careful cultivation to allow strong stems to develop uninterruptedly, especially if they are to be planted in avenues.

4. Shrubs — For the lists in this chapter, shrubs include all massing plants below 3 m in height, whether woody or herbaceous. Subdivision of each category would be very lengthy. In general, herbaceous plants are used in the same way as shrubs, for clumps or masses, and can be expected

to last as long as shrubs. Indeed, many shrubs require pruning or replacing well before herbaceous plants need to be thinned out. For design purposes shrubs and herbaceous plants are divided into three categories: large shrubs about 1.2–3 m or more height at maturity; medium shrubs from 0.5–1.2 m high at maturity; and ground cover shrubs less than 0.5 m high at maturity.

5. Climbers – The range and diversity of climbers in the tropics is immense. Many have the most exotic flowers imaginable. The list is broadly divided into foliage climbers, slender flowering climbers and heavy flowering climbers. Generally, climbers need good, deep soil, plenty of nutrient and strong rot-resistant supports. Few are self-clinging and most require strong wires or nets to twine up or for tendrils.

6. Bamboos – Ranging from giant *Dendrocalanus* to dwarf *Pseudosasa* the bamboo group is very extensive. Very fast growing and dense, most bamboos are short-lived and need regular cleaning out. Heavy leaf fall can be expected. The best bamboos for landscape work are the tall, slender bamboos that are used for screening or character planting, and smaller dense bamboos used for landscape massing and hedging.

7. Epiphytes – Abundant epiphytes festoon forest trees, and many can be used in landscape schemes.

No separate list is given, since this is a very specialized area of horticulture, but the following types can be considered either for tying on to trees or stumps, or planting in the ground.

(i) Orchids. A huge range of plants are available, but they are very difficult to grow without expert maintenance.

(ii) Bromeliads. Pineapples, *Aechmea*, *Tillandisa* and *Vreisia* and others are suitable as ground cover massing, but also for above ground soilless planting.

(iii) Ferns. *Asplenium* (bird's nest, Plate 14.15), *Platycerium* (stag's horn) and smaller ferns such as *Pteris* and *Davallia* are suitable for ground cover.

(iv) Aroids. *Arithurium* and numerous other forest aroids can be grown in the bark of trees or as ground cover in shady areas.

(v) Gesneriad. Flowering epiphytes with long trailing columns of tubular flowers, such as *Columnea* and *Aeschymanthus*.

8. Aquatics – Abundant aquatics are available and many produce beautiful foliage and flowers, as is shown in Plates 14.15 and 14.16. Many are extremely invasive and should not be used unless under very controlled conditions where their effect is important (for instance, in concrete pools on roof decks). Full sun is essential for flowering, and water management is required to keep algae,

PLATE 14.15 **The bird's nest fern** *(Asplenium nidus)* **in the fork of a tree.** *(Maurice Lee)*

PLATE 14.16 *Nymphaea* **spp. in full bloom.**

PLATE 14.17 **Plate-like leaves of** *Victoria amazonica*, **the giant waterlily, with** *Crimums* **in the background.** *(Maurice Lee)*

mosquitoes and rotting leaf litter under control. Water depth should be no less than 500 mm, with 1 m depth for larger aquatic plants such as the large lilies. Shallow water gets very warm and algal growth is then a more likely problem. Pool design should allow for water circulation, topping up of clean water and drainage for cleaning if necessary. The pH of the water is also important, and analysis in local water is important to determine what water treatment is needed for different species.

Marginal plants are also useful and soil bodies should be designed into ponds for these. The use of manures to keep the soil rich in ponds should be carefully controlled to avoid pollution, the killing of fish and any increase of algae. Generally, aquatics will not grow in chlorinated water.

Aquatic plants include the white-pink lotus (*Nelumbo nucifera*), lilies of many colours (*Nymphaea* spp.) and the giant water lilies (such as *Victoria amazonica* and *regia*) with yellow-pink flowers and leaves up to 6 ft in diameter. See Plates 14.16 and 14.17.

The marginal plants include avoids (such as *Spathyphyllum* and *Alocasia*), marantas (such as *Maranta* and *Calathea*), grass types (for instance, *Cyperus*, *Coix*, *Scirpus* and *Typha*), palm types (for instance, *Nypa* and *Pandanus*) and gingers and cannas (such as *Hedychium* and *Canna*).

## 14.8 PLANT LISTS

Tables 14.1 to 14.12 give a broad outline of the types of tropical plants that are available to the landscape designer. (Please note this list is essentially South-East Asian tropical and pan-tropical.)

TABLE 14.1
**Large trees**

| Species | Flowers | Characters | Comments |
|---|---|---|---|
| *Adenanthera pavonina* | Small with white clusters | Tall broad-headed light canopy | Pinnate leaves, light shade, scatters abundant seeds and pods |
| *Albizia lebbeck** | Small with yellow powder puffs | Umbrella-shaped, tall, dense canopy | Feathery leaves, rattling seed pods. Deciduous in dry areas |
| *Andira surinamensis* | Bunches of purple flowers | Upright dense foaming texture of foliage | Good shade with dark green dense foliage, messy flowers and fruits, poor soil-tolerant |
| *Bombax malabaricum* (Cotton tree) | Scarlet wax blooms, very spectacular | Very tall, open-tiered branching. Foliage not dense | Symmetrical-branching habit, fast growing. Messy flowers and seeds |
| *Calophyllum inophyllum* | White, fluffy, scented flowers | Broad-headed, dense, dark, glossy leaves | Good shade tree, salt-tolerant, for coastal situations. Invasive roots |
| *Couroupita guineensis* (Cannon ball tree) | Pink, white and yellow, fleshy | Tall, dense crown of light green leaves | Very large tree with peculiar cannon-ball like fruits on lower trunk |
| *Delonix regia* (Red flame/Poinciana) | Scarlet and white with massive seed pods | Umbrella-shaped tree with gnarled but smooth trunk | Beautiful tree with delicate light green foliage and spectacular flowers. Prefers seasonal climate. Light soil |
| *Erythrina variegata** | Scarlet clusters, like claws | Round-headed with dense crown of large leaves | Variegated leaf form and stripy trunk. Good shade tree |
| *Erythrophleum guineense* | None | Very large spreading crown, dense foliage | Good shade and light leaf colour. Dark contrasting bark. Deep soil |
| *Eugenia grandis** | White and cream powder puffs | Erect tree with dark, glossy leaves | Very tall, narrow tree, good for roadsides. Old trees drop branches. Good soil |

| Species | Flowers | Character | Comments |
|---|---|---|---|
| Eucalyptus deglupta | None | Erect tree with blue, very tall, dense foliage | Beautiful striated bark and bluish foliage. Good for roadsides and parks. Forestry tree. Poor soil tolerance |
| Fagrea fragrans (Tembusu) | Creamy white, very fragrant | Tall, vertical, branching habit | Light green leaves, very dark trunk. Elegant. Conical when young. Good soil |
| Ficus benjamina* | Insignificant | Drooping umbrella crown. Massive trunk and roots | Elegant weeping habit when young. Very large, shady tree when mature |
| Khaya senegalensis* (Mahogany) | None | Very tall, tight head, dense | Elegant, compact form, light coloured bark. Good shade. Deep soil |
| Peltophorum pterocarpum† (Yellow flame tree) | Brilliant yellow clusters over whole tree | Bushy, round-headed, dense foliage. Open branching | Good shade tree. Bright flowering followed by purplish pods. Good soil |
| Pterocarpus indicus† (Burmese rosewood) | Chrome yellow, short lived masses. Very fragrant | Huge, weeping, round-headed, dense foliage | Very fast growing, first class shade tree. Invasive roots. Brittle when old. Deep soil |
| Samanea saman† (Rain tree) | Pink powder puffs | Umbrella-shaped, short trunk, light foliage | Very fast growing, good shade tree. Invasive roots. Unsuitable for small areas |
| Swietenia macrophylla | Tiny white flowers | Tall, shaggy crown, thick trunk | Medium fast growing with unruly branching system. Good street tree |
| Tabebuia pentaphylla† (Tecoma/Pink poui) | Hugh masses of pink trumpets. Spectacular | Tiered-branching, tall, wide-spreading | Fast growing, dense, large leaves. Dramatic but messy flowering. Needs good soil |
| Tamarindus indica (Tamarind) | Small, yellow-brown, pea-like flowers | Round-headed, tall tree with light green foliage | Fast growing, feathery tree with strong, straight stem. Good shade tree. Pods used for cooking |
| Terminalia catappa† (Ketapang/Indian almond) | Small white flowers, abundant, constantly dropping | Very tall, tiered branches and large, shiny leaves. Autumnal | Fast growing, stately tree. Untidy perpetual leaf and nut fall. Autumn red tints. Invasive roots |

* Species warranting further research.
† Can be grown as an 'instant tree'.

TABLE 14.2
**Medium-sized trees**

| Species | Flowers | Character | Comments |
|---|---|---|---|
| Acacia auriculiformis | Small, yellow-scented powder puffs | Open-branched, shaggy-headed with coarse bark and twisted trunk | Pioneer tree, good for dry conditions. Drops acidic leaves and seeds all year round. Messy, short-lived and brittle |

| Species | Flowers | Character | Comments |
|---|---|---|---|
| *Amherstia nobilis* | Large red and yellow hanging sprays | Broad-headed, dense, with open branching inside | Spectacular tree with pinnate leaves drooping, pink when young. Moist, deep soil |
| *Caesalpinia ferrea* (Brazilian ironwood) | Small, yellow-brown clusters | Flat-topped, light foliage, open-branched habit | Graceful, slow-growing tree with peeling bark, light feathery foliage |
| *Cassia fistula\** (Golden shower) | Abundant yellow laburnum-like sprays | Broad-headed, open-branched, untidy shape | Large leaves, giving light shade, spectacular flowers, long, hard pods. Insect-prone. Needs good soil |
| *Cinnamomum iners\** (Wild cinnamon) | Creamy spikes | Upright, dense, bushy tree, rounded head | Slow growing with glossy leaves, flushing bright red. Good for tall hedge. Well drained soil |
| *Dalbergia oliveri* (Tamalan tree) | Small creamy flowers | Umbrella-shaped, light foliage with grey trunk | Light green, delicate foliage and slightly weeping form. Light shade. Good, well drained soil |
| *Dillenia indica* (Elephant apple) | White, magnolia-like, fragrant | Upright, conical tree with big leaves. Dense | Large, oramental, deep-veined leaves and huge, green, apple-like fruit. Fast growing. Shade |
| *Felicium decipiens* (Fern tree) | Insignificant | Dense, round-headed with dark green textured foliage | Attractive, slow-growing shade tree. Needs good soil and some shelter. Weak roots |
| *Hibiscus tiliaceus* (Tree hibiscus) | Large, lemon-yellow changing to red | Round-headed, dense, dark-leaved tree | Salt-tolerant, good for dry and coastal areas. Good shade. Attracts insects. |
| *Jacaranda filicifolia* | Bluish-purple in large clusters in dry seasons | Upright tree with very light, open foliage | Fast growing with spectacular flowers and delicate light green foliage. Best in drier areas, brittle |
| *Lagerstroemia speciosa\** (Rose of India) | Large, showy-frilled flowers in clusters, pink, mauve or purple | Round-headed, open-branched, dense foliage | Attractive flowers in drier seasons. Good shade. Prone to insect attack |
| *Mesua ferrea* (Ironwood tree) | Large white flower with yellow centre. | Dense, conical form, spreading when older, formal | New leaves crimson to white, leaves glaucous with light underside. Deep, moist soil |
| *Michelia alba* (Champaka, white jade tree) | Waxy, cream, upright flowers. Very heavily scented | Upright, conical when young, broad-headed later | Light green, large leaves, good shade. Exceptional fragrance. Rich, deep soil |
| *Pongamia pinnata* (Seashore mempari) | Pale mauve profuse clusters | Dense, round-headed, regular-shaped tree | Drought- and salt-tolerant, seasonal autumn colour and leaf fall. Prone to caterpillar attack |
| *Saraca thaipingensis* | Showy yellow clusters on trunk and branches | Dense, broad-headed tree with open underside | Good shade tree, soft pink flushing leaves. Purple seed pods. Moist soil |

TABLE 14.3
**Small trees**

| Species | Flowers | Character | Comments |
|---|---|---|---|
| *Baphia nitida* | Small white flowers | Bushy, rounded, small tree. Normally grows as hedge | Large green glossy leaves. Long lasting tall hedge, though slow to establish. Best in full sun. |
| *Bauhinia blakeana** | Large red–purple orchid-like flowers | Open-crowned, wide-branching, light leaf cover | Light shade tree, fast growing. Tends to be gnarled unless trained. Flowers mid-dry season. |
| *Calliandra surinamensis* | Delicate pink powder-puff flowers | Umbrella form, arching branches, light foliage | Fast growing, profuse flowers in morning only. Delicate leaves |
| *Callistemon viminalis** (Bottle brush) | Dense spikes of scarlet stamens | Weeping form with hanging foliage | Long thin leaves and weeping habit distinctive. Good feature tree. |
| *Cassia spectabilis* | Profuse yellow bunches | Rounded, bushy, dense foliage. Weeping habit, broad spreading form. | Profuse flowering. Good for massing and roadside use. Light green leaves |
| *Cordia sebestena* (Geiger tree) | Brilliant orange-scarlet crepy texture | Round-topped, regular form, dense leaves | Good shade tree, small white sweet edible fruit. Drought-tolerant |
| *Erythrina glauca* (Coral tree) | Deep red butterfly flower, profuse | Rounded, wide, spreading, gnarled branches. Open foliage | Glaucous foliage and distinctive branching. Very fast. Rather short lived |
| *Guaiacum officianale* (Lignum vitae) | Large blue clusters, orange yellow berries | Small, very compact. Rounded head | Very hardy, drought-tolerant, dense foliage. Flower and fruit at same time |
| *Gustava superba* (Stinkwood) | Few but showy pink flowers, waxy white inside | Rounded head, very dense, short trunk | Leaves emit peculiar odour. Yellow-green edible fruit. Shady. Needs good soil |
| *Plumeria spp* (Frangipani) | Large, fragrant, waxy flowers, wide variety of colours | Short, open-branched with round head. Gnarled trunk | Showy flowers, usually sparse leaves unless rich, moist, well drained soil. Check local superstitions |
| *Tabebuia pallida* (Pink trumpet tree) | Dense, pink clusters. Abundant | Upright growth with narrow, dense crown | Small, shiny leaves. Shade. Good for small spaces. Good soil and drainage |

TABLE 14.4
**Conifers**

| Species | Flowers | Character | Comments |
|---|---|---|---|
| *Agathis robusta* | | Stately timber tree. Very tall | Sub-tropical forest tree. Grey straight column to 30 m. Very narrow |
| *Araucaria columnaris** (Cook pine) | | Tall, pine-like, symmetrical tree. Very spiky foliage | Narrower than *A. heterophylla* (Norfolk Island pine). Architectural form |

| Species | Flowers | Character | Comments |
|---|---|---|---|
| *Casuarina equisetifolius** | | Feathery, upright, branching. Tall and open | Pioneer tree, very hardy. Pendulous, swaying branches. Wind and salt-tolerant |
| *Cupressus sempervirens* | | Conical cypress, dense and narrow | Dark green with greyish tint. Sub-tropical |
| *Juniperus chinensis** | | Conical, bluish tree, broad base | Traditional Chinese garden form. Fast growing. Messy leaf fall |
| *Pinus insularis** | | Tall, strong-growing tree. Typical pine form. | Fast growing timber tree. Fire-prone. Needs micorrhiza |
| *Podocarpus latifolius* and spp. | Catkin-like flower | Stiff, erect, with yew-like leaf texture | Bark sheds in long strips on older trees. Dark green rather sooty tree |

* Species in these groups warrant further research.

TABLE 14.5
**Palms (single)**

| Species | Flowers | Character | Comments |
|---|---|---|---|
| *Archontophoenix alexandrae* (Majestic palm) | Creamy-white | Tall palm with majestic crown. Slender stems | Arching fronds with narrow leaves. Attractive red fruit |
| *Areca catechu** (Betel nut) | Fragrant, white | Slender, straight palm with small crown | Reddish-orange olive-1shaped fruit containing betel nut. Dark green stem |
| *Bismarckia nobilis* | | Huge fan palm up to 60 m with large crown | Grey-green rigid palmate leaves. Female trees have brown fruits in plumes. Good soil |
| *Cocos nucifera* (Coconut) | Creamy-white panicles | Tall palm with large, feathery crown | Dwarf varieties available. *C. nucifera* (Golden Malay) has bright yellow coconuts. Good shade |
| *Elaeis guineensis* (Oil palm) | Separate clusters of male and female flowers | 18 m ringed trunk with graceful dark glossy crown | Palm oil produced from large clusters of red/dark fruit. Dense shade, wide spreading |
| *Licuala grandis** | | Small fan palm with distinctive leaves | Almost round bright green leaves. Glossy red fruit. Good texture plant |
| *Livistona chinensis** (Chinese fan palm) | Creamy-white panicles | Large spreading fan palm with stiff dense crown | Huge, bright green, glossy leaves. Metallic blue 1fruit. Good pot palm though can grow very large |
| *Phoenix dactylifera** (Date palm) | | Very tall palm with dense, stiff crown | Date palm species include *P. loureirii* and *roebelenii*. Both miniature pot palms |
| *Pritchardia pacifica* (Pacific sabal) | Fragrant, brown | Slender-trunked with large, round crown | Bright olive-green fan fronds. Glossy black-blue fruit. Distinctive formal shape. Good soil |
| *Roystonea oleracea** (cabbage palm) | Fragrant, creamy | Very tall feather palm with straight trunk | Large, glossy green, arching fronds. Small, purple fruit |

* Species warranting further research.

TABLE 14.6<br>**Palm-like Plants**

| Species | Flowers | Character | Comments |
|---|---|---|---|
| Cyathea spp. (tree fern) | | Single stem with flat, spreading crown | Brown, scaled trunk topped with huge, lacy, fresh green fronds. Needs shade and humidity. Rich, moist soil. Very decorative specimen |
| Cycas revoluta* (Cycad) | Woolly brown carpels | Palm-like rosette, prostrate, growing too small | Slow growing trunk. Stiff, glossy, green pinnate fronds. Specimen as in small groups |
| Ravenala madagascariensis (Traveller's palm) | White bird of paradise flower (monocarpic) | Palm-like trunk with with banana-like leaves in fan | Striking form of huge leaves. Can be planted in any direction. Good moist soil. Sky blue seeds |
| Pandanus sanden* | none | Thick stemmed ornamental screw pine with stilt-like roots | Spiral rosettes of long green glossy leaves, variegated with white and yellow. Tolerates dry soil |

* Species warranting further research.

TABLE 14.7<br>**Palms (multi)**

| Species | Flowers | Characters | Comments |
|---|---|---|---|
| Caryota mitis | | Fishtail palm with numerous suckers | Grey-green, trunks up to 8 m. Fruit red or black. Dense massing. Shade |
| Chamaedorea erumpens* | | Upright leafy dwarf palm | Erect bamboo-like stems with short, drooping pinnate leaves. Shade-tolerant |
| Chrysalidocarpus lutescens | | Graceful clump palm to 8 m | Slender yellow stems. Narrow pinnate foliage. Fruits purple or black. Tolerates wet or poor soils |
| Cyrtostachys lakka | | Beautiful clustering feather palm. Upright leaf form | Slender green trunks with large scarlet leaf bases. Black fruit on red stalk. Deep, moist soil |
| Licuala spinosa | | Fan leaf, dense cluster palm. Spiky stems | Glossy green leaves from top to bottom, petioles with black thorns. Red fruit. Tolerates sand and salt |
| Oncosperma tigillarum | Bright yellow | Very large, many-stemmed clump in excess of 20 m. Very spiny | Feathery fronds top trunks. Graceful oramental. Purple fruit. Mainly coastal |
| Ptychosperma macarthurii | | Dense, bushy, suckering feather palm to 8 m | Dense crown with toothed, pinnate leaves. Bright red fruit. Hedging |
| Rhapis excelsa* | | Miniature fan palm. Dense cluster form | Bamboo-like stems covered with coarse fibre. Glossy green leaves. Useful pot palm and dense hedge. |

★ Species warranting further research.

TABLE 14.8
**Large shrubs**

| Species | Flowers | Character | Comments |
| --- | --- | --- | --- |
| Ardisia elliptica | Small pink or white flowers | Evergreen shrub or small tree | Dark green leathery leaves provide dense screen. Red flushing. Glossy berries will stain paving |
| Caesalpinia pulcherrima (Peacock flower) | Orange–red flowers. Profuse | Open-branched shrub, prickly. Feathery form | Mimosa-like leaves. Free flowering even when young. Very hardy but needs good soil. Pink, yellow and red varieties also available |
| Calliandra haematocephala* | Red power puff. Profuse | Rambling shrub, dense dark foliage | Beautiful pinnate leaves. Forms attractive screen up to 3 m. Tolerates poor soil and dry conditions. |
| Cassia biflora* | Bright yellow clusters | Robust bush. Round head | Pinnate leaves. Very hardy, always in flower. Best in dull sun and thrives in poor soils. Road sider |
| Costus speciosus* (Spiral ginger) | Pineapple-like red spikes with large white, papery, yellow-centred flowers | Clustering, slender perennial herb. Lush | Spiral or drooping reedlike, green leafy stems. Forms a dense mass up to 2 m. Needs rich, moist soil |
| Duranta repens | Pale blue or white | Dense shrub. Rounded, vigorous | Ornamental orange-yellow berries. Makes good clipped hedge and massing plant. Best in full sun when it flowers abundantly |
| Ervatamia coronaria (Crepe jasmine) | Waxy, white, star-like flowers. Very fragrant at night | Spreading flat top. Dense form. Vigorous | Glossy green leaves. Double variety also available. Open sun in good soil. Good for massing or specimens |
| Euphorbia pulcherrima (Poinsettia) | Tiny yellow flowers surrounded by large scarlet bracts | Open, branching shrub with umbrella-form light leafing | Cream-coloured bract variety available. Seasonal flowering, prefers dry cool period to flower. Good soil required |
| Heliconia spp.* | Upright or pendulous inflorescence. Very showy | Clustering perennial herb. Dense and vigorous | Spectacular flowering plants, with banana-like leaves. Needs rich, deep, moist soil |
| Hibiscus spp.* | Large trumpet flowers. Most colours available. Single or double | Vigorous, free-flowering shrub. Upright habit | Very showy shrub used in mass or for hedging. Good soil |
| Ixora javanica* | Large dark red clusters in profusion | Bushy shrub. Very dense, rounded form | Rather slow growing, needs full sun. Yellow variety and other hybrids available. All flower continuously if fertilized |
| Kopsia fruticosa | Star-shaped, pale pink with crimson centres | Large, open, bushy shrub. Rounded habit | As specimen or in beds. Full sun and good soil |

| Species | Flowers | Character | Comments |
|---|---|---|---|
| *Malvaviscus arboreus* (Sleeping hibiscus) | Bright red, tubular, half closed flowers | Open-branched hibiscus-like shrub. Bushy, dense habit | Flowers remain half closed, hence name. Requires frequent pruning. Full sun or shade. Good for massing or hedge |
| *Murraya paniculata* | Small clusters of white, very fragrant flowers | Tree-like shrub with dense, bushy habit | Glossy green pinnate leaves. Can be clipped to tight hedge, or standard |
| *Mussaenda erythrochalmys** | Creamy-white flowers with deep red sepals | Spreading shrub or rambler | Full sun and rich, well-drained soil. Coloured sepals almost entirely cover the bush. Many varieties in pink, orange, white and cream |
| *Nerium oleander** | Large clusters of single or double flowers in white, pink or deep red | Willow-like stems with long, leathery leaves. Upright | Poisonous sap. Prefers sandy soil and flowers well on coast in dry seasons. |
| *Pisonia alba* | | Treelike foliage shrub. Open branched | Vivid yellow-green leaves provide interesting contrast to darker greens. Can be clipped to form hedge |
| *Sanchesia nobilis* | Yellow spikes with reddish-brown bracts | Bushy, foliage shrub. Very dense. Vigorous | Yellow stems turning red, dark green leaves with pale yellow veins. Can be cut back very hard to keep low. Forms dense solid mass in good soil |
| *Thevetia peruviana* (Yellow oleander) | Large, golden-yellow trumpets in small clusters | Large shrub or small tree. Open branched. Feathery form | Glossy, green, linear leaves are attractive. Also white and apricot varieties. Full sun and sandy soil. Poisonous |

* Species warranting further research.

TABLE 14.9
**Medium-sized shrubs and herbaceous plants**

| Species | Flowers | Character | Comments |
|---|---|---|---|
| *Acalypha* spp.* | Spikes red, white or cream and insignificant except in *A. hispida* | Bushy shrub | Ranging from very colourful red-copper leaves hedging plants with light green leaves. Vigorous, tolerant of poor conditions |
| *Alocasia sanderana** (Kris plant) | | Accent foliage plant | Metallic silver-green leaves with grey-white ribs and white margin. Back of leaf purple. Needs humidity. Accent plant, other varieties more hardy |

| Species | Flowers | Character | Comments |
|---|---|---|---|
| *Alpinia purpurata**<br>(Red ginger) | Crimson spathes in large<br>spikes | Leafy-stemmed<br>perennial | Good screen plant requires<br>part shade and good soil |
| *Asplenium nidus*<br>(Birds nest fern) | | Stiffly spreading<br>epiphytic rosette | Wide, leathery texture,<br>shining green leaves.<br>Commonly seen in tree<br>branches, also makes<br>good accent plant. Prefers<br>some shade |
| *Barleria cristata*<br>(Philippine violet) | Mauve tubes, dark to<br>near white or striped | Bushy, leafy shrub.<br>Vigorous | In borders, beds or as hedge,<br>does not flower well<br>when frequently trimmed.<br>Tolerates poor soil |
| *Bougainvillea* spp.* | Flower bracts range<br>through white, orange,<br>red, pink and purple | Perpetually flowering,<br>spiny shrub | These climbers also make<br>excellent shrubs in<br>masses. Requires heavy<br>pruning. *B. spectabilis*<br>(Mary Palmer) has red<br>and white bracts on same<br>plant |
| *Brunfelsia calycina*<br>(Lady of the night) | Deep lavender fading to<br>white, sweet scent | Slender spreading<br>branches | Especially fragrant at night.<br>Good for massing. Good<br>moist soil. Regular<br>compost needed |
| *Canna generalis** | Various, mostly red or<br>yellow. Spectacular | Erect, leafy-stemmed<br>perennial | Very free flowering. In beds<br>or as screen, fast growing.<br>Deep, rich, moist soil and<br>compost |
| *Clerodendron* spp.* | Various, most are free<br>flowering | Climbers, shrubs or small<br>trees. Vigorous. Hardy | *C. paniculatum*. Large genus<br>with wide range of habit<br>and form |
| *Codiaeum* spp.* | | Upright leafy bushes to<br>dwarf, slender ground<br>covers | Foliage plant with bright,<br>multi-coloured leaves.<br>Best in full sun. Many<br>striking cultivars |
| *Cordyline terminalis** | Panicles of lilac flowers | Slender, erect foliage<br>plant | Copper-green leaves with<br>red shading. Young<br>leaves bright red. Accent<br>plant or screen. Requires<br>shade. Cultivars in many<br>varieties of colour |
| *Crossandra undulifolia* | Apricot−orange with<br>prominent bracts | Fairly upright, bushy | Flowers almost con-<br>tinuously. Yellow variety<br>less common. Useful for<br>beds or as pot plant |
| *Dieffenbachia* spp.* | | Attractive, fairly upright<br>foliage plant | Striking leaves are green<br>with variegations and<br>splotches of colour.<br>Requires shade. Good<br>screen for interiors |
| *Dracaena* spp.* | Some species have<br>fragrant white flowers | Upright, strappy-leaved,<br>some trunked | Accent foliage plant<br>with striped or spotted<br>variegated leaves.<br>Many forms. Good<br>feature plants, hardy,<br>mostly drought-tolerant |

269

| Species | Flowers | Character | Comments |
|---------|---------|-----------|----------|
| *Excoecaria bicolor* | Small, narrow spikes | Bushy shrub with dense foliage | Shiny green leaves, red below provides an attractive foliage screen or hedge. Needs deep, rich, well drained soil |
| *Galphimia glauca* (Golden shower thryallis) | Abundant golden sprays | Upright, open shrub. Not dense | Free flowering, the terminal spray show well against the dark green or blue leaves |
| *Gardenia jasminoides* (Cape jasmine) | Large, white, fragrant | Spare-branched, spreading shrubs. Dense, rounded form | Can become taller if not pruned. Full sun. Glossy dark green leaves. Needs good rich soil. Very susceptible to insect attack |
| *Heliconia psittacorum** (Parrot flower) | Bright orange bracts | Perennial long stems and leaves | Bright green leaves, excellent in large groups. Invasive. Needs full sun and prefers damp soil |
| *Hymenocallis caribea* (Spider lily) | Elegant, fragrant, white flower, long petals | Free flowering perennial herb. Strappy clumps | Sword-shaped leaves. Good in large groups. Needs good soil. Shade-tolerant |
| *Jasminum sambac* (Arabian jasmine) | Very fragrant, white turning purple | Woody shrub. Bushy | Dark green leaves. Good for massing. Needs good soil. Very prone to insect attack |
| *Lagerstroemia indica* (Crape myrtle) | Abundant terminal clusters of crinkled pink or mauve flowers | Open branching. Sparse foliage | Needs pruning to retain shape. Profuse flowering if soil is good and well composted |
| *Malpighia coccigera* | White fringed star-shaped, flowers | Compact bush very dense | Dark green, prickly, holly-like leaves and red fruit. Makes excellent hedge or bonsai |
| *Pachystachys lutea* | Many creamy-white flowers in orange spike of bracts | Herbaceous shrub. Bushy upright form. | Dull green leaves. Good in masses. Light shade |
| *Pedilanthus tithymaloides variegata* | Red | Succulent branching bush, dense upright branches | Crooked fleshy stems with waxy pale green leaves variegated white and pink. Very good in large block, providing dense cover and foliage effect |
| *Plumbago capensis* | Azure blue. Profuse in dry weather | Bushy scandant shrub. Light green leaves | Good in borders or as trailing edge plant. Prefers some shade. Needs very free-draining soil. Seasonal dry period preferred |
| *Pseuderanthemum reticulatum* | Upright spikes of mauve-dotted flowers | Shrubby plant. Bushy, rounded form | Young leaves yellow, older leaves yellow-veined. Light shade, flowers after dry spell |
| *Schefflera arboricola* | Insignificant | Branching dwarf, dense foliage plant | Glossy green palmate leaves. Looks like a miniature *Brassaia*. Clusters of erect orange berries. Shade-tolerant |

| Species | Flowers | Character | Comments |
| --- | --- | --- | --- |
| Tecomaria capensis | Orange-scarlet flowers in loose clusters | Thickly sprawling shrub, dense foliage | Can be used for hedging. Deeply serrated, compound, fresh green leaves. Full sun for best flowering. Excellent massed |
| Thunbergia erecta | Deep violet funnel with yellow throat | Erect shrub, dense, bushy habit | Grows well in shade or sun. Flowers profusely about twice a year. Prefers damp soil. In mixed borders or as hedge |
| Wrightia religiosa | Fragrant, white, star-like flowers | Flat-topped shrub with horizontal branches | Excellent bonsai plant or in large masses |

* Species warranting further research.

TABLE 14.10
**Small shrubs and ground cover**

| Species | Flowers | Character | Comments |
| --- | --- | --- | --- |
| Aglaonema spp.* | | Striking leafy foliage plant | Attractive ornamental for shady conditions. Excellent in interiors. 'Silver Queen' gives best bushy effect and keeps well |
| Artemisia scoparia | | Shrubby perennial. Upright | Bright green distinctive foliage plant. Massing behind low plants |
| Asparagus sprengeri* | White | Fluffy-branched, dense plant | Rich green needle-like foliage in erect or drooping plumes. Needs shade |
| Begonia maculata* | Pink clusters | Herbaceous. Large soft leaves | Not in full sun. Needs rich, moist soil |
| Caladium hortulanum* (Fancy-leaved caladium) | Cream-coloured spathe, very infrequent | Tuberous herb with heart-shaped or lanceolate leaves | Many cultivars of striking colour and pattern. Full sun for best colour effect. The wild C. bicolor needs some shade |
| Calathea spp. | | Dense, leafy plant. Many forms and colours | Beautiful foliage plant for shady areas and interior use. Needs constant shade and moist soil conditions |
| Costus malortieanus | Yellow with red markings | Suckering perennial herb | Bright green, hairy, fleshy leaves provide excellent ground cover beds. Full sun or shade once acclimatized. |
| Cuphea hyssopifolia | Purplish-pink | Heather-like compact shrub | Small, dark green leaves. Full sun. Tolerates drier conditions |
| Dianella caerulea | Mauve | Perennial herb with upright lanceolate leaves | Excellent durable ground cover. Variegated form also available |

| Species | Flowers | Character | Comments |
|---|---|---|---|
| Euphorbia millii (Crown of thorns) | Salmon-red bracts with pale centre | Scandant, spreading, spiny shrub | Dull green leaves which drop if too dry. Can also be trained against trellis |
| Ixora (dwarf varieties)* | Bunches in various colours. Profuse | Very low, dense bush. Slow growing | I. sunkist bright red-orange flowers, continuously flowering. Excellent in large masses and full sun |
| Lantana sellowiana | Corymb of mauve flowers | Creeping shrub | Useful in borders or over low walls. Other dwarf varieties available in white, yellow or red. Well-drained soil, full sun. |
| Maranta leuconeura kerchoveana | Small, white, purple-striped raceme | Low-growing plant, folds up leaves in evening | Requires shade. Pale green leaves with chocolate markings in rows on either side of leaf |
| Nephrolepis spp.* | | Arching fern, rosette form | Many varieties from widely pinnate fronds to finely lacy fronds. Some tolerate sunny conditions. Most prefer shade |
| Ophiopogon spp. | Lavender | Grassy clustering plant | Forms dense cover of dark green leaves. Variegated and very dwarf forms available. Sun or shade |
| Pandanus pygmaeus | | Dwarf pandanus | Variegated yellow and green leaves. Provides dense glossy bed. Tolerates dry conditions |
| Phyllanthus myrtifolius | Tiny red | Low-arching shrub | Long flat green branches with dark green, leaf-like, wavy branches. Very useful in beds or as trailing edge plant. Very hardy |
| Portulaca grandiflora (Rose moss) | Bright pink-purple flowers | Succulent herb | Forms complete mat of colour. Dark green, cylindrical leaves. Full sun |
| Rhoeo discolor | White clusters like small mouths | Fleshy rosette | Stiff, lanceolate, dark green leaves, purple beneath. Dwarf variety available. Also variegated pink and yellow. Good in large masses. Best in full sun |
| Russelia equisetifolia | Bright red tubular flowers | Slender, pendulous, arching branches | Foliage effect produced by numerous branches. Good trailing over walls or in rockery. Full sun and dry soil |
| Sansevieria trifasciata* | Greenish-white fragrant flowers at night | Dwarf form of 'Mother-in-law's tongue'. Erect | Dark green leaves with grey bands. Full sun or shade |
| Scindapsus aureus | | Dense spreading ground cover or vigorous climber | Retains juvenile leaf form when used as ground cover |
| Selaginella uncinnata | | Robust, creeping fern | Metallic blue leaves in shade. Light green in sun |

| Species | Flowers | Character | Comments |
|---|---|---|---|
| *Spathyphyllum cannaefolium* | White, fleshy spathe with long cream spadix | Leathery, leafy plant | Dull green-black leaves. Good interior or pot plant, needs shady conditions and rich soil |
| *Stenotaphrum secundatum* 'Variegatum' | | Creeping stoloniferous grass | Stiff, flat, green leaves striped with cream. Very hardy. Forms dense cover |
| *Syngonium podophyllum* | | Creeping plant | Heart-shaped ornamental leaves, green with white marking. Many varieties. Needs shade |
| *Tradescantia fluminensis* | White | Succulent creeper | Rapid spreading with small blue-green leaves. Maroon below. Needs shade |
| *Vinca rosea* (*Catharanthus rosea*) | Rosy pink, purple or white | Branching-stemmed shrubby herb | Glossy dark green foliage. Can become very leggy and sparse. Well drained soil and full sun. Common on beaches. Poisonous |
| *Vriesia splendens* | Long sword-shaped spike of red bracts. Yellow flowers | Funnel-shaped rosette | Blue-green slender leaves with purple bands. Also epiphytic |
| *Wedelia trilobata* | Orange-yellow flowers | Vigorous ground cover or climber | Shiny green leaves. Full sun or deep shade. Will cover other plants it not controlled |

* Species warranting further research.

TABLE 14.11
**Climbers**

| Species | Flowers | Character | Comments |
|---|---|---|---|
| *Allamanda cathartica* | Large, yellow continuous flowering | Shrubby climber. Open branching | Glossy green leaves. Requires full sun. Can also be used as shrub or hedge |
| *Bauhinia kockiana** (Orange bauhinia) | Racemes of scarlet through to yellow flowers | Woody climber, very tall. Slow | Roots need shade, often seen wild in forest in trees. Needs deep soil |
| *Bignonia magnifica* | Bunches of large mauve flowers | Woody vine. Very vigorous. Open branching | Frequent flushes of flowers |
| *Bougainvillea* spp.* | Bracts in most colours. Select from hybrids | Scrambling shrub. Very bushy. Spiny stems | Requires full sun for good blooming. Some seasonal some year round bloomers. Free draining soil |
| *Congea tomentosa* | Silvery-white bracts. Very showy | Climbing shrub. Tall up to 20 m. Invasive | Woolly leaves, needs sun. Makes good large shrub. Can be clipped |
| *Ficus pumila* (Creeping fig) | | Woody climber. Self-clinging covers walls and rocks completely | Short roots cling for support enabling easy coverage of unsightly walls. Remove woody shoots to prevent untidy appearance |

| Species | Flowers | Character | Comments |
|---------|---------|-----------|----------|
| *Ipomoea* spp.* (Morning glory) | Pink through purple. Mostly morning flowers | Vigorous climber. Dense foliage | Best in sun or relatively poor soils. Can become invasive |
| *Lonicera japonica*\* (Honeysuckle) | White turning yellow | Rambling shrub. Vigorous climber, self-twining | Needs some shade and rich soil |
| *Mucuna bennettii* (New Guinea vine) | Huge scarlet pendant clusters, spectacular | Large woody climber. Slow to establish | Partial shade required. Will cover large pergola. Needs good soil |
| *Odontadenia speciosa* | Fragrant, apricot in large clusters | Woody climber. Bushy foliage | Prefers partial shade. Very beautiful |
| *Passiflora quadriglandulosa*\* (Passion flower) | Rose pink with corona | Vigorous climber, dense foliage | Good fence coverer. Full sun best |
| *Petrea volubilis* (Sandpaper vine) | Sprays of deep purple flowers with long lasting, mauve calyxes | Shrubby climber. Coarse, light green leaves | Very beautiful climber requiring partial shade and well drained soil |
| *Philodendron* spp. | | Heavy foliage, climber | Very decorative foliage. Needs shade |
| *Quisqualis indica* (Rangoon creeper) | White, becoming deep pink, fragrant | Vigorous climber. Heavy foliage | Useful for pergola or arch. Needs strong supports |
| *Strongylodon macrobotrys* (Jade vine) | Pendulous clusters of jade-green flowers. Spectacular | Heavy twiner, sparse leaves | A feature the rarity of colour of its metallic blue flowers in clusters up to 1 m or more. Partial shade preferred |
| *Thunbergia grandiflora* | Long strings of large blue flowers up to 1 m | Large climber. Very dense foliage | Requires sun and strong support. Fast growing. Deep soil |
| *Tristellateia australasica* (Maiden's jealousy) | Yellow, very free flowering | Vigorous climber, leafy | Full sun and damp soil. Excellent on fences or as edge trailer in planter boxes |

\* Species warranting further research.

TABLE 14.12
**Bamboo**

| Species | Flowers | Character | Comments |
|---------|---------|-----------|----------|
| *B. multiplex* (and multiplex variegata) | | 4 m high woody grass | Fern-like small leaves on grass reed-like hollow stems to 4 m. Good hedging |
| *B. ventricosa*\* | | Bushy-headed on multi stems | Swollen culms give it the name 'Buddha's belly bamboo' |
| *Schiyostachyum*\* *brachycladum* | | Erect open clumps, very tall | Canes yellow and green, long lanceolate leaves. Fresh green |
| *Thrysostachys siamensis* | | Light, feathery bamboo with slender, narrow leaves | Upright bamboo good for courtyards and narrow spaces. Breeze noise. Good soil required |

\* Species warranting further research.

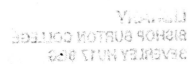

CHAPTER 15

# Planting in Hot, Arid Climates

## CHRISTOPHER DRIVER

The author would like to acknowledge his debt to Ann Willens, the author of this chapter in the first edition of *Landscape Design with Plants.* Her writing provided the basis for this new and updated chapter.

## 15.1 INTRODUCTION

The arid regions of the world – in North and South America, North and South Africa, Egypt, the Arabian Peninsula, India, Iran and Australia – occur where there is a deficiency of rainfull in relation to evaporation, and the annual amount of incoming radiation is greater than that which is reflected. This condition is most frequently encountered between latitudes 30° N and 30° S, where larger areas are dominated by high pressure systems and 'subsiding' air, that is air warmed adiabatically as it moves down towards the earth's surface so that clouds do not form and practically no rain falls. The arid and semi-arid regions of the world are shown in Figure 15.1.

Thirty-five per cent of the earth's land surface can be

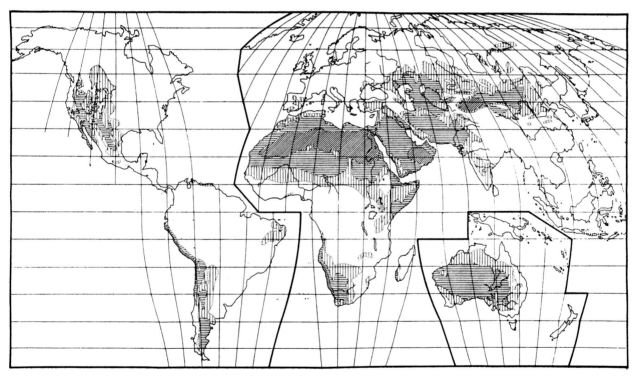

FIGURE 15.1 **The arid and semi-arid regions of the world.** *(Courtesy RIBA. Based on information prepared for UNESCO)*

EXTREMELY ARID (BASED ON RAINFALL RECORDS WHICH SHOW AT LEAST ONE YEAR WITHOUT RAIN).

ARID ⎫ BASED ON DEFICIT OF PRECIPITATION IN RELATION TO
⎬ POTENTIAL EVAPO-TRANSPIRATION USING THE INDEX
SEMI-ARID ⎭ DESCRIBED BY THORNTHWAITE IN 1948.

PLATE 15.1 **Minor wadi channel in the foothills of Jebel Akhdar, Oman, two months after the winter rains. The vegetation consists of herbaceous ephemerals, with permanent scrub** *(Acacia tortilis)* **in the background.** *(Christopher Driver)*

classified as arid or semi-arid, and although this characteristic unites the human inhabitants in their need to survive a generally hostile environment, there are many differences in their respective cultural histories and ecology. Of all the arid lands, those of the Arabian Peninsula have received most attention from landscape designers during the past thirty years. A large and relatively recent increase in prosperity has funded the technological advances necessary to lift the restrictions imposed by the harshness of the climate, and in doing so has encouraged the development of a more static, less nomadic style of life in the desert. Population increase and a parallel demand for permanent surroundings which simulate those of more temperate climates has provided many opportunities for experimentation in the establishment of plant material, not only in desert reclamation projects and agriculture, but also for urban beautification and amenity landscape design.

This chapter therefore attempts to define working parameters for the landscape architect in any hot, arid situation by describing the specific environmental and

practical constraints to landscape design in the Middle East. Knowledge of the prevailing physical characteristics of arid lands (for example, the climate, soils and vegetation types), of previous solutions to the problems of successfully establishing alien plant material and of the historical background of the country are essential if designers are to create a permanent new landscape and to respond effectively to the functional and aesthetic requirements of a commission.

## 15.2 LANDSCAPE HISTORY

Desert reclamation is not a new phenomenon, but many of the areas where settlement and agricultural extension are now being attempted were actually fertile in ancient times. Egypt, Sinai, Kuwait and North Africa were once forested, and a system of forest laws ensured the survival and protection of the natural vegetation in this region until the twelfth century AD. At the same time, desertification has been taking place for at least 2000 years. In fourth century BC Greece, for example, forest destruction, overgrazing and mismanagement

278

| Species | Flowers | Character | Comments |
|---|---|---|---|
| *Spathyphyllum cannaefolium* | White, fleshy spathe with long cream spadix | Leathery, leafy plant | Dull green-black leaves. Good interior or pot plant, needs shady conditions and rich soil |
| *Stenotaphrum secundatum* 'Variegatum' | | Creeping stoloniferous grass | Stiff, flat, green leaves striped with cream. Very hardy. Forms dense cover |
| *Syngonium podophyllum* | | Creeping plant | Heart-shaped ornamental leaves, green with white marking. Many varieties. Needs shade |
| *Tradescantia fluminensis* | White | Succulent creeper | Rapid spreading with small blue-green leaves. Maroon below. Needs shade |
| *Vinca rosea (Catharanthus rosea)* | Rosy pink, purple or white | Branching-stemmed shrubby herb | Glossy dark green foliage. Can become very leggy and sparse. Well drained soil and full sun. Common on beaches. Poisonous |
| *Vriesia splendens* | Long sword-shaped spike of red bracts. Yellow flowers | Funnel-shaped rosette | Blue-green slender leaves with purple bands. Also epiphytic |
| *Wedelia trilobata* | Orange-yellow flowers | Vigorous ground cover or climber | Shiny green leaves. Full sun or deep shade. Will cover other plants it not controlled |

\* Species warranting further research.

TABLE 14.11

**Climbers**

| Species | Flowers | Character | Comments |
|---|---|---|---|
| *Allamanda cathartica* | Large, yellow continuous flowering | Shrubby climber. Open branching | Glossy green leaves. Requires full sun. Can also be used as shrub or hedge |
| *Bauhinia kockiana\** (Orange bauhinia) | Racemes of scarlet through to yellow flowers | Woody climber, very tall. Slow | Roots need shade, often seen wild in forest in trees. Needs deep soil |
| *Bignonia magnifica* | Bunches of large mauve flowers | Woody vine. Very vigorous. Open branching | Frequent flushes of flowers |
| *Bougainvillea* spp.\* | Bracts in most colours. Select from hybrids | Scrambling shrub. Very bushy. Spiny stems | Requires full sun for good blooming. Some seasonal some year round bloomers. Free draining soil |
| *Congea tomentosa* | Silvery-white bracts. Very showy | Climbing shrub. Tall up to 20 m. Invasive | Woolly leaves, needs sun. Makes good large shrub. Can be clipped |
| *Ficus pumila* (Creeping fig) | | Woody climber. Self-clinging covers walls and rocks completely | Short roots cling for support enabling easy coverage of unsightly walls. Remove woody shoots to prevent untidy appearance |

| Species | Flowers | Character | Comments |
|---|---|---|---|
| *Ipomoea* spp.* (Morning glory) | Pink through purple. Mostly morning flowers | Vigorous climber. Dense foliage | Best in sun or relatively poor soils. Can become invasive |
| *Lonicera japonica** (Honeysuckle) | White turning yellow | Rambling shrub. Vigorous climber, self-twining | Needs some shade and rich soil |
| *Mucuna bennettii* (New Guinea vine) | Huge scarlet pendant clusters, spectacular | Large woody climber. Slow to establish | Partial shade required. Will cover large pergola. Needs good soil |
| *Odontadenia speciosa* | Fragrant, apricot in large clusters | Woody climber. Bushy foliage | Prefers partial shade. Very beautiful |
| *Passiflora quadriglandulosa** (Passion flower) | Rose pink with corona | Vigorous climber, dense foliage | Good fence coverer. Full sun best |
| *Petrea volubilis* (Sandpaper vine) | Sprays of deep purple flowers with long lasting, mauve calyxes | Shrubby climber. Coarse, light green leaves | Very beautiful climber requiring partial shade and well drained soil |
| *Philodendron* spp. | | Heavy foliage, climber | Very decorative foliage. Needs shade |
| *Quisqualis indica* (Rangoon creeper) | White, becoming deep pink, fragrant | Vigorous climber. Heavy foliage | Useful for pergola or arch. Needs strong supports |
| *Strongylodon macrobotrys* (Jade vine) | Pendulous clusters of jade-green flowers. Spectacular | Heavy twiner, sparse leaves | A feature the rarity of colour of its metallic blue flowers in clusters up to 1 m or more. Partial shade preferred |
| *Thunbergia grandiflora* | Long strings of large blue flowers up to 1 m | Large climber. Very dense foliage | Requires sun and strong support. Fast growing. Deep soil |
| *Tristellateia australasica* (Maiden's jealousy) | Yellow, very free flowering | Vigorous climber, leafy | Full sun and damp soil. Excellent on fences or as edge trailer in planter boxes |

* Species warranting further research.

TABLE 14.12
**Bamboo**

| Species | Flowers | Character | Comments |
|---|---|---|---|
| *B. multiplex* (and multiplex variegata) | | 4 m high woody grass | Fern-like small leaves on grass reed-like hollow stems to 4 m. Good hedging |
| *B. ventricosa** | | Bushy-headed on multi stems | Swollen culms give it the name 'Buddha's belly bamboo' |
| *Schiyostachyum* brachycladum | | Erect open clumps, very tall | Canes yellow and green, long lanceolate leaves. Fresh green |
| *Thrysostachys siamensis* | | Light, feathery bamboo with slender, narrow leaves | Upright bamboo good for courtyards and narrow spaces. Breeze noise. Good soil required |

* Species warranting further research.

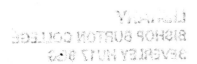

## ACKNOWLEDGEMENTS

I would like to thank Jennifer Steed for researching and compiling the plant lists.

## FURTHER READING

This book list makes no pretence to be exhaustive. Apart from the few books dealing with gardening in the tropics, the titles have been selected on the basis of useful comments about widespread tropical plants or contain good illustrations of mature specimens.

Adams, C. D. *Flowering Plants of Jamaica*, (Glasgow: University Press 1972) for University of the West Indies

Adams, C. D. *The Blue Mahoe and Other Bushes* (Singapore: McGraw-Hill Far Eastern Publishers Ltd 1971)

Bardi, P. M. The *Tropical Gardens of Burle Marx* (London: Architectural. Press 1964)

Bor, N. L. and Razada, M. B. *Some Beautiful Indian Trees* Bombay Natural History Society, 2nd edition, revised (Bombay: W. T. Stern)

Bruggeman, Tropical *Plants and Their Cultivation* (London: Thames and Hudson, 1962)

PLATE 14.18 **Asian Institute of Technology, Bangkok.** *(Maurice Lee)*

Chin H. F. *Malaysian Flowers in Colour* (Tropical Press Sdn Bhd. 1982)

Corner, E. J. H. *Wayside Trees of Malaya* (Singapore: Government Printing Office 1940) Vols. 1 and 2

Dale, I. V. and Greenway, P. T. *Kenyan Trees and Shrubs* (Nairobi: Buchanans Kenya Estates Ltd 1961)

Gibberd, A. V. and Gibberd, V. L. A *Gardening Notebook for the Tropics* (London: Longmans, Green & Co. 1953)

Graf, A. B. *Exotica* (N. J.: Roehrs, Rutherford, 1963) 3rd Edition

Graf, A. B. *Tropica* (Roehrs, Rutherford 1978)

Hargreaves, D. and Hargreaves, B. *Tropical Blossoms of the Carribean* (Portland: Hargreaves Industrial 1960)

Hargreaves, D. and Hargreaves B. *Tropical Trees* (Portland: Hargreaves Industrial, 1965)

Holttum, R. E. *Gardening in the Lowlands of Malaya* (Singapore: Straits Times Press, 1953)

Hutchinson, J. and Dalziel, J. M. *Flora of West Tropical Africa* (London: HMSO, 1954–1972) 3 Vols, 2nd edition, revised by F. N. Hepper

Kunkel, G. *Arboles Exoticos, Los Arboles Cultivados en Gran Canaria* (Edicias del Exemo Cabildo Insular de Gran Canaria 1969)

McCurrach, J. C. *Palms of the World* (New York: Harper & Bros. 1960)

Macmillan, H. F. *Tropical Planting and Gardening* (London: Macmillan, 5th Edition, 1956)

Menninger, E. A. *What Flowering Tree is That?* (Florida: Menninger, Stuart, Fla. 1958)

Menninger, E. A. *Flowering Trees of the World: For Tropics and Warm Climates* (New York: Hearthside Press 1962)

Menninger, E. A. *Seaside Plants of the World* (New York: Hearthside Press 1964)

Menninger, E. A. *Flowering Vines of the World* (New York: Hearthside Press 1970)

Millar, A. *Gardening with Andress Millar* (Port Moresby: South Pacific Post Pty Ltd. 1971)

Pertchik, B. and Pertchik, A. *Flowering Trees of the Caribbean* (New York: Rinehart & Co. Inc. 1951)

Polunin, Ivan *Plants and Flowers of Singapore* (Time Editions 1987)

Whitmore, T. C. *Palms of Malaya* (London: Oxford University Press 1973)

Williams, R. O. and Williams, R. O. *The Useful and Decorative Plants in Trinidad and Tobago* (Port of Spain: Guardian Commercial Printing, 4th edition, 1951)

PLATE 15.3 *Peltophorum pterocarpum* **planted as a street tree, with groundcover of** *Catharanthus roseus.* **Sultan Qaboos University staff housing, Oman.** (Architects: *YRM International*; Landscape Architects: *Brian Clouston International*; Photographer: *Ken Kirkwood*)

PLATE 15.4 **A slatted plant house at a nursery in Heliopolis, Cairo.** *(Maurice Lee)*

were identified as the probable causes. A similar pattern has emerged in present-day Sudan.

In general, the primary causes of widespread historic desertification are not precisely understood. While a change of climate was clearly responsible in part, other causes were due to human pressures and included deforestation and overgrazing followed by soil erosion, urbanization, irrigation and excessive water extraction. Lower levels of evapo-transpiration consequent on the loss of vegetation have resulted in decreased air humidity and precipitation.

## 15.3 CLIMATIC FACTORS

### Temperature

A summary of temperature readings taken in arid climates across the world gives a good indication of the extremes of recorded air temperatures.

| | |
|---|---|
| Mean maxima (Summer): | 43.6°C (Baghdad) |
| | 41.2°C (Sahara) |
| | 40.0°C (Arizona) |
| Maximum (Summer): | 55.0°C (Saudi Arabia) |
| Mean maxima (Winter): | 0.6°C (Kashgar, Asia) |
| | 30.0°C (Sahara) |

Low temperatures are not unknown in some arid areas — there are, for example, frequent severe frosts in Asia, snow has fallen on low ground in the Middle East in recent years and diurnal variations can be as great as 25°C in Saudi Arabia — but generally high temperatures create difficulties for imported vegetation in most arid lands. These difficulties arise for two main reasons. Firstly, high evapo-transpiration rates ensure that the potential for water loss exceeds the quantity of water available for use; and, secondly, certain chemical processes in plants are sufficiently intensified to cause plant death in non-adapted species. High radiation levels also lead to higher soil temperatures, which have a significant effect on plant growth rates.

Low temperatures, in areas where they do occur, may lead to chilling injury in plants, if below 10°C, or freezing injury if below 0°C. Chilling injury causes temporary cessation of growth, discoloration of the leaves and defoliation in landscape species such as *Cocos, Delonix, Moringa* and *Cynodon*, but the cellular damage caused by the cold is usually of limited effect and reversible. Freezing injury is unlikely to be a problem unless the drop to low temperatures is sudden,

since the salt content of cell sap is normally sufficient to resist damage, for instance *Thevetia* spp. and *Tecoma* can withstand a gradual descent to −4°C.

Local microclimatic influences, such as potential cold air pockets· and the reradiation of heat from buildings should be considered in planting design for arid areas where low temperatures have been recorded.

The average cloud cover in the Middle East is less than 40 per cent annually, and in the most arid areas this figure drops to less than 20 per cent annually. For six to eight months of the year in the desert there is likely to be no cloud cover at all.

Most arid land plant species require sun. While sun-obligate species will survive in shaded areas, with consequent poor growth and reduced flowering characteristics, shade-obligate species are unlikely to tolerate full sun.

### Rainfall

Quoted figures of less than 100 mm for average annual rainfall in the desert may be misleading, since the frequency of occurrence can be very erratic. Long periods of virtual drought are common. On arid and semi-arid lands the average annual rainfall is between 100 and 500 mm per year. In Saudi Arabia, the greater part

PLATE 15.2 **Characteristic** *Phoenix dactylyera* **plantation subsisting on ground water, in the rural town of Nizwa, Oman.** *(Christopher Driver)*

of annual precipitation falls between November and April. Individual falls are generally less than 25 mm, of which typically only 10 per cent reaches the soil, 20 per cent wets the ground surface, 20 per cent evaporates at once and the remaining 50 per cent is lost in surface run-off. As little as 10 mm is sufficient to cause run-off, and flash floods, when they occur, can be extremely destructive to new planting and landscape works unless extensive soil stabilization is carried out. Nor is light, infrequent rainfall beneficial in arid areas, since it may wash surface salts into the root zone, causing injury, scorch, defoliation and terminal dieback.

The lack of rainfall is compensated for, to some extent, by high relative humidity levels in certain areas. For example, readings of 60–90 per cent relative humidity are common on the west coast of Saudi Arabia and on the coast of the Arabian Gulf.

## Winds

Hot, drying winds are a regular feature of arid climates, and often develop into damaging sand storms. Wind causes sand abrasion, defoliation and plant burial, dune movement or blow-out, carries salt spray from the sea and increases evapo-transpiration rates. It sieves out and transports fine soil particles, creating soils of poor texture and structure. Topography and built form may exaggerate the damaging effects of strong, salt-laden winds on introduced plant material.

Winds are connected either with large scale disturbances in atmospheric circulation or occur at a local level. For example, the 'harmattan' of the southern edge of the Sahara develops when north-east trade winds dominate the area. In Saudi Arabia the 'shamals', four to five day long dust storms, occur most frequently in Spring. In the desert itself, winds with an average speed of 15 knots blow unceasingly, caused by the convection currents which result from fluctuating temperatures.

Almost all native plants are generally wind-resistant, but some introduced species are not. For example, *Albizia* spp., *Sesbenia* spp. and *Caesalpinia* develop brittle branches as they mature, and should be planted in sheltered locations. *Delonix regia*, *Ficus* spp. and *Cassia* spp. may lose foliage and damage may be caused to flowers and fruit.

Constant strong winds may lead to canopy deformation, which can be corrected by pruning or prevented by the use of protective fences or shelter belts of wind-resistant species. The drying effect of transportation on plants should also be noted. If a journey of more than 10 km is required, plants should be well watered, sprayed with anti-transpirant and covered before being moved, preferably in the early morning.

## 15.4 SOILS

Soils in arid areas are mostly calcareous and highly alkaline, and are usually characterized by immaturity, owing to the absence of water and biological activity, poorly developed horizons and a very low humus content. Any stratification is related to alluvial or sedimentation processes. High radiation levels are responsible for the accumulation of the soluble products of weathering, that is calcium carbonate and soluble mineral salts, in the upper parts of the soil profile.

The rainfall element in weathering and soil formation is of restricted importance, but the coincidence of high temperatures and favourable soil moisture conditions for a short season does much to offset the slowness of weathering. Some locations are wetter than mean rainfall figures would suggest, owing to local surface run-off conditions and seasonal or occasional flooding of alluvial plains by large through-flowing rivers.

Considerable variation is found in soil depth, texture, composition and fertility. Upward movement of soluble salts to the surface, coupled with the leaching of available nutrients following rain or irrigation, creates difficulties which must be overcome if new planting of non-adapted species is to be sucessful. The options for the landscape designer are to recommend modifications to the existing soil, to import soil which satisfies a rigorous specification or, if neither course of action is practicable, to choose plant species which will clearly tolerate the prevailing conditions. In practice, a combination of all three options will have the most satisfactory results.

## Soil types

It is a common misconception that soils in arid areas are dominated by shifting dunes and rocks. There is in fact a variety of arid soils, and a simplified indication of their characteristics is listed in Table 15.1.

Under the American system of soil classification most soils of arid areas are classified as aridisols. Entisols, only recently and slightly developed (e.g. dunes), are also common and mollisols, the typical grassland soils of prairie and steppe, are often associated with the cooler moister fringes of arid areas.

All of these soils can be affected by high contents of salts or highly alkaline conditions. These may be called halomorphic soils and can be developed by

(i) low humidity and a high mineral content of the parent material;
(ii) evaporation from saline ground water and capillary rise;
(iii) sea-water flooding.

It can therefore be seen that irrigation of such soils, or irrigation of non-saline soils with saline water can itself result in salinisation.

TABLE 15.1
**Examples of soils in arid areas**
(derived from the American system of soil classification)

| ARIDISOLS | Form where potential evaporation greatly exceeds precipitation and water rarely percolates through the soil except in extreme years. Lack of moisture inhibits chemical erosion and soil morphology is therefore related to the parent material. | ENTISOLS | Soils of slight and recent development; little or no horizon development. |
|---|---|---|---|
| | | Examples: | Dunefields exposed to bedrock areas, Hammadas, alluvial soils associated with wadi and sea-flooding loess. |
| Properties: | i) High base status (minerals) but low organic matter due to rapid oxidation; ii) a surface pavement of gravel; iii) a 'desert varnish' of manganese and iron oxide staining upper stone surfaces black; iv) 'caliche' layers of carbonate accumulation or gypsum banding. | Cultivation: | Fertility ranges from extremely low to very high depending on origin. The main problem is stability and most are susceptible to erosion by wind, water, or mass wasting. Can be salt affected. |
| Examples: | Grey and brown steppe soils; soils with calcareous and gypsum crusts; saline soils; hard calcium cemented silty sands. | | |
| Cultivation: | Limited chiefly by water availability; lack of internal permeability and percolation may cause problems of salinization and alkalinization. Nitrogen levels are usually low, phosphorus adequate, potassium high, trace elements adequate although often made unavailable by high alkalinity. Foliar applications of iron and trace elements may be necessary. | MOLLISOLS | Soils with deep, dark, relatively fertile topsoil formed under grassland vegetation; found where arid areas grade into steppe or prairie. |
| | | Properties: | Light coloured, salt affected patches often found in depressions. |
| | | Examples: | Brown soils of steppe, prairie and savannah; often alluvial and sometimes hydromorphic (e.g. high water table). |
| | | Cultivation: | Extensively used for food production although water availability is limited. |

PLATE 15.6 **Lush planting of** *Caesalpinia pulcherrima, Hibiscus rosasinensis, Bougainvillea spectabilis, Ipomoea palmata* **and** *Catharanthus roseus,* **shaded by** *Azedirachta indica.* **Riofinex Village, Jeddah.** (Landscape Architect: *Brian Clouston & Partners*; Photographer: *Robert Holden*)

PLATE 15.7 **Colour and structure in student residence courtyard provided by** *Ficus nitida,* **with underplanting of** *Catharanthus roseus* **and** *Alternanthera versicolor.* **Climbers on south-facing walls include** *Ipomoea palmata* **and** *Quisqualis indica.* **Sultan Qaboos University, Oman.** (Architects: *YRM International*; Landscape Architects: *Brian Clouston International;* Photographer: *Christopher Driver*)

In simplified terms, saline soils form where total salts are high, alkali soils result where the sodium percentage is high and the resultant sodium carbonate raises the pH.

Better quality soils are found in low-lying areas such as wadi channels, and result from the collection of finer sediments and water. Their nature is variable; in general, however, these soils are free-draining but nutrient-poor and low in organic matter. Areas of soil with a heavier texture may be subject to flooding after rain if drainage is poor. The increase in soil salinity, which results from surface and capillary action in these areas, makes them unsuitable for planting *in situ*, and potentially unusable as a source of imported soil. On steeper slopes, there are likely to be few significant deposits of soil.

## Soil salinity

Salinity makes absorption of water by the plant roots more difficult. Water may be present but unavailable to a plant, owing to high levels of soil water potential. The permanent wilting point for most species is at a soil water potential of around −15 bar.

Toxic ion effects are usually demonstrated by leaf damage, e.g. excessive chlorides by leaf tip burn, sodium by spot burns throughout the leaf and boron by tip and marginal burn.

Growth variations and smaller or thicker leaves are also signs of high salinity. Tolerances may be locally reduced or enhanced in adapted varieties of the same species. Germination may be affected by salt levels which are satisfactory for established plants.

Soil salinity is usually expressed by the electrical conductivity of an extract of the saturated soil paste, and the effect of electrical conductivity on plants is shown in Table 15.2

In testing for soil salinity the top 2.5 m should be sampled, since deep salts may rise up locally, particularly under uneven drainage conditions. Successful

TABLE 15.2
**US Department of Agriculture Scale**

| Electrical conductivity (mmhos/cm at 25°C) | Effect on plants |
| --- | --- |
| 0−2 | Mostly negligible |
| 2−4 | Yields of very sensitive crops may be restricted |
| 4−8 | Yields of many crops restricted |
| 8−16 | Good yield from tolerant crops only |
| > 16 | Only very few very tolerant crops give a satisfactory yield |

leaching and irrigation may result in a favourable redistribution of salts, given efficient drainage and good quality water. However, it will be necessary to consider the use of a soil amendment where low permeability and a high percentage of exchangable sodium (ESP) prevent the entry of water. The addition of gypsum (calcium sulphate), sulphur, sulphuric acid or ferrous sulphate, if available will increase the concentration of soluble calcium in the soil, with a consequent reduction in the ESP.

Where imported soil is used, the upward movement of salts in the soil, derived, for example, from irrigation water following leaching, can be prevented with the use of a simple capillary break consisting of a coarse stone drainage layer at the base of each planting bed.

## Soil fertility

Desert soils tend to contain high concentrations of sodium, potassium and calcium. The presence of sodium does not inhibit plant growth where it is counteracted by calcium. However, calcium and potassium, as well as magnesium, manganese, iron and boron are seldom available to plants in sandy soils, owing to lack of moisture and organic activity. Clay has a higher cation exchange capacity (CEC) than silt and sand and is therefore more nutrient-rich. Organic matter, too, is high in sites of cation/anion exchange, and the addition of 10−15 per cent (by volume) greatly improves the ability and potential of a soil for plant nutrient storage.

While leaching may disperse harmful salts and irrigation may free nutrients for uptake by plants, adding water in a free-draining medium will tend to wash out nutrients, and permanently irrigated soils will require adequate supplies of nitrogenous and phosphatic fertilizers. Irrigation water with a pH of 7.5 or more will eventually restrict the availability of iron, copper, zinc and manganese, and leaf chlorosis may result. This is counteracted by the use of fertilizer or foliar sprays or, if practicable, by adding up to 50 per cent of acid sphagnum peat to the soil mixture.

In general, soil nitrogen is not readily available to plants, since its primary sources, i.e. nitrate and ammonium, are rapidly assimilated by other soil organisms and are highly soluble. *Leguminosae* (for instance, species of *Acacia* and *Prosopis*), however, have a symbiotic relationship with nitrogen-fixing bacteria, from which they gain 50 per cent of their total nitrogen requirements. Some plants, e.g. *Casuarina*, *Eleagnus* and the Cycads, fix nitrogen with non-symbiotic bacteria. Drought-deciduous species draw back nitrogen and phosphorus from their leaves during dormant periods, and from leaf litter following rainfall or irrigation.

Planting media will usually consist of a mixture of imported wadi soil or 'agricultural' soil with structural and nutritional additives. Proportions of soil to organic matter vary, but typically between 5 and 15 per cent (by

PLATE 15.8 **Mixed street planting in staff housing at Sultan Qaboos University, Oman. Shade provided by** *Azedirachta indica.* **with loose hedges of** *Hibiscus rosasinensis* **underplanted with** *Lantana montevidensis,* **and** *Agave americana* **flourishing on the roundabout.** (Landscape Architects: *Brian Clouston International*; Photographer: *Christopher Driver)*

volume) of organic material is added. The use of organic matter greatly improves the water-holding capacity of sandy soils. Other additives include silt (to be used sparingly, as it may impede drainage), animal manure, sedge peat or nitrogen-stabilized bark, alginate and granular polyacrylamides. Ploughing in of a previously sown leguminous 'green crop' may also be advantageous.

## Soil analysis

Plants can be used to indicate the type and quality of existing soil, but it is essential that an accurate analysis of all soil components is obtained for the whole area of any site, and that it is obtained at different depths before planting.

If original soil is to be used, the choice of new plant species may be severely constrained by prevailing soil characteristics. However, existing soil in urban areas may be unusable due to previous uses, or to contami-

nation and despoliation resulting from typical construction techniques. Replacement to a depth of at least 1 m is essential, and it is usual in these cases to specify the importation of wadi soil or clean desert sand, for which a rigorous specification should be provided. The results of soil analysis should comply with the specification for imported soil.

A typical specification for good quality imported soil is as follows:

### (i) *Imported sweet soil*
Soil for use in tree pits and plant beds shall be approved imported sweet soil. The contractor shall ensure that an approved independent soil analyst will prepare a physical and chemical analysis of the imported soil, in accordance with the sweet soil specification together with a report and recommendations on fertilizer treatment. The soil analysis reports and fertilizer recommendations and soil source shall be made available for approval. Samples of the soil must be approved by the landscape architect before bulk delivery commences and all soil

285

thereafter brought on to site shall be of the same standard and quality as the approved samples. The landscape architect shall receive a soil analyst's report for each 500 m³ of soil materials prior to mixing, to be compared with approved sample test results. Soil brought on site without such approval and/or not complying with this specification will be deemed to have been brought in at the contractor's risk and he will be instructed to cart such soil off the site at his own expense.

## (ii) *Source*

Sweet soil shall be agricultural or wadi soil from an approved source, fertile, with a humus and fibre content and free of pernicious weeds, stones, sticks, subsoil and foreign matter. It shall be taken from a maximum depth of 400 mm from approved locations, having removed surface crusts and gypsiferous accumulations. Soil shall be treated as necessary to achieve the following characteristics:

1. pH of 6.5−8.0 saturated soil.
2. Electrical conductivity less than 4 mmhos cm−1 saturation extract.
3. Free carbonates less than 0.5 per cent air-dried soil.
4. Chlorides less than 200 ppm in saturation extract.
5. Sulphates less than 200 ppm in saturation extract.
6. Exchangeable sodium percentage (ESP) less than 15 per cent in neutral normal ammonium acetate.
7. Nitrates less than 75 ppm in saturation extract.
8. Phosphorus 10−25 ppm in 1.5 ammonium nitrate extractant (1/2 hour shake).
9. Potassium 100−400 ppm in 1.5 ammonium nitrate extractant (1/2 hour shake).

PLATE 15.9 **Mountain village at 5000 ft in Jebel Akhdar, N. Oman. Terraced agriculture, with** *Phoenix dactylifera* **(date palms) and fruit trees in blossom, watered by traditional** *Falaj* **(open channel) system.** *(Christopher Driver)*

10. Magnesium 25−100 ppm in 1.5 ammonium nitrate extractant (1/2 hour shake).
11. Boron less than 1.5 ppm, hot water soluble.
12. Sodium absorption ratio (SAR) less than 10 per cent.
13. Physical characteristics of loamy sand made up by particle size as follows:
    Sand − 2−0.05 mm; 70−85 per cent.
    Silt − 0.05−0.002 mm; 25−30 per cent max.
    Clay − less than 0.002 mm; 5 per cent max.

Failure of the soil to comply with one or more of the specification requirements should be investigated, since it may be due to shortcomings in sample collection or to localized aberrant characteristics.

## 15.5 WATER

## Rainfall

Rainwater harvesting, by levelling and compacting the ground and sealing the surface, can contribute to the efficiency of rainwater use in areas which receive significant precipitation. The size of a collection area relative to a planted area is inversely proportional to the ratio of rainfall to plant water requirements. In general, however, the contribution of rainfall to the water requirements of non-adapted species is negligible.

## Ground and surface water

Rivers, lakes, dams and shallow sub-surface flow (assisted by recharge dams) can all provide sources for natural irrigation, even in areas where occasional heavy storms are the norm. Sources of ground water in arid countries are often unsuitable for plants in both quality and quantity, except where there is substantial and regular annual recharge. High evaporation rates lead to high salinity in surface water in arid areas, and ground water may become saline if recharge is slow for reasons of over-use, low precipitation or if the water table is infiltrated by sea water.

## Process water

Sources of process water include desalination plants, solar stills and dew precipitation systems. None of these is likely to be a direct supplier of irrigation water, since production costs are generally considered to be too high, and available quantities of water are likely to be insufficient for large-scale use.

## Treated sewage effluent (TSE)

The quality of TSE is dependent on the quality of water used in mains distribution systems. Full treatment tends to increase salinity levels, but in hot countries the scope for the use of partially treated effluent in surface irrigation is greater than that in temperate countries because high temperatures accelerate the bacterial digestion of organic matter. The appropriate level of treatment will depend on the quality of water required. In general, primary effluents are suitable for afforestation schemes, secondary effluents for public parks and tertiary effluents for private gardens. Sludge may also be used, for example, in Kuwait, sludge-filled trenches generated growth rates of up to 2 m per year in pioneer species such as *Tamarix*, *Eucalyptus*, *Casuarina* and *Acacia*.

Effluent treated to a high standard (10/10) is frequently used in sub-surface irrigation systems in the Middle East. Objections to its use on medical and cultural grounds can usually be overcome, provided that adequate treatment and quality control can be demonstrated, and that full precautionary measures against contamination are taken during installation and operation. However, supplies may fluctuate, and supplementary sources should always be available.

## Water quality

Suspended solids that are often found in surface water, such as silt, mud, sticks and leaves, and organic material, such as seeds, algae and slime, must be removed by filtration and chlorination if irrigation is by means of a piped water supply. For health reasons, water will also have to be chlorinated to destroy viruses and bacteria. TSE may be safe (depending on the treatment process), but is generally high in inorganic substances, which will lead eventually to alkalinization and salinization of the soil.

Dissolved solids, such as mineral salts, create the most serious difficulties for plant material. Salinity levels are therefore critical and will determine whether a source of water is suitable for irrigation use or not. If there is no alternative source, irrigation methods and plant species must be selected to minimize the adverse effects of high salinity, and application rates adjusted accordingly.

## Water analysis

### 1. *Ground/surface water*
It is essential in arid areas to obtain a complete water analysis, and to calculate the rate at which water can be used without severe depletion of the water table reservoir. For example, perched water tables in sand dunes, formed from rainfall accumulating above an impermeable soil layer, can be quickly exhausted if they are used to irrigate large areas with little or no natural recharge. The water analysis should include:

(i) Quantity (and therefore numbers of wells to be dug).

PLATE 15.10 **Sharp, pointed leaves of** *Sansevieria trifasciata* **form a low hedge underneath** *Ficus retusa* **trees, Jeddah.** *(Maurice Lee)*

(ii)  pH value.

(iii) Total salinity (expressed in ppm, Me/litre or Ec values).

Critical values are (*c.f.* those for soil):

Low        0.0−0.25 mmhos/cm
Medium     0.25−0.75 mmhos/cm
High       0.75−2.25 mmhos/cm
Very high  >2.25 mmhos/cm.

(iv) Sodium content and SAR values. SAR (sodium absorption ratio) relates the concentration of $Na^+$ ions to other cations, and should be less than 10 per cent, although the tolerance of different species varies.

(v)  A measure of the alkalinity hazard or RSC (residual sodium carbonate). Critical RSC values are:

Safe        0−1.25
Marginal    1.25−1.5
Unsuitable  >1.5

(vi) Boron levels.

(vii) Concentrations of specific ions, noting those that might be too low or excessively high.

## 2. Treated sewage effluent (TSE)

A typical specification for TSE, assuming some quality control is possible, would be as shown in Table 15.3.

## 15.6 PLANT WATER REQUIREMENTS

Existing plants may either be dependent entirely on rainfall or be sufficiently established to tap available ground water. For example, phreatophytes such as *Prosopis* spp. grow tap roots up to 30 m long to reach deep water sources. Such water sources are unreliable, and native or unadapted species will be drought-resistant to varying degrees. Symptoms of drought include defoliation, loss of colour and terminal die-back. Water uptake is a function of the soil water potential, the root hair density and the upward transpiration process of the plant. Water vapour loss from the leaves is a side effect of the plant's need to photosynthesize and depends on the rate of water supply from the stem and roots, on climatic parameters such as solar radiation levels, temperature, vapour pressure and wind speed, and on the diffusion gradient between the interior of the leaf and the drier air outside. Changes in the stomatal pore size constitute the most significant barrier to the unlimited movement of water from the soil via the plant to the atmosphere.

## Calculation of water requirements

In assessing the survival chances of introduced plant species under arid conditions it is important to consider rates: of evaporation and potential evapo-transpiration (ETP).

Actual evapo-transpiration (ETA) in arid regions is difficult to determine, since it is considerably influenced by the moisture status and characteristics of the soil. However, ETP can be assessed from climatic data, as was originally postulated by Penman in 1948. The calculation is based on a measure of the quantity of heat available to evaporate water, and the capacity of the air around the plant to absorb it. ETP is therefore most simply defined as the 'maximum amount of water a plant could lose under prevailing climatic conditions' (Ricks, 1987).

Plant water requirements can thus be established in three ways:

(i)  Directly, using a lysometer to measure soil moisture content.

(ii) By simulation, using figures obtained from readings of evaporation from an open water surface ($E_o$). If an evaporation pan is used, a factor of 0.8 must be applied to convert readings to their $E_o$ equivalents. Thus $E_o = 0.8 \times E_{pan}$. For crops, a crop correlation factor gives adjusted E rates: for instance for citrus trees the factor is 0.6 but for grasses and alfalfa the factor may be as much as 1.95;

(iii) By correlation with climatic data (Penman's formula). In analysing ETP it should be recognized that annual ETP values are completely dominated by summer readings, and are not therefore relevant to conditions during the winter growing season.

In addition, real loss of water is likely to be less than the calculated values because of restrictions in the soil and resistances produced in the diffusion gradient of the plant. Information is lacking on the precise degree to which cultivated plants are able to restrict evapo-transpiration, and plant lists will necessarily include measures of drought-tolerance related to subjective experience rather than scientific record.

As a general rule, highly demanding species will require watering at 70 per cent of ETP, drought-tolerant species at 40–70 per cent of ETP, and drought resistant species at less than 40 per cent of ETP. Young plants may need 75–85 per cent of ETP until they are well established, at up to two years of age in Saudi Arabia (Ricks, 1987).

TABLE 15.3
**TSE quality**

| Chemical constituents | Max (mg/l) | Monthly average over four consecutive weeks (mg/l) |
|---|---|---|
| Aluminium | 5.0 | 1.0 |
| Ammonia ($NH_4$) | 45 | 30 |
| Arsenic | 0.2 | 0.05 |
| Beryllium | 0.3 | 0.1 |
| Boron | 2.0 | 1.0 |
| Cadmium | 0.03 | 0.01 |
| Chromium | 0.5 | 0.1 |
| Cobalt | 0.5 | 0.1 |
| Copper | 0.3 | 0.2 |
| Fluoride | 2.0 | 1.0 |
| Iron | 5.0 | 1.0 |
| Lead | 0.5 | 0.1 |
| Lithium | 10.0 | 2.5 |
| Manganese | 1.0 | 0.2 |
| Molybdenum | 0.05 | 0.01 |
| Nickel | 0.5 | 0.02 |
| Selenium | 0.02 | 0.05 |
| Vanadium | 1.0 | 0.1 |
| Zinc | 5.0 | 2.0 |
| Chloride | 350 | 250 |
| Free residual chlorine (after 60 min contact time) | 0.5  (min) | 0.5  (min) |
| Residual sodium carbonate | 0–1.5 | |
| Sulphate | 400 | 200 |
| BOD (5 days) | 15 | 10 |
| Sodium absorption ratio (SAR) | 0–10% | |
| Total dissolved solids | 1500 | 1000 |
| Total suspended solids | 15 | 10 |
| Temperature | 40 | 30 |
| pH | 8.5 | 7 (min 6.5) |

Soil moisture tension should be monitored continuously by a series of tensiometers. If required, these can be linked directly to the irrigation system to provide a fully automatic system. Typical SMT values are as follows:

Saturated soil 0–10 centibars
Field capacity 20–40 centibars
Wilting point 100 centibars

Good irrigation will maintain the SMT of sandy soils at 20–30 centibars, and that of loamy soil at 30–50 centibars. The holding capacity of coarse sand is around 38 mm per 300 mm, and infiltration rates may be greater than 40 mm per hour. Annual soil moisture deficit in the Middle East may be as much as 3 m, which means that an introduced species of tree with a canopy area of 36 m$^2$ could require up to 108 m$^3$ (108 000 litres) of irrigation water each year.

## 15.7 IRRIGATION SYSTEMS

The choice and design of suitable irrigation systems are primarily dependent on the following factors:

1. Plant water requirements.
2. Water quality and availability.
3. Site topography and soils.
4. Climate
5. Cost limitations.

The ideal irrigation system is one which minimizes plant stress and maximizes the efficiency of water use by providing water to the root zone at the same rate as it is used by the plants. Systems which maintain the soil at, or near, field capacity can use more saline water than those which allow the soil to dry out. It is important that control methods are sufficiently flexible to allow modification of the irrigation regime in response both to seasonal changes and to the varying requirements of different plant species. Systems should be unobtrusive, and simple to operate and maintain.

# Principal methods

## 1. Surface/flood systems
This is the traditional method, dating back 5000 years. The system works most effectively with small water basins or channels where the maintenance of low soil moisture tension is practicable.

The length of channel varies according to the soil permeability. A typical operating cycle would be between 10 and 21 days. Normal practice is to irrigate to field capacity, and wait until the soil moisture tension increases to an acceptable limit before irrigating again. Plants nearest the point of application are likely to be over-watered.

The advantages of this system are that it is simple and relatively cheap to install and operate. The disadvantages are as follows:

1. Regular channel maintenance is required to clear weeds and to avoid permanent standing water, which may harbour disease vectors such as bilharzia-carrying snails and mosquito larvae.
2. Soil is inaccessible following irrigation.
3. Uneven distribution and inefficient use of water (including rain), which is lost through run-off, seepage, evaporation and deep percolation below root zones. This method is 40 per cent efficient at best, and typically only 20 per cent efficient.
4. For health reasons this method cannot be used in public areas, except with potable or clean water.
5. Labour-intensive operation.
6. May cause plant stress.

Flood irrigation systems are generally unsuited to amenity landscape schemes, where strict control and the efficient use of water are the primary requirements.

## 2. Sprinkler systems
These were originally developed for agricultural use during the 1940s, and are designed to simulate rainfall. Large areas are watered on a 10 day cycle, with equipment moving, or being moved, up to three times a day. In contrast, modern sprinkler systems for amenity landscape use are fixed, operating sequentially over larger areas, once or twice a day. Advantages include the following:

1. Night-time use of fixed sprinkler systems achieves up to 80 per cent efficiency of water use in the Middle East and sprinkler systems are usually at least 70 per cent efficient.
2. Pop-up type sprinklers are the most unobtrusive and effective method of distributing water over large areas of grass, and do not interfere with the use of, for instance, playing fields.
3. Potentially uniform application rates reduce losses due to percolation (but may be difficult to achieve in odd-shaped areas).

Disadvantages include the following:

1. Wind causes drift, uneven application and wasted water in exposed locations (although designers can use knowledge of wind direction to their advantage).
2. For health reasons TSE cannot be used. Water must be clean, well filtered and of low salinity (to avoid foliage scorch)
3. Sprinklers are inappropriate for use in areas where plants have different water requirements.
4. High equipment and installation costs.
5. Emergency back-up systems will be required.

## 3. Drip/Bubbler irrigation
This system has been installed commercially since 1949, but was not developed widely for landscape use until the mid-1960s.

Fixed installations on, or just below, the ground surface deliver small quantities of water directly to the plants, typically via 2, 4 or 8 litre per hour pressure compensating drip emitters, or at a higher rate through adjustable stream bubblers. Although uninterrupted delivery of water is the most efficient and desirable irrigation regime, it is not practicable, owing to the potential for outlet blockage (caused by impurities in the water), which results from low volume/pressure application. However, the intermittent use of drip emitters (programmed to operate several times during the day or night) is the best method yet devised for maintaining constant low soil moisture tension. Effective filtration and flushing are vital in drip systems.

The advantages are that:

1. Drip systems are up to 90 per cent efficient and highly plant-orientated.
2. Losses due to percolation and evaporation are minimal, in particular when the system is combined with the use of a surface mulch, such as gravel, bark or PVC sheeting.
3. Precise application allows the control of root development if necessary.
4. Drip systems allow the use of TSE because the application method is unobtrusive and ground-based.
5. Similarly, saline water may be used because drip systems maintain a high soil moisture content in the root zone. Salts will build up outside the central wetted area, but water is less easily available to the plant in highly saline soil.
6. Direct controlled application of specific quantities allows the application of soluble fertilizers and pesticides via the irrigation system.

The disadvantages are that:

1. Installation costs are high, since drip systems require electrically-operated valves, extensive cabling, control panels and so on, as well as fail-safe devices such as low pressure shut-off valves to avoid down-drainage and backflow preventers to avoid contamination of main water supplies.
2. Failure, even in the short term, may lead to widespread movement of ground salts into the root zone.
3. Complexity of operation and repair, since the more technically complex a system is, the less likely it is to receive adequate maintenance and repair in the long term.
4. A relatively high risk of outlet blockage or failure due to pressure fluctuations and non-operation of self-cleansing services.
5. Emergency back-up systems will be required.

### 4. Sub-surface irrigation

This is a recently developed method which employs sub-surface rubber hoses with porous walls, and is theoretically very efficient in that water is delivered slowly, constantly and directly to the plant root zone, and hence soil moisture tension is maintained at ex-

PLATE 15.11 **Avenue planting of** *Peltophorum pterocarpum* **providing effective shade less than three years after planting, with neatly-trimmed ground cover of** *Carissa grandiflora 'prostrata'* **in tree pits. Sultan Qaboos University, Oman**. (Landscape Architects: *Brian Clouston International*; Photographer: *Christopher Driver*)

PLATE 15.12 *Lampranthus roseus* **planted as carpet ground cover, with** *Sansevieria trifasciata* **providing vertical accents. Sultan Qaboos University, Oman.** (Landscape Architects: *Brian Clouston International;* Photographer: *Christopher Driver*)

tremely low levels. No moving parts, or elaborate control systems are required, and low working pressure allows the use of extended pipe runs.

The disadvantages are the following:

1. This system has not been widely used or proven in 'difficult' conditions.
2. Application rates may vary in response to fluctuations in water pressure and soil temperature.
3. Saline water cannot be used because salts move into the root zone through capillary action.
4. Distribution pipes are prone to blockages caused by back pressure, and by salt or slime deposits in the pores.
5. Distribution problems are not easily identifiable at an early stage, nor can blockage or failure be precisely located without disturbance to plants and planting beds.

### 5. *Managed water tables and hydroponics*

These systems have been used, but require better quality water than is generally available. Water should be restricted to that supplied by desalination plants, solar stills and advanced effluent treatment plants.

Waterproof membranes creating artificial water table conditions assist in water retention and prevent the rise of salts from the water table. Salts from saline irrigation water may accumulate above the membrane.

The influence of a saline water table can be minimized if plant beds are raised, and capillary rise is interrupted with the use of a layer of graded stone above the water table at the base of the plant bed. Leaching can also be accomplished efficiently.

## 15.8 PLANTING DESIGN

Plants are symbolic of God's ability to sustain life in the desert in spiritual terms and are widely celebrated in Islamic decorative art. In spite of the fact that much of their traditional function in arid lands has been superseded by modern technology, plants continue to play an important part in assisting desert dwellers to tolerate the rigours of their surroundings.

The visual monotony of their natural environment and the often unbearable extremes of heat and aridity have always stimulated the inhabitants of arid lands to create oases of greenery, however small, where shade, colour, fragrance and a sense of security bring relief to the senses. Some of the earliest known parks and gardens were created by the inhabitants of ancient Mesopotamia and Egypt.

## The use and value of plant material

The creation of a favourable outdoor environment is the main objective of the landscape designer in arid areas, and the functional qualities of plant material in this respect are often more important than its selection on purely aesthetic grounds. Functional uses of plant material range from the large scale, such as the provision of green space for recreation and visual orientation in an urban context, to the amelioration of local microclimatic conditions. The functional uses are summarized in Table 15.4.

The use of any plant material will generate a strong visual and atmospheric contrast with the prevailing desert environment, and it is impossible in designing with plants to separate entirely the consideration of aesthetic qualities from that of functional requirements. Non-functional qualities include colour, patterns of light and shade, fragrance, textural variety, movement and attendant wildlife (birds, insects and so on). These qualities gain much of their value from being so rarely encountered in the desert.

In summary the most important design principles and objectives are listed below:

1. The creation of a favourable microclimate for people and plants.
2. Recognition and avoidance of problems caused by a general lack of water and sudden, heavy rains.
3. Plant selection to provide colour, and seasonal change based on flowering characteristics (rather than foliage).
4. Awareness of rapid growth rates, and equally of the poor habit of some commonly used species.
5. Restrained use of grass, which is intolerant of pedestrian wear and, more importantly, high in its water requirements.
6. Planting designs should bear in mind long-term maintenance limitations.

## 15.9 SUMMARY OF INFORMATION REQUIRED FOR DESIGN PROCESS AND PLANTING

1. Aerial survey and interpretation for large area surveys.
2. Investigation and analysis of surface and sub-surface geology.

TABLE 15.4
**Functional uses of plants**

| Function | Planting |
|---|---|
| 1. Shade<br>For pedestrians<br>For passive open-air activities<br>For buildings<br>For car parks | Trees in avenues and groups. Climbing plants on pergolas |
| 2. Shelter from wind, dust collection<br>On an urban scale, protection for new communities<br>For active and passive open-air activity<br>For highways<br>For agricultural areas<br>For establishment of more sensitive plant species | Belts of hardy trees and shrubs, combined with landform |
| 3. Screening<br>For privacy and security, e.g. where gardens are reserved for women and children<br>For reducing the bulk and impact of large or unattractive buildings | Fast-growing tree species |
| 4. Reduction of solar gain and glare<br>For ground level cooling, e.g. the use of ground cover in place of hard surfacing reduces temperatures in the open at ground level by up to 5°C | Grass and ground cover plants |
| 5. Cooling and directing air flow<br>For natural air-conditioning, particularly in urban areas | Trees and hedges, often in association with water |
| 6. Insulation and absorption<br>For buildings | Climbing plants on walls and roofs. Tall shade trees |
| 7. Space planning and movement control<br>For urban and suburban areas | All vegetation types combined with landform |

PLATE 15.13 **Detail of flowering stem of** *Caesalpinia pulcherrima. (Christopher Driver)*

3. Collection and analysis of soil samples.
4. Collection and analysis of meteorological data.
5. Determination and analysis of topography, drainage and soil conservation requirements.
6. Analysis of hydrology to determine water availability and quality.
7. Ecological analysis and selection of suitable planting material.
8. Analysis of present and proposed land use.
9. Recruitment and training of operating and maintenance personnel.
10. Choice of species, establishment of design criteria, preliminary and final design.
11. Design and establishment of tree and shrub nurseries and production of planting material.
12. Design and installation of irrigation systems for tree and shrub planting.
13. Establishment of shelter belts, dune stabilisation, soil amelioration and preplanting irrigation.
14. Establishment and management of planting.
15. Irrigation and plant maintenance.

PLATE 15.14 **Detail of flowers and foliage of** *Parkinsonia aculeata. (Christopher Driver)*

## 15.10 THE PLANTS

The warm climatic conditions and the prolonged sunlight of arid areas ensure rapid growth of plants when water is available. Non-adapted plant species absorb the higher levels of direct radiation and atmospheric heat which are found nearer the ground and, as a result, transpire more water than normal in attempting to keep cool.

Native plants are adapted to conserve water, and many reinforce this advantage by avoiding the heat altogether, by growing during the winter or by using the shade cast by the new growth of other species. Many species rely on a mat of lateral roots in the top 100 mm of the soil to collect moisture falling or collecting in the vicinity of the plant. This root system may extend up to ten times the length of the shoots. Shallow lateral root systems assist in keeping the soil in place and in conserving moisture at lower levels in the soil for use by plants with deeper roots. For the landscape designer this is an ideal combination to make maximum use of available water.

As little as 12 mm of rainfall will bring native shrubs out of dormancy, and many succulents will respond to even less. In wet soil, desert plants will develop new roots in as little as three days.

PLATE 15.15 **Detail of** *Nerium oleander,* **showing flower.** *(Gordon Bell)*

PLATE 15.16 *Delonix regia* **showing fine textured bipinnate leaves.** *Jacquemontia pentantha* **creeper and a hedge of** *Dodonea viscosa* **are also shown.** *(Maurice Lee)*

PLATE 15.17 **Magnificent specimen of** *Ficus retusa* **casting heavy shade, Cairo.** *(Maurice Lee)*

# Native plant life

The dominant species in desert vegetation may not have an ecological influence, as the dominant species tends to be the most abundant, so giving character and apparent homogeneity to the plant community. The characteristic communities that are found in arid areas are the following.

## 1. Accidental vegetation
This appears for a short growing season after heavy rain in areas where surface run-off accumulates, and may have a long dormant period of up to several years.

## 2. Ephemeral vegetation
This type of community makes up 50−60 per cent of all desert vegetation. It occurs where annual rainfall is recurrent and soil moisture is maintained during a season but not for the whole year. In arid habitats ephemeral vegetation persists, whereas in more temperate regions it would only be the pioneer type.

Succulent ephemerals store water in the plant tissues and the winter-growing types tolerate coarse ground surface conditions. Ephemeral grassland is found on shallow sand drifts and is important in warmer deserts. Herbaceous ephemerals form a mosaic pattern associated with patches of soft deposits in especially favoured locales which provide a briefly sustained water supply.

## 3. Suffrutescent perennial vegetation
A permanent framework of perennial vegetation occurs in two main layers − a suffrutescent layer (300−1200 mm high) and a ground layer. Succulent halfshrubs include plants such as *Haloxylon* and *Zygophyllum*; and salt marsh such as *Salicornia* and *Suaeda*. Perennial grassland communities are dominated by *Lasiurus hirsutus*, *Panicum turgidum* and *Pennisetum dichotomum*, and different communities indicate different soil types. Woody perennials are a transitional phase between succulent halfshrub and perennial grassland, and include community types dominated by *Zilla spinosa*, *Artemisia* spp. and *Astralagus* spp.

## 4. Frutescent perennial vegetation
This includes scrubland in three layers, with a frutescent layer 1200 mm−3 m high, a suffrutescent layer and a ground layer. The communities include the succulent shrub form, such as the cactus communities of American deserts and the *Euphorbia* spp. of tropical Africa and the Arabian deserts. Scrubland is the most highly-organized form of desert vegetation, indicating the

highest levels of water revenue in the desert, and also the most effective regime for water storage in the soil. Dominant species include *Acacia*, *Tamarix*, *Zizyphus* and *Prosopis*.

## Plant adaptations to arid conditions

Three main groups of plants show morphological and physiological adaptions, in response to arid conditions as follows.

### 1. Xerophytes

Xerophytes are protected from drought in a number of ways, including browning-off in the hot dry months, which is accomplished by species such as *Tamarix* and *Haloxylon*.

Some desert trees and shrubs actually drop their leaves for a few months of the year and others die back, restricting their activity to protected parts without becoming completely dormant. Wilting proceeds from the outermost leaves, through twigs to the trunk, and can reduce transpiration rates by as much as 90 per cent. Drought-deciduousness is a process that can be reversed if water becomes available.

Some species, such as *Acacia*, *Parkinsonia* and *Casuarina*, have small leaves; others, such as some of the *Ficus* spp., have heavy leaf cuticles; and some, like the *Euphorbias*, have no leaves at all. *Atriplex* avoids heat by reflecting sunlight, while *Tamarix* excretes salt via special glands in the stomata so that at high temperatures the salt crystallizes and reflects solar radiation. Other adaptations include deep root systems (*Tamarix*), wide-spreading roots (*Prosopis*), sunken stomata (*Oleander*), the capacity to absorb dew via salt crystals on the leaves in periods of low humidity (*Cactus* spp. *Euphorbias*) and the capacity to store water in the spines (*Acacia*).

The succulents have few leaves relative to their mass. Cacti and succulents store water in their leaf tissue, and have fewer stomata than other desert plants — about 2500/cm$^2$ compared with 10000/cm$^2$. As an example of evolutionary refinement, crassulacean acid metabolism (CAM) allows succulents to photosynthesize without opening their stomata during the day. However, succulents do not dominate arid areas as might be expected (except in areas where annual rainfall is less than 100 mm) because their intake of $CO_2$ is restricted and they are very slow-growing. In addition, CAM may not develop until the plants reach maturity.

Other relatively recent evolutionary developments, such as carbon-four photosynthesis, do not tend to give plants a competitive advantage in the natural situation, but C4 plants, such as Bermuda grass, are useful in a managed landscape where efficient use of scarce water resources is important.

### 2. Halophytes

Halophytes are protected from salt damage by the high osmotic values of their cell sap (increased by their

PLATE 15.18 *Ipomoea pescaprae* **makes a good climber or trailer.** (*Maurice Lee*)

uptake of salt), which retard transpiration. Up to 45 per cent of the dry weight of the leaves of halophytes may be salt. The halophytic plants include *Suaeda*, *Arthrocnemum* and *Nitraria* spp.

### 3. Hydrophytes

Hydrophytes are protected from possible flooding in high water tables by comparatively low osmotic values and high transpiration rates. These plants include *Atriplex*, *Tamarix* and *Prosopis* spp.

## The choice of plant species

Limiting factors to the choice of plants include the availability of irrigation water, the quality of irrigation water, design objectives, client preferences and cost. To a lesser extent site topography and climatic factors will also influence plant choice. Poor soils can always be modified or replaced entirely, drainage can be enhanced

and protection from marauding livestock can be provided.

An understanding of local ecology is essential, not only to ensure that the right species are selected, but also to make an assessment of the viability of introducing plants from equivalent environments elsewhere. Native plant material is adapted to climatic extremes, tolerant of high salinity levels, resistant to pests and diseases (except to new varieties or strains which may be introduced with alien material), and low in water requirements; and its cultivation will aid the development of subtle variations. There are also, however, possible objections to the use of native material, such as low visual amenity (owing to the insignificance of its foliage and flowers), thorns, client prejudice against 'weeds' and the ephemeral nature of many species. Some naturally tolerant species that are indigenous to arid areas are listed in Table 15.5. Table 15.6 describes some of the more common pests and diseases that affect plants in arid areas.

PLATE 15.19 *Quisqualis indica* **in flower, Jeddah.** *(Maurice Lee)*

TABLE 15.5
**Some naturally tolerant species indigenous to arid areas**

| Extremely tolerant of: | Species | Extremely tolerant of: | Species |
|---|---|---|---|
| 1. Poor soil structure<br>Gravel<br>Sandy | *Anabasis articulata, Haloxylon; Parkinsonia aculeata; Zizyphus spina-christi* | 5 High water table | *Arthrocnemum; Atriplex nummularia; Avicennia mariina; Casuarina* spp; *Prosopis juliflora; Tamarix* |
| Waterlogged, silty | *Acacia arabica; Eucalyptus* spp; *Tamarix* spp | 6. High soil moisture tension due to drought<br>Trees | *Acacia* spp; *Balanites aegyptica; Prosopis* spp; *Zizyphus* spp |
| 2. Wind damage<br>Trees | *Acacia mellifera; A. pendula; A. seyal; A. tortilis; Casuarina* spp; *Eucalyptus* spp; *Prosopis juliflora; Tamarix aphylla; Zizyphus* spp | Shrubs | *Calligonum; Capparis* spp; *Fagonia* spp; *Haloxylon; Parkinsonia aculeata; Salvadora persica;* cacti and succulents, and all included in the following salinity tolerant category. |
| Shrubs | *Calligonum* spp; *Dodonea viscosa; Haloxylon salicornicum; Nerium oleander; Parkinsonia aculeata; Pithecellobium dulce* | Trees | *Casuarina equisetifolia; Phoenix dactylifera; Prosopis juliflora; Tamarix aphylla; T. passerinoides* |
| 3. Grazing and over use | *Acacia; Haloxylon; Kochia indica; Prosopis; Salsola* spp; *Tamarix* | Shrubs | *Atriplex nummularia; Kochia indica; Nitraria* spp; *Suaeda* spp; *Zygophyllum coccineum.* |
| 4. Dune movement | *Acacia cyanophylla; Atriplex* spp; *Calligonum comosum; Citrullus* spp; grasses (e.g. *Cyperus glomeratus, Panicum turgidum*) | | |

These trees and shrubs show the greatest tolerance to highly saline conditions, even where soil and water table have been contaminated by sea water. The salinity of water or the soil solution may be measured directly as parts per million (ppm) of dissolved solids. It is more conveniently measured by the electrical conductivity (EC). The standard unit of electrical conductivity (mho/cm) is a large unit. It is therefore customary to choose a smaller subunit which gives a more convenient location of the decimal point. The units most commonly used are EC $\times 10^3$ (millimho/cm), EC $\times 10^6$ (micromho/cm). For example 3000 ppm is equivalent to an EC of 0·0047 mhos/cm or EC $\times 10^3$4·7 mmhos/cm or EC $\times$ $10^6$4700 mmho/km.

Salinity tolerances of the more decorative species are given, together with plant descriptions, in Table 15.7. These salinity figures are appropriate to plant survival under optimum conditions of shelter, water, drainage and humidity. Survival at salinities higher than stated can be possible under trickle irrigation with its continual leaching properties. Survival on a windy, arid site can be substantially lower, reducing salinity tolerance by as much as 1−2 mmhos/cm (60−400 ppm TDS).

These guideline figures should never replace on-site plant trials prior to final species selection.

TABLE 15.6
**Recognition of the more common pests and diseases**

| Symptoms | Probable cause | Affected species |
|---|---|---|
| *1. Pests* | | |
| Distorted foliage, flower buds | Thrips | Any |
| Dry, speckled yellow spots on leaf surfaces. Dusty, gritty appearance. Galls. March–September | Red spider mite, other mites | *Azediradicta indica, Terminalia catappa, Albizia lebbeck* |
| Stem, bark damage | Borers, cockchafer larvae | Palms |
| Wholesale damage to plants | Army worms | Any |
| Clouds of small white flies, black mould | Whitefly and sooty mould | *Lantana camara, L. c. nana, L. montevidensis* |
| Low vigour, small curled leaves, root nodules | Nematodes | Any |
| Scrawling white lines on leaf surfaces. Spring/autumn | Leaf miners | Any |
| Sudden wilting of healthy plants | Root damage by white ants, cutworms, wireworms, beetle grubs | Any |
| Malformed young shoots and leaves. Small green or black flies on leaf undersides and young shoots. Honeydew secretion. Galls | Green aphids, citrus blackfly | Any |
| Regular semi-circular pieces missing from leaf edges | Leaf cutter bees | Any |
| Irregularly-eaten leaves. Black droppings | Butterfly, moth larvae. Sod web-worms | *Citrus* spp., Bermuda grass |
| Yellow leaves. Wingless, soft-bodied insects, covered in white sticky cotton, on stem joints. Only in 28 °C and above | Mealy bug | *Citrus* spp., *Hibiscus rosasinensis* |
| White, yellow or brown waxy scales up to 5 mm long on leaf undersides. Honeydew secretion | Scale insects | *Ficus* spp., indoor plants |
| Irregular holes in foliage. Cream to brown-coloured insect, 15–20 mm long with projecting mouth parts | Weevils | Any |
| White mottled patches on leaves. Small yellow, pale-green insects on leaf undersides. April–October | Leafhopper | Any |

| Symptoms | Probable cause | Affected species |
|---|---|---|
| *2. Diseases*<br>Yellow or brown raised spots on both sides of leaves. Spring/autumn | Rusts | Any |
| White powder on stem, leaves | Powdery mildew | Any |
| Low vigour, dark core and roots | Pythium root core rot | Any |
| Soft decay of flowers, leaves, stems followed by brown-grey mould | Botrytis | Any |

TABLE 15.7
**Trees**

| Species (botanical name) | D (deciduous) / D/D (drought-deciduous) / E (evergreen) | Height (m) | Salinity-tolerance H, M, L (ppm if known) | Wind-tolerance H, M, L | Drought-resistance H, M, L | Flower colour | Native | Introduced | Use | Remarks |
|---|---|---|---|---|---|---|---|---|---|---|
| *Acacia* spp. incl. *A. arabica*, *A. cyanophylla*, *A. dealbata*, *A. decurrens*, *A. farnesiana*, *A. nilotica*, *A. saligna*, *A. tortilis* | D/D | 5–20 | M–H | H | H | Yellow | √ | √ | 2, 3, 4 | Thorny; fragrant flowers 500 + spp. |
| *Adenanthera pavonina* | Semi-D | 9 | M | L | M | Y | | √ | 3, 4, 5, 7 | Sandalwood |
| *Ailanthus altissima* | D | 15 | L | L | L | White | | √ | 2, 3, 4 | Only in least extreme climate |
| *Albizia lebbek* (also *A. julibrissin*) | D | 20 | 6000 | M | M | W/Green | | √ | 2, 3, 4, 7 | Untidy leaf/pod fall |
| *Arecastrum romanzoffianum* | E | 20 | M | M | M | | | √ | 3, 4, 5 | Palm |
| *Azedirachta indica* | D | 15 | 6000 | M | M | W | | √ | 2, 3, 4, 7 | |
| *Bauhinia purpurea* (also *B. variegata.*) | D | 6 | 1500 | L | L | Purple | | √ | 4 | |
| *Bombax malabaricum* | D | 30 | L | L | L | Red | | √ | 4, 7 | |
| *Boswellia carterii* | D | 3 | H | H | H | | √ | | 4 | Frankincense |
| *Brachychiton acerifolium* (also *B. populneum*) | E | 30 | M | M | M | Y | | √ | 4, 7 | Unusual form |
| *Carica papaya* (Paw-Paw) | E | 8 | M | L | L | | | √ | 3, 4 | Fruit |
| *Caryota mitis* | E | 3 | M | M | M | | | √ | 4, 5 | Palm |
| *Cassia* spp. incl. *C. fistula*, *C. nodosa* | D | to 10 | 1500 | L | M | Y | | √ | 1, 3, 4 | |

Use
1: Screen
2: Structure
3: Group
4: Specimen
5: Avenue
6: Shelter
7: Shade
8: Hedge
9: G. C.
10: Mass
11: Climber

| | | | | | | | | | |
|---|---|---|---|---|---|---|---|---|---|
| *Casuarina equisetifolia* (also *C. cunninghamiana, C. cristata, C. glauca*) | E | 15 | 20000 | H | H | | √ | 1, 2, 3, 5, 6, 8 | Topiary |
| *Cedrus libani* | E | 25 | L | H | L | | | 3, 4, 7 | Slow-growing, Pollution-tolerant |
| *Cercis silaquastrum* | D | 15 | M | M | M | Purple | √ | 4, 5, 7 | |
| *Ceratonia silaqua* | E | 15 | M | M | M | Green | √ | 4, 7 | Fruit |
| *Chorisia crispifolia* | D | 15 | L | M | L | | | 1, 3, 4, 5, 6 | |
| *Citrus* spp. | E | to 7 | 20000 | M | M | White | | 3, 4, 5, 7 | Fruit |
| *Cocos nucifera* | E | 15 | M | M | M | | √ | 1, 2, 6 | Palm, quick growing |
| *Conocarpus lancifolius* | E | 6.5 | M | M | M | | √ | 3, 4, 5, 7 | Forestry use |
| *Cordia sebestena* | E | 10 | L | M | H | Orange | √ | 1, 3, 4 | |
| *Cotinus coggygria* | D | 8 | L | M | M | Purple | √ | 3, 4, 5, 6 | Foliage colour |
| *Cupressus* spp. (incl. *C. sempervirens, C. arizonica, C. lusitanica*) | E | To 30 | | M | L | | √ | | More temperate zones |
| *Cycas revoluta* | E | 2 | L | M | M | | √ | 3, 4, 5 | Palm |
| *Dalbergia sissoo* | D/D | 25 | M | M | M | | √ | 1–6 incl | |
| *Delonix regia* | D | 15 | 1500 | M | M | Scarlet | √ | 1, 3, 4, 5, 7 | Dramatic flowers |
| *Dracaena* spp. (incl. *D. australis, D. indivisa, D. marginalis, D. sanderii*) | E | 5–10 | M | H | H | | √ | 3, 4 | Palm-like |
| *Erythrina christi-galli* (also *E. caffra,*) | D | 3 / 20 | 600 | L | L | Orange | √ | 3, 4, 5 | Not heat-tolerant under extreme conditions |
| *Eucalyptus* spp. (incl. *E. camaldulensis, E. citriodora, E. robusta, E. rostrata*) | E | To 40 | 9000 | H | L | | √ | 1–6 incl. | High water use and unmanageable growth rate; Best in shelter, belts, or not at all if water scarce |
| *Euphorbia* spp. incl *E. tirucalli* | E | 9 | M | H | H | Yellow | √ | 1, 2, 3, 6, 8 | |
| *Ficus* spp. (incl. *F. altissima, F. benghalensis, F. reliogosa, F. retusa, F. sycomorus*) | E | To 30 | 4500–6000 | M | M | | √ | 1, 2, 3, 4, 5, 7, 8 | *F. salicifolius* is a native species; Wide range of spp. for many uses, some very large |

TABLE 15.7
**Trees**

Use
1: Screen
2: Structure
3: Group
4: Specimen
5: Avenue
6: Shelter
7: Shade
8: Hedge
9: G. C.
10: Mass
11: Climber

| Species (botanical name) | D (deciduous) / D/D (drought-deciduous) / E (evergreen) | Height (m) | Salinity-tolerance H, M, L (ppm if known) | Wind-tolerance H, M, L | Drought-resistance H, M, L | Flower colour | Native | Introduced | Use | Remarks |
|---|---|---|---|---|---|---|---|---|---|---|
| Hyphaene thebaica | E | 10 | M | H | H | | ✓ | | 3, 4, 5 | Palm |
| Jacaranda mimosaefolia (syn. J. acutifolia.) | Semi-E | 12 | 1500 | M | M | Blue/Violet | | ✓ | 3, 4, 5, 7 | |
| Leucaena glauca | D | 9 | M | M | M | Yellow/ Green | | ✓ | 1, 2, 6, 7 | |
| Lagerstroemia indica | Semi-D | 8 | M | M | M | Red–white | | ✓ | 3, 4 | |
| Mangifera indica | E | 15 | L | H | L | | | ✓ | 3, 4, 5, 7 | Fruit |
| Manitoa gemnipara | D/D | 12 | 3000 | M | M | Cream | | ✓ | 2, 3, 4, 5 | |
| Melia azedarach | D | 12 | 2000 | M | M | Lilac | | ✓ | 3, 4, 5 | |
| Millingtonia hortensis | Semi-D | 15 | 3000 | M | M | White | | ✓ | 3, 4, 7 | |
| Moringa oleifera | E | 7.5 | M | L | M | Cream | | ✓ | 4, 7 | |
| Morus alba (also M. nigra) | D | 10 | L | M | L | | | ✓ | 4, 7 | Fruit |
| Olea africana (also O. europaea) | E | 8 | L | M | M | Yellow/white | ✓ | | 3, 4, 7 | Fruit (2 or more varieties for best results) |
| Parkia spp. | E | 15 + | M | M | M | Yellow | | ✓ | 4, 5, 7 | |
| Parkinsonia aculeata | D/D | 6 | 9000 | L | M | Yellow | | ✓ | 1, 2, 3, 4 | |
| Peltophorum pterocarpum (also P. africanum) | E | 24 | 3000 | L | M | | | ✓ | 4, 5, 7 | Not heat-tolerant under extreme conditions |
| Phoenix canariensis | E | 18 | H/M | H | M | | | ✓ | 3, 4, 5 | |
| P. dactylifera | E | 30 | H/M | H | M | | ✓ | | 3, 4, 5 | Dates |
| Pinus halapensis (also P. canariensis, P. pinaster, P. radiata, P. pinea) | E | 15 | H | H | H | | | ✓ | 1, 2, 3, 5, 6 | |

| Species | | Height (m) | | | | Flower colour | | | Uses | Notes |
|---|---|---|---|---|---|---|---|---|---|---|
| *Pistacia atlantica* | D | 10 | 3000 | M | H | | ✓ | | 1, 3, 4, 5 | Fruit |
| *Pithecellobium dulce* | E | 15 | H | H | H | | ✓ | | 1, 2, 6 | Edible seed pods |
| *Plumeria rubra acutifolia* (also *P. obtusa*) | D | 4 | L | L | M | Pink/white | ✓ | | 3, 4 | Fragrant flowers |
| *Pongamia glabra* | Semi-D | 8 | 1000 | M | M | Cream | ✓ | | 2, 3, 4, 6, 7 | |
| *Prosopis juliflora* | E | 10 | H | H | H | Yellow | ✓ | | 1, 2, 3, 6, 7 | |
| *P. cineraria* (syn *spicigera*) | E | 15 | H | H | H | Yellow | ✓ | ✓ | 1, 2, 3, 4, 6, 7 | Edible fodder |
| *Punica granatum* (also *P.g. 'nana'*) | D | 5 | 7000 | M | M | Red | ✓ | | 1, 2, 3, 8 | Fruit |
| *Ricinus communis* | E | 5 | 6000 | H | H | Green | ✓ | | 1, 2, 3, 4, 6 | |
| *Roystonea regia* | E | 30 | M | H | M | | ✓ | | 3, 4, 5, 7 | Palm |
| *Schinus molle* (also *S. terebinthifolius*) | E | 12 | 4500 | M | M | Yellow/white | ✓ | | 1, 4, 5, 7 | Fruits |
| *Sesbania grandiflora* | E | 6 | M | M | M | Red-white | ✓ | | 1, 3, 4, 7 | Beautiful flowers |
| *Spathodea campanulata* | E | 15 + | L | M | L | Red | ✓ | | 4, 7 | |
| *Tamarindus indica* | Semi-E | 25 | 3000 | M | M | Red | ✓ | | 4, 7 | Edible seed pod |
| *Tamarix aphylla* | E | 10 | 20000 | H | H | | ✓ | | 1, 2, 6, 7 | |
| *Terminalia catappa* | D | 18 | 4500 | M | M | Yellow | ✓ | | 3, 4, 5, 7 | Excellent shade tree |
| *Thespesia populnea* | E | 9 | 6000 | M | M | Yellow | ✓ | | 1, 3, 4, 5, 7 | |
| *Trachycarpus fortunei* | E | 12 | L | M | L | | ✓ | | 3, 4, 5, 7 | Palm |
| *Vitex agnus-castus* | Semi-D | 7 | 6000 | M | M | Blue | ✓ | | 1, 4, 7 | |
| *Washingtonia filifera* (also *W. robusta*) | E | 15 | 20000 | M | L | | ✓ | | 1, 3, 4, 5, 7 | Fan palm |
| *Yucca* spp. | E | To 15 | varies | H | H | White | ✓ | | 3, 4, 8 | |
| *Zizyphus spina-cristi* (also *Z. jujuba*, *Z. nummularia*) | E | 12 | 9000 | H | H | Green/ yellow | ✓ | | 1, 2, 4, 7 | |

TABLE 15.8
**Shrubs**

Use
1: Screen
2: Structure
3: Group
4: Specimen
5: Avenue
6: Shelter
7: Shade
8: Hedge
9: G. C.
10: Mass
11: Climber

| Species (botanical name) | D (deciduous) / D/D (drought-deciduous) / E (evergreen) | Height (m) | Salinity-tolerance H, M, L (ppm if known) | Wind-tolerance H, M, L | Drought-resistance H, M, L | Flower colour | Native | Introduced | Use | Remarks |
|---|---|---|---|---|---|---|---|---|---|---|
| Adenium arabicum | E | 1 | M | M | M | Pink | | √ | 4 | |
| Acalypha spp. (incl. A. hispadica, A. wilkesiana, A. marginata) | E | To 2 | M/H | M/H | M | | | √ | 2, 3, 8 | |
| Alocasia macrorhiza | E | 2 | | | | | | | | |
| Aralia spp. (incl. A. balfouri) | E | To 3 | M | L | M | — | | √ | 2, 3, 4, 8 | Protect from winds |
| Argyreia campanulata | E | 3 | M | L | M | Lilac | | √ | 1, 3, 8 | |
| Artemisia spp. (incl. A. absinthum) | E | 1 | M | M | M | Yellow | | √ | 3, 10 | |
| Atriplex spp. (incl. A. glauca, A. halimus, A. semi-baccata) | E | To 2 | 5–8000 | H | H | — | √ | | 2, 3, 8, 9, 10 | Silver-grey foliage |
| Barleria prionitis | D | 1.5 | M | M | M | Yellow | | √ | 3, 8, 10 | |
| Buddleia spp. (incl. B. alternifolia, B. asiatica, B. variabilis) | D | To 3.5 | L/M | L | M | Lilac/ Purple | | √ | 2, 3 | Protect from winds |
| Caesalpinia gillesi | E | 3.5 | 5500 | L | M | Yellow | | √ | 2, 3, 4 | |
| C. pulcherrima | E | 4.5 | 5000 | L | M | Orange | | √ | 2, 3, 4 | Straggly |

| Species | Habit | Height (m) | | Salt | Soil | Flower colour | | | Propagation | Remarks |
|---|---|---|---|---|---|---|---|---|---|---|
| Callistemon spp. (incl. C. citrinus, C. lanceolatus, C. viminalis) | E | To 6 | 9000 | H | H | Red | | ✓ | 1, 3, 4, 8 | Citrinus, slow |
| Calotropis procera | E | 3 | 6000 | H | H | Purple | ✓ | ✓ | 2, 3, 4 | Poisonous |
| Capparis decidua | E | 2 | M | M | M | White | | ✓ | 1, 3, 4, 10 | |
| Carissa grandiflora | E/D | To 6 | L | L | M | Yellow | | ✓ | 1, 2, 3, 4 | |
| Cassia spp. (incl. C. alata, C. glauca) | E | 3 | L | L | L | White | | ✓ | 4 | |
| Cestrum nocturnum | Semi-D | To 8 | 3000 | M | M | White | | ✓ | 1, 2, 3, 6 | Night fragrance |
| Chilopsis linearis | E | To 1.5 | M | M | M | Pink | | ✓ | 3, 4 | Willow-like |
| Cistus spp. (incl. C. hybridus, C. purpureus) | E | 3.5 | M | M | M | White | | ✓ | 3, 4 | |
| Clerodendron inerme | E | 3.5 | 8000 | H | H | White | | ✓ | 1, 2, 6, 8, 10, 11 | Excellent hedge plant |
| Codaieum spp. | E | To 3 | M | L | L | — | | ✓ | 3, 4 | Red/bronze/yellow foliage |
| Datura spp. (incl. D. candida, D. inoxia, D. saveolens) | E | To 3.5 | M | L | M | White | | ✓ | 2, 3, 4 | Poisonous |
| Dodonea viscosa | E | 3.5 | 7000 | H | M | Green | ✓ | ✓ | 1, 2, 8 | Excellent hedge plant |
| Duranta repens | E | 3 | M | M | M | Blue | | ✓ | 2, 3, 4 | |
| Eleagnus pungens | E | 4 | L | M | L | | | ✓ | 1, 2 | |
| Euphorbia spp. (incl. E. larica, E. pulcherrima) | E | To 4 | H/M | M | M | Red | ✓ | ✓ | 3, 4, 10 | |
| Gardenia jasminoides | E | To 2 | L | L | L | White | | ✓ | 4 | Protect from hot sun |
| Hibiscus rosasinensis | E | 4 | 1000 | M | M | Red/white/yellow | | ✓ | 1, 3, 4 | Good flowering shrub |
| Ixora spp. (incl. I. coccinea, I. chinensis, I. javanica) | E | To 3.5 | L/M | L | M | Orange/red | | ✓ | 3, 4, 8 | |
| Jasminum spp. (incl. J. officinale, J. sambac) | E | To 3 (or 15 if trained) | 600 | M | M | White/ yellow/pink | | ✓ | 4, 11 | Train as climber |

| Species (botanical name) | D (deciduous) / D/D (drought-deciduous) / E (evergreen) | Height (m) | Salinity-tolerance H, M, L (ppm if known) | Wind-tolerance H, M, L | Drought-resistance H, M, L | Flower colour | Native | Introduced | Use | Remarks |
|---|---|---|---|---|---|---|---|---|---|---|
| *Lantana camara* | E | 3 | 3000 | M | M | Yellow/orange/red | | √ | 1, 2, 3, 8 | Poisonous berries |
| *Lavandula* spp. (incl. *L. spica*, *L. stoechas*) | E | 1 | L | M | L/M | Purple | | √ | 3, 8, 9 | Fragrant |
| *Lawsonia inermis* | E | 2.5 | H | M | L/M | Pink/White | √ | | 2, 3, 8 | Henna |
| *Malvaviscus arboreus* | E | 3 | M | M | M | Orange | | √ | 3, 4 | |
| *Myrtus communis* | E | 2.5 | H/M | H | H | White | √ | | 2, 3, 8 | Fragrant |
| *Nerium oleander* | E | 6 | 9000 | H | L | Pink/White/Red | √ | √ | 1, 2, 3, 4 | Poisonous |
| *Plumbago capensis* | E | 3 | L | L | L/M | Blue | | √ | 2, 3, 4 | |
| *Rosa* spp. | D | To 1.5 | L | L | L | Various | | √ | 2, 3, 4 | Not heat-tolerant under extreme conditions |
| *Rosmarinus officinalis* | E | 1.5 | L | M | H | Blue | | √ | 3, 8, 9, 10 | |
| *Russellia juncea* | E | 1.5 | M | L | M | Orange | | √ | 3, 10 | |
| *Sesbania aegyptica* | E | 4.5 | 8000 | H | H | Yellow | √ | | 1, 2, 6 | Good pioneer/screen |
| *Tecoma* spp. (incl. *T. stans*, *T. smithii*) | Semi-D | 3.5 | 3000 | M | M | Yellow | | √ | 1, 2, 4 | Prune hard for good structure |
| *Tecomaria capensis* | E | 3 | L | M | M | Orange-Red | | √ | 2, 3, 4 | |
| *Tecomella undulata* | E | 3 | H | H | M | Orange | √ | | 2, 3, 4 | |
| *Thevetia* spp. (incl. *T. peruviana*, *T. thevetioides*) | E | To 4 | 7000 | H | M | Orange/Yellow | | √ | 1, 2, 3, 4 | |

*Use*
1: Screen
2: Structure
3: Group
4: Specimen
5: Avenue
6: Shelter
7: Shade
8: Hedge
9: G. C.
10: Mass
11: Climber

TABLE 15.9
**Groundcover**

| Species (botanical name) | D (deciduous) / D/D (drought-deciduous) / E (evergreen) | Height (mm) | Salinity-tolerance H, M, L (ppm if known) | Wind-tolerance H, M, L | Drought-resistance H, M, L | Flower colour | Native | Introduced | Remarks |
|---|---|---|---|---|---|---|---|---|---|
| *Acacia ongerop* | D/D | To 700 | 7000 | H | H | Yellow | ✓ | | |
| *Ajuga reptans* | E | 100 | M | M | M | Blue | | ✓ | Also for foliage colour |
| *Alternanthera versicolor* | D/E | 300 | M | M | L | White | | ✓ | For red/green foliage |
| *Arctotheca calendula* | Semi-E | 250 | M | M | M | Yellow | | ✓ | Invasive |
| *Carpobrotus edulis* | E | 250 | H | M | H | Pink/Yellow | | ✓ | Ice plant |
| *Catharanthus roseus* | E | 500 | L | M | M | Pink/White | | ✓ | |
| *Carissa grandiflora* 'prostrata' | E | 600 | L | M | M | White | | ✓ | |
| *Delaspermum alba* | E | 125 | H | M | H | White | | ✓ | Ice plant |
| *Drosanthemum hispidum* | E | 125 | H | M | H | Pink/Purple | | ✓ | Ice plant |
| *Gardenia jasminoides* 'radicans' | E | 600 | L | M | L | White | | ✓ | Fragrant, best in partial shade |
| *Gazania* spp. (incl. *G. splendens*, *G. uniflora*) | E | 300 | M | M | M | White to Red | | ✓ | Very showy |
| *Hedera canariensis* | E | 150 | L | M | M | — | | ✓ | |
| *Ipomoea palmata* *I. canariensis* | See 'Climbers' | | | | | | | | |

| Species (botanical name) | D (deciduous) D/D (drought-deciduous) E (evergreen) | Height (m) | Salinity-tolerance H, M, L (ppm if known) | Wind-tolerance H, M, L | Drought-resistance H, M, L | Flower colour | Native | Introduced | |
|---|---|---|---|---|---|---|---|---|---|
| *Lampranthus* spp. (incl. *L. aurantiacus*, *L. roseus*, *L. spectabilis*) | E | 100 | H | M | M | Pink/ Orange etc. | | √ | Ice plant |
| *Lantana* spp. (incl. *L. camara nana*, *L. montevidensis*) | E | 200–600 | M | M | L | Yellow, White Purple | | √ | White fly may be a problem |
| *Malephorea* spp. (incl. *M. crocea*, *M. luteola*) | E | 100–150 | H | M | H | Pink/ Orange | | √ | Ice plant |
| *Polygonum capitatum* | E | 150 | L | M | L | Pink | | √ | |
| *Portulaca* spp. (incl. *P. grandiflora*, *P. oleracea*) | E | 100 | H | M | M | Pink | | √ | |
| *Rhoeo discolor* | E | 500 | M | M | M | – | | √ | Purple/green foliage |
| *Rosmarinus officinalis* 'prostratus' | E | 600 | M | M | M | Blue | | √ | |
| *Sedum* spp. (*S. confusum*, *S. rubrotinctum*) | E | To 300 | M | M | H | Yellow | | √ | Small areas |
| *Setcreasa purpurea* | E | 300 | M | L | M | White | | √ | Dark purple foliage |
| *Trachelospermum* spp. *T. jasminoides* *T.j.* 'pubescens' | E | To 600 | L | M | L | White | | √ | |

TABLE 15.10
**Succulents**

| Species (botanical name) | Height (m) | Salinity-tolerance H, M, L (ppm if known) | Wind-tolerance H, M, L | Drought-resistance H, M, L | Flower colour | Native | Introduced | Use | Remarks |
|---|---|---|---|---|---|---|---|---|---|
| *Agave* spp. (incl. *A. americana*, *A. sisalana*) | 2 | H | H | M | Yellow/green | | √ | 1,3,4,8 | |
| *Aloe* spp. (incl. *A. arborescens*, *A. saponaria*, *A. variegata*) | To 6 | M | H | M | Yellow/green | √ | √ | 3, 4, 10 | Flowering spikes |
| *Cactus* (incl. *Echinocactus* spp, *Perocactus* spp, *Lemaireocereus thurberi*, *Opuntia* spp.) | To 5 | M | H | M | Various | | √ | 3, 4 | Slow-growing |
| *Sansevieria trifasciata* | 1.5 | H | H | M | Greenish/white | | √ | 3, 4, 8 | |

*Use*
1: Screen
2: Structure
3: Group
4: Specimen
5: Avenue
6: Shelter
7: Shade
8: Hedge
9: G. C.
10: Mass
11: Climber

311

TABLE 15.11
**Grass and grass substitutes**

| Species (botanical name) | English name | Remarks |
|---|---|---|
| *Anthemis nobilis* | Chamomile | Fragrant, yellow flowers |
| *Cynodon dactylon* (incl. vars: 'Tifway', etc.) | Bermuda grass | Most suitable lawn grass species. Hard-wearing, may brown off in winter and require overseeing with ryegrass for colour. |
| *Dichondra repens* | Ponyfoot | Hard-wearing, possible lawn substitute |
| *Lippia nodiflora* | Lippia | Good in full sun, but dies back in shade or cooler season, purple flowers, does not trample well |
| *Paspalum vaginatum* | Adelaide grass | Substitute for cynodon, salt- and drought-tolerant |
| *Pennisetum clandestinum* | | Drought-resistant, clump forming, pink/purple flower spikes |
| *Stenotaphrum secundatum* (incl vars: 'Common' 'Floratam' etc.) | St Augustine's grass | Coarser, less heat tolerant than cynodon, but widely planted in southern USA |
| *Zoysia tenuiflora* | Korean grass | Not hard-wearing, low maintenance |

N.B. – Lawns are a luxury.
They can be extremely effective in key locations but are costly in terms of water use, irrigation, installation and maintenance requirements.

## 15.11 SOME PROBLEMS OF PLANTING

Grazing of camels, goats, rabbits and Australian mammals can prevent the establishment of new plants and prohibit recovery of indigenous plants. Over-cultivation by man without replacement of plant nutrients and his collection of wood for fuel also degrade the soils and vegetation. Fencing, tree guards, education in crop rotation and public awareness of the reasons for planting all help to overcome this problem.

Most implementation problems can be overcome by proper management. Tree guards can protect new planting, sand must be cleared and stabilized, silts and clays must be hoed and mulching and fertilizers can be used to improve soil quality. It must be remembered that planting can only be carried out in the cooler months and that some form of pest control which does not break down in the heat will be necessary in the early growth stages. An efficient system of irrigation is essential, as one week's loss of irrigation can be fatal to young plants. Sand and salt can wear out or block any working parts of machinery and so regular pipe flushing and salt leaching must be carried out.

Motionless water surfaces that are exposed to the light will encourage algae which can block irrigation systems and make water features unsightly. Water should be continually moving and aerated to keep it clear. Polythene sheets and pvc pipes can be degraded in hot climates. They should be of heavy quality and sunk, covered or painted.

It will be easier to manage and maintain the planting scheme if workshops, stores and so on are erected close to the site and are easily accessible.

## 15.12 ADVANTAGES OF PLANTING IN ARID AREAS

1 .There is little need for expensive propagation units due to high temperatures and frost-free areas.

2. The growth rate per annum is very fast. Many plants grow at 2–3 m (6–10 ft)per year, and fast eucalyptus will grow 4 m per year.

3. There is a low level of pests and diseases in hot, dry climates.

4. There is a definite improvement of microclimate accompanied by increases in all types of wildlife, together with social and psychological benefits for the people living close to the planting.

5. Shelter belts assist in desert reclamation, growth of crops, and reduction of winds around housing.

6. Technological advances and research are stimulated by the urge to overcome climatic problems through methods such as desalination, plastic mulches, water table control and breeding of salt tolerant species.

Adverse effects will also occur and must be constantly monitored and corrected. Rapid depletion of sweet water for domestic use due to plant over-watering, salt accumulation in the soil and salt-pan developments due to irrigation wetting patterns are all likely to cause serious problems to plant establishment in arid areas unless the schemes are carefully managed.

TABLE 15.12
**Flowering plants — 1. Annuals, biennials and herbaceous perennials. (Mostly short-lived. For bedding and winter flowering display)**

| Species (botanical name) | English name | Species (botanical name) | English name |
|---|---|---|---|
| *Ageratum mexicanum* | | *Iberis* spp. | Candytuft |
| *Althaea rosea* | Hollyhock | *Impatiens balsamina* | Balsam |
| *Amaranthus tricolor* | Amaranth | *Kochia trichophylla* | |
| *Anthirrhinum majus* | Snapdragon | *Kniphophia ovaria* | Red hot poker |
| *Artemisia monosperma* | | *Lavandula vera* | Dutch lavender |
| *Aristida meccana* | | *Limonium sinuatum* | Sea lavender |
| *Arctotis* spp. | | *Linaria cymbalaria* | Ivy-leaved toadflax |
| *Aquilegia* spp. | Columbine | (*Cymbalaria muralis*) | |
| *Aster* spp. | Michaelmas daisy | *Linum* spp. | Flax |
| | | *Lobelia erinus* | |
| *Brachycome* spp. | | *Lobularia maritima* | |
| | | | |
| *Calendula officinalis* | Marigold | *Mathiola incana* | Stock |
| *Calliopsis bicolor* | | *Mesembryanthemum tricolor* | |
| *Callistephus hortensis* | China aster | *Mirabilis jalapa* | Four o'clock plant |
| *Celosia argentea* | Cockscomb | | |
| *Centaurea cyanus* | Cornflower | *Nicotiana* spp. | Tobacco plant |
| *Cheiranthus annuus* | Wallflower | | |
| *Chrysanthem bellum* | Chrysanthemum | *Ocimum basilicum* | Basil |
| *C. coronarium* | | *Oenothera missourensis* | |
| *Cineraria* spp. | | *Ononis variegata* | |
| *Clarkia elegans* | | | |
| *Cleome spinosa* | Spider flower | *Pelargonium* spp. | |
| *Cortaderia selloana* | Pampas grass | *Penstemon* spp. | |
| *Cosmos bipinnatus* | | *Petunia hybrida* vars | |
| *Coleus* spp. | | *Phlox drummondi* | |
| *Clianthus* spp. | | | |
| *Cyperus alternifolius* | Umbrella grass | *Salpiglossis* spp. | |
| | | *Salvia splendens* | |
| *Delphinium ajacis* | Rocket larkspur | *Saponaria calabrica* | |
| *Dianthus caryophyllus* | Carnation | *Saxifraga stolonifera* | |
| *Didiscus caeruleus* | Blue lace flower | *Scabiosa cancasia* | Scabious |
| *Dimorphoteca awianthiaca* | Cape marigold | *Sempervivum* spp. | Houseleek |
| | | | |
| *Gaillardia pulchella* | Blanket flower | *Tagetes erecta* | Marigold |
| *Godetia* spp. | | *Tropaeolum majus* | Nasturtium |
| *Gomphrena globosa* | Globe amaranth | *Tithonia* spp. | |
| | | | |
| *Hyssopus officinalis* | Hyssop | *Verbena hybrida* | |
| *Helianthus annuus* | Sunflower | *Viola tricolor* | Heartsease pansy |
| *Helichrysum bracteatum* | Everlasting flower | *Vittadina australis* | |
| | | *Zebrina pendula* | |
| | | *Zinnia elegans* | |

## 15.13 PLANT LISTS

The landscape designer requires colour, size, textural variety, and permanence. With careful selection and proper mitigation of the extremes of wind, soil erosion, heat and drought, many plants from non-arid lands have been introduced successfully into the hot, arid landscape.

Tables 15.7 to 15.14 list some of the plants which have been used in amenity planting throughout the Middle East. A few of the plants listed are in fact native; others are aliens but hardy enough to create the favourable conditions required by the least tolerant.

Selection of plants should always take more into account than obvious design suitability. Thus, while such checklists are useful in reminding the designer of the range of possible species, individual plants in particular locations must be considered in specific microclimatic terms. For example, if a plant grows locally, is it successful at an acceptable level, and how is this success achieved?

The plant checklists are not exhaustive. There will

**TABLE 15.13**

**Flowering plants – 2. Bulbs, corms, tubers etc. (Often better able to survive hot season than other perennials)**

| Species (botanical name) | English name |
| --- | --- |
| *Agapanthus africanus* | African lily |
| *A. orientalis* | |
| *A. umbellatus maximus* | |
| *Allium artemisietorum* | |
| *A. hierochuntium* | |
| *Alstroemeria* spp. | Peruvian lily |
| *Amaryllis belladonna* | |
| *Anemone coronaria* | Windflower |
| *Asparagus plumosus* | Asparagus fern |
| *Begonia* spp. | |
| *Canna indica* | |
| *C. edulis* | |
| *Colchicum ritchii* | Autumn crocus |
| *C. tuviae* | |
| *Crinum asiaticum* | |
| *C. americanum* | |
| *Dahlia* spp. | |
| *Freesia x hybrida* | |
| *Gladiolus* spp. | |
| *Gloriosa* spp. | Glory lily |
| *Hemerocallis littoralis* | Day lily |
| *Hymenocallis* spp. | |
| *Hyline gardneriana* | |
| *Iris nigricans* | |
| *Polianthes tuberosa* | Tuberose |
| *Zantedischia aethiopica* | Arum lily |

always be opportunities to experiment with the introduction of 'new' plants from climatically similar regions. However, availability may be a problem in that local suppliers and nurseries tend to stock only those tried and tested plants for which there is local demand (usually *not* from professional landscape designers). The solution, preferable in terms of both flexibility of supply and quality control, is to establish a site-based nursery for the propagation of plant material from seed and parent stock. Material grown from seed, in almost the final location, will be hardier and more vigorous, if properly acclimatized, than that which is freighted in from abroad. It may also be substantially cheaper.

## FURTHER READING

Adams, R. 'Technical Considerations of Salinity in Hot Territories', *ILA Journal* (1976)

Adams, R., Adams M., Willens. A. and Willens A. *Dry Lands: Man and Plants* (London: Architectural Press 1978)

Blatter, E. and Millard, W. S. *Some Beautiful Indian trees* (Bombay: John Bale and Curnow; 2nd ed., 1954)

Bor, N. L. and Raizada *Some Beautiful Indian Climbers and Shrubs* (Bombay: Natural History Soc. 1954)

Broun, A. F. and Massey, R. E. *Flora of the Sudan*, (Sudan Govt. Office, London 1929)

Cowen, D. V. (Mrs. Gardiner-Lewis) *Flowering Trees and Shrubs in India*, 4th ed., Bombay (1965)

Gubb, Alfred S. *La Flore Saharienne* and *La Flore Algerienne* (Algiers: 1913)

Moore, Eric *Gardening in the Middle East* (London: Stacey International 1986)

Palmer, E. and Pitman, N. *The Trees of South Africa* (Care Town: A A. Balkema, 1961)

Palmer, E. and Pitman, N. *The Trees of Southern Africa*, 3 vols. (Balkema 1972)

Post, G. E. *Flora of Syria, Palestine and Sinai*. American University of Beirut National Science Series No. 1, 2nd ed, 2 vols (Beirut 1932)

Rechinger, K. H. *Flora Iranica* (Akademische Druck and Verlagsanstalt, P. O. Box 598, A8010 Graz 1963)

Russell, E. W. *Soil Conditions and Plant Growth* (London: Longmans, 9th ed. 1961)

Stamp, L. Dudley *Asia* (London: Methuen, 1967)

*Flora of Iraq*. Iraq Min. of Agric. Several Volumes:
Guest, E. and Ali Al-Rawi, 1966, Vol. 1
Townsend, C. C. and Guests, E. 1966, Vol 2
Bor, N. L. with Ali-Rawi (ed. Townsend, C. C. and Guest, E.) (Baghdad 1968, Vol. 9)
Townsend, C.C. and Guest, E. (Baghdad, 1974, Vol. 3)

USDA *Soil Survey Manual*, Soil Classification and supplement (Washington: 1957)

## REFERENCES

Cochrane, T. and Brown, J. (Eds.) *Landscape Design for the Middle East* (London: RIBA, 1978)

Duble, R. and Kell, J. C. *Southern Lawns and Groundcovers*, (Houston: Gulf Publishing Co. 1977)

FAO UNESCO *Irrigation, Drainage and Salinity* (Rome: Hutchinson/FAO, 1973)

Hills, E. S. (Ed.) *Arid Lands – A Geographical Appraisal* (London: Methuen and Co. Ltd 1966)

Kelly, K. and Schnadelbach, R. T. *Landscaping the Saudi-Arabian Desert* (Philadelphia: The Delancey Press 1976)

Kwei, T. and Esmonde, T. *Landscape Plants in the United Arid Emirates* (New York: Teresa Kwei 1978)

Lanzara, P. and Pizzetti, M. *The Macdonald Encyclopaedia of Trees* (London: Macdonald and Co. 1982)

Ricks, G. 'Plants in arid areas', in *Landscape Design*, **166** pp 26–9 and**168**, pp 57–60, (London: Landscape Institute 1987)

TABLE 15.14
**Climbers**

| Species (botanical name) | D (deciduous) D/D (drought-deciduous) E (evergreen) | Tolerance (high, medium or low) | | | Flower colour | Remarks |
|---|---|---|---|---|---|---|
| | | Salinity | Wind | Drought | | |
| *Allamanda* spp. (incl. *A. cathartica*, *A. hendersonii*, *A. nereifolia*) | E | L | L | M | Yellow | Damp semi-shade |
| *Antigonon leptopus* | E | M | M | M | Pink | |
| *Aristolachia* spp. (incl. *A. elegans*, *A. frimbriata*, *A. grandiflora*) | E | L | L | M | Purple | |
| *Beaumontia grandiflora* | E | M | M | M | White | |
| *Bougainvillea* spp. (incl. *B. glabra*, *B. spectabilis*) | E | 500 | L | M | Red/white/yellow etc | |
| *Campsis grandiflora* | E | M | M | M | Orange/red | |
| *Clematis armandii* | E | L | M | M | White | |
| *Clerodendron splendens* | E | M | L | L | Red | Shade |
| *Clitorea ternatea* | E | M | M | M | Blue | |
| *Clytostama callistegioides* | E | L | L | L | Purple | Not in hot sun |
| *Cryptostegia grandiflora* | E | H | M | M | Rose/pink | |
| *Doxantha unguis-cati* | Semi-D | M | M | M | Yellow | |
| *Gelsemium sempervirens* | E | M | M | M | Yellow | |
| *Gloriosa rothschildiana* | E | M | M | M | Scarlet/Yellow | |
| *Ipomoea* spp. (incl. *I. horsfalliae*, *I. learii*, *I. palmata*, *I. pes-caprae*) | E | M | M | L | Purple | |
| *Jacquemontia martii* | E | M | L | M | Blue | |
| *Jasminum* spp. (incl. *J. grandiflorum*, *J. mesneyi*) | D/E | L | M | M | White/yellow | |
| *Lonicera* spp. (incl. *L. implexa*, *L. japonica*) | E | M | M | M | White/yellow | |
| *Luffa aegyptica* | Annual | H | L | M | Yellow | Seeds |
| *Passiflora* | D/E | M | M | M | Purple/white | |
| *Solanum* spp. (incl. *S. jasminoides*, *S. wendlandii*) | E | M | M | M | Blue/lilac | |
| *Quisqualis indica* | E | L | L | M | Pink/red | |
| *Thunbergia* spp. (incl. *T. alata*, *T. grandiflora*) | E | L/M | L/M | M | Blue-yellow | |
| *Vitis vinifera* | D | L | M | M | | Shade, fruit |

CHAPTER 16

# The Functional Uses of Australian Plants

## CHRISTINE AVIS AND JAMES MITCHELL

## 16.1 INTRODUCTION

Plants are the major element used in landscape design. Their constantly changing form enhances a design concept in a number of ways. Plants contribute not only to the visual quality of man's environment but also to the physical quality, and have relevant design features such as form, colour and texture that can be used by designers to generate the character of a landscape. They also have functional characteristics which can be used to affect the environment.

The natural Australian environment possesses unique vegetation that can be used as an inspiration in landscape design. Predominant qualities include the tall varied trunks of the eucalypts, the diversity of foliage, the varied colour of flowers, the blue-grey haze associated with massed Australian vegetation, and the hardiness and successful establishment of species indigenous

to an area. The functional characteristics of Australian plants include the capacity to articulate space, to provide screens, to control soil erosion, to achieve privacy, to ameliorate wind and to create shade.

This chapter presents the functional contribution of Australian plants in the landscape with specific listings of suitable species for each particular effect that is desired.

## 16.2 SPACE ARTICULATION

'Any element, natural or man-made, which is able to form a floor, wall or ceiling may be used to articulate space.' (Robinette, 1972, p. 16.) Therefore plant material can be an effective means of achieving this purpose, with the added asset of providing change and seasonal interest. (See Figure 16.1.)

Plants, by themselves or in association with others,

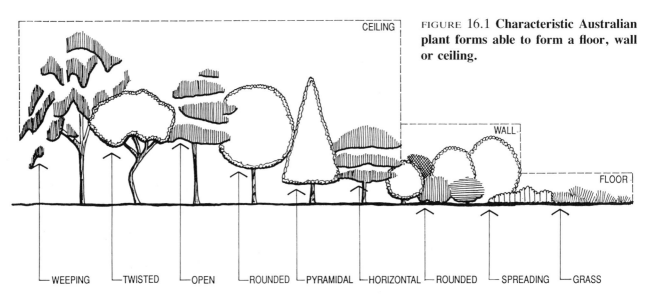

FIGURE 16.1 **Characteristic Australian plant forms able to form a floor, wall or ceiling.**

WEEPING — TWISTED — OPEN — ROUNDED — PYRAMIDAL — HORIZONTAL — ROUNDED — SPREADING — GRASS

316

PLATE 16.1 **A blue-grey haze is characteristic of the East Coast woodlands.** *(Christine Avis)*

PLATE 16.2 **The tall, varied trunks of the eucalypts** (here *Eucalyptus haemastoma*) **are charac-teristic of much of the Australian environment.** *(George Foster)*

can be used to define space A specific example of a plant that defines a space by itself is *Ficus rubiginosa*. As shown in Plate 16.3, this fig forms both a ceiling, with its domed spreading crown (often up to 25 m across), and walls, with its languid foliage. Alternatively, a series of single plants placed next to one another may form a ceiling, a solid visual barrier or wall, or may cover or give edge to an area.

As illustrated in Plate 16.4, tall eucalypts will provide a canopy or ceiling up high and allow for activity in the space below.

Many *Acacia*, *Callistemon* and *Melaleuca* species, with their dense foliage and outstanding flowers, will provide an interesting solid wall at eye height. Furthermore, native grasses and groundcover plants will serve as a good floor or give edge to a space. (See Plate 16.5)

Finally, the spaces that are created depend on the placement and selection of species. The form, scale, density and texture of plants will directly influence the character of a space. Table 16.1 lists a selection of Australian plants, with design characteristics that are useful in creating a variety of spaces.

## 16.3 SCREENING

A common need in landscape design is for plants that will provide a screen to block out the view of any unattractive feature, or enhance one's privacy.

There are numerous Australian plants suitable for screens. Many of these plants have the assets of being fast-growing and having unique forms that can create a

TABLE 16.1
**Space Articulation: representative Australian plants**

| Species | Habit (*size*) | Form | Height | Spread | Landscape function, potential and uses |
|---|---|---|---|---|---|
| **(a) Ceiling plants** | | | | | |
| *Acacia floribunda* | Small | Rounded | 6–8 m | 4–6 m | Adaptable, quick-growing species. Useful for windbreaks and screening |
| *Angophora costata* | Large | Twisted | 15–30 m | 8–15 m | Twisted limbs. Useful as shade or ornamental tree |
| *Banksia integrifolia* | Medium | Twisted | 10–20 m | 5–10 m | Twisted, knarled trunk. Good for screening when grouped |
| *Casuarina cunninghamiana* | Large | Pyramidal | 10–30 m | 10–12 m | Pendulous foliage. Useful as graceful shade tree |
| *Casuarina glauca* | Medium | Pyramidal | 8–20 m | 4–12 m | Pendulous silver-grey foliage. Useful as shelter tree when grouped |
| *Eucalyptus ficifolia* | Small | Rounded | 6–10 m | 5–8 m | Useful as shade and shelter tree |
| *Eucalyptus maculata* | Large | Rounded | 15–20 m | 15–25 m | Smooth, white-spotted bark. Useful as shade tree |
| *Eucalyptus elata* | Medium | Weeping | 8–25 m | 5–10 m | Species forms both a ceiling with its canopy up high and walls with its weeping foliage |
| *Eucalyptus tereticornis* | Large | Horizontal | 15–30 m | 8–15 m | Useful as shade and shelter tree. High branching |
| *Ficus rubiginosa* | Large | Rounded | 15–20 m | 15–25 m | Smooth, grey, heavily buttressed trunk. Domed spreading crown, walls of low branches and foliage |
| *Grevillea robusta* | Medium | Pyramidal | 10–25 m | 6–15 m | Feathery green foliage. Useful for open shelter |
| *Lophostemon conferta* | Large | Rounded | 10–35 m | 6–12 m | Useful for shade and as a screen when grouped. Good street and avenue tree |
| *Melaleuca linariifolia* | Small | Open | 6–10 m | | Graceful paperbark. Useful for low shelter |
| *Melaleuca quinquenervia* | Medium | Rounded | 15–25 m | 3–10 m | Paperbark, with twisted limbs. Gives dense shade |

318

| Species | Habit (size) | Form | Height | Spread | Landscape function, potential and uses |
|---|---|---|---|---|---|
| **(b) Wall plants: dense growing** | | | | | |
| *Acacia baileyana* | Small tree | Horizontal | 3−8 m | 3−6 m | Quick-growing, dense branching species. Useful for windbreaks and screens |
| *Callistemon citrinus* | Small tree | Rounded | 3−8 m | 3−6 m | Useful for low shelter. Pale green leaves, red flower spikes |
| *Grevillea longifolia* | Large shrub | Spreading | 2−4 m | 3−5 m | Open textured species. Useful for windbreaks and screens |
| *Hakea laurina* | Small tree | Rounded | 3−6 m | 3−5 m | Willowy foliage, outstanding red and gold flowers. Useful as a screen when grouped |
| *Melaleuca armillaris* | Small tree | Rounded | 3−6 m | 3−5 m | Low weeping branches. Needle-like foliage. Useful as dense hedge |
| **(c) Open growing** | | | | | |
| *Banksia marginata* | Small tree | Rounded | 3−10 m | 1−5 m | Spectacular flowers. Knarled trunk and open branch systems |
| *Callistemon viminalis* | Small tree | Weeping | 3−10 m | 2−6 m | Hardy, fast-growing species. Useful for low shelter and as ornamental specimen |
| *Eucalyptus leucoxylon* | Small tree | Horizontal | 5−8 m | 5−8 m | Irregular trunk and fine leaves. Useful ornamental and open shelter tree |
| *Hakea nodosa* | Large shrub | Rounded | 2−4 m | 2−3 m | Leathery foliage, showy flowers. Useful for traffic control |
| *Melaleuca elliptica* | Large shrub | Rounded | 2−4 m | 2−3 m | Open-growing with showy flowers and decorative bark. Useful screen |
| **(d) Floor plants** | | | | | |
| *Anigozanthos flavidus* | Low shrub | Spreading | 1−1.5 m | 1 m | Has outstanding paw-like flowers. Useful as a clumpy groundcover |
| *Boronia ledifolia* | Low shrub | Spreading | 1−2 m | 1−2 m | Dainty plant, with strong perfume. Fine foliage and flowers |
| *Darwinia fasicularis* | Low shrub | Spreading | 1−2 m | 1−2 m | Soft green foliage. Dainty red flower bells |
| *Eriostemon myoporoides* | Low shrub | Rounded | 1−2 m | 1−3 m | Native wax flower. Hardy and quick-growing |
| *Grevillea floribunda* | Low shrub | Spreading | 1−2 m | 1−3 m | Soft grey, strong foliage. Dense branching species |
| *Grevillea gaudichaudii* | Ground-cover | Spreading | 1 m | 1 m | Low, hardy groundcover with showy flowers |
| *Lomandra longifolia* | Herb | Spreading | 1 m | − | Erect and tufted perennial. Useful in defining space |
| *Themeda australis* | Grass | Spreading | 1 m | − | Kangaroo grass. Erect glabrous perennial. Stems and leaves, tinged with brown and purple |
| *Xanthorrhoea arborea* | Grass | Spreading | 1−2 m | 1 m | Grass tree. Erect perennial with tufted long, linear leaves. Outstanding tall, cylindrical flower spike |

PLATE 16.3 *Ficus rubiginosa* **here being transplanted to Darling Harbour Park will form both a ceiling, with its domed crown, and walls with its languid foliage, if it is transplanted.** *(James Mitchell)*

PLATE 16.4 *Eucalyptus citriodora* **stand provides a ceiling up high and a clearly defined room down below for activity.** *(James Mitchell)*

setting similar to an informal bushland. Uniform plantings of exotic species, for example *Cupressus* sp., tend to provide a formal screen not in character with the Australian natural landscape.

Screen plants may be required to form either a solid visual barrier or an open screen. Open screens are often necessary to allow the penetration of light.

For an effective dense screen, a combination of shrubs of different sizes is preferred, to ensure foliage growth to ground level. Mass planting of *Acacia*, *Callistemon* and *Melaleuca* species are suitable for this purpose. The open, graceful habitat of such species as *Callistemon viminalis* and *Melaleuca hypericifolia* is suited to partial screening, as is shown in Plate 16.6.

Table 16.2 shows a selection of fast-growing Australian plants suitable for dense screens, open screens and screening areas of limited space.

## 16.4 EROSION CONTROL

In the natural environment vegetation holds the shape of the land. Plant roots hold the soil in place and the leaves and branches form a cover on the ground that

PLATE 16.6 **The ornamental habit of** *Callistemon viminalis* **is useful for a partial screen.** *(James Mitchell)*

321

TABLE 16.2
**Screening: representative Australian plants**

| Species | Habit (size) | Form | Height | Spread | Landscape function, potential and uses |
|---------|-------------|------|--------|--------|----------------------------------------|
| **(a) Dense growing** | | | | | |
| *Acacia buxifolia* | Small tree | Rounded | 2–4 m | 2–4 m | Hardy wattle with low weeping branches. Useful for screen when grouped |
| *Hakea laurina* | Small tree | Rounded | 3–6 m | 3–5 m | Willowy foliage, outstanding red and gold flowers. Useful as a screen when grouped |
| *Melaleuca incana* | Large shrub | Spreading | 2–3 m | 2–3 m | Spreading shrub with grey-green, pendulous foliage |
| *Melaleuca nesophylla* | Small tree | Rounded | 3–6 m | 2–5 m | Dense branching plant. Good for shelter and screening |
| **(b) Open growing** | | | | | |
| *Acacia cardiophylla* | Large shrub | Rounded | 2–4 m | 2–4 m | Open shrub with light foliage and arching branches |
| *Callistemon viminalis* | Small tree | Weeping | 3–10 m | 2–6 m | Hardy, fast-growing species. Useful for ornamental screen when massed |
| *Melaleuca elliptica* | Large shrub | Rounded | 3–6 m | 2–5 m | Has blue-grey open foliage and strong red flowers. An attractive screen at eye level |
| *Melaleuca hypericifolia* | Large shrub | Rounded | 3–6 m | 2–5 m | Strong growing with arching habit. Useful for open screen |
| **(c) Screen plants for areas of limited space** | | | | | |
| *Hardenbergia violacea* | Climber | | | | Has attractive purple pea flowers |
| *Hibbertia scandens* | Climber | | | | Has shiny green leaves and bright yellow open-petalled flowers |
| *Kennedia rubicunda* | Climber | | | | Has attractive red flowers |
| *Pandorea jasminoides* | Climber | | | | White to pink trumpet-like flowers |

creates an effective barrier to water and air movement. In the course of urban development, roots, leaves and branches are normally removed, exposing the topsoil, which is subsequently eroded by the action of wind and water. It is this topsoil that provides anchorage, soil moisture and the most important nutrients for plant growth. Therefore it is essential to retain this soil for landscape works with plants.

For plants to be of benefit in controlling soil erosion, they should be quick-growing. A large number of Australian species have the advantage here. Additionally, as shown in Figure 16.2, the most useful species should have dense leaves or needles, dense branching systems and fibrous root systems.

Table 16.3 gives a list of Australian shrubs and ground covers that can be used to effectively control erosion.

## 16.5 TRAFFIC CONTROL

A further use of plants in landscape design is to assist in traffic control. Plants can provide definite patterns of direction to prevent dangerous random pedestrian and vehicle movement through an area which may damage and destroy the quality of an environment. The effectiveness of the barrier relies on the characteristics of the plants used, the height and spacing of plants and the width of the planting.

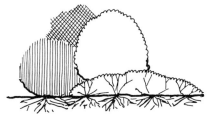

DENSE LEAVES OR NEEDLES CREATE EFFECTIVE BARRIERS TO AIR AND WATER MOVEMENT

EXAMPLE: LEPTOSPERMUM HORIZONTALIS
          GREVILLEA LONGIFOLIA

LOW DENSE BRANCHING AND MULTI-STEMS EFFECTIVELY CONTROL WIND

EXAMPLE: ACACIA BOORMANII
          EUCALYPTUS LEUHMANNIANA

FIBROUS ROOTS AND LEAVES ARE EFFECTIVE IN HOLDING TOPSOIL

EXAMPLE: KENNEDIA RUBICUNDA
          MYOPORUM PARVIFOLIUM

FIGURE 16.2 **Plant characteristics that effectively control erosion.**

TABLE 16.3
**Erosion control: representative Australian plants**

| Species | Habit (size) | Form | Height | Spread | Landscape function, potential and uses |
|---------|--------------|------|--------|--------|----------------------------------------|
| Acacia boormanii | Large shrub | Rounded | 3–5 m | 2–5 m | Hardy, quick-growing wattle with low branching. Useful for restricting wind and water movement |
| Eucalyptus leuhmanniana | Small tree | Rounded | 2–6 m | 2–4 m | Smooth barked mallee species with several trunks issuing from an enlarged rootblock. Useful in holding soil. |
| Grevillea longifolia | Large shrub | Rounded | 2–4 m | 3–5 m | Large low branching shrub with serrated leaves and pink or red flowers |
| Hakea purpurea | Low shrub | Spreading | 1–2 m | 2 m | Hardy spreading shrub with needle-like foliage and crimson flowers |
| Kennedia macrophylla | Low shrub | Spreading | 1 m | 2–4 m | Strong groundcover plant with fibrous root system. Useful in holding soil |
| Kennedia rubicunda | Climber | Spreading | 1 m | 2–4 m | Useful as groundcover with asset of being hardy and quick growing |
| Leptospermum horizontalis | Low shrub | Spreading | 1 m | 2–4 m | Dense spreading shrub with white tea tree flowers |
| Melaleuca wilsonii | Medium shrub | Spreading | 1–3 m | 1–3 m | Dense spreading species with narrow leaves and clusters of red flowers |
| Myoporum parvifolium | Low shrub | Spreading | 1 m | 1–3 m | Hardy groundcover that spreads by layering. Useful in restricting water and wind movement |
| Thryptomene saxicola | Low shrub | Spreading | 1 m | 1–2 m | Bushy, arching shrub with masses of pink flowers most of the year |

PLATE 16.7 **When grouped,** *Leptospermum scoparium* **forms an effective barrier to pedestrian movement.** *(James Mitchell)*

The unique characteristics of some plants make them more suitable for controlling traffic than others. Often dense, bushy shrubs with spiky, stiff foliage are most effective. Pedestrians tend to avoid plants that cause such discomfort when touched. Some Australian plants with the above features include many *Grevillea callistemon* and *Leptospermum* species, as are shown in Plates 16.7, 16.8 and 16.9.

In addition, plants are totally ineffective in controlling traffic if they are sparsely placed, as this will allow movement through openings through them. Plant material therefore should be grouped or massed together.

Finally, the width of the planting is important to consider. It may be that a combination of ground cover, shrubs and trees is required to form a wide, dense

PLATE 16.8 *Grevillea* **'Robert Gordon' forms a useful dense spreading hedge.** *(James Mitchell)*

PLATE 16.9 **A hedge of** *Callistemon* **sp. forms an effective barrier to pedestrian movement.** *(James Mitchell)*

TABLE 16.4
**Traffic control: representative Australian plants**

| Species | Habit (size) | Form | Height | Spread | Landscape function, potential and uses |
|---------|--------------|------|--------|--------|----------------------------------------|
| *Grevillea acanthifolia* | Low shrub | Spreading | 2.5 m | 2−4 m | Dense shrub with stiff foliage. Useful as barrier when grouped |
| *Grevillea juniperina* | Medium shrub | Rounded | 2−4 m | 2−4 m | Bushy shrub with spiky foliage |
| *Grevillea rosmarinifolia* | Low shrub | Spreading | 1 m | 1−2 m | Dense spreading shrub. Useful for low screen or hedge |
| *Hakea nitida* | Medium shrub | Rounded | 1−3 m | 2−3 m | Similar stiff foliage to that of *Hakea sericea*, thus a useful barrier |
| *Hakea sericea* | Large shrub | Rounded | 2−4 m | 1−3 m | Has stiff, spiky, needle-like leaves. Useful to control pedestrian movement |
| *Lambertia formosa* | Large shrub | Rounded | 2−3 m | 2−3 m | Shrub with serrated leaves and low, dense branching system. Useful pedestrian barrier |
| *Leptospermum scoparium* | Low shrub | Spreading | 1 m | 2−4 m | Bushy tea tree with stiff foliage, graceful habit and pink tea tree flowers |
| *Leptospermum squarrosum* | Medium shrub | Spreading | 1−2 m | 2−4 m | Useful dense shrub with stiff foliage and profuse flowers |
| *Westringia fruiticosa* | Medium shrub | Rounded | 2−3 m | 2−3 m | Useful as hedge, screen or groundcover on a large scale. Hardy foliage |
| *Woollsia pungens* | Low shrub | Spreading | 1−2 m | 1−2 m | Stiff, sharp leaves. Useful as barrier when grouped |

barrier to control vehicle movement. Alternatively, a panel of ground cover may be a sufficient barrier if it is wide enough.

Table 16.4 presents representative Australian plants that are useful for controlling traffic.

## 16.6 ACOUSTICAL CONTROL

Plants can generate sounds and attract wildlife which contribute diversionary sounds in a landscape. They can also provide an extra dimension as a result of wind moving through foliage or the rustle of fallen leaves on the ground. For example, wind may play through the long, pendulous, needle-like foliage of the *Casuarina* sp. producing a whistling noise. A further asset of this species is the sound created by crunching needles underfoot.

Alternatively, many Australian plants, such as *Anigozanthos* sp. and *Banksia serrata* (Plates 16.10 and 16.11), attract animals and birds which contribute diversionary sounds. Birds' singing can both enhance a space and assist in masking unpleasant noises.

Table 16.5 gives a listing of representative plants that encourages birdlife as a technique to ameliorate undesirable sound.

TABLE 16.5
**Acoustical control: representative Australian plants that attract birds (diversionary sound producers)**

| Species | Habit (size) | Form | Height | Spread | Landscape function, potential and uses |
|---------|--------------|------|--------|--------|----------------------------------------|
| *Acacia myrtifolia* | Medium shrub | Rounded | 1–3 m | 2–3 m | Profuse cream-yellow flower heads attract wildlife |
| *Anigozanthos flavidus* | Low shrub | Spreading | 1–1.5 m | 1 m | Tall kangaroo paw-like flowers of several colours attract birds |
| *Banksia serrata* | Medium shrub | Twisted | 2–4 m | 2–3 m | Blue-grey flower heads useful for attracting birds |
| *Epacris longifolia* | Low shrub | Rounded | 2 m | 2 m | Attractive red and white flowers for most of the year |
| *Eucalyptus sideroxylon* | Medium tree | Horizontal | 10–20 m | 5–10 m | Attracts birds with the honey present in the pink flowers |
| *Grevillea guadichaudii* | Groundcover | Spreading | 1 m | 1 m | Has red foliage and bristle-like flowers that attract birds |
| *Melaleuca hypericifolia* | Large shrub | Rounded | 2–4 m | 2–3 m | Red, brittle branches and coppery leaves attract birds |
| *Telopea speciosissima* | Large shrub | Rounded | 2–3 m | 1–2 m | The huge red flowers attract birds |

PLATE 16.11 **The outstanding flower heads of the** *Banksia serrata* **attract birdlife.** *(George Foster)*
PLATE 16.12 **The unique trunk forms and vertical leaves of eucalypts cast a mottled shade pattern.** *(James Mitchell)*

PLATE 16.13 **The pendulous needles of** *Casuarina cunninghamiana* **cast a soft tracery.** *(James Mitchell)*

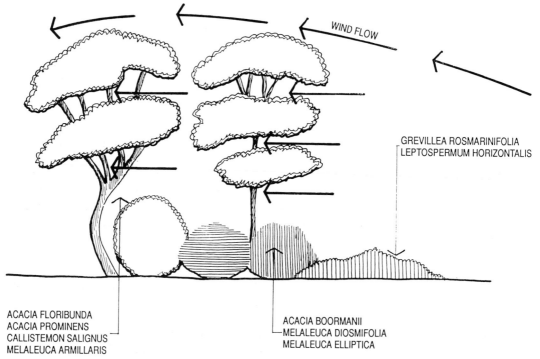

WIND FLOW

GREVILLEA ROSMARINIFOLIA
LEPTOSPERMUM HORIZONTALIS

ACACIA FLORIBUNDA
ACACIA PROMINENS
CALLISTEMON SALIGNUS
MELALEUCA ARMILLARIS

ACACIA BOORMANII
MELALEUCA DIOSMIFOLIA
MELALEUCA ELLIPTICA

FIGURE 16.3 **An effective windbreak using Australian plants that filter the wind, reducing its velocity without creating turbulence.**

TABLE 16.6
**Windbreaks: representative Australian plants**

| Species | Habit (size) | Form | Height | Spread | Landscape function, potential and uses |
|---|---|---|---|---|---|
| Acacia boormanii | Large shrub | Rounded | 3–5 m | 2–5 m | Low branching. Useful for windbreak |
| Acacia floribunda | Small tree | Rounded | 6–8 m | 4–6 m | Refer to Table 16.1. Provides filtered cover from ground level |
| Acacia saligna | Small tree | Rounded | 3–10 m | 3–6 m | Hardy wattle with low branching system |
| Acacia prominens | Medium tree | Horizontal | 5–20 m | 4–15 m | Dense tall shrub to medium tree. Useful for protection of slower growing plants |
| Callistemon salignus | Small tree | Rounded | 5–15 m | 3–5 m | Weeping branch habit. Useful when grouped |
| Casuarina glauca | Medium tree | Pyramidal | 8–20 m | 4–12 m | Refer to Table 16.1. Most effective for windbreaks when grouped |
| Grevillea rosmarinifolia | Low shrub | Rounded | 2–3 m | 2–4 m | Refer to Table 16.4. Useful bushy shrub |
| Leptospermum horizontalis | Low shrub | Spreading | 1 m | 2–4 m | Mat-forming groundcover. Useful when mass planted |
| Melaleuca armillaris | Small tree | Rounded | 4–8 m | 3–6 m | Refer to Table 16.1. Low branching habit, good for windbreaks |
| Melaleuca diosmifolia | Medium shrub | Rounded | 2–4 m | 2–4 m | Mat-forming shrub. Useful dense cover close to ground level |
| Melaleuca elliptica | Large shrub | Rounded | 3–5 m | 2–5 m | Refer to Table 16.2. Useful as windbreak when planted on a large scale |
| Pittosporum undulatum | Small tree | Rounded | 4–10 m | 2–6 m | Bushy tree with low branching habit providing dense cover from ground level |

## 16.7 WINDBREAKS

Plants can pay an important part in design for wind protection. They may be used by themselves or in association with landforms and architectural elements as a windbreak. Windbreaks have a marked effect on both the temperature within the landscape and around or through a building.

The most effective windbreak is one which filters the wind, reducing its velocity, rather than one which obstructs it completely. A dense barrier creates turbulence on both sides of it, thus failing achieve its objective of producing calm. If a windbreak is half solid and half void, it provides shelter from the wind on both sides. As is illustrated in Figure 16.3, the wind is filtered, thus reducing its velocity without creating unwanted turbulence.

For plants to be of maximum benefit in controlling wind, they should be quick-growing and able to tolerate the effects of strong winds. A large number of Australian species have these characteristics. Table 16.6 gives a representative sample of Australian plants that are suitable for windbreaks.

## 16.8 SHADE

Plants also contribute to the shading of a space reducing air temperature and improving man's microclimate. The most desirable plants to use are those that provide summer shade but also allow sunlight to pass through in winter. This benefit is usually associated with deciduous trees.

Most Australian plants are evergreen. Therefore species chosen to provide shade need to be positioned

329

TABLE 16.7
**Shading: representative Australian plants**

| Species | Habit | Form | Height | Spread | Landscape function, potential and uses |
|---------|-------|------|--------|--------|----------------------------------------|
| *Acacia baileyana* | Small tree | Rounded | 5–10 m | 4–6 m | Weeping branches and feathery foliage cast a light-filtered pattern on the ground |
| *Angophora costata* | Large tree | Twisted | 15–30 m | 8–15 m | The twisted limbs and vertical foliage cast a motley shade pattern |
| *Araucaria heterophylla* | Tall tree | Pyramidal | 25 m | 15 m | Straight trunk with almost horizontal branches cast a symmetrical pattern |
| *Banksia integrifolia* | Medium tree | Twisted | 10–20 m | 5–10 m | The twisted knarled trunk, serrated leaves and spectacular flowers cast a diverse contorted pattern |
| *Casuarina stricta* | Medium tree | Pyramidal | 8–20 m | 5–10 m | Spidery pendulous needles cast a filtered shadow |
| *Eucalyptus gummifera* | Large tree | Horizontal | 10–25 m | 5–15 m | Knarled branches and lustrous vertical foliage cast a motley pattern |
| *Eucalyptus microcorys* | Large tree | Rounded | 10–25 m | 5–20 m | Low branches and compact foliage cast a dense shade pattern |
| *Grevillea robusta* | Medium tree | Pyramidal | 10–25 m | 6–15 m | Pendulous divided leaves cast a wispy pattern |
| *Melaleuca elliptica* | Small tree | Open | 6–10 m | 4–6 m | Needle leaves cast a spiky shade pattern on the ground |

well and be of a form that allows winter sun to penetrate through the foliage. Some large Australian trees can contribute to a landscape in this way.

There are many higher branching eucalypts that allow sunlight to pass through their foliage. Eucalypts also have the asset of unique trunk forms and vertical leaves that cast mottled shade patterns. Often a mottled effect gives the ground much greater interest than the dense shade from more compact trees. Specific examples are *Eucalyptus scoparia* and *Eucalyptus citriodora*. (See Plate 16.12.)

Furthermore, the open and graceful habit of *Angophora costata* casts a unique shade pattern. The twisted limbs and vertically hanging leaves create quite a contorted pattern on the ground.

A third possible effect, as shown in Plate 16.13, is the pendulous foliage of *Casuarina* sp., which casts a soft, needle-like tracery. Table 16.7 lists species that will give shade in varying degrees and also cast interesting shade patterns.

## FURTHER READING

Beadle, N. C. W., Evans, O. D. and Carolin, R. C. *Flora of the Sydney Region* (Sydney: A. H. and A. W. Reed Pty Ltd 1972)

Child, J. *Trees of the Sydney Region* (Melbourne: F. W. Cheshire Publishing Pty Ltd and Lansdowne Press Pty Ltd 1968)

Child, J. *Wild flowers of the Sydney Region* (Melbourne: F. W. Cheshire Publishing Pty Ltd and Lansdowne Press Pty Ltd 1968)

Elliot, Gwen *The Gardener's Guide to Australian Plants* (Melbourne: Hyland House Publishing Pty Ltd 1985)

Elliot, R. 'It's more than visual', *Landscape Australia*, **1**, 31–3 (1980)

Lodder, M., Groves, R. H. and Wittmark B. 'Native grasses – the missing link in Australian landscape design', *Landscape Australia* **1**, 12–19 (1986)

Macoboy, S. *What Flower is That?* (Sydney: Paul Hamlyn Pty Limited 1980)

Maloney, Betty and Walker, Jean *Designing Australian Bush Gardens* (Sydney: Horwitz Publications Pty Ltd 1967)

Masters, Margaret *Landscaping for Australian Gardeners* (Sydney: Rigby Limited 1977)

Millet, M. *Australian Eucalypts* (Melbourne: Lansdowne Press 1969)

Oakman, H. *Garden and Landscape Trees in Australia* (Sydney: Rigby Limited 1979)

Robinette, G. O. *Plants, People and Environmental Quality* (Washington, DC: US Department of the Interior, National Park Service 1972)

Spooner, P. *Practical Guide to Home Landscaping* (Sydney: The Readers Digest Association Pty Ltd 1973)

Wilson, G. *Landscaping with Australian Plants* (Melbourne: Thomas Nelson (Australia) Limited 1975)

Wilson, G. 'Towards an Australian style of landscape design', *Landscape Australia* **1**, 39–42 (1979)

Wilson, G. 'Planting design using Australian species', *Landscape Australia* **1**, 30–2 (1983)

Wilson, G. 'Trees with clean trunks', *Landscape Australia* **2**, 150–51 (1983)

Wilson, G. 'Small trees that will stay small'. *Landscape Australia* **3**, 193–5 (1983)

Wilson, G. 'Trees in close stands and with multi-trunks', *Landscape Australia* **4**, 319–20 (1983)

Wilson, G. 'Towards more natural looking planting', *Landscape Australia* **1**, 57–8 (1984)

Wilson, G. 'Making pictures with flowers', *Landscape Australia* **2**, 119–21 (1984)

Wilson, G. 'Using clumping plants', *Landscape Australia* **4**, 310–11. (1984)

'The Work of Gordon Ford', *Landscape Australia* **2**, 79–84 (1979)

# CHAPTER 17

# Landscape Management and the Fourth Design Dimension

## RALPH COBHAM

## 17.1 INTRODUCTION

'To manage or not to manage?', that is not the question. Rather it is 'How and how much to manage plants?' This applies especially when plants are required to satisfy not one but a whole range of human needs, such as functional, commercial, cultural, aesthetic and spiritual requirements.

Like all living things which we value, plants when grown both as individual specimens and, particularly, in communities, require time in which to display their many virtues. Happily maturity cannot be designed or commanded at an instant. It comes with time, and only then if the plants have received the right type of treatment, which can range from intensive care to conscious neglect.

Of all the dimensions with which the landscape designer has to contend, time – the fourth dimension – invariably poses the greatest problems. Achievement of the visual effects ultimately desired is dependent upon so many factors which are beyond the designer's complete control at either the drawing board or initial contract stages of a landscape scheme.

The greatest ally of the landscape designer in confronting the challenge of time should invariably be the landscape manager, for it is the manager who is responsible for nurturing and looking after a design through its various phases of initial establishment, adolescence, maturity and regeneration or replacement. However, time does not stand still for the landscape management profession. Much has been learnt and written about this relatively new subject in the ten years since the first edition of this book was published. Thus, while this chapter retains essentially the same structure as before, it refers as much as possible to recent experience and published material.

It is rewarding to reflect on some of the main advances which have been made since the first edition was published. These include:

(i) The preparation of a National Conservation Strategy, to which the Government has pledged commitment and resources.

(ii) The advances made by Professor Tony Bradshaw and other researchers in identifying more appropriate techniques for establishing vegetation on alien substrates.

(iii) The introduction of the Wildlife and Countryside Act, which, despite a number of limitations, has led to significant changes in the attitudes of many different sectors of society towards the conservation of important historic, wildlife and visual features.

(iv) The restoration and associated management of several prestigious historic landscapes, including Painshill, Cadlands, Blenheim and Sutton Place.

(v) The impact made by NGOs and other organizations in restoring, conserving and managing urban, urban fringe and rural landscapes, especially the National Trust, The Farming, and Wildlife Advisory Group, the Groundwork Trust, The British Trust for Conservation Volunteers and The Manpower Services Commission, to mention a few.

(vi) The influence of CPRE in gaining greater public recognition for the importance of national conservation works.

(vii) The enlightened approach by several New Town and City authorities in commissioning consultants to prepare vegetation management strategies and plans in Britain and overseas (Hong Kong, The Middle East and USA).

(viii) The work of the DoE, Countryside Commission and Nature Conservancy Council in promoting the multiple use of land, especially through such recent initiatives as the establishment of Environmentally Sensitive Agricultural Areas. These are being administered by the Ministry of Agriculture, Fisheries and Food, in order to assist farmers to conserve particularly sensitive wildlife, historic and visual features by farming in less intensive ways.

(ix) The greater recognition by major nationalized industries and institutions of their responsibilities for the management of the land under their care, for instance by British Gas. British Rail is another notable example, having commissioned the preparation of a vegetation management manual covering the national rail network.

(x) The growing activities of the British Association of Landscape Industries in improving the standards of landscape design and plant care.

(xi) The pioneering work undertaken by Professor Chris Baines to promote a style of naturalistic gardening and public open space management.

(xii) The advances in technology made by the companies which manufacture herbicides, formulate growth regulating cocktails and design precision machinery.

(xiii) The writings of Tom Wright, John Parker, Alan Ruff, Peter Thoday and Richard Bisgrove.

(xiv) The establishment of Landscape Management courses at the Universities of Reading and Manchester.

The 'litany' is long and not without lustre.

It is significant that the preceding chapters all make reference, if not specifically at least by implication, to the importance of considering management and maintenance when designing and implementing landscape schemes. This is just as it should be. Without the involvement and sensitive support of these two activities, the efforts and money expended in the initial design and implementation work may not come to fruition. It is with the help of management and maintenance skills that the evolution of the physical and aesthetic effects intended by the designer and desired by the client can be achieved. These skills need to be applied as much in the broad rural landscape as in the intimate scale of a new town or refurbished housing estate.

The examples of landscape management and maintenance mentioned in this chapter are almost exclusively from British projects. However, experience has shown that the principles described are relevant for readers throughout other regions of the world.

In financial terms, management and maintenance usually involve relatively small annual outlays when compared with the capital expended at the outset, this annual figure amounting to between 5 per cent and 15 per cent of the initial cost. Such a seemingly insignificant figure may explain why in the past the two activities have either been overlooked or received inadequate attention. Yet when reviewed over the lifetime of a changed landscape, the annual management and maintenance costs will probably far exceed those of the initial works.

The broad components of a landscape design or plan vary widely in terms of capital and annual costs. Water bodies, while being expensive to install, generally require relatively little annual maintenance (£50–£220 per hectare). This compares favourably with average annual upkeep figures for areas of established amenity woodland and grazed parkland (£600 per hectare), urban recreation and sports grounds (£1620 per hectare) and highly manicured urban scenery such as municipal gardens (over £30 000 per hectare). In the case of some of the more prestigious schemes, the cumulative annual costs may soon outweigh the capital outlay.

Thus the design process calls not only for artistry in balancing physical and aesthetic considerations, but also in matching financial requirements and resources over the lifetime of the landscape scheme.

## 17.2 PROFESSIONAL ROLES

The approach to landscape management has advanced somewhat since the report of the Landscape Management Discussion Group, which was set up in 1973 to advise the ILA on the possible future role of the landscape manager in relation to the whole landscape profession.[1] In February 1987 a Landscape Management Discussion Forum was convened by the University of Manchester, at which a number of different views were expressed on the subject. One of these highlighted the essential diversity of landscape managers. This is a characteristic which needs to be retained. At the same time strenuous efforts are required to resist any attempts made to regiment the profession. One of the contributors to the Discussion Forum described the profession as follows:

'Landscape management is a hybrid profession or discipline. Members of the profession, both academics and practitioners alike, are involved in undertaking a multiplicity of tasks which draw upon a wide range of knowledge from both the sciences and the arts.'

Essentially, the hybrid profession has two parents. First, there is that body of knowledge and skills, drawn from the plant, land and other sciences, together with the arts, which are required to conserve, generate and perpetuate 'fine' landscapes. The second parent is, in essence, provided by those elements of the sciences and arts of business management which can beneficially be used in conserving, generating and perpetuating fine landscapes. Management is a discipline in its own right.

It is changing fast as the objectives of management and the subjects for study evolve. A wide range of management interests is involved, including business, corporate finance, personnel, planning, operation, organization, resources and many others. The skills required by a competent manager are growing. Increasingly, numeracy – aided by computing facilities – and psychology are required. Casework, as in medicine and law, also plays an important part.

These two parents, insofar as they affect or influence the nature of the profession, share a common focus, namely the wise functional, effective and often multipurpose use of land and associated resources.

Unless landscape management is firmly rooted in the functional aspects of land use, it can have little validity.

Progeny from the union of landscape and management skills can vary substantially, as is indicated in Table 17.1. One of the primary tasks of those responsible for training landscape managers is to determine the needs and demands of the market place for the different types of training which could and should be provided.

Official definitions of landscape management, which embraces, but is distinct from, 'landscape maintenance', have been available for several years. A definition of landscape management from the Landscape Institute (1983) in the *Register of Landscape Practices* is given below, followed by an older definition of landscape maintenance.

'*Landscape management* is the profession of landscape managers, who use their detailed understanding of plants and the natural environment to advise on the long-term care and development of the changing landscape. This involves them in the financial and physical organization of manpower, machinery and materials. Landscape management also involves consideration of statutory measures, such as planning lease and grant aid schemes, in order to preserve and enhance the quality of the landscape. The practitioners of the profession usually have a degree in horticulture, forestry or agriculture with further training in land management or other related disciplines.'

'*Landscape Maintenance* concerns the routine care of land, vegetation and hard surfaces in the manner prescribed for their satisfactory establishment and continued future performance.'

Such definitions provide no more than partial glimpses of reality. However, if recognized as such, they have their uses particularly as bench marks for students and other professions.

Through experience it has become clear that these definitions are inadequate, because they fail to describe the lineage of the hybrid and both the vigour and tensions which it can generate. Furthermore, just as the society and the landscapes which the profession seeks to serve change, so too does the profession itself. Both the parents are changing all the time, as is the nature of their relationship.

First and foremost, the professional landscape manager has a responsibility to the landscape itself. This responsibility is founded upon a fundamental understanding of two subjects:

1. The functions which the land and its associated resources that comprise the landscape are required to fulfil, including the procurement of food, timber, fish, fur, minerals and so on, the pursuit of leisure, the development of property for commercial and/or aesthetic gain and the conservation of visual, wildlife, historic and cultural features.

2. The ways in which these functions and resources themselves are changing. Over the last ten years substantial changes have been taking place in the forces that influence both rural and urban land uses and thus that influence landscape management.

The changes in the job of the landscape manager that are of particular note include the following:

(i) maximum food production policies have been replaced with the result that increasing importance is accorded to conservation;

(ii) forestry is in the ascendency;

(iii) major development projects, such as Kielder Reservoir, Stansted Airport, Severn Barrage and Channel Tunnel, have been and are being encouraged;

TABLE 17.1
**The hybrid nature of the 'landscape management' profession**

| Parent disciplines | Management Sciences and Arts | |
| | M | m |
| --- | --- | --- |
| | *Hybrids* | |
| Landscape Sciences and Arts | | |
| L | LM | Lm |
| l | lM | lm |

*Key* L = A profession in which great emphasis is placed upon the Landscape Sciences and Arts
l = A profession in which less emphasis than at present is placed upon the Landscape Sciences and Arts
M = A profession in which great emphasis is placed upon the application of Management Sciences and Arts
m = A profession in which little emphasis is placed upon the application of Management Sciences and Arts (although the maintenance skills may be well developed)

(iv) urban regeneration has recently captured the imagination of politicians and the religious and secular communities and institutions alike;

(v) tourism and leisure investment is increasingly associated with job creation;

(vi) garden festivals have become established as periodic, but sadly transitory, features of the British scene;

(vii) policies of privatization and the disposal of local authority land banks are being pursued.

Because longevity is a characteristic of many of the basic resources, the 'fourth dimension' is an aspect of management which demands both careful and continual attention by the profession.

The profession requires many different types of managers to fulfil the wide range of tasks in managing both large- and small-scale landscapes. These include:

(i) the formulation of policy, legislation and broad-scale planning;

(ii) the execution of design roles in rural situations;

(iii) all manner of practical tasks associated with the establishment and maintenance of landscapes through management of contractors, direct labour and/or volunteers;

(iv) the provision of popular leisure and recreation facilities, through the management of both visitors and the features themselves;

(v) procurement and deployment of the resources required for effective single or multi-purpose use of a landscape.

In undertaking these tasks, managers need to make a clear distinction between the large- and small-scale landscapes.

The profession, in short, is an important and essential part of the service sector of the national economy. There is no field of landscape work in which management activities do not play an essential part.

For landscape design to succeed it is essential that a number of professions should work together as a team. The activities of the landscape designer, the earth and social scientists, the landscape manager and the maintenance officer need to be closely related until landscape schemes are well on the way to maturity. One of the many benefits which has arisen from the burgeoning role of the Landscape Institute, through the involvement of landscape scientists and managers, is the greater scope for achieving better solutions to the landscaping problems of our changing society.

The remainder of this chapter is devoted to describing:

(i) the different skills which are required for the landscape management profession to be effective;

(ii) some of the ways in which the profession can help the designer;

(iii) a few of the many unresolved problems faced by members of the landscape profession collectively.

## 17.3 PROFESSIONAL SKILLS AND STRUCTURE

In the 1974 report of the Landscape Management Discussion Group, landscape management was described as a many-faceted profession, founded on various disciplines including horticulture, agriculture, ecology, estate management, design, surveying, planning, economics, sociology and administration. In short, a 'vascular bundle' of skills. It was stressed that to be successful, those practising landscape management should have considerable knowledge in at least one of the above disciplines, together with a sound appreciation of many more – particularly ecology. The landscape management profession is the concern of *three* groups of experienced people: the landscape clerk of works, the maintenance officer and the manager.

The main responsibility of the *landscape clerk of works* is for the correct short-term implementation of landscape designs and management plans. This calls for careful supervision to ensure that the landscape is treated and changed in strict accordance with the standards specified. Success depends on many practical skills, in particular horticulture and construction.

The chief concern of the *maintenance officer* centres on the development of landscapes according to the plans and standards agreed for one or more years. The key activity involves assisting with the preparation of annual landscape maintenance plans, followed by taking responsibility for their execution. One of the most important skills in the execution of these plans is the ability to deploy scarce manpower, materials, machinery and financial resources between the needs of several types of landscape in such a way as to best achieve the desired objectives. The relative economics of different maintenance methods and landscape treatments call for detailed attention by the landscape maintenance officer.

The *landscape manager* has a wide ranging responsibility for helping designers, planners and the members of several other professions and their clients to achieve the objectives which are agreed to be in the best *long-term* interests of the landscape and its users. 'Thus it is to be expected that the concern of professional landscape managers for the landscape will be wider than that of most farmers, estate managers, foresters, recreation managers . . .'

Table 17.2 attempts, in a simplified form, to indicate the types and sequence of involvement which are required from these three skills in the creation and evolution of new landscapes.

## 17.4 MANAGEMENT CONTRIBUTIONS

The most important situations which call for the services of the landscape manager and maintenance officer are those where existing or potential conflicts are greatest, namely:

(i) between the land users and the landscape;
(ii) between the plants to be established and their immediate environment.

Whilst there are usually no easy answers to these problems, at least a number of options frequently exist for their solution. The first type of conflict occurs in at least three forms, brief descriptions of which follow with examples.

## Changed land uses in the existing landscape

The major conflicts tend to occur where a radical change of use is proposed for a traditional and relatively undisturbed landscape. This is the case where new

TABLE 17.2
**Structure of the professional team during different phases of a large landscape scheme***

| | Site Appraisal & Resource Surveys | Initial Feasibility Study | Planning & Design Sketch Detailed | Preparation of Specification and B.o.Q. | Tendering | Contract | Establishment Maintenance Monitoring Regeneration |
|---|---|---|---|---|---|---|---|
| Land and social scientists | | | | | | | |
| Landscape Planner | | | | | | | |
| Economist | | | | | | | |
| Landscape Architect | | | | | | | |
| Engineer | | | | | | | |
| Quantity Surveyor | | | | | | | |
| Landscape Manager | | | | | | | |
| Landscape Maintenance Officer | | | | | | | |
| Landscape Clerk of Works | | | | | | | |

Approximate Relative Time Scale ←——————— 2–10 years ———————→ ←50–500→ years

\* In practice the structure is usually not so clear cut as the Table indicates.

Key:  ——————— period of close and regular involvement
      – – – – – – – period of observation and possibly occasional involvement

PLATE 17.1 **At New Ash Green the village is being constructed in an area of classic Kent countryside.** *(Ralph Cobham)*

settlements are built in the countryside.[2] Milton Keynes New Town[3,4,5] and New Ash Green 'Village'[6,7] are two such examples. The first, designated in 1967 and despite the most carefully laid plans, has had a considerable impact on the surrounding farmland. At New Ash Green the village has been constructed in an area of classic Kent countryside, consisting of chalk predominantly overlain by clay-with-flints and thin layers of sand or brickearth. Its vegetation is a mixture of semi-mature deciduous woodland, including neglected hazel coppice, herb-rich permanent pasture and arable land. All of this, despite the best intentions and plans of the parties involved, is vulnerable to an influx of primarily urban residents. Local participation in the upkeep of both the internal village areas and the surrounding landscapes is often the key to integration in such situations. At New Ash Green this has been fostered by a far-sighted group of residents, with the support of the progressive developer, the local authority, and the help of a number of management plans which identified the objectives, resources and operations required.

## Conflicts through increases in existing land uses

There are many areas of the countryside where recreational pressures, aggravated by weathering, have increased to such an extent that they threaten the very resources to which the visitors are attracted. Amongst the best known examples are the sites which were chosen by the Countryside Commission for conducting Experimental Restoration Projects, namely, Tarn Hows,[8] Kynance Cove, Box Hill, Snowdonia[9] and Ilkley Moor.[10] The landscape manager has much to contribute in such places, where the pressures of cars and feet, together with the accumulation of litter, combine to cause physical and visual deterioration on an unprecedented scale. The type of help which can be provided includes:

(i) identifying the areas which are most vulnerable to use by visitors, and conversely those which are resilient;

(ii) advising on the alternative strategies for solving the problems, ranging from the dispersal of visitors and their cars over a wider area, to their concentration in carefully selected sites equipped with litter collection and toilet facilities. By establishing a well-marked network of footpaths, and alternative transport systems, such as guided minibus and cycle services radiating from the chosen sites, the visitor pressures on the surrounding countryside can be contained;

(iii) specifying the restoration techniques which are likely to be most successful along footpaths, in car parks and in picnic areas;

337

PLATE 17.2 **Woodland fringes are vulnerable to pressures from the new residents, many of whom have come from urban areas.**

(iv) setting up the most effective system for managing and monitoring the areas, both during and after restoration. Such systems may involve at least one or more of the following: the establishment of a Management Committee, the appointment of Countryside Wardens, the use of local volunteers on a countywide scale, such as the County Durham Countryside Rangers, and the preparation of management and access agreements.

## Conflicts arising through the numbers of users and incompatible activities

Increasingly, situations are reported where there is competition between different interest groups for the same piece of land or the same resource. Conflicts are commonplace between:

(i) the ardent conservationists and those seeking recreation, particularly the flower pickers (including the amateur botanist!);
(ii) casual walkers and horse riders;
(iii) anglers and birdwatchers, on all but large water areas;
(iv) water skiers and other water-based sportsmen.

Methods of management, such as the spatial zoning or the rationing or rotation of uses, can help in some situations. Similarly, charging a fee for the use of

facilities can be a moderating influence. Nevertheless, it has to be recognized that there are some uses which are totally incompatible as far as the respective parties are concerned.

## Plant–environment conflicts

These conflicts are among those most commonly faced by landscape managers and maintenance officers. Climate and site conditions, particularly in exposed coastal situations (as at Teesmouth), often militate against the establishment and development of a successful vegetation cover. Experience, both in N.E. England and on the Dutch coast, has shown that the effects of an adverse climate – particularly prolonged drought in spring, due to a combination of low rainfall and persistently strong winds – can to a large extent be mitigated. The adoption of carefully conceived management and after-care operations ranks high in achieving success, along with important and closely related design features, such as:

(i) the wise choice of locally indigenous nurse and quick cover plant species;
(ii) the use of small stock, densely planted in large areas, which following selective thinning can be interplanted with long-lived species;
(iii) the use of protective ground contouring;

PLATE 17.3 & 17.4 **Wooden stakes prevent cars from driving all over The Plain at Shotover Country Park near Oxford, but the scars from previous misuse take several years to heal.** *(Dr D Steel)*

FIGURE 17.1 **'Hey, where's the ref?'** . . .**'The landscape manager don't you mean?'.** *(Brian Iley)*

(iv) the execution of planting operations earlier rather than later in the planting season.

Whilst the techniques of establishing and maintaining vegetation on reclaimed sites are well documented, success is by no means automatic. New problems continually arise. One example is that which was encountered on the site designated for the creation of a beach park on the coast of Irvine New Town in Scotland.[11,12] There, a diverse and interesting but vulnerable flora, including viper's bugloss (*Echium vulgare*), dwarf willow (*Salix repens*), sheep's bit (*Jasione montana*), wild thyme (*Thymus serpyllum*) and white flax (*Linum cartharticum*) colonized the site, the greater part of which was used for the tipping of chemical factory waste for many years. Whilst the vegetation was undoubtedly of educational value and a recreational asset in the area, it was not robust enough to withstand the public pressures normally associated with a beach park. The management task was to reconcile the desire to retain as much floristic interest as possible, both during and following the reclamation process, with the required function of the area. It was recognized that ultimately the vegetation might become increasingly difficult to maintain on account of public pressure and a gradual build-up of soil nutrients.

## The re-establishment of semi-natural habitats

Since the Second World War all categories of the country's rich and highly valued semi-natural wildlife habitats have been under increasing development pressure from a number of activities such as the reclamation for industrial use and the provision of drainage for more productive agriculture. Those categories subjected to greatest attack have been the estuarine (e.g. Teesmouth[13] and Merseyside), coastal and inland freshwater habitats. In the circumstances, it is natural that landscape managers should be involved in assisting other professions, notably ecologists and naturalists, to devise conservation and management measures which are most appropriate for the residual habitat areas. Their contribution is also important when opportunities arise for creating conditions in new locations suitable for re-establishing as closely as possible the habitats which are under threat or have already been lost. For many complex reasons, complete simulation is usually not possible. It is often for these very same reasons that the establishment and subsequent management of such areas undoubtedly present the greatest challenge to the professional skills of all the parties involved.

PLATE 17.5 **A woodland character and some feeling of maturity can develop within twenty years.** *(Richard Cass)*

PLATE 17.6 **The dune re-establishment trials undertaken at Irvine. (See also Plates 17.7 and 17.8.)** *(Ralph Cobham)*

PLATE 17.7 **The use of brushwood and chestnut paling fences to trap windborne sand.** *(Ralph Cobham)*

PLATE 17.8 **The planting of sea lyme and marram grass setts to stabilize accumulated sand.** *(Ralph Cobham)*

PLATE 17.9 **Way markers on a public footpath.** *(Ralph Cobham)*

PLATE 17.10 **Information board describing recreational facilities around the Suffolk Heritage Coast.** *(Kris Baker CRC)*

PLATE 17.11 **Experimental work undertaken by the National Trust at Tarn Hows to restore worn footpaths, using a single strand of nylon string.** *(Ralph Cobham)*

A challenge of this type also existed at Irvine, which although in certain respects not unprecedented, was probably unique in degree. A substantial area of sand dunes had been lost due to over-greedy sand-winning operations, further aggravated by strong onshore winds. As a result the public authority faced a problem of trying to re-establish a dune system within a time-scale which precluded sole reliance on probably the cheapest and in the long term most effective method, namely the man-aided process of sand accumulation using chestnut paling fences followed by the planting of sea lyme and marram grass setts. It unfortunately proved necessary to by-pass the semi-natural and inevitably slow processes and instead to fix appropriately graded and uncontaminated sand transported from inland areas of the site. As with many such problems, it became necessary to undertake on-site trials to evaluate which of the possible overall solutions and detailed establishment prescriptions were most likely to be most successful, before proceeding with the full scale operation. The trials at Irvine proved helpful in directing attention to the type of compromise solution which was most likely to succeed. This is a typical example of a situation where the land scientist, landscape architect and manager can benefit from close co-operation.

## 17.5 SOME MANAGEMENT AIDS

The range of 'tools' at the disposal of the landscape manager and maintenance officer for coming to terms with these and other problems is continually being increased. They fall broadly into four categories.

## Technical aids

There are growing numbers of agricultural, forestry and horticultural aids, such as slow release fertilizers, selective herbicides and precision machinery, which make many maintenance operations much simpler than has previously been the case. As the number of landscaped areas grows and the shortages of skilled men persist, such aids have an increasingly important role to play, just so long as they are used judiciously.

These aids are usually regarded as options which, in the case of grass management for instance, include cutting by machine or by hand, grazing, wearing by feet, using an infertile substrate both to minimize growth and to assist the diversity of species, applying herbicides, seeding with dwarf and prostrate growing species and controlling nutrient levels. One of the main tasks of the landscape manager is to select the most cost-

344

TABLE 17.3
**Plants as management aids**
Some of the main species best suited for either individual or mixed use as barriers which are difficult to penetrate

| | *Deciduous* (D) *or evergreen* (E) | *Appropriate for rural* (R) &/or *urban* (U) *Sites* | *Best time for trimming* | *General comments* |
|---|---|---|---|---|
| *Berberis darwinii* | E | U | May/June | Prickly. Normally used in semi-formal situations. |
| *Berberis stenophylla* | E | U | | |
| *Carpinus betulus* | D | R & U | July/Sept | Does well on heavier soils and withstands shade. |
| *Corylus avellana* | D | R & U | Sept/Oct | Good for chalk and dry situations. |
| *Crataegus monogyna* | D | R & U | Late summer | Prickly. Grows well in most soils and situations. Suitable for windy conditions. |
| *Crataegus oxyacantha* | D | R & U | | |
| *Fagus sylvatica* | D | R & U | Mid-summer | Does best on soils with pH higher than neutral. Suitable for windy conditions. |
| *Hippophae rhamnoides* | D | R & U | After flowering | Prickly. Salt tolerant. Think twice before planting because of its very vigorous growth. |
| *Ilex aquifolium* | E | R & U | Late summer | Prickly. Can be slow to establish, but succeeds better than many species in shade. |
| *Ligustrum ovalifolium* | E | U primarily | Sept | Quick growing and withstands pollution |
| *Lonicera nitida* | E | U primarily | Sept | Quick growing. Normally used in formal situations. |
| *Mahonia aquifolium* | E | U primarily | After flowering | Prickly points to the leaves. Normally used in informal situations. |
| *Prunus cerasifera* | D | R & U | July | Slightly thorny. Grows quickly. |
| *Prunus spinosa* | D | R & U | Late summer | Prickly. Particularly suitable for coastal and windy conditions. |
| *Pseudosasa japonica* | E | U | Early spring if required | Prone to damage by firing. |
| *Pyracantha angustifolia* | E | U primarily | May/July | Prickly and very hardy. |
| *Rosa canina* | D | R | After fruiting | Prickly. |
| *Rosa rugosa* | D | R & U | | Prickly. In urban areas used informally. |
| *Rubus fruticosa* | D | R | After fruiting | Prickly and vigorous. |
| *Sambucus nigra* | D | R & U | Early spring | Grows very quickly. Suitable for windy conditions. |
| *Taxus baccata* | E | R & U | Aug/Sept | Tolerates shade. |
| *Ulex europaeus* | E | R | After flowering | Prickly. Suitable for coastal and windy conditions, also for dry sandy soils. Prone to damage by firing. |

effective option for the particular site or circumstances concerned.

## Recreation management aids

The provision of facilities such as country parks, interpretive centres, nature trails and long distance walks enable large numbers of people to be attracted into areas specially designed and managed for their enjoyment. As a result, other places less able to withstand public pressure come to be both better respected and protected. Carefully designed and appropriately located waymarks and explanatory notice boards are essential in helping people to enjoy popular parts of the countryside in ways which are in the long-term interests of all parties. With such aids, worn footpaths and grassy areas can be rested, often using nothing more elaborate than a single strand of nylon string. Excellent examples of this type of management include the National Trust's work at Tarn Hows in the Lake District and that of Hampshire Country Council at Danebury Hill Fort.

Use of these and other aids is particularly helpful to the landscape manager where an area of land is required to accommodate multi-purpose activities, such as farming, forestry, recreation, sport and conservation. Grizedale Forest, the Beaulieu and Goodwood estates and the Kennermerduinen[14] and Veluwe National Parks in Holland are amongst the places where they can be seen to good advantage.

## Plant selection and other design aids

The way in which a landscape scheme is designed at the outset can do much to influence the subsequent management task. The influence of plant selection on the subsequently required levels of management and maintenance can be profound. As is well known, there are many different species which perform well with minimal maintenance, which through vegetative propagation can cover the ground quickly, which are tolerant of modern herbicides, which respond as required to growth retardants and which do well in association with other plants, owing to their compatible growth habits and life cycles. Plants themselves provide some of the most effective aids to management. Such is the wealth of plant material available that the landscape designer and manager are often faced with the difficult task of selecting those species which are most appropriate to plant for meeting needs such as the provision of either low cost groundcover or an effective prickly barrier against people and livestock (see Table 17.3). Both the species chosen and the variation in the height to which grass is allowed to grow are further well established techniques by which managers can save costs and persuade people to walk along certain routes. The use of the ha-ha was and still is a classic example of the way in which design of simple differences in ground level can aid the management task.

However, the role of plants needs to be seen in perspective since plant management is only one of the landscape manager's tasks. The management of people and visitors, of recreation facilities, of hard surfaces and water features, of utilities and of physical and financial resources all demand attention.

## Financial aids

Finally there are many financial aids upon which management can call. The assessment of external sources of finance available for assisting the establishment and aftercare of multi-purpose use and landscaping schemes

is a main responsibility of the landscape manager. These sources include:

(i) the sizeable D.o.E. grants for reclamation sites covering the establishment phase of both grass areas (3 years, normally only in situations where less than 10 cm (4 in) of topsoil have been used) and tree planted areas (5 years, amounting to a total equal to the value of the original sum of the contract),

(ii) the Forestry Planting grants which are now weighted significantly towards amenity considerations;

(iii) the Countryside Commission grants available to assist local authorities with tree planting and landowners entering into access or management agreements;

(iv) the grants available from charitable organizations, such as the Carnegie Trust, for the establishment and management of educational and interpretative facilities;

(v) the aid given by such organizations as the Tourist Board and Sports Council;

(vi) the wide range of grants offered by the Ministry of Agriculture, Fisheries and Food (MAFF).

## 17.6 PLANS AND SCHEDULES

Clearly, the responsibilities and contributions of the landscape manager are varied and diffuse. Yet there is usually a unifying or co-ordinating element. As with the solicitor and his deeds or the accountant and his balance sheet, the landscape manager and maintenance officer are required to prepare formal documents involving disciplined thought and calculation. For any major landscaping project these documents consist of the overall management plan and its essential companion, the short-term establishment or maintenance schedule. Tables 17.4, 17.5, 17.6 and 17.7 indicate some of the main features typical of these documents, though naturally the format and contents will differ according to the particular management problems that they are concerned with.

Such documents provide a basic reference for regular use by the managers, maintenance officers and designers concerned with the continuing evolutions of new landscapes. Preparation of these documents often means enlisting the help of an amalgam of skills, including those of the ecologist, agricultural and horticultural specialists, ornithologists and so on.

The preparation of these plans, especially for large-scale landscape areas such as urban parks, can be a somewhat laborious process, especially since it needs to be iterative in the interests of identifying the most cost-effective or optimum solution. Within recent years several computer programmes have been developed to assist both the preparation and regular appraisal of the

TABLE 17.4
**Features of a management plan**
A summary of the management task for a new London borough housing development area

| The main landscape maintenance areas | Levels of Council-financed maintenance recommended/required | Assumed/ estimated components (hectares) | Dimensions (hectares) |
|---|---|---|---|
| 1. GRASS | | | |
| Very high maintenance areas | 3−7 cuts per week during the season of use | 0.15 | |
| High maintenance areas | 18 cuts per season | 2.87 | |
| Intermediate maintenance areas | 7−11 cuts per season | 8.30 | |
| Low maintenance areas | 4−6 cuts per season | 4.56 | |
| Very low maintenance areas | 1−2 cuts per season | 10.47 | |
| TOTAL: GRASS | | | 26.35 |
| 2. TOTAL: HARD SURFACES | Daily/frequent attention | 1.03 | 1.03 |
| 3. FORMAL PLANTING | | | |
| Shrub areas | Low−intermediate levels of maintenance, | 2.13 | |
| Tree areas | but high standards | 1.89 | |
| TOTAL: FORMAL PLANTING | | | 4.02 |
| 4. TOTAL: INFORMAL TREE AND SHRUB PLANTING | Initially high levels of maintenance, but low thereafter | 9.14 | 9.14 |
| 5. TOTAL: LAKE | Intermediate level | 0.42 | 0.42 |
| 6. OTHER | | | |
| Maintenance area: depot and nursery | High level | 0.18 | |
| Allotments | High level | 0.40 | |
| Hedges | Low level | 0.24 | |
| School garden: cultivation area | High level during the holidays | 0.07 | |
| TOTAL: OTHER | | | 0.89 |
| GRAND TOTAL | | | 41.85 |

plans. Likewise several useful publications have appeared, which provide clear guidelines on the preparation of plans for a variety of urban, rural and urban-fringe situations.

The management plan usually commences with a statement of general aims and objectives, followed by a description of the levels and standards of maintenance which are desired for each of the main landscape areas. It is normal for there to be a review of the possible strategies whereby the objectives can be achieved. This involves an evaluation of:

(i) which maintenance operations should best be undertaken by direct, contract or voluntary labour;
(ii) whether machinery is best purchased, hired or

obtained by engaging a contractor. A description of the reasons for the choice of the preferred strategy is normally given, coupled with a summary (as indicated in Table 17.5) of the resources which it is estimated will be required.

Both the management plan and the maintenance schedule require the close involvement of the landscape designer concerned, since it is essential that these documents should relate specifically to the visual effects which the designer wishes to evolve over a particular time period. Figure 17.2 displays two examples of the types of illustration which are essential companions to the two documents. They should be the product of discussions between designer, manager and maintenance officer.

TABLE 17.5
**Features of a management plan**
Broad use and management recommendations for some main areas at New Ash Green

| Main land areas | Use | Level of maintenance/action to be taken (H = High; M = Medium; L = Low) |
|---|---|---|
| *Existing woodland* Nine Horse Wood | Walking; riding; visual amenity; adventure areas for children; (pillaging and dumping ground for residents as development proceeds and children grow up, unless careful). | H in accessible areas, M in protected areas where coppice being converted to standards. Woodland fringes allowed to grow wild and form impenetrable barrier. During development, high level of care for trees to be retained. |
| Redhill and Bowes Woods | Buffer framework/visual screen for housing developments; walking; tree-house style play areas; picnicking by adjacent residents; (motorized litter dump for residents, unless careful). | H wherever access is free. In all woods consideration should be given to the scope for zoning and rotating active and non-use areas. Protection of newly planted areas and fringes. Access points and routes to be well defined. |
| Bazes Shaw Wood | Nature reserve and nature trail/study area for use by local naturalist society and by children attending nearby school as an outdoor laboratory. | Management based on *conservation* practices and geared to the demonstration of ecological principles of vegetational succession, etc. Work by naturalist society and school volunteers. Protection from residents moving to and from meadow essential: access points to the wood should be counter to popular demand. |
| *New woodland* Redhill and Bowes Woods | As above. | Protection until established. H in any areas which are subsequently accessible. |
| Western and Northern Belts | Windbreak; visual screen/framework for future neighbourhoods. | L, after initial three years 'beating up' and weed control. |
| *Tree, shrubs and grass buffer zones between housing areas* | Increasing demand for informal 'let-off steam' play areas. The 'thread of Kent countryside...' | L, apart from twice annual tree survey and occasional grass cutting. Once trees established, grass within the drifts might be mown 2–3 times annually. Alternatively it can be left unmown. |
| *Grassland* Cricket square | Progressively increased match use as good sward and surface becomes established. | Relatively H to provide for enjoyable village class matches. |
| Outfield/soccer playing field | Increasing use for sports as population grows and good sward is established. (PLanting of tree groups and gentle earth contouring will give sense of enclosures.) | M, apart from *high* level of care in the case of worn areas, e.g. goal mouths; rotational siting of pitches and goal areas. |

| Main land areas | Use | Level of maintenance/action to be taken (H = High; M = Medium; L = Low) |
|---|---|---|
| Outer sports ground area | Area for tree screen planting and scout camping. Fair/gymkhana/bonfire ground. | L |
| The Minnis | Increasing use as the village green once reasonable sward and a more inviting character are established. | M |
| Nine Horse Meadow | Parkland for picnicking and walking. | L, involving removal of grass mowings to increase botanical variety and interest of the sward. |
| Apple Orchard | Apple trees retained but thinned to provide an attractive picnicking/playing area for local residents. | L |
| Woodland grass fringes and rides | Walking, riding and nature study. | L, involving a twice yearly mowing of *narrow* strip alongside paths. |
| *Hedges* | Increasing importance as visual screens and physical barriers. | H where gapping up or replanting required; H where sight lines involved and adjacent to houses. Other hedges require L or M according to whether or not they are in wilderness areas. |
| *Neighbourhood units – communal space* | An increasing range of active and passive uses as the population grows and its structure diversifies. | Generally H throughout. |
| *Prestige areas such as the Manor House, car parks and shopping centre* | | Generally H throughout. |

Source: *New Ash Green Master Plan*, Brian Clouston and Partners and Clouston Cobham and Partners, 1973

TABLE 17.6
**Features of a management plan: resource requirement appraisals**

| (i) *Estimated machinery requirements* | | | |
|---|---|---|---|
| | The Village Association £ | The Residents' Societies £ | Total £ |
| **A** Joint Village Associations/Residents' Societies requirements | | | |
| Tractor, MF 20 | 2 330 | 3 500 | 5 830 |
| Trailer | 630 | 940 | 1 570 |
| Flymo | 110 | 160 | 270 |
| 2 Knapsack sprayers | 70 | 110 | 180 |
| Hand tools | 360 | 540 | 900 |
| Sub Total: | 3 500 | 5 250 | 8 750 |
| **B** Village Association requirements | | | |
| 3 unit Gang mower for playing field and village green | 2 700 | | |
| Tractor mounted rotary for cutting meadowland and large rough fringe areas | 1 350 | | |
| Rotary mower 76 cm cut for pedestrian use in cutting woodland fringes and smaller rough fringe areas | 1 550 | | |

(i) *Estimated machinery requirements*

| | | | |
|---|---|---|---|
| Set of harrows | | | |
| Roller | 900 | | |
| Foreloader and bucket attachment | 1 100 | | |
| 1 Cylinder mower, 61 cm cut for the cricket square | 800 | | |
| 2 Hedge trimmers and generator | 540 | | |
| 1 Chain saw | 350 | | |
| Agricultural rake for meadowland | 670 | | |
| Auger/post hole digger | 540 | | |
| Sub Total: | 10 500 | – | 10 500 |
| C Residents' Societies requirements | | | |
| 1 Triple Ransome mower for neighbourhoods | | 4 500 | |
| 3 Cylinder mowers, 61 cm cut | | 2 400 | |
| 1 Rough-cut cylinder mower, 51 cm cut ⎫ for smaller lawn areas | | 400 | |
| 1 Tractor mounted sprayer with hand lances ⎭ | | 900 | |
| Sub Total: | – | 8 200 | 8 200 |
| TOTAL | 14 000 | 13 450 | 27 450 |

(ii) *Estimated total annual resource requirements*

| | The Village Association | The Residents' Societies | Total |
|---|---|---|---|
| Total hectares involved | 63.2 | 19.8 | 83.0 |
| Manpower: | £ | £ | £ |
| Estates Manager | 3 500 | 5 500 | 9 000 |
| Foreman | 4 500 | 6 700 | 11 200 |
| 3 permanent staff | 9 500 | 14 500 | 24 000 |
| 6 temporary staff | 8 000 | 16 000 | 24 000 |
| Sub Total: | 25 500 | 42 700 | 68 200 |
| Machinery: | | | |
| Depreciation (20% p.a.) | 2 800 | 2 800 | 5 600 |
| Maintenance/repairs | 2 700 | 2 700 | 5 600 |
| Sub Total: | 5 500 | 5 500 | 11 000 |
| Materials: | | | |
| Fuel, fertilizers, sprays, fencing, gravel, replacements, stakes etc. | 6 700 | 11 300 | 18 000 |
| Administration/overheads | 4 500 | 4 500 | 9 000 |
| TOTALS | 42 200 | 64 000 | 106 200 |
| COST PER HECTARE | 668 | 3 232 | 1 280 |

Source: *New Ash Green Master Plan*, Brian Clouston and Partners and Clouston Cobham and Partners, updated to 1989 values

## 17.7 BASIC DATA: AVAILABILITY AND SOURCES

The general advances in both the landscaping of many derelict and neglected sites and in the planning of large land areas for multiple use inevitably entail the supporting services of an efficient landscape management and maintenance profession.

To fulfil the essential management and maintenance functions there must be access to adequate data about technical performance and information on the costing of the project, the sources of which are at present unfortunately diffuse. The landscape manager is currently not as well served as either professional design or agricultural counterparts by a central pool of information. However, there is a growing body of reference data published by colleges and Government agencies (especially the Forestry Commission; the Countryside Commission and the Nature Conservancy Council). Some of the main information sources are listed in the bibliography, including the helpful D.o.E. Schedule.[15]

## 17.8 FUTURE DEVELOPMENTS

Provided that the landscape management profession organizes its information and other resources efficiently,

TABLE 17.7
**Features of a management plan: estimated annual costs for a London Borough**

| The main landscape maintenance areas | Ha. | Machinery £ | Materials £ | Manpower £ | Total £ |
|---|---|---|---|---|---|
| **1. Grass areas** | | | | | |
| Very high maintenance | | | | | |
| Bowling green | 0.07 | 672 | 642 | 4474 | 5788 |
| Cricket table | 0.08 | 614 | 327 | 3740 | 4681 |
| High maintenance | | | | | |
| Central precincts | 0.017 | 138 | 5 | 16 | 159 |
| Sports fields | 2.85 | 658 | 906 | 598 | 2162 |
| Intermediate maintenance | | | | | |
| Housing open space/occasional sports areas | 8.30 | 2291 | 403 | 1438 | 4132 |
| Low maintenance | | | | | |
| Open areas and verges | 4.56 | 791 | – | 1194 | 1985 |
| Very low maintenance | | | | | |
| Wildlife conservation and verges | 10.47 | – | – | 860 | 860 |
| Sub Total: Grass areas | 26.35 | 5164 | 2283 | 12320 | 19767 |
| **2. Hard surface sports facilities** | | | | | |
| Hard porous pitches | 0.90 | 3310 | | 11992 | |
| Tennis courts | 0.13 | 58 | | 501 | |
| Sub Total: Hard surface sports | 1.03 | 3368 | 2705 | 12493 | 18566 |
| **3. Formal planted areas** | | | | | |
| Shrub areas | 2.13 | 28 | 1911 | 9670 | 11609 |
| Tree areas | 1.89 | 28 | 3687 | 1113 | 4828 |
| Sub Total: Trees and shrubs | 4.02 | 56 | 5598 | 10783 | 16437 |
| **4. Informal trees and shrubs** | 9.14 | 23 | 3280 | 12682 | 15985 |
| **5. Lake** | 0.42 | 87 | 46 | 462 | 595 |
| **6. Other areas** | | | | | |
| Maintenance area | | | | | |
| Depot | | 2070 | | 8275 | |
| Nursery | 0.18 | | | 1656 | |
| Allotments | 0.40 | 138 | | 1592 | |
| Hedges | 0.24 | 269 | | 2157 | |
| School garden | 0.07 | 575 | | 478 | |
| Sub Total: Other areas | 0.89 | 3052 | 720 | 14158 | 17930 |
| **7. General site uses*** | | 2530 | 4600 | | 7130 |
| Total 1–7 inclusive | | 14280 | 19232 | 62898 | 96410 |
| plus overall contingency 2·5% | | 357 | 481 | 1572 | 2410 |
| GRAND TOTAL | 41.85 | 14637 | 19713 | 64470 | 98820 |

* Includes: Transport: 3-ton wagon, Tractor, Fuel

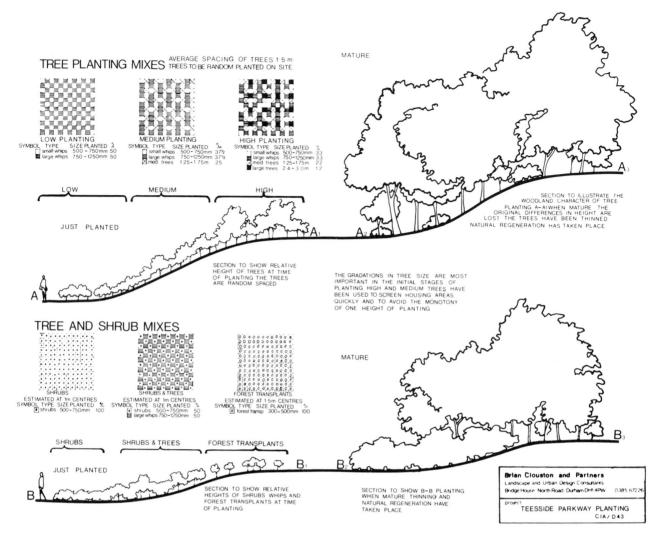

FIGURE 17.2 **Short- and long-term design and management guidelines for Teesside parkway planting.** *(Pam Hoyle)*

## Management plans

There is the need for management plans to be prepared, executed and monitored for a large number of areas, particularly those where the land is, or will be, used for a number of purposes. It is a difficult enough task to manage land where a single use is involved, but the difficulty is compounded considerably where competing activities, such as commercial farming, forestry, mining, recreation, education, field sports, conservation and human habitation, require to be carried out in juxtaposition. The complexity and challenge of this type of management exercise can be observed in practice in the National Parks[16] and other significantly large land areas, such as Upper Teesdale[17] (see Figure 17.4) and 'corridor landscapes' like Hadrian's Wall and the coastline. All such areas are managed with recourse to documented plans. This is not to imply that the areas are automatically well managed. However, the management plans are of benefit to the many disciplines involved in the sustainable use of important landscape areas. By its very nature, multiple land use is only likely to succeed where a balance is maintained between the interests concerned. As with semi-natural habitats, it is necessary to manage multiple land use areas in such a way as to maintain their wildlife and visual diversity. The richness of such areas, in both human and natural resource terms, lies in ensuring that no single interest or ownership becomes totally dominant.

## Research

Planning and management on their own are not enough, however. They need to be backed by a vigorous research programme. This is essential if multiple land use ventures are to be successfully established and managed. Much work has already been undertaken in a number of fields, such as the management of reclamation sites,

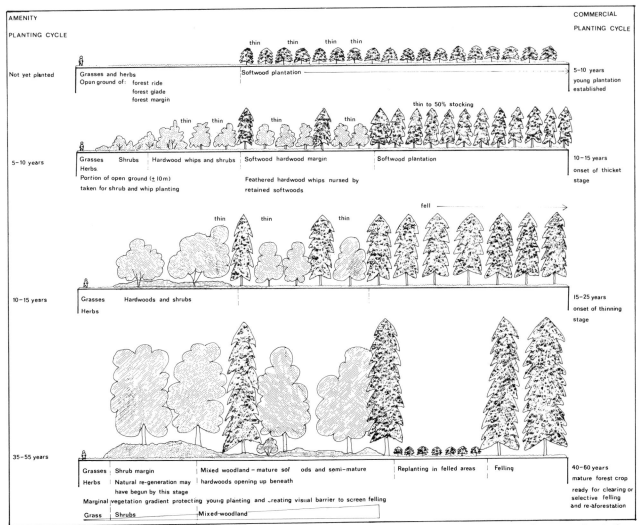

thin    thin    thin    thin

Not yet planted

Grasses and herbs
Open ground of:  forest ride
                 forest glade
                 forest margin

Softwood plantation

5–10 years
young plantation
established

thin to 50% stocking

thin    thin         thin         thin

5–10 years

Grasses    Shrubs    Hardwood whips and shrubs    Softwood hardwood margin    Softwood plantation
Herbs
Portion of open ground (± 10 m)                   Feathered hardwood whips nursed by
taken for shrub and whip planting                 retained softwoods

10–15 years
onset of thicket
stage

fell

thin         thin         thin

10–15 years

Grasses    Hardwoods and shrubs
Herbs

15–25 years
onset of thinning
stage

35–55 years

Grasses    Shrub margin          Mixed woodland – mature sof      ods and semi–mature      Replanting in felled areas    Felling
Herbs    │ Natural re-generation may  │ hardwoods opening up beneath
           have begun by this stage
Marginal │vegetation gradient protecting young planting and creating visual barrier to screen felling
Grass    │ Shrubs              Mixed-woodland

40–60 years
mature forest crop
ready for clearing or
selective felling
and re-aforestation

FIGURE 17.3 **Guidelines for the design and management of hardwood margins to commercial forestry plantations, in situations where visual, wildlife, sporting and informal recreation considerations are important.**

road verges, hedgerows, and recreation areas. However, many other fields are relatively untouched and what research results there are tend to be unco-ordinated. The following are amongst the topics meriting greater investigation:

(i) *The physical and financial implications of a range of different types of landscape schemes, using a variety of maintenance methods.* It is important that the capital and maintenance cost interactions, covering the lifetimes of all major types of landscape schemes, should become better known. Assuming that there is only a certain proportion of GNP available for land-scape and maintenance work it is important to know what types of capital and annual maintenance investment are likely to represent the best 'value'.

(ii) *The manner in which certain areas at present devoted primarily to recreation use might in future be simultaneously farmed or fished, if so dictated by national food requirements.* Possibly the resources of the relatively untrained recreators might be harnessed to ascertain this. It seems likely that a form of farming combined with recreational involvement will, in an age of public participation, come to have a greater place in the landscape of the future. Already visitors help to pick their own produce on some commercial farms, and this may possibly extend to activities associated with supervised farm holidays involving such tasks as planting up gappy hedgerows and otherwise idle areas of land. Research could help to provide management guidance for these and other important land

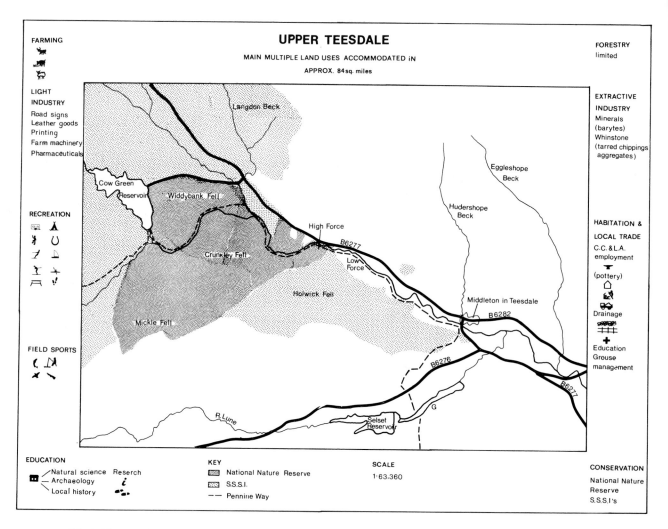

**FARMING**

**LIGHT INDUSTRY**
Road signs
Leather goods
Printing
Farm machinery
Pharmaceuticals

**RECREATION**

**FIELD SPORTS**

**EDUCATION**
Natural science  Reserch
Archaeology
Local history

**FORESTRY**
limited

**EXTRACTIVE INDUSTRY**
Minerals (barytes)
Whinstone (tarred chippings aggregates)

**HABITATION & LOCAL TRADE**
C.C. & L.A. employment

(pottery)

Drainage

Education
Grouse management

**CONSERVATION**
National Nature Reserve
S.S.S.I's

### UPPER TEESDALE
MAIN MULTIPLE LAND USES ACCOMMODATED iN
APPROX. 84 sq. miles

Langdon Beck

Cow Green Reservoir

Widdybank Fell

Crunkley Fell

Holwick Fell

Mickle Fell

R. Lune

Egglesbope Beck

Hudershope Beck

High Force

B6277

Low Force

Middleton in Teesdale

B6282

B6276

B6277

G

Selset Reservoir

**KEY**
National Nature Reserve
S.S.S.I.
Pennine Way

**SCALE**
1:63,360

FIGURE 17.4 **Conserving a sensitive landscape and maintaining a balance between multiple uses demands special management measures.**

areas such as the vast rural-urban fringes surrounding most conurbations,[18] including the ineptly named 'green belts'. In terms of land use, appearance and management these areas call for considerable improvement.

(iii) *The most effective forms of groundcover from a maintenance point of view*, in both open and tree or shrub planted areas, bearing in mind the now high costs of grass cutting due to rising fuel and labour charges. The many different shrub and groundcover communities which are being used in the landscaping of a variety of new public areas on housing estates merit investigation in relation to several factors, such as:

- their relative longevities under different environmental conditions;
- the total expenditure required for the initial

planting and subsequent maintenance over their lifetimes;
- their relative growth performances and resource requirements.

## 17.9 CONCLUSION

This chapter has contained a simple message: to 'design with plants' successfully requires careful attention to the fourth design dimension and thereby to management and maintenance considerations. It is a fitting conclusion to the chapter, since it stresses the need for close working relationships between like-minded professions and — just as importantly — with the nurserymen who produce the required plants and the contractors who carry out much of the work. In short, the subject concerns a family of skills.

PLATE 17.12 **The raw interface between residential and farming areas at Ashford.** *(Ralph Cobham)*

PLATE 17.13 **Motorized litter on British Rail line at Ashford.** *(Ralph Cobham)*

For the benefit of those many people in the modern world who enjoy landscapes abounding in a rich variety of plants of different ages, it is essential that the landscape managers and their counterparts in related professions should co-operate more closely with each other. Then there can be greater potential for establishing, maintaining and regenerating more places in which plants and people alike are able to thrive.

## ACKNOWLEDGEMENTS

In the preparation and presentation of this chapter, the author gratefully acknowledges the assistance received from the following colleagues and friends: Brian Iley (Figure 16.1); Mrs Pam Hoyle (Figure 16.2); Michael Thompson, Roger Lee and Tony Smith (Figure 16.3); Dr Tim Bines (Figure 16.4); George Cobham (Table 16.3); John Parker and Norman Leddy (Tables 16.6 and 16.7); Judy Snaith for assistance with selection of photographs. In preparing the second edition, the help of Russel Matthews, Julie Martin, Nick Burton, Alison Buckley and Kris Baker is gratefully acknowledged.

## FURTHER READING

Agricultural Development and Advisory Service, with the Countryside Commission. *Cowbyers Conference Report* July 1974

Aldridge, D. *Guide to Countryside Interpretation*: Part I 'Principles of Countryside Interpretation and Interpretative Planning' Countryside Commission, (HMSO 1975)

Arboricultural Association *Advisory Leaflets* No. 2 'A Guide to Tree Pruning', No. 3 'The Care of Trees on Development Sites' (1972)

Baines, J. C. 'Success with plants in housing rehabilitation', *Landscape Design* No. 137, pp. 18−19 (1982)

Baines, J. C. and Smart, J. *A Guide to Habitat Creation*. Ecology Handbook No 2 (London: GLC 1984)

Barber, D. (Ed) 'Farming and Wildlife: A Study in Compromise' *Silsoe Conference* 1970, RSPB in association with FWAG (1970)

Barrett, P. R. F. 'Aquatic herbicides in Great Britain, recent changes and possible future development'. *Proc Aquatic Weeds and their Control*, pp. 95−103, (Oxford: Association of Applied Biology 1981)

Biddle, P. G. 'Trees and Buildings', in *Advances in Practical Arboriculture*, Bulletin 65 (Edinburgh: Forestry Commission 1987)

Bradshaw, A. D. and Chadwick, M. J. 'The restoration of land: The ecology and reclamation of derelict and degraded land', *Studies in Ecology*, No. 6, (Oxford: Blackwell 1980)

Bradshaw, A. D. 'The biology of land reclamation in urban areas', in *Urban Ecology*, (Ed.) R. Bornkomm, J. A. Lee and M. R. D. Seaward (Oxford: Blackwell 1982)

Carter, E. S. 'Management of hedgerows and scrub', in J. M. Way (Ed.) *Management of Vegetation*, British Crop Protection Council Monograph No. 26, (Croydon: BCPC 1983)

Carter, R. W. G. 'A discussion of the problems associated with the restoration and management of sand dunes and beaches' Unpublished paper, *The New University of Ulster* (1975)

Cave, T. G. 'Management of vegetation in or near water', in J. M. Way (Ed.) *Management of Vegetation*, British Crop Protection Council Monograph No. 26 (Croydon: BCPC 1983)

CEGB 'Economy in landscape maintenance' *Symposium Summary* (1967)

CEGB *Landscape Code of Practice* Vol. 1 (1972)

Christensen, P. A. 'Management of national vegetation on farms', in J. M. Way. *Management of Vegetation*, BCPC Monograph No. 26 (Croydon: BCPC 1983)

Cobham, R. O. and Gill, C. J. 'Management and maintenance', *Gardener's Chronicle* Vol. 179 No. 26 pp. 39−43; Vol. 180 No. 2 pp. 16−19, Vol. 180 No. 3 pp. 16−18 (1976)

Cobham, R. O. 'The economies of vegetation management, in J. M. Way (Ed.) *Management of Vegetation*, British Crop Protection Council Monograph No. 26 (Croydon: BCPC 1983)

Cobham, R. O. 'Blenheim: Art and management of landscape restoration'. *Arboricultural Journal* Vol. 9 No. 2, pp. 81−100 (1985)

Conover, H. S. *Grounds Maintenance Handbook* (McGraw-Hill 1958)

Countryside Commission 'Landscape Agreements'. *CCP* 61 (1973)

Countryside Commission *Upland Management Experiment* (HMSO 1974)

Countryside Commission *Demonstration Farms*, *CCP*, No. 170 (1984)

Colvin, B. 'Landscape maintenance of large industrial sites', *ILA Journal*, No. 84 (1968)

Davison, J. G. 'Effective weed control in amenity plantings', in P. R. Thoday and C. H. Addison (Eds.) *Cost-effective Amenity Landscape Management*; HEA Conference Proceedings, Bridgewater: (HEA 1982)

Dawson, F. H. 'Ecological management of vegetation in flowing waters', in S. E. Wright and G. P. Buckley (Eds.) *Ecology and Design in Amenity Land Management*, Wye College, University of London (1979)

DOE and SDD *Housing Development Notes* II. 'Landscape of New Housing' (1973, 1974)

Duffey, E., Morris, M. G., Sheail, J., Ward, L. K., Wells, D. A., Wells T. C. E. (Editors) *Grassland Ecology and Wildlife Management* (London: Chapman and Hall 1974)

Duffey, E. and Watt, A. S. (Editors) *The Scientific Management of Animal and Plant Communities for Conservation* (Oxford: Blackwell Scientific

Publications 1971)

Dutton, R. A. and Bradshaw, A. D. *Land Reclamation in Cities* (London: HMSO 1982)

East Lothian County Council Planning Department *Dune Conservation — a twenty year record of work in East Lothian* (1970)

East Lothian County Council Planning Department *Dune Conservation 1970*, North Berwick Study Group Report (1970)

Eaton, J. W., Murphy, K. J. and Hyde, T. M. 'Comparative trials of herbicidal and mechanical control of aquatic weeds in canals'. *Proc Aquatic Weeds and their Control*, pp. 105–116 (Oxford: Association of Applied Biology 1981)

Evans, J. *Silviculture of Broadleaved Woodland*, Forestry Commission Research and Development Paper 62 (1984)

Fairbrother, N.*New Lives New Landscapes* (London: Architectural Press 1970)

Fairbrother, N. *The Nature of Landscape Design*, Chapter 7 (London: Architectural Press 1974)

Farming and Wildlife Advisory Group Essex Exercise *Farming, Wildlife and Landscape* (1975)

Gilbert, O. L. 'The Capability Brown Lawn and its management', *Landscape Design*, 146: 8 (1983)

Gilmour, W. N. G. 'The management of greenspace on a low budget', in C. H. Adison and P. R. Thoday (Eds.) *Cost Effective Amenity Land Management* (University of Bath 1982)

Grime, J. P. *Plant Strategies and Vegetation Processes*, (Chichester: John Wiley & Sons 1979)

Grime, J. P. 'Manipulation of plant species and communities', in A. D., Bradshaw, D. A. Goode, and E. Thorp, (Eds.) *Ecology and Design in Landscape*, The 24th Symposium of the British Ecological Society (Oxford: Blackwell 1986)

Grubb, P. J. 'The maintenance of species richness' in *Plant Communities: The Importance of the Regenerative Niche*, *Biological Review* 52, pp. 107–45 (1977)

Hebblethwaite, R. L. *Landscape Maintenance* (CEGB 1967)

Hewett, D. G. 'Human pressures on soils in coastal areas'. *Welsh Soils Discussion Group Report* No. 14 (1973)

Hookway, R. J. S. *The Management of Britain's Rural Land* (Countryside Commission 1967)

Hooper, M. D. and Holdgate, M. W. (Editors) *Hedges and Hedgerow Trees* (Symposium Proceedings Monks Wood Experimental Station 1968)

Hunt, R. and Rorison, I. H. (Eds.) *Amenity Grassland: An Ecological Perspective* (Chichester: John Wiley & Sons 1980)

Huxley, T. *Footpaths in the Countryside* (The, Countryside Commission for Scotland 1968)

ILA *Landscape Maintenance*, Report of Symposium, June 1963 (1963)

Insley, H. and Buckley, G. 'Some aspects of weed control for amenity trees on man made sites'. *Proceedings of Weed Control in Forestry Conference*, pp. 189–200, Wye College, University of London (1980)

Insley, H. 'The influence of post planting maintenance on the growth of newly planted broadleaved trees', in C. H. Addison and P. R. Thoday (Eds.) *Cost-effective Amenity Land Management* (University of Bath 1982)

Insley, H. 'Causes and prevention of establishment failure in amenity trees', in A. D. Bradshaw, D. A. Goode and E. Thorp (Eds.) *Ecology and Design in Landscape*, 24th Symposium of The British Ecological Society (Oxford: Blackwell 1986)

Institute of Recreation Management (Editors) *The Recreation Management Yearbook* (London: E. & F. N. Spon Ltd 1975)

Keenleyside, C. B. *Farming, Landscape and Recreation* (Countryside Commission 1971)

Kelcey, J. G. 'Weed control in amenity lakes.' *Proceedings of Aquatic Weeds and Their Control*, pp. 15–31 (Oxford: Association of Applied Biology 1981)

La Dell, T. 'The practical application of direct tree and shrub seeding', in C. Addison and P. R. Thoday (Eds.) *Cost-effective Amenity Land Management* (University of Bath 1982)

Laurie, I. C. (Editor) *Nature in Cities*, University of Manchester Landscape Research Group Symposium (1974)

Lovejoy, D. (Editor) *Land Use and Landscape Planning* (London: Leonard Hill Books 1973)

Lovejoy, D. & Partners (Editors) *Spon's Landscape Handbook* (London: E. F. & N. Spon Ltd, revised annually, 1956)

Lowday, J. E. and Wells, T. C. E. 'The management of grassland and heathland in country parks' *CCP* No. 105 (Cheltenham: Countryside Commission 1977)

McHarg, I. C. 'Can We afford open space? A survey of landscaping costs', *Architects' Journal*, March 8 and 15 1956, pp. 261–74

Malcolm, D. C. Evans, J. and Edwards, P. N. (Eds.) *Broadleaves in Britain* (University of Edinburgh Press 1982)

Marren, P. R. *Ecology and Recreation*: *A Review of European Literature* (University College, London 1975)

Matthews, J. R. (Ed) 'Countryside monitoring and management', *CCP*, No. 231, Countryside Commission (1987)

Murphy, K. J., Eaton, J. W. and Hyde, T. M. *The Management of Aquatic Plants in a Navigable Canal System for Amenity and Recreation*, Proceedings EWRS 6th Symposium on Aquatic Weeds, pp. 141–151, Novi Sad, Jugoslavia (1982)

Natural Environment Research Council *Amenity Grasslands — the Needs for Research*, Swindon: NERC Publications Series C, No. 19 (1977)

357

Nottinghamshire County Council *Sherwood Forest Study* (The Sherwood Forest Study Group 1974)

Parker, J. C. 'Mown grass: Techniques, costs and alternatives', in C. Addison and P. R. Thoday (Eds.) *Cost Effective Amenity Land Management* (University of Bath 1982)

Parker, J. C. *Quality Grass for General Landscape Functions*, NTC Workshop Report No. 4 (Bingley: NTC 1984)

Parker, J. C. 'Just keep on mowing for 300 years', in S. Harvey and S. Rettig (Eds.) *Fifty Years of Landscape Design* (The Landscape Press 1985)

Parker, J. C. 'Low cost systems of management', in A. D. Bradshaw, D. A. Goode and E. Thorp (Eds.) *Ecology and Design in Landscape*, The 24th Symposium of the British Ecological Society (Oxford: Blackwell 1986)

Penistan, M. J. and Laing-Brown, J. R. 'Copse and Spinney', *Landscape Design*, No. 127, pp. 26−9 (1979)

Pennyfather, K. *Guide to Countryside Interpretation*, Part II 'Interpretative media and facilities,' Countryside Commission (HMSO 1975)

Peterken, G. F. *Woodland Conservation and Management* (London: Chapman and Hall 1981)

Pollard, E., Hooper, M. D. and Moore, N. W. *The New Naturalist*, Chapter 16 (London: Collins 1974)

Pryce, S. 'Management problems of one to ten year old woody mass plantings', *Landscape Design* Vol. 2 No. 84, pp. 29−41 (1984)

Roberts, H. A. (Ed.) *Weed Control Handbook: Principles*, 7th edn (Oxford: Blackwell Scientific Publications 1982)

Rorison, I. H. 'The current challenge for research and development', in R. Hunt and I. H. Rorison (Eds.) *Amenity Grassland − An Ecological Perspective* (Chichester: John Wiley and Sons 1980)

Shildrick, J. (Ed.) (in press) *Wildflowers 87, Proceedings of the National Turfgrass Symposium*, University of Reading, September 1987, National Turfgrass Council

Speight, M. C. D. 'Outdoor recreation and its ecological effects' *Discussion Papers in Conservation* (London: University College 1973)

Steele, R. C. 'Wildlife Conservation in woodlands', Forestry Commission Booklet 29 (HMSO 1972)

Steele, R. C. 'Management of woodland and woodland vegetation for wildlife conservation', in J. M. Way (Ed.) *Management of Vegetation*, British Crop Protection Council Monograph No. 26 (Croydon: BCPC 1983)

Stewart, V. I. 'Soil drainage and soil moisture', in R. Hunt and I. H. Rorison (Eds.) *Amenity Grassland − An Ecological Perspective* (Chichester: John Wiley and Sons 1980)

Tandy, C. (Editor) *Handbook of Urban Landscape* (London: Architectural Press 1972)

Tandy, C. *Landscape of Industry* (London: Leonard Hill Books pp. 1975) 256−61

Thoday, P. R. (Ed.) *Weed Control in Amenity Plantings*, Conference Proceedings, University of Bath (1980)

Thoday, P. R. 'Ground cover − Factors determining its success', in P. R. Thoday and C. H. Addison (Eds.) *Cost Effective Amenity Landscape Management*, HEA Conference Proceedings. (1982)

Thoday, P. R. 'Tree establishment in amenity sites', in P. R. Thoday (Ed.) *Tree Establishment* (Bath University 1983)

Thompson, J. R. 'Roadsides: A resource and a challenge', in A. D. Bradshaw, D. A. Goode and E. Thorp (Eds.) *Ecology and Design in Landscape*, The 24th Symposium of the British Ecological Society (Oxford: Blackwell 1986).

Tregay, R. 'Design and ecology in the management of nature-like plantations', in A. D. Bradshaw *et al* (Eds.) *Ecology and Design in Landscape*, The 24th Symposium of the British Ecological Society, (Oxford: Blackwell 1986)

University of Newcastle upon Tyne *Landscape Reclamation*, Vols I & II (Guildford: IPC Business Press 1972)

Ward, L. K. 'Scrub dynamics and management', in S. E. Wright and G. P. Buckley (Eds.) *Ecology and Design in Amenity Land Management* pp. 109−27, Wye College, University of London (1979)

Warnock, T. 'A surveyor looks at landscape maintenance', *The Surveyor*, September 1967

Warren, A. and Goldsmith, F. B. *Conservation in Practice* (Chichester: John Wiley & Sons 1974)

Way, J. M. *Road Verges: The Function and Management* (Symposium Proceedings, Monks Wood Experimental Station 1969)

Way, J. M. 'Roadside verges and conservation in Britain: A review', *Biological Conservation* No. 12, pp. 65−74 (1977)

Weddle, A. E. *Techniques of Landscape Architecture* (London: William Heinemann Ltd 1967)

Weddle, A. E. and Pickard, J. 'Landscape Management: site conservation at Heriot-Watt University', *ILA Journal*, No. 94, May 1971

Wells, T. C. E. 'Management options for lowland grassland', in R. Hunt and I. H. Rorison (Eds.) *Amenity Grassland − An Ecological Perspective* (Chichester: John Wiley and Sons 1980)

Westmacott, R. and Worthington, T. *New Agricultural Landscapes* (Countryside Commission 1974)

Woodhouse, A. R. 'Further assessment of the effectiveness of a slow release nitrogen fertilizer on sports turf, *Journal of the Sports Turf Research Institute* No. 30 (1974)

Workman, J. 'Restoration of parks and subsequent management', *Landscape Research* Vol. 7 No. 1 (1982)

Wright, T. 'Landscapes: the state of welfare', *Gardeners' Chronicle*, Vol. 178 No. 24 pp. 26–8 (1975)

Wright, T. W. J. 'Design and management of semi-natural areas in historic gardens and parks in Great Britain', in S. E. Wright and G. P. Buckley (Eds.) *Proceedings of Ecology and Design in Amenity Land Management*, pp. 216–24, Wye College, University of London (1979)

Wright, T. W. J. and Parker, J. 'Maintenance and conservation', in A. D. Weddle (Ed.) *Landscape Techniques* (London: Heinemann 1979)

Wright, T.W.J. *Large Gardens and Parks, Management and Design* (St Albans: Granada 1982)

Wye College, Kent *Aspects of Landscape Ecology and Maintenance* (1972)

Wye College, Kent *Tree Growth in the Landscape* (1974)

## REFERENCES

1. 'Expansion of the Profession', Report prepared by the Ad Hoc Committee, ILA 1974
2. Boddington, M. A. B. 'Urban Pressure – coming to terms with the towns'. *Farm Business,* pp. 6–12 (1971)
3. *The Plan for Milton Keynes*, Milton Keynes Development Corporation (1971)
4. Boddington, M. A. B. 'Agriculture in Milton Keynes', *The Plan for Milton Keynes*, Technical Supplement No. 9 (1971)
5. 'Milton Keynes Revisited: 1971', University of Reading – Department of Agricultural Economics and Management, *Miscellaneous Study No. 51* (1972)
6. Best, R. H. and Rogers, A. W. *The Urban Countryside* (London: Faber 1973)
7. Brian Clouston and Partners, *New Ash Green Landscape Master Plan* (1973)
8. Barrow, G., Brotherton, D. I. and Maurice, O. C. 'Tarn Hows Experimental Restoration Project', The Countryside Commission, *Recreation News Supplement No. 9* (1973)
9. Leonard Manasseh and Partners *Snowdon Summit*, The Countryside Commission (1973)
10. Brian Clouston and Partners *Ilkley Moor Experimental Restoration Project*, Summary Report for The Countryside Commission and Ilkley UDC (1974)
11. Irvine Development Corporation *Irvine New Town Plan* (1971)
12. Brian Clouston and Partners and Irvine Development Corporation *Irvine Beach Park, Proposals for an Urban Park for Leisure and Recreation on the Clyde Coast* (1974)
13. Brian Clouston and Partners in Association with Teesside County Borough *Tees Riverside Plan*, Part I 'Landscape and Recreation' (1973)
14. Roderkerk, Dr E. C. M. 'Kennermerduinen National Park', *Nature in Focus*, No. 18, Council for Europe (1974)
15. *Schedule of Rates for the Preparation and Maintenance of Land* D. o. E. (HMSO 1973)
16. *Report of the National Park Policies Review Committee* D. o. E. (HMSO 1974)
17. Bradshaw, Dr M. E. (Ed.) *The Natural History of Upper Teesdale* (Durham County Conservation Trust 1976)
18. Rawling, J. T., Ratcliffe, J. E. and Shelton, A. J. *A Planning Study of Rural Leeds*, Vols. 1 and 2 (Civic Hall: Leeds 1972)

# CHAPTER 18

# The Establishment of Trees and Shrubs from Seed

## MARK SMEEDEN

## 18.1 THE ROLE AND HISTORY OF DIRECT SEEDING

The principal method for the natural regeneration of trees and shrubs is by seed. This method can be exploited by collecting the seed and sowing it directly into prepared sites where it is intended to establish woodland. The technique is known as direct tree and shrub seeding, and like many essentially simple landscape techniques has a long and widespread history of use. Direct tree seeding is not a new idea; it was practised extensively in Britain before the nineteenth century and in the twentieth century in some of the Crown Estate's woodlands. Outside Britain the technique has been employed for a variety of purposes, such as for forestry and land reclamation in the USA and Canada, shelter belts on the Russian steppe and for arid land revegetation in Australia. Closer to home, direct tree and shrub seeding along autobahn routes in West Germany during the 1970s helped to rekindle interest in the technique in Britain.

The principal interest in direct tree and shrub seeding has been in its potential for use on sites where the absence of topsoil or presence of disturbed soils and wastes make the establishment of plants difficult. Many areas of disturbed or derelict land have the capability to support woody vegetation, and yet many planting schemes are disappointing, for one reason or another, and fail to thrive.

One of the most common problems associated with the planting of nursery stock is the root to shoot ratio of the plant material supplied. In conditions where establishment is difficult this one factor is probably the most critical, and many plants that struggle to produce a root system to support their top growth fail. The root to shoot ratio developed by directly sown trees and shrubs is a natural balance resulting from the interaction of the seedling with its environment. Experience has indicated that in adverse growing conditions directly sown material produces proportionally greater root to shoot growth. This adaptability to changing conditions allows seedlings and saplings to survive until conditions are more conducive to producing greater shoot extension.

The genetic provenance of the plant or seed material becomes an increasingly significant factor on sites where establishment is difficult. A high proportion of nursery stock grown in Britain, and of stock imported through British nurseries from abroad, is grown from seed of continental provenance and origin. The genetic suitability of this stock to the conditions in which it is planted is debatable. The availability of tree and shrub seed from British genetic sources is continually improving. It is now possible with many species to specify British seed for growing in British conditions — in some instances seed collected in the region where a particular direct seeding scheme is proposed.

An additional factor that has stimulated direct seeding schemes in Britain is the interest in 'ecological' style planting using indigenous species. The naturalistic appearance of direct sown sites is sympathetic to this style of planting, and is of possible benefit where vandalism is anticipated. Vandalism can be a problem with some planting schemes, frequently because of the obvious target presented by regular patterns of trees and/or stakes. Any would be vandal facing the random pattern of a broadcast-sown direct seeding scheme is denied the opportunity of making an impression by destroying a pattern among the young seedlings. By the time the trees are large enough to be noticed, it is often too late for lethal damage to be casually inflicted. The slow, progressive development of the plant community

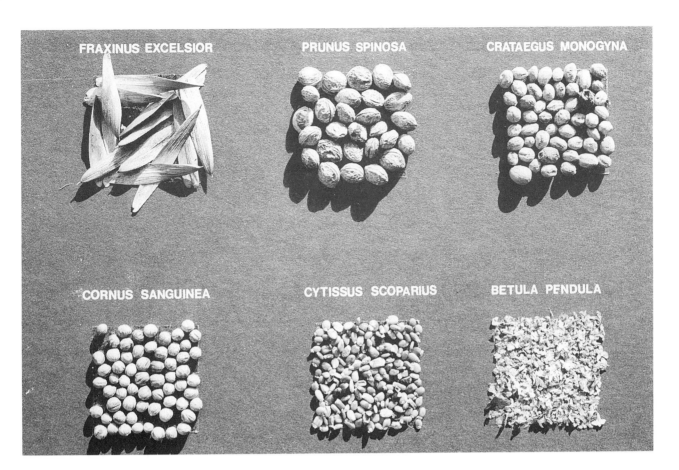

PLATE 18.1 **Tree and shrub seeds are as diverse as their adult parents.** *(Mark Smeeden)*

is a less obvious target. In areas close to habitation, where vandalism tends to be highest, the value of incorporating quick and colourful nurse companion crops may be that the 'garden' effect is sympathetic to a public perception of landscape, and the scheme more readily accepted.

## 18.2 TREE AND SHRUB SEED

Tree and shrub seed is a living material and must be both understood and cared for in order to give predictable germination.

The illustration in Plate 18.1 shows that the forms of tree and shrub seed are as diverse as their adult parents. These seeds not only look different but have different inherent characteristics, which have to be taken into account in a seeding specification. The most comprehensive single source of data on many aspects of broadleaved tree and shrub seed is the Forestry Commission Bulletin 59.[1]

## Seed storage

For storage purposes, seed may be broadly divided into two groups: recalcitrant and orthodox. The orthodox species can be stored successfully for long periods, providing that the seed can be dried down and main-

tained at a near 10 per cent moisture content and kept at a temperature of 3 to 5°C. Examples of these orthodox species are cherry (*Pronus* sp.), ash (*Fraximus* sp.) and hawthorn (*Crataegus* sp.). The recalcitrant species, such as oak (*Quercus* sp.), horse chestnut (*Aesculus* sp.) and sweet chestnut (*Castanea*), cannot be stored for long. Seed of these species collected in the autumn is best stored by mixing it with an equal volume of moist peat and putting it in hessian sacks, which allow the respiring seed to breath. The stored seed is best kept in a cold store a few degrees above 0°C and will need to be periodically wetted and remixed to maintain moist and aerobic conditions before sowing in the spring.

Many nursery men and landscape contractors, with cold stores for handling in-transit plant material, will be able to cater for successful seed storage. If these facilities are not available, then seed storage is best undertaken by established seed suppliers until the seed material is required for sowing.

## Seed handling

Care must be exercised when handling seed to prevent damage and loss of seed viability. Seed needs to be protected from temperature extremes, as both freezing and heating can cause death. It is also important to

361

PLATE 18.2 **A rich shrubby vegetation after three seasons on oil shale in central Scotland.** *(Mark Smeeden)*

control loss of moisture, especially with large, fleshy seeds such as acorns, which can quickly dry out if unprotected during transit or sowing. At all stages of direct seeding operations seed should be handled gently as heavy blows can cause obvious physical damage and lesser blows may well have a cumulative effect on seed viability.

## Seed treatments

Most native trees and shrubs have some form of dormancy mechanism which prevents germination until conditions are favourable for seedling survival, or which give a spread of germination over time to minimize the effects of unfavourable conditions. Seed dormancy mechanisms fall into three categories: exogenous and endogenous mechanisms, and combinations of the two.

Exogenous dormancy is caused by conditions in the outer seed coat, either physical or chemical. Most common is simple hardseededness, which forms the only barrier to germination for many woody legumes, such as broom (*Cytissurus scoporius*), tree lupin (*Lupinus arboreus*) and gorse (*Ulex* sp.). This dormancy mechanism is easily removed by a process of scarification, which consists of abrading the seed coat and thus allowing the seed to imbibe water. Small quantities of

seed can be treated by rubbing between two sheets of sandpaper. With larger quantities of seed scarification can be achieved by mixing it with an equal volume of brazil-nut-sized carborundum chips and rotating a moderately well packed container in an end-over-end shaker.

Other types of exogenous dormancy are generally exhibited by seeds in which germination is also controlled by endogenous factors. These endogenous mechanisms are associated with conditions within the seed embryo itself and are broadly either morphological or physiological. Morphological dormancy is exhibited by species like ash (*Fraxinus excelsior*), which have an underdeveloped embryo that needs a period of growth and development after the seed appears superficially mature. This condition is frequently associated with physiological dormancy.

Physiological dormancy of seeds varies in intensity from species to species and also within different seed lots of the same species. For many seeds, particularly Rosaceous species, such as hawthorn (*Crataegus* sp.) or crab apple (*Malus sylvestris*), a period of warm, moist treatment is needed before sowing. This pretreatment is intended to break down resistance in the seed coat to the effects of a period of cold, moist pretreatment during which chemical inhibitors can be leached from

362

the seed. Warm, moist pretreatment (WMP) is achieved by mixing seed with an equal volume of sieved peat and sharp sand or grit in a 1:1 ratio, moistened and stored at +20 °C in an open-necked polythene bag. Cold, moist pretreatment (CMP) is carried out as WMP but with a storage temperature of +1 to +3 °C. Some species, such as sea buckthorn (*Hippophae Rhamnoides*), rot easily, and should be mixed with sharp sand only for pretreatment. Other species, such as birch and alder (*Betulus* and *Alnus* sp.), are treated 'naked' without mixing with compost.

Forestry Commission Bulletin 59 gives recommended treatments for a wide range of species, although in the author's experience the upper end of most pretreatment periods gives the most reliable results. A typical entry from a direct seeding specification may appear as shown in Table 18.1

In the example given only 50 per cent of broom (*Cytissus scoparius*) is scarified. This is done to retain some of nature's strategy for seedling survival. The untreated part of the seed lot will germinate over a period of time, and thus prevent the total loss of the seed mix if environmental conditions are too harsh when the majority of seedlings emerge.

An additional seed treatment before sowing is the inoculation of all legume species (such as broom, gorse and lupin) with the appropriate strain of rhizobium bacteria to aid root nodulation and the plant's subsequent ability to fix atmospheric nitrogen into the soil.

## Seed testing

Seed suppliers and seeding contractors should be asked to provide current seed test certificates for each seed lot used. It is sufficient if these take the form of an estimate of quality per unit weight. This is available as the Quick Information Test service given for Great Britain by the Forestry Commission.[2]

PLATE 18.3 **Five-year-old alders sown on an oil-shale site in central Scotland.**

## 18.3 DATES FOR SEEDING

The range of seeding dates is dependent on species selection and regional climatic conditions. Generally, however, in the northern hemisphere the sowing season is from October to the end of May.

## Cultural factors

Autumn seeding has advantages on light soils, where early season seedling establishment may help to resist the effects of spring and early summer droughts. However, if there is an early emergence of seedlings before late frosts, then seedling losses may be expected. This is a situation in which beech (*Fagus sylvatica*) is exceptionally vulnerable.

Seed from an autumn sowing is also vulnerable to rotting in insufficiently aerated seedbeds, as well as being exposed to predators throughout the winter.

TABLE 18.1
**Seed treatment**

| Species | Seed treatment before sowing |
|---|---|
| *Alnus incana* | 4 weeks CMP (naked) |
| *Cytissus scoparius* | Scarify 50 per cent by weight, dress with rhizobium inoculum |
| *Fraxinus excelsior* | 10 weeks WMP and 10 weeks CMP |
| *Quercus robur* | None |

PLATE 18.4 **A one-year-old hazel spot-sown beneath a 600 mm acorn type D tree shelter on a subsoil covered landfill site.** (*Mark Smeeden*)

Spring sowing avoids all the disadvantages of autumn seedlings, but can mean that newly emergent seedlings are susceptible to drought conditions. Suggested optimum periods for establishing vegetation from seed (after R. N. Humphries) are given for the regions of England in Wells, Frost and Bell, 1986.[3]

## Seed supply and availability

Seeding dates depend upon a supply of the required seed being available in any stage of pretreatment required. If some degree of synchronous emergence is required in the spring of that growing season, it may not be wise to rely on warm autumn seedbed conditions to give a warm moist treatment (WMP) to physiologically dormant seeds.

In order to give WMP to such seeds before autumn sowing, stocks of seed stored from the previous year

need to be available, as current seed crops will often not be picked in time. This may well be a determining factor in such circumstances for rejecting autumn seeding dates.

If pretreated seed is required, it is important to take into account the total seed treatment time before sowing. For example, hawthorn seed (*Crataegus monogyna*) can take up to 24 weeks for complete pretreatment; in such a case any seeding contract would need to be let sufficiently in advance of sowing dates to allow seed supplies to be bought and placed in pretreatment.

## Predation

The effectiveness of animal predators, mostly rodents, in discovering and then consuming or damaging seed can never be overestimated. There is no simple cure to seedbed predation. The large seeded species, such as oak and hazel (*Quercus* and *Corylus* sp.), seem to be most susceptible, but this observation may be biased by the obvious visible evidence of a half-eaten acorn rather than the observation of more difficult to see smaller seeded species.

The use of strong smelling mulch material, such as forest bark, does not disguise the seed underneath it. Dressing the seed with red lead, or with rodenticides incorporated in latex emulsions, is more punitive than an effective deterrent. Even dipping acorns in bitumen emulsion is not a guarantee of protection from a hungry rodent. On some schemes well earthed-up tree shelters (Tuley tubes) seem to discourage predators, but this can only be practised where seed is sown in small units (spot seeding).

If direct tree and shrub seeding is proposed near almost any established vegetation, then a rodent population can be expected. In such instances a spring sowing date will minimize the period when the seed is vulnerable.

## 18.4 SEEDING PATTERNS

There are three seeding patterns currently employed for the direct seeding of woody vegetation:

(i)   Broadcast seeding.
(ii)  Row seeding.
(iii) Spot seeding.

The choice of seeding pattern is principally determined by the propensity of a site to develop competitive herbaceous growth. All topsoil sites, however cleaned they are by cultivation or herbicides, will contain reserves of weed seed in the soil. These weed seeds will germinate and plants emerge to compete with directly sown woody species. It is impossible to remove broadleaved weeds with herbicides from among broadleaved tree and shrub seedlings if they are intermixed. To

PLATE 18.5 **A wheat nurse crop providing an initial greening to the sides of a chalk cutting at a motorway junction.** *(Mark Smeeden)*

allow for herbicide control of weed species, seeding schemes must be implemented in a regular pattern. Broadcast seeding, with a consequent random distribution of seedlings, can only be employed on sites where a weed problem is not expected.

## Spot seeding

Spot seeding can be implemented in a regular pattern in the same way as is common for conventional planting schemes. A calculated number of seeds of one species is sown in one station, and through intraspecific competition one sapling or seedling of the species of tree or shrub sown dominates each spot. Spot seeding can be set out on a regular grid to allow easy herbicide application if a potential weed problem is suspected.

Spot seeding can be carried out by placing the seed directly into the substrate, or by seeding into degradable pots of compost off site and planting the pots of seed. This second method has several advantages: first the seeding depth can be accurately controlled by sowers working with a homogenous compost, secondly, time on site can be reduced, which is important in bad weather and, finally, the compost seems to improve the establishment of seedlings. Successful results have been given by using Finnish bottomless paper pots (Lannen Tehtaat Oy) of 64 mm diameter (size VS608) for large seed such as horse chestnut and 51 mm diameter (size VS508) for general use. A loam-based compost remains coherent in the pots, and the use of a special tool called a Pottipotki tube to plant the pots of seed ensures quick on site operations. If pots of seed need to be stored before planting out then they must be kept cool, well watered and well ventilated.

Spot seeding can also be combined with broadcast or rowseeding schemes to incorporate large seeded species, such as oak and hazel, without the need for additional machinery passes which would otherwise be needed to incorporate this seed to sufficient depth.

Tree shelters, or Tuley tubes, can be used with spot

cation of amendments such as mulch and fertilizer, localized application of materials over each seed spot may offer attractive cost saving.

## Row seeding

Row seeding is employed for much the same reason as spot seeding, the ease of herbicide application. Seeding is carried out by drilling parallel rows, between which herbicides can subsequently be applied. Each row should consist of only those species of a similar seed size, for instance, oak and hazel or blackthorn and hawthorn, so only one pass of the drill at the appropriate depth is needed for each row. Species diversity within a mix can be achieved by sowing alternate rows of species of the same seed size category. Variation of species of differing seed sizes in the same row may be achieved by drilling the row and then spot seeding seed of a different size into the row. Winged seeds, such as ash (*Fraxinus excelsior*), which will not pass through a seed drill, should also be incorporated into rows by spot seeding.

Precision drills that utilize perforated belts to carry the seed (for instance, the Stanhay Jumbo) can have cutsom-made belts for differing seed sizes. The adjustment of the speed to the belts in relation to the forward speed of the drill will determine the exact seeding rate.

Unlike spot seeding, row seeding cannot be carried out on steep slopes, on abruptly irregular surfaces or in very stony or rocky conditions. Localized placement of amendments and ameliorants, such as fertilizer and mulch, can be cheaper than whole site treatment, as was suggested with spot seeding, and additionally cannot be widely utilized by undesirable weed species between the rows.

## Broadcast seeding

Broadcast seeding provides the most exciting vegetation pattern, with trees and shrubs developing and interacting within a totally random distribution.

The fascinating visual effects achieved from a broadcast seeding are often closely interrelated with the use of companion species. There are several reasons for employing nurse crops and companion species to achieve the objective of developing the most advanced woody vegetation that a site will support. A quick initial effect will result from including a small cereal component in the seed mix. This will green the site and help to reduce the danger of soil erosion on slopes. This initial vegetation also, and most importantly, improves the microclimate for the developing seedlings of long-term species through a reduction in ground level wind speed, an increase in relative humidity between the stems and the provision of partial shade from the sun for developing seedlings.

Annual grass species, such as annual meadow grass (*Poa annua*) have been used as an alternative to cereals

PLATE 18.6 **Tree lupins dominating rows during their second season after sowing, providing shelter for long-term species that have been spot-sown between rows. Sand and gravel extraction site in south-east England.** *(Courtesy of Cambridge Direct Tree Seeding Ltd)*

sown schemes, with all the attendant cultural advantages recorded for planted stock. Shelters 600 mm high have been used mostly, and in many instances are used as an alternative to the plastic rabbit spiral, which needs a developed plant to support it. The comparative cost per tree of using tree shelters for rabbit protection instead of using rabbit-proof fencing will depend on local costs, size and shape of the plots and the desired density of seed spots. Compared with costs for whole site appli-

366

as an initial nurse crop. However, these grasses seed and spread rapidly and become a source of undesirable competition. Cereals do not present this problem, as only insignificant numbers of cereal seedlings grow from seed set from the previous year. In addition, the dead cereal stems help to supplement any original mulch material remaining during the second year after sowing.

Additional first year short-term interest can be provided by the inclusion of a small amount of the seed of colourful annuals such as the Corn Poppy (*Papaver rhoeas*).

In a typical broadcast-sown scheme the functions and visual impact of the cereal would be followed during the second year by leguminous perennials, such as perennial blue lupin (*lupinus polyphyllus*). In addition to carrying on the functions of the cereal nurse, the legumes can also fix atmospheric nitrogen into the soil.

The rich greens, bright flower colours and varied textures of the legumes are attractive and interesting. They also provide an early three-dimensional structure with potential for exploitation by wildlife. Woody leguminous shrubs, such as gorse, broom and tree lupin (*Ulex europeaus*, *Cytissus scoparius* and *Lupinus arboreus*), can be expected to add to, and continue the development of, a colourful and structurally varied vegetation during the third season of growth.

The microclimate amelioration provided by the nurse crops benefit the young tree and shrub seedlings that are developing concurrently with these companion species. A forestry-type thicket effect is achieved in three to four years with all the attendant benefits of shelter, weed supression and the beneficial drawing-up of tree and shrub growth. A typical scene during the fourth year of the development of a dynamic broadcast-sown community would be that of pioneer trees such as alder (*Alnus* sp.) starting to overtop the temporary herbaceous and shrub community and shade them out, to leave the longer term trees and shrubs, such as oak, ash and hawthorn (*Quercus* sp., *Fraxinus excelsior* and *Crataegus* sp.), to develop.

In order to achieve success, and a degree of predictability, for a complex exercise in four-dimensional design dynamics, the most detailed appreciation of site conditions and expected degrees of competition between species in the seed mix is needed. However, the degree of accuracy with which the percentage of different species within the mix can be predicted is limited. In many instances, the success with which sites that are difficult to plant can be vegetated outweighs this disadvantage.

The implementation of a broadcast-sown scheme is not reliant on any specialist equipment. Seed is divided into lots within the same seed size category (which determines seeding depth), it is then well mixed and if there is not very much of it, it will be bulked with a carrying medium like sand or sawdust to make even distribution easier. Small areas can be broadcast by hand, and larger areas with a tractor-mounted spinner. The largest seeds are sown first and incorporated with a harrow, followed by medium and then small sized seeds and further harrowing after each seed size group is broadcast. Very fine seed, such as birch and alder (*Betulus* sp. and *Alnus* sp.), is frequently surface-sown, and is subsequently washed into the soil interstices by the rain. If rain is not anticipated, then rolling the seed bed after sowing with a light roller will improve seed to soil contact.

Hydraulic seeding machines have been used for broadcasting tree and shrub seed on to steep slopes. High seeding rates are needed to compensate for possible seed damage in the machines and there is a resultant significant reduction in the predictability of results. Unless it is unavoidable, hydraulic seeding machines should not be used for broadcasting tree and shrub seed.

## 18.5 SITE TREATMENT

The seeding of woody vegetation on sites that are difficult to plant is a technique for seedling establishment. For the seedlings to develop into the desired scrub or woodland, the site conditions must be improved to the same degree as would be expected for a conventional planting scheme.

## Physical conditions

Compaction of the substrate is a common problem on sites where there is not a natural soil formation. There are two ways of dealing with this problem. Deep ripping with winged tine cultivators will be sufficient for most sites, commonly to a minimum depth of 450 mm at 1 m centres, although specific site conditions will determine the precise specification. When deep ripping may bring undesirable material to the surface, for example with some landfill sites, loose tipping of subsoil over the surface of the site may be the only practicable solution.

Excessive stoniness of the substrate will prevent the machinery operations necessary to drill seed for row-seeding schemes or to harrow the seed bed to cover broadcast-sown schemes. Moderate quantities of stone and rubbish can be picked off the seedbed to allow these operations to be carried out. Where this is not feasible, a spot seeding pattern should be employed.

Drought and high soil temperatures can be fatal to young tree and shrub seedlings. These conditions are most likely to occur on materials that are granular or texturally coarse, dark in colour and on steep slopes, particularly if they are south facing. The incorporation of bulky organic amendments into the seedbed should be considered where drought conditions are anticipated, as should the use of a mulch. A light-coloured mulch not only reduces evaporation from the soil surface but

**PLATE 18.7 A power-mulching machine applying chopped wheat straw and bitumen emulsion to a slope in a sand pit.** *(Courtesy of Cambridge Direct Tree Seeding Ltd)*

is important in ameliorating seed bed temperatures. Chopped wheat straw is a very effective mulch. This is used with straw lengths not greater than 100 mm, commonly applied at rates of about 4 tonnes per hectare and tacked down with 30 per cent bitumen emulsion at rates of approximately 1500 litres per hectare. Chopped straw, however, is difficult to handle as a localized application to seed spots, and a 10 mm depth of pulverized bark of at least 300 mm diameter is an easily applied solution.

## Existing vegetation

Herbaceous vegetation existing on a site before sowing should be killed with an appropriate herbicide. Even a small population of weed species can increase rapidly when seed bed conditions are improved for tree and shrub seeding.

## Chemical conditions

The chemistry of industrial wastes and spoils is a wide and complex subject. However, if there is one

generalization that can be made of spoiled land, it is that there will be deficiencies of available plant macronutrients. Nitrogen and phosphorus are the nutrients that are most commonly deficient, although deficiency of potassium also occurs. It is important to anticipate the extent of potential leaching of applied nutrients, and of possible fixation by reversion to insoluble compounds, before specifying seed bed ameliorants and amendments.

Nitrogen is readily lost from soils in which leaching is a problem. In such instances, the use of nitrogen-fixing legumes in seeding mixes is essential in order to avoid the need for continual applications of nitrogen fertilizer merely for maintenance. Initial application of nitrogen fertilizer, up to 50 to 75 kg N per hectare, is essential to establish cereal nurse crops, and subsequent applications may be needed until leguminous species are well enough established to be able to contribute to the soil nitrogen status.

Phosphorus is comparatively immobile in soils, and applications of superphosphate, usually at rates of 100 to 250 kg $P_2O_5$ per hectare, will be sufficient to remedy any deficiency. Phosphate applications should be made during seed bed cultivation to ensure an adequate distribution throughout the cultivated depth.

Potassium deficiencies are only occasional, and applications of 75 kg/ha as $K_2O$ are generally sufficient.

## 18.6 CALCULATION OF SEEDING RATES

The quantity of a particular species to be sown will depend on the proportion that it is to form of the total mix. To achieve the desired representation of any one species, calculations must take into account the quantities of the seed, the capacity of seedlings of that particular species to emerge from the seed bed and their interaction with the substrate into which they are sown, and thus their longer term survival.

### Spot seeding

The number of seeds sown per spot is calculated as:

$$\frac{100}{\% \text{ field emergence}} \times \text{Target seedling density}$$
$$= \text{total number of viable seeds required per spot}$$

In Table 18.2 is an example of a schedule of seeding rates for a spot-seeding specification on a clay sub-soil in central England. The seed is to be sown in paper pots of compost. It is assumed that all seed is pretreated to break dormancy as necessary.

TABLE 18.2
**Schedule of spot seeding rates**

| Species | Viable seeds per spot | Total seeds per spot[*] |
|---|---|---|
| Acer pseudoplatanus | 8 | 13 |
| Aesculus hippocastanum | 3 | 4 |
| Crataegus monogyna | 8 | 11 |
| Corylus maxima | 3 | 5 |
| Fraxinus excelsior | 10 | 14 |
| Malus sylvestris | 15 | 21 |
| Prunus padus | 10 | 14 |
| Prunus avium | 10 | 13 |
| Prunus spinosa | 7 | 8 |
| Quercus robur | 3 | 4 |

[*] Based on average viability of seed (Gordon and Rowe, 1982), adjustment is made to total number of seeds per spot after testing the viability of samples of each seed lot to be sown.[4]

### Broadcast and row seeding

The seeding rates for a broadcast or row-seeding scheme are reached by the following calculations:

PLATE 18.8 *Prunus avium* **or wild cherry reaching in excess of 1.8 m high during the third season after sowing on a topsoil site in northern England.** *(Mark Smeeden)*

$$\frac{\text{Percentage composition}}{100} \times \text{Target seedling density}$$
= Number of seedlings per $m^2$ (or linear m, for row seeding)

$$\frac{100}{\text{Percentage field emergency}} \times \text{Number of seedlings}$$
per $m^2$ (or linear m for row seeding) = Number of viable seeds per $m^2$ (or per linear m)

Number of viable seeds per $m^2$ × Area to be sown (or length of row) = Total number of viable seeds

$$\frac{\text{Total number of viable seeds}}{\text{Average number of viable seeds per kg}}$$
= Total weight of seed required

TABLE 18.3
**Example of a broadcast-sown scheme**

| Species | Composition (%) | Field emergence (%) | Number of seedlings per $m^2$ | Number of seedlings per $m^2$ | Average number of viable seeds per kg* | Weight of seed kg per hectare |
|---|---|---|---|---|---|---|
| *Acer campestre* | 15 | 20 | 2.25 | 12 | 8 900 | 13.58 |
| *Betula pendula* | 10 | 2.5 | 1.5 | 60 | 150 000 | 4.00 |
| *Crataegus monogyna* | 15 | 20 | 2.25 | 11 | 7 900 | 13.92 |
| *Cytisus scoparius* | 5 | 15 | 0.75 | 5 | 85 000 | 0.58 |
| *Fraxinus excelsior* | 10 | 20 | 1.5 | 8 | 7 800 | 10.25 |
| *Lupinus polyphyllos* | 15 | 15 | 2.25 | 15 | 29 750 | 5.04 |
| *Prunus spinosa* | 15 | 20 | 2.25 | 11 | 4 200 | 26.2 |
| *Quercus robur* | 15 | 60 | 2.25 | 4 | 220 | 181.00 |

Target seedling density = 15 per $m^2$

* Based on average viability of seed (Gordon and Rowe, 1982)[5] adjustment is made to total number of seeds per spot after testing viability of samples of each seed lot to be sown.

A calculated example is given in Table 18.3 for a broadcast-sown scheme for a clay sub-soil in Central England. It is assumed that all the seed is pretreated, that seeding will take place in spring, that no mulch is proposed and that the site is flat.

## 18.7 MAINTENANCE

Maintenance of directly sown schemes differs little from the correct maintenance for conventional planting schemes.

### Herbicide applications

Sites are either spot- or row-sown in areas where weed competition is expected to be a problem. In such situations applications of contact herbicide (for instance glyphosate as 'Round-up', a translocated contact herbicide) can be made to the areas surrounding the tree seedlings with guarded sprayers to maintain as large a weed-free area as is possible. Broadcast-sown schemes are only sown on sites where weeds are not expected to be a problem. However, the creation of a seed bed for tree and shrub seeding can produce conditions where herbaceous weed seedlings will be more successful than anticipated. Grass weeds have been successfully removed from broadcast-sown areas by winter applications of Kerb 50W (Propigamide) at rates of 1.75 to 2.5 kg/ha of wettable powder. However, this course of action should only be adopted if grasses are a serious risk to the saplings, as grass removal can leave a larger niche open to subsequent invasion by broadleaved weeds, which can only be removed by expensive individual treatment.

### Fertilizer applications

Although initial fertilizer applications may be made during or before seeding, plants may subsequently show a lack of vigour and exhibit leaf discoloration. In such instances, where there are no clear causes such as water-logging, disease or insect attack, a nutrient deficiency may be suspected. Foliar sampling and analysis for determining nutrient status should be carried out, as described in Arboricultural Research Note 50 83 SSS, issued by the DoE Arboricultural Advisory and Information Service. Nitrogen will be the most common deficient element on sites where adequate levels of fertilizer were initially applied. Additional fertilizer should only be applied in the minimum quantities needed, to avoid providing an excess above requirements which could be exploited by weeds.

### Thinning

Within seed spots, intraspecific competition will generally produce one dominant sapling, and no thinning of seedlings need take place. The thinning of any directly-sown area can be implemented on arboricultural or forestry principles, according to the objectives for the vegetation structure and composition.

However, broadcast-sown sites with a dynamic community of randomly distributed individuals are most likely to be sown on an impoverished or 'difficult-to-plant' substrate. The final, or most stable, form of vegetation on such sites is difficult to predict. The presence within the initial seed mix of a variety of herbaceous and woody plants will result in a complex interaction between individuals and species and the site. While observation and recording of such sites is comparatively recent, it may be expected that a degree of stability will be reached within the plant community corresponding closely to the greatest potential the site has for supporting vegetation. Any thinning or selection in such cases will most likely be implemented to achieve other design objectives rather than those that are purely cultural.

REFERENCES

1. Gordon, A. G. and Rowe, D. C. F. *Seed Manual for Ornamental Trees and Shrubs* (HMSO 1982)
2. Forestry Commission, Alice Holt Lodge, Wrecclesham, Farnham, Surrey
3. Wells, T., Frost, A. and Bell, S. *Focus on Native Conservation No 15, Wildflower Grasslands from Crop-sown Seed and Hay Bales* (Nature Conservancy Council 1986)
4. Gordon and Rowe, *op. cit.*
5. *Ibid.*

# CHAPTER 19

# The Establishment of Trees and Shrubs

## COLIN BROWN AND CEDRIC LISNEY

## 19.1 INTRODUCTION

This chapter is intended as an introduction to the technical subject of modern plant establishment. It does not attempt detailed specifications, but rather points the reader in the direction of current trends and techniques. Information has been drawn from a wide range of literature and research, as well as from practical experience gained over the last decade.

Throughout the chapter, good plant establishment practice is seen as operating at all levels in the design process, from site survey, through site planning, ground preparation and planting, to maintenance and management operations. Each stage is considered in relation to the whole.

## 19.2 SITE SURVEY

Site survey should aim to identify potential plant establishment problems at an early stage in the design process, so that provisions may be made in the landscape budget for alleviating them. The costs of carrying out the survey will be relatively small when compared with the cost of replacing failed plant material which has resulted from planting in unsuitable soil conditions. Experience has shown that if clients are made aware of potential problems at the outset, they are more likely to accept the higher costs associated with producing a workable landscape scheme on a difficult site. The site survey provides a logical and structured means of identifying existing site factors likely to inhibit plant establishment and, additionally, if well presented, provides a concise and convincing means of conveying the problems to the client.

The extent of the survey will vary according to the size and complexity of the individual site. A comprehensive landscape survey will cover a wide range of elements. Typical study areas include soils, geology, drainage, microclimate, topography and the nature and extent of existing vegetation. Even on the smallest of sites, the site survey should include a thorough investigation of soil characteristics with a view to their effect on plant growth.

Soil samples should be taken by digging small trial pits and the following information recorded: the depth and description of topsoil (including chemical and textural characteristics), the depth of subsoil, type of bedrock, presence of stones in the soil profile and the level of the water table and soil moisture content. Much of this information can be represented graphically on a diagram of the soil profile, annotated with notes and dimensions. On larger schemes, where funds allow, textural and chemical analysis of soil samples should be undertaken by one of the specialist agencies that provide a complete and detailed soil analysis service. On small sites, however, where funds may be low, this level of expenditure may not be justified, and in such cases perfectly acceptable results can be obtained in the field by means of relatively inexpensive equipment. Chemical analysis can be carried out with a portable soil-testing kit, which will contain the chemical reagents necessary to carry out the relevant tests, as well as information on correct sampling techniques and interpretation of results.

A simple chemical analysis will cover pH, nitrogen (N), phosphorus (P) and potassium (K) levels in the soil. The pH measurements indicate the degree of acidity or alkalinity in the soil. A pH of O denotes absolute acidity, pH7 neutrality and pH14 absolute alkalinity. Most soils are slightly acidic (around pH6.5) and most trees and shrubs will grow in soils with pH levels between 5 and 7.

Indications of N, P and K levels in the soil are useful, since these are the three main chemical elements necessary for successful plant growth. Their availability gives a good general indication of the inherent fertility of the soil on site. Deficiencies identified at this stage can be readily corrected through the application of a correctly balanced fertilizer before planting.

Soil texture refers to the physical characteristics of the soil, in particular the percentage distribution of clay, silt and sand particles present. This must be differentiated from soil structure, which refers to the arrangement of these particles within the soil profile. A soil's structural characteristic will be influenced to a great extent by its textural characteristics. A simple textural analysis can be carried out in the field by hand, and a simple classification is given here:

**Sand**   Gritty and does not soil fingers
**Sandy loam**   Gritty, can be pressed roughly into a ball and soils fingers
**Clay loam**   Sticky, easily moulded in fingers and quickly polished by sliding between finger and thumb
**Clay**   Sticky, becomes polished and stiff, but plastic enough to be rolled in long flexible 'worms'
**Silty loam**   Not sticky and cannot be polished but feels 'silky' or 'soapy'; is not cohesive, but can be moulded
**Medium loam**   Not gritty, sticky or silky

As a result of the survey information assembled, the landscape architect should have a good idea of the nature of the site he or she is dealing with and any problems that are likely to be encountered in establishing vegetation, such as poor fertility, poor drainage or exposed site. Strategies for alleviating any problems should be formulated at this stage, well in advance of any firm landscape proposals being drawn up. This information should be presented in report format to the client, together with some estimate of the costs associated with any ameliorative treatments required. Where appropriate, allowances should also be made in initial budget estimations for alleviating potential problems during building site operations, such as compaction of soils caused by the repeated passage of heavy machinery.

## 19.3 SITE PLANNING

If landscape architects have played a part in the development process at an early enough stage, then they may be able to maximize the protection of existing soil structure and vegetation by influencing the development of site layout plans.

The landscape architect should prepare a site protection plan for incorporation in the main building contract. This should detail the vegetation and ground to be protected while the site is being worked. It is important that these areas are identified at the pretender stage to enable the building contractor to allow in his tender for any restrictions.

Existing vegetation, if in reasonable condition, should be retained whenever possible. In addition to providing an immediate feeling of maturity to the landscape, it may be useful in providing important protection to new planting, especially on exposed sites.

Vegetation to be retained should be fenced off to the extent of its canopy before any other work is started on site, and the fencing should remain in place for the duration of the main contract works. If practicable, any site areas not directly affected by the construction works should also be fenced off. This will ensure that the soil structure in these areas is not irreparably damaged through compaction caused by the passage of heavy vehicles or through contamination of the soil by deleterious materials, such as diesel spillages. If these areas are to be planted up at a later date, the benefits of such protective action are immeasurable.

## 19.4 GROUND PREPARATION

In order that plants can be established in a particular situation, the soil into which they are to be planted must display certain characteristics:

1. It must be free from debris and herbage likely to be injurious to plant growth and/or an impediment to soil cultivation and maintenance operations.
2. There must be free drainage through the soil profile.
3. The soil must be mechanically stable.
4. Slopes must be of a grade that will not inhibit maintenance operations.
5. The soil surface must comprise a crumbly tilth or other finish suited to its intended planting.
6. Nutrient status and pH must be adequate.

These conditions can be achieved in most soils through techniques of soil cultivation and amelioration outlined below.

## Cultivation

There is no single soil cultivation specification that can be applied in all situations. The techniques used must always depend on the condition and nature of the site. On small sites and individual planting beds, hand operations may be appropriate. On larger sites machinery is required to enable the work to be carried out efficiently.

### (i) Cultivation of existing ground
Ground that is to be planted as part of a landscape contract but which is unaffected by engineering or building operations should generally be disturbed as little as possible. Before cultivation, herbicide should be applied to perennial weeds. Providing there are no significant hard pans in the soil profile, the ground may then be cultivated to a depth of 300 mm, using such

agricultural machinery as a plough or rotovator, followed by final cultivation by means of disc harrows to bring the soil surface to a condition suitable for planting. If hard pans have been identified, then these must be broken up by ripping to the required depth. The passage of machinery over the soil should be minimized to avoid compaction, and the work should ideally be carried out during the summer months when the soil is in a dry and workable condition.

On schemes where initial visual impact is unimportant, planting may take place directly through the sprayed out, dead herbage layer into the undisturbed topsoil beneath. The dead herbage acts as a surface mulch, retaining water, suppressing further weed growth and affording some degree of protection to young plants. This is a particularly cheap method of planting because of the limited cultivation required. However, it is only suitable on undisturbed soils where the soil profile is free from compaction and structure is good.

## (ii) Topsoil strip

Where topsoil cannot remain on site during the site development works, it should be stripped to its full depth and stored on site for later use. BS 3882 (1965) provides a detailed definition of topsoil. It is important that topsoil stripping operations are monitored closely by the landscape architect, as topsoil depths frequently vary over relatively short distances, and it is vital that topsoil is not inadvertently mixed with the underlying subsoil during stripping operations.

If trees and shrubs are to be successfully established on soils that have been stripped and respread, then it is important that soil damage, especially to the soil structure (the arrangement of individual soil particles within the soil profile), is minimized during stripping operations. Two types of damage commonly occur: smearing and compaction. Smearing of soil is caused by the movement of a blade across the soil or by slipping or spinning wheels. Compaction is caused mainly by the pressure of vehicles running over the soil (Plate 19.1). Both processes inhibit free drainage, causing surface waterlogging, and also make it difficult for plant roots to penetrate deeply into the soil. Under such circumstances plant establishment is severely inhibited. Both compaction and smearing are related to the wetness of the soil. Damage increases as soils become wetter, and for this reason it is most important that soil handling is only carried out during dry periods of the year and that operations are suspended during and immediately after spells of wet weather.

Compaction during stripping can be reduced by using vehicles with low ground pressures. If repeated movement over the soil is necessary, then vehicles should run in the same wheel track ruts whenever possible rather than compacting new, still loose, areas of soil. To reduce damage further, vehicles should always run over the lowest layer of soil available, that is not over topsoil when a route over subsoil can be used.

Most damage to soil during stripping takes place as the soil is picked up and laid down. If the amount of handling can be reduced, then soil damage will also be reduced. Thus, the direct movement of soil from a stripped area to restored land is preferable. Double handling of soil from a stripped area into stockpiles followed by later respreading increases the likelihood of damage. While single handling is sometimes possible on large, phased jobs, smaller jobs usually require the intermediate storage of soil on site in mounds. These should not exceed 2 m high and should be fully surrounded by temporary protective fencing to prevent vehicular access and contamination from pollutants. Herbicides should be used to keep mounds free from weed growth.

## (iii) Subsoil cultivation

Before topsoil is replaced in the areas where it is required, the subsoil must be thoroughly prepared. This is essential if sustained plant growth is to be achieved, as plant roots must be able to penetrate the subsoil layer easily in order to gain anchorage and obtain a ready supply of mineral nutrients. Failure to prepare the subsoil properly may result in hard pans and compacted layers beyond which the plant roots cannot penetrate. In such cases plants become effectively pot-bound and growth will be retarded. Since water cannot move downwards through the soil profile in these circumstances, the soils may become waterlogged, cold and anaerobic, which will result in high plant failure rates.

Site supervision by the landscape architect is most important at this stage, as future problems caused through lack of care during subsoil cultivation become quickly masked below a layer of cosmetic topsoil, and will only manifest themselves at a later date when plants may fail to develop properly. Good subsoil cultivation is the key to successful plant establishment.

Subsoil should be graded to smooth flowing contours and to achieve the tolerances specified for the finished level of the topsoil. Local excavations should be carried out as necessary in areas where thicker topsoil depths are required. Light, non-cohesive subsoils should be loosened by a three-tine ripper, a minimum of 300 mm deep at 600 mm centres. Stiffer clay and other cohesive subsoils should be loosened with two winged-tine rippers pulled so as to follow in the tracks of the machinery, a minimum of 500 mm deep at 1.0 m centres. The winged tines shatter the soil, breaking up hard pans and improving drainage and root runs. Fairly large machinery may be required to pull the tines at the required depth. In order to avoid root damage, ripping must not be carried out within the branch spread of trees which are to be retained.

### (iv) Topsoil spread

Topsoil that has been stored on site may not be sufficient for all needs, and so additional topsoil may have to be brought in from elsewhere. Imported topsoil should be specified to BS 3882 and should be neutral pH. It must be inspected and approved by the landscape architect before being spread on site. Topsoil should be spread over prepared subsoil in layers not exceeding 150 mm depth and each layer should be firmed before spreading the next one. The minimum recommended topsoil depths after light consolidation are 100 mm for grass areas, 400 mm for shrub areas, and 600 mm for tree pits. Following spreading, the topsoil should be cultivated and graded by reducing the top 100 mm to a tilth suitable for blade grading to particles of 10 mm diameter or less. Stones larger than 75 mm should be removed. When the topsoil is reasonably dry and workable, it should be final graded to smooth flowing contours with falls for adequate drainage, removing all minor hollows and ridges. Smaller beds may be hand dug. As with subsoiling operations, timing is vitally important. Topsoiling must only be carried out during favourable weather conditions under the supervision of the landscape architect or appointed Clerk of Works.

### (v) Drainage

Ensuring adequate drainage throughout the soil profile is essential if plants are to establish themselves successfully. Good cultivation techniques will improve natural soil drainage, but even in soils which have been well prepared before planting high water tables or the existing ground conditions may mean that waterlogging is likely to be a problem. In such instances the landscape scheme must incorporate an adequate field drainage system. This can be costly to implement, and adequate budgetary provision at the pre-tender stage is essential. Drainage layouts should always aim to intercept excess water at source, that is before it reaches the site. The field drain system is usually composed of a number of main field drains linking smaller diameter laterals, the main drains connecting into an open ditch or surface water drainage system which takes water off the site.

A variety of types of land drains are commercially available. Most systems comprise clay tiles or porous plastic pipes laid in trenches backfilled with soil or drainage stone, depending on the nature of the soil. The diameter of the pipes to be used and exact details of the drainage layout will depend on the soil and water characteristics peculiar to each individual site. These are best determined by specialist drainage consultants. On sloping sites, natural drainage can be improved by cultivating at right-angles to the contours, that is downslope. This encourages the downslope movement of water under gravity. Drains located at the top and bottom of the slope remove excess water as it occurs.

PLATE 19.1 **Waterlogged conditions arising from the repeated passage of heavy machinery over subsoil under unsuitable conditions. This soil will require a programme of ripping and cultivation to alleviate compaction before topsoiling.**

## Soil amelioration

If the procedures outlined for topsoil stripping, subsoil cultivations and topsoil respread are carefully followed under ideal weather conditions, and the site is well drained, then most soils are perfectly capable of sustaining some form of woody plant growth. In addition to these operations, however, some soils benefit from further ameliorative treatment if they are to support a wide range of plant species. The structure of heavy clay soils may need to be improved, so that they become more free-draining and friable, while light, sandy soils will benefit from having their water-retaining capacities

375

PLATE 19.2 **Typical earth-moving plant. With such heavy machinery in operation it is important that soils are only worked under suitable conditions if structural damage is to be minimized.**

increased. Problems with pH or nutrient deficiency identified in the site survey may also need correcting. This may be done with the aid of soil ameliorants. These fall into three basic categories:

1. Fertilizers.
2. Lime (pH).
3. Manures and soil conditioners.

### (i) Fertilizers

Soil nutrient deficiencies can be alleviated simply and economically by using correctly balanced inorganic fertilizers in measured amounts. The relative balance of nutrients to be added will be apparent from the results of chemical analysis conducted as part of the site survey. Agricultural fertilizers are characterized by their quick release action and are not ideal for woody plants such as trees and shrubs. General purpose, slow acting, slow release fertilizers are available under a variety of trade names and are more useful to the landscape architect. These are usually incorporated into the soil at the time of planting.

### (ii) Lime

Lime is added to the soil for two purposes: to raise pH

and to improve the physical structure of clay soils by causing flocculation (grouping) of the clay particles. In the latter case, excess application should be avoided, since at high pH levels the nutrient phosphate becomes unavailable and other elements, such as iron and aluminium, become toxic to plants.

### (iii) Manures and soil conditioners

It is almost impossible to alter the texture of a soil economically (that is to alter its particle size composition). However, the structure of a soil (the arrangement of the soil particles within the profile) can be altered through the addition of bulky organic or inorganic materials. If incorporated correctly, these will improve structural soil properties by allowing air, water and plant roots to penetrate the soil more freely.

Depending on the type of conditioner that is used, its application may have the additional benefit of providing certain important plant nutrients. Spent mushroom compost, for instance, contains nitrogen (but also contains lime, so its use near lime-hating plants such as rhododendrons should be avoided). In most cases, however, the benefits are purely physical. In landscape work the type of soil conditioner to be used on a particular job will depend to some extent on the availability of suitable cheap local materials, such as mushroom compost, peat, waste paper pulp, sawdust or dried sewage sludge. There are, however, problems associated with using some of these materials. For example, paper pulp may be high in aluminium, and therefore toxic to plants, while sewage sludge from industrial areas may be high in heavy metals.

Ameliorants are usually spread over the soil to a specified depth (100–150 mm) following topsoiling, and ripped into the soil to a depth of 450 mm during final cultivation. Alternatively, soil ameliorants may be incorporated into the soil at the time of planting (see 19.6).

Careful consideration should be given to the need for incorporating such materials. Recent work carried out by the Forestry Commission (Davies 1987) suggests that the use of soil ameliorants to improve soil structure is of questionable benefit in aiding plant establishment.

## Planting into subsoil

Establishing vegetation directly on to prepared subsoil is now recognized as a cost-effective and successful alternative to traditional methods of topsoiling. There is a growing awareness that soils need not resemble carefully cultivated garden tilth to support active woody growth.

In their basic state, subsoils are typically low in organic matter and lacking in structure. Clay subsoils may be waterlogged in winter and subject to drying and cracking in summer. They generally contain good levels of almost every nutrient except nitrogen.

Compaction during building works, caused by the repeated passage of heavy machinery over the site, often leads to the formation of impervious hard pans at depth in the subsoil. These provide potential barriers to natural drainage processes as well as inhibiting penetration by plant roots.

Given good techniques of cultivation and preparation and the right size and choice of plant material, trees and shrubs can establish themselves after being planted directly into subsoil. This removes the necessity of importing large amounts of costly topsoil.

The basic technique employed is to cross-rip the subsoil by means of winged tines to shatter the soil profile and relieve any compaction that may be present. The tines should follow in the tracks of the machinery that is pulling them. Deep ripping to 600–700 mm is desirable. This requires the use of fairly large machinery. When ripping on demolition sites, the operator must be careful to avoid creating new problems by dragging large quantities of rubble to the surface. The specification and budget must make provision for a degree of site clearance following the ripping operations.

To be successful, the work must be carried out during the summer months when the subsoil is in its most workable condition (Plate 19.2). If operations are attempted when the soil is wet and sticky, then irreparable damage may occur. In areas where waterlogging or poor drainage is a problem drainage systems should be incorporated.

If the soil structure is particularly poor, there may be some benefit in incorporating such bulky organic matter as peat or spent mushroom compost into the profile at the time of ripping. The material is simply spread to 150 mm depth and cross-ripped into the subsoil. This has the effect of opening up the soil profile, improving drainage and aeration. A final cultivation, using tractor-mounted machinery, may be carried out to achieve fine mixing.

Planting can take place directly into this medium. Small-sized, predominantly native stock should be used and slow release, high nitrogen, high phosphate fertilizer incorporated at the time of planting. Repeat applications of fertilizer at the beginning of subsequent growing seasons are also beneficial. If planting pits are dug, they should be backfilled with excavated subsoil rather than imported topsoil to prevent differential shrinkage between the backfilled material and the surrounding soil during periods of drought.

Problems of weed control are reduced when planting into subsoil, since the initial seed bank is far smaller than that in the topsoil. Nevertheless, programmes of maintenance and aftercare are essential if plants are to establish themselves successfully.

The cost of planting into existing subsoil averages out at about one-third of that for importing and spreading a 300 mm layer of topsoil. The technique is appropriate in areas where the aim is to establish predominantly native stands of trees and shrubs, using small-scale vigorous plant material, such as transplants or whips. It is, however, inappropriate where less robust or ornamental species are to be established. In these situations the traditional 'topsoil' approach is more likely to result in successful establishment, but only if good cultivation practices are followed and a reasonable depth of topsoil is provided.

## Planting on mounds

Mounding is increasingly being incorporated along new road corridors and on large construction sites in order to utilize excavated material that would otherwise be extremely costly to remove from the site and dispose of. If they are sensitively designed, mounds can add diversity and interest to the landscape as well as providing some degree of shelter on exposed sites.

Principles of good cultivation on mounds are much the same as for any other soil. Use of the right machinery at the right time of the year under the right kind of conditions is essential. Where ground is to be ripped, this should take place at right-angles to the contours,

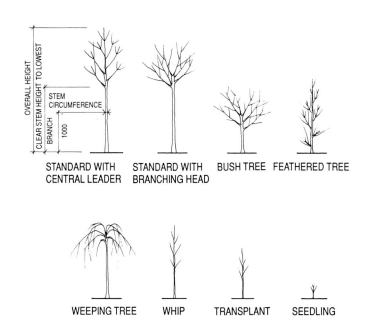

FIGURE 19.1 **Examples of forms of trees,** *BS 3936* **(1980).**

that is downslope, to allow free water drainage under gravity. Land-drainage runs to the front and rear of large mounds are important if waterlogged conditions around the base of the mounds are to be prevented. Careful contouring of the mounds is important if low spots and hollows are to be avoided. Because mounds, by their very nature, are generally situated above the surrounding water table, they may be prone to drying out in summer. Associated problems, such as shrinkage and cracking of clay soils, make successful plant growth difficult. Because of this, surface mulches which help to retain moisture are particularly useful on mounded areas.

Conversely, in very poorly drained areas mounding may aid the establishment of plants by raising the plants' root zones above the waterlogged areas, thus improving conditions for plant growth.

## 19.5 PLANT SPECIFICATION

### British Standards

There are several British Standards (BS) relating to the specification of trees and shrubs:

1. BS 3936 – Specification for nursery stock
   (1980) Part  1 Trees and shrubs
   (1978) Part  2 Roses
   (1978) Part  3 Fruit
   (1984) Part  4 Forest trees
   (1985) Part  5 Poplars and willows
   (1981) Part 10 Groundcover plants
2. BS 4043 (1978) Recommendations for transplanting semi-mature trees
3. BS 5236 (1975) Recommendations for the cultivation and planting of trees in the advanced nursery stock category

By providing a nationally recognized standard of production and specification the British Standards aim to reduce any misunderstanding that may arise when nursery stock is bought and sold. BS 3936 Part 1, for example, gives definitive descriptions of tree sizes and habits (Figure 19.1), together with definitions of container grown and containerized, root-balled and open-ground-grown shrubs. Minimum recommended sizes and dimensions of selected commonly available shrubs

TABLE 19.1
**Dimensions of standard trees**

| Designation | Circumference of stem measured 1 m from ground level | Min. overall height from ground level | Approximate max. height from ground level | Clear stem height from ground level to lowest branch |
|---|---|---|---|---|
| | cm | m | m | m |
| Short standard | Not specified | Not specified | Not specified | 1.00 to 1.20 |
| Half standard | Not specified | 1.80 | 2.10 | 1.20 to 1.50 |
| Light standard | 6 to 8 | 2.50 | 2.75 | 1.50 to 1.80 |
| Standard | 8 to 10 | 2.75 | 3.00 | 1.80 min. |
| Tall standard | 8 to 10 | 3.00 | 3.50 | 1.80 min. |
| Selected standard | 10 to 12 | 3.00 | 3.50 | 1.80 min. |

Note. Minimum overall heights do not apply to weeping trees.

are listed and the standard also contains brief information on root systems, plant origin, condition, packaging and labelling. See Tables 19.1 and 19.2.

Plant material should always be specified by its full Latin name to the relevant BS covering it. The specification should include information about the size of the stock required and whether it is bare-rooted or container-grown. Nursery trade catalogues list plant sizes that are most commonly available. Wherever possible, young stock should be specified in preference to larger, older stock. Any loss of initial impact is quickly compensated for by the vigorous, healthier growth of the younger stock.

## Container-grown and bare-rooted stock

Shrubs grown in the open ground which are then lifted out and sold are known as bare-rooted stock. BS 3936 (Part 1) states that they shall 'have been transplanted to produce fibrous roots and the branches shall have been cut back or trimmed as necessary for the species, so as to produce bushiness'. Most trees, native plant stock and some ornamental species are specified as bare-rooted material.

Plants which have been wholly or partly grown in pots before sale are described as container-grown. The supply of container-grown stock is now widespread and most ornamental shrubs may be specified in this manner (Plate 19.4). Under BS 3936 (Part 1) container-grown plants shall 'at whatever time of year they are sold, have been established in the container long enough for substantial new root growth to have been produced within the container. The shrubs shall have been cut back or trimmed (according to species) and grown with sufficient space to have encouraged bushiness. The size

TABLE 19.2
**Dimensions of other tree forms**

| Designation | Circumference of stem measured 1 m from ground level | Min. overall height from ground level | Max. overall height from ground level. | Clear stem height from ground level to lowest branch |
|---|---|---|---|---|
| | cm | m | m | m |
| Seeding | – | – | – | – |
| Transplant | – | – | 1.20 | – |
| Whip | – | 1.20 | 1.50 | – |
| | – | 1.50 | 1.80 | – |
| | – | 1.80 | 2.10 | – |
| | – | 2.10 | 2.50 | – |
| Feathered | – | 1.80 | 2.10 | – |
| | – | 2.10 | 2.50 | – |
| | – | 2.50 | 3.00 | – |
| Bush | – | – | – | 30 to 60 |

of the container shall be in reasonable proportion to the size and mass of the plant'. The main advantages of container-grown stock are:

1. It can be used to extend the traditional planting season.
2. The larger size of container-grown stock compared to bare-rooted stock provides greater initial impact on planting schemes.
3. The continual, year-round production of container-grown stock for sale commercially is attractive to nurseries, as it improves their cash-flow and ensures a steady workload throughout the year.

For these reasons it seems likely that trends towards greater production of container-grown plant material will continue in the future.

There are drawbacks associated with the use of container-grown plants, however. Four are listed here:

1. Container-grown stock can cost up to five or six times as much as bare-rooted plant material to supply and plant. As bare-rooted stock is now less readily available, this means that planting schemes inevitably cost much more to implement.
2. Plants may become potbound if grown for too long without potting on, or, alternatively, the roots may be too loose if the plants have not established properly in the pots before arrival on site.
3. Container-grown material is often protected from exposed conditions in nursery tunnels, and once planted out on exposed sites is subject to severe dieback and even death in extreme cases.
4. There is evidence to suggest that young, healthy, bare-rooted stock establishes itself faster and better than older, larger, container-grown stock.

For these reasons it is recommended that good quality bare-rooted material is specified in preference to container-grown stock wherever possible.

## Plant selection

The landscape architect is faced with a bewildering selection of plant material to choose from. There is a wealth of nursery catalogues, trade literature and plant dictionaries available, many of which provide useful information on the growing habits and requirements of plants.

Not all species are suitable for large-scale landscape work. Some species establish themselves only very slowly; others require annual maintenance if they are to grow satisfactorily, are difficult to obtain in large numbers or are simply too expensive to use.

Many local authorities and private practices produce their own plant lists, comprising a selection of reliable, robust plants which grow well under a variety of conditions, are readily available commercially and require little aftercare once established. Growth habits, ultimate size and shape, special requirements and so on are all listed in order to aid the designer in choosing the plant that will achieve the desired effect for the particular job in mind. Several lists may be drawn to cover a variety of planting situations that are likely to be encountered. These may include lists of ecologically balanced plant assemblages, lists of plants for use on difficult sites, ornamental planting lists or lists of plants suitable for use in heavily vandalized sites. Such lists should not be allowed to become so restrictive or inflexible that only a narrow range of plants is constantly being planted to the exclusion of all others.

Some establishment failure on sites is undoubtedly due to incorrect species selection rather than the inability of a particular site to support woody growth. Thoday (1983) notes that on difficult sites it is important to match plant selection with the soil conditions prevailing at the end of the construction phase. In cases where soils have been severely damaged this may require the use of resilient pioneer species, such as *Salix*, *Alnus*, *Betula* and *Acer*, rather than such climax species as *Quercus* or *Fagus*. Clearly, under such circumstances the designer must be prepared to tailor his design aims to suit the nature of the site.

On sites where soil conditions have been protected throughout the contract works, the success and vigour of any existing on-site vegetation may give some indication of species likely to establish themselves effectively on the undisturbed soils. In general, native species, particularly pioneers, will always establish themselves more successfully than exotics.

## Specification of tree sizes

Trees are available in a wide range of sizes. The standard tree has traditionally provided the backbone to many landscape schemes. On difficult or large sites, however, where conditions are poor, recent trends lean towards the establishment of dense stands of trees and shrubs, using small-size plant material, such as transplants and small whips (Plate 19.3). Techniques of cultivation, planting and maintenance used in agriculture and forestry can be employed, with more money being invested in soil preparation than in the plant material itself. Growth rates are such that the smaller material will outstrip the larger stock in size within three to five years.

Associated with this approach is a growing recognition of the unacceptable failure rate resulting from traditional techniques of standard tree planting. The results of a survey of standard and larger trees planted in 1979 revealed that only 54 per cent survived after five years (see Skinner, 1986).

There is undoubtedly still a place for standard tree planting on schemes where individual specimen trees are called for or in groups among smaller size plantings to create immediate effect while the smaller plant material establishes itself, but frequently such trees should not be relied upon for the final desired effect. There is a need to educate both the client and the public to accept smaller plant material initially, in return for much more effective plant massing within two or three years. The proposition is attractive on the grounds of cost alone: the cost of one standard tree supplied and planted would purchase and plant around 25 transplants, which will cover an area of about 25 square metres.

## Sources of plant material and availability

The basic cost of plant material varies enormously, both between species and also anually because of differences in the availability of particular species caused by fluctuating demand. Budget constraints often mean that there is a need to specify cheap plant material on landscape schemes. It is difficult to predict annual species costs and availability in advance, since the nursery industry in Britain is so fragmented. In general, however, small-sized common native stock provides the cheapest source of plant material, followed by other small-sized bare-rooted stock.

Nowadays, much stock is brought in from the continent and grown on in British nurseries, as it tends to be cheaper and more uniformly grown than British stock. BS 3936 Nursery Stock Part 1 states that the supplier must declare whether or not the plants offered for sale are UK grown or not. Imported stock may not be as hardy as British grown stock and may fail unless it is hardened in the nursery well before planting. Similarly, stock which has been grown in southern England may struggle if planted in the north. Thus, nurseries growing their own stock in similar climatic conditions to those of the site are preferable sources of supply, and the landscape architect should therefore consider specifying local sources of supply for a particular scheme if at all possible. Before doing so, he should check with the nurseries that the plants he requires are in stock.

Some nurseries allow labelling of plants, so permitting the designer to select plants individually. This is particularly useful on schemes requiring specimen plants. On large schemes it is sometimes possible to ask nurseries to grow plant stock on for the job. This ensures availability and a certain degree of quality control over the plant material that is being produced. If it is left to the contractor to obtain plants for a particular scheme, then the specification should require approval of the source from the landscape architect before proceeding.

## Considerations of plant hardiness

On schemes in which the ornamental planting content is high, plant hardiness will affect species choice, especially where landscape schemes are being undertaken in areas prone to late frosts. Some plants, such as varieties of *Hebe*, are notoriously susceptible to frost damage, and the landscape designer should think carefully before including them in his specification. *Frost damage to trees and shrubs*, a technical paper published by the Joint Council for Landscape Industries in January 1985 came to the following conclusions:

1. Designers must plant the right species in the right situation. This requires a thorough knowledge of plant hardiness and factors affecting

PLATE 19.3 **Young hornbeams** (*Carpinus betulus*) **lined out in young stock such as this generally transplant more successfully than larger, more expensive stock. Comparative growth rates may be such that the smaller material outstrips the size of the larger stock within two to three years of planting.**

plant susceptibility. Most reference books indicate frost-susceptible species.

2. Designers must check whether plants have been winter-protected by polythene, net tunnels or cold glass in the nursery. Such species will not be wind-hardy and may suffer in severe winters, particularly on exposed sites.
3. Designers should consider nominating suppliers of plant material and inspecting stock prior to supply.
4. Plants should be inspected on arrival at the site.
5. In the case of nominated suppliers, designers should check the suppliers' replacement policy.
6. Adequate cultivation, preparation and drainage are essential if plants are to survive in severe winters.
7. Plants should be well protected in transit and properly planted under suitable conditions.
8. Designers should use the CPSE *Code of Practice for Plant Handling* in their specifications and ensure that suppliers and contractors adhere to it.
9. Consideration should be given to pruning certain species to remove tender growth.
10. Good stock, good handling, good planting and good ground conditions are the major factors leading to successful establishment and growth.

Although specifically relating to frost damage of trees and shrubs, these conclusions are of relevance to plant establishment in general.

## 19.6 PLANTING TECHNIQUES

### Planting season

In the northern hemisphere the planting season for deciduous trees and shrubs traditionally runs from the end of October to the end of March. This is when the plants are in a dormant condition and are least susceptible to damage during handling. Early planting, before the end of the year, is more successful than planting from January onwards. Late plantings are particularly vulnerable to spring droughts and should be avoided unless adequate watering can be carried out. Evergreens establish more readily if they are planted in early autumn or late spring. Establishment may also be improved if a stock that is planted particularly late is sprayed, before lifting, with an anti-transpirant to reduce water loss from the plant and to ease transplant shock.

There are periods within the normal planting season when planting should be delayed. The three main hazards are:

1. Frost.
2. High winds (especially during periods of low temperature and low relative humidity).
3. Excessive water (after periods of heavy rainfall or snow).

Frost may kill exposed roots or root systems held in containers. It will also prevent good planting practice, since the soils become lumpy when frozen and cannot be mixed intimately with plant roots. Drying winds quickly kill exposed roots and will cause desiccation of young shoots and leaves of evergreens. Plants in transit or on site waiting to be planted are most susceptible to this kind of damage.

Cultivation of soils containing excess soil water during planting can cause severe structural damage and compaction, creating conditions that are unsuitable for plant growth. The planting specification should prohibit planting under such conditions, and the landscape architect must ensure that the specification is enforced.

There is a need to make the client aware of the constraints of the planting season at an early stage in the contract process and to co-ordinate the site programme in such a way that ground becomes available for planting at the optimum time. Ideally, soil cultivation and amelioration procedures should be carried out during the late summer months when the ground is dry and workable, and should be followed by late autumn or early winter planting.

### Plant handling

It is essential that nursery stock is handled correctly between being lifted in the nursery and arriving on site for planting. Equally important is the period of time that the material spends on site before planting. Unless correctly lifted, packaged, transported and stored on site, then even the most healthy plant material will fail. In recognition of this and in an attempt to define recommended procedures, the Committee for Plant Supply and Establishment has produced a booklet on plant handling (CPSE 1985). This contains information on liability, lifting stock, bundling, packaging, labelling, protection, temporary storage, transport and receipt by the purchaser.

The landscape architect should always inspect plant material that arrives on site. It is important to check that plants are carefully labelled and packaged in accordance with the code of practice. Root systems on individual bare-rooted plants should be checked, with particular attention to any dryness at the roots.

If there is to be a short period between plants arriving on site and being planted out (up to 48 hours), then a temporary covering of the roots with damp sacking, straw or peat is acceptable. Where longer delays occur, then bare-rooted plants should be heeled in in moist, friable soil, placed in an indirect or humidified cold store or supported upright on a well drained site and the roots immersed in a deep layer of moist straw, peat or other suitable material. The material should be firmed to exclude air and watered periodically, as the condition of the material requires. Protection should be given against damage by small mammals. Bundled plants may need cutting open and spreading out so that intimate contact between the roots and the plunging medium is achieved. Stout rails will be needed to support standard trees and other large stock. Container-grown plants should be maintained upright and watered as required.

On sites where this treatment is not possible the landscape architect should arrange for a staggered delivery, so that plants can be planted immediately on arrival.

## Preplanting weed control

Stock should always be planted in weed-free soil. Any perennial weeds present should be sprayed out with an appropriate herbicide, applied in strict accordance with the manufacturer's instructions. Since January 1989 all persons engaging in the use of herbicides must hold the relevant Certificate of Competence for the use of herbicides required under the Control of Pesticides Regulations (CPR 1986).

## Planting densities

The way in which plants are to be physically arranged and spaced on the ground will vary according to the aim of the designer. Two basic approaches to planting out may be identified.

### Single species beds
Where plantings are largely ornamental in character, plant material is generally planted in species groups to form interwoven beds of species displaying differing characters of form, texture and colour. Larger selected specimen shrubs or trees may be planted as individual highlight features (Figure 19.2).

Initial plant spacing will depend on consideration of the growth habit of individual species (for instance, spreading or upright, arching or clumping) and also of their vigour. In landscape planting the aim must always be to achieve close canopy conditions as quickly as possible, while at the same time planting economically with sufficient spacing between the plants to avoid interspecific competition, which will result in unattractive, weak and spindly growth of individual plants.

### Mixed species beds
In more natural plantings, where the aim is to establish blocks of woodland, hedgerows or shelter belts, small-sized plant material (feathers, whips and transplants) is planted in mixes at regular spacings to form a mutually supportive, fast-growing matrix of trees and shrubs that is easily maintained (Figure 19.3). As with all planting, mixes should always be designed with specific site conditions in mind. Most mixes incorporate a percentage of fast growing 'nurse species', such as willow and alder, which establish quickly to create more favourable sheltered conditions for the slower growing, eventually dominant species such as oak and ash.

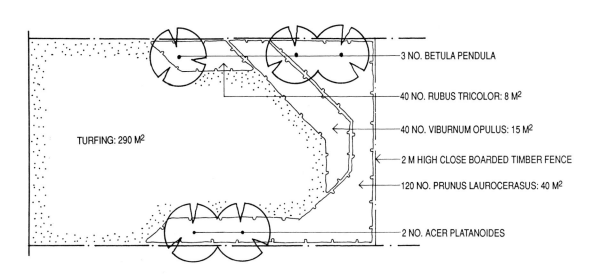

TURFING: 290 M²

3 NO. BETULA PENDULA

40 NO. RUBUS TRICOLOR: 8 M²

40 NO. VIBURNUM OPULUS: 15 M²

2 M HIGH CLOSE BOARDED TIMBER FENCE

120 NO. PRUNUS LAUROCERASUS: 40 M²

2 NO. ACER PLATANOIDES

FIGURE 19.2 **Typical planting plan for single-species bed.**

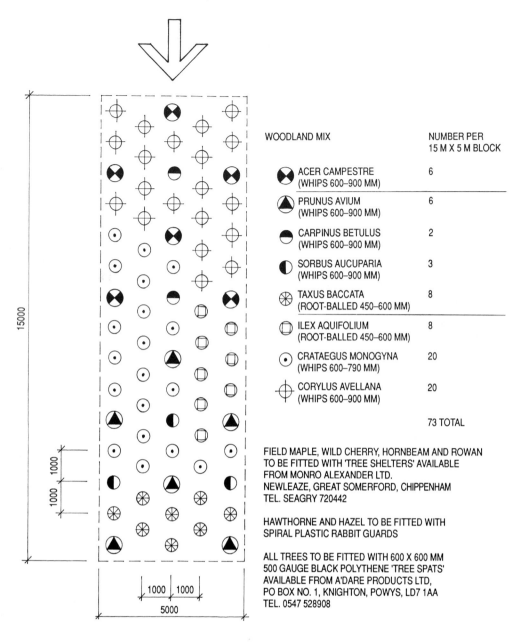

WOODLAND PLANTATION PLANTING MODULE

FIGURE 19.3 **Woodland plantation planting module.**

Good ground cultivation, healthy plant material and a comprehensive maintenance regime are important factors in the successful establishment of this type of planting. Management plans are essential if long-term design aims are to be achieved. Plantations are usually fenced, and it is usually necessary to protect stock against damage from rabbits and small rodents. In landscape work, plants are typically spaced at 1 m centres. However, recent work by the Forestry Commission suggests that 2–3 m spacing for broadleaf plantations is optimum, resulting in favourable growth rates, more easily maintainable stock and a reduction in the need for long-term thinning.

## Planting techniques

### Container-grown stock

Container-grown stock must be pit-planted. Pit size should always be slightly larger than the root ball.

The basic planting operation is simple. The plants should be removed from their containers with as little disturbance to the root ball as possible. Any roots

PLATE 19.4 **Container-grown conifers. Most ornamental plant material is now available as container-grown stock. Most woodland-type planting is carried out using cheaper, bare-rooted stock.**

coiled around inside the containers should be carefully loosened and spread before planting. The sides and bottom of the planting pits should be lightly forked and loosened to enable early root penetration. It is important that plants should be planted to the same depth as they were growing at in the nursery. This can be determined by soil marks on the necks of the plants. Finally, soil should be lightly firmed around the root ball, ensuring that no air spaces remain. Excess compaction around the planting area must be avoided, especially on heavy clays. Mechanical soil augers are sometimes used to dig the planting pits; these should be avoided in heavy soils as they may result in glazing of the pit sides, with poor root penetration and reduced establishment rates.

### Root-balled stock
Most conifers and a variety of other plants have fibrous roots. Consequently, if they are field-grown, they are usually lifted with soil attached and wrapped with hessian to keep their root balls intact.

Procedures for planting root-balled stock are similar to those employed for planting container-grown stock. The hessian need not be completely removed before planting, as it will eventually rot in the soil. It should, however, be loosened or cut from around the roots to avoid unnecessary root constriction. It is good practice to soak the root ball in water before planting out.

### Bare-rooted shrubs, transplants and whips
Most smaller sized tree material, native shrubs and bush roses are supplied as bare-rooted stock. Container-grown material may be available, but tends to be more expensive to obtain and plant than bare-root stock, and is therefore not generally used. The two basic methods of planting bare-root stock of this size are pit planting and notch planting.

The procedure for pit planting differs only slightly from that adopted for container grown plants. The pit should be excavated to a size and depth large enough to accept the plant's root stock, and the sides and bottom of the pit should be loosened to promote free drainage and early root penetration. Any subsoil that is excavated should be discarded. When backfilling, it is essential to

385

avoid air spaces around the roots of the plant, and this is best achieved by shaking the plant gently, while backfilling with good quality fine topsoil. This may be mixed with a soil conditioner and/or fertilizer if required. The soil should be gently firmed around the roots, the final soil level being both at the general level of the adjacent ground and also at the level of the nursery soil mark on the plant. If the plant is set too deep or not deeply enough in the soil, then death is likely to occur.

Where stock is planted directly into subsoil, the hole should be backfilled with the excavated subsoil rather than with imported topsoil. This avoids problems associated with differential shrinkage between the material in the backfilled pit and the surrounding ground, such as water stress or torn roots.

With notch planting a spade is inserted into the soil and levered to create a notch into which the bare root plant is placed; the spade is then removed and the notch closed by firming around the hole. This is by far the quickest and cheapest method of planting, and may be the only practical planting method on large schemes that use large amounts of small plant material. Wherever possible, however, pit planting should be specified in preference. There is a danger that spade leverage will cause compaction and smearing of the soil immediately adjacent to the root zone, reducing the plant's chances of survival. Failure rates among notch-planted stock are in any case inevitably higher than among pit-planted material, simply because less care is taken during the planting process. Trees planted as transplants or whips should not require staking.

### Bare-rooted, feathered and standard trees

With the exception of some semi-mature specimens which are supplied root-balled, most trees for use in landscape work are still specified as bare-rooted stock. Planting takes place into specially prepared tree pits excavated to specified dimensions (450 x 450 x 450 mm, for feathered trees and 600 x 600 x 600 mm for standard trees) and backfilled with good quality topsoil. This may be mixed with a soil conditioner or fertilizer as required. Any subsoil dug out during pit excavation should be removed from site.

Before backfilling, the bottoms and sides of the pits should be broken up to a depth of 200 mm to aid root penetration. If pits are excavated into heavy clay subsoils which are prone to waterlogging, then individual tree pits should be drained by field drains leading from each pit. Failure to do this can lead to a build-up of water around the tree roots, with eventual waterlogging and death.

The tree should be planted to the depth of the soil mark on the root collar, the soil being lightly firmed during backfilling to ensure intimate contact with the roots. Because of the volume of soil, successive layers of soil need to be firmed as backfilling proceeds. It is

important to avoid overfirming, which will inhibit root growth and prevent adequate moisture penetration through the soil.

It is usual to stake feathered and standard trees to prevent wind rock, which can break new roots and create an air pocket at the base of stems. Under most conditions single staking is sufficient. Stakes should be pointed at one end and treated with a non-injurious wood preservative. The stake should be positioned close to the tree on the windward side before backfilling and driven vertically into the bottom of the pit, taking care to avoid damage to the roots, until the top of the stake is at the required height. Material should be consolidated around the stake during backfilling and the tree secured firmly to the stake by means of at least two adjustable tree ties. The top tie on a tree stake should be at the very top of the stake in order to prevent damage to the tree by rubbing. Tree ties are available commercially from a variety of sources.

There has recently been much discussion about the necessary height of tree stakes. The main function of the stake is to prevent wind rock at the roots, not to support the stem of the tree. There is evidence that prevention of trunk movement by staking up to the crown prevents the tree from developing a natural resistance to wind blow through formation of secondary tissue. Thus, wherever possible, it is desirable to use short stakes, sufficiently long to anchor the base of the tree firmly while allowing the rest of the plant to move. There are instances where long stakes are desirable, for example in areas prone to vandalism. Stakes that extend some way into the crown of the tree are thought to discourage the breaking off of the main head of the tree through bending. In areas of strong prevailing winds it may be useful to angle stakes at 45° to the tree to be supported, in the direction of the prevailing wind, fixing the tree at the top end of the stake only.

### Semi-mature trees and extra heavy nursery stock

These are referred to under BS 4043: 1966 (1978), 'Recommendation for transplanting semi-mature trees', and BS 5236 (1975), 'Recommendations for the cultivation and planting of trees in the advanced nursery stock category'.

In certain situations, such as courtyard planting, it may be desirable to use extra large trees for immediate effect. Such trees are costly and careful consideration should be given to the use of smaller stock before including them in a specification. Plants should be individually chosen at the nursery well in advance of planting on site. Lifting and transporting semi-mature trees is a specialist job. Machinery can dig, lift and transplant large trees with a minimum of human effort, and specialist subcontractors should be used to carry out the task.

Preparing the site for the arrival of the tree follows much the same procedures as are outlined above for the planting of standard tree stock. A tree pit is dug to accept the root ball of the transplanted tree. Backfilled material should comprise good quality topsoil. During backfilling operations soil should be firmed around the rootball and the tree well watered. On poorly drained sites each tree pit should be individually drained. Trees should be firmly fixed by underground or aerial guying to prevent wind rock. Staking may be sufficient on extra heavy nursery stock. Regular maintenance, particularly watering, is an essential requirement in the successful establishment of large plant stock.

## Soil additives at planting

### Bulky soil ameliorant
On ground that has already been improved by ripping in bulky organic material there is no need to incorporate further soil ameliorant at the time of planting. Where initial soil amelioration has not been carried out, however, then the operation may have some value, particularly if the soil is particularly coarse or very heavy. The ameliorant is normally dug into the soil or, in the case of trees requiring tree pits, incorporated with topsoil backfill.

There are a wide range of suitable materials, ranging from peat and spent mushroom compost to proprietary products, such as tree planting compost, produced specifically for the job. Recent research has cast doubt on the value of the use of soil ameliorants as an aid to tree establishment (see Davies 1987).

### Non-bulky ameliorants
Several products, capable of absorbing many times their own weight in water, can be mixed into the soil at the time of planting. When turgid they provide a potential water source for plants that is readily exploitable.

Bare plant roots may also be dipped in proprietary liquid root dips, which aim to prevent dehydration of the root system and help the plant in the uptake of water and nutrients, thereby stimulating new root production. The manufacturers recommend that the dip is most effective when applied to bare-rooted stock as soon as possible after lifting.

Opinion seems to be divided as to the value of these treatments. It seems likely that during prolonged periods of drought these products may be of value in reducing plant losses, but under normal conditions where good techniques of cultivation, planting and aftercare are practised, their worth is limited.

### Fertilizer
It is good practice to incorporate fertilizer at the time of planting, particularly in impoverished soils in which specific deficiencies have been identified by chemical analysis at the survey stage. The fertilizer composition may be tailored to meet the specific needs of the deficiency where it is particularly acute. In other cases a general, slow-release inorganic granular type of fertilizer is adequate.

There is a great deal of current debate as to how fertilizers should be applied. One school of thought holds that the fertilizer should be scattered around the base of the plant, so that nutrients percolate down through the profile to the roots, while the other holds that fertilizers should be thoroughly incorporated into the soil at the time of planting, since the relative immobility of phosphate in the soil means that it is unavailable to plants if not placed in an area directly exploited by plant roots. More experimental investigation is needed into this topic. By its very nature, notch planting requires that the fertilizer is scattered on the soil surface.

Experiments have shown that fertilizer application is generally of little benefit unless competitive weed species are adequately controlled, since the faster growing weeds are likely to be stimulated to the detriment of the trees and shrubs.

## Cutting back newly planted stock

Many trees and shrubs, particularly bare-rooted stock, may benefit from pruning at planting, especially on difficult sites. Crown pruning of standard trees goes some way to redressing root to shoot ratios and reduces water stress when plants are in leaf. Newly planted native shrubs may be hard pruned to promote young vigorous growth and bushiness. Bush roses also benefit from hard pruning.

It is important to explain the reasons for such operations to the client. Hard pruning is not appropriate in all situations. On schemes where ornamental planting is the main component, ground conditions are good and plant stock healthy, any benefits associated with cutting back at the time of planting are likely to be outweighed by the need to achieve initial impact.

## Mulching

When correctly specified and implemented, mulching will fulfil the following functions:

1. It will suppress weeds, thus reducing maintenance costs.
2. It will aid retention of soil moisture during periods of drought.
3. It will provide an attractive surface finish, which is particularly useful in areas where planting has taken place into less than perfect soil conditions.
4. Over a period of years the mulch will gradually break down and become incorporated into the soil, providing a long-term source of organic soil matter.

Mulches are expensive and may not be appropriate

Mulches are usually specified to 75 mm compacted depth and are spread after planting operations have been completed. They should only be spread over damp soils.

An effective alternative mulch treatment over small areas is provided by pegging 500 gauge black polythene sheeting over the soil and covering it with a thin layer of gravel or soil. The polythene completely suppresses weed growth while retaining soil moisture during periods of drought. Planting takes place through slits cut in the plastic. Subsequent maintenance requirements are minimal, mainly confined to ensuring that the polythene remains well pegged.

Black polythene circles of various diameters, each circle slit to the centre, are also available. These are placed around the bases of individual trees, and are particularly useful in plantations, where total surface mulches are too costly to apply. Forestry Commission experiments have shown that the larger the area covered by the circle, the more benefit to the plant concerned in terms of vigour and growth. A minimum ground coverage of 1 m$^2$ is recommended.

## Protection

### Tree guards

Tree guards are used in urban areas to give some measure of protection against vandalism and accidental damage, and in rural areas to protect newly planted trees against grazing by stock (Plate 19.5). Tree guards are usually only used on plant material of standard size or above in urban situations, but are available in much smaller sizes for use in plantations. Their design and specification will vary according to the task that they have to perform, for instance they may be strong, visually attractive and vandal-proof in towns and practical, inexpensive and stock-proof in rural areas.

### Rabbit guards

Newly planted stock, even in many urban areas, is susceptible to damage from both rabbits and such other small rodents as voles. Where these are likely to be a problem, plant material must be protected from the outset. Rabbit guards comprise spirals of plastic which provide some protection against grazing by rabbits when wrapped around the bases of young trees. They are relatively inexpensive to supply and to fix, but are visually unattractive. They should not be used on plants that are less than 1.2 m in height. Secure rabbit-proof fencing is a more desirable alternative.

On some schemes voles also present a problem, causing widespread grazing damage. The maintenance of a 1 m$^2$ weed-free area around the base of each plant will deter the animals to some extent. Where losses are unacceptable, the base of young plants should be protected with a 150 mm length of split piping.

PLATE 19.5 **An appropriate tree guard design for rural or parkland areas. The function of this guard is to provide protection from grazing animals and accidental damage from maintenance machinery. Young plant stock would need the additional protection of spiral rabbit guards at their base.**

over large areas of woodland-type planting or in areas where a high quality visual finish is not required.

The types of material most commonly used for mulching in landscape work are shredded bark (available commercially in a variety of grades and finishes), spent mushroom compost, well rotted manure and peat. Wherever possible, local sources should be used, since transport costs have a large bearing on unit costs.

## Temporary fencing

Temporary fencing is used to define and protect large areas of newly planted, young trees and shrubs until they are fully established. Depending on the nature of the site, the fencing may provide protection against grazing animals, vandalism and construction site damage. Access must be provided for maintenance purposes. In rural areas posts, wire and netting are appropriate. If necessary this can be designed so as to be rabbit-proof. In urban areas and on building sites chestnut pale fencing may suffice. In all situations the fencing should be well constructed, sturdy and robust enough to fulfil its function.

## Shelter fencing

On particularly exposed sites, where successful plant establishment is likely to be inhibited by strong winds, windbreak fencing is recommended. This is commercially available and comprises plastic netting constructed in such a way as to reduce and deflect strong winds, therefore affording valuable plant protection. It has the additional benefit of being stock-proof.

## Tree shelters

Tree shelters are a relatively new idea, of use in matrix-type planting areas. Initial research and development into their use has been carried out by Graham Tuley of the Forestry Commission. Several types are now commercially available.

All types of tree shelters basically consist of a clear plastic tube which is placed over newly planted, small-size stock (whips and transplants) and fixed to a ground-driven stake (Plate 19.6). Microclimatic conditions within the tube are particularly favourable for plant growth, leading to better establishment and faster growth rates in the years immediately following planting. Additional major benefits are protection against animal browsing, rabbit grazing and spray damage caused during weed-control operations.

Some disadvantages have also been identified, for instance some tree species establish poorly or only moderately successfully when shelters are used and some trees are unable to support themselves if the shelter is removed earlier than the first five years.

Shelters can look unsightly in the landscape and there is some evidence of damage by abrasion to emerging shoots. More research is needed to monitor these problems. For a comprehensive overview of tree shelter development see Browell and Mead (1987).

## Direct tree seeding

This is a relatively recent, still largely experimental technique, which provides a potentially cheap method of establishing seemingly natural scrub and stands of woodland trees and shrubs in areas where initial visual impact in unimportant. Seed mixes, together with nurse crops of winter wheat or such woody legumes as tree lupin or broom, are sown on to bare ground and the seeds are buried by the use of conventional agricultural machinery. To facilitate germination some seeds require dormancy to be broken by special treatment before sowing. On steep slopes where cultivation is not possible, seeds are covered with a suitable mulch in place of soil.

Maintenance regimes are the minimum necessary to ensure that weeds do not become rampant and the nurse crop does not become over dominant. Selective thinning may be necessary to achieve this. Percentage germination of tree species is variable but generally low. Growth rates vary between species and according to site conditions. More experimental work is needed before this approach can be widely used with any degree of confidence.

## 19.7 MAINTENANCE

Careful maintenance following the completion of the planting contract is fundamental to plant establishment and the successful achievement of long-term planting objectives. Planting contracts should include a maintenance period that begins after practical completion of planting works. This should ideally run for at least two years on most sites, and up to five years on difficult sites. Operations should include replacement of dead and dying plant material, keeping the site weed-free, adjusting tree ties and watering adequately during periods of drought. It is important that the maintenance that will be needed is clearly defined in the specification, so that the contractor can allow for it fully when pricing the works.

### Weed control

Weed control is possibly the most important maintenance operation of all. Newly planted trees and shrubs are very susceptible to competition from weeds, which compete for water and to a lesser extent light and nutrients. Growth rates of plants are severely reduced by weeds and if weed growth is particularly rank, plants may die altogether. Even the growth rates of trees that have been planted for several years are reduced by vegetation growing around the tree base. It is therefore clearly important to control weeds if the natural vigour of newly planted stock is to be encouraged (Plate 19.7).

Several techniques for controlling weeds are available. On small urban sites hand weeding is a possible method. On larger sites it becomes impractical because it is so slow and labour-intensive. It is possible to control weed growth through the use of soil mulches applied immediately after planting. Mulches with the addition of herbicides (chemical weedkillers) or herbicides alone are, however, more reliable. In order to control weed growth successfully on a particular site it may be necessary to specify the use of a number of different types of herbicide, together with a programme for their application. This is because there is, as yet, no single herbicide on the market capable of killing all weed species. Most herbicides will also cause damage to trees and shrubs and so must be applied extremely carefully by skilled operators.

Good application of herbicides is the key to safe and effective weed control. Manufacturers' recommendations regarding the mode of application of herbicides must be followed carefully, and appropriate protective clothing worn at all times. It is generally desirable to maintain a weed-free area around the base of each plant to a diameter of 1.0 m. In most situations this means total weed control over the entire planted area. For more detailed information on the use of herbicides and their mode of action, see Wright (1982).

### Watering

Assuming that the material has been well planted into reasonable soil, then moisture availability becomes a critical factor in determining plant success. Both heavy (clay) and light (sandy) soils are prone to drying out in summer, causing severe stress to newly planted stock. Effective weed control reduces the competition for the available moisture in the soil and mulches may further aid soil moisture conservation by reducing evaporation. If possible, ornamental schemes should be designed with mains supply watering stations which allow on site irrigation to be carried out by the landscape contractor. Particularly in southern Britain, regular irrigation will have a positive effect on plant establishment and may make the difference between the success and the failure of plants in drought years. Particular emphasis should be given to watering large stock, and regular watering is usually necessary between June and August. The topsoil should be thoroughly soaked to its full depth. If watering points are not available then the landscape contractor should arrange to have water delivered to the site.

In drought conditions, when the provision of water is restricted by legislation, contractors should be required to inform the landscape architect of the cost of second-class water from sewage works or other approved sources.

### Plant replacements

Dead or dying plant material should be replaced as part of the general maintenance process. It is not always necessary or reasonable to require the contractor to replace every plant that dies in reclamation schemes, for example, initial plant quantities are deliberately over-specified to allow for the high losses of plants that are often associated with such schemes.

### Adjustment of tree ties and stakes

Tree ties and stakes should be regularly inspected and adjusted to prevent rubbing and wind rock, and to allow for growth of the tree. Tree stakes should be removed as soon as the tree is growing strongly and able to support itself adequately. Under good growth conditions this should be within 2–3 seasons.

**PLATE 19.7 Oak trees excavated three seasons after planting as 38 cm transplants in a weeding experiment near Cambridge. (a) The tree on the left had no weeding. (b) The tree on the right grew in a 0.5 m diameter weed-free plot.**

### Mulching

Mulches should be topped up as necessary to retain the original specified depth of material.

### Damage

If rabbit or rodent damage was not anticipated at the time of planting and has since become a problem, then appropriate guards or fencing will have to be provided to prevent further loss of plant material. It is unreasonable to expect the contractor to bear the cost of these.

## 19.8 LONG-TERM MANAGEMENT

The management programme should follow on continuously from the maintenance period and should aim to ensure the continuing health and vigour of the newly established stock. Maintenance operations are often neglected by the client, who is frequently reluctant to spend further money on the post-establishment phase of a scheme. This can be disastrous in the long term,

and it is vital that the importance of a long-term management plan, together with its financial implications, is impressed on the client from the outset.

Because of their extended nature, management programme areas often run under a separate contract or series of contracts to the main planting contract. If the client has his own maintenance staff, then they should be informed of the architects' long-term design intentions, so that situations like that shown in Plate 19.8 can be avoided. The landscape architect should outline the design aims, the management operations necessary to achieve them, and a recommended timetable for action, and issue them in a management schedule.

The following work should be included in the schedule.

### Watering

Continued regular watering becomes less important as stock establishes itself, but remains critically important during times of drought, particularly on schemes which are predominantly ornamental.

391

Thinning should always be selective and should be carried out with the landscape architect's long-term design aim in mind. Selective thinning may also be necessary in ornamental planting, where initial plant densities were deliberately high to create an instant visual impact.

### Coppicing

Coppicing may be a long-term objective in a woodland-type of planting, in which case a coppicing programme should be detailed in the management plans.

### Replanting climax species

On difficult sites, conditions may have restricted initial species selection to pioneer species. Once they are successfully established, these may be thinned and the gaps replanted with climax species such as beech and oak, which should be able to establish themselves under the more favourable conditions that will have been created by the pioneer species. In this way species diversity may be built up over time, and the long-term design aims of the landscape architect satisfied in stages.

## 19.9 CONTRACT SPECIFICATION

Contract procedures are beyond the scope of this chapter. For a comprehensive overview of the subject see Clamp (1986).

A well written and well presented specification is essential to the successful establishment of plants. Specifications for ground preparation, planting operations, maintenance and management should be directly relevant to each individual site, and must be carefully worded to be as precise and clear as possible.

Many offices use standardized specification clauses which can be used under a variety of situations. Clauses may be deleted or added to build up a specification suitable for use on a particular scheme. If the clauses can be stored on a word processor linked to a printer, then specifications can be built up quickly and efficiently without the need for the document to be completely retyped each time. Extreme care must always be taken to ensure that the clauses are of direct relevance to the site. If standard clauses are not appropriate for a specific situation then new clauses must be drafted.

## 19.10 SITE SUPERVISION

Site supervision is essential at all stages of the contract works if the standards and operations described in the specification are to be translated into acceptable results

### Weed control

Once closed canopy conditions are achieved, most weed growth is naturally suppressed, and weed control can be reduced to spot treatments applied infrequently to control persistent perennial weed species.

### Tree ties and stakes

Once trees are well established and are growing strongly, tree ties and stakes should be removed. This operation may take place as part of the general maintenance works.

### Thinning

Thinning is carried out in situations where matrix planting at fairly close centres has been used to establish dense stands of vegetation. Such plantations may need thinning several times over a period of years before management is complete. Without thinning, individual plants will become spindly and weak, and species that were intended only as nurse crops during the initial stages of establishment will suppress the growth of the intended dominant species.

on site. The landscape architect or an appointed specialist Clerk of Works should be on hand to check and approve all stages of operations, for instance ground preparation, topsoil spread, arrival of plants on site, storage on site and planting operations. The architect should also keep a close check on the site during the subsequent maintenance period. Standards of work or materials not in accordance with the specification should be rejected at once. The client should be made aware of the need for supervision at an early stage in the design process, so that allowances can be made in the design budgets for regular site visits, and, if necessary, the implementation of supervisors' reports.

## FURTHER READING

Addison, C. H. and Thoday, P. R. (Eds) *Cost Effective Amenity Landscape Management*, H E A Conference Proceedings (University of Bath 1983)

Binns, W. O. and Fourt, D. F. *Reclamation of Surface Workings for Trees, 1 Landforms and Cultivation*, Arboricultural Research Note, Issued by the DoE Arboricultural Advisory and Information Service (1981)

Bradshaw, A. D. 'Topsoil Quality — Proposals for a new system', *Landscape Design*, **141**, February pp. 27—34 (1983)

Browell, M. and Mead, H. 'Tree shelters', *Landscape Design*, **166**, April, pp. 57—60 (1987)

Campbell-Lloyd, R. 'Mulching — Doing it right', *Landscape Design*, **163**, October, p. 75 (1986)

Clamp, H. *Spons' Landscape Contract Manual*, (E. & F. N. Spon Ltd 1986)

Committee for Plant Supply and Establishment *Code of Practice for Plant Handling* (Horticultural Trades Association 1985)

Davies, R. J. *Trees and Weeds: Weed Control for Successful Tree Establishment*, Forestry Commission Handbook, No. 2 (HMSO 1987)

Davies, R. J. *A Comparison of the Survival and Growth of Transplants, Whips and Standards With and Without Chemical Weed Control*, Arboricultural Research Note, Issued by the DoE Arboricultural Advisory and Information Service (1987)

Davies, R. J. *Do Soil Ameliorants Help Tree Establishment?*, Arboricultural Research Note, Issued by the DoE Arboricultural Advisory and Information Service (1987)

Evans, J. *Silviculture of Broadleaved Woodland*, Forestry Commission Bulletin No. 62 (HMSO 1984)

Evans, J. and Shanks, C. W. *Tree Shelters*, Arboriculture Research Note, Issued by the DoE Arboricultural Advisory and Information Service (1987)

Hacket, B. *Planting Design* (E. & F. N. Spon 1982)

Holden, R. 'Topsoil Specification', *Landscape Design*, **141**, February, p. 35 (1983)

Insley, H. 'The use of container-grown broadleaved trees', *Landscape Design*, **137**, February, pp. 38—40 (1982)

Joint Council for Landscape Industries *Frost Damage to Trees and Shrubs* (The Landscape Institute 1985)

La Dell, T. 'An introduction to tree and shrub seeding' *Landscape Design*, August, pp. 27—31 (1983)

Pepper, H. W. *Plastic Mesh Tree Guards*, Arboricultural Research Note, Issued by the DoE Arboricultural Advisory and Information Service (1987)

Pryce, S. 'Management problems of one to ten year old Woody Mass planting', *Landscape Design*, **147**, February, pp. 39—41 (1984)

Ruff, A. and Tregay, R. *An Ecological Approach to Urban Landscape Design*, Department of Town and Country Planning (University of Manchester 1982)

Skinner, D. N. *Planting Success Rates — Standard Trees*, Arboricultural Research Note, Issued by the DoE Arboricultural Advisory and Information Service (1986)

Stephens R. J. and Thoday, P. R. *Weed Control in Amenity Plantings*, Conference Proceedings, University of Bath (1980)

Tandy, C. (Ed) *Handbook of Urban Landscape* (Architectural Press 1973)

Thoday, P. R. (Ed) *Tree Establishment*, Conference Proceedings, University of Bath (1983)

Tregay, R. and Gustavvson, R. *Oakwoods New Landscape; Designing for Nature in the Residential Environment* (Warrington and Runcorn Development Corporation 1982)

Tregay, R. 'A sense of nature', *Landscape Design*, **156**, August, pp. 34—38. (1985)

Weddle, A. E. (Ed) *Landscape Techniques* (Heinemann 1979)

Wright, T. 'Weed control in landscape maintenance', *Landscape Design*, **139**, August, pp. 37—40 (1982)

Wright, T. 'Mulches and weed control', *Landscape Design*, **140**, November, pp. 27—9 (1982)

# CHAPTER 20

# Design and Management of Interior Landscape

## ALAN CORNFORD AND STEPHEN DALE

## 20.1 INTRODUCTION

The growth of interior landscape in Britain over the last ten years has been dramatic. The reason for this is not immediately clear, but one can surmise that the general increase in building and office refurbishment since the problems of the early 1970s has coincided with an increased awareness of the exploratory schemes carried out in the United States in the late 1960s.

A recent visitor to Britain from Belgium questioned why it should be that so much interior landscape was evident in the United Kingdom when there was so little of any importance in the rest of Europe. Again, we can only surmise on the reasons, but it would seem that our common language and positive links have brought many ideas more quickly to this country from America.

Many architects visit sites in North America (Plate 20.1), and many of the schemes that they have seen have been well documented in recent years. Their successes have given designers in the United Kingdom greater confidence to try to produce similar design schemes.

## 20.2 HISTORY

To achieve scale, an interior landscape must have the space and environment in which to survive, and these can only be achieved with an atrium or conservatory. Many interior landscape schemes in the US are based on a theatrium or a covered courtyard, an approach which has found favour with building architects in recent years, while in Britain we have a long standing awareness of the conservatory, so beloved by the Victorians. This approach is used mainly in the domestic market, but also, to a lesser degree, in commercial buildings.

The origins of the atrium are to be found in the Mediterranean owing to the climate. Here a courtyard enclosure, often with a central water feature, provided a cooling atmosphere for the building as a whole. The design developed as a direct response to the climate, and our modern northern equivalents are based on exactly the same design, but related to our somewhat harsher climate.

Covered internal spaces can be dated from the early nineteen hundreds, with Warren and Bucklin's Arcade in Providence, Rhode Island and Charles Barry's Reform Club in Pall Mall (1837). Scale and effect were increased with Paxton's Great Exhibition Crystal Palace (1851) which spawned many winter garden equivalents, and Mengonis' Galleria in Milan (1867). These were built possibly due to the opulence of the age, since little of significance in the form of internal clear covered space was evident until the 1960s.

In the 1960s, it was America that was at the forefront of developing the space for interior landscape that was to take the industry away from the small-scale limitations of office planting. John Portman's Regency Hyatt in Atlanta (Plate 20.2) and Roche and Dinkeloo's Ford Foundation Building in New York, both built in 1967, were to set a precedent for the current generation of designers; the former for the atrium, the latter for the concept of an internal garden, designed by the landscape architect Dan Kiley. At about the same period, Roache and Dinkeloo designed the John Deere building in Moline, Illinois. This had an even more extensive landscape, and created a further precedent of scale. These landscapes survive still. They have developed and plants have changed, but they are no less dramatic now than when they were first unveiled.

In this country, with a nation's consciousness influenced by botanic garden spectacles such as the Palm House at Kew and the Tree Fern House in Glasgow (Plate 20.3), large-scale landscape in interiors has been accepted and developed very quickly. True scale was

achieved in the Skyline Hotel at Heathrow and the Redditch Shopping Centre, where date palms were used in the malls. To an extent, the conservatory philosophy survives in the use of date palms and similar exotica in leisure pools and display gardens. The difficulty in controlling this form of space other than at high temperatures has seen perhaps greater success with the enclosed atrium, which will allow a direct response to the climate and with correct balance give year round use.

Our modern city space is dictated to an extent by economics rather than art, in that it has to be economical to run, the landscape must be a feature to aid the selling or the letting of the building and the 'safe' design is preferred. We are, however, growing aware of the internal park principle, since the landscape is less domestic and is generally permanent. When handled professionally, the true internal landscape is now a feature of large-scale buildings which we can look forward to over the next decade.

## 20.3 DESIGN CONSIDERATIONS

Much of the current potential for interior landscape design exists thanks to the early efforts of the small-scale office 'scapers' – those who supplied plants and planters for offices and, more importantly, maintained them in good health. They created the awareness of plants and proved that plants could survive in the often inhospitable environment of an office, with its low light, low humidity, variable heat and erratic air flow.

Through necessity, a hardy mixture of plants providing colour and variegation tended to appear. They were often changed and rarely matched. If this seems a cruel analysis, I stress again that the office environment places severe limitations on what plants can be used, and that the client's request is often for something 'cheerful'.

With the current improvement in the quality of the office environment and, more importantly, the creation of larger scale landscape interiors, we need, with due regard to the environmental limitations, to apply our basic design approach strongly. With attention to style and scale, a simple approach will often be more successful than the busy gardenesque approach of the near past. An appreciation of the total internal space, with an earlier entry into the design process, will enable landscape designers to create a solution with true longevity, rather than a display which provides no more than a momentary diversion.

## Scale

There is a need to develop beyond the traditional attitudes towards the scale of an entire landscape when thinking about the design of internal atria and, indeed, any large space. An awareness of the potential of the internal height and volume is essential, and we must make use of this dramatically increased third dimension, which is only occasionally presented to those dealing with exteriors, for instance on building perimeters and quarry faces.

Within the practical limitations of maintenance, the interior space can include the planting of very mature trees, the use of terracing to emphasize the height, the planting of balconies and void edges and planting at high level to trail or flower with the full benefit of natural light. The use of some or all of these elements will not only create a true impact for the client, but will also enable the designer to utilize all aspects of the three-dimensional void.

395

PLATE 20.2 **The Atlanta Regency Hyatt — the arrival of the large-scale atrium in the USA. Recent problems with the *Ficus* have resulted in the addition of intrusive artificial illumination, which had not been envisaged.** *(Steve Dale)*

PLATE 20.3 **The Victorian conservatory. The UK has a traditional awareness of interior landscape from the Victorian era — the Glasgow Botanic Garden Tree Fern House, dating from 1873.** *(Steve Dale)*

**PLATE** 20.4 **Redditch — a bold use of large-scale plant material in a shopping mall, with** *Phoenix* **date palms grouped informally in ground pits.** *(Steve Dale)*

## Style

The style of an internal space is often predetermined by the character of the building, and we must accept this limitation. In conjunction with the design team, however, it is often appropriate, if not required, to design the landscape to a style or character type. Whether to emphasize the building, or as a relief to it, style will need to be varied far more frequently in the internal space, for example a quality shopping mall (Plate 20.4) will require elegance, a control square simplicity, a conservatory lushness or a 'garden' food court (Plate 20.5) attention to detail. It is the variation of plant types, numbers, scale and, above all, an appreciation of the intention that are important.

## Colour

The landscape designer will find that colour is far more intense in an internal space that it is outside, and much more frequently apparent. The multiple use of building materials, the intensity of the light and the inclusion of people themselves tend to create a busier, more vibrant space in an interior, only equalled in bazaars and busy urban squares on the exterior.

Because of this, the traditional mixture of green foliage and colour, using crotons and cordyline, for example, can appear confused and insignificant. Better perhaps is to create strength through simplicity and careful use of blocks of colour that can then be changed periodically to provide relief. In North America, the careful use of intense colour, such as in the IBM Building, New York (Plate 20.6), has proved extremely effective and should be considered more favourably in this country.

## 20.4 INTERNAL SPACE POTENTIAL

### Climate

The traditional atrium in a Roman villa, although unglazed, was designed to cool the internal space and protect against the heat of the Mediterranean. The modern atrium can similarly act to moderate the external weather, be it the heat of Florida or the cold of Scandinavia, and at the same time it will enable people to move freely in a pleasant environment. The design potential of this should not be missed.

### Temperature control

Environmental engineers have long recognized the value of a covered atrium as a low cost equalizer against the elements, reducing the cost of heating, the need for high grade external glazing and as a means of balancing heat exchange from the office environment. Given the importance of an atrium as an important light well and consequent internal focus, the interior landscape designer should grasp the opportunity to create, within the space, a landscape worthy of the focus.

### Work space

Through the experience of office landscaping, we should understand the importance of the work space to those who inhabit it from morning until night. People may spend more of their working lives in a place of work than they do in their homes, so that the importance of the quality of that space cannot be overemphasized.

The extension and continuation into a central atrium must be recognized as it becomes the relief, the focus of interest and the pleasant 'exterior' that we all need. It

397

PLATE 20.5 **Food court landscape –
highly stylized landscape, which has to
respond to themes and characters. A
simple elegance is sometimes the most
effective, as shown here, where** *Cocos
plumosa* **have been used almost exclusively.** *(Steve Dale)*

PLATE 20.6 **The IBM building, New York – excellent use of scale to create an internal park for public use, with
bamboo, simple groundcover and massed seasonal colour.** *(Steve Dale)*

becomes the park that so rarely exists outside our window. See Plate 20.7.

## Leisure box

Given that the covered atrium provides a controlled environment through which we can all pass freely, the scope for design is tremendous. Whether it is to be designed as a garden to be viewed, a park to be enjoyed or a café to sit in, the internal space should become an extension of the external environment to which we are often denied pleasant access through the vagaries of our climate. If we view the interior space as a landscape 'leisure box' (Plate 20.8) into which we can freely move, we can begin to make better use of that space. It will attract the public, possibly extend the length of their visit to a retail surrounding and enhance their desire to return at a future date. Thus, there can be commercial reasoning behind the provision of a pleasant landscape. Above all, however, must be the concept that it is a landscape with the inclusion of other elements and not the mere dressing of a space with plants.

## Interior and exterior landscapes

As building technology has improved, so has the ability to create lightweight structures and translucent structures of hitherto unknown delicacy. With this improved technology, despite an unhealthy fascination for mirror finishes, architects and engineers have used glass as a vertical face more than at any time since Paxton first conceived his Crystal Palace. The relevance of this trend to the interior landscape designer is that it helps us to reinforce a fragile visual link between the interior and exterior landscapes, leading the public logically from one to the other.

At the domestic scale, the conservatory is seen as the 'garden room', and public acceptance of this slight transition is not in doubt. The unimpeded movement from one to the other, depending on the vagaries of the climate, is fundamental to the future of large-scale landscape interiors, and a visual linking of feature and scale, using similar height trees and surfacing materials, should be explored whenever possible.

## 20.5 REQUIREMENTS IMPOSED BY THE DESIGN

### The limitation of environmental conditions

Having established the range of environmental conditions that are required to support the interior landscape, the landscape designer must ensure that the environmental engineers, and above all the client, are aware of the need to maintain these conditions for as long as the scheme remains in that form. History has given us a precedent in the winter-garden landscapes of the Victorian era, which through financial decline and loss of public interest were removed or survived in limited, frost-tolerant form.

The importance of the accuracy required in the per-

PLATE 20.7 **The internal park principle. Robert Fleming building in Copthall Avenue, City of London – a fine example of large-scale** *Ficus* **with simple ground cover to create the impression of a park.** *(R. Macmillan)*

PLATE 20.8 **The leisure box principle – an interior that captures active and passive recreation in a true landscape setting. The Embassy Suite Hotel, Fort Lauderdale.** *(Steve Dale)*

formance of service equipment and the intention to ensure that this is maintained should be the initial responsibility of the landscape designer. His professional credibility, and indeed liability, may depend on all parties' acceptance of the consequences of the support machinery failing.

## Design for permanency

The scale of interior landscape has taken it subtly away from the temporary nature of office interiors. Where a true 'landscape' is designed, it is unlikely to be in mobile containers; the planters are likely to be drained and the sheer size of the installation will render it a permanent feature. In addition to the need for continuity in environmental conditions, as previously mentioned, the landscape designer should be aware of the practical requirements for maintenance, and should always consider this 'fourth dimension', which is so important to interior landscape.

When seeking tenders or negotiating a contract, the landscape designer should either provide a specification personally, or seek an exact specification from the selected contractor as to the range of operations and frequency of visit that is expected. On renewal of a maintenance contract, the client should always seek prices on a comparative basis and, ideally, the landscape designer should participate in the long-term evaluation of the landscape management.

Above all, the client should be advised against the simple approach of 'How much would you charge to maintain this?', which can result in the rapid decline and demise of an original design.

## Structural implications

When presenting the range of effects that are possible within an interior space, the landscape designer should be aware of the structural implications that large-scale landscapes can have. Frequently, the floor of an atrium or reception foyer will be on a raised slab, and the general design approach will have to be one of caution. The structural engineer and architect may not have envisaged the scale, and once the slab is cast, it is a

400

PLATE 20.9 **Skyline Hotel, Heathrow — an early use of large-scale plant material in an internal landscape.** *Ficus* and *Phoenix* **give an exciting scale to an 'internal courtyard', with low-level, fully glazed roof providing good natural light.** *(Steve Dale)*

costly and difficult operation to increase the structural capacity.

## Long-term technical risks

Interior landscape, generally requiring large-scale plant material (Plates 20.9 and 20.10) and water, requires an awareness of failure that is seldom experienced with exterior schemes.

The problems arising in interior landscape can be manifold, and the ability to overcome these should be considered in the initial design. For instance, a mature tree may have to be installed before a building is occupied; it may even require the removal of a glazing panel at an upper level for entry into the building; and at some stage it will also require replacement, and the landscape designer must ensure that this is feasible.

Similarly, a water feature (Plate 20.11), desirable in so many instances, may fail in its waterproofing, or an irrigation system may become ineffective, owing to the build-up of calcareous deposits within the outlets. These management problems can be overcome, and design should not bow unnecessarily to them, but it is essential

PLATE 20.10 **Large-scale plant material at a Florida nursery of trees up to 10 m in height — in this instance a** *Bucida bucerus* **(black olive).** *(Steve Dale)*

to consider the consequences of any design action from the outset of the project.

## Living material

There is no doubt that a living scheme tends to be more successful than an imitation one, and public appreciation has proven this. However, having established an environment suitable for healthy plant growth, the landscape consultant must make the client aware of the long-term consequence of looking after the scheme.

Interior planting tends merely to survive in a healthy state rather than grow as freely as an exterior scheme. However, given suitable conditions, trees may put on considerable growth, and this must be controlled by the maintenance team by thinning and pruning. The necessity to carry out these operations should be accepted from the outset and the clients advised accordingly, so that they know what they are letting themselves in for.

Chemical or biological control of pests and diseases is a vital aspect of plant care in interior landscape, and acceptance of this fact is equally important. Whereas an infestation of greenfly is an evil which can be controlled without undue disturbance on an exterior scheme, an outbreak of blackfly can cause extreme concern to

office staff in an interior scheme before there has been time to deal with it.

In all instances, it is the responsibility of the landscape consultant to make the client and managing agents aware of the potential problems when the scheme is still under discussion.

## Specification

The need for accurate specification is essential when designing large-scale interior landscape, to ensure that the end result equates to the conception. With a variety of professions that have no specific training in landscape design dealing with interior landscape, poor specification is often the case. This weakness is not only unfair to the client, who expects a high level of professionalism, but also to the contractor, who will be unable to accurately price the design and may produce a poor installation as a result.

The supply of interior plant material suffers from numerous sources, resulting in a lack of standardization, in contrast to the high standards achieved with exterior stock. Thus, exact specification is necessary to ensure that the required form of plant is achieved. Any generalization will result in contractors putting in prices for a different product. The price variation will then be greater and the lowest cost will often unwittingly result in an inferior installation.

It should be the responsibility of the landscape consultant to ensure that a full specification is produced. The client's responsibility is to ensure that the appropriate professional is appointed to undertake this aspect of the work.

## Conclusion

Interior landscape design is a specialist aspect of our profession which as yet has not been fully accepted. The consultant will need to be aware of many aspects of the building professions, knowledge of which hitherto has been unnecessary. It is fair to say that the knowledge of a landscape architect must be increased before dealing with interior space, and few of our educational establishments have seen fit to include a detailed study programme on interior design within their syllabus. The landscape architect still remains, however, the professional most suited to dealing with interior landscape design.

Before applying basic design principles, the landscape consultant has to build on awareness of the interior space, the specialist environmental requirements, the appropriate professional consultants who will be required and the particular problems associated with

PLATE 20.11 **Water features — a visual and design asset but a long-term technical risk. This example at the Edmonton Mall provides a fine focus, but many others were out of commission on the same visit.** (*Steve Dale*)

PLATE 20.12 **Plants for covered, unheated spaces –** *Podocarpus mackii*, **widely used in the USA, tolerant of low temperatures and available up to 10 m in height.**

building programme. The end results can be spectacular, and failures can be dismal, but in this rapidly expanding element of our profession, the time is right for a concerted and co-ordinated approach to this new area of design potential that lies ahead.

## 20.6 ENVIRONMENTAL REQUIREMENTS

### Types of environment

Interior environments vary enormously, and it is essential to understand the inbuilt environment to enable correct plant specification. In designing with plants internally one is likely to experience any of the following environmental types:

1. Traditional office environment – lighting level 300 to 800 lux. By virtue of the low light level within the average office, only a very limited range of plants from the tropical plant range is applicable.
2. Enclosed, heated, low light environment. This environment is typical of the average atrium space within a multi-storey building, requiring additional plant lighting to support large tree material. Only limited tropical plants will be suitable for specification within this environmental type.
3. Enclosed, heated, medium to high light environment. An environmental type now quite commonly found in shopping centres and low rise office buildings. Tropical plant material will be very happy within this environment, as will certain sub-tropical species.
4. Enclosed, unheated, high light environment. This environmental type, reminiscent of the orangery and conservatories of the past, is sometimes found within a new office development, but is becoming more evident in the refurbished shopping centres, where a glazed roof is put on a previously open mall, but full heating and air conditioning are considered prohibitive. This environment will only support sub-tropical material. See Plate 20.12.
5. Enclosed, unheated, low light environment. This is probably the most difficult space to handle as, in general, low temperature tolerant plant material requires a higher light level, and very substantial artificial illumination will be required for plant life support.

### Light

Recommended light level categories based on a 12 hour lighting period per day for 7 days per week are given here.

    (i) Low – 400–750 lux.
   (ii) Medium – 750–1000 lux.
  (iii) High – 2000 lux.
  (iv) Very high – 3000–5000 lux.

Light is the major stimulant to the life cycle of plants, because it is the energy source that triggers the process of photosynthesis for the manufacture of food. Interior foliage plants can make use of either natural or artificial light. Clearly, natural lighting is to be encouraged, as it provides energy-efficient, pleasant and ambient lighting

403

and because of its full spectrum. Ideally, natural daylight should be the primary light source for any internal plant material. For the standard range of tropical plants, however, quality of light is less important than intensity of light, and artificial illumination should be programmed to provide a continuous 12 hour per day minimum for plant material, 7 days per week, with at least a 6 hour dark period.

It must be understood that light levels required to support major trees within interior space will rarely be greater than the compensation point that provides sufficient energy only to produce growth to replace dying tissue. It is therefore vitally important that the lighting specification is at least adequate for this purpose, to guarantee long-term survival for the plant material. When calculating supplementary artificial illumination, the lighting engineers must allow for bulb degradation and dust, and so a planned bulb replacement programme should be initiated.

## Temperature requirements

The temperature preferences for each plant variety must be taken into account in any planting specification. These preferences are basically an indication of the temperatures that the plant varieties would find in their natural habitat, and represent the ideal temperature for the plant to live in. Most tropical, interior, foliage plants have the ability to tolerate and even thrive in the indoor temperature ranges that are most comfortable for human beings.

It should be mentioned here that the temperature of the atmosphere affects the moisture intake of the plant. Temperature affects the stomata and therefore controls the photosynthetic process, as does the light intensity. A higher atmospheric temperature will promote greater moisture use by the plants. Conversely, a lower temperature will cause a slower photosynthetic rate and hence a slower moisture use rate, but also slower growth rates.

## Relative humidity

Although interior foliage plants naturally experience 60 per cent to 90 per cent humidity, they can easily tolerate conditions in which humans thrive. Problems of low humidity will not normally occur until the reading dips below 35 per cent. Such conditions are, however, extremely uncomfortable to humans. For most tropical plant material, if human inhabitants are comfortable, the majority of interior foliage plants should be able to thrive.

## Heating, ventilation and air conditioning

In most interiors, carbon dioxide ($CO_2$) levels are normally high enough that only adequate ventilation is required to replenish the $CO_2$ used in photosynthesis, and to prevent stagnation of the air around the foliage. Ventilation is also required to prevent heat build-up around foliage in high light intensity which could result in foliage burn. Air-conditioned air will usually neither harm nor help unless the air is extremely cold or extremely hot. Because this may be the case and may harm plants you should avoid placing plants in the direct path of the airstream from the supply grills. This is especially important when the AC system is in heating cycle, as direct heat blasts will almost certainly burn the foliage. Localized directioning of air from AC grills should be considered.

## Drainage and irrigation

In small-container planting drainage is of course not practical, but in large, built-in planters, drainage should be inbuilt wherever possible. This is particularly important in the case of large tree material in excess of 3 m height, so that a surfeit of water can be made available to ensure the growing medium remains moist, as large interior trees do consume significant amounts of moisture, and in an undrained planter underwatering can be a serious problem. For the sake of controlling maintenance costs, irrigation is recommended wherever possible, but any form of automatic or drip-fed irrigation system must of course be limited to planters that are drained. A variety of subterranean irrigation systems are available, including inter-linking systems that are all applicable to soil culture plants.

Hydroponic culture is an alternative to soil culture, and hydroculture, by its very nature, has its own irrigation system. Harmful buildup of salts is avoided by either drainage or sub-irrigation.

## Growing medium

With the growing acceptance and understanding of subterranean irrigation, greater care is required in the general understanding of the solid/air/water relationship. A medium providing 50 per cent solid, 25 per cent water and 25 per cent air is the ideal, but you often find media with 25 per cent available water and 25 per cent unavailable water, with a resultant decrease in available air.

With a growing medium we must consider:

(i) capillarity and water-holding properties;
(ii) air space and gas exchange;
(iii) physical stability over time;
(iv) chemical stability and number of contaminants;
(v) nutrient-holding capacity and low salts.

## Water supply

The general contraction of industry in the United Kingdom favours either manual watering or assisted

404

subterranean irrigation rather than fully-automated watering systems. The convenience of water supply outlets is therefore very critical. Convenient sinks are appropriate for free-standing plant installations, while landscape planters should wherever possible have a water supply to the inbuilt planter to coincide with the drainage that is already present.

## 20.7 PRODUCT AVAILABILITY AND SOURCES

As the product we are dealing with is either tropical or sub-tropical in origin, it will either come from those regions that have appropriate climates or be grown under glasshouse conditions in Northern Europe.

### Supplies from Europe
Supplies of material that are grown under glass are plentiful as regards ground cover and small feature plants up to 1 m in height, but the costs of growing plants in Northern Europe, particularly the energy costs, prohibit the production of large material on a regular commercial basis. Energy costs have dictated that growers in Northern Europe look for faster-growing material as production items to secure their own business future, and this has led to a limitation in the species available in commercial production.

Northern European tropical plant production is mainly based in Holland, Denmark and Belgium, with the UK production of tropical plants having declined significantly over the past decade. Unlike exterior shrub production, there are not common production standards, and specification by pot size is not practical. The specifier of interior plant material must accurately specify height, spread and stem or cane numbers to give the contracting industry the opportunity of pricing the contract correctly.

### Sources of large tropical trees
We shall describe large material as being 3 m and above in height. The UK contracting industry is forced to look to Florida as the main source of large tropical products. Production in Florida has developed to satisfy the demand of Northern American industry for large tropical trees and is the largest area from which acclimatized containerized trees can be brought. The climate in Florida is not truly tropical, and the occurrence of winter frosts has increased in recent years, causing quite severe damage, particularly to the citrus plants. Of late, large tropical trees undergoing acclimatization for the internal landscape have had to be overwintered in shade houses and covered with polythene for further protection.

In the last few years great strides have been made in the understanding of shipping plants from Florida. Shipping time has been reduced from 21 days to 14 days, and current thinking favours shipping temperatures of about 55°F to reduce transpiration during the passage.

Experiments have also proved that drenching the plant with water before shipment in an effort to avoid dehydration gives very good protection. The shorter shipping time has the benefit of reducing the acclimatization time in the United Kingdom, and, providing the product is available in Florida, it is now possible to operate within a 6 month time span from the point of ordering the material to its installation on site.

Malaysia and Singapore are rapidly becoming alternative areas of supply. But shipping times of between 21 to 28 days limit the varieties that can be brought over from the Far East to palm species at present.

### Sub-tropical plant material
Particularly well used sources of sub-tropical plants are Spain and Italy. Florida is trying to start to supply colder, more tolerant plants, which are brought down from such areas as the Carolinas, and the anticipated demand for cold, tolerant material in the North American market could well proved interesting over the next few years.

There is a belief within the industry that parts of Southern Europe could well develop to become the Florida of Northern Europe by providing both sub-tropical and tropical plants.

### Future developments
Of late, vast production of small plants has been developing in tropical locations and, with the exception of production of flowering plants and soft tropical material, Northern European nurseries are being progressively turned over to the acclimatization and final preparation for marketing of the smaller, tropical material. There is a clear need for further development in the availability of cool, tolerant conservatory-type plants, and early signs of this development can be seen in the shipping of young plants from New Zealand to cater not only for the increase in commercial conservatory-type space, but also to satisfy the huge resurgence of conservatories as part of our environment.

## 20.8 PLANT LISTS

# 'Top 25' interior landscape plants

*Spathiphyllum*
*Aglaonema*
*Syngonium*
*Philodendron scandens* and *pertusum*
*Dracaena studneri, massangeana, fragrans*, Janet Craig, *marginata* and *deremensis*
*Ficus benjamina*, Gold King and *nitida*
*Schefflera arboricola* and *actinophylla*
*Anthurium* (Plate 20.13)
*Croton*
*Sansevieria*
*Chamaedorea*
*Howea forsteriana*

PLATE 20.13 *Anthurium scherzerianum* – **a good example of a tolerant foliage groundcover with flower interest.** *(Steve Dale)*

*Scindapsus*
*Dieffenbachia*
*Rhoicissus rhomboidea*
*Nidularium*

## Flowering plants for interior landscape

*Chrysanthemum*
*Azalea*
*Kalanchoe*
*Begonia*
*Cyclamen*
*Gerbera*
*Cineraria*
*Aphelandra*

## Tropical trees for interior landscape in general production

*Ficus nitida*
*Ficus benjamina*
*Bucida buceras*
*Phoenix roebelinii*
*Cocus plumosa*

PLATE 20.14 *Podocarpus gracilior* **in a shade house, ready for shipment to Europe and ideal for shopping mall use.** *(Steve Dale)*

PLATE 20.15 *Veitchia* **and** *Ptycosperma (Adonidia* **and** *Alexander)* **palms, good examples of the tolerant and impressive range of palm species available for internal use at 9 or 10 m in height.** *(Steve Dale)*

*Podocarpus gracilior* (Plate 20.14)
*Chrys lidocarpus (areca) and lutescens*
*Howea (kentia) forsteriana*
*Ptycosperma elegans*
*Veitchia (adonidia) merrillii* (Plate 20.15)
*Livistona chinensis*
*Phyllostachys nigra hennon*
*Dracaena marginata*
*Phoenix dactylifera*
*Schefflera actinophylla* (Plate 20.16)
*Aralia elegantissima*

# Sub-tropical trees for interior landscape

*Eriobotrya*
*Magnolia*
*Olea europaea*
*Cupressus cashmireana*
*Araucaria (Norfolk Island pine)*
*Ragoshomia*
*Pittosporum*
*Carinocarpus*
*Phoenix canariensis*

PLATE 20.16 **Traditional plants, such as** *Schefflera actinophylla,* **are available up to 9 m in height and are potentially of great use in varying the visual form of internal plant material.** *(Steve Dale)*

## FURTHER READING

BALI *Guide to Specification for Interior Landscape,* Second edition (Keighley: British Association of Landscape Industries 1983)

Blombery, A. and Rodd, T. *Palms* (London: Angus and Robertson 1982)

Graf, A. B. *Exotica* (Rutherford, N. J: Roehrs 1978)

Gaines, R. L. *Interior Plantscaping* (New York: McGraw-Hill 1977)

Hessayon, D. G. *The House Plant Expert* (Waltham Cross: PBI Publications 1980)

Huxley, A. J. *The Macmillan World Guide to House-plants* (London: Macmillan 1983)

*Interior Designers Handbook* (London: Grosvenor Press 1987)

Manaker, G. H. *Interior Plantscapes: Installation, Maintenance and Management* (Englewood Cliffs, N. J: Prentice-Hall 1981)

Saxon, R. *Atrium Buildings* (Guildford: Architectural Press 1986)

Scrivens, S. *Interior Planting in Large Buildings* (Guildford: Architectural Press 1980)

Wright, M. (Ed.) *Complete Indoor Gardener* (London: Pan Books 1980)

# General Index

# Plants, Index to Latin Names

411

412